PEACE, CONFLICT, AND VIOLENCE

Peace Psychology for the 21st Century

Daniel J. Christie

OHIO STATE UNIVERSITY

Richard V. Wagner

BATES COLLEGE

Deborah Du Nann Winter

WHITMAN COLLEGE

Prentice Hall

Upper Saddle River, New Jersey 07458

Library of Congress Cataloging-in-Publication Data

Peace, conflict, and violence / [edited by] Daniel J. Christie, Richard V. Wagner, Deborah Du Nann Winter.
   p. cm.
  Includes bibliographical references and index.
  ISBN 0-13-096821-8
   1. Conflict management. 2. Peace–Psychological aspects. 3. Social justice. 4. Violence. I. Christie, Daniel J. II. Wagner, Richard V. III. Winter, Deborah Du Nann.

HM1126.P4 2001
303.6'9–dc21
                                                00-059830

This book is dedicated to Ralph K. White, with gratitude and admiration.

VP, Editorial Director: Laura Pearson
Executive Editor: Stephanie Johnson
Managing Editor: Sharon Reinhardt
Managing Editor, Production: Mary Rottino
Production Liaison: Fran Russello
Project Manager: Pine Tree Composition
Prepress and Manufacturing Buyer: Tricia Kenny
Art Director: Jayne Conte
Cover Designer: Bruce Kenselaar
Cover Art: Bill Fitzpatrick/White House Photo Office; Library of Congress; Ken Karp/ Pearson Education/PH College; United Nations; Jay Ullat/Stearn/Black Star; David R. Frazier Photolibrary, Inc.
Marketing Manager: Sharon Cosgrove

This book was set in 10/12 Baskerville by Pine Tree Composition, Inc. and was printed and bound by RR Donnelly & Sons Company. The cover was printed by Phoenix Color Corp.

Text credits appear on p. 425, which constitutes a continuation of the copyright page.

© 2001 by Prentice-Hall, Inc.
A Division of Pearson Education
Upper Saddle River, New Jersey 07458

Printed in the United States of America
10 9 8 7 6 5 4 3 2 1

ISBN 0-13-096821-8

Prentice-Hall International (UK) Limited, *London*
Prentice-Hall of Australia Pty. Limited, *Sydney*
Prentice-Hall Canada Inc., *Toronto*
Prentice-Hall Hispanoamerica, S. A., *Mexico*
Prentice-Hall of India Private Limited, *New Delhi*
Prentice-Hall of Japan, Inc. *Tokyo*
Pearson Education Asia Pte. Ltd., *Singapore*
Editora Prentice-Hall do Brasil, Ltda., *Rio de Janeiro*

CONTENTS

Contents

FOREWORD

Unlike much trendy writing that has been cashing in on the change of centuries and millennia, this splendid book very appropriately links its treatment of peace psychology to the special date of its issue. The threats and opportunities presented to a psychology of peace, conflict, and violence are so radically different in the twenty-first century than they were until the very last decade of the bloody twentieth century. Responding to the new challenges, the editors and authors present a reconceptualization of peace psychology as a field of research and practical intervention, filled out with contributions that represent the best ongoing work. This book unquestionably becomes the best single resource for psychologists, students, other social scientists, and concerned citizens to turn to for orientation to psychology's present and potential involvement in these important matters. I see it as giving enduring shape to the field.

In the second half of the twentieth century, the top priority for people concerned with war and peace was preventing the catastrophe of nuclear war between the giant nuclear powers around which world politics were polarized. Ralph White, the stalwart elder statesman of peace psychology, edited a fine book, *Psychology and the Prevention of Nuclear War* (New York University Press, 1986), which brought together a representative selection of the best psychological thought on the topic. Since I wrote the Foreword to that volume, I am keenly aware how greatly the present book contrasts in conception. My thinking was shaped by the intellectual climate of the Cold War era, of which I am a survivor. It may be useful to readers of the present book for me to comment briefly on matters about which its editors and authors have really changed my thinking.

At a time when embarrassingly few psychologists saw fit to give priority to what seemed to them to be a matter of sheer world survival, I regarded it as a distraction to include the agenda of social justice under the same banner as avoidance of nuclear war. I thought that Psychologists for Social Responsibility, in which I was active, ought to concentrate its efforts on mobilizing psychologists to the absolutely critical issue of survival—especially since I had come to think they would use any excuse to avoid attending to the prospect of nuclear annihilation—an avoidance resulting from well-learned helplessness. So I did not warm to Johan Galtung's proposal (which plays a major role in the conceptualization developed here) to refer to the various forms of social injustice that harm people as "structural violence," thereby pairing structural violence with direct violence as social evils to be combated. I had a strong continuing commitment to the struggle against injustice, but thought the distinction between direct violence and social injustice conceptually and politically important. It even seemed to me that the idea of structural violence was a kind of rhetorical tactic to get people more concerned with injustice—a worthy objective but one that sets the wrong priorities when the likelihood of nuclear catastrophe was so great.

But the Cold War ended more than a decade ago, and although the risks of nuclear war remain so long as enormously destructive nuclear armament is stockpiled, the avoidance of nuclear war is no longer the preemptive issue. And the violence characterizing our post–Cold War era is not primarily between nation states engaged in the anarchic power plays of Realpolitik; it is increasingly between ethnic or religious groups, often within nation-states. In this new situation, I find the four-fold scheme on which this book is organized very appropriate.

In their brilliant introductory chapter, which also gives a sound review of the history of Peace Psychology in the Cold War era, Christie, Wagner, and Winter pull together much emerging consensus in their four categories. There is direct violence and structural violence, in the sense of Galtung's distinction. And there are ways of stopping or preventing violence: peace-making including conflict resolution in the case of direct violence, peacebuilding in that of structural violence. Since direct violence at both the individual and group levels gets instigated or augmented by the thwarting of human needs (yes, there is something to the old frustration-aggression hypothesis), the link between peacebuilding and social justice is explicitly argued. The merit of the scheme is especially clear in the authors' call for a systems orientation in which the reciprocal influence of direct and structural violence is recognized.

The chapters deal with conflict and violence at the interpersonal and intergender as well as intergroup and interstate levels, affording valuable perspectives on such currently active research areas as child and spousal abuse. The editors properly note that whether conflict and violence at different levels follow similar patterns of relationship and respond to similar interventions is a questions for empirical research.

The book's emphasis on peacebuilding and social justice will inherently make it controversial. Research on structural violence and social justice, let alone activism in the promotion of social justice, inherently challenges the status quo, in which injustice is structurally embedded. So be it. If psychologists are to involve themselves in the attempt to reduce the human carnage that follows from urban destitution or poverty in what we used to call the "Third World," they are likely to find themselves in the intellectual company of emancipatory radicals like Paolo Friere or Ignacio Martín-Baró.

The general direction of the book's marshalling of current knowledge and wisdom, as I sense it, does not support Utopian expectations of a final solution for the human problems of conflict and violence, expectations so often shattered in the past. I see the prospect of an empirically grounded Peace Psychology with an activist wing, which can contribute substantially to the never-ending effort to keep the human world livable for human beings. This book makes a large contribution to the identity of such a discipline.

M. Brewster Smith
Santa Cruz, California

PREFACE

Psychologists have been interested in psychological aspects of war and peace since the beginning of modern psychology. Early in the twentieth century, William James challenged the overly simplistic and misguided view that war was an inevitable result of human nature (James, 1910). He also cautioned about the allure of the military in the military-industrial-university complex. Military service emphasizes duty, conformity, loyalty, and cohesion, virtues that are likely to attract well meaning conscripts unless suitable civic substitutes are found. It seems appropriate that Morton Deutsch (1995) referred to William James as the first peace psychologist in an article that appeared in the first issue of *Peace and Conflict: Journal of Peace Psychology*.

Peace psychology as a distinct area of psychology did not begin to emerge clearly until the latter half of the twentieth century, when the United States and Soviet Union were locked in a nuclear arms race that had compelling psychological features and threatened the survival of humankind. The nuclear threat peaked in the mid-1980s, igniting a counter-reaction by a generation of psychologists who began to identify themselves as peace psychologists. These psychologists were trained in traditional areas of psychology, typically, social, developmental, cognitive, clinical, and counseling psychology, and they were eager to apply concepts and theories that held the promise of preventing a nuclear conflagration.

Two events helped to establish the legitimacy and value of peace psychology. In 1986, Ralph K. White published an important volume on "Psychology and the Prevention of Nuclear War" which helped identify some of the content of peace psychology. The destructive consequences of mutual enemy images was focal in the book and approaches to peace emphasized tension reduction strategies. In 1990, institutional support was forthcoming when the American Psychological Association recognized a new division, the Division of Peace Psychology (Division 48).

As the Soviet Union began to unravel, leaving only one superpower in the world that could claim economic and military supremacy, the threat of nuclear war seemed greatly diminished, at least from the perspective of scholars in the United States. Nonetheless, the Cold War left in place institutions and professional affiliations that supported research and practice aimed at the reduction of violence and the promotion of peace. The general contours that would form the content of peace psychology were becoming clear as peace psychologists turned their scholarly tools toward an examination of the psychological dimensions of the continuing and ubiquitous problems of peace, conflict, and violence.

Our purpose in editing this volume is to bring together in one place international perspectives on key concepts, themes, theories, and practices that are defining peace psychology as we begin the twenty-first century. We share with our international colleagues a broad vision of peace psychology, covering a wide range of topics such as ethnic conflict, family violence, hate crimes, militarism, conflict management, social justice, nonviolent approaches to peace, and peace education. In addition to providing a useful resource that integrates current research and practices for scholars and practitioners, we wanted the book to be accessible enough to introduce a new generation of students, both graduate and upper-division undergraduate, to the field. When organizing the topics in the book, we have tried to capture the four main currents in peace psychology: (1) violence, (2) social inequalities, (3) peacemaking, and (4) the pursuit of social justice.

In the first section of the book, contributors examine violence at various levels of analysis, from the micro to the macro, reflecting the wide range of interests in peace psychology. For example, at the micro level, we examine violence in intimate relationships. At the macro level, we consider nationalism and interstate war. At intermediate levels, we include violence against gays and lesbians, and various forms of intergroup violence. We draw a sharp distinction between conflict and violence, emphasizing the distinction between thought and action. Conflicting viewpoints are not inevitably linked with violence and may even lead to constructive conflict resolution.

In the second section of the book, we distinguish direct violence from structural violence: direct violence refers to events that harm or kill individuals or groups as contrasted with structural violence which is manifest in social inequalities. In structural violence, hierarchical relations within and between societies privilege those who are on top while oppressing, exploiting and dominating those who occupy the bottom. Like direct violence, structural violence also kills people but does so slowly, by depriving people of basic necessities. There are important psychological reasons why people tolerate and rationalize structural violence and we identify some of these reasons in this volume. We examine structural violence within societies but also include in our analysis the problem of militarization, which contributes to structural violence globally, most often depriving those with the fewest resources, usually women, children and indigenous people. The organization of the book reflects our bias that violence is best understood from a systems perspective with overt forms of violence manifest in micro and macro contexts, and conditioned by structural and cultural configurations.

While the first half of the book deals with systems of violence and links direct and structural forms of violence, the second half examines systems of peace. In the third section of the book, we examine peacekeeping and peacemaking, both of which are methods that are designed to stop or prevent direct violence. The section on peacemaking emphasizes positive approaches to peace in which rules for cooperating are added to the repertoire of adversaries in a conflict situation and conflict resolution is achieved when the adversaries arrive at mutually agreeable outcomes. In nearly all the chapters on peacemaking, the authors emphasize the importance of being sensitive to cultural differences.

In the fourth section on peacebuilding, the authors present psychologically informed approaches to social justice that are designed to reduce structural violence. Structural peacebuilding matters to peace psychologists because the roots of direct violence can often be traced to structure-based inequalities. Accordingly, chapters in the fourth section identify psychological concepts and processes involved in the nonviolent pursuit of socially just ends. Taken together, the sections on peacemaking and structural peacebuilding offer a roadmap for peace psychologists who are dedicated to theory and practices that promote peace with social justice.

Daniel J. Christie
Richard V. Wagner
Deborah Du Nann Winter

ACKNOWLEDGMENTS

No book emerges singlehandedly, but this one rests on the creativity and hard work of more people than most volumes we've seen. First, we owe hearty thanks to our 44 authors who worked tirelessly through many drafts, and sometimes against impossible deadlines to submit material when we needed it. Special thanks to Mike Wessells, who recommended many of the authors and helped shape the content of this volume. Also, thanks are due to two "pros" who helped with rewriting—Maria Boza and Nancy Maclean—and to Paula Brown, without whose expertise and hard work half the book would never have made it out of Lewiston, Maine.

Most importantly, we want to thank our students, who teach us more than they know, and whose insightful comments over the years helped clarify important concepts and streams of ideas; they include Dan Christie's students at The Ohio State University, Marion Campus: Jennifer Swain, David Boyer, Barbara Stickel, Paula Burnside, Kay Hendricks, P.J. Mullins, Tricia Murphy, Peter Bermudez, Tracy Miley, Stefanie Stoner, Katrina Cortolillo, Leigh Anne Doyle, Shirley Saksa, Christina Sisson, Curtis Tuggle, and classes in psychology and international studies that field-tested parts of the book; Dick Wagner's students at Bates College: Jonathan Horowitz, and "Chile 96" and "Chile 98"; and Deborah Winter's students at Whitman College, who helped enormously on earlier drafts of the manuscript: Laura Boston, Sara Houck, Dana Leighton, Matthew Lee, Afifa Ahmid, Heather Waite, Anne McCullough, Lisa Okuma, Megan Hekelwrath, Calon Russell, Mariah Lebwohl, Sarah Alexander, Marianne Brady, and Nikki Addison.

Many eminent scholars provided the groundwork on which this volume builds. Perhaps the first was William James, but no less important are the many people whose work during the Cold War period inspired and guided the first generation of peace psychologists, including Ralph K. White, Herbert Kelman, Morton Deutsch, Charles Osgood, Irving Janis, Jerome Frank, Urie Bronfenbrenner, Thomas Milburn, and political scientists Robert Jervis, Ned Lebow, and Johan Galtung. We are especially grateful to the late Jeffrey Rubin for encouraging collaborative publication in the field. And we honor the feminist scholars who have enriched our analyses: Ethel Tobach, Betty Reardon, Elise Boulding, Birgit Brock-Utne, Cynthia Enloe, and Susan McKay.

Others helped put the field of peace psychology on the political and scholarly map with their tireless work both in publication and in political arenas. We owe special appreciation to

M. Brewster Smith for his brilliant work in helping the Division of Peace Psychology become a new division of the American Psychological Association in 1990. We offer particular thanks to Milt Schwebel for his work in founding the Division's journal: *Peace and Conflict: Journal of Peace Psychology,* and for serving as its gracious first editor. And we are indebted to our international colleagues, particularly Andy Dawes (South Africa), Di Bretherton and Ann Sanson (Australia), and Abelardo Brenes (Costa Rica) who have hosted biennial meetings on the Contributions of Psychology to Peace under the auspices of the Union of Psychological Sciences. These forums have facilitated collaborative linkages and broadened the field of peace psychology immeasurably.

All proceeds are donated to The Society for the Psychological Study of Peace, Conflict, and Violence: Division of Peace Psychology of the American Psychological Association.

Contributors

NAOMI ABRAHAMS is Chair of the Department of Sociology at Mount Hood Community College in Portland, Oregon. She received her Ph.D. in Sociology from the University of California, Santa Barbara. She is the author of numerous articles on gender and power relations in families, communities, and politics. Her current areas of research include: community responses to domestic violence, domestic violence and the courts, and gender and ethnic inequality in welfare reform.

INGER AGGER is Associate Research Professor of Psychology at the University of Copenhagen where she also received her Ph.D. in cultural sociology. She is the author of *The Blue Room: Trauma and Testimony among Refugee Women* (1994), and *Trauma and Healing under State Terrorism* (with Soeren Buus Jensen) (1996), as well as numerous articles and book chapters on the psychology of human rights violations. She has done research in Latin America and Africa, and served as European Union coordinator for psychosocial projects from 1993 to 1996 in the Balkans during the war.

ANNE ANDERSON has been National Coordinator of Psychologists for Social Responsibility since 1984. She has been a feminist therapist since 1972, joining the Washington Therapy Guild in 1976. She also works with seriously emotionally disturbed children and their families at the Episcopal Center for Children. She is part of an International Technical Assistance Group for Christian Children's Fund, whose mission is to integrate psychosocial perspectives into the traditional community-building work of CCF. She has been a civil rights, women's rights, and peace activist for much of her life.

LAURA BOSTON graduated with Honors in Psychology from Whitman College in 1999, and is a graduate student at Colorado State University.

DI BRETHERTON is Director of the International Conflict Resolution Centre at the University of Melbourne, in Australia, where she offers courses and supervises research in the Psychology Department. She has worked on conflict management projects in a number of countries, including Vietnam, Sri Lanka and the Philippines. During 1998 to 2000 she worked with UNESCO in Paris to help plan and implement the International Year for a Culture of Peace.

She is Chair of the Committee for the Psychological Study of Peace of the International Union of Psychological Science and President Elect of the Division of Political Psychology of the International Association of Applied Psychology.

MICHAEL BRITTON is a psychologist and practicing psychotherapist, consultant to the Social Security Disability Determinations Services in New Jersey, co-founder of NJ Psychologists for Social Responsibility, a member of the Academy of Registered Dance Therapists and former Board member of the American Dance Therapy Association. He has done interview research with retired military officers who served during the Cold War nuclear arms buildup, and research on kinds of parental love that enable children to grow up and be successful in love.

ED CAIRNS teaches psychology at the University of Ulster and has been a visiting scholar at the Universities of Florida, Cape Town, and Melbourne. Most of his work has investigated the psychological aspects of the conflict in Northern Ireland. He is a Fellow of the British Psychological Society and a member of the Division of Peace Psychology of the American Psychological Association.

DANIEL J. CHRISTIE is Professor of Psychology at Ohio State University. He is a former president of the Division of Peace Psychology of the American Psychological Association, and serves on the editorial board of its journal. His research explores children's perceptions of violence, models of intercultural sensitivity, and structural peacebuilding. He teaches courses in psychology and international studies at the OSU Marion campus, has served as president of Psychologists for Social Responsibility, and does applied work on local and international programs that enhance the educational and economic opportunities of minority and indigenous ethnic groups.

PETER T. COLEMAN holds a Ph.D. in social/organizational psychology from Teachers College, Columbia University. He is an Assistant Professor of Psychology and Education and Director of the International Center for Cooperation and Conflict Resolution at Teachers College. He currently conducts theoretical and applied research on conflict resolution training, conflict resolution and difference, intractable conflict, and on the conditions for the constructive use of social power. His most recent publication is *The Handbook of Conflict Resolution: Theory and Practice,* co-edited with Morton Deutsch.

LUCIAN GIDEON CONWAY III is a doctoral student at the University of British Columbia. He has a broad range of research interests, including the emergence and change of culturally-shared beliefs (especially stereotypes), the psychology of political leaders, and anything relevant to cognitive complexity. He has authored or co-authored seven articles, comments, and book chapters on these and other topics. He has recently been awarded an Izaak Walton Killam Memorial Pre-Doctoral Fellowship to support his doctoral research.

ANDY DAWES is an Associate Professor in the Department of Psychology at the University of Cape Town, where he teaches developmental and clinical psychology. He has studied the impact of war and other forms of violence on children and adolescents, and has investigated the effects of South Africa's political transition on levels of intergroup tolerance among young people. He also has an interest in the promotion of tolerance among young people in newly democratized societies.

CHERYL DE LA REY is a Senior Lecturer in the Department of Psychology at the University of Cape Town, where she obtained her Ph.D. She is on the editorial boards of the *South African Journal of Psychology* and *Agenda,* and is a member of the International Advisory Group of the journal *Feminism and Psychology.* Her research and publications cover issues of gender, race, and social policy. Recently she has worked on a project on women and peacebuilding in South Africa in collaboration with Susan McKay.

MORTON DEUTSCH is E.L. Thorndike Professor Emeritus at Teachers College, Columbia University. He is well-known for his pioneering research on cooperation-competition, inter-group relations, conflict resolution, and social justice. His work has been honored by many prizes and awards as well as by election to the presidency of various psychological societies. His most recent book is *The Handbook of Conflict Resolution: Theory and Practice,* co-edited with Peter Coleman.

DANIEL DRUCKMAN is Professor of Conflict Resolution at George Mason University's Institute for Conflict Analysis and Resolution, where he also coordinates the doctoral program. He has published widely on such topics as nationalism, negotiating behavior, peacekeeping, political stability, nonverbal communication, and modeling methodologies, including simulation. He received the 1995 Otto Klineberg award for Intercultural and International Relations from the Society for the Psychological Study of Social Issues for his work on nationalism, and a Teaching Excellence award in 1998 from George Mason University.

JOHAN GALTUNG, Professor of Peace Studies and Director of TRANSCEND, a peace and development network, has tried to work for peace along two parallel tracks. One is as a re-searcher, author of 85 books, and teacher in 50 countries; another is as a conflict worker in more than 40 conflicts. His nomadic life has brought him to most of the world's countries, and he is now "at home" with his Japanese wife, Fumiko Nishimura, herself a researcher, in five of them: Japan, the United States, France, Spain, and Norway.

JAMES GARBARINO is Co-Director of the Family Development Center and Elizabeth Lee Vincent Professor of Human Development at Cornell University. Prior to his current position, he served as President of the Erikson Institute for Advanced Study in Child Development (1985–1994). He has authored numerous books including *Lost Boys: Why Our Sons Turn Violent and How We Can Save Them* (1999), *Raising Children in a Socially Toxic Environment* (1995), and *Let's Talk About Living in a World with Violence* (1993). His awards include the American Psychological Association's Award for Distinguished Professional Contributions to Public Service.

SOLVEIG HÄGGLUND is Associate Professor of Education and Vice Dean of the Faculty of Education at Göteborg University, Sweden. Her research focuses on socialization, develop-ment, and learning in different settings. She has conducted studies on gender socialization, prosocial development, and social responsibility in preschool and school settings. Recent re-search concerns social inclusion and exclusion in formal educational settings. She teaches post-graduate courses in socialization theories, children's rights and realities, and human ecology. She is co-director of the Cross-cultural Research Programme on Children and Peace.

ILSE HAKVOORT is a Visiting Scientist in the Department of Education at Göteborg Univer-sity, Sweden, with a postdoctoral stipendium from STINT (Swedish Foundation for Interna-tional Cooperation in Research and Higher Education). She is co-coordinator of the Cross-cultural Research Programme on Children and Peace since its establishment in 1996. Her research interests focus on the development of children's conceptualization of peace and war, learning and development in different socio-cultural contexts, peace education, and storytelling. She is involved in courses on conflict resolution and communication.

SARA HOUCK graduated with Honors in Psychology from Whitman College in 1999.

KATHLEEN KOSTELNY is Senior Research Associate and Director of the Project on Children and Violence at the Erikson Institute in Chicago. Her work has taken her to war zones and areas of political conflict including Mozambique, Angola, Nicaragua, the West Bank and Gaza Strip, Cambodia, Kosovo, and East Timor, as well as communities struggling with violence in the United States. She is the co-author of *Children in Danger: Coping with the Consequences of Community Violence* (1991) and *No Place to Be a Child: Growing Up in a War Zone* (1992). She is the recipient of fellowships from the Kellogg National Leadership Program and the Fetzer Institute.

HARVEY LANGHOLTZ is an Associate Professor of Psychology at the College of William & Mary and is the Founding Director of the United Nations Institute for Training and Research Programme of Correspondence Instruction in Peacekeeping Operations. He has authored or edited twelve books, among these *The Psychology of Peacekeeping, Principles for the Conduct of Peace Support Operations,* and *International Humanitarian Law and the Law of War.* He is on the Executive Committee of the Division of Peace Psychology of the American Psychological Association.

MATTHEW LEE graduated from Whitman College in 1999.

PETER LEENTJES was born in the Netherlands and emigrated to Canada as a young boy. He served a career in the Canadian Armed Forces in peacekeeping, humanitarian operations, and training. Deployments included peacekeeping in Cyprus, exchange with the French Cavalry, Commandant of Canada's Armour School, and a tour in Bosnia-Herzegovina setting up military relief operations as Chief of Staff Operations. In 1995, he was appointed Chief of Training for the United Nations Department of Peacekeeping Operations. In 1999 he retired from the Canadian Armed Forces and assumed his current position with the U.S. Army Center of Excellence in Disaster Management and Humanitarian Assistance.

DANA LEIGHTON is an undergraduate Psychology Major at Whitman College.

M. BRINTON LYKES is Professor of Community/Social Psychology at the University of the Witwatersrand in Johannesburg, South Africa, and is on leave from the School of Education at Boston College. Her participatory action research explores the interstices of indigenous cultural beliefs and practices and those of Western psychology, towards creating community-based responses to the effects of war and state-sponsored violence. She is co-author/editor of four books, including *Myths about the Powerless: Contesting Social Inequalities* (1996) and *Trauma psicosocial y adolescentes Latinoamericanos: Formas de acción grupal* (1994).

DANIEL M. MAYTON II is Professor of Psychology at Lewis-Clark State College in Lewiston, Idaho, where he has taught for 24 years. For the past decade-and-a-half he has taught courses on nuclear war, peace, and nonviolence and has published research on nuclear war attitudes, nonviolent predispositions, and the value underpinnings of activism and nonviolence. He is a member of the editorial board of *Peace and Conflict: Journal of Peace Psychology.*

DYAN ELLEN MAZURANA is a Research Associate and Adjunct Assistant Professor in Women's Studies and International Studies at the University of Wyoming in Laramie. In the fall of 2000, she joined the faculty of Women's Studies at the University of Montana, Missoula. She is co-author of *Women and Peacebuilding* (1999), as well as several articles on women, peacebuilding, and armed conflict. Her latest work includes training U.N. peacekeepers and research on the gendered experiences of child soldiers.

SUSAN MCKAY is Professor of Nursing, Women's Studies, and International Studies at the University of Wyoming and is a psychologist in private practice. She is past president of the Division of Peace Psychology of the American Psychological Association and an editorial board member of *Peace and Conflict: Journal of Peace Psychology*. In collaboration with Dyan Mazurana, her current research focuses upon gender and peacebuilding. Other recent scholarship has explored the relationship between gender and peace psychology.

CARLINDA MONTEIRO is an Angolan social worker who serves as Regional Technical Advisor for Christian Children's Fund. In Angola, she has developed training curricula and oversees psychosocial projects in multiple Angolan provinces that build resilience, assist youth and displaced children and families, and link health and psychosocial well-being. She often advises UNICEF and the Angolan Government on psychosocial programming for children affected by violence and for former underage soldiers. Her research focuses on traditional healing, Bantu cosmology, and ways of integrating Western and local approaches to assisting children and families.

CRISTINA JAYME MONTIEL is Associate Professor of Psychology and Senior Fellow of the Center for Social Policy and Public Affairs at the Ateneo de Manila University. She has published articles on political trauma, citizen-based peacemaking, bargaining for peaceful terminations of unsuccessful coup attempts, and attributional analysis of poverty. She received the Outstanding Service Award from the Division of Peace Psychology of the American Psychological Association, and the Distinguished Contribution Award from Psychologists for Social Responsibility. During the Marcos dictatorship, she chaired *Lingap Bilanggo* (Care for Prisoners), a movement for political prisoners' general amnesty.

BIANCA CODY MURPHY is Professor of Psychology and currently holds the Dorothy Reed Williams Chair in the Social Sciences at Wheaton College in Massachusetts. She has published articles about peace education, atomic veterans, families exposed to environmental toxins, and clinical issues with women, and lesbian and gay clients. She is the co-author of *Interviewing in Action: Process and Practice*. She is a past president of Psychologists for Social Responsibility and is the current Chair of the Board for the Advancement of Psychology in the Public Interest of the American Psychological Association. She is a licensed psychologist practicing with Newton Psychotherapy Associates.

ULRIKE NIENS is a graduate of the Free University of Berlin in Germany. She is currently pursuing a doctorate in Psychology at the University of Ulster in Northern Ireland. She has done fieldwork on ethnopolitical conflict in both Northern Ireland and South Africa. Her research interests revolve around broad social science perspectives on social change and social identity theory.

SUSAN OPOTOW is Associate Professor in the Graduate Programs in Dispute Resolution at the University of Massachusetts, Boston. Her scholarship addresses the psychology of injustice and conflict. Her research examines moral exclusion in everyday life, predominantly in environmental and school contexts, in order to gain insight into the social psychological factors fostering more virulent, widespread moral exclusion in state-sponsored violence, torture, and genocide. She has edited two issues of *Journal of Social Issues*—"Moral Exclusion and Injustice" (1990), and "Green Justice: Conceptions of Fairness and the Natural World" (1994, co-edited with Susan Clayton).

PAUL PEDERSEN is Professor at the University of Alabama at Birmingham. He was a visiting faculty member for six years at universities in Indonesia, Malaysia, and Taiwan. He was a Senior Fellow at the East West Center for four years and a Senior Fulbright Scholar in Taiwan for one year. He has written 35 books, 62 chapters, and 92 journal articles, mostly on multicultural counseling and communication. He is particularly interested in reframing conflict into cultural categories and learning more about how conflict is managed across cultures.

DOUGLAS PERKINS is Associate Professor of Family and Consumer Studies at the University of Utah, and a Fellow of the Society for Community Research and Action. His research and service-learning courses focus on community and environmental psychology applications to citizen participation and empowerment, neighborhood revitalization, crime and fear, prevention programs for youth, housing, and urban land use. Much of his community service focuses on state and local advocacy and planning for affordable housing.

MARC PILISUK is a Professor of Psychology and Human Sciences at the Saybrook Graduate School and Research Center. He is the author of six books, including *The Healing Web: Social Networks and Human Survival* (with Susan Hillier Parks, 1986), as well as over 120 articles. He has served as President of the Division of Peace Psychology of the American Psychological Association and currently serves on the board of its journal, *Peace and Conflict: Journal of Peace Psychology*, as well as on the National Steering Committee of Psychologists for Social Responsibility.

ANN SANSON is an Associate Professor in Psychology at the University of Melbourne. Her teaching and research cover developmental psychology and conflict and its resolution. Among her publications, she has guest-edited two issues of the *Australian Psychologist*—"Psychology of Peace and Conflict" (July 1993), and "Psychology and Indigenous Issues" (July 2000). She is a member of the Committee for the Psychological Study of Peace, and has held positions as convenor of Psychologists for the Promotion of World Peace, and Director of Social Issues of the Australian Psychological Society. She is currently a Principal Research Fellow at the Australian Institute of Family Studies.

MILTON SCHWEBEL, a clinical/counseling psychologist, is Professor Emeritus of Psychology at the Graduate School of Applied and Professional Psychology and former Dean of the Graduate School of Education, Rutgers University. He is former president of Psychologists for Social Responsibility and current editor of *Peace and Conflict: Journal of Peace Psychology*. Among his many books, as author or editor, are *Behavioral Science and Human Survival*, and a forthcoming book on educational policy and structural violence.

ERVIN STAUB is Professor of Psychology at the University of Massachusetts, Amherst. His primary areas of work have been on altruism and helping behavior in children and adults and on harmdoing, especially genocide and other collective violence. His books include a two-volume treatise, *Positive Social Behavior,* and *The Roots of Evil: The Origins of Genocide and Other Group Violence.* He also edited and co-edited a number of volumes, the most recent in 1997: *Patriotism in the Lives of Individuals and Groups.* He served as president of the Division of Peace Psychology of the American Psychological Association from 1999 to 2000.

MANFRED B. STEGER is Associate Professor of Political Theory at Illinois State University. Recent publications include: *The Quest for Evolutionary Socialism: Eduard Bernstein and Social Democracy* (1997), *Engels After Marx* (1999), *Nonviolence and Its Alternatives: An Interdisciplinary Reader* (1999), and *Gandhi's Dilemma: Nonviolent Principles and Nationalist Power* (2000). He is currently working on a book titled *Globalism: The New Market Ideology* (forthcoming 2001).

PETER SUEDFELD taught at the University of Illinois and Rutgers University before becoming Head of the Department of Psychology and later, Dean of Graduate Studies at the University of British Columbia. His research focuses on coping and adaptability in challenging environments. He is the author or editor of eight books and over 200 journal articles and book chapters. He is a Fellow of the Royal Society of Canada and the American and Canadian Psychological Associations. He has served as President of the latter, and in 1996 received its Donald O. Hebb Award for distinguished contributions to psychology as a science.

PHILIP E. TETLOCK is Harold Burtt Professor of Psychology and Political Science at the Ohio State University. He received his Ph.D. in Social Psychology from Yale University in 1979 and was Professor of Psychology at the University of California, Berkeley between 1979 and 1995. He has received scientific awards from the National Academy of Sciences, the American Association for the Advancement of Science, the American Psychological Society, the American Political Science Association, and the International Society for Political Psychology. His current research focuses on criteria people use to evaluate the quality of judgment and choice in various spheres of life.

FINN TSCHUDI has recently retired from his position as Professor of Psychology at the University of Oslo, Norway, where he taught for 36 years. While primarily responsible for methodology, he has also been teaching and publishing in the fields of personality and cognitive and social psychology. As a consultant to the Conflict Council in Oslo, he is helping to introduce models for conflict transformation from Australia. He is also working to perfect computer programs for studying homo/heterogeneity in how different groups of people construe social and personal issues.

RICHARD V. WAGNER has been Professor of Psychology at Bates College in Lewiston, Maine since 1970. He received his Ph.D. in social psychology from the University of Michigan. He is a past president of the Division of Peace Psychology of the American Psychological Association, and is incoming editor (2001–) of *Peace and Conflict: Journal of Peace Psychology.* His current interests include political psychology and conflict resolution, and he is a mediator for the court system in Maine.

LINDA WEBSTER is an Assistant Professor at the University of the Pacific in Stockton, California, where she is the director of the school psychology program. Her research has focused on child maltreatment and attachment, and addresses systemic change for these children and their families. She also maintains a private practice with her husband which provides services to children and families in poverty.

MICHAEL G. WESSELLS is Professor of Psychology at Randolph-Macon College and Psychosocial Advisor for Christian Children's Fund. He has served as President of the Division of Peace Psychology of the American Psychological Association and of Psychologists for Social Responsibility. His research examines the psychology of humanitarian assistance, post-conflict reconstruction, and the reintegration of former child soldiers. In countries such as Angola, Sierra Leone, East Timor, and Kosovo, he helps to plan, evaluate, and train in community-based, culturally grounded, holistic programs that assist children, families, and communities affected by armed conflict.

DEBORAH DU NANN WINTER is Professor of Psychology at Whitman College in Walla Walla, Washington, where she has taught for 26 years. She is the author of *Ecological Psychology: Healing the Split Between Planet and Self* (1996) as well as numerous articles on the psychology of peace and environmental issues. She serves as President of Psychologists for Social Responsibility, and is on the Editorial Board of *Peace and Conflict: Journal of Peace Psychology*.

INTRODUCTION TO PEACE PSYCHOLOGY

Daniel J. Christie, Richard V. Wagner,
and Deborah Du Nann Winter

I urge you to beware the temptation . . . of blithely declaring yourselves above it all and label both sides [United States and Soviet Union] equally at fault, to ignore the facts of history and the aggressive impulses of an evil empire, to simply call the arms race a giant misunderstanding and thereby remove yourself from the struggle between right and wrong and good and evil . . . [The Soviet Leaders] are the focus of evil in the modern world (Ronald Reagan, 1983, pp. 363–364).

What became known as the "Evil Empire Speech" reflected the sentiment of many people in the United States during the 1980s. The United States and Soviet Union were locked into a *Cold War,* a contest for global power and military advantage (Lippmann, 1947). Both sides exchanged heated rhetoric, amassed weapons, and instilled fear in one another. Shortly after Reagan's "Evil Empire Speech," survey research registered a peak in anti-Soviet sentiments by U.S. citizens (Yatani & Bramel, 1989), and a peak in the level of fear people reported in connection with the threat of nuclear war (Schatz & Fiske, 1992). Interviews with children in the United States, Soviet Union, and other countries revealed widespread fear (Chivian et al., 1985; Schwebel, 1982) and other reactions that could be categorized as hopelessness, powerlessness, and futurelessness (Christie & Hanley, 1994).

Fear not only fuelled the nuclear arms race but also ignited the countervailing forces of activists and scholars in psychology who sought ways to reduce the threat of a nuclear holocaust (White, 1986). The Cold War wound down with the collapse of the Soviet Union in the late 1980s, but not before galvanizing a generation of psychologists who formed the Division of Peace Psychology within the American Psychological Association (Wessells, 1996), and began to identify themselves as peace psychologists.

Although the emerging discipline of peace psychology is a product of the 1980s, throughout the twentieth century, psychologists have been interested in theory and practice related to social conflict and violence. The level of interest has waxed and waned in parallel with the intensity of conflicts and threats faced by the United States (Morawski & Goldstein, 1985). Interest among psychologists was especially high during the Cold War but also during the "hot wars" of World War I and II.

PSYCHOLOGY'S ROLE IN WORLD WAR I AND II

The concerns of peace psychologists are deeply rooted in the field of psychology, not only because the promotion of human well-being is central to the mission of psychology (APA Bylaws I.1, http://www.apa.org/about/mission.html) but also because psychologists have long been concerned about war and peace. William James, a founder of psychology in the United States, has been regarded as the first peace psychologist (Deutsch, 1995). Just prior to World War I, James gave an address on "the moral equivalent of war" in which he highlighted the enthusiastic readiness of humans to rally around the military flag (James, 1995), a social psychological phenomena akin to "nationalism" that has played out repeatedly for generations, especially when relations between nations become hostile. James argued that militaristic urges are deeply rooted in humans and that societies must learn to channel the satisfaction of their needs in productive directions.

Psychologists did not follow James' advice, but they did become involved in U.S. military affairs during the First World War. Among the more important contributions of psychologists to the war effort was the development of group intelligence tests that were used to select and classify new recruits, a development that "put psychology on the map" (Smith, 1986, p.24).

Psychologists had even greater involvement during the Second World War. A number of specialties in psychology emerged and supported the war effort. *Clinical psychologists* developed and administered tests to place personnel within the military establishment and they also treated war-related emotional problems. *Social psychologists* contributed their expertise, developing propaganda designed to promote the war effort by boosting morale at home and demoralizing the enemy abroad. A number of psychologists worked with the Office of Strategic Services, the precursor of the Central Intelligence Agency, selecting and training people involved in "undercover" activities in Europe and the Far East. *Human factors psychologists* participated in the design of weaponry and other instruments used by the military, and *experimental psychologists* trained nonhumans to perform human tasks. The best-known example of the latter was B. F. Skinner's research in which he trained pigeons to guide pilotless missiles to targets, a program that was ultimately discarded (Herman, 1995). In all these activities, psychologists were enthusiastic participants in the effort to win World War II, a war that was regarded by most people as a just war.

PSYCHOLOGY'S ROLE IN THE COLD WAR

The ideology of Realpolitik has guided the conduct of foreign policy worldwide for nearly three centuries (Klare & Chandrani, 1998). *Realpolitik* is the belief that politics is reducible to three basic goals: keeping power, increasing power, and demonstrating power (Morganthau, 1972). The international politics of the United States was, and continues to be, primarily guided by the ideology of Realpolitik. From a Realpolitik perspective, one sees security in the international system as the balanced capacity among states to use coercive power. Furthermore, because it is assumed that all sovereign states seek to maximize their power, and they operate within an international structure that is anarchical, the best way to ensure security is to be militarily strong and to adopt a policy of *deterrence*. According to the logic of deterrence, each state can best ensure its security by threatening any would-be aggressor with a retaliatory blow that would be unbearably costly to the aggressor. By the conclusion of World War II, a tidy bipolar superpower arrangement had emerged in the world. The United States and Soviet Union were locked into an adversarial relationship in which they competed and concentrated their resources in an arms race, a Cold War that resulted in enormous stockpiles of conventional and nuclear weapons.

During the early years of the Cold War, psychologists continued to support the policies of the U.S. government. Tensions between the United States and Soviet Union grew, as did the arsenals of nuclear weapons that were aimed at each other. There were scattered attempts by committees of the American Psychological Association (APA) and the Society for the Psychological Study of Social Issues (SPSSI) to analyze the implications of the new atomic warfare capability on future international relations, as well as the potential psychological effects on populations experiencing atomic bombardment. Generally, these early committees lacked focus but agreed that the major psychological concern was citizens' attitudes toward atomic warfare and energy. They "emphasized the need to accurately assess and control public opinion in order to achieve public consensus regarding foreign relations and atomic war" (Morawski & Goldstein, 1985, p. 278). On the whole, the public was quite supportive of government policies. Although survey research indicated that Americans were well aware of the bomb, and expressed little hope about the potential for international agencies to harness the spread of atomic energy and bombs, very few Americans expressed worry or fear (Cottrell & Eberhart, 1948). The usual psychological interpretation of the public's low level of concern in the face of the atomic threat was that ordinary Americans felt helpless, relied on the authorities to deal with the problem, and used a psychological defense that was called "fear suppression" (Harris, Proshansky, & Raskin, 1956). No one in the psychological community suggested that fear might be an appropriate response to the threat of nuclear annihilation (Morawski & Goldstein, 1985).

During the 1950s, a growing number of psychologists were employed as scientists and practitioners by the federal government and the military. Psychologists used their expertise to assess and change the public's attitudes toward atomic warfare, to deal with emotional problems experienced by persons exposed to atomic testing, and to reduce soldiers' fear and reluctance to participate in atomic maneuvers (Rand, 1960; Schwartz & Winograd, 1954). Although the activities of psychologists were many and varied, most psychologists shared the common goal of preparing the country—civilians and military alike—for the anticipated nuclear confrontation with the Soviet Union.

The ideology of Realpolitik prevailed, despite the efforts of a few individuals within the psychological establishment (such as Gordon Allport, Hadley Cantril, and Otto Klineberg) who argued that the atomic age required a new form of diplomacy and the abolition of war (Jacobs, 1989). Policy makers were not particularly receptive to the advice of psychologists, especially in matters of foreign policy. Besides, most psychologists in the post–World War II era were preoccupied with the development of psychology as a profession and those who wanted to speak out knew they would be putting themselves at professional risk. Marked by the "McCarthy era," in which anyone opposed to government policy could be branded a communist and brutally punished, the U.S. political climate in the early 1950s was not conducive to voices that opposed government policy.

In the late 1950s and early 1960s, however, several challenges to the Cold War mentality and its embrace of Realpolitik emerged in the field of psychology. Important publications signaled an incipient shift from planning for war to proposing policies designed to promote the chances for peace (Wagner, 1985). In 1957, *The Journal of Conflict Resolution* began publishing articles on conflict reduction in international relations. Another publication was a special issue of the *Journal of Social Issues,* which was critical of the U.S. policy of nuclear deterrence (Russell, 1961). Two edited volumes were particularly noteworthy: one by Wright, Evan, and Deutsch (1962), *Preventing World War III: Some Proposals,* and another one by Schwebel (1965), *Behavioral Science and Human Survival.* As Morawski and Goldstein (1985) assess the significance of these appearances:

> First, the level of analysis was shifted from an exclusive focus on the behavior of individuals to a more inclusive focus on the behavior of nations. Second, psychologists began to emphasize the prevention of war rather than preparations for war. And third, whereas previous research had attempted to document or generate public consensus with government policy, the new work was critical of U.S. foreign policies. (p. 280)

In other ways psychologists began breaking from the tradition of promoting government policy. Instead of analyzing ways of ensuring that public opinion coincided with Realpolitik considerations, Soviet citizens were humanized when interviews with them revealed that their views of the United States were similar to the views that U.S. citizens had of them, forming a *mirror image* of one another (Bronfenbrenner, 1961). At about the same time, some of the pioneers in peace psychology such as Jerome Frank and Ralph K. White were articulating the dangers of developing *diabolical enemy images* (Frank, 1967; White, 1966), which people tend to create, especially when they feel threatened. Even deterrence, the centerpiece of U.S. foreign policy, came under scrutiny as scholars noted the logical and empirical inconsistencies in the policy (Milburn, 1961). The argument applies even today because there is no logical or empirical way to prove whether deterrence actually keeps an enemy from attacking. One can only know when deterrence fails to deter an enemy.

Instead of analyzing methods of treating soldiers' resistance, Osgood (1962) proposed Graduated and Reciprocated Initiatives in Tension-reduction (*GRIT*), a method of defusing international tensions by having each side take turns at initiating tension-reducing actions. Not unlike standing on the outer edges of a teeter-totter, both superpowers could move toward the center of the teeter-totter in small steps, taking turns all the way. There have been suggestions that President Kennedy and Soviet Premier Khruschev drew from the GRIT model back in the early 1960s when they took a series of initiatives that culminated in a nuclear arms control treaty (viz., the Limited Test Ban Treaty). Etzioni (1967) identified the steps that were taken by both sides, and they neatly conformed to a GRIT pattern.

From the mid-1960s until the late 1970s, domestic concerns took precedence over international issues and U.S. psychologists gave less attention to the Cold War and the threat of nuclear war. Topics that appeared with some regularity in the *American Psychologist* and the *Journal of Social Issues* included student activism, population growth, changes in sex-roles, and a range of problems related to race relations. Meanwhile, political scientists continued their scholarship on war and peace. Looking at the world through a Realpolitik perspective, political scientists and those who specialized in international relations analyzed the Vietnam War, casting the war in the bipolar East-West struggle in which the United States sought to contain the spread of communism. The policy of containing communism was driven by *Domino Theory,* the belief that the fall of Vietnam to Soviet influence would make it likely that another domino would fall, producing a chain reaction and ultimately leading to the spread of communism all over the world.

As the United States withdrew troops from the hot war in Vietnam, a second round of the Cold War ensued. In lockstep, the superpowers enacted the well-known *"security dilemma"* with one side's attempt to gain security through more military armaments threatening the other side, which responded in turn by increasing its armaments. During the 1970s, the policy of deterrence was taken to the height of logical absurdity as the arms race backed both superpowers into a corner and stuck them with the reality of *MAD*, "mutually assured destruction." Now, no one would begin a nuclear war, it was reasoned, because no one could win. Both sides' excessive stockpiles of nuclear weapons meant that if an all-out nuclear war did occur, the result would be not only the total destruction of the superpowers but an end to life as we knew it.

In the early 1980s, public concern about the threat of nuclear war increased dramatically as the rhetoric grew more hostile on both sides and the U.S. government began to openly discuss plans for achieving nuclear superiority and for waging and prevailing in a protracted nuclear war (Scheer, 1982). Citizens' concern about nuclear war continued to rise, especially in the United States and in Europe, as the U.S. Defense Department proposed to build a nuclear capability that would enable the United States to fight a range of nuclear wars, from a limited strike to an all-out nuclear exchange (Holloran, Gelb, & Raines, 1981). The threat of nuclear war loomed large, especially for Western Europeans because the United States deployed "intermediate range missiles" on their soil and there was talk in the Reagan administration about the possibility of keeping a nuclear war in Europe limited to tactical exchanges with the Soviet Union. A limited nuclear war would not require the use of missiles from the U.S. strategic arsenal, thereby keeping the war at a distance from the U.S. mainland (Scheer, 1982). Not surprisingly, the increasing levels of tension and the escalation of the arms race activated peace movements in both the United States and Europe.

As tensions peaked, reactions of the scientific community in psychology were varied. Some social and behavioral scientists took policy positions (White, 1984), or advocated political activism (Nevin, 1985), while others cautioned that taking positions on such issues required extrapolating far beyond existing psychological knowledge (Tetlock, 1986). A useful analysis of the problem was offered by Deutsch (1983) who underscored the interdependence of the United States and Soviet Union and made it clear that any attempt by one side to pursue security without regard for the security of the other side was self-defeating.

Despite the thoughtful analyses of some psychologists, psychological theory and practice had little if any influence on the course of the Cold War. From the perspective of policy makers, the Cold War was fundamentally an interstate problem, not an intrapsychic problem that was amenable to psychological analyses. Instead, international relations specialists, steeped in the tradition of Realpolitik, were called on as the experts who were best equipped to address most of the scenarios that were likely to lead to a nuclear war.

In order to have credibility, psychologists who wanted to develop theory and practice related to the prevention of nuclear war had to begin by understanding and challenging a Realpolitik framework. Ralph K. White's (1986) edited volume, *Psychology and the Prevention of*

Nuclear War, provided a compendium of articles written by psychologists and political scientists who gave coherence to the perspectives of political psychologists and also added a measure of legitimacy to psychological analyses of the nuclear threat. Likely psychological and political antecedents of a nuclear holocaust were identified and elaborated upon. Emphasis was placed on the problems of an unbridled arms race, mutually distorted perceptions, destructive communication patterns, coercive interactions, competition for allies around the world, and other psychological and political processes.

With few exceptions (Frank, 1967; Wagner, 1988), psychologists and political scientists stayed close to the Realpolitik framework when analyzing large-scale conflict during the Cold War. Moreover, policy recommendations were largely reactive and narrowly focused on the superpower relationship as attempts were made to prescribe ways of diminishing the intensity of the superpower conflict.

The Cold War was a conflict on a grand scale that spawned a great deal of research and practice on methods of resolving conflicts. The groundwork for the practice of conflict resolution was laid many years earlier when Follet (1940) introduced conflict resolution methods in organizational settings. But it was in the midst of the Cold War that Fisher and Ury's (1981) very practical and highly readable little book, *Getting to Yes,* became a bestseller. To this day, the book is a useful guide on how to negotiate and resolve conflicts. Some of the concepts they introduced, such as "win-win outcomes," are still part of the everyday vocabulary of professional negotiators and laypersons alike.

The late 1980s saw the Cold War end, with little assistance from conflict resolution procedures. Instead, the Soviet Union's power diminished under the crush of its own economic problems, which were largely caused by its overextension on international commitments around the world far beyond its capabilities (Kennedy, 1986). The West could rejoice as Soviet influence sharply declined and the Berlin Wall, a symbol of the great global, superpower divide, began to fall. At the conclusion of the Cold War, only one superpower remained, and concerns about the nuclear arms race and the possibility of nuclear annihilation subsided dramatically (Schatz & Fiske, 1992).

THE POST-COLD WAR ERA: PEACE PSYCHOLOGY COMES OF AGE

The Cold War was a power struggle of global proportions that made certain categories of violence salient. Using the state as the focal unit of analysis, scholars concentrated their attention on interstate wars, wars of liberation, secessionist movements, civil wars, and wars in which the superpowers directly intervened militarily (i.e., interventionist wars). Although many other forms of violence were prevalent, from a state-centered perspective, what mattered most were those struggles that had a direct bearing on the strategic, U.S.–Soviet balance of power (George, 1983).

Since the end of the Cold War in the late 1980s, the planet's bipolar superpower structure has reconfigured dramatically and entirely new categories of security concerns have emerged. To be sure, the sovereign states of the international system will still have conflicts to manage, but increasingly, patterns of violence are not neatly following the contours of our inherited system of sovereign states. In the post–Cold War era, a complex pattern of interlacing schisms is emerging, which divides people not so much by state boundaries but by ethnicity, religion, economic well-being, population density, and environmental sustainability (Klare, 1998). A small sample of what we are now observing globally is the outbreak of ethnic violence and other forms of identity group conflict and violence, a growing number of economic and political refugees, ecological devastation and pockets of food insecurity, concentrations of drug-related violence, and international terrorism. These problems are within and across international boundaries and underscore the need to reorient peace psychology and enlarge its scope of practice. The current volume was conceived within the context of these new challenges and represents an attempt to reinvigorate the search for psychological analyses that can inform theory and practice in peace psychology for the twenty-first century.

DEFINING THE SCOPE OF PEACE PSYCHOLOGY

The waning of the Cold War made it possible for peace psychologists to step back from a preoccupation with a single issue—nuclear annihilation—and begin to consider a broader range of threats and opportunities that bear on human well-being and survival. Our intention in this volume is to capture some of the new currents in the field by offering a sample of scholarship that reflects the breadth of research and practice that is being undertaken and shaping peace psychology in the twenty-first century. We have tried to include the work of scholars from around the world because peace psychology aspires to be international in scope and grounded in a multi-cultural framework. As the chapters will make clear, peace psychologists in the post–Cold War era remain concerned about the problem of violence but they are enlarging the radius of their concerns to include the insidious problem of *structural violence,* which occurs when basic human needs are not met and life spans are shortened because of inequalities in the way political and economic structures of a society distribute resources (Galtung, 1969). Moreover, the "peace" in peace psychology is being cast in a far more comprehensive framework, requiring an ambitious agenda that attends not only to traditional concerns about the nonviolent resolution of conflict but also to growing concerns about the pursuit of socially just ends. These new emphases in peace psychology require nothing short of a redefinition of the field. Accordingly, we offer the following definition that captures the thrust of the current volume:

> Peace psychology seeks to develop theories and practices aimed at the prevention and mitigation of direct and structural violence. Framed positively, peace psychology promotes the nonviolent management of conflict and the pursuit of social justice, what we refer to as peacemaking and peacebuilding, respectively.

Our working definition of peace psychology is used to frame the organization of the book, which conforms to a four-way model focusing on direct violence, structural violence, peacemaking, and peacebuilding.

ORGANIZATION OF THE BOOK: THE FOUR-WAY MODEL

Section I: Direct Violence

The current volume retains the traditional focus of peace psychology on international relations by applying psychological concepts and theory to problems of interstate violence and the threat of nuclear war. In addition, because direct violence does not neatly follow the contours of the sovereign state system, chapters in Section I reflect a wider radius of violent episodes that vary in scale from two-person intimate relations to the large-scale violence of genocide. While different in scale and complexity, these varied forms of violence share several features: They all engender direct, acute insults to the psychological or physical well-being of individuals or groups, and they erupt periodically as events or episodes.

The analytic tools of peace psychologists are central to understanding many forms of direct violence. For instance, in Section I, many of the contributors from around the world underscore the importance of *social identity* processes, which are manifest when individuals begin to identify with particular groups and favor their ingroups over outgroups. Quite naturally, the basic need to have a sense of who we are is inextricably woven into the fabric of our identity groups. Conflict and violence often erupts when two or more groups of individuals have different identities and see each other as threats to their identity group's continued existence. These identity-based conflicts are central to many forms of violence including hate crimes, gang violence, ethnic conflicts, and even genocide. Sovereign states have been woefully inadequate in dealing with identity-based problems.

Also reflected throughout the text is peace psychologists' growing appreciation for the structural roots of violent episodes. For example, patriarchal structures in which males dominate females play a role in intimate violence. Similarly, cultural narratives that denigrate gays, lesbians, and other marginalized identity groups are predisposing conditions for direct violence. Section II looks closer at some forms of violence that are deeply rooted in the structures of a society, what we are calling "structural violence."

Section II: Structural Violence

Today, an increasing number of peace psychologists are concerned about structural violence (Galtung, 1969), an insidious form of violence that is built into the fabric of political and economic structures of a society (Christie, 1997; Pilisuk, 1998; Schwebel, 1997). Structural violence is a problem in and of itself, killing people just as surely as direct violence. But structural violence kills people slowly by depriving them of satisfying their basic needs. Life spans are curtailed when people are *socially dominated, politically oppressed,* or *economically exploited.* Structural violence is a global problem in scope, reflected in vast disparities in wealth and health, both within and between societies. Section II examines a number of forms of structural violence, all of which engender structure-based inequalities in the production, allocation, and utilization of material and non-material resources.

Galtung (1969) proposed that one way to define structural violence was to calculate the number of avoidable deaths. For instance, if people die from exposure to inclement conditions when shelter is available for them somewhere in the world, then structural violence is taking place. Similarly, structural violence occurs when death is caused by scarcities in food, inadequate nutrition, lack of health care, and other forms of deprivation that could be redressed if distribution systems were more equitably structured. The chapters in Section II make it clear that structural violence is endemic to economic systems that produce a concentration of wealth for some while exploiting others, political systems that give access to some and oppress others, and hierarchical social systems that are suffused with ethnocentrism and intolerance.

In Table 1, we outline some differences between direct and structural violence based in part on Galtung's (1996) pioneering work in peace studies.

As noted in Table 1, direct violence refers to physical violence that harms or kills people quickly, producing somatic trauma or total incapacitation. In contrast, structural violence kills

Table 1

Direct Violence	Structural Violence
Kills people directly	Kills people indirectly
Kills quickly	Kills slowly
Somatic harm	Somatic deprivation
Dramatic	Commonplace
Personal	Impersonal
Acute insult to well-being	Chronic insult to well-being
Intermittent	Continuous
Subject-action-object observable	Subject-action-object unobservable
Intentional and immoral	Unintentional and amoral
Episodes may be prevented	Inertia may be mitigated

indirectly and slowly, curtailing life spans by depriving people of material and non-material resources. Direct violence is often dramatic and personal. Structural violence is commonplace and impersonal. Direct violence may involve an acute insult to the physical well-being of an individual or group. Structural violence is a chronic threat to well-being. Direct violence occurs intermittently, as discrete events, while structural violence is ongoing and continuous. In direct violence, the subject-action-object relationships are readily observable while political and economic structures of violence are not directly observable, though their deadly results, which are delayed and diffuse, are apparent in disproportionately high rates of infant and maternal mortality in various pockets of the world. Because it is possible to infer whether intentionality is present in cases of physical violence, the morality of an act can be judged and sanctions can be applied. Direct violence is often scrutinized by drawing on religious dicta, legal codes, and ethical systems. Intentionality is not as obvious in impersonal systems of structural violence, and considerations of punishment are seldom applicable. Finally, direct violence can be prevented. In contrast, structural violence is ongoing, and intervention is aimed at mitigating its inertia. Fundamentally, structural violence occurs whenever societal structures and institutions produce oppression, exploitation, and dominance. These conditions are static, stable, normalized, serve the interests of those who hold power and wealth, and are not self-correcting.

A psychological question, posed in Section II on structural violence, is how people, who are morally principled, can live their lives without giving much attention or thought to the pervasive problem of structural violence. To answer this question, research is presented that identifies psychological processes people employ routinely and by so doing, limit their *scope of justice* to include only certain people, thereby perpetuating the socially unjust conditions of structural violence. Authors in Section II also look carefully at the targets of structural violence, especially women and children, because they are disproportionately harmed by structural violence worldwide. An emerging problem of the twenty-first century is globalization, which refers to the worldwide push for free markets that leave in their wake enormous inequalities on a large scale. Globalization is fuelling vast disparities in wealth and a global division of labor in which people in some countries profit and engage in the work of the head while others suffer and toil with their hands. At the dawn of the twenty-first century, militarization continues to be an important source of structural violence, generating vast inequalities in coercive power and fuelling the potential for episodes of violence, as big powers supply arms to smaller countries around the world.

Although we have highlighted distinctions between direct and structural violence, the relationship between direct and structural violence is *circular*. For example, the man who physically abuses a woman is enacting a dominance hierarchy that is supported by patriarchal narratives in a society. At the same time, his violent act reinforces the structural arrangement that puts men in a dominant position over women. Hence, direct violence is not a stand-alone phenomenon; instead, direct and structural violence operate together forming an interlocking *system of violence*. The challenge for peace psychologists is to become systems analysts, which requires an effort to simultaneously focus on the individual as the locus of the problem while also transforming the structural and cultural context within which violent behavior is embedded.

In the last two sections of the book, we look at two kinds of peace processes which form a *system of peace* that is well suited for the prevention and mitigation of direct and structural violence. We begin with *peacemaking,* an attempt to prevent or mitigate direct violence by promoting the nonviolent management of conflict.

Section III: Peacemaking

Peacemaking is designed to reduce the frequency and intensity of direct violence. The section on peacemaking begins with a chapter on U.N. peacekeeping, an approach in which would-be combatants are separated by neutral forces. Peacekeeping may be used flexibly, either before or after episodes of direct violence, that is, to prevent or mitigate episodes of violence. Peacekeeping has traditionally focused on managing, rather than resolving, conflicts. Several chapters in Section III are given to the topic, *"conflict resolution,"* reflecting the emphasis in peace psychology on the prevention of violent episodes by using procedures that encourage dialogue, empathy, and win/win outcomes. Contemporary theorists and practitioners in conflict resolution view conflict as a perceptual event, arising when two or more parties perceive their goals as incompatible with one another. By convention, psychologists separate thought and action, which allows conflict practitioners to decouple the perception of incompatible goals (conflict) from violent behavior, and deal with the former before the outbreak of the latter. Therefore, although conflicts may lead to direct physical violence, the perception of incompatible goals does not make violence inevitable. What matters most is whether or not the parties in a conflict use the situation as an opportunity for creative problem solving that can benefit both or alternatively, mismanage the conflict in ways that damage the relationship (Rubin & Levinger, 1995). Because the meanings of conflict and resolution are always embedded within the context of a particular culture, we also have included a chapter that highlights the importance of cultural contexts.

Although conflict resolution procedures attempt to prevent episodes of violence, in many instances, when violence is not prevented, other efforts are needed that are better suited for post-war interventions. Several chapters in Section III address the aftermath of violence and the importance of addressing psychological, political, and economic dimensions of the problems that arise in the wake of violent episodes. Topics include the problem of post-war trauma, reconciliation in divided societies, and the broader problem of societal reconstruction. Even though these post-war interventions take place after-the-fact, they can interrupt repeated episodes or cycles of violence, and thereby serve as a form of violence prevention.

Although peacemaking is often very useful, the approach has limitations, not least of which is the problem that peacemaking can be used as a tool by those with power who can insist on peaceful means of resolving disputes, while ignoring socially just ends. The dialogue process that characterizes peacemaking approaches is important but a sustainable peace requires structural and cultural peacebuilding, actions and supporting narratives that redress the deeper and more permanent roots of the problem.

Section IV: Peacebuilding

While preventing and mitigating episodes of destructive conflict and violence are familiar moorings for peace psychologists, we seek to enlarge our scope of inquiry and practice by mitigating the inertia of structural violence. Just as we found it useful to distinguish direct and structural violence, we also see merit in distinguishing peacemaking (Section III) from peacebuilding, the latter of which refers to the pursuit of social justice (Section IV). The issue of social justice (Deutsch, 1985) and positive approaches to peace that emphasize human interdependence and the satisfaction of needs is not new to the field of psychology (Wagner, 1988), nor to the interdisciplinary field of peace studies (Smoker, Davies, & Munske, 1990). But once again, we are particularly indebted to Galtung's (1996) work in the multidisciplinary field of peace studies, where the distinction between peacemaking and peacebuilding is central to the discourse. In Table 2, we delineate a number of differences between peacemaking and peacebuilding.

As noted in Table 2, the term "peacemaking" refers to a set of actions that reduce the likelihood of violent episodes. In contrast, peacebuilding is designed to reduce structural violence. Peacemaking emphasizes nonviolent means while peacebuilding emphasizes socially just ends. Peacemaking tends to be reactive, arising from the threat or actual use of direct violence. Peacebuilding can be proactive, addressing long-term structural inequalities that may become antecedents of violent episodes. Peacemaking is temporal and spatial, satisfying the current interests of conflicted parties who occupy a particular geopolitical space. Peacebuilding is ubiquitous and less constrained by time and place. Peacemaking emphasizes the prevention of violence while peacebuilding emphasizes the promotion of social justice. Peacemaking may support the interests of the status quo while peacebuilding often threatens the social order.

Peacebuilding has cultural, political, and economic dimensions (Galtung, 1996). Culturally, peacebuilding requires the transformation of cultural narratives or beliefs that justify and

Table 2

Peacemaking	Peacebuilding
Reduces direct violence	Reduces structural violence
Emphasis on nonviolent means	Emphasis on socially just ends
Reactive	Proactive
Temporally and spatially constrained	Ubiquitous
Prevention of violent episodes	Promotion of social justice
Interest in the status quo	Threat to status quo

legitimize the dominance of one group over another. Politically, peacebuilding occurs when political systems that oppress people are transformed so that there are equal opportunities for political representation and voice. Peacebuilding includes transforming economic structures that exploit and deprive people of resources needed for optimal growth and development so that everyone has adequate material amenities such as decent housing, jobs, education, and health care. Although transformative processes are cultural and structural, progress in peacebuilding can be observed indirectly with measures that tap the degree to which there is equity in basic need satisfaction within and between societies. *Quality of life* indices are particularly useful and typically include mortality, lifespan, and levels of literacy (see, for example, United Nations Development Programme, 1997).

Peacebuilding is important in and of itself, to redress structural inequalities that deprive people of choices, health, and wealth. But peacebuilding also is essential to root out the structural bases of direct violence. A theme we advance in the present volume is that sustainable peace requires peacemaking efforts within the context of longer term efforts to promote macro level changes that produce more equitable social structures, that is, both peaceful means of dealing with differences and socially just ends. Indeed, from our perspective, peace is indivisible, including not only the absence of violence but also a continually crafted balance of structurally organized equality that satisfies basic human needs.

Peacebuilding shifts the emphasis from extreme individualism to institutional change and community based solutions, as exemplified in participatory action research, a methodology which places social transformation and empowerment at the center of the research process (Brydon-Miller, 1997; Lykes, 1997). Section IV deals with various conceptualizations of peacebuilding and applications throughout the world. Emphasis is placed on promoting human rights, Gandhian principles of nonviolent social change, the role of women as peacebuilders, and roles for psychologists as practitioners and policy change advocates.

The four-way model we introduce employs conceptual distinctions between direct and structural violence and between peacemaking and peacebuilding. In practice, however, direct and structural violence form a larger *system of violence*. Similarly, peacemaking and peacebuilding, while conceptually distinct, can be treated as an interlocking *system of peace*.

SYSTEMS OF VIOLENCE AND PEACE

Although it may be useful for peace psychologists to distinguish direct and structural violence, we are beginning to see more clearly a *circular relationship* between both types of violence, forming an interlocking system of violence. The system operates at various levels, from the interpersonal level to the large-scale violence of genocide as we illustrate with the following examples.

In intimate relations, for example, the direct violence of men on women continues worldwide, in part because women's low socioeconomic status constricts choices and keeps women in a position of vulnerability and dependency vis-à-vis men, a structurally violent condition that sets the stage for more episodes of direct violence. The cultural dimension is also present as violence is justified by patriarchal narratives about a "woman's place" (Bunch & Carillo, 1998).

At another level, genocide cannot be easily explained away as the resurfacing of ancient hatreds. Although a number of familiar psychological dynamics are at play in ethnicity-based genocide, including oppositional group identities, group polarization, and fear of one another, the deeper, structural roots also matter. For example, the genocide that took place in Rwanda and left nearly three-quarters of a million people dead can be traced back to colonial policies that gave preferential treatment to one group (Tutsis) over another group (Hutus), and by doing so produced a hierarchical arrangement in their society (Mays, Bullock, Rosenzweig, & Wessells, 1998). These differences are then exacerbated by contemporary structural forces such as crushing poverty, large class inequalities, pressure from the International Monetary Fund (making the poor even poorer), and a variety of others structural factors (Smith, 1998).

Not only does structural violence play a role in direct violence but the converse also holds, thereby completing the circle. For example, militarization, the degree to which nations rely on weapons, is treated in this volume as a form of structural violence. We appreciate that there is a large political constituency in the United States that embraces a robust military budget because it believes that the best way to ensure peace is through military strength. At the same time, militarism produces enormous profits for weapons developers and drains resources from other sectors of the economy that could satisfy human needs more productively and equitably. Moreover, the United States supplies more weapons to the world than any other country and most of the recipients are Third World countries that feel threatened by their neighbors. Like the United States, these Third World countries are pursuing security by accumulating weapons (Renner, 1998). In essence, militarization produces structural violence within the United States and provides the means by which internation rivalries can become deadly, organized, direct violence.

On a global scale, resources are distributed unevenly with the poverty in the global south contributing indirectly to drug-related crimes and deaths in the global north. Interdependence is apparent as poor farmers cultivate the coca plant in order to generate income to survive. On the demand side, drug traffickers in the global north find it far more lucrative to move drugs than to work at minimum wage jobs that offer no health care benefits or opportunities for advancement (Crosby & Van Soest, 1997).

Not only is violence systemic but peace processes also can be viewed from a systems perspective. Peacemaking, as exemplified by conflict resolution procedures, can be used to deal directly with part of a violent system, encouraging nonviolent dialogue instead of overt forms of violence. However, from our perspective, the deeper roots of these problems require an integration of peacemaking with peacebuilding. To root out the structural bases of these problems previously mentioned requires a transformation of the socioeconomic status of women worldwide, the elimination of militarism, and the elimination of disparities in wealth that divide people by ethnicity and geography. In short, problems of violence on any scale require the promotion of a system of peace that emphasizes the nonviolent management of differences combined with the pursuit of socially just ends.

In the last chapter of this volume, we revisit the four-way model and then delineate some perennial tensions in the field of peace psychology. We conclude with a discussion of the challenges that are likely to face peace psychologists throughout the twenty-first century, emphasizing the centrality of environmental sustainability (Winter, 1996) as we pursue structural and cultural changes that are capable of delivering the equitable satisfaction of human needs for current and future generations.

SECTION I

DIRECT VIOLENCE

Introduction by
Richard V. Wagner

Violence derives from conflict, but conflict does not inevitably result in violence. Conflict can often be constructive. Only under certain extreme conditions does conflict ultimately result in violence. Conflict, defined as "perceived divergence of interest, or a belief that the parties' . . . current aspirations cannot be achieved simultaneously" (Rubin, Pruitt, & Kim, 1994, p. 5), can be dealt with in a variety of ways, including cooperative problem solving, yielding by one of the parties, and inaction, as well as various nonviolent contentious tactics such as ingratiation, persuasive arguing, and threats. Alternatively, the conflict can be handled by violence.

There are certain preconditions for a violent response to conflict: (a) that a party care more about its own interests than about the interests of the other, a basic principle of the dual concern model of conflict (Blake & Mouton, 1979), and (b) that a party believe it will be successful if it acts violently in pursuit of its goals. In addition, there are factors which increase the probability that conflict will result in violence, among them the perception that nonviolent means will be ineffective, that violence will have few negative repercussions for the aggressor, and that violence will prevent the adversary from gaining an advantage if it were to initiate violence first. Furthermore, there are certain contextual factors that predispose a party to act violently, including social norms that condone violence and the availability of means (e.g., weapons) of executing a violent act.

In this first section, we consider direct violence, the most obvious, overt form of violence, perpetrated by one or more disputants directly upon those with whom they are in conflict. In our introductory chapter, we distinguished between direct violence and the structural violence that is built into the social, political, and economic institutions of a society. Direct violence requires no intervening social structures for the violence to occur. It is the violence we read and hear about daily. It is parents fighting, one spouse battering the other or their children; it is children beating up other children in school or gangs attacking customers at a gay bar; it is ethnic cleansing, it is terrorism, it is war.

Direct violence and structural violence (which is the subject of the succeeding section of this volume) are highly interdependent. The existence of structural violence, such as unequal distribution of resources or a corrupt political system, inevitably produces conflict, and often direct violence. People who live in substandard conditions and see themselves as unable to satisfy their needs in the face of a political system that they cannot otherwise influence, may resort to direct violence to address their needs. Often the process is circular: structural violence leading an oppressed group to direct violence, which in turn leads to further oppression to curb the direct violence. For example, if the political establishment feels threatened by the people protesting substandard living conditions, they may respond with further oppression to curb the direct violence.

There are three themes that appear in the majority of the chapters in this section: our ability to generalize from one level of analysis and one type of violence to another; the critical role that protecting one's identity plays in promoting violence; and the cultural values that influence violent action.

GENERALIZATION

In the introductory chapter, we stated that "peace psychology seeks to develop theories and practices aimed at the prevention and mitigation of destructive conflict, violence, domination, oppression, and exploitation." The authors of the chapters in this section engage in this process by presenting concepts and examples pertaining to violence in a variety of settings and at different levels of analysis, from the interpersonal to the international. It would be valuable to know to what extent the principles applied in one setting can be profitably generalized to other settings. Can we, for example, generalize from bullying on the playground to bullying in sub-Saharan Africa, or from anti-gay/lesbian hate crimes to ethnic cleansing?

Levinger and Rubin (1994) provide a helpful typology and set of principles that can guide us through the process of generalization. They suggest that all conflicts have some features in common, such as their derivation from perceived divergence of interests and the presence of a mixture of motives. However, in the case of the number of parties in the conflict and the number of issues involved, we should generalize with caution. When a conflict is between two people, determining the parties' interests may be quite simple; when the conflict is among nations, their interests may be quite complex and, further, may involve a number of constituencies, each with its own interrelated set of interests. It would, therefore, be extremely inappropriate to take a model developed from analyses of domestic disputes and apply it uncritically to international disputes.

IDENTITY

A second theme you will find in a number of the articles is the central role identity plays in conflict and violence. Abrahams, for example, notes that low self-esteem and self-efficacy are associated with wife batterers, and Staub asserts that one group devalues another in order to strengthen its own identity. Three chapters use social identity theory and its successors to explain conflict and violence: Murphy argues that social identity leads to bias in favor of one's own group, which in the case of gender is a background factor in anti-gay/lesbian violence; Niens and Cairns use self-categorization theory and relative deprivation theory as explanatory components for intrastate violence; and Druckman uses social identity and self-categorization theory to explain ways in which nationalistic sentiments can lead to war.

CULTURAL CONTEXT

The third theme incorporated in most of these chapters is that cultural norms provide the background for violence. Cultural norms and values are evident throughout: gender role expectations in the case of intimate violence, homophobia in anti-gay/lesbian violence, cultural devaluation and an "ideal of antagonism" in genocide, nationalistic sentiments in interstate conflict, and political and moral values in the use of weapons of mass destruction. Clearly, peace psychologists must understand the dynamics of conflict in a wide variety of contexts, from the interpersonal to the international levels of analysis.

OVERVIEW OF THE CHAPTERS ON DIRECT VIOLENCE

We begin this section focussing on conflict and violence at the most basic social level of analysis—two-person intimate relationships. In the first chapter, Naomi Abrahams argues that the major underlying issue in domestic violence is dominance and control. She describes various psychological factors involved—attitudes, behavior, and social learning—and then moves up a level of analysis to consider domestic violence in the context of family systems theory.

Bianca Cody Murphy analyzes anti-gay/lesbian violence in the United States. Many of the explanations she reviews, such as the authoritarian personality, frustration and scapegoating, and social identity theory, derive from earlier psychological analyses of racial and anti-semitic violence in the community. She includes an attitudinal analysis of the development of homophobic views and behavior. Then, like Abrahams, she steps beyond purely psychological analyses with a description of political and feminist perspectives on anti-gay/lesbian violence and proposes legal, cultural, and educational responses to such hate crimes.

Moving beyond the community, ethnic violence is the focal theme in Ulrike Niens and Ed Cairns' analysis of intrastate violence and Ervin Staub's examination of genocide and mass killing. Niens and Cairns describe how relative deprivation, social identity, and self-categorization theories help explain intrastate conflict and then they apply their analysis to the conflict in Northern Ireland. Staub uses a variety of constructs in his analysis of genocide, from individual processes such as just-world thinking, bystander apathy, and scapegoating to societal variables like traditions of obedience, unhealed group trauma, and an "ideology of antagonism."

Interstate conflict is addressed in Daniel Druckman's chapter on nationalism and war, and in Lucian Conway, Peter Suedfeld, and Philip Tetlock's chapter on how integrative complexity may influence, or be influenced by political decisions that lead to war and peace. Druckman considers basic needs underlying nationalist sentiments and discusses our understanding of how nationalist images may lead to war. He is acutely aware of the problems of levels of analysis, asking whether we understand how people transfer their sentiments from small membership groups to larger, national entities. Conway, Suedfeld, and Tetlock review the literature on integrative complexity, that is, the degree to which people understand multiple perspectives on a particular problem and are able to integrate those perspectives coherently. They list a variety of political contexts in which low integrative complexity has been associated with a drastic deterioration in interstate relations, and note the uncertainty about the role of low integrative complexity: is it a symptom or a cause of worsening relations?

Finally, Michael Britton's chapter on nuclear, biological, and chemical weapons of mass destruction discusses weaponry in the context of the massive mutual fear that developed during the Cold War. He asks how long it will be before there is universal recognition that weapons of mass destruction will ultimately make war obsolete.

I conclude this introduction with a caveat. Many of the articles acknowledge that psychological analysis provides only a part—perhaps a small part—of the explanation of direct violence. Niens and Cairns, for example, see psychology as "modest but critical" and recognize political, economic, and religious bases of intergroup violence. Similarly, Murphy acknowledges the importance of political explanations of anti-gay/lesbian violence. Small or large, psychology's contributions to understanding the bases of direct violence are relevant—as are all potential explanations—and therefore should be understood and further developed to the greatest extent possible.

CHAPTER 1

INTIMATE VIOLENCE

Naomi Abrahams

The prevalence of intimate violence has become frighteningly apparent: Current statistical estimates suggest that 28 percent of marital relationships in the United States include incidents of physical violence (Gelles & Straus, 1988; Straus & Gelles, 1990). Further, the rates of dating violence are at least as high (Gelles, 1997). Clearly, the magnitude of intimate violence suggests that a slap, punch, or kick within couples cannot be fully understood solely in terms of individual pathology, though it may be tempting to do so. While individual behavior is certainly shaped by psychological factors, it is simultaneously influenced by social structures such as the family, religion, law, and power relations particular to gender, race, and class. In this way, psychology's focus on the individual, and sociology's focus on groups and society, are both important in coming to terms with the awesome problem of intimate violence.

Consider the following case study of Lisa reported in Barnett and LaViollette (1993):

> I believe that you stay with your partner for better or for worse. I didn't know what "worse" was when I made that promise, but I promised. I believe my husband loves me, and I'm starting to believe he could kill me.

> I'm not sure how long I should stay and how "bad" is "too bad." I know I don't believe I should be hit. But I do believe if my relationship is a mess, I should stay to help make it better. (p. 2)

Through her statement, Lisa reveals a discourse surrounding gender and marriage; namely, that it is important to work on a marriage, even if that marriage involves violence. Her experience as an individual is wrapped up in cultural expectations surrounding commitment in relationships. Linking the individual and social structure is important in making sense of intimate violence.

Peace psychology may contribute to understanding and transforming intimate violence because it traverses difficult bounds between individual, organizational, and societal levels of analysis in addressing conflict and violence. At its core, intimate violence rips away security, identity, and self-determination. Intimate violence often centers on power and control over another person. Let's take a look at the case history of Betty and Henry reported by Barnett and LaViollette (1993):

> Betty and Henry were married and had a 14-month-old daughter, Melissa. Henry was self-employed but unmotivated. When Betty's independence got the better of him, he be-

came abusive. Betty had gone to work on numerous occasions with bruises on her face and arms. For the most part, nobody talked about what was happening. (It is often easier for friends and family to deny abuse, to minimize the severity of discord, and to ignore evidence.)

Betty's friends and financial security were a threat to Henry. He became more controlling, and he threatened to kill her if she tried to leave. His obsession culminated in Betty's 2-week "confinement." He stayed at home to watch her. Eventually, he needed money and took her to the bank to make a withdrawal from her savings account. Betty and Melissa escaped to the Long Beach Battered Women's Shelter.

Henry threatened to sue Betty for custody of the baby unless he was allowed to visit her. A third-party visitation was set up by the shelter through her attorney. No one at the shelter felt good about this arrangement, but everyone felt compelled to go ahead with the plan because of the legal ramifications of noncompliance. Betty and the baby were to go to her attorney's office accompanied by a male friend of Betty's (the father of one of her friends). While they were in the parking lot, Henry grabbed the baby and told Betty to get into his car or she would never see Melissa again.

Betty's body was not discovered for several months. Henry was charged with murder. He had taken Betty to an isolated spot in the desert where he beat and shot her. Her body had to be identified by her dental records. Melissa had been in the car.

At Henry's trial, one of his previous wives admitted to the abuse she had experienced at his hands. She was still afraid of him. Henry was eventually convicted of second-degree murder. Betty's last words to one of the authors as she left to meet Henry were: "If I don't come back, it is because he killed me." (p. 49–50)

Nearly 700 husbands and boyfriends are killed by their girlfriends or wives each year,

whereas more than 1,500 wives and girlfriends are killed by husbands and boyfriends each year (U.S. Department of Justice, 1995). Murder constitutes an extreme form of intimate violence: it represents the tip of the iceberg of a problem that is widespread in intimate relationships.

Since peace psychology identifies and promotes conditions that favor human needs for security, identity, and self-determination, peace psychology can and should concern itself with the daunting problem of intimate violence. Research on violence for the twenty-first century must develop a language that adequately addresses *power relations* as they relate to intimate violence. Psychology must be more closely melded with sociology in research on intimate violence. In so doing, we will be afforded the opportunity for a more integrated response to the questions: What are the dynamics underlying an adequate explanation for intimate violence? What can be done to reduce intimate violence?

For more than twenty years, researchers, activists, and survivors have struggled with the dynamics underlying intimate violence. Psychologists and sociologists have contributed to an understanding of intimate violence. In this chapter, I review approaches to intimate violence within the fields of psychology and sociology. I discuss the problems with early research, particularly in the field of psychology. In addition, I examine ways in which dominance and control are central to addressing intimate violence. For the purpose of this chapter, I focus on physical violence among adults. Physical violence is one form of intimate violence along with emotional abuse and sexual abuse. In addition, child abuse within families is a huge problem in its own right. I narrow the focus here not because other forms of intimate violence are less important, but simply to allow some depth in my discussion of this aspect of intimate violence.

PSYCHOLOGICAL APPROACHES TO INTIMATE VIOLENCE

There are a variety of approaches within the field of psychology to intimate violence. In particular, intimate violence has been studied in relation to abnormal psychology and personality theories, behavioral and attitudinal approaches, and social learning theory.

Abnormal Psychology and Personality Approaches

Early psychological research tended to emphasize the unique, abnormal characteristics of individuals who engaged in intimate violence. For example, physically assaultive husbands were deemed sadistic (Pizzey, 1974) or suffering from brain lesions resulting in sporadic outbursts of violence (Elliot, 1977). Sometimes, researchers suggested that battered women were masochistic (Snell, Rosenwald, & Robey, 1964). In part, early research relied on small samples of violent relationships with particularly skewed groups, such as men who had been convicted of assault. And, violence was understood to be a rare occurrence in families. Most of the research, past and present, has focused on violence against women by men in heterosexual relationships.

Within the realm of psychological literature, recent research benefits from the understanding that violence cannot be adequately explained solely on the basis of personality traits. While some researchers still look to personality disorders, they explain only a fairly small proportion, estimated at 10 percent, of cases of intimate violence (Straus, 1980). Clinical research is more likely than survey research to empha-

size the characteristics of individuals that might lead to violence. Hamberger and Hastings (1986), for example, suggest that assaultive men may have borderline personalities, they may be anti-social, and/or may suffer passive-dependent/compulsive disorders. In a later comparative study of violent and non-violent men, Hamberger and Hastings (1991) report that non-violent men are more comfortable in intimate relationships and experience greater control over their emotional states. Other researchers report low self-esteem among men who batter their wives (Neidig, Friedman, & Collins, 1986), as well as feelings of inadequacy and powerlessness (Weitzman & Dreen, 1982). Dutton (1995) finds that borderline personality disorder is positively related to assaultive behavior among men in intimate relationships. He argues that men who experience absent, abusive, or cold parental upbringing develop fear and anger with respect to attachment, resulting in borderline personalities as well as intimate abuse. One exciting area of research in psychology looks at a variety of different profiles of abusers. Dutton and Golant (1995) outline a variety of types of physically assaultive men. One type of physically abusive man they discuss is the psychopathic assaulter who experiences no remorse for the abuse he inflicts and who is often violent outside as well as inside the family. Another type of abuser is overcontrolled, emotionally withdrawn, and passive-aggressive. Finally, cyclical abusers are emotionally volatile and experience an extreme need to control intimacy.

The growing recognition of a variety of psychological profiles of batterers will lead to more sophisticated, and hopefully effective, remedies for violence. In addition, the psychological complexity of battery contributes to sociological research, thereby bridging the gap between psychological and sociological approaches to intimate violence. For example, recent sociological research on the widespread practice of arresting batterers shows that only some types of batterers are likely to be deterred by arrest. Indeed, arrest may provoke further violence among batterers who are not easily shamed and who commit other types of violent acts (Sherman, 1992). In this manner, it is important to combine an analysis of psychological profiles of batterers with deterrence strategies in order to implement effective policies for reducing intimate violence.

Behavioral and Attitudinal Approaches

In addition to considerations of self-esteem, self-efficacy, and personality disorders as contributors to intimate violence, Riggs and O'Leary (1989) have considered behavioral and attitudinal predictors of violence. They suggest that acceptance of violence, past use of violence, partner aggression, and relationship conflict are important predictors of violent behavior in intimate relationships. Another important behavioral correlate is alcohol consumption. Considerable research has demonstrated a correlation between alcohol abuse and family violence (Coleman & Straus, 1983; Gelles, 1974; Leonard & Jacob, 1988). On the other hand, Song (1996), in her study of wife beating in Korean immigrant communities, found that alcohol consumption had no relationship to rates of violence. Instead, traditional cultural values predicted greater levels of violence. Indeed, the cultural expectations associated with alcohol may have a greater impact on behavior than the drug itself. From his examination of survey, police, cross-cultural, and experimental research, Gelles (1993a) also argues that alcohol does not cause family violence. In particular, cross-cultural and experimental research indicate divergent behavioral outcomes from

alcohol consumption. It seems that as it relates to aggression, the effects of alcohol are less physiological than they are based on social expectations regarding cultural definitions of the effects of alcohol. As Gelles writes: "In the end, the social expectations about drinking and drinking behavior in our society teach people that if they want to avoid being held responsible for their violence, they can either drink before they are violent or at least say they were drunk," (1993a, p. 84).

Behavior is organized and explained in relation to the culture in which it exists. In her work on behavioral cycles of violence, Lenore Walker recognizes that behavioral patterns exist within particular cultural contexts (Walker, 1999). Walker (1979) outlines a behavioral cycle that she calls the "cycle of violence" to explain intimate violence. The cycle includes a tension-building phase, an acute battering phase, and a tranquil, nonviolent phase. During the tension-building phase, the abuser may engage in psychological and/or relatively minor physical assaults. The victim of assault, generally a woman, "walks on eggshells" to assuage her partner and prevent an escalation of violence. Escalation is inevitable, however, and at some point, an explosion of violence occurs, during which time the victim has no control over ending the violence and generally feels trapped. Following the acute battering stage, the abuser is often remorseful and loving in the tranquil phase:

> During the third phase, the battered woman may join with the batterer in sustaining the illusion of bliss. She convinces herself, too, that it will never happen again; her lover can change, she tells herself. This "good" man, who is gentle and sensitive and nurturing toward her now, is the "real" man, the man she married, the man she loves. Many battered women believe that they are the sole support of the batterer's emotional

stability and sanity, the one link their men have to the normal world. Sensing the batterer's isolation and despair, they feel responsible for his well-being. (Walker, 1989, p. 45)

The inherent loss of control of physical safety through the cycle of violence leads to a type of Post Traumatic Stress Disorder, according to Walker. Battered women may stay in violent relationships in part because they feel they have at least some control in the situation they are in. Escape would hurl them into the unknown. The psychological effects of the cycle of violence also help explain why battered women kill their abusers. Walker describes Battered Women's Syndrome as a form of Post Traumatic Stress Disorder triggered by intimate violence in which battered women kill their abusive partners. Walker is quick to point out that psychological dynamics cannot be understood apart from the societal sanctioning of intimate violence and the lack of adequate protection or response from the state (i.e., police). Battered women are trapped not only in a psychological sense, but also through the lack of support they receive culturally, economically, and from the criminal justice system.

Social Learning

Social learning provides another important area of research into intimate violence. Children who observe violence and/or are victims of violence in their family of origin are more likely than others to engage in violent behavior or to become victims of violence as adults (Herrenkohl, Herrenkohl, & Toeder, 1983; Steinmetz, 1977). In other words, through modeling, individuals may develop an acceptance of, and propensity to engage in, violence (O'Leary, 1993). The effects of witnessing violence as a child are more likely to predict violence for men than

for women (Straus, 1980; Ulbrich & Huber, 1981). However, Kaufman and Zigler (1993), Straus (1980), and O'Leary (1988) warn that the effects of observing violence are easily overestimated. Growing up in violent households does not determine that an individual will become violent. As a result, understanding intimate violence must extend beyond an modeling approach.

While research on the psychological processes involved in intimate violence are important, the problem of intimate violence spills beyond individual characteristics and dispositions and relationship conflict into social structure. In order to understand what ties people to violent relationships, it is important to consider societal constructions of the family and gender. To fully explore the structural dimensions of intimate violence, sociological approaches to intimate violence must be considered.

SOCIOLOGICAL APPROACHES TO INTIMATE VIOLENCE

Within sociology, there are two primary and conflicting approaches to intimate violence. One approach emphasizes the construction of the family as a system and as a social institution. As Gelles points out, "The family, with the exception of the military in times of war and the police, is society's most violent institution" (1993b, p. 35). The other approach centers on gender inequality. I discuss each approach in turn.

Family Systems

What is it about the family as an institution that fosters high rates of violence? Gelles and Straus (1979, 1988) suggest that a number of characteristics of families contribute to intimate violence. In part, contemporary American culture encourages very high expectations for intimacy within romantic relationships and families. High expectations regarding family intimacy may also engender disappointment over unmet desires. Violence may result from frustration over a sense of a lack of reciprocation of rewards within the family (Gelles, 1983).

Research on courtship violence suggests that dating relationships contain somewhat higher levels of violence than do marital relationships (Gelles, 1997). Perhaps even more disturbing is the finding by Henton et al. (1983) that one-quarter of victims of intimate violence and a little less than one-third of offenders viewed physical violence as a sign of love. Clearly, cultural definitions of romantic love and family intimacy feed into high rates of intimate violence.

Intimacy may combine with stress to produce intimate violence in families. Stress is an inherent outcome of ever-changing family life as families grow throughout the life course (Gelles & Straus, 1979). Stress experienced outside of the family may be projected onto the family. One source of stress is financial: Intimate violence is more common in low-income households, and in families where men are unemployed or employed part-time (Prescott & Letko, 1977; Rounsaville, 1978).

Further, societal norms of family privacy also contribute to violence. What goes on in the family is easily hidden from public scrutiny (Gelles & Straus, 1979). Gelles (1983) suggests that people engage in family violence because the rewards of violence (for example, producing a desired result from a family member, gaining control) outweigh the costs of violence such as negative labeling in the larger community.

Straus (1973) argues that families operate as systems that feed off of the normalization of violence in the larger culture and minimize, ignore, and thereby stabilize violence that occurs within the family itself.

Gender Inequality

For many feminist researchers, the family as an institution is also deemed to contribute to intimate violence, though here we begin to touch on one of the major divisions within sociological schools of thought regarding intimate violence. Language differences reveal divergent perspectives: Family systems theory sociologists write about "domestic violence" whereas feminist researchers write about "battered wives" and "battered women." Feminist researchers emphasize gender inequality as the basis for violence (Dobash & Dobash, 1979; Yllo & Bogard, 1988). As Yllo writes: "Violence within the family is as complex as it is disturbing . . . Despite this complexity, the most fundamental feminist insight into all of this is quite simple: Domestic violence cannot be adequately understood unless gender and power are taken into account" (1993, p. 47). In essence, intimate violence is one manifestation of patriarchy. Patriarchy, or male domination, is deeply encoded in religious traditions as well as other cultural expectations that emphasize men's dominance and women's submission. Social definitions of love, nurturance, and caretaking encourage women to remain in violent homes (Barnett & LaViollette, 1993; Pagelow, 1981). This encouragement occurs both in the form of women's identities and perceptions of violence as well as in social systems surrounding women such as family, clergy, and other support systems in women's lives. Indeed, cross-cultural research suggests that cultural expectations condoning marital violence and emphasizing gender inequality contribute to high rates of intimate violence (Fawcett, Heise, Isita-Espejel, & Pick, 1999; Horne, 1999). Around the globe, high rates of wife-beating occur in patriarchal societies (Walker,

1999). From the many thousands of women burned alive by in-laws when dowry endowments are not deemed high enough in India (Narasimhan, 1994), to Chilean rates of intimate violence against woman reaching 60 percent of heterosexual relationships (Larrain, 1993), wife-beating is deeply enmeshed in the "common sense" of patriarchal cultures.

The economic structuring of society is woven into cultural traditions supporting intimate violence against women in families (Dobash & Dobash, 1992). In Western industrialized nations, women are still primarily responsible for domestic labor including child care (Berk, 1985; Hochschild, 1989) and are more likely to have interrupted career trajectories to care for small children (Huber & Spitze, 1983; Steil, 1995) while being paid less than men for the work that they do in the paid labor force across racial categories (Thornborrow & Sheldon, 1995). Interviews with women who are survivors of intimate violence indicate that economic dependence is one important bind to domestic assault (Barnett & LaViolette, 1993; Pagelow, 1981). In this way, patriarchal structures of the family and labor force contribute to wife-battering. One avenue for addressing the problem of intimate violence involves promoting economic as well as domestic equality.

At the same time, some research suggests that when husbands have lower status educationally and occupationally than their wives they are more likely to engage in intimate violence (Gelles, 1974; Hornung, McCullough, & Sugimoto, 1981). In this case, wife battery may provide a means to control and retaliate against women for infringing upon men's position of dominance. Economic, cultural, law enforcement, and legal empowerment of women must operate in conjunction with one another to achieve

meaningful change with regards to intimate violence.

The lack of support for women in situations of intimate violence from the criminal justice system relates to a disjuncture between cultural meanings of violence and legal codes prohibiting domestic assault (Ferraro & Pope, 1993; Abrahams, 1998). Despite important legal changes as well as growing economic resources from the state to aid victims of intimate violence in the United States, battered women still experience a lack of support from the police, courts, and support services (Barnett & LaViolette, 1993; Hoff, 1990). As a result, battered women are left in violent homes in states of fear. Feminist research on battered women also reveals that fear holds women in families in which they experience intimate violence (Hoff, 1990). This fear is far from irrational. Indeed, the greatest likelihood of serious injury and death occurs after women have left their violent partners (Saltzman et al., 1990). Women are not adequately protected from violence by the state. In particular, Hispanic and African-American women are likely to be discouraged from calling on the police or Anglo-dominated social services for protection (Ashbury, 1993; Gondolf, Fisher, & McFerron, 1988). As a result, continued educational work with law enforcement and court officials is necessary to transform the cultural "common sense" that contains racist and sexist beliefs and practices.

One area of controversy in intimate violence involves the question of violence against men by women. While some family systems sociologists engage in national surveys and find virtually identical levels of violence between men and women in families (Berk, Berk, Loseke, & Rauma, 1983; Gelles & Straus, 1988), hospital, police, survey, and homicide data all indicate that women are harmed by intimate violence in vastly greater proportions than are men. As Gelles writes:

> Unfortunately, almost all of those who try to make the case that there are as many battered men as battered women tend to omit or reduce to a parenthetical phrase the fact that no matter how much violence there is or who initiates the violence, women are as much as 10 times more likely than men to be injured in acts of domestic violence.
>
> It is quite clear that men are struck by their wives. It is also clear that because these men are typically larger than their wives and usually have more social resources at their command, that they do not have as much physical or social damage inflicted on them as is inflicted on women. (1997, p. 93)

Thus, while the issue of violence against men has been controversial and heated within sociological discourse and popular culture, the fact that men encounter violence inflicted by women does not erase gendered power relations of intimate violence. Still, it is important to recognize the reality that men are beaten, and that gender is not the sole determinant of violent behavior.

MOVING INTO THE TWENTY-FIRST CENTURY: EXPANDING THE DISCOURSE

Feminist research on intimate violence contributes a great deal to an understanding of the patriarchal structures that produce intimate violence. Clearly, cultural constructions of gender play a central role in such violence. Gender is not, however, the entire explanatory framework necessary for intimate violence. Men are sometimes victims of intimate violence in heterosexual couples. And, violence occurs in gay and lesbian relationships (Letellier, 1994; Renzetti & Miley, 1996). While international perspectives on intimate violence highlight the importance of gender inequality (Walker, 1999), we must both acknowledge the importance of gender and avoid the insistence that gender is the only important dynamic underlying intimate violence.

Further, this new discourse must somehow bind more adequately sociological and psychological approaches to violence. That is, psychological factors contributing to violence must be understood in a sociocultural context. For example, Dutton (1994) takes us in the wrong direction when he suggests that gay and lesbian violence demonstrates the explanatory power of psychological rather than social-structural factors (such as gender) in intimate violence. A strictly psychological approach to intimate violence is akin to attempting to solve the problems of war through personality theories and counseling. No doubt, psychological processes are important in making sense of intimate violence, but psychological processes are wrapped in cultural practices and power relation structures.

How can we expand the discourse? Renzetti (1997) provides an example, integrating power relations and social structure in her discussion of internalized homophobia as it relates to violence in gay and lesbian couples. In this regard, she writes:

> Internalized homophobia occurs when gay men and lesbians accept heterosexual society's negative evaluations of them and incorporate them into their self concepts . . . Clinicians report that internalized homophobia causes homosexuals to experience lowered self-esteem, feelings of powerlessness, obsessive closeting of sexual orientation, denial of difference between themselves and heterosexuals, and self-destructive behavior such as substance abuse. It may also lead to aggression against members of one's own group, which could take the form of partner abuse. Thus, societal homophobia (a

social structural variable) generates internalized homophobia (a psychological variable), which, in turn, may lead to partner abuse in same-sex relationships. (1997, p. 290)

Alternatively, or in addition, the psychological profile of a dependent and controlling batterer across lines of sexual preference and gender may also represent individual-level manifestations of social structural values, that is, socialization in cultural traditions valuing control and dominance.

Bodies are the vessels through which systems of inequality are achieved and maintained. Bodies that are hacked apart and stomped on interpersonally and institutionally produce and reinforce inequality. At the same time, violence cannot be solely understood in relation to power. That is, psychological factors interact with sociological variables in relation to intimate violence. Sociological discourse is not easily melded with that of psychology, and yet, an expanded discourse on intimate violence requires just such a move. The danger in relying too heavily on psychological approaches to intimate violence is that it misses the "big picture," the social structures in and through which people act. On the other hand, the danger in relying solely on sociological explanations for violence is that it may overgeneralize structural categories as explanations for violence and miss out on individual-level variables that contribute to violent behavior in intimate relationships. The problem of intimate violence requires that we develop a new, integrated language for explaining and understanding the dynamics underlying such violence: a language that weaves together psychological and sociological approaches to intimate violence.

CHAPTER 2

ANTI-GAY/LESBIAN VIOLENCE IN THE UNITED STATES

Bianca Cody Murphy

During the Gulf War, a Los Angeles delicatessen owned by an Arab-American was set ablaze. Before igniting the fire the arsonists scribbled a message on a wall "You Fuckin' Arab, go home."

On December 19, 1986, a group of white teenagers in Howard Beach shouting "There's niggers on the boulevard. Let's kill them," chased three black men. One escaped, another was severely beaten, and a third was beaten and while trying to escape his pursuers he was run over by car on the Belt Parkway.

In 1990, in Madison, Wisconsin, unidentified vandals smashed the windows and cut the brake lines of a bus that was supposed to take Jewish children to a day camp. The sabotage was discovered but the climate of anti-Semitism became so dangerous in Madison that armed police had to be stationed outside local synagogues during Rosh Hashanah.

HATE CRIMES

Violent acts, such as those described above by Jack Levin and Jack McDevitt (1993), are often called *hate crimes*. "Hate crimes are words or actions intended to harm or intimidate an individual because of her or his membership in a minority group; they include violent assaults, murder, rape, and property crimes motivated by prejudice, as well as threats of violence and other acts of intimidation" (Finn & McNeil, 1987, p. 2). In the United States, hate crimes are committed against racial, ethnic, religious, and sexual minorities. According to official reports, racial bias results in approximately 60 percent of all hate crimes in the United States, with African-Americans being the most vulnerable to hate crimes. Crimes committed against people because of their religious affiliation rank second, while crimes committed against people because of their sexual orientation rank third. It should be noted that according to FBI statistics, most hate crimes based on religion are property crimes directed at religious institutions, i.e., vandalism of synagogues, churches, and cemeteries (Garofalo, 1997). Formal reports from the Department of Justice and other law enforcement agencies as well as informal reports from such groups as the Southern Poverty Law Center's Klanwatch, the Anti-Defamation League, and the National Coalition of Anti-Violence Programs indicate that hate and bias crimes and acts of violence are on the rise.

Hate violence is *a form of terrorism*. Hate violence traumatizes not only the direct victim but all members of the targeted group. Richard Berk, Elizabeth Boyd, and Karl Hamner (1992) note that a key ingredient of hate-motivated violence is the "symbolic status of the victim" (p. 127). As Greg Herek points out, bias crimes "are especially serious because they potentially victimize an entire class of people . . . they assail the victim's identity and intimidate other group members" (1989, p. 948).

ANTI-GAY/LESBIAN HATE CRIMES: OVERT, DIRECT, EPISODIC VIOLENCE

In Nashville, Tennessee vandals ransacked the home of a gay minister, scrawling "homo" and "fag" on his possessions. (National Gay and Lesbian Task Force, 1989)

In Los Angeles, a man yelling "sick mother-fucker" threw a beaker of acid into the face of a lesbian employee of the local Gay and Lesbian Community Services Center. (National Gay and Lesbian Task Force, 1986)

A 21-year-old University of Wyoming student was pistol whipped and then left lashed to a fence in the near freezing cold outside of Laramie. He was found after 10 hours and died after five days in a coma.

Gay men and lesbian women, as well as other sexual minorities, including bisexual and transgendered men and women, are frequent targets of hate crimes in the United States. The Southern Poverty Law Center has estimated that gay men and lesbians are six times as likely to be physically attacked as Jews and Hispanics in America, and twice as likely as African Americans. Valerie Jenness and Kendal Broad note: "By many accounts, violence motivated by homophobia and heterosexism represents the most visible, violent, and culturally legitimated type of 'hate crime' in this country" (1994, p. 402). (See Comstock, 1991, for a good historical review of the ebbs and flows of anti-gay/lesbian violence in the United States.)

Official statistics on hate crimes are an inaccurate measure of anti-gay lesbian violence. Many gay men and lesbian women do not report verbal harassment or physical violence against them to the authorities because they fear that they will be subjected to *secondary victimization* at the hands of police or others who may learn of their sexual orientation and subject the victim to a second round of mistreatment (Herek & Berrill, 1992). Greg Herek, Roy Gillis, Jeanine Cogan, and Eric Glunt (1997) found that while approximately two-thirds of lesbian and gay victims of non-bias crimes reported the incident to law enforcement authorities, only about one-third of the hate crime victims did so. In a study on sexual orientation hate crimes in Los Angeles, Edward Dunbar (1998) reported that gay and lesbian people of color were both more likely to be victimized and less likely to report the hate act than European white gay men and lesbian women.

On November 11, 1996, a young gay teenage boy, who had just come out to a friend earlier that morning, was verbally harassed and physically assaulted by three youths as he walked home from school. He sustained injuries to his neck, head, and chest from being kicked, punched, and spit upon for being a "sissy" and "a fucking fag." He told his parents that he received the injuries during a soccer game. (National Coalition of Anti-Violence Programs, 1997)

In El Paso, Texas, a gay man was assaulted by his cousin, brother, and father during a wedding reception because of his sexual orientation. The man drove himself to the hospital for x-rays and emergency treatment. When asked why he was there, he told a male nurse what had happened and was advised not to disclose his sexual orientation to anyone else at the hospital because "they won't treat you right." The victim declined to report either incident to the police or hospital administration. (National Coalition of Anti-Violence Programs, 1997)

Since official statistics only record those who have reported the attack, many researchers survey samples of gay and lesbian communities to determine the rates of hate violence. Reviewing these surveys, Greg Herek (1989) reports as many as 92 percent of lesbian women and gay men responded that they have been the targets of anti-gay verbal abuse or threats, and as many as 24 percent report physical attacks because of their sexual orientation. In a survey of Sacramento-area adults, Herek, et al (1997) found that, since age 16, 11 percent had experienced assault with a weapon, based on their sexual orientation; 14 percent had experienced assault without a weapon; 17 percent vandalism; 45 percent had been threatened with violence; 32 percent had been chased or followed; 33 percent had objects thrown at them; and the overwhelming majority had been verbally harassed. However, Herek and his colleagues (Herek & Berrill, 1992; Herek, Gillis, Cogan, & Glunt, 1997) note the methodological problems of these types of self-report surveys, including memory limitations, difficulties in question interpretation, and variations in how one decides if a crime was motivated by sexual orientation. Furthermore, most studies of anti-gay/lesbian violence have adults as their subjects. (For a discussion of violence against lesbian and gay youth see Hershberger and D'Augelli, 1995.)

CHARACTERISTICS OF ANTI-GAY/ LESBIAN HATE VIOLENCE

A number of studies have been conducted to understand the nature of hate crimes. These studies have focused on the characteristics of the perpetrators and the circumstances in which hate crimes occur.

1. The perpetrators of anti-gay/lesbian violence (and most hate crimes) are pre-dominately male teenagers and young adults (Herek et al., 1997; LeBlanc, 1991). In a survey of almost 500 community college students, Karen Franklin (1998) found that 18 percent of the men said that they had physically assaulted or threatened someone they thought was gay or lesbian compared to 4 percent of the women. Thirty-two percent of the men and 17 percent of the women said that they were guilty of verbal harassment.

2. Anti-gay/lesbian violence frequently happens in groups (Comstock, 1991; Garofalo & Martin, 1993). Groups increase violence through social contagion (LeBon, 1896) and deindividuation (Festinger, Pepitone, & Newcomb, 1952; Zimbardo, 1970). People in groups don't feel personally responsible for their behavior—often thinking, "It is the group, not me, who is doing this."

3. The targets of anti-gay and lesbian attacks are often unknown to the perpetrator and chosen at random (Garofalo & Martin, 1993; Lane, 1990). This randomness may make it harder for the person to cope with the consequences than if he or she was a victim of some other crime. Victims may feel that there is nothing they could have done to prevent the attack, especially since they were attacked for something over which they feel they have no control and which may be a key aspect of their personal identity—their sexual orientation (Garnetts, Herek, & Levy, 1990; Herek, Gillis, Cogan, & Glunt, 1997).

4. Anti-gay/lesbian violence is particularly brutal. Kevin Berrill, formerly the director of the Anti-Violence Project of the National Gay and Lesbian Task Force (NGLTF), reports that homosexual murder victims are less likely to be shot

than to be "stabbed a dozen or more times, mutilated and strangled" (Miller & Humphreys, 1980, cited in Berrill, 1992, p. 25). The director of Victim Services at Bellevue Hospital in New York City has stated that "attacks against gay men were the most heinous and brutal I encountered. They frequently involved torture, cutting, mutilation and beating, and showed the absolute intent to rub out the human being because of his [sexual] preference" (M. Mertz, cited in Berrill, 1992, p. 25).

STRUCTURAL VIOLENCE AGAINST GAY MEN AND LESBIAN WOMEN

But overt acts of violence against lesbian women and gay men are only the most visible and heinous offenses in a pattern of discrimination and oppression. Gay men and lesbian women face *structural violence* as well as direct episodic violence. The structural violence against gay men and lesbian women is the result of heterosexism. Herek (1992) defines *heterosexism* as "an ideological system that denies, denigrates, and stigmatizes any nonheterosexual form of behavior, identity, relationship, or community" (p. 89). Herek distinguishes between psychological heterosexism which is manifested "in individual attitudes and behaviors" and *cultural heterosexism* which is manifested "in societal customs and institutions, such as religion and the legal system" (p. 89). It is this cultural heterosexism that results in structural violence against lesbian women and gay men.

As a result of cultural heterosexism, gay men, lesbian women, and other sexual minorities suffer *discrimination* in many areas, including housing and employment.

Margarethe Cammemeyer, a Bronze-Star winner and 28-year military veteran, was dis-

missed from the army despite a stellar record of service to her country (Cathcart, 1998).

Sherry Barone faced a cold-hearted cemetery which refused to include the epitaph "life partner" on the tombstone of her late partner, Cynthia Friedman, despite a legally executed request by Cynthia to do so. (Cathcart, 1998)

Only ten states currently offer *civil rights protections* to lesbian women and gay men. In most states, they have no legal recourse if they are discriminated against. In the last 20 years, with the rise of the gay rights movement, there have been attempts to pass legislation that would protect gay and lesbian civil rights. However, for every effort to increase protections for gay and lesbian civil rights, there have been countermoves to take them away. A recent Vatican statement to U.S. bishops supports discrimination against gay men and lesbian women and urges Catholics to oppose the passage of civil rights for gay men and lesbian women. In 1992, the state of Colorado passed a referendum which prohibits the state and all its agencies from acting on any claim of discrimination by a lesbian or gay man. (Note that the Supreme Court has issued an injunction against it.) That same year, a stronger initiative in Oregon stating that public institutions including the schools "shall assist in setting a standard for Oregon's youth that recognizes homosexuality . . . *as abnormal, wrong, unnatural and perverse and . . . to be discouraged and avoided*" [italics added] was defeated but received support from 44 percent of the voters. And, in 1998, opponents of lesbian/gay civil rights successfully sought to repeal a gay civil rights law in Maine.

Not only do gay men and lesbian women have few laws to protect them from discrimination, but many laws themselves are discriminatory. Gary Comstock (1991) points out that U.S. laws have enabled legalized violence against homosexuals. In the past, *sodomy laws* made same-gendered sex punishable by the death penalty. Although capital punishment for same-sex relations was removed from the books and corporal punishment is no longer in use, engaging in same-gender sexual acts is still illegal in 22 states. In 1986, the Supreme Court upheld the right of states to prosecute adults for engaging in consensual sexual acts with each other in the privacy of their own home (*Bowers vs. Hardwick,* 1986).

In addition to legal sanctions against lesbians and gays for engaging in same sex acts, there are other *discriminatory laws.* Gay men and lesbian women have no legal right to marry. Laws prohibit them from disclosing their sexual orientation in the military. They can be denied family health insurance policies and visiting rights in hospitals since they are not legally "family members."

SOME PSYCHOLOGICAL EXPLANATIONS OF ANTI-GAY/ LESBIAN VIOLENCE

Psychologists have a long history of attempting to understand what causes prejudice and violence. These approaches have focused primarily on intrapsychic and interpersonal psychological processes.

Authoritarian Personalities

In keeping with psychology's emphasis on understanding individual behaviors, one of the earliest explanations of prejudice was based on individual personality. People who were prejudiced shared characteristics referred to as an *authoritarian personality* (Adorno, Frenkel-Brunswik, Levinson, & Sanford, 1950). The characteristics included a submissiveness to the authority of the ingroup, a tendency to punish others who violated conventional values, preoccupation with domi-

nance, exaggerated concern with sex and repression of sexual feeling, and rigid thinking. While it may be argued that the leaders of organized hate groups may demonstrate these "authoritarian" characteristics, very little research has been done on the perpetrators of anti-gay/lesbian hate crimes.

Frustration, Scapegoating, and Realistic Group Conflict

Another early psychological explanation of prejudice and aggression comes from the work of John Dollard and his colleagues at Yale University (Dollard, Doob, Miller, Mowrer, & Sears, 1939). They suggested a theory of *scapegoating* or *displaced aggression:* Frustrated people often direct their anger toward members of another group. Racial prejudice, for example, was seen as related to economic insecurity. Between 1882 and 1930, there were more lynchings of African-Americans in the South in years when cotton prices were low (Hovland & Sears, 1940).

Related to the frustration-aggression theory, is Muzafer Sherif's (1966) *realistic conflict theory* (RCT). The realistic group conflict theory can be seen in Levin and McDevitt's (1993) description of zero-sum thinking. "They view two or more individuals or groups as striving for the same scarce goals, with the success of one automatically implying a reduced probability that others will attain their goals . . . Zero-sum thinking engages the individual in a competitive struggle to upgrade himself and downgrade others" (pp. 54–55), which can set the scene for hate violence. For example, Jeanine Cogan (1996) suggests that marginalized groups, the poor, immigrants, ethnic minorities, and sexual minorities are being scapegoated by society-at-large for the growing disparity between the very rich and the rest of society in the United States. "The victims are blamed for the offender's personal or economic plight" (Spillane, 1994, p. 245).

Social Identity Theory and Ingroup Bias

According to *social identity theory* (Tajfel & Turner, 1986), people have both an individual and a social identity. Seeing one's group as superior increases personal self-esteem. People have a tendency to enhance their self-esteem by evaluating more favorably the groups to which they belong (ingroups) compared to other groups (outgroups). Simply being placed in a group can create ingroup bias. Michael Billig and Henri Tajfel (1973) found that even if the us-them categorization is based on trivial issues, such as the toss of a coin, people still favor their own group.

Ingroup bias means favoring one's own group, but it can also, although not always, mean devaluing the other. A sense of belonging and comradeship increases when there is a common enemy. Studies have shown that those ingroup members who have an experience which lowers their self esteem, are more likely to highly rate the ingroup and denigrate the outgroup (Cialdini & Richardson, 1980). Bias against the outgroup is also more common if there are social supports for degrading the outgroup. In the United States there are social, religious, political, and legal supports for prejudice against gay men and lesbian women.

Karl Hamner (1992) suggests that the tendency to devalue the other is particularly true of specific members of an ingroup who have low ingroup status. "This may help to explain the young age of man gay-bashers . . . young people often have not yet had sufficient chance to achieve their own status. Consequently, they turn to group identification and social comparison to boost their self esteem" (p. 185). Joseph Harry (1992) suggests that "gay-bashing offers a nearly ideal solution to the status needs of the immature male . . . It provides immediate status rewards in the eyes of one's peers because, unlike verbal reports of sexual conquest, it provides direct and corroborated evidence of one's virility" (p. 115).

Theories about Anti-Gay/Lesbian Attitude Formation

Much of the psychological research specifically focused on anti-gay/lesbian violence has been on attitude formation. The majority of people in the United States see gay men and lesbian women as sick, immoral, or criminal (Davis & Smith, 1984). In a study that distinguished between attitudes toward lesbian women and gay men, Herek (1988) reported that 68 percent of respondents agreed with the statement that "sex between two men is just plain wrong" and 64 percent said that they agreed with the statement that "sex between two women is just plain wrong." Over two-thirds (69.9 percent) agreed with the statement "I think male homosexuals are disgusting," and 59.9 percent agreed with the statement "I think lesbians are disgusting." Attitudes toward gay men and lesbian women have changed over time. According to a 1997 Gallup Poll, 84 percent of the population believe that homosexuals should have equal job opportunities, but 59 percent believe that homosexual behavior is morally wrong (Berke, August 2, 1998).

Early psychological research on anti-gay/lesbian bias studied the correlations between negative attitudes toward gay men and lesbian women and other personal characteristics. Mary Kite (1984) offers a nice summary of these early studies.

(P)eople who hold negative attitudes toward homosexuals are likely to support the maintenance of traditional sex roles . . . , are more likely to stereotype the sexes than those who hold positive attitudes . . . , and favor preserving the double standard between men and women . . . (are) less likely to know a homosexual . . . may be status conscious, authoritarian, and sexually rigid. . . . (Others) reported a strong positive correlation between attitudes toward women and attitudes toward homosexual and reported that negative attitudes toward homosexuals are positively correlated with negative attitudes toward blacks. (pp. 69–70)

Other studies showed that men exhibit significantly more negative attitudes toward homosexuals than do women (Nyberg & Alston, 1976–1977). Men are more negative toward gay men than they are toward lesbian women, whereas women are no more negative toward lesbian women than they are toward gay men. (Kite & Whitley, 1998)

Herek (1984) has defined three functions of attitudes towards homosexuals: ego defensive, experiential, and symbolic. The function of *ego defensive attitudes* can be seen in the use of the term "homophobia." It is commonly believed that those who hold negative attitudes toward gay men and lesbian women do so because they feel personally threatened by their own unconscious conflicts about either sexual orientation or gender identity. From a psychodynamic perspective, prejudiced attitudes toward gay men and lesbian women serve to decrease tension aroused by these unconscious conflicts. Franklin (1998) found that many of the perpetrators in her study reported assaulting gay men and lesbian women "to prove their masculine identity by displaying toughness and an endorsement of heterosexuality" (p. 4).

Experiential attitudes are based on past interactions with known homosexuals. "Experiential attitudes develop when affects and cognitions associated with specific interpersonal interactions are generalized to all les-

bians and gay men" (Herek, 1984, p. 8). Herek notes that most people develop their beliefs about gay men and lesbian women from stereotypes and ignorance without any contact with gay men and lesbian women. Franklin found that the largest number of assailants in her study claimed that they were reacting to perceived advances by a person. "Assailants interpret their victims' words and actions based on their belief that homosexuals are sexual predators. . . . once someone is labeled as homosexual, any glance or conversation by that person is perceived as sexual flirtation. Flirtation, in turn, is viewed as a legitimate reason to assault" (1998, p. 3).

Symbolic attitudes are ways of expressing abstract ideological concepts that are closely linked to one's notion of self and to one's social network and reference groups. Symbolic attitudes are developed through socialization. "(E)xpressing their attitudes reinforces their self-conceptions publicly, identifies them with important reference groups, and probably elicits acceptance or avoids rejection from significant others" (Herek, 1984, p. 12). This is similar to Franklin's finding that many of the perpetrators she studied reported assaulting gay men and lesbian women because of "ideology," viewing themselves "as social norm enforcers who are punishing moral transgressions" (1998, p. 3).

A POLITICAL EXPLANATION OF ANTI-GAY/LESBIAN VIOLENCE

Anti-gay/lesbian violence is complicated and multi-faceted with numerous, interacting causes. Psychological theories provide useful ways of understanding anti-gay/lesbian violence from an intrapsychic and interpersonal perspective. However, psychological explanations are not sufficient. A *political analysis* of violence against lesbian women, gay men, and other sexual minorities considers power dynamics and social institutions rather than just individual attitudes and behaviors.

A *feminist perspective* understands violence against lesbian women and gay men in terms of gender politics. Gay men and lesbian women (as well as other sexual minorities, most notably transgendered men and women) are seen as gender outlaws who threaten male patriarchal hegemony. In a very clear and articulate argument, Suzanne Pharr (1988) says that homophobia is *"a weapon of sexism."* Heterosexism and homophobia serve misogyny and sexism. Heterosexist attitudes and institutions keep women in subordinate relation to men, preserving male dominance and female dependence. Heterosexism maintains the view that women need men to function properly, to be fulfilled and secure. Women bonding together in any way that threatens male dominance and control—political, economic, or sexual—are at serious risk of retaliation. Homophobia is the ultimate weapon against women's empowerment.

Pharr argues that gay men are also perceived as a threat to male dominance by "breaking rank with male heterosexual solidarity" and "causing a damaging rent in the very fabric of sexism," as they are "betrayers," "traitors . . . who must be punished and eliminated" (1988, p. 18). Gay men threaten white male supremacy because they challenge what it means "to be a man." This idea is supported by the fact that "gay men who described themselves as 'a little feminine' or 'very feminine' were twice as likely as other gays to experience gay bashing" (Harry, 1992, p. 119).

Children learn the penalties of being *gender non-conforming* at a young age. They are harassed at school and in the playground. The link between gender non-conformity and anti-gay and lesbian violence it

quite apparent. "Anti-gay slurs target non-aggressive boys, tomboyish girls, children with lesbian or gay parents, and even children who befriend these youngsters. Surveys of school children indicate that anti-gay slurs are the most dreaded form of harassment" (Franklin, 1998, p. 6).

Barbara Perry (1998) has studied *hate groups* and ideologies of power in the United States. She maintains that hate groups are based on preserving "the hegemony of white, heterosexual, Christian, male power" (p. 32). "The conclusion that hate activists reach is that it is not minorities who are oppressed and persecuted, but the shrinking white majority" (p. 47). Gay men and lesbian women are seen as threatening the continued survival of the white race because it is assumed that they recruit youth, do not reproduce, and spread AIDS. "Those who recruit for homosexual sodomy are a factor pushing us ever closer to the edge of racial suicide" (Strom, online cited in Perry, 1998, p. 25). "White race faces certain extinction in the near future, unless we identify and destroy our executioners" (Northern Thunder cited in Perry, 1998, p. 47).

Only a small percentage of anti-gay/lesbian violence is committed by members of hate groups (Garofalo, 1997). But, incendiary hate group rhetoric, combined with cultural heterosexism, create the context in which individual acts of violence against gay men and lesbian women occur; a cultural context in which people can "justify" or "downplay" the violent acts they commit. Many people who would find racist and sexist jokes offensive have no trouble with anti-gay/lesbian humor. Our legal system has said that we must protect the "civil rights" of racial, ethnic, religious, and gender minorities but that gay men and lesbian women do not need "special privileges." Schools recognize the need to "teach tolerance" but find anti-bias curricula controversial because it is assumed that any conversation about gay and lesbian issues—even anti-bias work—would talk about and thus promote sex.

A feminist analysis of anti-gay and lesbian violence means looking at all forms of *oppression,* those based on class, race, ethnicity, age, gender, disability, religion, as well as sexual orientation. While gay men, lesbian women, and other minorities do not threaten the survival of white men, they are in fact a threat to white, able-bodied, heterosexual, patriarchal rule—a threat to patriarchy, not men.

RESPONSES TO ANTI-GAY/ LESBIAN VIOLENCE

Legal Responses

One of the first responses to anti-gay/lesbian violence has been what Valerie Jenness and Ryken Grattet (1996) refer to as "the criminalization of hate." There are currently two federal *hate crime laws,* and numerous state hate crime statutes.

The Hate Crimes Statistics Act (P.L. 101-275), which became law in 1990, requires the U.S. Department of Justice to maintain statistics on hate crimes. However, it doesn't require local or state agencies to report the statistics to the FBI, nor does it provide any funds to local police agencies or the FBI to help with this task. The second federal law, The Hate Crimes Sentencing Enhancement Act, (P.L. 103-322), requires that the U.S. Sentencing Commission provide sentencing enhancements for crimes that are determined beyond a reasonable doubt to be hate crimes. This only applies to hate crimes committed on federal property, but many states have sentencing enhancement acts. Congress is currently considering the Hate Crimes Prevention Act of 1998 (S.1529/H.R. 3081) which would amend current federal

criminal civil rights laws to provide authority for federal officials to investigate and prosecute cases in which the violence occurs because of a victim's gender, sexual orientation, or disability. However this law is also provoking much controversy.

There has been a struggle to include sexual orientation in hate crimes legislation on both the federal and state level. Forty-one states have hate crimes statutes; however, only 19 states and the District of Columbia include sexual orientation. This is significant given the fact that the largest number of prosecutions for hate crimes occurs at the state level (Spillane, 1994).

There are a number of problems with current hate crimes legislation. It is often difficult to tell what is and what isn't a hate crime (Berk, Boyd, & Hamner, 1992; Gerstenfeld, 1992). Not all jurisdictions are required to report hate crimes. Many gay men and lesbian women fear secondary victimization if they disclose their sexual orientation (Berrill & Herek, 1992). Enhancement laws may in fact increase hostility (Gerstenfeld, 1992). Finally, calling anti-gay harassment a hate crime puts it into the jurisdiction of the criminal justice system, "which may not be well prepared to deal with deep-seated intergroup animosities" (Garofalo, 1997, p. 142)

However, hate crime legislation does send a symbolic message. "The laws then serve a *symbolic* purpose, and the punishment of offenders acts as a denunciation of their evil acts . . . The primary difference between symbolism and denunciation is that symbolism focuses on the law itself, whereas denunciation focuses on the punishment for violating the law" (Gerstenfeld, 1992, p. 267).

Social Responses

Levin and McDevitt assert there is "a growing *culture of hate;* from humor and music to religion and politics, a person's group affiliation—the fact that he or she *differs from people in the ingroup*—is being used more and more to provide a basis for dehumanizing and insulting the person" (1993, p. 34). Rather than helping counteract the growing culture of hate, the media contributes to its spread. Eliminating portrayals of others that are racist, sexist, ableist, ageist, and heterosexist would be an important step toward reducing hate crimes in U.S. society.

The *contact hypothesis* suggests contact between members of hostile groups will reduce intergroup hostility. Allport (1979) notes that intergroup contact decreases hostility between groups when it meets four necessary conditions: "Prejudice (unless deeply rooted in the character structure of the individual) may be reduced by equal status contact between majority and minority groups in the pursuit of common goals. The effect is greatly enhanced if this contact is sanctioned by institutional supports (i.e., by law, custom or local atmosphere), and provided it is of a sort that leads to the perception of common interests and common humanity between members of the two groups" (p. 231).

Numerous studies have shown that heterosexuals who have more contact with lesbian women and gay men have more positive attitudes toward them than those who believe they have not had contact or do not know lesbian women or gay men (Herek & Capitanio, 1996). Gay men and lesbian women can be encouraged to come out to others, breaking stereotypes, and fighting the forces that would keep them hidden and invisible. (See Niens and Cairns in this volume for a further elaboration of contact theory.)

Educational Responses

It is possible to change social norms through educational campaigns. Schools can combat the dominant cultural norm that says that it is okay to harass someone for being different. Franklin suggests a "(p)roactive intervention against school based harassment and violence. *Anti-bias curricula* must be introduced as early as kindergarten and must continue through high school" (1998, p. 8). Anti-bias curricula help teachers learn how to recognize such violence and intervene to eliminate it. Children are taught how to work collaboratively, how to have empathy for others, and how to handle feelings of frustration and anger.

Many teenage perpetrators of anti-gay/lesbian violence are thrill seekers who commit crimes because of frustration and boredom (Levin & McDevitt, 1993; Franklin, 1998). Afterschool programs and activities that provide activities and challenges for adolescents may help decrease all forms of crimes by giving adolescents the chance to develop new skills and feel a sense of opportunity and hopefulness.

Combating Interlocking Systems of Oppression through Coalition Building

Valerie Jenness and Kendal Broad (1994) note that, "Unlike feminist activism around violence against women . . . activism around anti-gay and lesbian violence has ignored patriarchy and the gender relations that sustain and reflect it" (p. 419). They cite the work of Carole Sheffield who notes that the "linkage between race-hate, gay-hate, and misogyny is evident" (1987, p. 89), and point out that gay and lesbian anti-violence activism rarely recognizes the centrality of race and gender.

Anti-lesbian/gay violence must be understood within the context of *interlocking systems of oppression*. Structural violence against racial and ethnic minorities and the poor creates an environment ripe for all kinds of frustration and aggression. The widening gap between the rich and poor in the United States and the sense of despair that it engenders create a context in which violence becomes endemic. A more equitable society in which individuals do not feel that they are competing with others for a smaller piece of the pie will help to decrease frustration and aggression.

CONCLUSION

As the United States enters the twenty-first century, hate crimes and violence against racial, ethnic, religious, and sexual minorities are on the rise. Anti-gay/lesbian violence is similar to violence against other minority groups but differs in some important ways. Anti-gay/lesbian violence is more socially sanctioned. The structural violence of sodomy laws and other discriminatory laws creates a context that supports the dehumanization and demonizing of gay men and lesbian women. Lesbian women and gay men are more likely than other minority group members to experience physical assaults and attacks that are particularly vicious. Anti-gay/lesbian violence seems to be rooted more in gender politics than difference politics, although racial politics have an effect.

While a psychological perspective offers us some understanding of what contributes to individual attitudes and behaviors, we must not ignore the political nature of anti-lesbian/gay violence and all hate crimes. If the twenty-first century is to see a reduction in hate crimes and violence, then it is essential that people (1) attend to structural violence and the social and power dynamics of the patriarchal system in which such violence occurs; (2) recognize that much of what is considered anti-gay/lesbian violence is in fact based on gender politics; (3) acknowledge and affirm the incredible diversity in the lesbian and gay communities in terms of race, ethnicity, age, class, education, disability, and political ideology; (4) use our psychological knowledge to construct interventions to prevent all forms of violence; and, (5) work in coalitions with other oppressed groups using our strengths and training in human behavior and systems theories to create radical social change.

CHAPTER 3

INTRASTATE VIOLENCE

Ulrike Niens and Ed Cairns

Despite the fact that the Cold War has ended, the world faces a new problem that threatens global peace and security. This is because "fierce new assertions of nationalism and sovereignty" have sprung up and the world is threatened by "brutal ethnic, religious, social, cultural, or linguistic strife" (Boutros-Ghali, 1992). Not all of these are strictly new conflicts, because while the end of the Cold War has spawned many of them, it has also aggravated others, and exposed older ones as essentially ethnic rather than between hostile political ideologies. Unlike international wars, the combatants in ethnic conflicts inhabit the same battlefield. Therefore, even when the actual fighting fades, their lives are intermeshed with those of their opponents. As a consequence, intrastate violence is often characterized by viciousness rather than by the more impassive slaughter of international wars. Group loyalty and the maintenance of group boundaries are dominant features of such conflicts, as are communal memories of victimization. Together they create psychological processes that contribute to further violence and genocide.

This chapter will examine the contributions that psychology has made, and can make, to understanding intrastate/intergroup conflict, through an examination of the three most influential theories in this area, and in particular the attempts that have been made to use these theories to understand one such conflict—that in Northern Ireland. This will be followed by a brief review of psychology's contributions to the management and resolution of such conflicts. Again we will attempt to set this work within the context of Northern Ireland.

THEORETICAL EXPLANATIONS FOR INTERGROUP CONFLICT

Background

In the late 1950s and early 1960s psychological explanations for intergroup conflict were based largely on psychodynamic thinking, tested mostly by researchers from the United States. These theories contained ideas often loosely based on the notion of the displacement of aggression.

Using this basic idea, theories have been developed to explain intergroup conflict involving unconscious processes such as projection and scapegoating. Other more complex schemes have hypothesized the development of a particular personality type, central to which is authoritarianism, which in turn is related to outgroup hostility. Put simply, these theories see the attitudes and behavior of people towards outgroups as "ways of working out individual emotional problems in an intergroup setting" (Tajfel, 1978). One might think of this as a sort of sophisticated group form of "kicking the cat." These views of intergroup conflict based on some form of individual pathology became very popular, especially after the Second World War when people were trying to come to terms with the horrors of the Holocaust.

In the 1970s, however, European psychologists in particular began to be disenchanted by this approach. While acknowledging that these ideas might play a role in explaining interpersonal conflict, the problem was how to extrapolate directly from interpersonal conflict to intergroup conflict. These social psychologists suggest that although the primary explanation for intergroup conflict is psychological, anyone who has studied an *identity-based* conflict knows that other factors also play a role. In Northern Ireland, for example, where people derive part of their self-concept from identifying with one of the two rival communities, factors such as religion, history, demography, politics, and economics are also important to understanding the conflict.

The development of a new theory, known as social identity theory, overcame many of the theoretical problems inherent in theories of the displacement of agression (Tajfel & Turner, 1986). Social identity theory has several advantages over earlier theories in that it: (1) is firmly based in social theory, (2) makes no assumptions about abnormality or irrationality, (3) leaves room for the role of other disciplines, such as politics, history, religion, and demography, and (4) has informed the debate over cures as well as causes of social conflict.

Before considering these issues in more detail, the present chapter will review two other major theories that psychologists have used to explain intergroup conflict. The first of these is authoritarian personality theory, which is a more sophisticated version of earlier Freudian theories, and the second is relative deprivation theory (RDT). Both of these theories are important for their heuristic value. We will then focus on social identity theory (SIT) in more detail, including some relatively new ideas about how it may be possible to incorporate the other theories into SIT and so develop a unified theory. The chapter will then move on to consider how psychologists have contributed to ideas about peace and reconciliation in the context of intrastate violence and the impact SIT has had on this debate.

Authoritarian Personality Theory

According to Adorno et al. (1950), the individual's personality structure provides the basis for the development of intolerant attitudes. The hypothesis was that there is a link between the development of negative intergroup attitudes and the type of family in which a child grows up. Specifically, an authoritarian upbringing is one in which parental discipline relies upon harshness, few freedoms, strict adherence to social norms, and punishment in case of disobedience. The belief was that growing up in this type of family caused intrapersonal conflict that led to hostile attitudes against the parents and in turn against authorities in general. Adorno and his co-authors believed that the child's hostility is transferred to individuals or groups that appear to be weak, different in terms of social norms, or lower in status (e.g., ethnic minorities). Hence, this offers the basis for intergroup conflict.

Adorno et al.'s theory of the authoritarian personality was undoubtedly one of the most important catalysts for social psychological research in authoritarianism, ethnocentrism, prejudice, and intergroup conflict. However, most scientists today share the opinion that neither the theory nor its operationalization is tenable in the original form.

Relative Deprivation Theory (RDT)

The central thesis of relative deprivation theory (Gurr, 1970; Runciman, 1966) is that relative deprivation is not necessarily equal to actual deprivation because relative deprivation refers to the individual's *feeling* of being deprived. The hypothesis is that this feeling of deprivation is the result of a difference between the individual's expectations of attainment and his/her actual achievement. The individual's expectations of attainment may arise from social comparisons either with other social groups, with other individuals, or with the self in the past. Runciman (1966) refers to feelings of deprivation resulting from a negative outcome, as the result of comparisons with other *groups*, as "fraternalistic" deprivation, and negative feelings resulting from comparisons with other *individuals,* as "egoistic" deprivation. Because fraternalistic deprivation is linked to social behavior, the assumption is that, in contrast to egoistic deprivation, fraternalistic deprivation can lead to outgroup hostility (Brown, 1995).

There are several major conceptual and methodological problems with relative deprivation theory (Walker & Pettigrew, 1984). One is that much of the existing research deals largely with egoistic relative deprivation, ignoring fraternalistic relative deprivation. A second is that research in this area has often failed to operationalize RD at the appropriate levels. Finally, much work in the RD area has often failed to specify the person or groups that individuals are using for comparison purposes, and it has failed to specify the dimension or dimensions along which the comparison process is being made. In other words, do people just feel somehow generally relatively deprived or do they feel deprived in terms of some specific dimension such as power or money?

Social Identity Theory

There has been little interest in either authoritarian personality theory or relative deprivation theory as explanations of the conflict in Northern Ireland. One possible reason is that neither theory appears to account for the psychological forces at work "which intensify the strength of feeling beyond what the real conflict of interest would appear to justify" (Whyte, 1990, p. 102). Only social identity theory (SIT) (Tajfel, 1969, 1981; Tajfel & Turner, 1979) and its more recent version, self-categorization theory (Turner et al., 1987) appear to offer this level of insight. SIT suggests that *individuals use social categories not only to simplify their environment, but also to identify and to define themselves.* By identifying with a specific social category, a person defines him/herself as a group member, thereby developing a social identity.

The central thesis of SIT is that individuals strive for a *positive self-concept,* in part by trying to achieve a *positive social identity.* This positive social identity in turn depends on (social) comparisons with other social groups. The goal of the social comparison process, therefore, is to find comparative dimensions that provide a positive outcome for the *ingroup* (the group the individual identifies with) in order to enhance the group's and the individual's self-esteem.

SIT allows for temporal changes, which gives the theory a vital dynamic quality. In order to cope with both the positive and negative outcomes resulting from comparison processes, the theory proposes that individuals develop *identity management strategies.* Such identity management strategies become most important when intergroup comparison results in a *negative social identity.* When this happens, SIT suggests that an individual may re-sort to (1) individual mobility (i.e., exiting the group), (2) social creativity (including changing the comparison group or changing or re-evaluating the comparison dimension), or (3) engaging in social competition.

The individual's or group's choice of specific identity management strategy depends on the perception of the existing intergroup context and on the strength of ingroup identification. More specifically, *permeability* of group boundaries, and *stability and legitimacy* of intergroup relations determine the individual's or group's preference for particular identity management strategies. When individual mobility is not possible (because of perceived "impermeable" group boundaries), intergroup identification becomes stronger and the collective strategies of social competition and social creativity become important. Consequently, the situation is more likely to lead to negative outgroup attitudes and in turn to intergroup conflict.

To sum up, SIT claims that people derive part of their self-image from the social groups to which they belong and that individuals strive to maintain a positive self-image, in relation to their group membership, through comparisons with other outgroups. If this social comparison process results in a negative outcome, SIT argues that the perceived type of intergroup context (in terms of permeability, stability, and legitimacy) will determine the individual's or group's choice of identity management strategy. In certain situations, particularly when group boundaries are seen as impermeable, intergroup conflict is the likely outcome.

THE CONFLICT
IN NORTHERN IRELAND

Despite the fact that it is possible to trace the Irish conflict with the English to at least the sixteenth century, Ireland really only came to the world's attention because of the violence that has spanned the last 25 years and which has led to some 3,000 deaths and tens of thousands of injuries due to increasing community divisions. At its most basic, the conflict in Northern Ireland is a struggle between those who wish to see Northern Ireland remain part of the United Kingdom (the Protestant/Unionists) and those who wish to see the reunification of the entire island of Ireland (the Catholic/Nationalists). Complicating this, however, is the fact that underpinning the conflict are important historical, religious, political, economic and psychological elements (Cairns & Darby, 1998).

Several attempts have been made to apply authoritarian personality theory to explain the conflict in Northern Ireland. Various writers have suggested that Irish social attitudes (including those of Northern Ireland) are more conservative than those of Britain. Heskin (1980) for example, claims that people in Northern Ireland "are raised with traditional and conservative political and religious values" (p. 84), making them rather (more) authoritarian in their outlook. Despite this, social psychologists in Northern Ireland did not find this exclusively psychological analysis of the conflict convincing. There has therefore been only one attempt to apply authoritarian personality theory to the conflict, and that study (Mercer & Cairns, 1982) failed to find a clear relationship between authoritarianism and intergroup conflict in Northern Ireland. Mercer and Cairns suggested that authoritarianism, rather than being an underlying personality syndrome, is probably determined, in Northern Ireland at least, by exposure to conservative ideas which in turn are related to sociocultural variables such as education, social class and religiosity.

Other social scientists have applied relative deprivation theory to explain the conflict in Northern Ireland, which is not an affluent area, given its combination of large families, poor standards of health, high prices, low earnings, high unemployment, and poor housing. This situation was exacerbated by Protestant domination that led to unemployment rates that are higher for Catholics than for Protestants. As a result, most commentators would agree that Catholic aspirations to join their co-religionists in the Republic of Ireland is fueled at some level by their relative deprivation, that is, the way Catholics have been treated in Protestant-dominated Northern Ireland over the last seventy years.

Over the last two decades, significant progress has been made in tackling the inequalities experienced by Northern Ireland's Catholics. Yet disparities still remain, especially in the area of employment. However, despite the apparent face validity of relative deprivation theory as an explanation for conflict in Northern Ireland, few researchers have been sufficiently convinced to actually put it to the test.

Birrell (1972) was the first person to apply RDT, examining in detail economic, social, and political factors in Northern Ireland, concluding that there were widespread feelings of relative deprivation in the Catholic community. However, Birrell focused virtually exclusively on actual inequalities between Catholics and Protestants and made no attempt to show that Catholics actually *perceived* these inequalities or felt them to be important.

Subsequently, Willis (1991), in an unpublished doctoral dissertation, attempted to test the theory in Northern Ireland more directly. Willis concluded that (1) in Northern Ireland fraternalistic relative deprivation is more strongly related to social protest than egoistic relative deprivation, (2) increasing the perception of inequality does not necessarily lead to an increase in feelings of discontent, and (3) Tajfel's (1978) theory of social identity can be used with relative deprivation theory to shed light on the Northern Ireland situation.

These results were later confirmed by Willis and Cairns (1993) who interviewed Catholics living in the city of Derry in Northern Ireland. Analysis of the interviews produced clear evidence for the existence of feelings of relative deprivation among Catholics. However, what was particularly interesting was that while respondents indicated that they believed that they were not discriminated against individually, they also confirmed that Catholics and Protestants at a group level do practice intergroup discrimination. Willis and Cairns hypothesized that respondents distinguished between individual and group level discrimination in order to distance themselves from the situation in Derry. Once again, this study highlighted the importance of *group* feelings of relative deprivation (fraternal relative deprivation). As SIT is the only theory that persuasively accounts for the fact that individuals act in terms of group as well as self, this suggested a link between relative deprivation theory and social identity theory as a fruitful area for further research.

Social Identity Theory and Northern Ireland

Social identity theory (SIT) has provided a useful underpinning to much sociopsychological research in Northern Ireland (Cairns, 1982; Gallagher, 1989). Undoubtedly this theory's popularity has stemmed from the fact that SIT recognizes that psychology has only a modest role to play in explaining what was happening in Northern Ireland because "the social, historical, political and economic causality of the present situation must undoubtedly remain prior to the analysis of any of its psychological concomitants" (Tajfel, 1982, p. 9). However while the amount of variance accounted for by SIT is modest, it is significant. SIT, as Cairns and Darby (1998) have pointed out

. . . captures the phenomenon better than individually based cost-benefit analyses of such behaviors as, at one extreme, the hunger strikers, or at a more prosaic level the intense group loyalty represented in election results. SIT is above all a dynamic theory in which the relationship between groups is seen as fluid, and provides insight into the social changes which have occurred in Northern Ireland and which are still underway (p. 756).

In Northern Ireland social categorization (or "telling") plays an important role in everyday life. Burton (1979), an anthropologist, has suggested that people in Northern Ireland are almost obsessed with what he describes as the most fundamental and overwhelming question about someone: Which denomination do they belong to?

To answer this question, people in Northern Ireland have developed the skill of using cues such as school attended, first name, and area of residence. When this information is denied, they may fall back on less reliable cues such as surname, facial appearance, or even type of swear words used (Cairns, 1987). The concept of social categorization has stimulated empirical research to determine the age at which children in Northern Ireland learn to use first names (Cairns, 1980; Houston, Crozier, & Walker, 1990) or faces (Stringer & Cairns, 1983) to categorize others as ingroup or outgroup members. Generally this work points to the fact that, on average, this skill is not mastered until about age ten to eleven years.

Not only is categorization of others in this way important but so is self-categorization. In survey after survey, when people in Northern Ireland are asked to state whether they are Catholic or Protestant, the majority are willing to answer the question. Indeed people in Northern Ireland see no problem in stating that they are Catholic or Protestant

and then stating that they never attend church. This is of course also related to the very old joke—which has some psychological truth in it—about the Jewish person being asked if he was a Catholic Jew or a Protestant Jew. Self-categorization is also a well-researched area, the results of which make it clear that the situation in Northern Ireland is a complex and dynamic one which does not preclude fluctuations in identity salience nor the exclusion of private as opposed to public identities (see Benson & Trew, 1995). Further it provides an insight into the fact that in Northern Ireland the boundaries between the two groups are seen for the most part as impermeable.

The operation of social comparison process in Northern Ireland, which individuals and groups apply to achieve positive identity, has been less well researched. Social comparison processes however are not difficult to observe because the only way to achieve a more positive social identity is to ensure that one's social group, put simply, scores points over the other social group. This explains why people in Northern Ireland are apparently often more concerned with differentials than with ultimate end goals. This can range from arguments about who started the current conflict to which group actually came to Ireland first in prehistoric times. On a more everyday level the flag-flying and marching and the opposition to it, for which Northern Ireland has become a byword on television screens throughout the world, is undoubtedly best understood as part of the exercise to maintain a sense of group superiority.

MANAGING AND RESOLVING CONFLICT: NORTHERN IRISH EXPERIENCES

Psychology has not only been involved in trying to explain intergroup conflicts but in attempting to manage, resolve or even prevent them. In this context, the *contact hypothesis* has been one of the influential paradigms used by psychology to understand the way in which conflict between groups can be reduced (Allport, 1954; Amir, 1969).

The contact hypothesis states that contact between people will allow them to communicate with each other and thus to discover that they share similar basic attitudes and values, and to appreciate each other's way of life. The product of this, it is claimed, will be positive attitudes, not only towards the specific outgroup members with whom contact occurred but towards the outgroup in general and hence a reduction in conflict.

Unfortunately, despite its obvious intuitive appeal, the contact hypothesis has received only limited empirical support. The problem is that even when intergroup contact takes place under what are thought to be ideal conditions, positive attitudes formed towards individual members of the outgroup with whom one comes into contact often fail to generalize to the outgroup in general.

The Contact Hypothesis and Northern Ireland

Northern Ireland is a relatively segregated society, especially for children, the vast majority of whom attend denominational schools. For many, this is the problem. Therefore, encouraging some form of cross-community contact, in the main involving children, is often seen as the solution. Initiatives in this area have ranged from more informal contacts in the form of summer camps, to setting up a third (integrated) school system. However, people in Northern Ireland already co-exist individually on a day-to-day level, whereas a social psychological analysis suggests that the conflict exists at an *intergroup* level. A criticism, therefore, that can be leveled at many of these contact schemes, is that they encourage contact on an inter-individual basis rather than on an intergroup basis as suggested by social identity theory.

One of the earliest programs involved bringing children together from the two communities for holidays, often in the United States. These schemes have been criticized because they only reach a small number of children and involve only short-term contact. More recently, in recognition of the fact that most pupils will continue to be taught in segregated schools, the government has introduced a common curriculum for all schools, which includes two compulsory cross-curricular themes with a community relations thrust, Education for Mutual Understanding (EMU) and Cultural Heritage. This has been done in the hope that it will end the mutual ignorance which many feel characterizes Northern Irish society. A second strategy has been to encourage and finance (but not make compulsory) inter-school contacts between Catholic and Protestant schools. The most radical option involves developing new integrated schools. Since 1980 some 40-plus elementary and secondary schools have opened which share a common aim of reflecting both communities in their pupil and staff compositions while reflecting cultural pluralism in their curriculum (Dunn, 1989). These schools continue to grow in number but only serve a small proportion of Northern Ireland's children.

THE FUTURE

In this last section we will discuss future developments in the three areas we have examined so far, theoretical explanations for intergroup conflict, the contact hypothesis, and ending with some speculation about intrastate violence in general and psychology's role in combating this dangerous threat to world stability.

Theoretical Explanations for Intergroup Conflict: A Unified Model

As the number of empirical investigations in this area has started to undergo a rapid expansion, the search for a model unifying authoritarianism, relative deprivation, and social identity has now become critical (Kawakami & Dion, 1995). One place to start such a search is to examine the obvious links between social identity theory and both authoritarian personality theory and relative deprivation theory.

Authoritarian Personality Theory and Social Identity Theory

Efforts have already begun to reconceptualize authoritarian personality theory. According to Duckitt (1992), the basic construct underlying the three attitudinal clusters found by Altemeyer—conventionalism, authoritarian submission, and authoritarian aggression—reflect the intensity of an individual's feeling of social identity. Duckitt presumed that with increasing *ingroup identification* and stress on *group cohesion* the individual would show an increase in conventionalism, authoritarian submission, and authoritarian aggression. As a result, he suggested that with increasing ingroup identification the emphasis on behavioral and attitudinal conformity with ingroup norms would increase. Furthermore, this should enhance the emphasis on unconditional obedience to ingroup leaders and the intolerance of not conforming to ingroup norms.

As a result of this, Duckitt has produced a new definition of authoritarianism: ". . . authoritarianism is simply the individual's or group's conception of the relationship which should exist, that is, the appropriate or normative relationship, between the group and its individual members" (1989, p. 71). Duckitt's new perspective has the added advantages that it is bipolar, with authoritarianism as one extreme and liberalism as the other, and that it views authoritarianism as easily influenced by situations and different group contexts.

Relative Deprivation Theory and Social Identity Theory

Several authors have already commented on the correspondence between RDT and SIT (Brown, 1995; Tajfel, 1981; Walker & Pettigrew, 1984). SIT and RDT both involve social (intergroup) comparisons as the basic mechanisms underlying ethnocentrism and the individual's development of prejudice. However, SIT additionally emphasizes the importance of group identification as a necessary process prior to social comparisons. Furthermore, SIT is more focused on cognitive processes ("How do people think about their ingroup in comparison to the outgroup"). In contrast, RDT, at its best is more concentrated on the emotional aspect of intergroup relations ("How do people feel about their group in comparison to other groups or individuals") (Brown, 1995, p. 202). If a rapprochement of these two positions were possible it would help to overcome one of the main criticism of SIT noted above, namely that SIT is too focused on cognitions, neglecting emotions in intergroup conflict.

The parallels between SIT and RDT are particularly obvious in a more recent version of RDT known as Folger's (1987) referent cognitions model (RCT). According to RCT, individuals compare actual social comparison outcomes between groups (perhaps in terms of power or money) with other possible alternatives. The individual's awareness of these other possible or "referent" outcomes may arise from social, temporal or imaginative comparisons. The author suggests that those referent outcomes individually perceived as more positive than reality may lead to discontentment and resentment and in certain situations ultimately to intrastate conflict.

Additionally, the variables *justification* and *likelihood of amelioration* are included in the model. Justification is the individual's perception of the legitimacy of the actual comparison process—"is it just/fair that we have less money/power?" The hypothesis is that the individual's resentment against other individuals or groups should increase the more the actual outcome is seen as being illegitimate (i.e., unfair or unjust). Situations where the referent outcome is seen as "obviously" just and the actual outcome as "obviously" unjust are most likely to lead to intrastate conflict.

The concept "likelihood of amelioration" refers to the individual's perspective on the stability of the actual outcome. Folger assumes that the perceived possibility of future change to a more positive referent outcome will decrease resentment. In contrast, no hope for a change to the better will increase resentment. Justification and likelihood of amelioration are conceptualized as mediating the relationship between referent outcomes and resentment.

As noted above, SIT hypothesizes that how the individual perceives relations between his/her ingroup and an outgroup, in terms of permeability of group boundaries, stability of intergroup relations, and legitimacy of intergroup relations, will determine the actual identity management strategies that individual will adopt. In turn, which identity management strategy is adopted will have a major bearing on whether intrastate conflict is likely to arise. In RCT terminology, the concepts "referent outcomes," "justification," and "likelihood of amelioration" determine the degree of resentment. Both theories assume that outgroup hostility (which underlies intrastate

conflict) is determined by the perceived rightness of the group's position in relation to a comparison group and the perception of future change of the group's position to the better. While SIT suggests identification with the ingroup as a mediating variable, RCT suggests relative deprivation.

In conclusion, there are similarities between SIT and RDT and/or RCT, respectively. Folger's (1987) RCT shares basic assumptions with SIT and RDT (e.g., social comparisons as the underlying process for intergroup hostility and hence intrastate conflict). In addition, the variables claimed by RCT to determine different levels of resentment match well with the variables mentioned by SIT as determining the individual's or group's choice of different identity management strategies.

Contact Hypothesis: Recent Developments

Despite the disappointment engendered by the contact hypothesis, social psychologists have resisted the temptation to throw the baby out with the bath water. As a result, work in this area is leading to promising new avenues of research (Pettigrew, 1998).

In particular, recent research in social cognition, taken in conjunction with some of the ideas on SIT outlined above, has begun to provide clues as to more effective ways that contact can be used to alter stereotypes. What this research has shown is that stereotypes are highly resistant to change, i.e., stereotypic beliefs show considerable inertia in responding to discrepant information. In order for stereotype change to occur, it is necessary for the stereotype disconfirmers to be seen as typical of the *group*, rather than of individuals. This is where social identity theory comes in, because what this means is that contact must takes place, not between individuals as individuals, but rather between members of respective groups. In other words, the contact must occur at the intergroup end of the continuum rather than at the interpersonal end.

Paradoxically therefore, part of the solution may be to make people's group affiliations more salient in the contact situation and not less (Brown, 1988), thereby ensuring that the participants see each other as representatives of their groups and not merely as exceptions to the rule. In this way, contact should ideally aim towards changing people's minds about what constitutes a typical group member (Werth & Lord, 1992).

To summarize, the most recent thinking is that for contact to successfully disconfirm key stereotypic beliefs it not only has to involve interpersonal contact, it must also involve intergroup contact with a member or members of the outgroup who are prototypical in all respects with the exception of the one key factor to be disconfirmed. In addition, the contact should take place over a long period of time and in order for the specific disconfirming stereotyped behavior or belief to be expressed the contact should optimally take place under highly structured conditions in which the interactions may need to be loosely scripted (Desforges et al., 1991).

Intrastate Conflict

As we noted at the beginning of this chapter, intrastate conflicts have become more common in the last decade. There is no reason to believe that this trend will diminish in the near future. While all such conflicts are to some extent unique, nevertheless they do contain commonalities. For this reason it is possible to make some tentative suggestions, based on experience in Northern Ireland as to the best way psychologists might contribute to the search for peace.

To begin with, psychologists must understand that in intrastate conflicts their role in the overall peace scheme is a *modest but critical* one. During the conflict itself, they may serve to give people hope and perhaps lower tensions, while clinicians can of course provide necessary psychological first-aid. As the conflict moves toward a settlement, psychologists may play an important role in facilitating negotiations. Ultimately, however, they depend upon the success of the political process in creating a setting within which peace and reconciliation may be achieved. It is during the post-political settlement period that psychology's role will most likely take precedence.

Another lesson that all psychologists must learn is that, even post-settlement, their goal may be to manage or reduce conflict, not necessarily to eliminate it entirely. For example, the government in Northern Ireland, which for many years encouraged contact between the two communities, has recently come to acknowledge the need for pluralism in Northern Ireland (Cairns & Darby, 1998). This has led to government policies encouraging cultural diversity through support for activities that are traditionally associated with Catholics only or Protestants only.

Finally we can envisage a time when psychology will play a role, not just in helping to intervene in ongoing intrastate conflicts or to reconstruct societies torn apart by such conflicts, but also in preventing intrastate conflicts. As political scientists and political psychologists develop the ability to detect the early warning signs that hindsight tells us precede most conflicts, psychologists must develop techniques to counter and ameliorate intrastate conflicts before they are inflamed and out of control. In doing so psychologists can help to end cycles of violence which have plagued many parts of the world for centuries and in the twenty-first century will be a major threat to world peace.

CHAPTER 4

NATIONALISM AND WAR: A SOCIAL-PSYCHOLOGICAL PERSPECTIVE

Daniel Druckman

The study of nationalism is a social-psychological phenomenon to the extent that individuals express sentiments or emotions towards and have attitudes about their own and other nations. Focusing their attention primarily on individuals and small interacting groups, social psychologists have sought basic knowledge about the ways that people relate to groups and nations. Central to this focus are the conditions that arouse or reduce feelings of attachment toward ingroups as well as feelings of enmity toward outgroups.

Nationalistic sentiments must be part of any explanatory framework of intergroup or international relations. The etiology and manifestation of these sentiments are important research issues, addressed by studies reviewed in this chapter. More perplexing, however, is the way that they influence collective behavior at the level of ethnic groups, states, or nations. It is this connection between micro (small groups) and macro (nations) level processes that poses the greatest challenge to students of nationalism. Only a few attempts have been made to develop the connections and few social psychologists have developed the implications of their experimental and survey find-

ings for actions taken by nations. Plausible mechanisms for connecting sentiments to national actions were discussed in earlier articles (Druckman, 1994, 1995). In this chapter, my goal is to situate social-psychological variables in a larger framework of factors that lead toward or away from war.

NEEDS, TYPES OF INVOLVEMENT, AND ORIENTATIONS

The bases for group and national attachments are widely assumed to be lodged in human needs: "Groups in general are organized to meet human needs; their structures and processes are in part molded by these needs" (Guetzkow, 1957, p. 47). At the level of the nation, the group fulfills economic, sociocultural, and political needs, the last including security, group loyalty, and prestige. While these needs are regarded as universal, their strength varies in different nations and in different individuals. The needs are not limited to national identifications but are regarded as being the basis for group identification in general: "The ways by which an individual relates to his nation have aspects in common with the ways in which an individual relates to

any group of which he is a member..."
(Terhune, 1964, p. 258). Basic underlying
needs for attachment and the nation as a
(type of) group are central themes in the
social-psychological approach to nationalism.

A variety of types of needs have been
proposed by researchers investigating the
social-psychological aspects of nationalism.
Most taxonomies distinguish between the
affective and *instrumental functions* served by
nations. For Terhune (1964), the nation
achieves relevance for the individual in
terms of affective (sentimental attachment
to the homeland), goal (motivation to help
one's country), and ego involvement (sense
of identity and self-esteem derived from national identification). DeLamater et al.
(1969) proposed a triad of needs for national involvement which they refer to as
symbolic, functional, and normative where
sanctions and role expectations are emphasized. Parallel concepts are found in the lit-
eratures on individual motivation and small
groups: for example, need for achievement
(goal involvement), need for affiliation (affective involvement), and need for power
(ego involvement); member attraction (affective involvement), task orientation (goal
involvement), and status attraction (ego involvement). Stagner's (1967) answer to the
question why citizens often respond so enthusiastically to appeals by national leaders
consists of the following "universal" desires:
autonomy, power, prestige, altruism, morality, and the will to survive. Many of these desires can be subsumed under Kelman's
(1988) dichotomy of a need for self-protection and a need for self-transcendence.

The questionnaire surveys conducted
by Terhune (1964) and by DeLamater et al.
(1969) suggest that any of the types of involvement can bind the individual to the nation, but for many national groups there
may be a preferred type of involvement.

Terhune, for example, found differences
between the foreign and American samples
used in his study: goal involvement correlated most strongly with a nationalism measure for the foreign students, while affective
involvement correlated more strongly with
nationalism for the American students. Nationalism was strongest overall for students
from underdeveloped countries.

Orientations toward conflict resolution
have also been thought about in terms of
development. Gladstone's (1962) distinction between *egoistic* and *integrative orientations* emphasizes the difference between
being strongly motivated to win (viewed as
an earlier stage of development) and recognizing the importance of collaboration for
mutual benefit (viewed as a later stage).
They are similar to the progression from decreasing egocentricity to increasing socio-
centricity as discussed by Piaget (1965). As
children progress along this dimension they
are increasingly able to take the points of
view of people from other nations and de-
creasingly ready to depict other nations in
terms of simplified enemy images (Silverstein & Holt, 1989). Such a progression may
also have implications for the current recognition of a need for mutual or collective security: Increased concern for the welfare of
other nations is essential to the realization
that no nation is secure until all nations are
secure (Hicks & Walch, 1990). Whether applied to the development of individuals or to
decision-making elites, these concepts contribute the dimension of growth through
time. Individuals may develop more sophisticated ways of relating to their nations as they
progress from egocentric to sociocentric orientations. More direct implications for a nation's foreign policy derive from the inference that national decision-makers also
progress along this growth dimension.

The developmental trend from self to
other orientation should be seen in in-

creased *prosocial behavior,* which includes helping others, sympathy for them, empathy toward them and, even altruism on some occasions (Wispe, 1972). Such positive forms of social behavior may have adaptive advantages. It has been argued, from the perspective of evolutionary psychology, that cooperative behavior promotes individual survival (Caporeal et al., 1989), and that cooperative groups are more effective than less cooperative groups (Brewer & Kramer, 1985). It also contributes to a person's sense of identity by distinguishing between others who are like them and those who are not, between friends and foes (Volkan, 1988). The cooperative behavior displayed between members of one's own group, strengthened by pressures of conformity to group norms, are rarely seen in relations between members of different groups. It is in this sense, as Ross notes, that "sociality promotes ethnocentric conflict, furnishing the critical building block for ingroup amity and outgroup hostility" (1991, p. 177).

Of particular interest are the *conditions* that influence why a person identifies with his or her group. Findings from numerous studies, (e.g., Druckman, 1995) suggest that neither "personality" nor group loyalty is a sufficient explanatory construct. It appears that *group representatives* respond to broad aspects of the situation, aspects that can be manipulated by groups or their leaders to produce the "desired" behavior. They can also be manipulated by third parties who are asked to mediate conflicts between groups.

Research shows that representatives who make a spirited defense of their group to gain resources in negotiations will develop feelings of increased commitment to the group and its perspectives. The perceptions or feelings are aroused by the situation, such as a competitive confrontation (or a joint problem-solving task) between the groups, and lead to such actions as in-transigence in negotiation (Zechmeister & Druckman, 1973).

Of particular concern, however, is the relevance of these laboratory findings for the behavior of citizens in their role as national representatives (Perry, 1957). More generally, to what extent do laboratory findings apply to non-laboratory settings? One approach to this issue is to assume that the more similar two situations are, the more likely will findings obtained in one apply to the other. In more technical terms this involves the *ecological validity* of the findings. Similarity between settings can be judged in terms such as culture, group structure, immediate situation (e.g., crisis vs. non-crisis), and the types of conflict among the parties. Another approach is to ask whether sentiments developed for (or behaviors shaped by) groups transfer to the larger context of intergroup and international relations. This is a matter of linkage where relevance is shown by recurring patterns of identification with groups whether they are defined at a micro or macro level of analysis.

At issue is the way that sentiments are developed in relation to different units of identification. From one perspective, the expression of sentiments is similar whether the group consists of interacting individuals or abstract entities: Sentiments expressed toward small groups need not precede those expressed toward such larger entities as nations and may, in fact, be contradictory. Much social-psychological experimentation is guided by the assumption of similar processes that can be invoked simultaneously; that is, national loyalties do not depend on the prior development of communal loyalties. A competing perspective on this issue assumes that loyalties transfer from smaller to larger entities: Sentiments expressed toward small groups or communities form the basis for those expressed toward nations.

PATRIOTISM AND NATIONALISM

Findings reviewed in the section above make evident the ease with which ingroup attachments are developed and competitive behavior is aroused in intergroup situations. They do, however, raise questions about the relationship between positive ingroup and negative outgroup sentiments or attitudes. Whether attitudes of enmity toward other (out) groups are a direct result of positive emotional attachments to one's own group or are aroused by competitive features of tasks or situations remains an issue: Can enmity (or competitiveness) be aroused in representatives who do not have strong attachments to their group? Can group representatives whose attachments are strong have favorable attitudes toward and engage in cooperative behavior with outgroups? These questions are addressed by the research reviewed in this section.

Implications for the link between ingroup amity and outgroup enmity are developed in the factor analysis studies reported by Feshbach (1990). He found that it is possible to distinguish among different kinds of ingroup orientations and identifications. Analyses of responses to items in a questionnaire about attitudes toward one's own and other countries revealed two relatively independent factors. One factor concerns attachment to one's country: Strong loadings were obtained on such items as "I am proud to be an American." This factor was labeled *patriotism*. A second factor concerns feelings of national superiority and a need for national power and dominance: Strong loadings were obtained on such items as "In view of America's moral and material superiority, it is only right that we should have the biggest say in deciding U.N. policy." This factor was called *nationalism*. Correlations between these factors and such variables as

early familial attachments, attitudes toward nuclear arms, and readiness to go to war suggest distinct patterns. "Nationalists" indicated stronger support for nuclear-armament policies and were more ready to go to war but less willing to risk their lives than "patriots." "Patriots" showed a stronger early attachment to their father than did "nationalists."

Feshbach's research also suggests that attitudes toward own and other groups or nations develop early in life. Studies of children's acquisition of attitudes, reviewed by Sears (1969), indicate that nationalism, at least in the United States, develops first as highly favorable affect without supporting cognitive content. The content may be a rationalization for the feelings which may linger after the cognitive component of attitudes have changed: Since the feelings develop earlier than the content, they are likely to be more resistant to extinction. It is those feelings, reflected in the distinction between patriotism and nationalism, that render debates between hawks and doves so vociferous and difficult to resolve. Attempts to mediate the differences are made difficult by the deep-rooted needs served by the attitudes: Policy consensus is more likely to result from compromises in positions than changes in the underlying feelings. Less clear, however, is the source for nationalistic attitudes: Do they emerge, as Feshbach's data suggest, from weak parental attachments? Or, do they emerge as a transfer of sentiments developed in a strong nuclear family unit?

According to Feshbach, patriotism is less likely to create public pressure for war than nationalism and is, thus, a more desirable orientation for citizens. Given that the tendency for ingroup attachments is probably universal (e.g., Tajfel, 1982), he suggests taking advantage of the positive elements of such attachments (namely, patriotism) and deemphasizing the negative elements (namely, nationalism). It should be possible to have pride in one's nation, recognize shortcomings, and be willing to cooperate with other nations, an orientation referred to by Feshbach as a "patriotic internationalist."

Feshbach's findings and recommendations suggest that ingroup amity is not always linked with outgroup enmity. Certain kinds of ingroup orientations are associated with a tendency to denigrate outgroups, while others are not (Berry, 1984). This distinction is made also in the well-known work of Adorno et al. (1950) on the authoritarian personality: They distinguished between a healthy patriotic love of one's own country not associated with prejudice against outgroups, and an ethnocentric patriotism (like Feshbach's nationalism), which would be. Much more recently, Duckitt (1989) suggested that insecure group identifications would be associated with prejudice and secure group identifications would not (see also Tajfel, 1981). This work calls into question an overall relationship between ingroup and outgroup attitudes—that attitudes toward the ingroup explain attitudes toward outgroups. The relationship may vary with a number of aspects of the situation as discussed in the next section.

The labeling of factors, such as patriotism or nationalism, reflects an assumption that these are relatively stable attitudinal-dispositions which are difficult to change. Conceivably, the orientations are not stable across situations but are aroused (or ameliorated) under certain well-defined conditions. For example, patriotic orientations may occur frequently in non-competitive situations while nationalistic attitudes are expressed more strongly in competitive situations. An experimental approach is better suited to identifying the conditions that arouse attitudes and behavior. A large number of experimental studies have been designed to explore these issues.

INGROUP BIAS[1]

Results obtained from many experiments leave little doubt that the mere classification of people into different groups evokes biases in favor of one's own group; for example, "my group is better, friendlier, more competent, and stronger than other groups" (Brewer, 1979; Messick & Mackie, 1989). Further, the bias is obtained even under conditions of cooperative interdependence between groups (Brewer & Silver, 1978). These results challenge the theory that ingroup bias is caused by intergroup competition or conflicts of interest as suggested by the early experiments conducted by the Sherifs (1965) and Druckman (1968a), among others. More recent studies suggest that competition is *not* a necessary condition for ingroup bias, although it can result from competition and is probably stronger in competitive situations.

The most prominent explanation for ingroup bias is Tajfel's (1982) social identity theory (SIT). This theory claims that people's self-evaluations are shaped in part by their group memberships so that viewing their group in positive terms enhances their

---

[1]The experimental work reviewed in this section refers to laboratory groups. Relevance of these findings to nationalism is based on the assumptions that group identification subsumes national, cultural, and other identifications and that the experimental methodologies provide insights about some influences on such identifications. Further, the problem of relevance may not depend on methodology. A more complex rendering of the concept of nationalism can also be explored in laboratory settings. The laboratory does not restrict an investigator's focus to face-to-face groups. It is possible to explore the sentiments aroused by identifications with abstract constituencies and "imagined communities" as well. Whether it is possible to reproduce the *scale, intensity,* and *salience* of national identifications is an empirical issue that can also be evaluated systematically.

self-esteem, which is further enhanced by making a favorable comparison between their own and another group: An analogous concept is Feshbach's *nationalism* discussed above; also analogous at the group level is the concept of *ethnocentrism,* which refers to the concomitance of ingroup amity and outgroup enmity (LeVine & Campbell, 1972). If this theory is correct, it should be demonstrated that intergroup discrimination increases a member's self-esteem. Studies by Oakes and Turner (1980) and by Lemyre and Smith (1985) support this hypothesized relationship. However, many other studies designed to test key implications of SIT provide mixed evidence for the theory. Such experimental variations as degree of ingroup identification, saliency of group membership, security of group identity, and group status failed to produce consistent results from one study to the next. (Messick & Mackie, 1989). Taken together, the studies indicate that such single-factor explanatory concepts as self-esteem do not seem sufficient to explain ingroup bias.

A broader theory proposed initially by Turner (1987) is referred to as self-categorization theory (SCT). SCT places greater emphasis than SIT on the way people categorize others into groups. The theory suggests that people evaluate their own group as superior only when they clearly see differences between members of their own and other groups. Without the categorizations of similarities and dissimilarities, real or distorted, the evaluative biases would not occur. However, the research has not illuminated the relative importance of perceived differences and self-esteem as sources of intergroup discrimination. A more complex explanation would include the combined or interactive effects of both elements.

The focus of most of the studies reviewed above is on *attitudes* toward members of ingroups and outgroups. A related body of work has examined how people *behave* in terms of their group memberships. Many studies, conducted within the framework of matrix games (notably the Prisoner's Dilemma Game), show that groups play more competitively than individuals, and show that group representatives are more competitive bargainers than nonrepresentatives. At issue in all of these studies is whether the competitiveness is a function of group identification per se. Insko et al. (1988) offer a different explanation. They showed that the increased competitiveness of groups was attributed to an intragroup consensus about the group's strategy: When groups acted in lockstep, enhanced competition occurred. A similar finding was obtained by Druckman (1968b). The most competitive groups in that study were those that agreed in prenegotiation sessions on the relative importance of the issues under discussion. It may be that a consensual strategy, rather than group identification per se, produces the observed increased competition. Whether it also produces ingroup biases in noncompetitive or minimal groups remains to be determined. Conceivably, intragroup consensus contributes to the perceptual discrimination that seems to precede evaluative biases.

It is clear that better-designed experiments are needed to isolate the factors responsible for the bias (Messick & Mackie, 1989). Particularly important are studies that identify the motivations of group members. Such clarification would bring us full cycle from studies that identify underlying needs for nationalism, reviewed earlier, to situations that arouse bias, reviewed in this section, and back to identifying the motives that are responsible for the biases expressed in attitudes and behavior. There is, however, a difference of perspective and methodology between the two types of studies. The former, intended to identify underlying needs, use questionnaires to assess attitudes that serve needs considered to be universal and relatively unchanging; the latter, intended to identify the conditions, assess attitudes and behavior that may also reflect needs, but the needs (goals or strategies) are aroused by the situation and are complex and changing. These different perspectives also reflect an age-old issue of whether we have a need for enemies or whether enemies are constructed by policy elites to serve political purposes (Volkan, 1988). From either perspective, however, it will be necessary to conduct experiments that begin to unravel the causal path from needs or attitudes (expressions of bias) to behavior (competitive choices, aggression).

The role of competition in arousing ingroup bias has not been clarified. Many of the experiments cited above show that bias can be aroused by mere categorization, while others link bias to a competitive situation. Is the bias stronger in competitive situations? Is it stronger on measures of behavioral choices than in expressions of attitudes? The studies to date have concentrated on assessing the bias in the context of an ingroup and an outgroup. Also interesting is the question whether the bias occurs in the context of multiple groups, where non-membership groups can serve as reference groups.

SENTIMENTS TOWARD MULTIPLE GROUPS

Much of the laboratory research reviewed above, and much of the earlier sociological theories, distinguishes only between ingroups as *membership groups* and outgroups as *non-membership groups*. Largely ignored in this work are *multiple group memberships* and a different array of outgroups for each of these memberships: overlapping and cross-cutting group memberships are part of the landscape of intergroup relations within or between nations. For nationalism, however, these complex patterns apply primarily to outgroups, not ingroups: most people are citizens of one nation, even if there is wide variation in the strength of identification with that nation.

From the standpoint of a nation's citizens, other nations can be scaled on a dimension from positive to negative orientations as well as the intensity with which these orientations are expressed. Of interest are the characteristics of nations that determine where they are placed on these dimensions.

Evidence for the "scaling hypothesis" is provided by results reported in the 1960s: e.g., Druckman (1968a), Singer et al. (1963), and Brewer (1968). The results suggest that sentiments expressed in favor of one's own group's members or against another group's members are a function of the nature of the comparison. For some outgroups—those that are allies, perceived as being similar and advanced, eligible for membership—the extent of bias is small. For other outgroups—those that are enemies or renegades, perceived as dissimilar and "backward" or distant, not eligible for membership—the bias is likely to be rather large. The evaluative bias is likely to be quite small or even reversed for outgroups that are emulated (Swartz, 1961).

Reference Groups

Reference group theory, as developed by Kelley (1952), Sherif and Sherif (1953), Merton (1957), and others, takes into account the often-overlooked cases of positive sentiments expressed toward non-membership groups. Applied to national identification, reference group theory highlights varying orientations that may be taken toward one's own and other nations.

Positive orientations toward non-membership groups are necessary, but not sufficient, conditions for making them reference groups. Liking for another group (or person) does not indicate *identification* with that group (or person). More is required, such as adopting its values or aspiring to membership. An interesting analytical problem is to discover the conditions for moving from positive sentiments *toward* identification *with* a non-membership group. Varying degrees of identification with non-membership groups can be scaled in terms of the way one relates to the group, for example, as follows:

High Identification	1) Motivated toward becoming a member
	2) Assimilating the group's norms and values
	3) Using the group's standards for evaluating performance
	4) Taking a positive orientation toward the group
	5) Understanding the group's norms and values
Low Identification	6) Recognizing the group's existence

The critical threshold that renders a non-membership group a reference group is between steps 4 (positive orientation) and 3 (evaluating performance): The further one goes up the ladder, from steps 6 to 1, the stronger the identification with the group. Reference-group identifications are maintained to the extent that those groups satisfy certain basic needs such as Kelman's (1988) self-transcendence or self-protection or needs related more closely to self-esteem (Tajfel, 1982). To the extent that these needs are not satisfied in membership groups—or satisfied better by non-membership groups—nationalistic or ethnocentric feelings are reduced.

The studies reviewed above provide limited insight into the conditions for group identification. They do, however, suggest some *independent variables* that may be relevant. For example, strength of identification with one's own or a reference group may vary with characteristics that lead to emulation (wealth, political power, military prowess, human rights); extent of visibility or knowledge of customs or living conditions; the type of contact experiences with members of other groups; extent to which boundaries are open or closed; extent to which needs are satisfied by one's own-group membership; and the extent to which one's own group is isolated. These variables may be hypothesized to influence sentiments toward and identification with both membership and non-membership groups. Their impact remains to be explored.

ROLE OF COGNITION IN IMAGES OF OWN AND OTHER NATIONS

To this point we have concentrated primarily on nationalistic sentiments. In this section, we are concerned with the distinction between descriptive, cognitive content, and the evaluative emotional aspects of images, as well as the extent to which they are *stereotypes*. An image is a stereotype if there is widespread agreement among individuals about its content or evaluations of own and other nations.

Content and Evaluational Aspects of Images

The distinction between content and evaluative aspects of images was made in Lambert and Klineberg's (1967) study of children's views of foreign peoples. Separating content diversity (e.g., reference to the political or economic system or to the nation's demography) from evaluative diversity (e.g., they are kind, naive, talkative), they found that a national group with a friendly orientation toward another group was well-informed about the group and described them with a diversity of *descriptive* terms and a minimum number of *evaluative* terms. In contrast, those groups with an unfriendly orientation toward other groups were relatively uninformed about them—used few terms to describe them—and showed a proliferation of evaluative references. This finding was also obtained by Druckman, Ali, and Bagur (1974) in each of three cultures, India, Argentina, and the United States.

Both aspects of images, the descriptive and evaluative content and the diversity of terms used, were shown to be influenced by one's orientation toward (friendly or unfriendly) and familiarity with the target nations. An implication of this research is that motivational factors underlie the findings on friendliness and evaluative categories—friendly nations were stereotyped more than unfriendly nations on evaluative terms—while cognitive factors underlie the findings on familiarity and descriptive categories—familiar nations were stereotyped less than unfamiliar nations on descriptive terms. The distinction between motivational and cognitive mechanisms is not meant to imply single-factor explanations of stereotypes. Rather, it refers to the relative emphasis placed on the one or the other type of mechanism in specific contexts. Any stereotype or image is the result of an interplay among cognitive and affective factors. Cottam's (1987) theory on the relationship between motives and the content of images proposes that the content can be predicted from three factors: a) perceptions of threat and opportunity, b) power distance, and c) cultural distance. To illustrate how this

works, Cottam discusses two examples, referred to as the "barbarian" analogue and the "degenerate" analogue.

The "barbarian" image reflects a perception of a threatening nation, superior (or equal) in terms of military capability but "inferior" in terms of culture. It takes the form of describing the nation in diabolical terms similar to Reagan's view of the Soviet Union as the "evil empire." The content of the stereotype includes: 1) a simple, single-minded, and aggressive enemy; 2) a monolithic decision structure; 3) a conspiratorial decision-making process; 4) a judgment that the enemy's advantage in capability is attributed to one's own inability, for moral reasons, to use one's own capability to optimal advantage in countering the "morally-inferior enemy"; and 5) citizens in one's own nation who disagree with this portrayal are "dupes at best, traitors at worst." The stereotyped enemy is seen as being dangerous, a view that would temper hasty aggressive action against them.

The "degenerate" image is based on a perception of opportunity coupled with a view that the other nation is comparable in strength but vulnerable. The content of the stereotype includes: 1) an enemy that is uncertain, confused, and inconsistent; 2) a diffuse and uncoordinated decision process; 3) decisions not guided by a strategic framework; 4) a lack of will that prevents them from being effective; and 5) citizens who disagree with this image are "effete and weak," much like those in the enemy nation. Based on this portrayal, the other nation is seen as being "ripe for the picking," a view that would encourage or rationalize aggression against them. The Bush administration's portrayal of Saddam Hussein's Iraq prior to the Gulf War had many of these features.

Cottam takes his analysis further by suggesting strategies that may effectively deal with these sorts of simplistic images. For example, when dealing with an opportunistic aggressor's "degenerate" image, he suggests conveying a tough posture, referred to in the foreign policy literature as *containment;* when dealing with national leaders who perceive threats, he advises a cooperative strategy, referred to as *détente*. These strategies are intended to disconfirm the other's images and, by so doing, create *dissonance,* which the other nation's leaders must resolve.

But, Cottam's theory does not take into account the apparent rapid swings in sentiment that occur under the influence of events and leadership. Notice how rapidly the Chinese became "good guys" after Nixon went to China, how fast Saddam Hussein became "a devil," or how sentiments expressed by Americans toward the U.S. military changed dramatically following the war in the Persian Gulf. Although generally consistent with a situational approach to nationalism, most social-psychological theories have not explained this phenomenon.

Content of Images as Theories of War

Cottam's typology corresponds in some ways to alternative theories of war as described by Silverstein and Holt (1989). For these authors, enemy images are not isolated phenomena but are best understood as part of a theory of war. They describe the "folk or Rambo theory," the "Realpolitik theory," and the "scientific or systems theory."

The *folk theory* posits a contest between good and evil, a world of dichotomous certainty without ambiguity. The demonic image of the enemy, which includes both Cottam's "barbarian" and "degenerate" images, is a central feature. This theory is closest to the traditional meaning of stereotypes as oversimplified images of one's own and other nations, referred to also as "mirror

images" when citizens in both nations hold these views of one another (Bronfenbrenner, 1961). Polarized thinking in both nations prevents debate and impedes conflict resolution on issues related to the opposed ideologies. Of particular interest are the conditions under which such thinking occurs in national representatives and in large segments of a nation's population. With regard to representatives, it has been shown that statements made by negotiators are less varied during periods of stress in an international negotiation (Druckman, 1986). Osgood (1962), Milburn (1972), and others have shown that, under external threat, populations tend to lapse into simplified stereotypes of the enemy.

The *Realpolitik worldview* is depicted as an oversimplified theory of war based on the game of power politics. While seen as being less simple than the folk-theory view, this approach is regarded by many psychologists, as being dangerous: It was the prevailing view attributed to American politics and to academic political science during the Cold War era. The game metaphor used by the realist school places a premium on winning a contest that is played without a framework of agreed rules; a focus on the self prevents concern for the possibility of joint gains or fair resolutions. But this characterization of the realist position may also be an oversimplification. (Here we encounter the interesting case of stereotyped thinking by psychologists who lament the dangers of stereotyped views of other nations.) Although some realist thinkers do indeed present a simplistic, albeit cynical, view of international relations, many other realists present a complex theoretical framework built on the assumptions of power politics in an anarchic international system. Nowhere is this complex rendition more evident than in the work of the most influential realist, Hans J. Morgenthau. A careful reading of Morgenthau reveals considerable complexity in the way that power is defined, assessed, and used (Morgenthau & Thompson, 1985). While power is the centerpiece of his framework, it is not a unidimensional concept. The issue then is not the complexity of realist approaches but their assumptions.

Other complex approaches to foreign policy focus more on cognitive processes than on power politics, and may be subsumed under the heading of *systems perspectives:* for example, the complex imagery described by cognitive mapping approaches (Bonham & Shapiro, 1986) or the ranked hierarchy of values approach to debate described by Rokeach (1979). The key point made here is that there is value in complex imagery, whether that imagery is based on realist or liberal assumptions. By reducing the temptation to stereotype other nations, it prevents pitting own nations against others in ways similar to Cottam's (1987) depicted views of the world. Since complex cognitive structures are assumed to underlie attitudes, values, and images, it should be possible to create the conditions for eliciting them.

Less clear in these treatments are the effects of sentiments on the content and structure of argumentation or values. The earlier discussion suggested that strong nationalist sentiments or intense group identification may produce simplified images of ingroups and outgroups. It was also shown, however, that a positive orientation toward one's own nation may not, by itself, result in stereotyped (oversimplified) images of an enemy nation. It should be possible to create the conditions for complex imagery without reducing one's attachment to a nation. Although difficult to sustain in all circumstances, especially during periods of high stress, complex imagery of the sort described by Silverstein and Holt's (1989) systems theory of war, by Bonham and Shapiro's (1986) cognitive mapping approach, or by Rokeach's (1979) values analysis can be taught, though the precise mechanisms underlying the learning process need extensive research.

NATIONALISM AND WAR

Psychological research has concentrated primarily on the *conditions* that arouse nationalist sentiments or stereotyped images of other nations. Less attention has been paid to the *connection* between those sentiments or cognitions and actions taken by nations. In this section, I attempt to spell out these connections, beginning by conceiving them in sequence, as stages toward or away from warfare.

The first stage consists of pressures brought by citizens on decision makers. A few studies show that national policies concerning defense spending are influenced by public images of adversaries (e.g., Burn & Oskamp, 1989) which are, in turn, influenced by changed relations (e.g., Trost et al., 1989). A second stage consists of the decision-making process engaged in by policy makers. From a psychological perspective, structural factors are not simply viewed as direct causes of collective action, as in the link between power and actions, but are the factors to be weighed by decision makers as they *consider* alternative courses of action. Included in the decision-making process is the propensity for misperception. A number of studies have shown that exaggerated national self-images can lead to miscalculations of likely outcomes from collective actions (e.g., Lebow, 1981).

The third stage consists of the actions that follow from the decision to commit resources, to mobilize, and to act. Actions, once taken, are likely to be influenced by such group characteristics as cohesion.

Group loyalty is usually regarded as a defining aspect of cohesion (Zander, 1979) and is emphasized in the literature on the motivation of soldiers (Moskos, 1970; Lynn, 1984). Less clear is the distinction between loyalty as cause or consequence of cohesion, and the role of cohesion in sustaining troop motivation over time (Druckman, 1995).

By making these connections, we can situate social-psychological factors in a framework of the causes and consequences of war. These factors are construed largely at the micro level of individuals (decision-makers) and small groups (decision-making and combat units) and, thus, provide only a partial explanation for collective action. A more comprehensive framework would also include macro (societal) level factors. In addition to identifying the factors at micro and macro levels, the framework would arrange them in time-ordered sequence which specifies the paths taken toward or away from war. Building on recent literature, the discussion to follow takes a step toward developing a framework that connects nationalism to war.

The distinction between a human, liberal-prone nationalism and a virulent, aggressive form, made by Gellner (1995), is relevant. Most treatments of nationalism focus on the former: the political, social, psychological, and economic development processes that influence the formation of national identities (Posen, 1993). Considerably less scholarship has been devoted to the more aggressive aspects and, thus, to the connection between nationalism and war (except the edited books by Kupchan, 1995, and Comaroff & Stern, 1995). This may be due to two dilemmas about the relationship. One concerns the confusion between causes and consequences: leaders use nationalism to mobilize public support for military preparation; nationalism is aroused by the conflict and intensified by victory.

Another dilemma concerns whether to focus analytical attention on citizens or decision-making elites: Are elites influenced by citizen pressure to act or are citizens' views and sentiments manipulated by elite machinations?

Regardless of the causal sequence, however, it is clear that intense nationalism can be aroused, in elites and citizens, easily and quickly. It plays an important, although not sufficient, role at each stage in the decision-mobilization processes leading to and sustaining violent intra- and international conflicts. Rather than resolving the directionality dilemmas, I place nationalistic sentiments in a framework that elucidates the conditions and processes leading toward or away from war.

Conditions, Background Factors, and Processes: A Framework

The literature on nationalism and war calls attention to variables that can be organized in such categories as conditions, background factors, processes, and outcomes. Included in the category of *background factors* are a nation's political structure as authoritarian or democratic (Kupchan, 1995), relations with minorities who live within the state (Van Evera, 1995), balance of power between ruling elites and ethnic minorities (Druckman & Green, 1986), and availability of alternatives to conflict or war. The link between these factors and nationalism is regime legitimacy, summarized in the form of an hypothesis: The less legitimate a government, the greater the incentive to provoke nationalistic sentiments that support conflict.

The process of provoking nationalist sentiments by decision-making elites involves constructing myths about the state in relation to foreigners. Van Evera notes that "myths flourish when elites need them most, when opposition to myths is weakest, and when publics are most myth-receptive" (1995, p. 151). Elites need them most when their legitimacy is in question and when they are faced with external or internal threats. Opposition to myths is weak when the society lacks independent evaluative institutions such as the media and universities. The citizenry is most receptive to myths in periods of transition and when they are faced with external threats. Ready acceptance of myths constructed by ruling regimes facilitates mobilization for collective action. Mobilization is also easier when national identification is relatively fluid. Bienen (1995) emphasizes the advantages (to elites) of dealing with a malleable citizenry. However, just as a fluid nationalism can be stirred up in the service of conquest or defense, its intensity can also be lessened through the experiences accompanying participation in combat. For this reason, a more durable nationalism may sustain combat even if it is more difficult to manipulate to serve the hegemonic goals of ruling elites.

The discussion above on reference groups emphasizes multiple group identities. Some of these identities are stronger or more durable than others. More durable identities are harder to manipulate, but provide a source of stable support for military mobilization. More fluid identities are easier to manipulate to serve the short-term goals of hegemonic leaders. Whether durable or fluid, identities are based on illusions of the distinction between "us" and "them." Connor (1994) discusses the myths of hemispheric, continental, regional, and state unity. For example, regions of Southeast Asia, the Far East, the Middle East, and sub-Sahara Africa are noted more for their distinctive than common characteristics, and the myth of intrastate unity has been exposed in the divisions between Croats and Slavs, Czechs and Slovaks, Quebeçois and

Canadians, and Flemish and Walloons. For leaders intent on sustaining unity at any of these levels, the challenge is to perpetuate the image of a common historical culture among different language communities. For leaders intent on exploiting divisions between communities within a region or state, the tactical challenge is to engender and sustain the image of distinctive ancestral roots and cultures among the different language communities. For scholars, according to Connor, the challenge is to resist the misperceptions of homogeneity that have influenced analysis and public policy.

But, plausible as these warnings and tactics seem, some scholars have contended that widespread nationalism is not an important precondition or influence on decisions to fight or sustain combat. In his analysis of the war in Serbia and Bosnia, Mueller (1998) claims that it was carried out largely by small bands of "thugs" or criminals. Leaders did not rely on mobilizing citizens to prosecute the war. He argues further that nationalism was either not widespread in these countries or that it did not provide sufficient incentives to fight. In fact, his analysis portrays citizens as victims rather than benefactors of elites' ambitions. Although limited to the case contexts studied, such analyses raise questions about the connection between nationalism and war. Nationalism is widely seen as a motivating factor for decisions to fight. It may not, however, be either necessary or sufficient to initiate or sustain combat.

Rather than to impute a causal role to nationalism, even in its aggressive or virulent form, I prefer to place these sentiments or variables in a larger framework of conditions that may lead to decisions to initiate or avoid war (including both civil and international conflicts). The framework shown in Figure 4.1 distinguishes among antecedent, concurrent, and consequent variables and includes the factors discussed in this section. Myth-

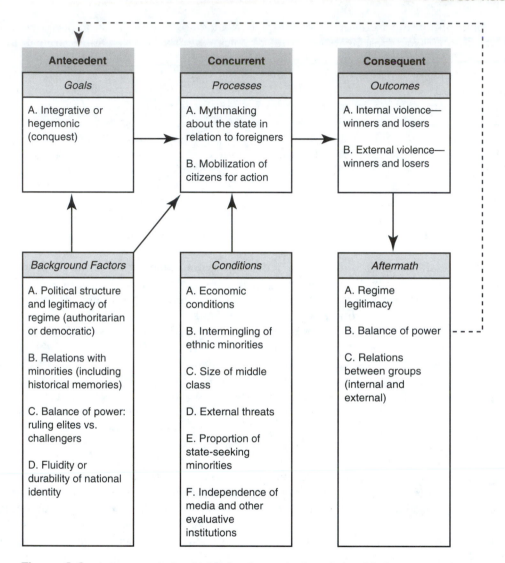

Figure 4.1 A framework that highlights factors in the relationship between nationalism and war.

making and mobilization, processes that
support conflict, are understood against the
background of goals, structures, relations
with minorities, and legitimacy as well as a
variety of internal and external conditions.
Nationalism is construed in this framework
in terms of fluid or durable identities (a

background factor) and responsiveness to
myths created usually by decision-making
elites (a process): New myths are easier to
create among citizens with fluid identities;
older myths are more likely to be sustained
when citizens have relatively durable identities that coincide with the images. These fac-

tors converge on an outcome, which can be regarded as a decision to fight or to sustain combat, with implications for changes in legitimacy, power, and relations (referred to in the framework as the "aftermath"). The feedback loop—from consequents to antecedent factors—indicates that the adjusted evaluations (following conflict) of legitimacy, power, and relations lead to another cycle of decisions about continuing the conflict. For example, combat victories may increase citizens' aggressive nationalism as well as reinforce leaders' hegemonic goals, both of which fuel further violent conflict.

At the heart of the framework is elite manipulation of nationalistic sentiments and identities. Citizens are vulnerable in times of economic and political transition leading to social disintegration (Kupchan, 1995; Mueller, 1998). But, disintegration is not a sufficient condition for conflict. Citizens must also be mobilized for action. This is easier to accomplish in nondemocratic societies with a small middle class. It is also more likely when there is an external threat (imagined or real) and when members of the same ethnic background are subject to discrimination in other lands, such as Turks living in Cyprus or Germany (Van Evera, 1995). When thought about in this way, the conditions and processes take the form of a rough time-ordered pathway starting with the society's political structure and culminating in the aftermath of the conflict and nation rebuilding as follows:

> 1) Political structure → 2) size of middle class → 3) extent of economic and political transitions → 4) extent of social disintegration → 5) extent of external threat → 6) manipulation of nationalistic sentiments → 7) fluidity of national or ethnic identification → 8) mobilization of citizens → 9) intra- or interstate conflict or violence → 10) outcomes of conflict → 11) post-conflict changes → 12) nation rebuilding.

EMPIRICAL GAPS: TOWARD A RESEARCH AGENDA

While contributing to our understanding of the connection between nationalism and war, the framework also reveals gaps in our knowledge that can be addressed by further research.

a) Group sentiments may be distributed among many different groups, both membership and non-membership. Of particular interest are the conditions under which citizens identify with a non-membership group or nation, the extent to which such contra-identifications occurs, and its implications for collective action.

b) To what extent do national sentiments, and the accompanying biasing tendencies, hinder the development or articulation of complex images or explanations of another nation's policies and actions?

c) It is important to specify further the roles played by perceptual and structural variables in influencing a nation's decision to act, its attempts to mobilize resources and citizens, and the actions taken.

d) What is the relationship between social disintegration and external conflict? While disintegration may motivate elites to manipulate enemy images, it may also reduce citizens' nationalism or their receptivity to enemy images.

e) What is the relationship between the fluidity of national identifications and external conflict? While citizens with a relatively fluid identity may be more vulnerable to elite manipulation, those with more durable identities may be more stable in supporting their nation's military campaigns.

f) What are the relationships between nationalism, mobilization, and sustained
combat? How often (and in which
types) are wars fought by mercenaries?
Can national combat be sustained with
mercenary armies in the absence of
widespread citizen support?

g) When settlement does not result in resolution, conflict continues in the aftermath of war. What conditions influence
continued conflict between parties who
concluded a war or agreed to a cease
fire? What role does heightened nationalism (usually expressed by victorious
nations following war) play in fueling
further conflict?

h) What is the relationship between intra-
and international conflict? Do intranational divisions interfere with attempts
to prosecute international wars? What is
the influence of nationalism on cohesion and mobilization for external conflict? Do cohesion and mobilization further strengthen nationalism?

PROSPECTS FOR NATIONALISM IN THE TWENTY-FIRST CENTURY

In considering prospects, I summarize some
implications from the social-psychological
studies in relation to the macro-level variables in the framework. Many laboratory
studies demonstrated the ease with which
identities and accompanying ingroup–outgroup images can be established. Identities
may be more fluid than durable, changing
with changes in the situation such as a reeval-
uation of incentives and goals, shifting alliances, superordinate goals, the discovery of
new reference (non-membership) groups,
and third-party interventions. Changing conditions can increase or decrease ingroup attachments just as they can intensify or reduce the negative sentiments expressed

toward outgroups. A challenge is to understand the conditions that increase (or decrease) the positive elements of ingroup attachments, referred to earlier as patriotism,
while decreasing (or increasing) the negative aspects of outgroup enmity, referred to
as nationalism. This challenge has important implications for mobilizing citizens for
collective action, including war.

The framework shown in Figure 4.1
identifies some factors that can trigger aggressive nationalism. The processes of
image- or mythmaking and mobilization engaged in by some decision-making elites,
are understood in relation to certain political and economic conditions. Citizens in nations with authoritarian regimes during periods of economic transition are more
vulnerable to elite manipulation of nationalist sentiments than those in prospering
democratic societies. Incentives for such
manipulation are increased when the
regime faces challenges (from state-seeking
minorities) to its authority and legitimacy
and when it effectively controls the media.
Prospects can then be projected from
trends in these conditions, notably toward
or away from democratization and self-suffi-
cient economies. The variables can be used
as a checklist of indicators for monitoring
these trends.

Although there is reason to offer opti-
mistic prospects—namely, toward more liberal-prone nationalisms—based on current
international trends, two dilemmas serve to
reduce the confidence in any forecast. One
is that citizens' nationalism may be less important in authoritarian than in democratic
political systems. While authoritarian elites
can more easily manipulate popular sentiments, they may have less need to do so.
Mueller's (1998) work on mercenary armies
in Bosnia and Lynn's (1984) analysis of soldier motivation suggest that nationalism or
patriotism may not be important incentives

to sustain combat. While democratic regimes have more difficulty in manipulating popular sentiments—in large part because of the role of an independent media—they may have more need to do so, especially in countries with all-volunteer militaries. Thus, the trend toward democratization may not reduce nationalistic sentiments but may make it increasingly difficult to mobilize and sustain those sentiments for war.

The second dilemma consists of an apparently increasing tension between globalization (larger, supra-national identities) and fragmentation (smaller, national and ethnic group identities). In commenting on trends in European nationalism, Periwal (1995) noted that, on the one hand, an increasingly cosmopolitan and integrated Europe is an antidote to the perils of exclusionary nationalism. On the other hand, this consolidation may give rise to reactive sentiments from those who feel excluded. Blocked mobility or assimilation can lead to a sense of humiliation which makes people vulnerable to nationalistic appeals. Within Poland, and perhaps other Eastern European nation-states, a tension exists between a desire to assimilate into a greater Europe and a desire to retain an historic national identity. This may well be an unresolved tension well into the twenty-first century, making us wonder whether the balance will tip in favor of the one—cosmopolitanism—or the other—nationalism.

CHAPTER 5

INTERGRATIVE COMPLEXITY AND POLITICAL DECISIONS THAT LEAD TO WAR OR PEACE

Lucian Gideon Conway, III, Peter Suedfeld,[1]
and Philip E. Tetlock

And the war began, that is, an event took place opposed to human reason and all human nature. (Tolstoy, cited in Huberman & Huberman, 1964, p. 391.)

From the dawn of history down to the sinking of the Terris Bay, the world echoes with the praise of righteous war . . . I am almost tempted to reply to the Pacifist as Johnson replied to Goldsmith, "Nay Sir, if you will not take the universal opinion of mankind, I have no more to say. (C. S. Lewis, 1949, pp. 64–65.)

As suggested by comparing the above reflections, a striking duality about war is that it is at once both seemingly aversive to humans and yet nearly universally accepted and practiced. Virtually all humans would agree that war is, if not inherently bad, at least highly disagreeable and the cause of much suffering. Indeed, the act of killing another human being—even in war—may well, as Tolstoy suggested, go against human nature. For example, examination of the 27,000 muskets retrieved from dead soldiers at the Battle of Gettysburg during the American Civil War, and reports by American riflemen during World War II, show surprisingly low percentages of weapon use, even with enemy soldiers in plain view (Grossman, 1996, 1998). This suggests that humans may have a built-in aversion to the very thing that defines war—killing other humans.

On the other hand, this general aversion to war makes it all the more puzzling that, for practically as long as there have been nations or societies, there has been war, and that certain wars are accepted as necessary. Why, given that peace seems so psychologically preferable to war, is international peace so difficult to maintain?

Wars have multiple levels of causes. The historian studies political maneuvering and the rise and fall of particular leaders; the philosopher may explore moral and ethical causes of war in general; the sociologist may be concerned with such causes as mass

---

[1]During the writing of this paper, Peter Suedfeld was a Visiting Scholar at the Mershon Center, The Ohio State University.

movements and competing loyalties; the economist may assess the distribution of resources among the various antagonists. Some political scientists argue that war is the inevitable outcome of nations each pursuing their own rational self-interest in an international environment characterized by anarchy, where guns are indeed *ultima ratio regis* (the final argument of kings: traditional slogan of the artillery). All of these approaches have merit, but the psychologist has a distinctly different task: to understand, as much as possible, what sorts of things those responsible for war think and feel that makes them send their own countrymen into battle, and why ordinary citizens obey, often enthusiastically. In doing so, the psychologist hopes to explain more precisely and at a deeper level exactly what factors contribute to the rise of particular wars, and, conversely, what factors contribute to a peaceful compromise in certain situations that, on the surface, closely resemble a build-up to war.

THE APPROACH OF THE AUTHORS TO WAR AND PEACE OUTCOMES

There is a tendency in the psychological literature to assume that war as an outcome is bad and that peace is good (see Suedfeld, 1992). Our own view is that this is a philosophical issue that generally lies beyond the scope of psychology. It may well be that wars are best judged, in the moral sense, as "good" or "bad" on a war-by-war basis. Whatever the case, however, the goal of the psychologist is to focus on the processes that lead to particular, predictable outcomes—and not to assign normative values to those outcomes.

INTEGRATIVE COMPLEXITY

The purpose of the present chapter is to investigate the role of a particular psychological construct, integrative complexity, in political decisions that lead to war or peace. *Integrative complexity* involves both (1) the degree to which people differentiate among aspects of or perspectives on a particular problem ("differentiation"), and (2) the degree to which people then relate those perspectives to each other within some coherent framework ("integration"). Differentiation is necessary but not sufficient for integration; one can differentiate without integrating, but not integrate without first differentiating. Integrative complexity is measured by coding verbal passages (in most of the research discussed here, this entails coding public addresses or documents of political leaders) on a 7-point scale, where 1 equals low differentiation and low integration, 3 equals high differentiation and low integration, 5 equals high differentiation and moderate integration, and 7 equals high differentiation and high integration (for scoring details, see Baker-Brown et al., 1992).

AN INTEGRATIVE COMPLEXITY PERSPECTIVE ON SOME MAJOR CRISES

Consider what might happen to political leaders during a time of intense international conflict when war is a real possibility. The leaders might adopt one of two different hypothetical approaches to resolve the crisis: (1) they might stand unyielding by their position, refusing to see (or admit they see) any merit in that of the opposition, or (2) they might be (or at least appear) flexible and willing to compromise. It seems reasonable that when leaders adopt the first strategy during a crisis, the situation is more likely to end in war, while leaders who adopt the second approach are more likely to have that crisis end in peace. If leaders refuse to see any merit in their opposition's arguments during crises, they are more likely to end up "sticking to their own guns"—both figuratively and (sometimes) literally. Conversely, if leaders attempt to be flexible and cooperative, they should be more likely to work out a peaceful resolution. Given this, to the degree that low integrative complexity is associated with an unyielding strategy and high integrative complexity is associated with a more flexible strategy, it seems theoretically reasonable to expect that integrative complexity could serve as a useful *predictor* of the outbreak or avoidance of war.

Let us now look at the evidence pertaining to the link between the integrative complexity of the statements of political leaders and eventual war or peace. We will then explore the possible explanations for this link, and consider the limitations of this literature.

THE AMERICAN CIVIL WAR

More Americans were killed during the bitterly fought Civil War than during any other war in history (of course, it was the only war in which both opposing armies were made up of American soldiers). Interestingly, although it was fought from 1861 to 1865, the war very well could have begun about ten years earlier. Around 1850, there was a great debate in the U.S. Senate concerning the slavery status of any new states entering the Union. Would such states be allowed to have slavery or not? This debate ended in 1850 with a peaceful compromise. Why, given this, did the very similar Senatorial debates in 1860 to 1861 end in the incredibly violent Civil War?

One answer may be that the North and the South were driven to war by two increasingly influential extreme political factions— factions that tended to be lower in complexity than more moderate groups. Based on historical writings, prominent political figures before the Civil War were classified as either abolitionists, free-soil Republicans who would tolerate slavery but not allow it to

spread into new states, Buchanan Democrats who would permit slavery in new states if the within-state majority approved it, and outright supporters of slavery who wanted it to be legal throughout the nation. Results indicated that the two moderate groups (free-soil Republicans and Buchanan Democrats) were higher in complexity than both extreme groups (abolitionists and slavery-supporters; Tetlock, Armor, & Peterson, 1994). This suggests that the groups that were most likely driving the nation towards war were indeed lower in complexity. This interpretation is partially supported by the fact that the group highest in complexity, the Buchanan Democrats, was also highest in "war avoidance" as a central value, suggesting an association between high complexity and peace (although it should be noted that the other moderate group, the free-soil Republicans, was only moderate in "war avoidance").

The above results do not directly compare integrative complexity levels prior to the 1850 compromise and the 1861 war. One would expect that, if complexity were a key factor in the outbreak of the Civil War, the integrative complexity of the 1850 debates would be markedly higher than the 1860 to 1861 debates. To our knowledge, no such direct comparison exists using an integrative complexity score. However, using a less sophisticated measure of complexity, Winter (1997; see also Winter & Molano, 1998) found that complexity was indeed lower during the Senate debates of 1860 to 1861 than during the Senate debates of 1850.[2] Taken together, this evidence sug-

[2]This difference was just short of conventional levels of significance (one-tailed $p = .055$). However, the authoritarianism score, comprised in part of the complexity measure, did achieve conventional levels of significance (Winter, 1997; Winter & Molano, 1998). (Authoritarianism is negatively correlated with complexity: Persons high in authoritarianism do not want to think about new and unconventional ideas.)

gests a link between the integrative complexity of the prominent political players of the day and the ultimate beginning of the Civil War.

WORLD WAR II

Neville Chamberlain was the Prime Minister of Great Britain during the latter 1930s, and he faced a difficult dilemma: Nazi Germany was a burgeoning military power making often difficult international demands. Should he negotiate or stand firm? His choice was to use a highly flexible appeasement strategy. Chamberlain's primary political opponent on this matter was Winston Churchill, who dogmatically maintained that Hitler and the Nazis must be dealt with by arms buildups and stern displays of force. Churchill claimed that appeasement through flexible negotiation was simply encouraging further aggression (most historians agree, with the 20/20 vision that hindsight affords, that Churchill was right). As we might expect of one with such an unyielding position, Churchill's integrative complexity scores on Germany-related issues were quite low throughout the 1930s.

More to our present purpose, Chamberlain had consistently higher complexity levels than Churchill until very near the actual beginning of World War II, when he showed a major drop in complexity (Tetlock & Tyler, 1996). This is further evidence that a downward shift in integrative complexity is often a signal that war is imminent.

Analyses of statements made by Japanese policy-makers in 1941 prior to their attack of the United States at Pearl Harbor revealed a pattern that was only partially consistent with this hypothesis. The complexity of three key Japanese policy-makers, analyzed in both early and late 1941, did not reliably differ in complexity between the two time periods (Levi & Tetlock, 1980). Why?

It may be that certain unique cultural differences caused the Japanese to exhibit less consistent responsiveness to a looming war than the other nationalities that so far have been placed under the complexity microscope. Similarly, chronic personality differences between the three men could have caused them to react differently. Or, the truncated range of time examined may have been relevant: The earlier time frame may have been too near the December 1941 attack for the predicted downturn in complexity to be detected. Indeed, a study of nine surprise attacks from 1941 to 1982, including the Japanese attack on Pearl Harbor, was more supportive of a hypothesized link between integrative complexity and war or peace (Suedfeld & Bluck, 1988).

This suggests that complexity is a useful predictor of impending aggressive military actions even when the explicit content of the attacking nation's statements successfully hides the imminent attack.

THE COLD WAR

In the years between the end of World War II and the fall of Communism in Eastern Europe, the United States and the Soviet Union were the primary opponents on the international political and military scene. This time period was dubbed the "Cold War" because, although never officially at war, these two superpowers spent a great deal of military and political energy on interventions around the globe, designed to expand their own influence and limit that of the opponent. Consequently, this era has proven a useful context for exploring the link between integrative complexity and hostile vs. cooperative outcomes in international conflicts.

Tetlock (1985, 1988) assessed the integrative complexity of official Soviet and American foreign policy statements from 1945 to 1983. Time series and regression analyses revealed that the Soviets' complexity tended to be lower during the quarter-year prior to an aggressive intervention (such as the military intervention in Afghanistan, the Soviet-supported invasion of South Korea by North Korea, and the installation of Soviet nuclear weapons in Cuba), and higher during the quarter-year prior to an agreement with the United States that peacefully resolved a difficult international issue (such as the agreement to lift the Berlin blockade, the truce agreement which ended the Korean War, and the Soviet withdrawal of their nuclear missiles from Cuba). Similarly, the United States' integrative complexity levels were lower during the quarter-year of an aggressive intervention (such as American support for the Bay of Pigs invasion of Cuba, the American invasion of Cambodia, and American military support of Israel during the Yom Kippur War) and higher during the quarter-year before a peaceful agreement with the Soviet Union.

That the Soviets and Americans differed in terms of the exact time of the complexity shift relative to the aggressive or cooperative act probably reflects something unique about each nation's approach to foreign policy; indeed, the Soviets tended to be more premeditative in their foreign policy during the Cold War (Adomeit, 1981; George, 1969; Leites, 1953; see Tetlock, 1985, for a discussion). However, for our purposes it is the striking similarity that is most informative: Both the Soviets and the Americans showed decreased complexity prior to (or during) an aggressive act, and increased complexity prior to (or during) a peaceful agreement.

SADDAM HUSSEIN DURING THE PERSIAN GULF CRISIS

During the summer of 1990, Saddam Hussein ordered a successful Iraqi invasion of the oil-rich country of Kuwait, surprising the rest of the world. In response to this action, a coalition of nations—led by the United States—brought their collective military forces to bear on the Iraqis. A dramatic military showdown ensued.

Several interesting findings from studies of this time period (Suedfeld, Wallace, & Thachuk, 1993; Wallace, Suedfeld, & Thachuk, 1993) suggest that the integrative complexity of the leaders, especially Saddam Hussein, was an important aspect of the crisis. The Western media has often depicted Saddam as the power-mad Butcher of Baghdad, who had his mind unyieldingly set on world conquest (see Bulloch & Morris, 1991; Darwish & Alexander, 1991). Interestingly, though, during the two months prior to Iraq's invasion of Kuwait, Saddam's integrative complexity scores were actually relatively high; this suggests that perhaps Saddam did not have his mind uncompromisingly aimed towards war. However, consistent with the surprise attacks reported above, his complexity fell markedly immediately prior to the invasion. This is further evidence that aggressive international acts are preceded by lower complexity in the attacking nations.

Immediately after the invasion occurred, his complexity rose, and it became higher yet once the invasion had been accomplished with complete success. In the few months following the invasion, international pandemonium broke out as many nations and the U.N. Secretary General tried diplomatically and through economic sanctions to convince Saddam to evacuate his troops from Kuwait. None of these ploys worked. Interestingly, although Saddam's integrative complexity levels were higher during these months than immediately after the successful invasion, they were only slightly so—much less than would generally be expected during such a complicated international negotiation. One inference from this is that Saddam never really intended to compromise his position, and that by this time he either viewed war as inevitable or did not believe that the Western world would go to war over Kuwait.

REVOLUTIONARIES FROM CROMWELL TO CASTRO

International crises relevant to war and peace come in different shapes and sizes. One generally non-peaceful event in a nation's history is a revolution, that is, the violent overthrow of a government to establish an entirely new one. Successful revolutionary leaders (like Oliver Cromwell, George Washington, and Fidel Castro) generally showed low complexity during the attempted revolution. Interestingly, however, those leaders who remained low in complexity after taking over the government tended to be ousted from power. Leaders who were able to increase their integrative complexity after gaining power were more likely to remain in power (Suedfeld & Rank, 1976). These findings again suggest that high complexity is associated with relative peace, while low complexity is associated with armed hostilities.

THE MATCH BETWEEN COMPLEXITY LEVEL AND THE SITUATION

For many activities, it is true that "it takes two to tango." But while it is certainly true that many wars are mutually entered into by the various participants, war does not require the consent of all parties involved. Nations can simply be forced into war by a foreign attack; once that happens, they must defend themselves or surrender. Although it has been consistently found that the attacking nation typically decreases in complexity when an aggressive action is imminent, that does not mean that the defend-

ing nation necessarily likewise decreases. What might the pattern be for a nation on the receiving end of an unwanted war?

One might guess that nation's leaders would also decrease their complexity as they prepare for the coming onslaught, or to match the complexity levels of their opponents. The available evidence, however, suggests that the opposite is the case. In their study of nine surprise attacks, for instance, Suedfeld and Bluck (1988) found a marked increase in the complexity of the defending nations between two to four weeks and one week prior to the attack. Similarly, although showing a decrease prior to the other three military conflicts from 1947 to 1976, Egypt and Syria slightly increased in complexity before the surprise invasion of the Suez Canal zone by Britain, France, and Israel in 1956 (Suedfeld, Tetlock, & Ramirez, 1977). In addition, although Saddam Hussein decreased in complexity prior to his own invasion of Kuwait, his complexity increased in the weeks before the deadline given by the Security Council for his withdrawal (Suedfeld, Wallace, & Thachuk, 1993; Wallace, Suedfeld, & Thachuk, 1993).

Why might a nation forced to defend itself show a pattern opposite to that of the attacker? Perhaps the most intuitively appealing explanation is that the defending nation increases its complexity in hopes of reaching a compromise and averting the crisis (Wallbaum, 1993).

This suggests an interesting psychological template for a one-sided war. Evidence from the Soviet-American Cold War era (Tetlock, 1985) suggests that, in general, enemies will typically match each other's complexity during crises. The evidence reported above, however, implies that in any heated international crisis where one nation adopts a low-complexity stance while the other nation, presumably in an attempt to win reconciliation, adopts a high-complexity position, military conflict may be imminent. This underscores the important point that simply evaluating complexity out of the historical context is not particularly informative: Just because a nation's leaders are high in complexity at a given time does not mean that nation will find a peaceful agreement. Agreements, unlike wars, require acceptance by both sides (Raphael, 1982).

Indeed, being highly complex could be a very dangerous enterprise if one's opponents are low. When confronting an implacable and determined antagonist, it may be necessary to present an equally impervious front to the enemy. Simply maintaining high complexity will guarantee neither peace nor success. Rather, the ability to apply different levels of complexity to different situations may play a greater role in success or failure in a variety of contexts, including maintaining peace against a determined antagonist (Suedfeld, 1992).

WHAT ACCOUNTS FOR THE COMPLEXITY–WAR/PEACE LINK?

As discussed earlier, it seems intuitively credible that a highly competitive negotiating strategy will likely lead to war. But is integrative complexity a *symptom* or a *cause of* the type of diplomatic bargaining that leads to war or peace? Do leaders who decide to force their enemies into submission do so because their integrative complexity decreases, or does the fact that they have determined to force their enemies into submission cause their complexity to reflect a decrease? Do persons who try to make peace do so because their integrative complexity increases, or does the fact that they are determined to make peace cause their complexity to reflect an increase?

There is evidence from a laboratory setting that actual cognitive differences in com-

plexity can causally contribute to aggressive or peaceful decision-making. "Inter-Nation Simulation" studies revealed that persons low in integrative complexity are three times as likely to rely on competitive actions such as war than persons high in complexity. In addition, players who were low in complexity were more likely to use violence when frustrated (Driver, 1965; Schroder, Driver, & Streufert, 1967; Streufert & Streufert, 1978). Conversely, negotiating pairs high in complexity are more likely to reach mutually beneficial compromises (Pruitt, 1981; Pruitt & Lewis, 1975), thus suggesting that those low in complexity use negotiating tactics less likely to end in peaceful resolutions. Although this research suggests a direct causal relationship between complexity and war/peace outcomes, it cannot answer a critical question: in historical crises, what causes the *changes* in complexity in the first place?

Stress is one possibility. Crises are stressful—and stress has predictable effects on integrative complexity. The *disruptive stress hypothesis* suggests that although low to moderate levels of stress can increase complexity, high levels of stress (such as those probably caused by international crises) decrease complexity because of the fact that stress depletes the cognitive resources necessary for complex thinking (e.g., Suedfeld, Corteen, & McCormick, 1986; Suedfeld & Rank, 1976). Indeed, consistent with the predictions of the disruptive stress hypothesis, major political leaders' integrative complexity scores do tend to decrease notably during international crises. In one study, measurements of integrative complexity levels before, during, and after international crises between 1958 and 1983 revealed that 15 of the 16 leaders decreased in complexity during the crises (Wallace & Suedfeld, 1988).

Group dynamics may also play an important role in the relationship between complexity and war. The influential group-think model posits that psychological pressures toward consensus within groups can, during times of crisis where a decision is required, lead high-level group members to unequivocally accept the opinion of their leader—even if they really disagree with it (see Janis, 1982, 1989). Signs of groupthink include a reluctance to criticize other members' opinions, ignoring input from qualified persons outside the group, and failing to explore potential alternative options to the leader's viewpoint.

Perhaps not surprisingly, there is evidence of a link between groupthink and integrative complexity. Tetlock (1979) found that decision-makers in cases classified as groupthink scenarios demonstrated less complexity than cases classified as non-groupthink scenarios. On the flip side, Bordin (1998) found in an experimental study that military officers low in integrative complexity were more prone to the influences that lead to groupthink in the first place when responding to an imaginary crisis caused by a terrorist attack on a United States embassy. This evidence suggests not only that shifts in group organizational strategies will affect complexity, but, conversely, that groups in which the members are low in complexity will be more likely to be affected by such group dynamics processes. To the degree that the impending crisis affects most or all members of a leadership group, this suggests that group processes may multiply the effects of low complexity on decision-making relevant to war and peace.

Of course, factors other than stress and group dynamics can affect the level of complexity of a nation's policies. Certain individuals seem to have chronically higher (or lower) levels of complexity than others; thus, the complexity of a nation's policies may shift when the leadership of that nation changes. For example, Mikhail Gorbachev displayed decidedly higher complexity scores than his Soviet predecessors (Tetlock, 1988; see also Tetlock & Boettger, 1989). There may also be an individual difference in the ability to recognize and act upon the need to shift complexity levels, as was observed among the group of revolutionary leaders mentioned earlier.

THE COGNITIVE AND IMPRESSION MANAGEMENT INTERPRETATIONS

It could be that the decision to take either an aggressive or peaceful tack in international crises is arrived at entirely independent of integrative complexity, and complexity as revealed in diplomatic statements merely reflects those decisions. For example, the complexity of such statements could be the result of an intentional rhetorical strategy designed to create a particular impression on one's antagonist. If a nation's goal is to simply bend another nation to its own desires, then one way to accomplish this is to issue low-complexity statements that get the no-compromise message across. Conversely, a nation's leaders may feel that flexible maneuvering can better accomplish their own selfish ends, and thus issue statements that are higher in complexity. Thus, the public statements of these official representatives do not necessarily reflect the private or actual complexity levels of these individuals, but rather simply result from fully intentional strategies designed to leave a particular impression on their antagonists (see, e.g., Tetlock, 1985).

Is the cognitive approach (which assumes that complexity causally contributes to decisions leading to war or peace) or the impression management approach (which assumes that complexity merely reflects an intentional strategy to engage in competitive or cooperative rhetoric) more adequate?

Direct tests of cognitive vs. impression management explanations of complexity in historical documents are difficult; indeed, it has been argued that such tests are very hard to interpret even when performed in a controlled laboratory setting (Tetlock & Manstead, 1985). The most direct attempt to disentangle the two explanations with regards to war and peace decisions comes in research on Neville Chamberlain prior to World War II. Tetlock and Tyler (1996) were able to use both public and private documents of Chamberlain for these analyses. To the degree that Chamberlain's private documents really reflected his sentiments, the researchers were able to assess his actual thoughts. As previously mentioned, Chamberlain's generally high complexity took a steep dive as the outbreak of the war approached. The impression management approach would predict that Chamberlain's public documents would particularly show this drop, while his private documents (since they reflect his real thoughts) would not. This did not occur; in fact, the drop was much larger for his private than his public documents (which did not attain conventional levels of significance; Tetlock & Tyler, 1996). This suggests that, as a cognitive approach would predict, the association between integrative complexity and decisions that lead to war or peace reflects a *real* difference in the complexity levels of the various major players on the diplomatic scene. Suedfeld and Rank (1976) reported that they found no differences in the complexity of public vs. private documents generated by revolutionary leaders during and after the revolution.

Not all of the evidence is so favorable to the cognitive approach. And of course, these two approaches are by no means mutually exclusive. The deliberate use of rhetoric does not preclude real cognitive change, and vice versa. At this point, it is premature to take a firm position as to the relationship among impression management goals, complexity of information processing, and war or peace outcomes. Indeed, we consider it highly probable that both real cognitive changes and intentional impression management contribute to this link.

CONCLUSION

As we have seen, the evidence suggests that integrative complexity is a powerful predictor of whether an international crisis will end in war or peace. However, a number of alternative interpretations for this consistent relationship must be considered.

One possibility is that complexity level may be susceptible to conscious manipulation as leaders wish to project either an image of flexibility and open-mindedness, or of firm resolve, independently of their actual thought processes. Another is that the nature of the crisis may dictate complexity: intractable conflicts over important goals may be so stressful that complexity levels drop (disruptive stress), whereas complexity may remain or become high when the individual actually sees an acceptable compromise resolution.

The centrality of the role of individual statesmen, the focus of most analyses, is another moot issue. For example, Chamberlain exhibited a relatively sharp decline in complexity during confidential, high-level decision-making sessions about how Britain should cope with Hitler's Germany. It may be that Chamberlain, increasingly demoralized and discouraged, was showing disruptive stress as it became more and more obvious through the grim months of 1939 that his policy of appeasement had failed. Alternatively, it is possible that the European world was becoming an integratively simpler milieu as the pace of rearmament accelerated and alliance structures became increasingly sharply defined. In this view, Chamberlain represents a relatively powerless mediating variable serving merely as a conduit for the shifting features of the geopolitical environment.

In our view, it is premature to take a strong position on whether the complexity of leadership thinking or communication is a key causal construct, or is a sign of the operation of other, more fundamental, causal forces. The level of proof leaves us with an open, if not completely neutral, mind. An interesting possibility is implied by a recent study (Santmire et al., 1998). In a simulated hostage negotiation, it was not the level of complexity of the negotiators that made the difference. Rather, negotiators whose levels of complexity were moderately close to each other were more likely to achieve mutually beneficial outcomes than negotiators who were either very close or very diverse in complexity. This finding needs to be tested in real-life situations.

We began by posing the question: Given how aversive war is to people in general, why does war happen at all? An integrative complexity perspective offers one potential answer. Consider the different psychological makeup of the paths to war and peace. Perhaps war, because it is in some respects more difficult for humans to engage in than peace, requires the unitary commitment to an ideal that is the hallmark of low complexity. Complex processing may be largely incompatible with war, because once one begins processing many perspectives, one is likely to hit upon persuasive solutions that do not include war. Negotiating peace demands that one be very attentive to multiple perspectives. At the very least, peaceful compromise requires thinking about one other viewpoint—that of the opposition. At the most, it requires balancing the many different complicated issues generally inherent in an international crisis. Thus, integrative complexity theory offers one psychological explanation of some of the causes of war in general, as well as being a useful predictor of whether a specific crisis is likely to lead to war or to peace.

As is perhaps obvious, the scoring of integrative complexity has some practical implications. Assessing the complexity levels of opponents and allies may be fruitful in understanding their position, but whether or not increased complexity among leaders would be a good thing (and the reader will recall that we do not prescribe it as the cure for all evils), it does not appear to have occurred. Comparisons of current and recent world leaders with those of earlier times show no particular pattern of change. Thus, at least to the extent that it depends upon individual propensity for integratively complex thinking, even under stress, world peace in the early part of the twenty-first century will probably be no more stable than in previous eras.

CHAPTER 6

GENOCIDE AND MASS KILLING: THEIR ROOTS AND PREVENTION

Ervin Staub

The U.N. Genocide Convention, passed on December 9, 1948, has defined genocide as "acts committed with intent to destroy in whole or in part, a national, ethnical, racial or religious group . . ." In this chapter, I will explore the roots of and, briefly, some approaches to the prevention of genocide as well as mass killing, the killing of large numbers of people without the intention to destroy the whole group. Genocide and mass killing have fuzzy boundaries. Mass killing is frequently a waystation to genocide. Most importantly perhaps, genocide and mass killing have similar roots, and their prevention requires similar approaches. I will refer to them simply as group or collective violence.

The chapter will engage the central goals of peace psychology: understanding the roots of collective violence and its destructive consequences and exploring how such violence can be prevented and how individuals can contribute to its prevention and to the creation of peaceful societies and a peaceful world. I will discuss the following topics: (1) instigators of collective violence, such as difficult life conditions and group conflict; (2) psychological processes that arise from them, such as scapegoating and antagonistic ideologies; (3) the evolution of increasing violence that may end in geno-

cide; (4) characteristics of cultures that make these processes more or less probable; (5) group conflict as a source of collective violence; (6) the role of bystanders and the effects of their passivity; (7) the need for bystanders to intervene to halt violence once it has begun, together with useful modes of intervention; and finally, (8) proposals for preventing such violence before it begins.

THE ROOTS OF GROUP VIOLENCE

How do human beings develop the motivation to kill large numbers of people or even to exterminate a whole group? How do the inhibitions that normally stop us from killing other people decline? Understanding the roots of genocide and mass killing requires us to look at social conditions, culture, political systems, relationships between groups, individual and group psychology, and the behavior of "bystanders."

Difficult Life Conditions as a Source of Group Violence

Intense life problems in a society, as a starting point for group violence, include severe economic problems, great political conflict, rapid and substantial social change and their combinations. For example, Germany faced tremendous life problems before Hitler came to power. In Rwanda, a very poor, overpopulated country, preceding the genocide of the Tutsis and the massacres of "moderate" Hutus in 1994, there was further increase in population, great increase in economic problems, a civil war, and political conflict among the Hutus who ruled the country (Kressel, 1996; Prunier, 1995; Smith, 1998).

Difficult life conditions create social upheaval and frustrate fundamental human needs (Kelman, 1990). Especially important are the following needs: for physical and material security, including the belief that one will be able to feed oneself and one's family; for defense of one's identity or self-concept, including one's values and ways of life; for a feeling of effectiveness and control over important events that affect oneself; for a comprehension of reality, especially as social disorganization and change make people's world views ineffective in understanding the world and their place in it; for connection to and support by other people, especially in difficult times when connection is disrupted by people focusing on their own needs (Staub, 1996b).

Psychological Responses

In response to difficult life conditions, people often scapegoat a particular group, blaming the group for life problems (Allport, 1954; Staub, 1989). They adopt new *ideologies,* conceptions or visions of how to organize society or the world. People need positive visions, especially in difficult times, but the ideologies they adopt are often *destructive,* in that they identify "enemies" who supposedly stand in the way of the ideology's fulfillment. Many authors suggest that scapegoating and destructive ideologies are created *by* leaders in an effort to gain followers or solidify their influence over followers.

Another theory, however, is that when people cannot find ways to fulfill their basic needs constructively, they act to fulfill them in destructive ways, such as turning to and even seeking leaders who initiate or encourage scapegoating and offer destructive ideologies.

By scapegoating others, people come to feel better about themselves and their group: The difficulties they face are not their fault. By adopting destructive ideologies, they adopt a new understanding of what reality is and should be. The Nazi ideology told Germans that while others, especially Jews, are inferior, they themselves are superior people and have a right to more "living space," to the territories of other people. The ideology of Cambodia's communists, the Khmer Rouge, proclaimed *total social equality,* identifying those who previously had power and educated people in general as enemies unable to contribute to an equal society. Thus, some must be destroyed to create a better world for "all." Both scapegoating and ideology strengthen identity and connect people to others who join them in working for a shared cause against a targeted group. Both create hope.

The Evolution of Destructiveness

Genocide does not directly result from turning against others. Its motivation and psychological possibility evolve gradually. In most instances, there is a progression of actions and a psychological evolution along a continuum of destruction. Sometimes the evolution starts long before those who commit genocide appear on the scene. For example, long before the genocide in Turkey in 1915 to 1916, the Armenians were discriminated against as a subject people and suffered repeated attacks. In one period during the late nineteenth century, at least

200,000 Armenians were killed (Hartunian, 1968; Kuper, 1981).

Both research with individuals (Buss, 1966; Goldstein et al., 1975) and my analysis of group violence (Staub, 1989) indicate that people learn by doing. Engaging in harmful acts changes individual perpetrators, by-standers, societal norms and institutions, and the entire culture. Such changes not only make possible but also often encourage in-creasingly harmful acts. *Just world thinking* (Lerner, 1980), the tendency to believe that the world is a just place, makes perpetrators and bystanders see the suffering of victims as deserved, either because of their actions, or their character, or both. Victims are further devalued and ultimately excluded from the realm of moral values and rules (Opotow, 1990; Staub, 1990). Ordinary moral and human consideration no longer applies to them. This enables perpetrators to engage in greater and greater violence. Some develop a fanatic commitment to fulfill the ideology and eliminate its enemy. Many German Nazis developed this fanaticism and continued to kill Jews long after it was evident that Germany was going to lose the war.

Cultural/Societal Characteristics

A number of cultural/societal characteristics predispose a group to respond to difficult life conditions by thoughts and actions that lead to violence. Most societies possess these characteristics to some degree; they become dangerous, however, when they are present in combination and to a substantial degree.

Differentiating between "us" and "them," and devaluing "them," are essential, central roots of people turning against others. Such devaluation often becomes part of a culture and societal institutions. *Cultural devaluation* evolves because it serves a number of functions, like strengthening identity by elevating one's group over another or justifying the lesser status or rights of some group. There was a history of devaluation of Jews by Germans; of Tutsis by Hutus; and of Serbs, Croats, and Muslims by one another. There was a rift, suspicion and antagonism in Cambodia between the ruling classes and wealthier people living in the cities and the peasants working the land in the countryside. (See Niens and Cairns in this volume for a review of the social identity theory explanation of causes of devaluation of others.)

A *monolithic society, in contrast to a pluralistic society,* is another important predisposing characteristic. In a monolithic society, the range of values and beliefs and the freedom to express them are limited—either by the political system or by the nature of the culture. In such a society, it is less likely that members of the population will speak out against policies and practices that inflict harm on some group. In a pluralistic society, by contrast, many voices intermingle in the public domain. The public dialogue makes scapegoating, the widespread adoption of destructive ideologies, and progression along a continuum of destruction less likely.

A strong respect for and *obedience to authority* is another predisposing cultural characteristic. For example, long before Hitler came to power Germans were regarded as extremely respectful of and obedient to authority (Girard, 1980). In societies that are strongly oriented to authority, people will be more affected by difficult life conditions, as their leaders and society fail to protect them. They will also be less likely to speak out as leaders move the society along the continuum of destruction.

The nature of the political system is also important. Extensive analysis of democratic and authoritarian/totalitarian systems shows that democracies seldom engage in genocide or start wars against other democracies (Rummel, 1994). Democracy, however, can range from being superficial to deeply rooted in culture and social institutions. Germany was a democracy during the Weimar Republic, but it became a totalitarian system under the Nazis. In Argentina, military dictatorships regularly replaced elected governments. The institutions of a "civic society," moderate respect for authority, and the right and opportunity for all groups to participate in public life are important aspects of a pluralistic, democratic society.

Finally, *unhealed group trauma* can be a source of collective violence. Trauma creates insecurity and mistrust (Agger, this volume; Janoff-Bulman, 1992). Members of victimized groups will see the world as a dangerous place. During periods of conflict, they will tend to focus on their own vulnerability and needs, making it difficult for them to consider the needs of others. Individuals and groups that have experienced great suffering, especially violence at the hand of others, are more likely to respond to a renewed threat with violence, which they will view as defensive aggression.

However, it is far from inevitable that survivors of group violence will become perpetrators. Many individual survivors devote themselves to the service of other human beings (Valent, 1998). Most likely, these are people who have experienced genuine human connections to others or have had protective or healing experiences and want to make sure that others won't suffer as they have.

GROUP CONFLICT AS THE SOURCE OF COLLECTIVE VIOLENCE

Histories of Ethnic and Group Conflict: Ideologies of Antagonism

The evolution of destructiveness may take the form of mutual antagonism and violence over an extended period. With the psychological groundwork already laid, a sudden flare-up of violence can take place. A history of conflict, hostility, and mutual violence leads to perceiving the "other" as an enemy who represents a danger to one's existence. At the same time, each group's identity is partly defined by its enmity to the other. I call this an *ideology of antagonism* (Staub, 1989). Examples of ideologies of antagonism include the French and Germans during some of their history and the parties in the former Yugoslavia at the end of World War II, as well as the relationship between Hutus and Tutsis in Rwanda (Kressel, 1996; Prunier, 1995).

Conflicts over Status, Power, and Rights

Difficult life conditions can lead subordinate groups in a society to demand greater rights and opportunities. Protest can turn into revolt. If successful, it can turn into mass killings or genocide *against* the dominant group, as happened in Cambodia. More often, though, demands, acts of self-assertion, and violence by the subordinate group lead to increasing persecution, mass killings, or genocide *by* the dominant group. State response to rebellion by "ethnoclasses" excluded from power has been the most frequent cause of genocide (Fein, 1993) and other group violence since the Second World War.

The disappearances in Argentina (*Nunca Más,* 1986) as well as in a number of other South and Central American countries are examples of mass violence emanating from the dominant group. In Colombia, guerillas rule segments of the country and kidnap people for ransom, a practice that has spread so that about 50 percent of all kidnappings in the world now take place in Colombia. In response, paramilitary groups and the military itself have killed many people (Human Rights Watch, 1996; U.S. State

Department, 1996), including peasants suspected of supporting the guerillas and members of political parties and organizations identified as leftist, especially their leaders.

Violence perpetrated against those who try to change the social system is frequently not just a matter of defending self-interest. It is also the defense of "hierarchy legitimizing myths" (Sidanius, in press), or what may be called "ideologies of superiority" by those who possess power, wealth, and influence, and come to see societal arrangements as "right" (Staub, 1989).

The Role of Leaders and Elites

The combination of difficult life conditions (or other instigators) and culture affects the kind of leaders a population is open to. Although leaders have some latitude in how they deal with difficult life conditions or group conflict, they often intensify already existing hostility (Kressel, 1996). They not only do this to gain and strengthen influence, but also because they themselves are affected by the combination of culture and difficult life conditions. Leaders often magnify differences between groups in power and status, adopt or create destructive ideologies, and use propaganda to enhance devaluation of and fear of the other. They create organizations that are potential instruments of violence—for example, paramilitary organizations, which have been used as tools of collective violence in many countries, including Bosnia and Rwanda (Kressel, 1996), Argentina (Nunca Mas, 1986), Turkey, and Germany.

Some leaders have been especially important in creating great violence: Hitler, Stalin, Idi Amin, Saddam Hussein, probably Milosevich in Yugoslavia, and warlords in Africa, like General Aidid in Somalia (Farer, 1996) are among well-known names. The

combinations of societal conditions and cultures discussed above may allow individuals who would not be accepted under "normal" conditions, to come to the fore. However, at least some of these leaders are not initially motivated to bring about the destruction and violence they create. But the personality of the leaders, the culture of the group, the ideology that is created or adopted and resulting actions, lead to an evolution that produces unfortunate changes in both the group and the leaders themselves.

The Passivity and Complicity of Bystanders

Both internal bystanders (members of a perpetrator group who are themselves not perpetrators) and external bystanders (outside groups and nations) have great potential to influence events and inhibit progression along the continuum of destruction. Their active opposition can reawaken the perpetrators' moral values, challenge the exclusion of victims from the moral universe, cause concern about retaliation or punishment, and make harm-doing costly. Unfortunately, internal bystanders normally remain passive and, over time, many of them come to support the perpetrators. External bystanders usually also remain passive, proceed with business as usual, or actively support the perpetrators. For example, in 1936 the world affirmed Nazi Germany by holding the Olympics in Berlin, and U.S. corporations continued doing business in Germany (Simpson, 1993). When the killings of Armenians began in 1915, Germany, Turkey's ally in the war, remained passive (Dadrian, 1996). Articles in German newspapers even justified Turkish actions (Bedrossyan, 1983). More recently, while Iraq was using chemical weapons against its Kurdish citizens, many countries, including the United States, continued to provide military equipment and economic aid to it. The United States saw Iraq as a counterweight to a fundamentalist, hostile Iran. France provided military support to the government of Rwanda in the early 1990s and continued to do so without objecting to the sporadic killing of thousands of Tutsis before 1994, when the genocide was perpetrated (Gourevich, 1998).

Perpetrators are confirmed in the rightness of their cause by the passivity of bystanders (Taylor, 1983), and even more by their support. By the same token, substantial evidence shows that individuals have great potential influence on the behavior of other bystanders, and even on perpetrators. How a person acts—remaining passive or taking action—and what a person says can lead others to help or not help someone in distress (Latane & Darley, 1970). At Le Chambon, the Huguenot village in France, heroic actions by the villagers during World War II in saving Jewish refugees changed some of the perpetrators, who in turn helped the villagers (Hallie, 1979).

The potential of groups of people, states, and the international community to exert influence is great, though rarely used. But witnessing the suffering of others is painful, and bystanders who remain passive tend to reduce their empathic suffering and guilt by distancing themselves from victims. This may make later action by them even less likely.

THE POTENTIAL OF BYSTANDERS: BYSTANDER ACTIONS TO HALT VIOLENCE

The Issue of Intervention

The further a group has progressed along a continuum of destruction, the more committed perpetrators become to their violent course. Bystanders must exert influence if

the evolution toward mass killing or genocide is to stop. Many types of bystanders can play important roles—for example, nongovernmental organizations (NGOs) and citizen groups (Rupesinghe, 1996). Beyond a certain point in the evolution of violence, however, the influence and power of nations and the community of nations is required. The earlier that nations respond to human rights violations, the less committed will perpetrators be and more likely it is that they can be stopped without the use of force.

Even in cases where intervention is clearly justified, or even demanded by current international law, it has rarely occurred. Nonintervention in the affairs of sovereign states is a longstanding tradition, dating at least from the Treaty of Westphalia in 1648. The principles of state sovereignty and nonintervention have become part of the U.N. charter, and they greatly limit the potential of the United Nations to respond to human rights violations.

For nations and the community of nations to become active bystanders, it is necessary that the pursuit of national interest, national obligation, and nationhood itself be defined to include the protection of human rights and the safety of human beings. This would require a moral vision about shared responsibility for the protection of human rights and the development of *standards* for *when* nations should act, *who* should act, and *what* actions should be taken. The existing system mandates action only in the most extreme situation, genocide, and even this mandate is not followed. The United Nations pulled its peacekeepers out of Rwanda when the violence began. As it became evident that a genocide was in progress in Rwanda, attempts to send back peacekeepers were slowed by a refusal to invoke the U.N. Genocide Convention and by a lack of cooperation among nations, particularly the United States (Gourevich, 1998). Effective response requires the creation of *institutions* to provide early warning and, even more importantly, to *activate* responses. The creation of standards and institutions would contribute to a responsible international system in which effective action could be implemented.

The Types of Actions Required

Early warning is extremely important. A conceptual system like the one described here can indicate the need for action, based on the assessment of life conditions, group conflict, movement along the continuum of destruction, and cultural characteristics. Others have also proposed ways to determine the need for action, focusing not only on existing levels of discrimination and violence but changes in them (Bond & Vogele, 1995; Charny, 1991; Harff & Gurr, 1990).

However, in the past, early warning often has not led to action. Human Rights Watch publicized the impending danger of violence in Rwanda and the head of the U.N. peacekeeping force received information about the impending plans for genocide, but no action occurred.

The United Nations needs to act more *before* a genocide occurs. At this time, the United Nations has to rely on nations for military force, for sanctions, and even for powerful condemnation. Since the passivity of nations is a central issue, there ought to be institutions or offices within nations working with the United Nations that have the responsibility to initiate action in response to danger signs. The process of developing procedures and institutions can itself contribute to changing the international climate, to values, commitments, and operating procedures related to the rights and well-being of people everywhere.

If reactions occur early enough, they may start with high-level *private communication*. Such communication enables leaders to change a violent course without losing face. *Public demands* can cause leaders who do not want to appear weak in front of their followers to resist policy changes. Nations and the community of nations, speaking with a firm and unified voice when persecution and violence begin, can reaffirm—and to some degree reinstate in the eyes of perpetrators—the humanity of the victims. Intervening groups can raise concern among perpetrators about their own image in the eyes of the world, and about possible consequences of their actions, which could move some internal bystanders to action.

In times of crisis, the leaders of the international community should get directly involved. The course of action in the former Yugoslavia might have been different if, for example, critical foreign ministers had traveled to Zagreb and Belgrade immediately after the Serbs attacked Croatia and bombed the ancient city of Dubrovnik. They could have offered help with mediation, with negotiations in resolving issues, as well as economic and other types of assistance. At the same time, such a delegation could have firmly and forcefully communicated a resolve not to tolerate further violence, specifying actions they would take if it continued.

If words and warnings are ineffective, nations can intensify their response by withholding aid and can progress, if necessary, to sanctions and boycotts. The earlier such actions are taken, and the more uniformly nations abide by them, the more effective will they be. The participation of many nations helped make the boycott of South Africa effective. Sanctions that pressure leaders directly, for example, by freezing their assets in foreign banks, can be especially useful. More problematic are long-term sanctions that deprive a population of the essentials of everyday life, like food and medication, as in the case of Iraq and Cuba.

When violence is already at a high level, the time for sanctions as the only response will have passed. When no other means exist to save human lives, using an international force can become unavoidable. By the time force was used in Bosnia, it seemed the only option available to bring a halt to violence.

Preventing Collective Violence

Even when there is no imminent danger of intense violence, instigating conditions and culture may make future collective violence probable. In such instances, prevention is extremely important. The role of outsiders, of bystanders, of "third parties" is crucial here as well (Staub, 1996c).

A number of organizations, like Peaceworkers and Peace Brigade International, send foreign volunteers into countries where the government or the military appears ready to perpetrate violence against some group. Usually, perpetrators do not want the world to know about their violence and do not want other countries involved. As a result, the simple presence of foreign witnesses can sometimes stop violence at demonstrations or against individuals whom the perpetrators consider undesirable. For example, in the fall of 1997, a coalition between Peaceworkers and a new youth-led human rights organization, Global Youthconnect, sent American college students to be present at student demonstrations in Kosovo. No violence occurred at these demonstrations.

Healing and Reconciliation

Helping previously victimized groups heal is essential to preventing later violence by them. Acknowledgement of the group's suffering and expressions of empathy from outsiders promote healing. So does people writing about and talking about what has happened to them, their family and their group, and providing support to each other (Pennebaker & Beall, 1986; Pennebaker et al., 1987). Writing and talking about painful experiences, in small groups, in a context of mutual empathy and support can help replace the turning inward and disconnection that come from victimization with connections to other people (Staub & Pearlman, 1996).

Testimonials, memorials, and ceremonies commemorating victimization and suffering can also promote healing. However, many groups memorialize their suffering in ways that recreate injury and fuel nationalism. For example, Serbs have focussed on the tremendous injury they suffered in the defeat of Serb forces by Turks in the fourteenth century. The sense of injury is understandable in that Turkey subsequently ruled Serbia for centuries. But the continued focus on deep national wounds has been a source both of hostility to Serbs who in earlier centuries converted to Islam and of destructive nationalism. It is important, instead, to create ceremonies that help people grieve and at the same time form connections with others in building a better, peaceful future.

Frequently, members of the perpetrator group feel wounded, either because they had been previously victimized, or because the violence has been mutual. They may also be wounded because killing and making people suffer are actions that wound (Browning, 1992; Kelman & Hamilton, 1989), as does belonging to a group that has done that. Both groups may need to heal, assume responsibility for their actions, and reconcile. This is extremely difficult soon after intense group violence. It is easier if at least important perpetrators are punished.

In places like Rwanda and Bosnia, the way groups are geographically intertwined makes reconciliation essential for avoiding continued cycles of violence. See Agger (this volume) for a further discussion of trauma reduction in Bosnia.

Dialogue, Problem-solving Workshops, and Other Contact

Dialogue between members of hostile groups can help them heal and reconcile if it addresses past wounds and fosters mutual empathy. It can help them find solutions to practical problems the groups have to resolve in order to live with each other. Researchers and practitioners of conflict resolution have found that bringing members of hostile groups together who are ready to talk to each other can lead to mutual acceptance and commitment to improve group relations (Fisher, 1997; Kelman, 1990; Rothman, 1992).

Creating contact is a significant achievement by itself. Deep engagement with the "other," ideally under supporting conditions like equality, is important to overcome negative stereotypes and hostility (Allport, 1954; Pettigrew, 1997). Identifying joint goals and shared effort in their behalf are extremely valuable. People can join to rebuild houses destroyed in the course of violence, as some have done in Bosnia. They can join to help children who lost parents or have been traumatized by the violence around them. Healing and reconciliation can facilitate such contact, while positive contact itself contributes to healing, resilience (Butler, 1997), and reconciliation. See Murphy, as well as Niens and Cairns (both in this volume), for further discussion of how contact can be constructive in helping perpetrators and previously victimized people engage in efforts to prevent further violence.

Truth Commissions and Tribunals

Truth commissions and tribunals, by establishing what has actually happened, make it less likely that perpetrators will be able to consider themselves victims, which otherwise might lead to renewed violence by them. A significant contribution of the Nuremberg tribunals to the creation of German democracy was to show the German people the horrendous actions of their own nation, extensively using materials gathered by the Nazis themselves.

Truth commissions and tribunals, by acknowledging victims' suffering, can promote healing. Affirming that the violence against them was neither normal nor acceptable can help victims feel safer. The punishment of perpetrators, especially of leaders, communicates to the world and to the formerly victimized group that violence against groups is not acceptable.

The best way for truth commissions to operate to achieve these positive ends, and the right relationship between establishing the truth and assigning punishment, are still in the process of evolution. The latest and best-known example of a truth commission, in South Africa, was effective in enabling some people to tell their stories and to make the actions of perpetrators public knowledge. However, some of the people who were victimized during the apartheid regime have felt deeply hurt that many perpetrators who confessed what they had done seemingly without regret or apology could get amnesty (Hamber, 1998). This is a complicated matter as well: whom to punish and for what crimes for the sake of justice and healing, without punishing so many people that it creates new wounds that may interfere with reconciliation. Truth and reconciliation processes established in South Africa at the end of *apartheid* are discussed in detail in this volume by de la Rey.

Culture Change: Democratization

By changing aspects of cultures, the likelihood of genocide and mass killing may be reduced. But groups do not welcome others' attempts to interfere with their culture. Helping countries with democratization has been one of the few acceptable ways to create culture change. For example, after the fall of communism, Eastern European countries welcomed Western help in developing the institutions that maintain democracy: a well-functioning, fair judiciary, free and fair voting practices, party politics, and the creation and strengthening of nongovernmental organizations (Sampson, 1996). Democratic institutions and practices, in turn, promote pluralism and reduce overly strong respect for and obedience to authority.

Children: Inclusive Caring and Moral Courage

While institutions have a life of their own, it is individuals who maintain both culture and institutions. Raising children with humane values who care about the welfare of human beings is an essential avenue to prevention. However, such caring has to be inclusive, has to extend to people outside the group, in order to make genocide less likely and active responses to the persecution of people outside the group more likely. Children also need to develop moral courage, the ability to stand up for their values. Essential are warmth and affection, positive guidance by parents and other socializers, and encouragement of children to actually help other people, so that they learn by doing (Eisenberg, 1992; Staub, 1996a).

Other chapters in this volume discuss in detail programs concerned with the care and education of children. Hakvoort and Haglund consider children and peacebuilding, and Coleman and Deutsch describe school programs designed to promote education for a peaceful world.

Prospects for the Twenty-first Century

The twentieth century saw many genocides and mass killings. Will these horrors continue into the twenty-first century? Unfortunately, without a system of prevention, this is likely to be the case. We live amidst tremendous changes in the world, for example, in technology, modes of communication, the nature of jobs and the globalization of the world economy and culture. Because of these changes and the spread of belief in individual rights, including the rights of women, there will be changes in social roles, family life, and parenting in traditional societies.

As I have noted in discussing difficult life conditions, great social change puts great demands on people. This is even true of positive change. But some of the changes that are likely to occur, and the reactions they evoke in traditional societies, will not be positive. In addition, the discrepancy between rich and poor has been increasing, adding to the potential for violence. Global communication that makes poor people aware of others' wealth is likely to intensify their sense of injustice.

These conditions are likely to frustrate basic needs to a substantial degree. They are likely to intensify a trend that has been already evident in our century; namely, individuals turning to some group, often an ethnic, religious, or national group, or an ideological movement that is capable of fulfilling their needs for security, identity, and connection.

To make genocide and mass killing unlikely, prevention becomes essential. The United Nations' focus on economic development and the improvement in quality of life as a central avenue to prevention, while important, may not be fast enough or, by itself, sufficient.

The U.N. General Assembly has identified eight principles essential to the promotion of a culture of peace: non-violence, respect for human rights, democracy, tolerance, promotion of development, education for peace, free flow of information, and wider participation of women. While some of these are processes and actions that need to be created, others are outcomes, or end products. To bring them about requires some of the preventive efforts I have suggested (and others that are discussed in the section of this book on peacebuilding). It requires positive visions about the future and the creation of communities that provide people with identity and connection, not separation or opposition. These may best be smaller communities rather than larger, potentially violent ones. To create positive visions in difficult times requires support and help to leaders by "bystanders" of many kinds. Concentrated efforts by the community of nations, the United Nations, and nongovernmental organizations are all needed. But individual citizens must exert influence on all these systems and must, on their own or as members of nongovernmental organizations, directly engage in preventive efforts if genocide and mass killings, which have devastated the twentieth century, are to end.

CHAPTER 7

WEAPONS OF MASS DESTRUCTION

Michael Britton

In this chapter, I will examine weapons of mass destruction from a psychological perspective. Thanks to modern science, very large numbers of people can be killed with just one of these (nuclear, chemical, or biological) weapons. I will consider psychological dynamics common to many people, focusing on two questions: Why was the buildup of nuclear weapons so massive in the Cold War that they became central to that era? What can we expect in the future? To answer those questions, I will use concepts from clinical psychology, a field that has had to confront violence and the triumph of rage and hate over empathy, concern, and love for self and others.

A BRIEF HISTORY

Biological weapons have not actually been used so far (B. H. Rosenberg, personal communication, November 15, 1998). Chemical weapons (gas) have been used sporadically, in World War I, in the 1980s Iraq–Iran War, again by Iraq in killing Kurdish civilians (A. Smithson, personal communication, November 15, 1998), and by a religious sect leader in a Tokyo subway (Lifton, 1997). Nuclear bombs were used by the United States to destroy two Japanese cities near the end of World War II. In short, the actual use of

weapons of mass destruction has been limited. But tens of thousands of nuclear weapons were built during the Cold War. Their destructive power is staggering: The first thermonuclear bomb had a force equivalent to twenty billion pounds of TNT (Rhodes, 1995). The four countries involved, the United States, Britain, and France on one side and the Soviet Union on the other, targeted those bombs on each other's industry, mining, communications, transportation, political, and military sites. Many such targets were located in or near cities, so that war plans in effect targeted cities (Arkin & Fieldhouse, 1985; Herken, 1985, 1992). It was not just cities that were targeted to disappear, however, but whole countries. Each side's nuclear war plans were designed to end the other's functional existence; the nuclear arsenals were known as "nation killers" (Rhodes, 1995). The two sides created a situation termed "Mutually Assured Destruction," meaning a nuclear attack by either guaranteed a nuclear counterattack by the other. The arsenals would have acted in concert to destroy the countries that made up Western civilization, from the United States and Canada in the west, across Europe to the far reaches of the Soviet Union in the east.

How did these countries come to make those weapons a central feature of their relations with one another? The answer involves looking at three principles: (1) Understanding behavior in a social system requires looking at the system as a whole; (2) behavior is not driven by reality, but by our interpretations of reality; and (3) violence reinforces the belief that the world belongs to the strong.

Systems

A system is a set of social groups (countries, classes, etc.) with so much ongoing interaction that you can't understand the behavior of any one party without looking at the interactions among them all. Those interactions are the context within which each decides what to do next. The parties approach each other with particular expectations/beliefs; once a pattern of interaction fits with everyone's expectations, interactions tend to stabilize. The parties try to maintain what is working for them, a process called homeostasis. Each then appears to have its own role in the collective "drama" in which the system is engaged. Systemic dramas tend to have overarching themes, such as "Empire Building" or "Globalization."

The Cold War was the overarching drama of the second half of the twentieth century. Understanding how that came to be requires looking at Western civilization as a single social system. The people in the Cold War had a very hard time doing that. To them "The West" and "The Communist Bloc" were separate worlds. But, in fact, the countries involved had a history of extensive interaction and exposure to each other's ways of thinking; they really were a single civilization at "war" within itself.

Beliefs Create Behavior

What was it that led the parties to build nuclear weapons? Both sides would have answered that the realities they faced left no alternative. The implication is that behavior is a straightforward response to reality. Clinical psychology suggests otherwise: What determines our reactions to a situation is not so much the reality before us, but our understanding of that reality. Cognitive therapy, for example, focuses on the thoughts that automatically come to mind about given situations. Taken together, such thoughts form a *cognitive schema* or set of assumptions by which we interpret what's going on, what we expect to happen, and what we decide to do (Beck, 1976; Beck et al., 1979).

Milgram's (1974) research on obedience is instructive. He told research subjects they would be part of a scientific investigation laying the groundwork for medical advances; their role would be to administer electric shocks to people (who in fact only pretended to feel pain) to study certain effects. His subjects saw their "subjects" writhing in (simulated) pain from (simulated) electric shocks; many struggled to set aside emotional distress at the pain they believed they were causing. They did all this because they believed the situation involved accomplishing a good objective in a legitimate manner. This research has a disturbing implication: If we or others understand weapons of mass destruction to be urgently needed to advance a vital cause, we will build them, deploy them, and quite possibly use them.

If people in four major countries became involved in building nuclear bombs during the Cold War, we can suspect they, too, believed they were involved in an urgent, beneficial project requiring them to do so. And we can suspect that many of them, like Milgram's subjects, struggled to set aside feelings they might have had about endangering hundreds of millions of lives. There were many other factors that led them to behave as they did, including domestic politics in the various countries, organizational/bureaucratic dynamics, international competition, etc. But there is another factor overlooked in those explanations.

Consider the following: In the aftermath of the world wars, the countries of Western civilization could have looked back on the violence in which they'd been embroiled and could have decided the task before them was to work together to construct a world in which their many peoples could live safely. Their domestic political campaigns would then have been about who could do that best, and their bureaucracies would have tried to increase their budgets in service of those ends. But that was not how they interpreted the post-war situation. They concluded they were in imminent danger from one another, danger that could be held at bay by building nuclear weapons. Clinical psychology would suggest the basis for that interpretation of the situation had as much to do with the assumptions each held about the world of intergroup relations as with any other factor. What then were those assumptions? And how did a set of assumptions leading the parties to be so dangerous to one another catch on so widely?

UNDERLYING/CORE RELATIONAL SCHEMA

You're a member of a country; what goes on in the world of countries may impact you. You're a member of an economic-social class; changes in the class system, and your location within it, may affect such things as how much you'll earn and where you'll live. You may be part of a national or ethnic group whose future will shape yours as well. Your skin color locates you in widely differing mindsets people have about "race." Each of those role-worlds (country, class, etc.) involves a mental "map" of the parties

that make up that world, the ways you can expect them to behave, and your options for dealing with them. Cognitive therapists use the term *schema* (or *assumptive set*) to refer to assumptions that might underlie your behavior in all those different situations. A parallel term from psychoanalytic thinking is *core relational theme.* I will use a slightly different language. A *surface schema* "maps" one of the role-worlds I just listed. A set of assumptions underlying a number of those schemas is an *underlying/core relational schema.* I am suggesting two things. A core relational schema developed in the thinking in Western civilization in regard to all kinds of intergroup relations. Second, that underlying assumptive set played a large role in creating the World Wars and the Cold War.

If you examine the history of Western civilization in the centuries leading up to World War I, you'll find themes of coercion and resistance had been evolving for a long time in the interactions between countries; social/economic classes (monarchs, aristocrats, middle classes, working classes, underclasses); traditional regimes and revolutionaries; national groups and the governments from whom they sought autonomy; imperial powers in relation to each other and those they fought to colonize; and between Whites and other races in the course of imperialism. No matter which kind of relationship was involved, the protagonists readily saw themselves as involved in struggles over power, with power viewed as "zero sum" (what one party gained another necessarily lost). They often believed the decision about which party would have its way would be settled by force. That core set of assumptions was summed up by Morgenthau (1948): "[I]nternational politics, like all politics, is a struggle for power" (p. 31). People assumed (a) governments are determined to get their way even if it means going to war to do so; (b) conflict is inevitable, the world is dangerous; and (c) the more military force you can wield, the safer you will be.

It's not that there weren't *competing* core relational schemas; there almost always are. Within psychoanalytic thinking, the Kleinian model sees competing underlying schemas as expressions of one or the other of two fundamental core schemas (Ogden, 1989). The first involves destroying inner concern for others in order to pursue our own agenda; the second involves keeping a reign on action because it might be harmful to others. The first focuses on self without concern for others, the second inhibits self because others matter. The world obviously becomes a very different place depending on which of these underlies how the members of a system treat one another.

There is a relationship between the two Kleinian core relational schemas (my language) and systemic dramas. Those dramas (e.g., "industrialization," "empire-building," "globalization") are used to organize social systems. But they involve choices about which Kleinian intent to act on: concern for one's own agenda or concern for others. Normally the two exist in a kind of balance. But the more frequently one or the other is chosen throughout a system, the more it moves to the foreground and defines the collective drama.

SYSTEMIC SPIRALS

As the twentieth century dawned, the zero-sum readiness to deprive, exploit, or kill others in pursuit of an objective was certainly not the only intent motivating leaders in the circles of power across Western civilization. It was one schema competing with others of more benign intent. But there was a gathering momentum to emphasize that assumptive set. It was understood that government leaders in various countries would

resort to military force "when necessary" to get their way, a belief that became more entrenched as it was acted on in more spheres of life, from handling urban riots, to small wars, to conquering Africa and territories in the Pacific, etc. With actions provoking counter-actions, the "drama" of the early twentieth century was being defined as a set of power-struggles to be settled by force. As countries, colonies, national groups, and classes tried to impose their own objectives, they reinforced each other's belief that the world belonged to those with the power to impose their will. With many parties treating each other in accordance with that schema, a momentum developed in the system that made it hard for any one party to stop, a dynamic referred to as a *vicious spiral* (Senge, 1990).

Escalating Violence

We have learned from the field of domestic violence counseling that each act of violence can set the stage for more extreme subsequent violence. An analogous process took place in Western civilization, in part as a result of developments in the organization of armies and in the power of weapons. The development of the nation-state produced large citizen armies, blurring the line between civilians and the military (Adas et al., 1996; Anderson, 1991). Industrialization of warfare led to half a million soldiers being killed in single battles lasting several weeks (e.g., the Battle at Somme) and blurred the civilian/military distinction further. Bombing factory workers to demoralize them was regarded as a way to break an enemy's will to wage industrialized war. Hitler ordered the bombing of civilian England; the Western allies pursued the bombing of German cities to the point of firebombing Dresden, killing 200,000, though the city had no military value. The Allies firebombed 74 Japanese cities, and destroyed the cities of Hiroshima and Nagasaki with atomic bombs (Rhodes, 1995). By the time the warring that began in 1914 finally ended in 1945, 60 million had been killed (Sivard, 1988). Killing hundreds of thousands of civilians in cities had come to seem normal. Adding nuclear weapons to the picture seemed like an extension of a now-standard practice. With each crossing of the line as to what was acceptable militarized violence, more extreme violence had become thinkable, until even "nation killing" seemed to make sense.

POST-TRAUMATIC THINKING

The survivors of World War II had lived through the nightmare of 38 countries at war, punctuated by horrific atrocities and genocidal assaults (Balakian, 1997; Chang, 1997; Lifton, 1986), and then got the news about the development of nuclear weapons and the devastation they create. Clearly governments could have seriously murderous intent, and now they could implement that intent with nuclear weapons. People on both sides of the Iron Curtain had the kinds of thoughts and feelings people could be expected to have in the wake of horrific violence (Herman, 1992): They were in dread of being unprepared for a surprise attack, and they felt a need to amass superior force in order to feel safe. Given existing beliefs that the world of intergroup relations was about power, and having witnessed such violence, it was easy for the different parties to assume the worst about each other and to believe the only way to be safe was to build nuclear weapons. In fact, neither side intended to invade the other, but neither could bring itself to trust the other (Organski & Kugler, 1980). Fear fueled angry determination to build more weapons; more weapons fueled more fear and anger

(Wessells, 1995). It seemed a spiral with no escape.

ANALYSIS

By acting on the intention of setting aside concern for others in order to pursue an agenda, people in Western civilization built up a tradition of resorting to that schema in their dealings with one another as countries, classes, national groups, etc. With so many people included in those groups, and with the value of coercion in one area reinforced by what was going on in other areas, momentum grew to conduct intergroup relations according to this belief. The violence of the resultant world warring further reinforced their belief in the danger posed by potential adversaries. Adoption of coercion as a way of life in intergroup relations thus reinforced itself in a vicious spiral, producing a widely accepted expectation of the worst and a belief in building as powerful a set of weapons as one could. While there were many historical influences, interactive missteps, and psychological processes involved, it was the widening and deepening of belief throughout the system that led its members to fear and hate each other so much, and to build nuclear weapons against each other on such a massive scale.

IMPLICATIONS

This analysis of the psychological dynamic that made nuclear weapons central in the Cold War can guide our thinking about whether such weapons will play a central role in the future. The depth and pervasiveness of the assumption that the world is about who can impose their will on others is the key to the role weapons of mass destruction will play in the century ahead. The greater the pervasiveness of that core relational schema, and the greater the violence surrounding it, the more rigidly it will be accentuated and the greater the risk of a vicious spiral accompanied by widespread building of those weapons.

A CHANGING DRAMA

With the demise of the Cold War, it was not clear whether the momentum toward more of these weapons would increase or decrease. After the collapse of the Soviet Union, regional enemies on its borders who hadn't feared each other in the past (because their actions were contained by Soviet influence) now had to face each other unprotected. Nuclear weapons held appeal as a means of guaranteeing safety, but the enemies being feared would have the same idea. There was little confidence that international controls for preventing proliferation would keep these enemies from building such weapons (Wessells, 1995). The weapons also held allure as ways to infuse struggling countries with pride as "real" global players (Ghosh, 1998; Roy, 1998). In addition, a number of former Soviet republics had nuclear weapons on their soil; Soviet scientists were out of work. The incentive to sell nuclear weapons or anything related to them seemed great. If nuclear weapons had been widespread during the Cold War, the concern was that they would become even more widespread after its end.

The effort to retard the momentum toward nuclearization had begun in the 1960s with the Partial Test Ban Treaty. Subsequent treaties banned atomic weapons in Antarctica, Latin America, the South Pacific, Southeast Asia, the ocean floor, and outer space. Nuclear risk reduction centers were created, the Anti-Ballistic Missile Treaty and the Comprehensive Test Ban signed (Sivard, 1996), along with the Nuclear Non-Proliferation Treaty, which required the nuclear powers "to pursue . . . cessation of the nuclear arms race at an early date . . .

[along with] nuclear disarmament, and . . . general and complete disarmament under strict and effective international control" (U.S. Department of State, 1971).

While the nuclear powers regard their weapons as critical to maintaining geopolitical status, the defining global theme seems to be shifting from superpowers and geopolitical conflict to super-corporations, globalized economic competition, and information technologies. That shift in the surface schema may also involve change in the core assumptions underlying intergroup relations: Maybe the world will not be about power and danger; maybe weaponry will not define the future. Iraq and North Korea are viewed as pockets where the old mindset still holds sway and weapons of mass destruction still pose a threat. There is hope that as the Cold War continues to recede in time, the residual presence of the old schema (violence as the path to safety and prestige) will fade in these pockets as well.

A second kind of concern also exists. I have described how a schema that is fairly ruthless in nature can dominate people's conception of intergroup relations, even though they personally may be oriented to positive social relationships in everyday life. But there are individuals whose personality structures are organized around belief in exploitation, danger, and the utility of killing, regardless of whether the larger social drama supports such themes or not. Individuals whose personalities contain a large component of psychopathy (predatory behavior, a preference for being dangerous to others) or delusional paranoia (sense of others as dangerous) at a level where killing is regarded as potentially useful, can organize extremely dangerous projects if given the chance, including the development of weapons of mass destruction. Those high in psychopathy are more likely to lead organizations in which psychopathic themes persist on the social level, such as criminal cartels. Those high in delusional paranoia (with religious content) are more likely to organize religious cults.

The potential threats from "residual pockets," criminal cartels, and cults involve the risk of a small number of weapons of mass destruction. What about the potential for their large-scale deployment? Will the nuclear powers eventually disband their still immense arsenals? Will there be a build-up of such weapons on a large scale in the future? The answers depend on whether the core assumptions that led to their widespread deployment in the past change or not. If the underlying relational schema that the world is about achieving objectives at whatever cost to others continues to be pervasive, "globalization" will be susceptible to deteriorating into another vicious spiral, replete with large numbers of nuclear, chemical, and/or biological weapons. If the core schema survives on a pervasive basis, such weapons will be widely built. If it does not, they won't. The question is how to detect whether the underlying relational schema is changing or not.

INDICANTS OF CHANGE

Adapting the Kleinian model (Ogden, 1989) to this problem, we should be looking to see how widely intergroup relations are based on assumptions that: (a) groups (countries, classes, national groups, etc.) are absorbed in making relationships mutually empowering; (b) with a resultant sense that the world is safe (from threats of coercion, intimidation and violence); and (c) with no one thinking that accumulating means for violence is a path to safety or success. To the degree these assumptions underlie the surface schema in intergroup relations and generate a self-reinforcing momentum (Senge's *virtuous spiral*), weapons of mass destruction will likely not play a large role in the future. Determining

which set of core assumptions underlie intergroup relations is the key to predicting the future role of these weapons.

MOVING FROM A DANGEROUS WORLD TO A SAFE WORLD

Herman's (1992) model of recovery from trauma suggests a set of indicants of change from an underlying belief in the world as dangerous to an underlying belief in safety, with indicants grouped in three categories. The first group indicates movement out of the old schema (with their absence suggesting a lack of change in core assumptions despite changes in the surface historical drama). The second indicates a transition between assumptive sets, while the third indicates consolidation of the new set.

Category I: Establishing Safety

The first signs of substantive change from assuming the world is about coercion involve concrete actions that undo investment in intimidation. Four such indicants will be outlined.

First, are the existing nuclear arsenals still ready for launch on short notice? Do nuclear, chemical, and biological weapons still exist? "Yes" answers indicate a continued assumption that the world is organized around coercion. Their elimination (Schell, 1998) would indicate a government no longer worried that this is so.

Second, building and deploying weapons of mass destruction draws substantial resources away from projects that could keep people alive. The United States spent some $10.5 trillion on the Cold War military effort (Markusen & Yudken, 1992); the four nuclear powers spent an estimated $8 trillion on their nuclear weapons (Sivard, 1996). As of 1996, the United States continued to spend $26 billion to $39 billion per year on nuclear weapons (Sivard, 1996). Millions could have lived had those resources been allocated to projects needed to keep them alive (Christie, 1997). Current annual U.S. expenditures for nuclear weapons, for example, could pay the yearly cost of the following life-saving measures *globally:* elimination of starvation and malnutrition ($19 billion); basic shelter ($21 billion); health care and AIDS control ($21 billion); refugee relief ($5 billion); removal of land mines ($2 billion) (World Game Institute, 1997). Should major governments shift investment of that magnitude from these weapons to programs that keep people alive (rather than, for example, the next generation of high-tech products unrelated to survival), that reallocation would indicate a shift in the core sense of the meaning of relationships. The more resources shift from militarization to keeping people alive, and the more parties engage in that reallocation, the greater the indication of substantive change in the intentions being brought to intergroup relations.

Third, critical to breaking the pattern of dangerous interactions among governments is their relating to each other differently, including accepting mutual responsibility for the danger they jointly create (Blight & Lany, 1995; White, 1984). That process was modeled in research interventions by Blight and Lany, in which Americans, Russians, and Cubans examined together their roles in the Cuban Missile Crisis of 1962. The greater the shift by government leaders from jockeying for advantage to trying to understand together what went wrong and what each party could themselves do to make things collectively work better, the more likely governments will be able to stop making the world as violent as they have made it in the past.

Fourth, the surface focus of the global drama is shifting from conflicts among governments to globalization of economic competition. In economics, worst-case scenarios

involve economic collapse rather than nuclear war. That step away from military violence may reflect small but positive movement. If the driving intent behind globalization remains at the level of epic business projects pursued at the expense of others, little substantive change will have occurred at the core schema level, and the global system will be at risk of remilitarizing relationships. If the shift to an economic drama is the first step in an ongoing evolution such that the driving intent behind economic endeavors becomes helping everyone (globally) stay alive and have a decent life, that would indicate substantive change in the underlying relational schema. It is important to remember that global enterprises not only perform the tasks at hand, they enact one or another core schema and thereby move it to the fore. The objectives pursued by these enterprises and by countries will define for our children and grandchildren the answer to this question: Is this a world of coercers and predators (in which only weapons ultimately create safety), or a world of collaborative good intent that actually works? Projects like the U.N. effort led by Graca Machel to end the impact of war on children (United Nations, 1996; Wessells, 1998) answer that our relationships can be driven by a concern to be protective of one another, or at least protective of one another's children. The more that global enterprises are driven by that primary purpose, the less likely the future will involve widespread deployment of weapons of mass destruction.

Category II: Narration, Remembrance, and Mourning

Category II indicants mark the subtle shifts that occur during the transition between assumptive sets. These indicants have to do with the narratives (media reports, political speeches, history texts) produced by the various parties to global relations. As people move from one assumptive set to the other, the nature of their narratives goes through changes that reflect those shifts.

The core schema in which parties pursue their own gain with little regard for the cost to others generates narratives driven by the agendas of various parties to dominate or resist domination. Narration is *propaganda.* Narratives of nationalism become epic tales of timeless glory from which ignoble moments are erased and the experiences of enemies dismissed. The public voice of the dominated is silenced.

A shift from forging words and images as instruments in struggles over power and justification to reflectively putting into words one's historical experience (*narratives of identity*) indicates some shift at the core schema level. That shift can be seen in two different kinds of identity narratives, those of the intimidated or oppressed and those who have dominated. Signs of change in the latter include admission of wrongdoing, recognition of the impact of past (or present) actions on others, reflection with compassion for their own experience, and exploration of the practices and ideas used to harden them against empathy so that domination could be a "livable" way of life. In both cases, the indicant of change is a shift in what preoccupies the authors from establishing justification for further power struggles to struggling to get a clear sense of identity in the context of intergroup history, with the moral complexity of what has been taking place.

Further change is indicated by a shift from narratives of identity to *multi-sided narration* which involves the principle that leaders and ordinary people from all sides must be interviewed or quoted, and that each side must be presented as having a story to tell. Genuine multi-sided narration can be recognized by a concern to present the history of interactions and intentions in such a way that all sides can find their own dignity in what they hear or view. It entails giving voice to the hopes and suffering of all the sides, with a reflection of their intentions and efforts, as well as actions they took that obstructed peace, unintentional or otherwise.

Serious desire to understand self and others in context, with both goodness and moral flaws, leads to a shift in tone as well. Multi-sided remembrance carries an undertone of poignancy, as suffering and loss are revisited, given dignity and context. Righteous belligerence can have an exciting ring, but multi-sided remembrance faces difficult questions: How is it that they, who were agents of so much of our pain, were also only human? How it is that we who were so good hurt innocent others? What might life have been, had we all been more generous to each other? There is a poignancy to the fact that, despite righteousness and even rightness, much has been lost. Perhaps the most difficult shift has to do with hatred (conscious or unconscious) that is completely identified with, whether it involves determined suppression/deprivation of others by people in power, or unremitting hatred by people out of power. Letting go of hate and control as centers around which identity is organized, and allowing for sorrow and less emphasis on control, along with forming relationships with those who were hated, is very painful and takes time. But without that shift, re-creating danger comes easily. What should be evident behind the words and images in the narrative struggling through these issues is a sense of care to help the parties have a more complex understanding and a deeper feel for themselves and for each other, so they can go forward into the future more constructively.

The emergence of multi-sided narration signals a shift from being locked in the drama (and core schema) of the past, to looking back upon both with a growing sense that "it is behind us, it is over." Ebbing of belief in pursuing agendas no matter who gets hurt is a harbinger of assumptive sets in which kinder possibilities can come to life. Transit between underlying schema can be recognized in the movement from propaganda to narratives of identity to thoughtful efforts at understanding together how life works and how together it can be made to work better.

Category III: Building Relationships on New Values

Category III indicants reflect consolidation of the assumption that the primary interest of all parties in the global drama is making life a good experience together. What are the signals of that shift?

Beyond the effects associated with dominance and resistance (fear, anger, shame, contempt, moral hostility) lies a very different kind of feeling for life. Ezrahi (1997) focused on a change in personal psychology among "ordinary people." A self that can resist epic calls to die in war for a "great cause" begins with individuals wanting not to die, i.e., with experiencing personal life as a precious gift to be cherished. He suggests a person who loves her/his own aliveness can feel a compelling affection for life in others and make of relationships something other than the calculus of power. Sustaining love of life, he suggests, requires working to identify and give voice to personal experience, which in turn makes possible empathy for the personal experience of others. Krystal's (1988) work on trauma focuses on change from the sense of catastrophic danger to a renewed capacity to feel emotions (vs. alexithymia) and to love life (vs. anhe-

donia). He redefined the central affect in life not as anxiety (as Freud held) but as love, seeing it as the basis for empathy. By implication, both authors suggest looking for a sustained tone of delight in the organization of life.

We can extend this to looking for the building of public purpose out of supporting a life well-loved by all parties. For example, Jervis (1976) postulated a politics of "generosity" in which a group gives what another needs even though it is not compelled by power considerations to do so. Markusen and Yudken (1992) wrote about "nurturing" economics, raising the question of what the economic world would be like if decisions and policies were primarily driven by a desire to see others do well in life. Nelesson (1993) developed an urban planning methodology for helping people envision their community's physical structure in ways they experience as beautiful as well as evocative of pleasure and affection, and then assists them in bringing that vision to fruition. This involves regaining shared control over life (effective democracy) and gives a message that people should value/love their own feelings about beauty, affection, and pleasure in life enough to act on them. Alexander's (1979; Alexander et al., 1977) work on architecture conveys the sense that public life can focus on supporting the interactions in which life is loved. The administration of Jamie Lerner, an architect-mayor in Curitiba, Brazil, provides a demonstration of putting such intentions and attitudes in practice on a city-wide level, along with the impact on the populace's feel of life (Mc Kibben, 1995).

Indicants that the alternative Kleinian assumptive set underlies global intergroup relations involve a shift in the intent driving public institutions and a resultant change in the affective tone in public life. There needs to be a predominance globally, in political and economic problem-solving and deci-sion-making, of an underlying feel for the gift of life, and evidence that the formulat-ing and implementation of public purpose centers on all parties responsibly making a life together that they love. That would be the strongest indicant of core change and the strongest predictor that weapons of mass destruction will not be a central fea-ture of the future.

CONCLUSION

This chapter examined the underlying as-sumptive set that led to building weapons of mass destruction on a large scale and the processes that give that set the power to dominate the Cold War era. The key to whether such weapons will be widely built in the future lies in whether the dominant as-sumptive set changes or not. Indicants for recognizing the degree of change have been presented.

SECTION II

STRUCTURAL VIOLENCE

Introduction by
Deborah Du Nann Winter
and Dana C. Leighton

Direct violence is horrific, but its brutality usually gets our attention: we notice it, and often respond to it. Structural violence, however, is almost always invisible, embedded in ubiquitous social structures, normalized by stable institutions and regular experience. Structural violence occurs whenever people are disadvantaged by political, legal, economic, or cultural traditions. Because they are longstanding, structural inequities usually seem ordinary—the way things are and always have been. But structural violence produces suffering and death as often as direct violence does, though the damage is slower, more subtle, more common, and more difficult to repair. The chapters in this section teach us about some important but invisible forms of structural violence, and alert us to the powerful cultural mechanisms that create and maintain them over generations.

Johan Galtung originally framed the term "structural violence" to mean any constraint on human potential caused by economic and political structures (1969). Unequal access to resources, to political power, to education, to health care, or to legal standing, are forms of structural violence. When inner-city children have inadequate schools while others do not, when gays and lesbians are fired for their sexual orientation, when laborers toil in inhumane conditions, when people of color endure environmental toxins in their neighborhoods, structural violence exists. Unfortunately, even those who are victims of structural violence often do not see the systematic ways in which their plight is choreographed by unequal and unfair distribution of society's resources. Such is the insidiousness of structural violence.

Structural violence is problematic in and of itself, but it is also dangerous because it frequently leads to direct violence. The chronically oppressed are often, for logical reasons, those who resort to direct violence. Organized armed conflict in various parts of the world is easily traced to structured inequalities. Northern Ireland, for example, has been marked by economic disparities between Northern Irish Catholics—who have higher unemployment rates and less formal education—and Protestants (Cairns & Darby, 1998). In Sri Lanka, youth unemployment and underemployment exacerbates ethnic conflict (Rogers, Spencer, & Uyangoda, 1998). In Rwanda, huge disparities in both income and social status between the Hutu and Tutsis eventually led to ethnic massacres.

While structural violence often leads to direct violence, the reverse is also true, as brutality terrorizes bystanders, who then become unwilling or unable to confront social injustice. Increasingly, civilians pay enormous costs of war, not only through death, but through devastation of neighborhoods and ecosystems. Ruling elites rarely suffer from armed conflict as much as civilian populations do, who endure decades of poverty and disease in war-torn societies.

Recognizing the operation of structural violence forces us to ask questions about how and why we tolerate it, questions that often have painful answers. The first chapter in this section, "Social Injustice," by Susan Opotow, argues that our normal perceptual/cognitive processes lead us to care about people inside our scope of justice, but rarely care about those people outside. Injustice that would be instantaneously confronted if it occurred to someone we love or know is barely noticed if it occurs to strangers or those who are invisible or irrelevant to us. We do not seem to be able to open our minds and our hearts to everyone; moral exclusion is a product of our normal cognitive processes. But Opotow argues convincingly that we can reduce its nefarious effects by becoming aware of our distorted perceptions. Inclusionary thinking can be fostered by relationships, communication, and appreciation of diversity.

One outcome of exclusionary thinking is the belief that victims of violence must in some way deserve their plight. But certainly it is easy to see that young children do not deserve to be victims. The next two chapters in this section address the violence experienced by children. In the first, "The War Close to Home: Children and Violence in the United States," Kathleen Kostelny and James Garbarino describe the direct and structural violence which children in Chicago and other urban areas of the United States endure, paralleling that experienced by children who live in countries at war. Children who endure these environments often become battle weary, numb, hopeless, and/or morally impaired. But children not only suffer directly from violence, they also suffer from the impaired parenting and communities which poverty inflicts. The authors describe how community and family support mechanisms can mitigate these effects. For example, home visitation and early childhood education programs provide crucial family and community support.

While Kostelny and Garbarino focus on community intervention techniques, Milton Schwebel and Daniel Christie, in their article "Children and Structural Violence," extend the analysis of structural violence by examining how economic and psychological deprivation impairs at-risk children. Children living in poverty experience diminished intellectual development because parents are too overwhelmed to be able to provide crucial linguistic experiences. Schwebel and Christie's discussion concludes that economic structures must provide parents with living-wage employment, good prenatal medical care, and high-quality child-care if we are to see the next generation develop into the intelligent and caring citizens needed to create a peaceful world.

If children are the invisible victims of society's structural violence, so are their mothers. In the chapter "Women, Girls, and Structural Violence: A Global Analysis," Diane Mazurana and Susan McKay articulate the many ways in which global sexism systematically denies females access to resources. From health care and food to legal standing and political power, women and girls get less than males in every country on the planet. Mazurana and McKay argue that patriarchy-based structural violence will not be redressed until women are able to play more active roles making decisions about how resources are distributed.

Patriarchal values also drive excessive militarism, as Deborah Winter, Marc Pilisuk, Sara Houck, and Matthew Lee argue in their chapter "Understanding Militarism: Money, Masculinism, and the Search for the Mystical." The authors illuminate three motives fueling excessive military expenditures: money, which, because of modern market forces, leads half the world's countries to spend more on arms than on health and education combined; masculinism, which leads societies to make soldiering a male rite of passage and proof of manhood; and the search for the mystical, as men attempt to experience profound human processes of self-sacrifice, honor, and transcendence through war. Like William James, these authors argue that we will need to find a moral equivalent to war, in order to build lasting peace.

The global economy that drives weapons production and excessive militarization produces structural violence on a planetary scale, especially in developing countries, which Marc Pilisuk argues in his chapter "Globalism and Structural Violence." As global markets grow, income disparity increases around the world. Relaxed trade regulations and increased communication networks are creating powerful multinational conglomerates that derive huge profits from exploiting underpaid laborers in developing countries. The result is horrific structural violence to workers who toil under brutal conditions. Globalism also produces a monoculture, in which people throughout the world learn that "the good life" is based on consumer values. Pilisuk shows how nongovernmental organizations at the local level can organize globally to reclaim workers' dignity.

Finally, Brinton Lykes's chapter, "Human Rights as Structural Violence," shows how structural violence is invisible when human rights are conceived simply in civic and political realms. She argues for the expansion of human rights to include collective, cultural, and indigenous rights, which guarantee people their traditional culture and relationship with their land. Using two case studies, Guatemala and Argentina, she shows how collective rights help people heal and reclaim their cultural identities.

Lykes's discussion, as well as each of the chapters in this section, help us see the limitations of psychology as it is traditionally conceived, that is, the study of individuals and their responses to their environments. These papers require that we examine the political and economic institutions that psychologists typically ignore. In this respect, the thinking in both Sections II (Structural Violence) and IV (Peacebuilding) of this book go beyond traditional psychology, illuminating the sociological, economic, political, and spiritual dimensions of violence and peace.

As insidious as structural violence is, each of these papers also point out that it is not inevitable. Learning about structural violence may be discouraging and overwhelming, but all the authors in this section note that the same processes which feed structural violence can also be used to address it. Reducing structural violence by reclaiming neighborhoods, demanding social justice and living wages, providing prenatal care, alleviating sexism, organizing globally while celebrating local cultures, and finding non-militaristic avenues to express our deepest spiritual motives, will be our most surefooted path to building lasting peace.

CHAPTER 8

Social Injustice

Susan Opotow[1]

SOCIAL INJUSTICE

Social injustice challenges us to recognize the ordinarily invisible harms that are inflicted but not seen, and the rationalizations and justifications that support them. This chapter shows how both direct and structural violence depend on distorted perceptions, thoughts, and moral decisions, and suggests a framework for fostering inclusion, social justice, and peace in the twenty-first century.

DIRECT AND STRUCTURAL VIOLENCE

Violence is the exertion of physical force so as to injure or abuse. Johan Galtung (1969) directs our attention to overt vs. more subtle forms of violence. *Direct violence* is immediate, concrete, physical violence committed by and on particular, identifiable people. Even when it is committed from afar, as in missile launches, particular people decide what to do, particular people activate weaponry at a particular moment, and particular people are victims.

Structural violence, in contrast, is less obvious than direct violence. It is gradual, imperceptible, and normalized as the way

things are done; it determines whose voice is systemically heard or ignored, who gets particular resources, and who goes without. In structural violence, agency is blurred and responsibility is unclear; there may not be any one person who directly harms another. Structural violence normalizes unequal access to such social and economic resources as education, wealth, quality housing, civic services, and political power.

Direct and structural violence have different manifestations, but they are clearly related and interdependent. *Ethnic cleansing*, a euphemism for mass murder motivated by ethnic conflict, is direct violence that results from many kinds of structural violence, forces which have intertwined in "a long-forgotten history coming back to haunt us, a history full of thousands of economic, social, ethical, territorial, cultural and political problems that remained latent and unnoticed under the surface of totalitarian boredom" (Vaclav Havel, quoted by Burns, 1992, p. 3).

On the other hand, direct violence can give rise to long-term structural violence. Rape as a weapon of war has long-lived effects on victims and their society. Raped individuals are often reluctant to come forward because they fear exacerbating the debasement they and

[1]The author would like to thank her graduate student, R. Kirk Fallis, and the three editors of this volume.

their families have already experienced. In some societies, mass rape has produced social, economic, and political inequalities; for example, in 1998, rape directed at Chinese women in Indonesia was tactically employed to wrest control of Indonesia's commerce away from Chinese citizens (Mydans, 1998).

MORAL EXCLUSION

Both structural and direct violence result from moral justifications and rationalizations. *Morals* are the norms, rights, entitlements, obligations, responsibilities, and duties that shape our sense of justice and guide our behavior with others (Deutsch, 1985). Morals operationalize our sense of justice by identifying what we owe to whom, whose needs, views, and well-being count, and whose do not. Our morals apply to people we value, which define who is inside our *scope of justice* (or "moral community"), such as family members, friends, compatriots, and coreligionists (Deutsch, 1974, 1985; Opotow, 1990; Staub, 1989). We extend considerations of fairness to them, share community resources with them, and make sacrifices for them that foster their well-being (Opotow, 1987, 1993).

We see other kinds of people such as enemies or strangers outside our scope of justice; they are *morally excluded*. Gender, ethnicity, religious identity, age, mental capacity, sexual orientation, and political affiliation are some criteria used to define moral exclusion. Excluded people can be hated and viewed as "vermin" or "plague" or they can be seen as expendable non-entities. In either case, disadvantage, hardship, and exploitation inflicted on them seems normal, acceptable, and just—as "the way things are" or the way they "ought to be." Fairness and deserving seem irrelevant when applied to them and harm befalling them elicits neither remorse, outrage, nor demands for restitution; instead, harm inflicted on them can inspire celebration.

Many social issues and controversies, such as aid to school drop-outs, illegal immigrants, "welfare moms," people who are homeless, substance abusers, and those infected with HIV are essentially moral debates about who deserves public resources, and thus, ultimately, about moral inclusion. When we see other people's circumstances to be a result of their moral failings, moral exclusion seems warranted. But when we see others' circumstances as a result of structural violence, moral exclusion seems unwarranted and unjust.

Psychological Bases for Moral Exclusion

While it is psychologically more comfortable to perceive harm-doers to be evil or demented, we each have boundaries for justice. Our moral obligations are stronger toward those close to us and weaker toward those who are distant. When the media reports suffering and death in Cambodia, El Salvador, Nicaragua, the former Yugoslavia, and Rwanda, we often fail—as a nation, as communities, and as individuals—to protest or to provide aid. Rationalizations include insufficient knowledge of the political dynamics, the futility of doing much of use, and not knowing where to begin. Our tendency to exclude people is fostered by a number of normal perceptual tendencies:

1. *Social categorization*. Our tendency to group and classify objects, including social categories, is ordinarily innocuous, facilitating acquisition of information and memory (Tajfel & Wilkes, 1963). Social categorizations can become invidious, however, when they serve as a basis for rationalizing structural inequality and social injustice. For example, race is a neutral physical characteris-

tic, but it often becomes a value-loaded label, which generates unequal treatment and outcomes (Archer, 1985; Tajfel, 1978).

2. *Evaluative judgments.* Our tendency to make simple, evaluative, dichotomous judgments (e.g., good and bad, like and dislike) is a fundamental feature of human perception. Evaluative judgments have cognitive, affective, and moral components. From a behavioral, evolutionary, and social learning perspective, evaluative judgments have positive adaptive value because they provide feedback that protects our well-being (Edwards & von Hippel, 1995; Osgood, Suci, & Tannenbaum, 1957). Evaluative judgments can support structural violence and exclusionary thinking, however, when they lend a negative slant to perceived difference. Ingroup-outgroup and we-them thinking can result from social comparisons made on dimensions that maximize a positive social identity for oneself or one's group at the expense of others (Tajfel, 1982).

3. *Fundamental attribution error.* We tend to attribute our own behavior to situational factors but attribute others' behavior to their personalities or dispositions (Jones & Nisbett, 1971). This attribution bias occurs because situational factors influencing others are less obvious to us than the nuances of our own social situation. As a result, our characterological attributions about others can be harsh or unflattering because we do not see the complex contextual factors that influence their behavior. In interpersonal feuds and in intergroup wars, an adversary's position and interests are depicted as more simple than the complex contingencies and extenuating circumstances influencing our own behavior.

4. *Self-serving biases.* Social comparisons often result in moral judgments with egocentric biases (Messick & Sentis, 1979). Self-serving perceptions and judgments magnify others' imperfections and lead us to cast others as less deserving than ourselves (Miller & Ross, 1975). Research on enemy images (cf., Holt & Silverstein, 1989; Volkan, 1988; White, 1984) and ethnocentric conflict (cf., Brewer, 1979; LeVine & Campbell, 1972) document our tendency to see adversaries as frightening, untrustworthy, or immoral.

5. *Zero-sum thinking.* Although many conflicts can be resolved with some mutual gains for disputants, we tend to view conflicts as zero-sum so that gains for one mean losses for the other (Deutsch, 1973). This perceived—but often exaggerated and inaccurate—incompatibility of interests can generate negative attitudes, prejudice, bias, and hostility (Campbell, 1965).

6. *Attributive projection.* Our tendency to perceive our own views as correct and universal can make it difficult to prevent them from intruding on and interfering with our inferences about others (Higgins, 1981; Ross & Fletcher, 1985). Imagining others' views as indistinguishable from our own supports the belief that our own social reality is correct and helps us avoid intrapsychic tensions that could result from realizing that others' beliefs may be in opposition to ours (Markus & Zajonc, 1985; Ross & Fletcher, 1985). Although we assume that age increases our ability for perspective taking and understanding others' thoughts and concerns, research on social perception, attributive projection, and false consensus indicate that adults continue to perceive others' beliefs and perceptions as more similar to their own than they actually are (Holmes, 1968; Ross & Fletcher, 1985; Ross, Greene, & House, 1977). Consequently, when others hold views that are different from our own, attributive projection leads us to view people who hold them as wrong and outside our moral community.

7. *Just world thinking.* Our need to perceive the world as fair and to believe that peo-

ple get what they deserve results in *just world thinking* (Lerner, 1970, 1980). In just world thinking, either evidence that victims are suffering is denied or their fate is perceived as just (Lerner & Simmons, 1966; Rubin & Peplau, 1975; Ryan, 1971). The view that the world is just because those who suffer deserve their suffering assuages our guilt (Austin & Hatfield, 1980; Utne & Kidd, 1980; Walster & Walster, 1975). Just world thinking masks structural inequality by reducing distress resulting from perceived social injustice. Bystanders to structural and direct violence are more psychologically comfortable when they perceive that exploiters deserve their good outcomes and victims deserve their suffering. During World War II, surveys conducted in the United States indicated a rise in anti-Semitism, rather than increased sympathy or concern for victims of the Holocaust (Selznick & Steinberg, 1969). Bystanders were able to maintain their belief in a just world by seeing victims as blameworthy people who deserved their fate.

Each of these tendencies toward perceptual distortion has adaptive, innocuous, and self-protective aspects, but each also fosters moral exclusion, structural and direct violence, and, ultimately, social injustice.

Dimensions of Moral Exclusion

Like violence, moral exclusion takes a variety of forms. The forms of moral exclusion can be described on three dimensions: 1) *intensity,* from subtle to blatant; 2) degree of *engagement,* from active to passive; and 3) *extent,* from narrow to wide in scope.

Intensity. The intensity of moral exclusion ranges from subtle to blatant. At the mildest end of the intensity dimension, we have rude or degrading behavior, then mild injury, severe injury, torture, irreversible injuries, mutilation, and murder. More subtle forms of moral exclusion relegate some people to social roles that undermine human dignity and allocate resources so that they receive less. Subtle forms of exclusion include such forms of structural violence as inadequate health care, sanitation, enforcement of housing codes, and police protection; substandard civic services can cause injury and death, even when direct violence is not intended. Blatant forms of moral exclusion include intentionally injurious, destructive behavior such as inflicting disfigurement, pain, injury, and death on people and destroying homes, communities, crops, and businesses.

Engagement. Participation in moral exclusion ranges from unawareness to ignoring, allowing, facilitating, executing, and devising. At the more passive end of the engagement dimension, crimes of ignoring and allowing occur when people have the social, intellectual, or financial resources to hinder moral exclusion, or aid those who are harmed, but remain aloof, uninterested, or uninformed. At the more active end of this dimension, are crimes of devising and executing violent acts. Architects of genocide, despots such as Pol Pot of Cambodia, are at the extreme end of the engagement scale, even when they themselves do not carry out the policies they devise and set into motion.

Extent. Moral exclusion ranges in extent from narrowly focused, to widespread and prevalent within a society. Narrowly focused moral exclusion affects small segments of a society, targeting those viewed as marginal, deviant, or nonentities, such as people having minority religious views or minority sexual orientations. Widespread moral exclusion affects most of a society; for example, during dictatorships or inquisitions, human rights violations and persecutions become the norm (cf., Moore, 1987).

Table 14.1 Dimensions of moral exclusion

	Subtle manifestations		Blatant manifestations	
	Narrow in extent	**Wide in extent**	**Narrow in extent**	**Wide in extent**
Passive engagement	1 Ignoring or allowing rudeness, intimidation, and derogation, such as bullying and sexual harassment	2 Ignoring or allowing domination and structural violence, such as slavery, racism, sweatshops, poverty, domestic violence	3 Ignoring or allowing persecution and violence directed at particular subcultures, such as hate crimes, witch hunts	4 Ignoring or allowing direct violence and rampant violations of human rights, such as ethnic cleansing, mass murder, inquisitions
Active engagement	5 Participating in, facilitating, executing, or devising such forms of rudeness, intimidation, and derogation as bullying, sexual harassment	6 Participating in, facilitating, or devising domination and structural violence, such as slavery, racism, sweatshops, poverty, domestic violence	7 Participating in, facilitating, executing, or devising persecution and violence directed at particular subcultures, such as hate crimes, witch hunts	8 Participating in, facilitating, executing, or devising such forms of direct violence and rampant violations of human rights, such as ethnic cleansing, mass murder, inquisitions
Perceptions of those excluded	Invisible, nonentities	Expendable, less than human	Reprehensible, vermin, a contaminating danger, a plague	

Table 14.1 describes eight forms of moral exclusion that emerge from interactions among these dimensions. While each form is quite distinct, on a deeper level, all forms have much in common. Whether moral exclusion is blatant or subtle, active or passive, and wide or narrow, it is characterized by a psychological orientation that:

- views those excluded as psychologically distant.
- lacks constructive moral obligations or responsibility toward those excluded.
- views those excluded as nonentities, expendable, and undeserving of fairness, community resources, or sacrifices that would foster their well-being.
- approves of procedures and outcomes for those excluded that would be unacceptable for those inside the scope of justice.

Like direct and structural violence, multiple forms of moral exclusion simultaneously exist within a society and, like direct and structural violence, one form of moral exclusion can give rise to others. For example, moral exclusion which is characterized by passive engagement, subtle manifestation, and wide extent (Cell 2) creates a social climate that nurtures more virulent forms of exclusion, such as homophobic hate crimes and lynching (Cell 7) or "ethnic cleansing" (Cell 8).

DETECTING SOCIAL INJUSTICE

Moral exclusion fosters structural and direct violence. Even when moral exclusion and structural violence are widespread and severe, they can be invisible when they are institutionalized. Before they can be addressed and deterred, they require detection. Detection, however, can be difficult for several reasons:

1. *Social injustice does not surface as a moral issue.* Harm and suffering that others experience is less obvious and painful than harm we ourselves experience. How we understand others' situations determines what we believe can or should be done. Different kinds of obligations ensue from construing others' experiences as morally relevant or not (Berkowitz, Guerra, & Nucci, 1991). Structural violence such as dangerous, brutal, degrading, and ill-paid work can be perceived as a matter of personal discretion (e.g., "It's her choice to work here") or social convention (e.g., "This is how these factories operate or they will close and people will be out of work") rather than a moral issue (e.g., "Poverty-level wages and insufficient safety mechanisms are exploitative and should be illegal").

2. *Social injustice is hard to see up close.* It is easier to detect injustice and moral exclusion in the past or in distant cultures than it is in our own. Self-deception occurs when people encounter evidence that contradicts their worldview. Psychologically, it is easier to question the credibility of evidence, dismiss its relevance, or distort it to fit one's views (Bandura, 1991). To avoid discovering evidence that disconfirms important beliefs, people keep themselves intentionally uninformed, failing to ask questions that would reveal unwanted information (Fingarette, 1969; Haight, 1980), "leav[ing] the foreseeable unforeseen and the knowable unknown" (Bandura, 1991, p. 95). For example, information on the widespread use of child labor in the production of rugs, clothing, and footwear was available many years before public opinion was mobilized to combat it.

3. *Indecision and inaction abets social injustice.* Eldridge Cleaver's aphorism from the 1960s, "you are either part of the problem or part of the solution," emphasizes non-neutrality of inaction. In malevolent social contexts, failing to perceive violence or act against injustice has important individual

and collective social consequences. Failing to perceive or oppose moral exclusion in contexts of widespread, severe, active violence, such as slavery or political repression, may be expedient and self-serving, but is a non-neutral decision with political implications for victims, perpetrators, and bystanders. Since moral exclusion narrowly directed at one group is more likely to spill over and spread than it is to abate, large portions of a society can become collaborators in persecution, as happened during the Spanish Inquisition, the witch trials in Europe, and McCarthyism in the United States (Moore, 1987).

4. *Combating social injustice consumes resources.* Constricting the scope of justice can lead to harmful outcomes. Enlarging the scope of justice, however, is not always possible or desirable. Although we like to think of ourselves as fair, moral, and upstanding, our capacity for justice is finite. Considering, attempting, and achieving fairness incurs real costs in time, energy, and resources. These costs increase during conflict, as resource availability diminishes and claims on scarce resources expand (Lerner, 1981; Leventhal, 1979; Staub, 1989). Under adverse conditions, excluding others from one's scope of justice is adaptive and simplifies difficult choices. Thus, moral exclusion is not a simple problem, but raises profound, complex questions about justice (Crosby & Lubin, 1990).

FOSTERING SOCIAL JUSTICE

Structural violence and moral exclusion can be narrow in scope, relatively subtle in outcome, and result from passive complicity. They can be perceived as acceptable, normal, and the way things are done. Structural violence may offer some members of society protection against competing claims on our scarce social or physical resources. Yet structural violence is not inevitable. While our society is characterized by many

forms of direct and structural violence, inclusionary thinking also flourishes. As previously unrecognized injustices gain attention, now more than ever we support the civil and human rights of such disadvantaged people as children, the aged, and people with HIV, and increasingly, the effects of destructive environmental behavior on the natural world (Opotow & Clayton, 1994). Fostering inclusionary thinking can be accomplished by:

1. *Welcoming open dialogue and critique.* Change and resource scarcity are a fact of social life, but they increase the sense of threat and danger and consequently narrow the scope of justice (Opotow, 1990). Therefore, tolerance for and encouragement of discussion and critique is a first step in recognizing structural violence and identifying its causes and cures. Supporting open dialogue and valuing pluralistic perspectives not only can help us identify unfair and divisive procedures for distributing social resources, but can also help social groups (e.g., political entities, citizen organizations) develop sufficient flexibility to withstand the stresses of social change and conflict (Coser, 1956).

2. *Establishing procedures that keep communication channels open during increased conflict.* Dialogue and critique are especially difficult and particularly important in those difficult times characterized by conflict and resource scarcity. Therefore, establishing communication channels and keeping them open is important if open dialogue and critique are to be encouraged. Foresight in establishing and maintaining these channels before they are needed is essential if they are to function when conflicts escalate (DeRidder, Schruijer, & Tripathi, 1992).

3. *Valuing pluralism and tolerance.* The need to view situations from perspectives other than one's own is axiomatic in conflict resolution, but the ability to do so is not

innate (Opotow, 1992). Understanding others' needs and positions means quieting one's own views so that they do not interfere with our ability to perceive the perspectives of others. Benefits that result from pluralism and tolerance include an increased ability to take others' perspectives; an increase in fresh, novel, and creative approaches; personal growth; and constructive societal change. Perspective taking and tolerance can be learned, and are more likely to become normative when they are modeled throughout the society by leaders, teachers, and parents in their relationships with each other (Opotow & Deutsch, 1999).

4. *Being alert to symptoms of moral exclusion.* Although it is more comfortable to see others as the ones perpetrating structural and direct violence, we are all skilled at moral exclusion. Exclusionary thinking is promoted by prevailing myths that allow us to take a righteous stance, deny negative outcomes that accrue to others, deny the validity of their perspective, and deny our own contributions to the problems of social living. Awareness of the symptoms of moral exclusion can help individuals, groups, institutions, and nations take actions consistent with the moral principles they cherish.

CONCLUSIONS: PEACE PSYCHOLOGY FOR THE TWENTY-FIRST CENTURY

The direct violence of hate crimes, ethnic tension, and war are the visible effects of unseen, pervasive, and long-lived structural violence, such as poverty, unemployment, and discrimination. Structural violence is sustained by social, psychological, economic, and political conditions that privilege some but exclude others. Differential access to effective schools, health care, safe and affordable housing, employment, sanitation services, and transportation are social, economic, and political issues, but they

are fundamentally moral issues as well. What is traditional, affordable, and expedient cloaks implicit moral choices that privilege some with access to social and physical resources while rationalizing others' lack. Moral exclusion makes structural violence probable, "logical," and invisible.

Although moral exclusion, direct and structural violence, and social injustice are ubiquitous, they are not inevitable. Inclusionary thinking is fostered by valuing one's connections to and interdependence with others, while seeing the mutually constructive possibilities of those connections as beneficial. Maintaining relationships depends on being committed to extending considerations of fairness, being willing to make sacrifices, and being willing to allocate and share resources to preserve those relationships with distant as well as close people. While we tend to envision peace as an outcome, peace is an inclusionary process. In the long run, cultures of peace, characterized by human rights, tolerance, democracy, free flow of information, non-violence, sustainable development, peace education, and equality of men and women will depend upon moral inclusion.

Social conflicts can foster injustice, but they also motivate social change that advances social justice. Constructive conflict processes can maximize social outcomes, but they are not intuitive and need to be learned (Colelman & Deutsch, this volume; Deutsch, 1973; Opotow & Deutsch, 1999). Appreciation of diversity, trust, and respect are difficult to achieve, taking considerable skill, effort, maturity, and patience to accomplish. To achieve these constructive outcomes, communication needs to unflinchingly address rather than suppress real structural inequalities that take some people's needs into account while disregarding, disrespecting, and excluding others. By so doing, we can enlarge the scope of justice, foster equality, and promote peace in the twenty-first century.

CHAPTER 9

THE WAR CLOSE TO HOME: CHILDREN AND VIOLENCE IN THE UNITED STATES

Kathleen Kostelny and James Garbarino

INTRODUCTION

For an increasing number of American children, growing up in the midst of violence is a tragic fact of life. Addressing the causes of violence and helping children who experience such violence is at the core of peace psychology. This chapter provides an overview of children's experiences of violence in the communities where they live. We begin by assessing the scope of violence that children experience in their day-to-day lives, and then examine the risk factors that contribute to the problem of violence at the family, community, and cultural levels. Next, we describe the psychosocial and developmental effects of violence as well as issues affecting children in the twenty-first century. In conclusion, we present six promising prospects for intervention, prevention and peacebuilding, designed to break the cycle of violence for children in the United States.

THE SCOPE OF VIOLENCE IN THE UNITED STATES

The United States is the most violent country in the industrialized world—especially for children and youth. Community violence has become such a problem that in 1992, the Surgeon General declared violence a public health emergency (Koop & Lundberg, 1992). Each year, millions of American children and adolescents are victims of violence in their own communities (Garbarino, Dubrow, Kostelny, & Pardo, 1992). Many more witness violence directed at others. Still others are the perpetrators of violence. Some youth are all three: victims, witnesses, and perpetrators.

More than 2,500 youth were killed nationwide in 1994—an 82 percent increase from 1984 (OJJDP, 1997). In a moderately violent community in Washington, D.C., 61 percent of first- and second-grade children and 72 percent of fifth- and sixth-grade children reported witnessing one or more incidents of community violence (Richters & Martinez, 1993). In high-violence communities in Chicago, 89 percent of third- and fifth-grade children have heard gunfire where they live, 38 percent have seen a dead body outside, and 21 percent have had someone threaten to shoot them (Kostelny & Garbarino, 1998). These statistics are closer to what children living in war zones experience than they are for children living "at peace."

For example, during the brutal war in Lebanon, research conducted from 1990 to 1991 found that 45 percent of Lebanese children had witnessed violent acts (Macksoud & Aber, 1996). In comparison, our Chicago study conducted during 1995 to 1996 found that 43 percent of the children in our sample had witnessed the violent event of seeing someone shot (Kostelny & Garbarino, 1998). Furthermore, many schools are no longer safe havens for children, but rather settings where violence is rampant. Data from a 1993 survey of third- to twelfth-grade children in the United States revealed that 23 percent of the children had been victims of violence in and around schools (Harris & Associates, 1994). In 1996, students ages twelve through 18 were victims of more than 250,000 incidents of violent crime while at school (Kaufman, Chandler, & Rand, 1998).

In addition to being victims of violence, children and youth are also increasingly the perpetrators of violence. According to a Justice Department report, youth aged ten to 17 committed 2,800 homicides in 1995 (an 84 percent increase from 1986) and 205,500 aggravated assaults (an increase of 137 percent) (OJJDP, 1998). Gangs, the majority of whom are youth, commit a large part of the violence that pervades many urban communities and an increasing number of rural communities. Miller (1992) estimated that

there were approximately 2,000 gangs and nearly 100,000 gang members in the United States in 1980. By 1996, the number escalated to more than 31,000 gangs and approximately 846,000 gang members (OJJDP, 1997). In recent studies, adolescent gang members in various locations committed from 68 percent to 89 percent of all serious violent offenses. While the typical age range for gang members is twelve to 24, and the average age is 17 years, younger members are becoming more common. In a 1998 survey of eighth-graders, 9 percent reported they were currently gang members, and 17 percent said they had belonged to a gang at some time in their lives (OJJDP, 1998, May).

Not only are gangs becoming more prevalent, but they are also more violent than in previous decades. The rise in gangs and gang violence has been attributed to the increasing availability of semiautomatic and high-powered weapons. In Chicago, gang homicides more than doubled from 1987 to 1990 (Block & Block, 1993; Spergel, 1995). Moreover, because the rate of U.S. children experiencing clinical levels of adjustment and developmental problems doubled from the 1970s to the 1990s, gangs increasingly include significant numbers of youth who are psychologically impaired, increasing their dangerousness (Garbarino, 1995).

RISK FACTORS

The risk of developmental harm from exposure to violence increases when other biological, cultural, psychological, and social risks are present in a child's environment. While a single risk is not more likely to cause developmental harm, when risk factors accumulate, the likelihood of damaging consequences increases dramatically (Rutter, 1987). We briefly discuss four of these risk factors: family violence, depressed mothers, media violence, and easy accessibility to firearms.

Family Violence

A growing number of children experience violence within their family. Research on child abuse rates in high-crime communities in Chicago found that these communities had rates four times higher than the city average (Garbarino & Kostelny, 1992, 1994). When children already vulnerable from experiencing community violence are then exposed to family violence, they show increased risk of developmental harm. In studies of children living in violent communities, children who also experienced violence at home had significantly more behavioral and psychological problems than children who did not experience family violence (Garbarino & Kostelny, 1996b; Kostelny & Garbarino, 1998).

Depressed Mothers

Parents who live with the chronic stress of poverty and violence are often depressed and overwhelmed, and thus may not be able to care for and nurture their children adequately (Halpern, 1990). Such parents are often socially isolated because they live in high-crime communities; they isolate themselves and their children by not leaving their homes to seek supportive networks for themselves and their children. In such dire circumstances, parents easily transmit feelings of powerlessness, futility, and hopelessness to their children.

Media Violence

Television is a powerful influence in the lives of children. While educational and social programs can have a positive influence on children, programs which contain violence and aggression can have long-lasting negative consequences. Nearly all children are exposed to violence in the mass media, particularly television. For example, by the time they reach 18 years of age, U.S. children have witnessed over 200,000 violent acts on television. Eighty percent of television programs contain violence, with an average of five acts of violence per hour during prime-time viewing, and an average of 25 acts of violence per hour during Saturday morning children's programs (Gerbner, Morgan, & Signorielli, 1994).

Research has found that a steady diet of violent and aggressive television has negative effects on children's social, emotional, and moral development (Murray, 1997; Eron, Gentry, & Schlegel, 1994). These effects include: (1) increased aggressiveness and antisocial behavior, including developing favorable attitudes and values about the use of violence to solve problems and an increased appetite for more violence in entertainment and real life; (2) desensitization to real-life violence, including less sensitivity to the pain and suffering of others, and more willingness to tolerate increasing amounts of violence; and (3) belief that the world is as mean and dangerous in real life as it is on television (Murray, 1997).

Accessibility to Firearms

The easy availability of firearms in the United States is a major factor in the deaths and serious injuries to children and youth. Every two hours a child is killed by a gun, and five others are seriously injured. More children were killed by guns in the last decade than there were U.S. soldiers killed during the Vietnam War. Unless gun violence is curbed, the U.S. Department of Health and Human Services projects that within the next 15 years, gun fatalities will become the leading cause of death in the United States. In a study conducted by the YWCA, 54 percent of young people reported they had access to a firearm

(Harris & Associates, 1994). Moreover, every day, nearly 270,000 students carry guns to school. Research has found that the increase in homicides by juveniles in the late 1980s was related to crimes committed with handguns (Butterfield, 1998). Many children and youth, particularly boys, are fascinated with and drawn to guns because of the power and status they convey (Garbarino, Dubrow, Kostelny, & Pardo, 1992). While some youth are drawn to the power of guns, many believe they must carry guns for protection.

MEDIATING EFFECTS OF VIOLENCE

A number of factors mediate, or influence, how children and youth will respond to the violence they experience in their communities. These factors include a child's individual characteristics, the social context established by a child's family, community, and larger society, as well as the particular characteristics of the violence (Garbarino & Associates, 1992). Individual factors include a child's developmental level, temperament, and the quality of attachment to the parent or caretaker. Family factors include the level of support and the quality of interactions among family members. Community factors include the ties within the neighborhood, employment opportunities, and other resources or support systems. Societal factors include laws, institutions, and values, especially society's attitudes toward violence and punishment. These factors can either serve as risks—increasing the likelihood of negative developmental outcomes from violence, or protective factors—buffering the stress and trauma of violence for children. Finally, the characteristics of the violence—for example, the amount and type of violence, the child's relationship to the perpetrator and victim, and proximity to the incident—also affect the child's response to that violence (Marans & Adelman, 1997).

Individual Characteristics: Developmental Level

Where a child is developmentally influences how that child will respond to stressful and traumatic incidents of violence. A child's development ranges across many domains—linguistic, cognitive, affective, and physical. Development is also the process by which children form a picture, or draw a map of the world in their mind, and their place in it. These representations, or social maps of the world, reflect the cognitive competence of the child. But they also indicate a child's moral and affective inclination—characteristic ways of feeling about the world. Does the child trust others? Does the child expect the protection of adults? Does the child see a safe and secure place in the world? The child's social map is primarily the result of experience, but increasingly it becomes the cause of behavior.

Family Support

While the primary caretaker is an important factor in buffering stress and trauma for children, other family members can also protect a child from developmental harm. In her study of children at risk, Werner (1990) found that secure attachments in infants were related to the presence of a supportive family member, but not exclusively the primary caretaker. The extended family can lessen stress, encourage coping behavior, and facilitate the child's working through violent experiences by providing additional adult nurturing and positive models of identification.

Community Support

Belonging to a community where one is valued and esteemed, cared for and loved, acts as a potent protective factor in the lives of children. Such social support comes from friends, neighbors, and teachers, who encourage self-esteem and promote competence. Children need coherent experiences and the help of concerned, competent adults to meet new demands, to cope with new stresses, and to achieve higher levels of functioning. Although violent events can disrupt significant social relationships, some social networks are able to maintain children's belief that they are secure and cared for. This belief affects the degree of stress children experience, as well as their subsequent psychological adjustment.

Cultural Factors

Violence has so permeated life in the United States that to a large degree certain types and amounts of violence have come to be accepted and expected as solutions to problems. The message is reinforced in much of our entertainment—television, movies, and video games portray heroes who excel at violence. Often, these violent acts are glorified, and powerful messages—that violence is an acceptable and admirable way of resolving conflict—are sent to children. Furthermore, a relationship exists between children's belief in the legitimacy of aggression and their own aggressive behavior. Children who believe that aggression is justifiable are three times as aggressive as children who do not approve of such aggression (Erdley & Asher, 1994; Tolan & Guerra, 1994).

Acute vs. Chronic Violence

Acute violence and chronic violence impact children in different ways. While a child's response to a single episode of violence often includes a normal shock reaction, which is marked by severe anxiety, it usually lasts only a short time (Garmezy & Rutter, 1983). Moreover, children are usually able to assimilate a single, isolated violent event into their existing world view and see the

event as an accident (Garbarino, Kostelny, & Dubrow, 1991a). Unlike acute violence, which is short-lived and where children can go back to their usual routines after the stressful event, chronic violence requires developmental adjustment, including major personality changes, changes in patterns of behavior, and the adoption of an ideological framework for making sense of the ongoing violence (Garbarino, Kostelny, & Dubrow, 1991b).

Furthermore, the effects of violence are cumulative; the more children experience violent events, the more vulnerable they are to developmental harm and traumatization (Pynoos & Nader, 1988). In our study of children in high-violence communities in Chicago, children who experienced four or more types of community violence displayed more than twice the aggressive behavior as children who experienced only one type of violence in the community (Kostelny & Garbarino, 1998). Moreover, children having personal experiences with violence at a low or moderate level, or living in communities with moderate violence, responded better to a violence-prevention program than did children who experienced high amounts of violence or lived in communities with high levels of violence. This finding suggests a threshold effect in terms of the amount of violence a child can experience, and still be able to change aggressive attitudes and behavior. Once that threshold is passed, it may be extremely difficult to change children's thinking and behavior.

THE IMPACT OF VIOLENCE

Experiencing chronic violence can shape children's development in multiple negative ways, including mental health disturbances years after the violence occurred (Kinzie, Sack, Angell, Manson, & Rath, 1986). Many children cope with violence by adopting behavior that is adaptive in a vio- lent setting but is dysfunctional in "normal" settings in which they participate (Gar- barino & Kostelny, 1993, 1996a). For exam- ple, adapting to chronic violence by becom- ing hypervigilant and hyperaggressive may be a useful strategy on the streets, but is detrimental to being successful in school (Garbarino, Dubrow, Kostelny, & Pardo, 1992).

Preschool children frequently regress to earlier developmental levels in response to violence—bedwetting, anxious attachment to their caretaker, and a decrease in talking can result. Other symptoms include phobic reactions, difficulties with sleeping, social withdrawal, aggressive play, and a severely limited capacity for exploration and think- ing (Garbarino & Kostelny, 1997a, 1997b). School-age children often develop symp- toms including somatic complaints, cogni- tive distortions, trouble concentrating, learning difficulties, inhibitions, increased aggression, disruptions in peer relation- ships, and erratic behaviors in response to violence. On the other hand, adolescents often display acting out and self-destructive behavior such as increased risk-taking, delinquent and criminal behavior, life- threatening reenactments of violent epi- sodes, aggressive actions, and involvement in gangs (Eth & Pynoos, 1985). For some of these children, the psychological con- sequences are particularly devastating, in- cluding fear, desensitization, hopelessness, impaired moral development, and the per- petration of violence.

Fear and Loss of Safety

Experiences of violence destroy a child's perception of home, school, and commu- nity as traditional bastions of safety. Vio- lence threatens a child's sense of secure at- tachment to caretakers, thus jeopardizing

the formation of a stable base from which a child can venture forth in exploration of the surrounding world. Danger replaces safety as the organizing principle, and the child comes to believe that there is no order and continuity in life. As a result of adults who hurt or fail to shield them from vio- lence, young children may not trust any adults to help and protect them. Such chil- dren may turn inward in an attempt to draw on their own internal resources. Or, they may turn outward in fear, hatred, or in an effort at self-protection (Garbarino, Kostelny, & Dubrow, 1991b). For example, children who do not feel safe may adopt ag- gressive and violent behavior towards others in an attempt to protect themselves from harm by taking the offensive.

Psychic Numbing

When violent stressors continually occur, denial and numbing can result. When ex- treme situations become unpredictable, these "battle weary" children attempt to block out stressful or traumatic events by ig- noring reality (Terr, 1990). While such a re- sponse may be socially adaptive in the short run, it becomes a danger to the next gener- ation, when the child becomes a parent. This phenomenon has been observed in studies of some families of Holocaust sur- vivors (Danieli, 1985). The emotional numbing that initially helped them to cope with the horrors of the concentration camps on a day-to-day basis put them at risk for emotionally neglecting their own children in the long run.

Futurelessness

Some children develop a sense of futureless- ness, or a profound fatalism about their lives. They come to expect more violence di- rected at them and death at an early age (Bell, 1991; Osofsky et al., 1993). When asked where they see themselves in ten years, such children often reply "Dead" or "I don't think I'll make it that long." In a survey of twelfth graders in U.S. cities, 35 percent did not expect to live to old age. For minority adolescents, the percentage rises to 50 percent (Garbarino, 1995).

Aggressive Attitudes and Behavior

Exposure to violence increases the acceptance of violence and the likelihood of a child engaging in future violence and other antisocial acts. One way to feel safer is to align oneself with those who are frightening; some children come to identify with the aggressor. These children often join gangs and model themselves and their behavior on those powerful, aggressive individuals and groups in their environment who caused the danger in the first place. Aggressive behavior during childhood is likely to lead to aggressive violent behavior as an adult. Eron and colleagues (1994) found that aggressive behavior at age eight predicts aggressive behavior at age 30 unless there is intervention.

ISSUES AFFECTING U.S. CHILDREN IN THE TWENTY-FIRST CENTURY

While recent trends indicate that violent crime is decreasing, violence by and to U.S. youth is increasing. In 1995, 25 percent of all known juvenile homicides were located in five cities: Chicago, New York, Los Angeles, Detroit, and Houston, although only 10 percent of the nation's population live in these areas. These cities contain large numbers of vulnerable youth who live in families with multiple risk factors. The combination of poverty, drugs, racism, deteriorated physical and social resources, and concentrations of vulnerable families with multiple problems have created hotspots of lethal violence—"inner-city war zones." This syn-

drome became particularly evident in the 1970s and achieved epidemic proportions by the mid-1980s, spreading to urban and rural areas throughout the United States (Garbarino, 1999).

While these vulnerable populations don't cause the epidemics, their impoverished position makes them good hosts for "infection." Such was the case with the Black Plague of the Middle Ages which started in the homes and neighborhoods of the lowest levels of society, where sanitation conditions and nutrition were most primitive, but eventually reached into the palaces of the nobility. Unmarried teenage pregnancy over the past 30 years has shown the same pattern: The high rates observed among inner-city minority girls in the 1960s were found throughout the U.S. in the 1990s among girls who lived in small-town, suburban, and rural areas.

The same epidemic model can describe lethal youth violence in schools. Homicides committed by youth in schools first peaked in 1992 to 1993, the first stage of an epidemic, when 50 people died, mostly in urban schools and involving low-income, minority youth. In 1997, a second stage of the epidemic began in rural and suburban areas. According to data compiled by the federal government, the rate of juvenile murders in suburbs and in small towns and rural areas increased 25 percent in 1997.

INTERVENTION, PREVENTION, AND PEACEBUILDING: SIX PROPOSALS

Despite these grim statistics, there are sources of health and resilience that offer hope for children and youth in the twenty-first century. Identifying and then acting on these sources of health and resilience are essential to peacebuilding. We present six approaches that can counteract youth violence, approaches that begin in infancy and continue throughout adolescence.

Home Visits

The first approach is insuring healthy babies and positive parent-infant relationships beginning in the earliest days, months, and years of life—in pregnancy, childbirth, and infancy. This approach reduces the likelihood of children coming into the world at a biological disadvantage and prevents them from being maltreated by their parents. Chief among such approaches is home health visits that begin prenatally and continue through the first years of life.

Home visiting programs involve a caring person who represents the community in the life of a child before the child is even born. When done best, these programs make contact with families soon after conception and enter into a long-term, supportive relationship with them. The home visitor comes to the family's residence on a regular basis throughout the first two years of the child's life, providing information and a caring that all prospective parents need, but which prospective parents with risk factors accumulated in their lives particularly need. The home visitor establishes a relationship to address needs of both the mother and the unborn child. Positive and durable results of home health visiting have extended from birth into adulthood. For example, babies are born with fewer health problems; they experience dramatically less child maltreatment (infants who did not have home visiting experienced four times the amount of child abuse in the first two years of life); and as adolescents they are significantly less involved in the criminal justice system (Olds et al., 1997).

Care-giving Relationships

A second approach lies in programs that promote a healthy child-caretaker relationship. A crucial goal for such programs is to ensure that difficult children will be ac-cepted rather than rejected by their parents (and later by their teachers). Such rejection is the primary route through which many children develop conduct disorders and gravitate to anti-social peers. One of the foundations for resilience is at least one strong, secure attachment; having none puts a child at risk. Young children who evidence impaired attachment relationships with their caregivers need help repairing relationships. Children are better able to endure the emotional stress and physical disruption of chronic violence if they remain with their primary caretaker and are taken care of in a stable, routine manner (Garbarino, Kostelny, & Barry, 1998). Parents who are "models of resilience," available with reassurance and encouragement during adversity, helping their children understand and process stress and trauma, are more likely to have resilient children (Anthony & Cohler, 1987).

Early Childhood Education

A third approach is high-quality early childhood education programs—preschools, Head Start centers, nursery schools, and day-care centers that promote positive child development and prevent the likelihood of early violent behavior. These programs serve as focal points for parent education and support programs that improve the ability of parents to care for children in nurturing and accepting ways. This intervention is particularly important if the family is at risk for maltreating and rejecting the child. Early childhood education programs can be an informal early warning system for children who are developing problems with aggressive behavior. One of the most famous long-term follow-up studies of a high-quality early childhood education program (the Perry Preschool Program) reports that for every dollar spent on the program, at least seven were saved years later because the program's graduates showed less involvement in the criminal justice system (Garbarino & Associates, 1992).

Elementary School Programs

The fourth approach includes a growing number of violence prevention programs at the elementary-school level. These programs are based on the observation that by age eight, patterns of aggressive attitudes and behavior become crystallized, and without intervention such patterns continue into adulthood. Evaluations of violence prevention and reduction programs reviewed by Tolan and Guerra (1994) indicate that the most effective strategies are those that begin in childhood and combine "cognitive restructuring" (changing ideas about aggression) with "behavioral rehearsal" (practicing alternatives to violence).

One such program is *Let's Talk About Living in a World with Violence* (Garbarino, 1993). This workbook-based program was developed to stimulate child-adult and child-child dialogue about the meaning, rationale, effects of, and alternatives to violence in all domains of a child's life. The program provides help to school-aged children, to change the way they think about violence (i.e., that violence is acceptable and justifiable), to change their aggressive behavior, and to promote pro-social values. When used by a teacher who received training and support, integrated the program with other topics, and used concepts in actual conflict situations, students were able to change aggressive attitudes and behavior (Kostelny & Garbarino, 1998).

Character Education

The fifth approach is character education. Modern character education programs involve mobilizing schools and the community to endorse and promote a set of core values of trustworthiness, respect, responsibility, fairness, caring, and citizenship. The key to such efforts is that the programs provide concrete opportunities for children to experience honorable behavior, integrity, and caring in their relationships with adults. Additionally, these programs promote spiritual development in activities like caring for dependent beings—infant children, the infirm elderly, growing plants, and baby animals.

Conflict Resolution Programs

Finally, conflict resolution programs focus on middle schools and junior high schools and teach mediation, conflict resolution, and peace education activities. One of the largest and longest-running school-based programs focusing on conflict resolution and intergroup relations is the Resolving Conflict Creatively Program developed by Educators for Social Responsibility (Aber, Brown, & Henrich, 1999). The program attempts to change the entire culture within schools to become peaceable and effective communities of learning. Components of the program include classroom instruction that teaches students key skills and concepts in social and emotional learning, provides training for teachers, parents, and administrators, and trains students as mediators who then help their peers resolve conflicts that arise.

CONCLUSION

Peace for U.S. children will challenge us intellectually, economically, politically, and spiritually. Our efforts need to be situated within a larger social context and be aimed at violence prevention and constructive system change. Peace and healthy development do not occur automatically when community violence ceases. As long as systemic inequities exist and other pressures toward violence operate at the family and cultural levels, children will suffer from structural violence, and cycles of violence will continue (Wessells & Kostelny, 1996). Making peace is much more than simply "getting tough on crime" or "conflict resolution programs." Peace requires leadership and vision to assess the role of each and every institution, each and every child's development, and each and every public policy to understand its contribution to the larger problem of violence in American life. Peace will require years of dedicated and informed work by professionals from varied backgrounds, working closely with grassroots organizations and political leaders to transform America into a truly "kinder and gentler" society, a transformation which must be the core agenda for the twenty-first century.

CHAPTER 10

CHILDREN AND STRUCTURAL VIOLENCE

Milton Schwebel and Daniel J. Christie

The reduction of direct violence requires not only interventions aimed at individuals, but also structural changes aimed at how societies operate, as Kostelny and Garbarino have outlined in their chapter. In this chapter, we examine the effects of structural violence on children. *Structural violence* is the unequal distribution of power and wealth within and between societies, and it has insidious effects on the health, intellectual development, education, and general welfare of millions of children. The cruelties of structural violence on children are often subtle, unspoken, unrecognized, and even *normalized*, regarded by many people as natural or "just the way things are." This chapter focuses on how children suffer the cruel effects of structural violence, and why it has long-lasting consequences on their intellectual, social, and emotional development.

THE GLOBAL PICTURE

We can gauge the extent to which children are victims of structural violence by comparing the conditions that would be ideal for optimal growth and development against those children actually experience. Albee (1992) concluded that an ideal environment or prevention program would

ensure that every baby born anywhere in the world would be a healthy, full-term infant weighing at least eight pounds and welcomed into the world by economically secure parents who wanted the child and had planned jointly for her or his conception and birth. . . . The baby would be breast-fed by an adequately nourished mother who was not on drugs [and there would be] good health care for expectant mother and child (p. 313).

Although other experts might add to these criteria for an ideal environment, few would dispute the significance of the features Albee identified. We do not have to look far to realize that we are a long way from providing optimal conditions for the world's children. More than a quarter of the world's population, about 1.5 billion people, are considered poor (Renner, 1998) and most of the poor live in so-called "developing countries" in the southern hemisphere. These countries, which are sometimes referred to as Third World countries, contain more than two-thirds of the world's population but possess only 16 percent of global income (Renner, 1998; UNDP, 1997). The gap between the rich and the poor countries is staggering: the richest one-fifth of the world's population has 82.7 percent of the global income while the poorest one-fifth has only 1.4 percent (UNDP, 1992). Small wonder that there are tensions between the global South and the global North.

Throughout the world, children suffer from structural violence. About twelve million children under five years old die each year in developing countries, most often from preventable causes. The deaths of over six million children, or 55 percent, are caused by malnutrition, not because there is a shortage of food in the world but because food is unequally distributed. Gandhi's terse comment is relevant here: "There is enough in the world for man's [sic] need but not for his greed" (as quoted by Ostergaard, 1990, p. 206). Other preventable causes of malnutrition include poor health services, unsafe water, inadequate sanitation, harmful child-rearing practices, and a lack of maternal support. More than 2.2 million children under the age of five die each year from infectious diseases, including childhood diarrhea. We know these diseases are primarily caused by unsafe drinking water and inadequate sanitation and are thus preventable (UNICEF, 1998).

Besides the twelve million children who die from preventable diseases each year, even more disturbing is the fact that each year 160 million children survive the dire conditions of crushing poverty, but end up chronically malnourished and suffer from severe developmental disabilities both physically and mentally. Given the poor health status of so many children, it is not surprising that over 100 million children of school age fail to attend school (UNDP, 1997), and most of them are girls (Kagitcibasi, 1998). These children pay a great price because education is the most certain way to increase human potential, as measured by intelligence tests, and to raise human capital, measured by lifetime earnings. In countries where studies have been conducted, the

more schooling children receive, the higher their IQ and earnings (Brody, 1997).

While it has long been recognized that the education of men is important, it is becoming increasingly clear that when women are deprived of education, everyone pays an enormous price. Recent research has linked well-being of children to well-being of women (Buvinic & Yodelman, 1989; UNDP, 1997). In comparison to men, women have a more profound and direct impact on children's survival, health, and quality of life (El-Mouelhy, 1992). Despite the important link between women and children, there is no society in the world where women enjoy the same opportunities as men, whether measured by enrollment in school, literacy, preparation for careers, political participation, earned income, or any other measure that reflects *quality of life* (see Mazurana & McKay, this volume; UNDP, 1995). Worldwide, women receive only 54 percent of the years of schooling as men, even though more education for women translates into multiple benefits to societies, such as lower rates of fertility and child mortality (UNDP, 1996). Women with more education tend to marry later in life, begin childbearing later in life, and have fewer children (Belsey & Royston, 1987). Literacy also matters because, like education, higher levels of maternal literacy are associated with lower infant mortality and fertility rates; maternal literacy levels are also associated with better family nutrition and lower overall population growth (Bunch & Carillo, 1998). Clearly, the well-being of women, particularly their educational attainment, serves the interests of children and society as a whole. More broadly, all countries ought to invest generously in education, especially because those societies that invest the most in education also demonstrate the most rapid growth in economic development (McGranahan, 1995).

STRUCTURAL VIOLENCE IN DEVELOPED NATIONS

The structural violence of poverty is not limited to developing countries. There is a Third World inside many First World countries. Countries with high average incomes do not necessarily provide a high quality of life for all of their citizens. In industrial and information-based societies, more than five million people are homeless, more than 37 million people are unemployed, and more than a third of the adult population fail to complete secondary education (UNDP, 1997).

In the United States, the gap between the rich and poor is larger than in 17 other industrialized countries. Children living in wealthy U.S. families are among the most affluent children in the world, but children living in poor U.S. families are among the poorest of all the industrialized countries (Gottschalk & Smeeding, 2000).

The Psychosocial Costs of Structural Violence

Poverty has huge negative impacts, but especially on those who are most vulnerable: women and children. Compared to families that are not in poverty, families in poverty have higher levels of infant mortality, child abuse, children in out-of-home placements, school truancy, and child homelessness (Brown, 1983; Edelman, 1983). Poverty puts both the expectant mother and the developing fetus at risk in a variety of ways. Mothers in poverty are less likely to receive medical care during pregnancy, are more likely to have complications during delivery, and are more likely to have a premature newborn or a full-term baby who has a lower than normal birth weight. Both premature birth and pregnancy complications affect children because these problems are associated with developmental disabilities, which include a host of physical, emotional, and learning problems. Low birth weight is a particularly important consideration because it puts the infant at risk for a wide range of disabilities including cerebral palsy, seizure disorders, visual-motor coordination problems, learning disabilities, and mental retardation (Bradley et al., 1994; Crooks, 1995).

Like poverty, the problem of *unemployment* is also rooted in the economic structures and policies of a society. Unemployment directly affects parents' well-being, which, in turn, affects children's well-being. At the time of this writing, unemployment in the United States was low in comparison to typical levels, affecting fewer than 5 percent of the labor force but still a large number of people, in total about six million. The effects of unemployment on families are enormous. Brenner (1976) found that in the United States, an increase of only one percentage point in unemployment was associated with increases of 5.7 percent in homicides, 4.1 percent in suicides, 4.3 percent in mental hospital admissions for men, 2.3 percent for women, and nearly 2 percent in deaths from stress-related disorders. Communities affected by major lay-offs show significant increases in marital conflict, parent-child conflict, and child abuse, because unemployment affects the whole family. Marital satisfaction also tends to be low when employment is unstable (Cherlin, 1979).

Underemployment is a related problem. People who are underemployed tend to feel like victims of fate (Burris, 1983). As Schwebel (1997) has noted: "The rapid increase (over 200% between 1992–1994) in the U.S. in the use of temporary workers is likely to exacerbate feelings of insecurity, undermine self-esteem, and increase stress in spousal and parental relationships" (pp. 339–340).

The Impact of Structural Violence on Parenting

Some of the impacts of poverty and other forms of structural violence affect children directly, but many of the effects are mediated by the way parents interact with their children (Toomey & Christie, 1990). Structural violence jeopardizes both mediated learning and parenting styles.

Mediation in Learning and Development.

To appreciate how structural violence impedes intellectual development, we draw from Vygotsky's (1978) theory of mediated learning and the work of others who have extended and applied his thinking, including Feuerstein (1980) and Wertsch (1998). In Vygotsky's view, maturation is secondary in the development of the mind. He compared maturation, which is passive, to what he called the practical activity of children—playing, exploring, eating, observing, smiling, and much of the time, in all of this activity, *interacting with others*. Children, he pointed out, make enormous advances in their abilities when they can understand and use speech, which gives them greater power and control over their activities.

To illustrate the point, picture four scenes, each separated in time. In the first, we see mother and her two-year-old daughter who, with mother's guidance (or mediation), has just succeeded in completing a jigsaw puzzle. Mother says, "Good girl." In the second scene, a few months later, the little girl, playing with her doll, helps the doll place the jigsaw pieces in their appropriate places, and then the girl says to the doll, "Good girl." In the third scene, six months later, playing alone, after solving a child's puzzle, she says *aloud* to herself, "Good girl." She has learned to cue herself about various aspects of how to fit puzzle pieces together, just as her mother had done earlier as a mediator (e.g., "look for a place for a small piece" or "this piece looks like a ball"). In the final scene a year later, after she has successfully read a picture book story, she *thinks* to herself, "Good girl."

In this manner, thought is a sequence of learned verbalizations. The words of the adult become the child's egocentric speech, i.e., the words spoken aloud in play or spoken aloud to oneself. Later, those words become the child's inner thoughts. What starts as an interpersonal process ends as an intrapersonal one. In Vygotsky's terms: "Every function in the child's cultural development appears twice: first, on the social level, and later, on the individual level; first, between people or *interpsychological,* and then *inside* the child or *intrapsychological.* All the higher functions originate as actual relations between individuals" (1978, p. 57). Hence, the child's intellectual development is in part a result of the skilled mediation of adults.

Vygotsky (1978) further refined his theory of mental development with the concept of the "zone of proximal development." The zone is the difference between two developmental levels: the *actual* level at a given time, which can be established by assessing the child's independent problem-solving ability, and the *potential* level, which can be assessed by observing the child's problem-solving performance when guided by an adult. To illustrate, if a child who is looking at a picture and working independently cannot differentiate "up" and "down," "left" and "right," but with the mediation of an adult learns them readily, then these concepts are within the child's zone of proximal development. We can expect that with instruction, i.e., the mediation of an adult, the child could master the concepts. All through infancy and childhood, the individual has zones of proximal development. Children in poverty are at a disadvantage because of the lack of mediated learning experiences and cultural tools that support success in school.

Parenting Styles. In addition to underscoring the importance of mediated learning experiences, research in developmental psychology has identified parenting styles that are conducive to children's growth and development. During the early years of life, the quality of parenting has an effect on the kind of attachment an infant will form with the primary caregiver (Ainsworth, Bleher, Waters, & Wall, 1978; Bee, 1997). Securely attached infants behave differently from insecurely attached infants. *Securely attached* infants prefer the primary caregiver to other adult figures, use the primary caregiver as a secure base from which to explore strange or unfamiliar settings, seek regular and frequent contact with the primary caregiver, and can be soothed by the caregiver when the infant experiences distress. *Insecurely attached infants* demonstrate an array of negative emotional responses to the caregiver: anger, detachment, ambivalence, apprehension, etc. Studies that have examined parent-child interactions suggest that secure attachments are causally linked with a parental characteristic called *contingent responsiveness* (Isabella, 1993). Parents who are contingently responsive towards their children are sensitive to the cues their children use to signal various needs. Not only are the parents sensitive to the child's needs but they respond to needs promptly and appropriately. Very often a dance ensues in which the baby's smile elicits a smile from the parent; then, the child's vocalization invites an oral response from the parent, and so on. The multiple stressors of poverty make it difficult for parents to behave in a responsive way to their children's needs (Toomey & Christie, 1990). Not surprisingly, insecurely

attached infants are much more likely to be found in conditions of poverty than in non-poverty situations (Bee, 1997).

The degree to which parents provide warmth and guidance has been associated with positive developmental outcomes (Baumrind, 1972; Maccoby & Martin, 1983). *Warmth* consists of parental affection, empathy, and contingent responsiveness. Parents who provide *guidance* set high but reasonable goals, use rules consistently, and monitor their children's behavior. When parental warmth is combined with high levels of guidance, *authoritative parenting* (not authoritarian) takes place. Children raised in authoritative families tend to have high levels of self-esteem, self-reliance, achievement, and, at the same time, tend to comply with parental requests.

Poverty makes it difficult for parents to provide guidance, warmth, and responsiveness. Parents in poverty lack resources, struggle to meet their children's needs, and are left with a narrow range of choices when they have to make decisions that affect the well-being of their children. For instance, poor parents have fewer choices than middle-class parents about day care, housing, health care services, and education (see Webster and Perkins in this volume). In addition, parents in poverty environments often experience multiple stressors and chaos (McLoyd & Wilson, 1991), as crises arise unpredictably and repeatedly. Stress also takes its toll on parents' emotional well-being. Poverty and unemployment often leave parents depressed, emotionally unavailable, and, therefore, unresponsive to their children's needs (Leana & Ivancevich, 1987). Problems are compounded because children of parents in poverty are more likely to have learning difficulties and physical disabilities, which place additional stress on the parent-child relationship.

Bee (1997) summarized some of the contrasting features of parents in poverty and parents who are not. Parents in poverty tend to talk to their children less often, give explanations less often, spend less time doing intellectually stimulating activities with their children, are less warm, and more punitive in their discipline. The consequences of parenting styles that lack warmth and structure are particularly problematic, because they often lead to negative outcomes in children, including aggressive behavior, lack of self-reliance, and low levels of self-esteem and achievement.

The Impact of Structural Violence on School Achievement

McLoyd (1998) has reviewed a number of studies that demonstrate the impact of poverty and socio-economic status (SES) on children's school performance and related variables. Children's SES is related to their performance on IQ tests and other measures that predict school performance. Once in school, poor children perform lower than non-poor children on achievement test scores, number of years of schooling completed, and high school graduation rates. Poor children are higher on course failure, grade retention, placement in special education, and dropout rate. In addition to problems related to school performance, McLoyd cites studies suggesting that poor children exhibit more emotional and behavioral problems than middle-class children.

Once again, *parenting styles* are important. As reported by Frisby (1998), Kellaghan (1994) identified family processes associated with high achievement in school. These included "opportunities provided to children for thinking and imagination in daily activities . . . availability and quality of help provided by the family on matters re-

lated to school work . . . opportunities for language development and the use of complex levels of language" (p. 68). In addition, low-SES children tend to lose ground in their academic skills during the summer. Entwistle, Alexander, and Olson (1997) have provided a detailed analysis of the problem. During the school year, comparable gains in reading and math were demonstrated by low- and high-SES children. However, during the summer, low-SES children showed a decline in their academic skills while high-SES children posted gains.

The *quality of schools* also impacts children's performance. Some schools achieve good outcomes consistently, year after year, when compared to other schools, even when both sets of schools are operating under similar levels of neighborhood affluence. A variety of measurable variables have been used as indices of "good outcomes," including attendance rates, standardized test scores, levels of delinquency, and proportion of college-bound graduates. Bee (1997) has reviewed the findings of a large number of studies and concludes that the characteristics of the most effective schools bear a striking resemblance to the authoritative parenting style. Among other features, these schools are characterized by "clear goals and rules, good control, good communication, and high nurturance" (p. 406).

CONFRONTING STRUCTURAL VIOLENCE: A CALL FOR MULTI-DISCIPLINARY APPROACHES IN THE TWENTY-FIRST CENTURY

Reducing structural violence is no easier than confronting the structures that propagate direct violence, war, and the nuclear threat. One place to begin, however, is for scholars to recognize that the mere existence of structural inequalities is a form of violence. Galtung's (1996) pioneering work in the 1960s was a beginning, and more recently we have seen a reemphasis on structural violence by Galtung (1998) and others (Christie, 1997; Pilisuk, 1998; Schwebel, 1997).

Most psychologists are not trained in macro-level interventions, but failing to engage with structural problems and focusing only on the individual unit of analysis and change places peace psychologists in the role of helping people maintain the status quo. To the extent that we help people adjust to the stresses of poverty, unemployment, and inadequate health care and education, we unwittingly contribute to the inertia of structural violence. Dryfoos (1997) makes a similar point when suggesting we ought to de-emphasize the individual attributes of children and adolescents and move the locus of our attention "toward the settings that so profoundly influence [child] outcomes—families, neighborhoods, schools, health and welfare systems, employment and training, and the justice system" (p. 41).

Accordingly, we recommend five policies for mitigating structural violence. From a psychological perspective, we are comfortable with these policy recommendations because research indicates that each of these recommendations would have desirable psychosocial outcomes. However, the policies should be rigorously evaluated in a multidisciplinary context, giving attention to both individual and structural variables. In addition, we are aware that the recommendations are based on research conducted in the United States, so caution should be exercised when generalizing to other contexts.

Guaranteed Employment

We have discussed the detrimental effects of unemployment on parents and children. The meaning, value, and importance of work has been elucidated by psychologists and others. Reviewing research on happiness, Myers and Diener (1995) argued that work provides personal identity and helps us define who we are. It gives us a "sense of pride and belonging to a group [that] helps people construct their social identity. And work can add focus and purpose—a sense that one's life matters" (p. 15). Wilson (1996), refers to the effects of disappearing work from urban ghettoes this way:

> Work is not simply a way to make a living and support one's family. It also constitutes a framework for daily behavior, it imposes discipline . . . In the absence of regular employment, life, including family life, becomes less coherent. Persistent unemployment and irregular employment hinder rational planning in daily life. (p. 30)

In the United States today, unemployment is relatively low, but from a psychological point of view, it is clear that every increment in unemployment reverberates through society and has a toll on human well-being. We are quite aware that there are many questions associated with a full-employment strategy. For example, who should be counted among the unemployed (i.e., only those seeking work; only those able to work, etc.)? Does income have to be above the poverty level to be counted as employed? Does merely having an income based on a 40-hour work week qualify as employment? Should temporary or part-time workers who want full-time jobs be counted among the unemployed? Would full employment impact adversely on investments and job creation? Clearly, many of these questions go beyond the scope of psychology and require multidisciplinary teams working at various units of analysis (for a more detailed analysis, see Schwebel, 1997). The point we make here is that the harmful effects of unemployment and underemployment of parents on children is well documented from a psychological perspective. A concerted effort on the part of psychologists to mitigate this form of structural violence is needed.

A Minimum Wage above Poverty Level

As we noted earlier, unemployment and poverty leave a family with a narrow range of choices in matters of vital importance to the child's well-being. But guaranteed employment is not a panacea if the compensation for work is so minimal that there is no appreciable effect on one's quality of life. In many ways, underemployment poses threats to individuals, many of whom feel as if they are victims of fate (Burris, 1983). The exponential increase in the hiring of temporary workers in the United States can produce a variety of harmful psychological effects and can damage relationships. As Schwebel (1997) asserts:

> For the "temps," as for all the others in disadvantaged positions in the labor market (or for those who have given up and are no longer in that market), the consequences due to insecurity about the future, not only about a job but also about health insurance and other supports, can undermine a sense of efficacy (Bandura, 1997), affect coping mechanisms (Lazarus & Folkman, 1984), and induce learned helplessness (Seligman, 1975). (pp. 339–340)

When wages do not have a palpable effect on well-being, it makes little rational sense to work. Indeed, some of our most vexing problems in the United States are inextricably woven into the fabric of an economic system that is highly punitive to those who lack the technical skills required for a high quality of life in an information-based society. Underemployment can be harmful not only to the individual but also to society. For instance, it is not surprising

that from a global perspective, a symbiotic relationship has developed between the supply of illegal drugs by the global South and the demand for drugs by the global North. While poor farmers in the global South cultivate the coca plant to generate income and feed their families, drug traffickers in the global North find it far more advantageous to move drugs that can quickly yield high monetary returns instead of struggling at minimum-wage jobs that fail to satisfy basic human needs (Crosby & Van Soest, 1997).

High-quality Child Care for All Children

Kostelny and Garbarino (in this volume) underscored the importance of high-quality child care as a means of reducing the impact of violence on children. Here, we emphasize research suggesting that high-quality child care could benefit children's cognitive development, particularly for children who come from families in poverty (Scarr & Eisenberg, 1993). Even middle-class children show significant cognitive gains if experience is sufficiently enriching (Clarke-Stewart, Gruber, & Fitzgerald, 1994). Moreover, intensive enrichment during the preschool years can produce enduring effects on children's school performance. As McLoyd (1998) notes, such a finding "argues for making Head Start a full-day rather than a half-day program, five days per week, year-round" (p. 198).

Certain activities seem particularly worthwhile for the developing child. For instance, it is especially important that children hear others read stories because, as reading experts such as Gerald Coles (1998) have argued, storybook reading contributes to eventual reading success, expands oral vocabulary, and strengthens the child's eagerness to read.

Prenatal Medical Care and Parent Training for All

Although the United States is by some measures the wealthiest nation in the world, the wealth is spread unevenly, which is one reason why the United States has a high infant mortality rate, ranking twenty-first when compared to other developed countries (UNDP, 1997). Infant mortality is one indication of how well people take care of one another.

Lack of support for prenatal care not only contributes to high mortality rates but is associated with a host of developmental problems, many of which cannot be remediated and eventually become a burden on health care and public education systems in the long term. Support for preventive efforts during the fetal period would be highly cost effective, as Kostelny and Garbarino have argued (earlier in this volume). But paying up front for long-term solutions does not neatly coincide with two-, four-, and six-year political cycles. Moreover, we do not yet have political consensus that all children have the "right" to the best start they can get in life.

Again, social sciences have illuminated the policies and programs that are likely to be effective. One widely cited program, for instance, is the University of Rochester Nurse-Home Visitation Program (Olds, Henderson, Tatelbaum, & Chamberlin, 1986). The program provides home visits by nurses that begin when the mother conceives and continue until the child is two years old. During the prenatal period, nurses discuss nutrition and health matters with expectant mothers. After birth, greater emphasis is placed on infant development, how to build support networks, and the use of community services. When compared to partial implementations of the program, the full program showed higher levels of maternal employment and a reduction in the incidence of direct violence as reflected in the reports of child abuse and neglect. We concur with Kostelny and Garbarino that the first line of defense in preventing youth violence is a healthy baby combined with a positive parent-infant relationship.

The importance of effective parenting from conception through childhood cannot be overemphasized. Authoritative parenting styles not only produce desirable developmental outcomes, as we have pointed out, but can serve a protective function, helping poor, inner-city children resist peer pressure and other influences that are detrimental to healthy development and school performance (McLoyd, 1998).

Equity in Public Education

Hawkins (1997) has argued that it is feasible to provide a "high-quality public education that guarantees success for all children, regardless of race or socioeconomic status" (p. 300). Yet enormous inequalities exist in the quality of schools and instruction in public education across the United States, a condition that reinforces and exacerbates inequalities in school achievement and, in the long term, inequalities in society as a whole.

Earlier, we emphasized the importance of students staying in school. We cited research indicating that years of schooling is associated with the economic well-being of individuals. In light of research suggesting that one of the best predictors of dropout rates is a low level of academic success (Cairns & Cairns, 1994), the problem of school quality becomes paramount. Clearly, improving the quality of education can have a significant impact on students' success (Mortimore, 1995) and, as a result, remove an important risk factor related to many problems, including dropping out of school.

Mortimore (1995) has identified specific features of schools that promote positive student outcomes, including high expectations of the student, the use of joint planning and consistent approaches toward students (i.e., consistent expectations), an academic emphasis and a focus on learning, a high level of student involvement in schooling and school life, parental involvement in the life of the school, monitoring of students' progress, the use of rewards for desirable behavior, and strong positive leadership of the school.

CONCLUSIONS

Enough social science research has accumulated for us to offer some specific, empirically supported policy recommendations that can have a wide range of positive effects. What is needed is the political will, a commitment to implement policies that we know produce positive developmental outcomes.

We are only at the beginning stages of a social science revolution that can mount a serious challenge to structural violence against our children. While the task might seem formidable, we are reminded that a wide range of large-scale social changes have taken place in the recent past. Just over a century ago, it seemed unlikely that dueling would ever be delegitimized as a means of settling disputes. Nor did it seem likely that slavery would be abolished; that women would have the right to vote; or that compulsory education would become law in most countries of the world. Remarkable changes have also occurred recently: Forty years ago there was no ecology movement and now large-scale recycling efforts are commonplace. Within the past ten years, laws have been enacted that rule out cigarette smoking in many public areas. In fact, a number of stunning changes that bear on human security have occurred very recently: the fall of the Berlin Wall, which signaled the end of the Cold War; the establishment of war tribunals that hold rogue leaders accountable for war crimes; the movement to ban landmines; the dismantling of apartheid in South Africa. These profound societal changes give us reason to hope that the problems of structural violence against children will not always be normalized. Even though poverty, and all forms of structural violence, are fueled by powerful vested interests, we have seen that major social change is not only possible, but inevitable.

CHAPTER 11

WOMEN, GIRLS, AND STRUCTURAL VIOLENCE: A GLOBAL ANALYSIS

Dyan Mazurana and Susan McKay[1]

Given that the natural birth ratio is 106 males to 100 females, and that females tend to have longer life expectancies, it is shocking to learn that "more than 100 million girls and women are missing" (Sen, 1990, p. 61). Birth ratios of males and females would predict that there should be *more* women living today, particularly in Asia (Bunch, 1995). But in some parts of the world, men outnumber women by 20:1 (United Nations, 1996). To comprehend this staggering problem, 100 million "missing" women is equivalent to the total number of war-related deaths of 100 Pol Pot–initiated famines and massacres in Cambodia (1975 to 1978), 200 of the genocidal civil wars recently witnessed in Rwanda (1994 to 1995), and 2.5 times the deaths of World War II (1939 to 1945) (Sivard, 1996). But how many have even noticed, let alone demanded accountability for, this killing of girls and women? A primary reason for this disregard is that much of the violence against women results from structural violence.

In this chapter, we document and analyze socio-cultural, economic, and political structural violence against women from a feminist perspective. For our purposes, structural violence can be divided into two categories: premature death attributed to inequitable life opportunities, and a reduced quality of life in which human potential is diminished (Brock-Utne, 1989). When structural violence happens to girls or women because of their gender, *patriarchal structural violence* takes place (Brock-Utne, 1989). *Patriarchy* can be defined as systems or structures of exploitation that normalize socially constructed gender differences in ways that reproduce and legitimatize male domination (Ebert, 1996). Oppressions are normalized when they are presented as "the way things are"; then, one does not need to be curious about them, let alone try to change them, because they are "typical" or "normal." Feminist theory is useful here because it seeks to reveal and de-

[1]The authors would like to thank the editors, two anonymous reviewers, and Daniel J. Isaak for thorough reviews of this manuscript.

construct human systems and beliefs that are naturalized, paying specific attention to constructions and manipulations of gender, masculinity, and femininity (Enloe, 1993). Understanding patriarchal structural violence means locating and analyzing the socio-cultural, economic, and political systems that perpetrate or condone physical, sexual, and psychological violence against women (Galtung, 1969).

SOCIO-CULTURAL SYSTEMS

Socio-cultural systems are numerous and diverse. In this chapter, we limit our discussion to patriarchal structural violence in systems and institutions that maintain son preference, inequalities in the allocation of food and health care, and educational discrepancies.

Son Preference

The threat of violence begins prior to birth for many females. Social preference for male children is strong in many societies and can result in the premature death or killing of female infants—termed *female infanticide*—a form of direct violence resulting from structural violence. Structures and institutions that play continuing roles in the strengthening of son preference include economic systems such as dowry payments or "bride price" (the payment by the bride's family to the groom's), or cultural beliefs in which sons are seen as the providers for parents in their old age. In much of Asia where the dowry system remains strong, "a family with three girl children might well face financial ruin" (Mongella, 1994, p. 31). Girls therefore are considered a burden, while the birth of a boy is celebrated as good fortune.

Systems and institutions that perpetuate an early devaluation of, and violence against, girls are strengthened by economic systems that pay women less for equitable work, fail to account for nearly half of women's work worldwide, and routinely discriminate against women in the labor market (Waring, 1988). Cultural and religious systems and institutions also perpetuate systems of discrimination against girls through promoting beliefs that privilege males with the perpetuation of the family name, and by mandating male-only roles in the rites of deceased parents and ancestors as, for example, in Pakistan and India. The combination of male preference and political policies can contribute to female infanticide. For example, to curb population growth in China, the government penalizes families with two or more children through tax penalties and state sanctions. In selecting the gender of their child, many Chinese families strongly favor boys over girls; of the 100 million missing women in the world, 50 million of them are from China—a result of both female infanticide and selective abortion (Sen, 1990).

Systems and institutions that maintain son preference and early violence against girls often beget others that perpetuate violence. For example, the combination of male preference, the devaluation of female lives and labor, and technological advances such as sex determination tests and access to safe abortion have been used to detect the presence of female fetuses. In many such cases, women either choose or are forced by husbands or relatives to abort (Narasimhan, 1993). One study of abortions in Maharashtra, India, revealed that 7,999 out of 8,000 fetuses aborted were female (Jaising, 1995). Some clinics offering sex determination tests and abortion promote the use of these forms of medical technology for patriarchal structural violence. Billboards advertising these services read "Better to spend Rs500 today [the price of a sex determination test and abortion] rather than Rs500,000 at the time of the girl's marriage [the dowry price]" (Narasimhan, 1994, p. 51). Patriarchal structural violence is so normalized in India that advertising campaigns advocating the death of girls was supported by a cabinet minister and many physicians before ultimately being dropped because of the protests of women's rights groups (Narasimhan, 1994).

Food and Health Care Distribution

Structural violence against girls and women is also evident in food and health care distribution. According to the World Health Organization, girls and women often receive less food and health care services than male counterparts, particularly in developing countries (Bunch, 1995; Mongella, 1994; Newland, 1979; Sullivan, 1995). In India, for example, "girls are fed less and for shorter periods and are not given [more expensive] foods like butter or milk, which are reserved for boys" (Jaising, 1995, p. 51). This practice incurs a health risk because the fats in foods like butter and milk are imperative for the proper development of a child's brain, cognitive abilities, and spinal cord. Along similar lines, 40 percent of women in the developing world suffer from high levels of anemia, in part because meats and protein-rich foods are reserved for males (Mongella, 1994). This phenomenon occurs not only in the developing world: In both World Wars I and II, American and British governments set up ration plans that reserved meat for (male) soldiers (Seager, 1993).

Governmental policies and practices by large multinational corporations can also contribute to structural violence against women and their families in the area of food production and distribution. In the Philippines, for example, with the government's and the World Bank's blessing, multinational, mono-crop plantations pro-

duce enough crops to rank the Philippines the 14th-largest food exporter in the world. However, 80 percent of Filipino children go hungry every day, with 70 percent of the population living beneath the poverty level (Largoza-Maza, 1995). Rates of malnutrition and poverty are intensified for the typical Filipino woman, who has an average of eight children and no access to birth control, family planning, or divorce. Consequently, rural women throughout the world practice subsistence farming. Although there is no exchange of money, subsistence farming does increase the odds that a woman and her children will eat. But according to the World Bank, the way to improve these women's lives is to increase export growth through structural adjustment policies. These "unproductive" women and their children are driven off the land to make room for the new multinational corporations and expanding mono-crop plantations. The women and their families then migrate to urban areas where they contribute to growing unemployment and help fill the pool of cheap labor from which the multinationals draw (Waring, 1988).

In addition to unjust systems of food and land distribution, girls receive fewer health services than boys. Although girls in some locales, such as rural Mexico, suffer from more disease and illness, boys are taken to the hospital and are given medication and vitamins at a significantly higher rate than girls (Brock-Utne, 1989). Other studies on equitable household distribution of health care provisions show that compared to boys, girls have a mortality rate that is 12 percent higher under one year of age, and 8 percent higher between one and five years old (Jaising, 1995). These rates are exacerbated when the girl comes from groups that experience the most poverty and discrimination, such as the indigenous peoples of Guatemala, 50 percent of whose children are dead before the age of five because of malnutrition and overwork (Schirmer, 1993).

Education

One of the most effective ways of increasing girls' access to food and health services is by improving their education. Education has proven the most effective means to address the poverty, malnutrition, and poor health conditions that affect one-fifth of the world's population (Sivard, 1993, p. 31). Throughout the world, education is a means to a better and longer life. However, girls receive less education than boys, even though according to the United Nations Children's Fund (UNICEF), educating girls "is one of the most important investments that any developing country can make in its own future" (1994, p. 20). Girls are not educated because of beliefs that they will only become wives and mothers and because scarce familial education resources are reserved for boys (another form of son preference); young girls are kept at home to help raise younger siblings and perform other forms of labor to assist their mothers (Narasimhan, 1993; Sivard, 1993, 1996; UNICEF, 1994). Consequently, educational rates are gender biased. Around the world, of all living school-aged children, 14 million more boys than girls are in primary school (UNICEF, 1994), and of the nearly billion illiterate adults worldwide, two-thirds are women (Sivard, 1996).

It is widely recognized that high-quality, basic, universal education is the foundation of world health and economic security. Over time, nearly all other indicators of progress—including nutrition, infant and maternal mortality, family planning, child health, and women's rights—is "profoundly affected by whether or not a nation educates its girls" (UNICEF, 1994, p. 20). While not a panacea, education provides women and girls with at least the knowledge for im-proving nutrition and sanitation in their homes. Education also enhances women's status in their relationships at home, which increases decision-making regarding family planning, contraceptive choices, and finances. The global results of educating girls and women are lower fertility, lower population rates, lower infant mortality rates, healthier children, and a more productive economy (Mongella, 1994; Sivard, 1996).

ECONOMIC SYSTEMS

Structural patriarchal violence is apparent in economic and labor systems worldwide. Women make up more than half of the world's population, and perform 66 percent of the world's work, often in jobs more physically demanding and time-consuming than jobs held by men. However, women "earn only 10% of the world's income and own 1% of the world's property" (Elliott, 1996, p. 17), and they account for "70% of the world's 1.3 billion absolute poor" (United Nations Development Fund for Women [UNIFEM], 1995, p. 1). Why?

Women's (Invisible) Work

One of the primary reasons women are poor is that the majority of women's work literally counts for nothing. Feminist economist Marilyn Waring (1988) has demonstrated how most governmental accounting systems do not recognize the majority of women's labor because the rules of the United Nations System of National Accounts (UNSNA) only count that which passes through the marketplace, i.e., anything that has currency-generating capacity. All countries wishing to be members of the United Nations, or borrow money from the World Bank, or acquire a loan from the International Monetary Fund (IMF), must adhere to rules set down in the UNSNA. Yet these systems' economic policies place no value on peace, the preservation of natural resources, or unpaid labor, including that of reproducing and nurturing human life. Important decisions are made using figures generated from the UNSNA about whose needs are met, how to allocate taxes, which programs receive support and which do not. Some of these decisions literally determine who will live and who will die (Waring, 1988).

While states may not publicly acknowledge women's labor in informal economies, they nevertheless rely upon it. For example, the Philippine's 2000 plan, a joint project of the Filipino government, the IMF, and the World Bank, relies on Filipino women staying in their jobs in the garment and electronic industries, sending home foreign currency from their jobs overseas as domestic and contract workers, and working as prostitutes or exotic dancers. For example, with the closure of U.S. military bases, the Filipino government is now counting on Filipino prostitutes and exotic dancers to switch their client base from soldiers to tourists and international businessmen, in order to continue the flow of foreign currency (Largoza-Maza, 1995). Thus, we can see that governments are often reluctant to challenge patriarchal structures of violence against women because economic and political systems rely on them.

Military and Social Expenditures

What work *do* governments value? How *do* they spend their treasuries? When governments allocate resources, especially in large amounts, they provide insights to their priorities. For over half of the world's countries, maintaining a military and buying weaponry are higher priorities than the health needs of their citizens; for 25 countries, military expenditures exceed those for education, and for 15 countries, defense is more important than health and education combined (Sivard, 1993). The privileging of militaries over people has staggering consequences (Winter, Pilisuk, Houck, & Lee, this volume). Money spent on armaments in just two weeks worldwide would provide the entire world's populace with safe drinking water.

The U.S. government provides an illuminating example of military spending at the expense of its citizens' welfare. Although the United States accounts for less than 5 percent of the world's population, it spends more than 40 percent of the world's defense outlays. The United States ranks first in the world in military expenditures, military technology, military bases worldwide, military training of foreign forces, military aid to foreign countries, naval ships, combat aircraft, nuclear reactors, nuclear warheads and bombs, and arms exports. Three years after the end of the Cold War, U.S. arms exports were the highest of any country, higher in fact than all "the 52 other arms exporting countries combined" (Sivard, 1996, p. 41). This emphasis on military expenditures comes at a price to the U.S. citizenship. Despite being one of the richest countries in the world, the United States lags behind in social protection, ranking poorly by world comparison in maternal and infant mortality rates (12th and 13th), mortality rates under the age of five (18th), and percentage of school-age children in school (18th). The United States has been sliding steadily downward in these categories since the 1980s (Sivard, 1993, 1996).

Women in particular pay the price for war economies. Inflated military budgets often come as a result of reductions in social services, where worldwide women are most often employed (Turpin, 1998). For example, for the price of 20 MiG-29 fighter planes from Russia, India could have furnished basic education to all 15 million of its girls who are out of school (UNDP, 1994). When women are employed in the military, it is largely in low paying, assembly-line factory jobs (Enloe, 1993).

Military practices such as maintaining prostitution for servicemen, dropping chemical weapons on rural areas, and targeting civilian populations during conflicts, cause specific harm to women, through disease, cancers, birth defects, and psychological and reproductive disorders (Enloe, 1993; Herman, 1992; McKay, 1998; Seager, 1993). For example, because of the U.S. military's systematic poisoning of Vietnam during the war through the dumping of massive amounts of Agent Orange and Dioxin, Vietnamese women today have the world's highest rates of spontaneous abortions. Rates of birth defects have markedly increased and fetal death rates are now 40 percent higher than before the war (Seager, 1993). Vietnam is not an anomaly: Throughout the world women and their children suffer disproportionately to men in war. Worldwide, they account for 80 percent of refugee and displaced populations, are often targets of rape and genocide, as in the wars in the former Yugoslavia and Rwanda, and suffer from multiple forms of gender-based violence (McKay, 1998).

POLITICAL SYSTEMS

Political and legal systems in non-democratic countries often maintain and perpetuate structural, as well as direct, violence. Consequently, many liberation struggles are fought to enact changes towards democratic systems. With the collapse of the Eastern Bloc and the Soviet Union, and struggles for independence and justice throughout Africa and Latin America, the world has recently seen an unprecedented number of emerging democracies. Unfortunately, democratic systems also have ways of perpetuating structural violence, wherein women and minorities are particularly impacted.

Engendering Democracy

Despite the potential of democratic governance, patriarchal structural violence is often embedded in democracy. In the eighteenth century, democracy meant not merely a form of government but a principle of social equality (Arblaster, 1987). However, even the most vocal advocates of social equality in the seventeenth and eighteenth centuries could only conceive of equality among propertied white men. Indeed, "it was their interests that government had been created to serve," and the idea that men could and should represent women was widely accepted and promoted (Phillips, 1992, p. 25). Citizenship was created in the male image. Even today, democracy as a political ideology too often normalizes the male image as "citizen" and encourages others to deny aspects of themselves to conform to some unitary norm, which itself was never gender-neutral. For example, many South African feminists working in the early 1990s to reconstruct their nation were acutely aware that "the universal standing in society which we have been fighting for is that of a 'being with masculine characteristics engaging in masculine activities'" (Bazilli, 1991, p. 11). Clearly, the gendering of democracy and citizenship must be on the agenda if women are to truly benefit from democratic systems of governance.

Women and the Private Sphere

The male bias inherent in (patriarchal) democracy has led to forms of patriarchal structural violence that relegate "women's issues" to the "private" realm where they become "private matters" that the state does not address. This bias is perhaps nowhere clearer than in the issue of domestic violence, where male bias greatly impairs the ability of police, judges, and lawmakers from recognizing the violent behavior in the family. "The view that 'as a family matter' battery is less important, is based on men's, not women's perceptions" (Murray & O'Regan, 1991, p. 45). The multiple forms of domestic violence that women suffer have profound physical and psychological effects (Herman, 1992; Kelly, 1993), prompting international calls for domestic violence to be recognized as a form of torture (Copelon, 1994). Governmental support of patriarchal structural violence through its inattention to "private" matters is apparent throughout the world. Until 1991, the murder of a wife in Brazil was legal—it was considered an honor killing and was done to preserve the family's honor because of a woman's transgression. In many areas of the world, men are free to rape their wives with no threat of legal repercussions (Mertus, 1995).

Other examples of government-sponsored patriarchal structural violence include laws and systems that condone particular forms of violence against women, deny women control over their bodies, provide no assistance with child care and maternity leave, make no attempt to remedy child support defaults, and fail to provide unemployment protection to women who work within the "private" realm in domestic service or farm work (Waring, 1988; Murray & O'Regan, 1991). Because governments rarely address patriarchal structural violence or fight for women's rights, progress for women is largely made by women working for the recognition and enforcement of women's rights. As a result, in countries such as Australia, Brazil, Britain, Columbia, India, Sri Lanka, and the United States, violence against women in the home has been identified and some forms of it criminalized (Fineman & Mykitiuk, 1994).

Women in Decision-making Bodies

Women must actively participate in creating, executing, and enforcing the laws (Zama, 1991). Feminists continually acknowledge the necessary steps between theory and practice, urging that action must follow critiques and recommendations. A law may concede a right to freedom from violence, decent health care, legal representation, a clean environment, or a living wage, but if the state refuses to fund or enforce these polices then the right exists only on paper (Bazilli, 1991). The question then becomes, to what extent do women have access to, and control over, the state, its policies, laws, and coffers?

Relative to the proportion of the population they comprise, women are consistently underrepresented, if not absent from positions of political power, all over the world. For example, only recently has women's representation at the national level in the United States climbed to 11 percent, ranking it well below Seychelles (46 percent), Finland (39 percent), Norway (36 percent), Sweden (34 percent), Cuba (23 percent), China (21 percent), and others, and about on par with Angola (15 percent), and Italy (13 percent), both of whose proportions of women in parliament recently fell by 5 percent to reach these numbers. In Australia, Costa Rica, and Greece, as elsewhere, when women are elected and given cabinet posts, their appointments tend to be in the more feminized (and devalued) arenas of family or community concerns, and not in the more the masculinized, powerful, and prestigious departments of finance, treasury, foreign affairs, and defense (Watson, 1990). Such consistent underrepresentation of women in the upper-levels of government cannot be accidental (Phillips, 1991).

Likewise, in the newly democratic nations of East Central Europe, "women's citizenship rights are deemed to be of secondary importance in the current democratization process" (Einhorn, 1993, p. 149). Not only are women forced to take a back seat, but the total number of women in governmental positions is dramatically decreasing because there are no longer party quotas that specify how many women should hold office. In former socialist parliaments, where women once occupied up to 30 percent of the seats, they now hold as little as 7 percent in the new democratic parliaments. As a result, women are almost completely invisible at the highest levels of government, and at the parliamentary level little discussion takes place about the protection or enhancement of women's rights (Einhorn, 1993; Renne, 1997).

The exclusion of women from national decision-making bodies is a form of patriarchy. The men who benefit from their monopoly on power often meet challenges to the status quo of governmental power with strong resistance. For example, the women's movement in India has been pushing for a bill to set a quota of 30 percent for women's representation at the national level. On July 15, 1998, it appeared the bill's supporters had the two-thirds majority needed to pass, and supportive women members of parliament (MPs) attempted to bring it to a vote. Opposing male MPs caused such disruptions, including grabbing the bill from the speaker's hand and tearing it up, that the speaker shelved it for a later vote. Supporters of the bill protested, and failing, tried to have a date set for the bill to be reintroduced, but the speaker would not recognize the women MPs. When a male MP supporter tried to push the case, he was beaten by the opposing male MPs, removed from the floor by security officers, and taken away bleeding in an ambulance (Sullivan, 1998). In this case and others, supporters of a patriarchal status quo literally fight to keep women out.

Electing women who will strive for women's empowerment by dismantling patriarchal structures and effectively participate in government is a necessary, though not sufficient, condition. Male bias in political structures also perpetuates obstacles to women's political involvement based on access to and control of wealth, sexual divisions of labor in the household, division of "public" and "private," and a lack of government programs to support working mothers. In the highest levels of government, such obstacles include, but are not limited to, working hours, the conditions of assemblies and councils and, particularly in the United States, the financial burden of running for election (where the average U.S. Senate seat now costs five million dollars). Discrimination that limits women from political participation is a form of patriarchal structural violence against women, and these barriers should be addressed and removed by the state.

While governmental efforts are critical, the civil and domestic spheres must change as well. Because constraints on women's political activity result from psychosocial, economic, and political structures, equal representation in legislature or parliament without considerable transformation in social relations is impossible (Phillips, 1991).

CONCLUSION

The denial of girls' and women's right to food, health care, education, and life, as well as the undermining of their political, economic, and social rights are some of the most damaging and egregious forms of direct and structural patriarchal violence.

Women and girls deserve to have their human rights recognized and enforced. The global community must reject all efforts to justify abuse on the basis of culture. While global women's movements have had some effect in confronting violence and reducing inequality, structural violence against women and girls remains pandemic (Basu, 1997). Peace cannot be achieved until both indirect and direct forms of violence are dismantled. As we have seen throughout this chapter, patriarchal systems that discriminate against women and girls contribute to the eventual expression of direct violence. If we are serious about achieving peace, then we must be committed to women's empowerment. As a result, research and activism on women's issues are key elements of any serious peace agenda.

CHAPTER 12

UNDERSTANDING MILITARISM: MONEY, MASCULINITY, AND THE SEARCH FOR THE MYSTICAL

Deborah Du Nann Winter, Marc Pilisuk, Sara Houck, and Matthew Lee

Militarism does not consist of any army, nor even of the existence of a very great army. Militarism is a spirit.
Woodrow Wilson, 1916 (as cited by Berghahn, 1984, p. 108)

Like Woodrow Wilson, we define militarism in this chapter as a psychological rather than a physical process: *Militarism* is a set of values that support military activities and enable countries to mobilize for war. Militarism is as important during peace as it is during war. In fact, wars cannot be conducted unless militarism is nurtured long before wars begin. In democracies, somebody must provide a rationale for military expenditures and possible threats. The importance of military readiness must be articulated and that rationale must be persuasively communicated to the public. Legislative decision-makers must agree to allocate funds for the military, rather than to other forms of social spending.

In this chapter, we argue that the preparation for war is as problematic as war itself.

Because militarism is a global form of structural violence, we begin by analyzing the excessive financial costs and social injustice caused by militarism. Our central concern is why people decide to pay these exorbitant prices. To answer this question, we examine underlying psychological processes that are not always obvious. We assert that money, masculinism, and the search for the mystical drive militaristic sentiments beyond logical ends. Finally, we suggest that psychologically valid mechanisms to address these motives are required before structural violence from excessive militarism can be curbed. Because militarism calls on some of the deepest and most cherished of all human capacities, we believe that salvaging the best of militarism while redirecting the military's focus is a crucial task for the twenty-first century.

THE THIN LINE BETWEEN WAR AND PEACE

In modern societies, support for military matters is often covert until armed conflict erupts. When soldiers fight wars, they must leave their families and join scores of other displaced persons to march, kill, and die for the sake of some political objective they often know little about. Because, as we have long known, war is not instinctual, people must be socialized to kill (May, 1943). The media helps the public understand the need to fight by objectifying the enemy and portraying it as evil (Hesse & Mack, 1991), and often even subhuman (Reiber & Kelly, 1991). Such treatment communicates dire predictions of what might happen should the enemy prevail. For example, in the early stages of the Vietnam War, the public was continually warned that a communist government in Vietnam would only be the first of a line of falling dominoes that would eventually threaten the United States. Strong feelings of nationalistic identification get aroused, creating an "us vs. them" dichotomy that is oversimplified and rigid (Tetlock, 1988). Military leaders on our side are depicted as heroes, and people questioning the wisdom of military action are portrayed as unpatriotic.

Yet sudden psychological support of military actions cannot arise in a vacuum. Along with a well-rehearsed army, government leaders and the media build militaristic value systems between wars so that militaries can be instantly activated. In peacetime, such values are often latent. Large numbers of citizens passively condone, if not support, their militaries, in order for them to function effectively when called upon. In this way, the line between peace and war becomes blurred. The first peace psychologist, William James, noted that "battles are only a public verification of the mastery gained during the peace interval . . . [The] preparation for war by nations is the real war, permanent, unceasing" (James, 1910/1995, p. 19).

STRUCTURAL VIOLENCE OF MILITARY PREPAREDNESS

Preparation for war is a form of structural violence, since its social, political, and economic structures cause avoidable injury or deaths (Christie, 1997; Galtung, 1969). Structural violence is insidious because it has no active agent, no conscious intent, and no clear point of origin (see Chapter 1). But inevitably, national decision-makers choose between military and social spending. When countries spend precious income on military matters instead of food, health care, or environmental protection and restoration, injuries and deaths to civilians occur. As Eisenhower put it a half century ago, "the problem in defense spending is to figure how far you should go without destroying from within what you are trying to defend from without" (1956, as quoted by Sivard, 1996).

Half of the world's governments spend more to guard their citizens against military attack than to protect them against the enemies of good health, such as contaminated water, poor nutrition, and lack of medical care (Sivard, 1993). World military expenditures reached an all-time high of $1.3 trillion in 1987. Despite significant decreases since the close of the Cold War, however, global expenditures in 1995 still amounted to more than $1.4 million per minute. The United States became the world's military superpower during World War II, when its military budget sky-rocketed from under $13 billion a year to $530 billion (Sivard, 1996). The United States currently eclipses the rest of the world by a huge margin, spending over five times that of the second-biggest spender (Russia); more than the combined budgets of the 13 countries ranking below it (Sivard, 1996); and over 18 times the combined spending of those countries often identified as its biggest threats (North Korea, Iran, Iraq, Libya, Syria, Sudan, and Cuba).

Even redirecting relatively small amounts of military expenditures could significantly impact social well-being (see Mazaruna and McKay, this volume; Pilisuk, this volume). For example, just 4 percent of the world's military budget could raise global literacy to 50 percent, and redirecting 8 percent of military budgets for family planning would stabilize global population by the year 2015. The cost of one nuclear-powered submarine ($2.5 billion) could immunize the world's children for one year. Clearly, excessive military expenditures constitute great structural violence.

TRADITIONAL EXPLANATIONS FOR EXCESSIVE MILITARISM

Psychological explanations for militarism have for several decades focused on fear, pride, and logic. Let us examine these in turn.

Fear

White (1984, 1986) argued in his classic volume on the psychology of war that "fear is what fuels arms races [along with] an exaggerated preoccupation with power" (1986, p. 242). White used Freud's distinction between objective and neurotic anxiety to argue that most wars are caused by exaggerated, unrealistic fear. Arms races are Freudian compulsions, which have a "symbolic reassuring function [and] serve to keep the underlying neurotic anxiety from reaching the surface of consciousness" (1986, p. 245). From White's perspective,

militarism is primarily an unconscious process through which decision-makers try to reduce their vulnerability by excessive arms buildup. Militaries soothe national fears (at least those of the elites), which is one reason the expression of fear by military personnel is taboo, especially in wartime.

Pride

Closely related to fear is pride, which also serves as an important motivator of military activity (Frank, 1986). Ribbons, stripes, and uniforms symbolize glory and honor. War originally undertaken out of fear can be easily continued by pride because so often, "proving one's courage and determination by continuing to fight becomes an end in itself, more important than gaining the object of the fight" (Frank, 1982, as cited in Frank, 1986, p. 226). Weapons builders have often given affectionate names to their products and displayed them in their glory. For example, one German manufacturer termed the artillery of World War I "Big Bertha," after his wife (Pearson, 1994). Military leaders have marched in parades for centuries, showing off their grandeur. Even in peace-time, military leaders can easily become attached to their big budgets and prestige.

Status needs are clearly at stake in the nuclear arms race. For example, developing countries like India and Pakistan yearn to become part of the "nuclear club" (Wessells, 1995). Their recent nuclear tests and willingness to pay high costs through economic sanctions demonstrate the powerful psychological factors of both fear and pride that commonly operate. Although Pakistan is one of the ten poorest countries in the world, its Prime Minister Nawaz Sharif happily announced on May 28, 1998, that "the big powers have never taken us seriously . . .

[but] . . . today . . . we have become a nuclear power." As Pakistanis celebrated in the streets, one university student commented, "we are ready to pay any price and make any sacrifice to live as a self-respecting nation" (Burns, 1998).

Logic

While the emotional dimensions of fear and pride are important, so are the more cognitive dimensions of logic and choice. War can be seen as a decision to maximize gains and minimize losses. One way to understand the logic of excessive arms buildup is through *game theory* (O'Neill, 1989), a mathematically formal approach for examining decision-making that assumes people rationally choose to maximize outcomes. The Prisoner's Dilemma Game (PDG), for example, employs a set of pay-off contingencies that frequently result in self-destructive behavior (Rapoport, 1962; Rapoport & Chammah, 1965). When two people are faced with a choice to cooperate or compete, their decision is greatly affected by the costs of being betrayed. In thousands of laboratory studies (Dawes, 1991), people got trapped into self-destructive behaviors by trying to avoid risks. When the repercussions of being betrayed by one's enemy are too great, trust is unlikely, and choices that seem defensive quickly become self-defeating. From the perspective of game theory, nuclear planners in the United States and Soviet Union became caught in a set of contingencies, whereby attempts to maximize gains and minimize risks led to irrational choices on both sides.

The competitive aspect of such a game has its historical roots in *Realpolitik,* a political philosophy that assumes nation-states operate in a competitive system of threats (see Chapter 1, this volume). The logic of Realpolitik predicts that nations with inadequate arsenals will be attacked, and the only

way to assure deterrence is to build a mightier set of threats than one's adversaries. Clearly fear and pride are at stake in these decisions, but from the perspective of game theory, excessive nuclear weapons production is also an outcome of logic, when that logic is based on presumed competitiveness and hostility of other nations. When the stakes of being betrayed are horrendous, defensive choices are logical, even when they produce great costs.

Although presumed competitiveness of the other may sometimes be accurate, countries often interpret an adversary's actions as offensive, when the adversary perceives its own actions as defensive (Bronfenbrenner, 1961; Pilisuk, 1972.) We call this paradox the *offense/defense ambiguity.* An example is the U.S. bombing of Iraq during the late 1990s. While the United States claimed that its actions were designed to prevent Iraq's future use of weapons of mass destruction (thus a defense), Iraq clearly saw the U.S. actions as offensive (*Newsday,* January 18, 1998). A second example of the offense/defense ambiguity is the Cuban Missile crisis. When the Soviets sent a ship with nuclear materials to protect Cuba in 1962 (regarded by the Soviets as a defensive action), the United States quickly interpreted the move as offensive and sent a blockade to surround the ship. Tensions mounted as the two countries came as close to nuclear strikes as any time before or after. Further demonstrating the tendency to see one's own actions as purely defensive, the United States changed the name of its "Department of War" to "Department of Defense" in 1948.

This offense/defense ambiguity is an example of the *fundamental attribution error* (Ross, 1977), by which we explain our own behavior in situational terms, but others' behavior as an outcome of their intentions and dispositions. Behavior by a perceived adversary that is poorly understood is easily interpreted as intentional aggression (Jervis, 1976), whereas the action of our own country seems a natural self-protective reaction to a dangerous situation. Unfortunately these misperceptions quickly accumulate and lead to armed conflict (Stoessinger, 1998), undertaken out of defense rather than offense. Charles Osgood (1962) noted this proclivity in his theory about reciprocated aggression. When one's moves are seen as offensive, they stimulate reciprocated aggression; when one's moves are clearly seen as an attempt to de-escalate tension, they can be reciprocated and armed conflict can be avoided (Pilisuk & Skolnick, 1968).

THE MONETARY BASIS OF MODERN MILITARISM

With or without perceived threat from adversaries, military expenditures soon develop a life of their own. Though they may have originally been formulated on the basis of fear and competition, continued militarism can only thrive if societies are able and willing to pay the financial costs. In modern bureaucracies, budgets develop self-sustaining power.

The U.S. defense budget, for example, is often justified on the basis of economic, rather than security reasons. Jobs, it is argued, are the reason we need bigger budgets. Budget cutbacks are dangerous not because of national security, but rather for economic reasons. For example, when the 1998 U.S. Congress allocated an additional $7 billion to the Defense Department beyond what the Pentagon requested, legislators argued that jobs would be threatened if orders for weapons and base operations were diminished (Kreisher, 1998).

The job argument is fallacious, however, because spending on infrastructure creates more jobs than spending on defense. For example, in the United States,

$1 billion pays for 9,000 guided missile production jobs; 21,600 local transit jobs; 63,000 educational services jobs; or 16,500 jobs in pollution control (Renner, 1990). Thus three times as many jobs are created when federal monies are directed toward domestic programs than toward weapons. Similar figures have been generated for Germany, India, and other countries (Renner, 1990).

Industrialized countries increasingly build and sell weapons because bureaucratic conservatism and vested interests are strongly reflected in military spending patterns (Pearson, 1994). Weapons are big business. Over a quarter of the top 500 multinational corporations are licensed to produce and export arms (Buzuev, 1985). Governments need weapons industries to maintain their arms businesses, and often parcel out contracts to various manufacturers and laboratories to keep them going. In this way, the United States has sustained numerous aerospace firms, including McDonell-Douglas, Northrop, Boeing, General Dynamics, and Lockheed (Pearson, 1994).

Efforts to control the manufacture and distribution of arms produce a dynamic tension between economic forces and long-range security. Unfortunately, the increasingly global production system makes arms control more difficult than ever. Big arms firms work under multinational structures, where cross-border military/corporate collaboration leads to foreign investments, international subcontracting, international licensing, and joint ventures. If one country has regulations that forbid arms sales to a certain customer, a deal can still be closed by using a foreign partner-firm (Pearson, 1994). Moreover, well-educated but unemployed engineers and scientists can offer their services to potential enemies abroad. Such internationalization of the arms industry is eclipsing the power of national governments to maintain regulations of any sort (Greider, 1998). Consequently, arms firms can continue producing weapons long after their utility for national security has waned.

Thus, arms manufacturers' quarterly reports illuminate more about the militarization of the world than any one political ideology, Realpolitik included. Most of the wars around the planet are now fought within nations, with small arms supplied by developed countries. Almost 90 percent of all war deaths are caused by guns, rather than missiles, bombs, or tanks. Small arms are cheap: for $50 million (the price of one modern fighter jet), 200,000 assault rifles can be purchased. Small arms sales are largely unregulated, but rampant: $3 billion worth of small and light weapons are shipped across borders each year (Renner, 1998). Moreover, small arms feed private security units, which are increasing in number and size, just as national armies are shrinking. In some countries, such as South Africa and Australia, private security forces are larger than national armies (Renner, 1998).

Thus, while Realpolitik may have provided the logic for massive military expenditures between the superpowers during the Cold War, market forces contribute to its healthy survival long after the reasons for creating them have faded. But market forces cannot be the whole story because market forces exist for all human endeavors, whereas militarization has thrived when social spending has dropped. To answer why, we turn to the question of just who is responsible for making decisions to buy bombs instead of butter.

MASCULINISM AND THE MILITARY CULTURE

Arms dealers, makers, producers, designers, and users are almost universally male. Feminists ask about the gender of those making important decisions (Seager, 1993) and find it consequential that militaries and state departments are almost entirely made up of men, working in highly masculinist institutions that glorify and promote the traditional male values of strength, power, and competitive advantage. From a feminist perspective, male dominance of military and arms industries is no coincidence. As Cynthia Enloe (1993) notes, universally, "masculinity has been so intimately connected to militarism that it is no wonder there have been questions about whether the two are analytically separable" (p. 52).

War is always, in some way, a test of gender, and soldiering a test of manhood (Elshtain, 1987). Drill sergeants are hired to make boys into men. Boot camp recruits are called "ladies," "girls," or "fags," until they are toughened up for their role as killers—then they become men (Ruddick, 1995). These homophobic, misogynist labels are justified as a means to prevent troops from displaying feminine traits and affections that might threaten the place of ritualized masculinity (Reardon, 1985).

From their position of control in militarized institutions, men enhance their power over women by defining and conducting war, as well as most functions of the state. In the Pentagon, logic and reason are cherished, emotions and caring are disparaged. The gendered dimension of reason vs. caring is well-established—males are socialized to display reason, and females to display caring (Bem, 1981; Gilligan, 1982; Tannen, 1994). The most "hard-nosed" and coldly "logical" men are the ones promoted in the defense establishment (Cohn, 1987). Those men who demonstrate the most masculine values get to define national security.

Conventional military mechanisms are saturated in sexual dynamics in which male power is often expressed through violence against women. Sexual assaults and harassment are common occurrences in the military, as seen in the military colleges of the

United States throughout the 1990s. The Tailhook scandal, in which naval officers were convicted of sexual harassment during an officers' party, is exceptional, not for its crimes, but for the willingness of the women officers to press charges (Zimmerman, 1995).

Likewise, domestic violence is three times higher among U.S. military than non-military families (Thompson, 1994), and domestic violence escalates when soldiers return to their homes after war (Edmonds & Castaneda, 1992). Guatemalan indigenous women have reported more domestic violence during the civil war in their country (Enloe, 1993), as have Yugoslavian women (Nikolic-Ristanovic, 1996). The sexual warfare in former Yugoslavia is not new: Rape of women has always occurred in armed conflict.

That military men should be so easily prone to sexual violence is not surprising when militaries systematically condone the objectification of women by providing prostitutes for their troops. Military planners see such services as legitimized rewards that the hardships of soldiering require. Ubiquitous in militarized settings, prostitution is officially approved and supported by governments and banks around the world to aid military personnel. For example, in 1967, the U.S. military signed a treaty with the Thai government that allowed soldiers from Vietnam to visit Bangkok for "recreational services." That Thailand is now considered a world center for the sex industry can be attributed to the various American banks that loaned the necessary $4 million to build the massage parlors and brothels (Seager, 1993).

The normalization of prostitution in the military culture was clearly illustrated during an incident in 1995 in which three U.S. soldiers were charged with raping a schoolgirl in a car near the Army base in Okinawa, Japan. Their commanding officer said that the rape could have been avoided if the soldiers had simply paid for a prostitute. "For the price they paid to rent the car they could have had a girl," he explained (Molotsky, 1995). Entangled in the system of military prostitution, women learn to "interpret womanhood as acceptance of themselves as militarized service objects" (Enloe, 1989, p. 214).

Ritualized masculinity fuels military institutions, and weapons engineers and war strategists use explicit sexual imagery to describe their powerful technologies. Defense intellectuals inside the Pentagon use eroticized language, discussing warheads in terms of "penetration dynamics" with "weight to thrust ratios" (Cohn, 1987). Nuclear warheads are referred to in sexual terms, as strategists ask each other if they got to "pat" the missile? Cohn explains that "patting is an assertion of intimacy, sexual possession, affectionate domination. The thrill and pleasure of 'patting the missile' is the proximity of all that phallic power, the possibility of vicariously appropriating it as one's own" (p. 695). With overtly gendered imagery which celebrates male power, scientists at Los Alamos Laboratory called the first atomic bomb "Oppenheimer's baby," and referred to those that were successfully detonated as male babies, whereas duds were called girls.

These explicit sexualized images portray identification with male power, a God-like control over the forces of life and death. The first atomic bomb test was called Trinity—the unity of the Father, the Son, and the Holy Spirit—to symbolize the male forces of creation. One physicist witnessing the first test commented that "It was as if we stood at the first day of creation." Robert Oppenheimer, lead scientist of the team which designed the first atomic bomb, thought of Krishna's words in the Baghavad

Gita: "I am become death, the shatterer of worlds" (Pilisuk, 1999).

EXPERIENCING THE MYSTICAL

At Lawrence Livermore National Laboratory in the United States, nuclear scientists refer to their club as "the priesthood" (Gusterson, 1991). Those with great seniority preside over a set of ritualized rites of passage for the novices. These rituals include years of study in the esoteric and secret classified language, competitive jousting for the role of designer of the next weapon test, grueling months of hard work for the chosen, and limited access to the sacred test site for the cloistered elite.

That many nuclear engineers both portray and experience their work in spiritual terms illuminates the third and perhaps most elusive dimension of militarism: that of *mystical experience,* which we define here as the experience of absolute or ultimate forces beyond human control. Mystical experience is at the core of religion, and militarism calls upon deeply religious sentiments. William James acknowledged this argument in his lecture on "The Moral Equivalent of War" when he noted that "reflective apologists for war at the present day take it religiously. It is a sort of sacrament. Its profits are to the vanquished as well as to the victor; and quite apart from any question of profit, it is an absolute good, we are told, for it is human nature at its highest dynamic" (1910/1995, p. 20).

More recently, Barbara Ehrenreich (1997) has put mystical experience at the center of her theory about war. War, she claims, is a kind of sacrament, a blood ritual that has drawn on humankind's deepest and oldest impulses. Although militarism is not an instinct, the religious sentiment underlying it may be. The religious passions of war are easily observed throughout history:

in the more militarized forms of Islamic *jihad,* in the Christian Crusades, and in twentieth-century Nazism, where religious rituals were manifestly incorporated. Less obvious but equally potent are the contemporary religious sentiments in the form of nationalism. Nationalism elicits spiritual strengths of self-sacrifice, courage, and honor. Ehrenreich posits that "the passions of war are among the 'highest' and finest passions humans can know: courage, altruism, and the mystical sense of belonging to 'something larger than ourselves'" (1997, p. 238). James noted that these sentiments are not bad; indeed they represent the more virtuous dimensions of human existence: "conceptions of order and discipline, the tradition of service and devotion, of physical fitness, of unstinted exertion, and of universal responsibility" (1910/1995, p. 26).

With such sentiments, large numbers of people may be swept into an altered state of consciousness, marked by emotional intensity and a fixation on the collectivity. For example, World War I brought on the ecstasy of taking part in great events and joy of overcoming the pain of death. People became socially intoxicated, feeling a part of a whole, and the sense of being lost in that greater whole (Partridge, 1919). Even during peace, war monuments and cemeteries stimulate religious sentiments where civil worship may take place in sacred places. According to Arnold J. Toynbee, humans require "spiritual sustenance which can be found in militant nationalism in which the glorification of War is a fundamental article of faith" (Toynbee, 1957, p. 18).

Like monks, initiates into military institutions undergo stringent training, deprivation from normal sources of social contact, and systematic education on the moral dimensions of service. If infantry soldiers do not always feel a religious conviction about their soldiering, they at least feel the bond of the platoon as a primary motivation for putting themselves at risk. Feeling oneself part of the greater unit, even if it is only the platoon, rather than the nation, is the spiritual fuel of battle.

The search for the mystical helps us understand why the countervailing forces, such as the dissolution of the Cold War, increasing gender parity, and informed discussions about budgets and jobs, have not seriously impeded militarism. Militaries will continue to train people for killing, and others will design, build, and sell weapons, until other mechanisms for militarism's spiritual dimensions are provided, because these motivations are not only deeply seated, but represent some of the most valued sentiments of human beings. Given the depth and value of these religious dimensions, we must ask: What alternatives could possibly provide an alternative to militarism?

ALTERNATIVES TO MILITARISM

What alternatives can we find to militarism? Many might claim that the best alternative to militarism that contemporary industrialized societies offer is sports. In peace-time, no other single activity draws the collective embrace of victory, ecstatic crowds, big money, and national attention as professional and collegiate sports teams. But sports are more likely to be a predictor of war than a substitute for it. A connection between sports and militarism was well established by Mangan (1981), who demonstrated the way team sports in the nineteenth century flourished in British boarding schools and socialized boys for the British military. Sports are an efficacious teacher of militaristic values because they are inherently competitive and strategic. War imagery is frequently laden with sports metaphors, e.g., in Vietnam, a bombing campaign was named "linebacker I"; and

sports imagery is frequently laden with war metaphors, e.g., football players are referred to as "weapons" who must "obliterate" the "enemy" (Shields & Bredemeier, 1996). Most boys view successful participation in sports as tests of masculinity, whose links to militarism we have already discussed. Empirical research has shown that more violent societies engage in more aggressive forms of sports. For example, Sipes (1973, 1975, 1976) found a strong link between wars and popularity of contact sports. In another demonstrated link between athletics and militarism, the number of months a country had been at war correlated positively with the probability of participation in Olympic games (Keefer, Goldstein, & Kasiarz, 1983). Sports more likely teach militarism than provide or teach alternatives to it.

We believe that a better substitute would be to use militaries for domestic programs rather than wars. Long before the U.S. Job Corps program began, William James argued that a youth corps should be substituted for mandatory military service:

> Instead of a military conscription, a conscription of the whole youthful population . . . to coal and iron mines, to freight trains, to fishing fleets in December, to dish-washing, clothes-washing, and window-washing, to road building and tunnel-making, to foundries and stoke-holes, and to the frames of sky-scrapers, would our gilded youths be drafted off, to get the childishness knocked out of them, and to come back into society with healthier sympathies and soberer ideas. . . . [Then] . . . no one would remain blind as the luxurious classes now are blind, to man's [sic] relations to the globe he lives on" (1910/1995, pp. 24–25).

Almost a hundred years ago, James argued that the values of military service are worth retaining: self-sacrifice, discipline, and work for a common goal. But elites had lost touch with the working poor, and also lost awareness of their problematic relations with the planet. Social service and experience with physical labor would be good for them, and good for society.

We agree with James. And we would like to extend his argument by noting both Ehrenreich's (1997) and Greider's (1998) similar thoughts about how to retain the best of militarism, while using it for peace. Both argue that enormous amounts of human and financial capital should be freed from excessive militarism for fighting that which will be the largest peril of the twenty-first century: environmental degradation, climactic changes, and the depletion of natural resources. Worldwide, militaries use one-third of research and development resources (Renner, 1990). Just when we need to reduce excessive expenditures on militarization, we need funding for environmental reclamation, for new technologies for sustainable culture, including renewable forms of energy, water conservation, non-polluting agricultural practices, and sustainable urban planning.

Converting "swords to plowshares" will not be an easy task but it is imperative and it is underway. In Indiana, an Army ammunition plant was converted to parkland and a small business center (Wade, 1994). The California State University at Monterey Bay opened in 1995 on former Fort Ord (Hartigan, 1995). Citizen groups have worked on converting San Francisco's Presidio (Ruben-

son, 1996). Most defense contractors are studying ways to convert weapons technologies to consumer goods.

Meanwhile it is also appropriate to nominate nonviolent direct action (see Steger, this volume) for the moral equivalent of war. Such activities have brought independence to India, the overthrow of a violent dictator in Haiti, and a revolution in the rights of African Americans in the United States. The teachings of Gandhi and Martin Luther King, Jr. both illuminate how nonviolent action enlists people's energies in great contests of strategy, and provide an opportunity for identifying with causes that affirm the spiritual. Because most wars are now fought within, rather than between, nation-states, the prospects for allegiance to symbols of hope are more decentralized. The same human strengths tapped by militarism could be directed to social action.

The challenges for human survival in the twenty-first century are great, but so have been the inordinate expenditures on militarization in the twentieth. Rechanneling our money, attention and commitment from destroying enemies to combating environmental decline and building sustainable societies (see concluding chapter) will be our greatest and most challenging project. Yet we are entitled to feel hopeful because the powerful motivations of money, masculinism, and mystical experience are still available and we can chose to direct them toward building peace, instead of war.

CHAPTER 13

GLOBALISM AND STRUCTURAL VIOLENCE

Marc Pilisuk[1]

Sometimes in history we witness so dramatic a change in the way human beings live that it affects almost every aspect of how we define what it means to be human. Globalism is such a phenomena. I have chosen the term *globalism* to emphasize the condition of a highly interdependent planet. One aspect of globalism refers to a global culture in which all people are exposed to similar ideas through the media. Globalism leads people to wear Western-style clothing, seek greater consumption regardless of what they already have, and to work hard to get money. Under globalism's influence, people learn to equate the process of holding elections, however biased, with democracy, and equate corporate expansion and technological development with progress. As I shall argue in this paper, globalism is a pernicious form of structural violence which creates poverty, diminishes the human sense of agency or control, and harms the environment.

The chapter begins with a review of one of the most vital of human characteristics, our capacity for making attachments to other people and to the settings where we live. I show first how the capacity for human bonding, essential to human development, has evolved historically and how the settings for such development have changed. I then focus upon those aspects of globalization that have the most profound effects on us, including structural violence in the workplace, in women's health, and in domestic terrorism. Finally, I point to the striking resiliency of people trying to retain and protect the values of caring for each and for their planet in a growing global community.

To understand globalism, it is useful to examine the opposite condition of localism. For most of human history, meaningful social interactions occurred in a limited geographic area among a small local band. People in these groups were typically linked to each other by kinship, but also economically, socially, and spiritually (Demos, 1970). People valued the lives of others and the ecology in which they lived because they were directly sustained by kin and local resources. Connection to other people and to a special place produces a sense of identity and of security (Proshansky, Fabian, & Kaminoff, 1995; Winter, 1998). The mechanism that assured fulfillment of their ties was *caring* (Pilisuk & Parks, 1986). Families

[1]The author wishes to express thanks to Jennifer Tennant, Jan Arnow, and Jolaine Beal for assistance with documentation and research.

and local communities created norms limiting violence that might undermine their continuity. These pre-industrialized groups should not be romanticized. These societies were often rigid, highly stratified, and characterized by the exploitation of the majority for the few. Close living and scarce resources sometimes resulted in some anger and violence. Local units often preclude privacy and demand conformity from their members. Those who found themselves in oppressive families or communities often had no way to leave or to improve their lot. Some families did not survive. But those kinship groupings that best provided for the care and safety of their members were able to endure and pass on their methods of assuring supportive behavior.

As corporations become the social group commanding major portions of the waking day, the mechanism that assures interactive behavior is not *caring*, but rather *marketability*. Individual identities are no longer created solely in small units. Increasingly, identities and measures of success become the ability to sell oneself to a large corporate entity. Although family and community life are still retained outside of the corporation, participation in the marketplace often weakens the feeling of belonging and meaning (Bellah, Madsen, Sullivan, Swidler, & Tipton, 1985; Pilisuk & Parks, 1986). One anthropologist writing in 1936 expressed the hope that growing industrialization would not further transform society into a collection of rootless individuals searching in vain for the bands they had lost (Linton, 1936).

HUMAN COSTS OF GLOBALIZATION

The weakening of ties to special people and places has produced more than a nostalgia for simpler times. First, globalization has come with serious violence to health and well-being. The change from caring to marketability is harmful first because it has in-

creased poverty and social marginality. The poor are at a greater risk for every form of affront to physical health and mental well-being (Browne & Bassuk, 1997; Syme & Berkman, 1976).

Second, globalization harms us psychologically. The cultural capacities that evolved to provide people with particular human identities and attachments to other people were developed and passed on largely in direct, face-to-face contacts. The study of how people learn to make bonding attachments is one of the major themes both of developmental psychology (Ainsworth, 1982; Bowlby, 1973) and of feminist theories of psychological identity (Belenky, Clinchy, Goldberger, & Tarule, 1986). Appreciation of special people and of special places is still a human need, but such needs are increasingly met by what corporations will sell us for recreation, leisure, and escape. These alternatives cater to a basic narcissism, or seeking of pleasure for oneself (Kanner & Gomes, 1995). For most people, these marketed outlets are not sufficient. They provide only temporary respite from the pressured activity of the competitive workplace, and they fail to address the need for intimate social ties, or for finding creativity in the activities of everyday life.

Third, globalization devastates the natural environment. While global corporations require growth, the resources of the earth are finite. Corporate growth and the consumption patterns create harmful accumulations of waste, jeopardizing health and local communities. For example, toxic wastes from more than 40 countries are shipped to a single company, Chemical Waste Management in Emelle, Alabama, where the contamination takes a toll on the mostly Afro-American and extremely poor citizens who live in the area. (Political Ecology Group, 1994). While contaminated environments have been most harsh for impoverished people of color, problems of ozone depletion, global warming, depletion of rainforests, loss of fish and other wildlife, diminished access to clean water, and the presence of airborne contaminants are problems affecting all people. Solutions to these environmental dangers are no longer possible within a single country.

POVERTY: ITS PSYCHOLOGY AND ITS DISTRIBUTION

The global market has created winners and losers, a polarization of income greater than at any time since records have been kept. In 1997, the world's 477 billionaires (up from 358 the year before) had combined earnings greater than the poorer half of the entire world's population (Korten, 1999). Corporate growth increased 11 percent, and CEOs from the major corporations increased their incomes by 50 percent. Of the 100 largest economies in the world, 51 are now corporations rather than nation-states (Hacker, 1997; Korten, 1995). Between 1950 and 1997, the world economy grew six-fold, to a total of $29 trillion. Yet each year, twelve million children under five years of age die—33,000 per day—the overwhelming majority from preventable illnesses. An equal number survive with permanent disabilities that could have been prevented (U.N. Development Programme, 1997).

Wealthy nations like the United States are not immune from devastating economic polarization. In 1996, the top 5 percent of U.S. households collected 21.4 percent of the national income, the highest level ever recorded. The income of the lowest 20 percent decreased by 11 percent (Hacker, 1997; U.S. Census, 1997a). In that time period, approximately 20 million Americans did not have enough to eat—a 50 percent rise since 1985 (U.S. Census, 1997b). Twenty-one million people used food banks or soup kitchens, but 70,000 people were turned away when supplies ran out (Alaimo,

Briefel, Frongillo, & Olson, 1988; Lamison-White, 1997). Close to 2 million people become homeless each year (Fagan, 1998).

Limited material resources are not the only plight of poor people. Poverty inflicts psychological scars as well; it is an experience of scarcity amidst affluence. For many reasons, such as those discussed by Opotow (this volume), poverty produces the scorn of others and the internalized scorn of oneself. Indigence is not just about money, roads, or TVs, but also about the power to determine how local resources will be used to give meaning to lives. The power of global corporations in local communities forces people to depend on benefits from afar. Projected images of the good life help reduce different cultural values to the one global value of money. Meanwhile, money becomes concentrated in fewer hands. The world is dividing into a small group of "haves" and a growing group of paupers. This division of wealth inflicts a level of structural violence that kills many more persons than have died by all direct acts of violence and by war.

STRUCTURAL VIOLENCE IN THE WORKPLACE

Modern trade agreements have released giant corporations to move where environmental restrictions are absent, taxes low, and labor cheap. As a result, workers suffer. For example, in an Indonesian factory contracting for Nike, the working conditions are hot and crowded, yet drinking water is rationed. A worker must get a permission slip to use the bathroom. She also has to come in when sick to get permission from the company doctor to stay home. If she cannot do so—even with a note from her own doctor—she is forced upon her return to undergo a two-hour public scolding. A worker of 28 is considered old for the work and can expect to be dismissed. The women suffer sexual harassment from guards touching their bodies to verify that they are not stealing shoe parts (Rhodes, 1997a). People who have no other alternative seek these jobs in Indonesia. Bad as the situation is, people suffer even more as these jobs are being lost to people who will work for even less in Vietnam, Haiti, China, and Pakistan.

For example, of the 1,000 employees of the Keyhinge Toys factory in Da Nang, Vietnam, 90 percent are women 17 to 20 years old. They make the giveaway toy characters from Disney films for McDonald's "Happy Meals." These workers are exposed to acetone fumes, while management refuses to pay health insurance. Women at Keyhinge received six to eight cents an hour in 1997. Wages failed to cover 20 percent of the daily food and travel costs for a single worker, let alone her family (Pilisuk, 1998). The CEO of Disney, by contrast, earned $203 million in the same year (Rhodes, 1997b).

Like most of the countries permitting sweatshops, Indonesia forbids independent unions. The official government union, run by retired military officers, deducts dues from paychecks and suppresses workers who express grievances. When conditions become intolerable, massive walkouts occur. After the workers negotiate an agreement and return to work, the police interrogate suspected leaders. For example, Cicih, a young woman, worked at a Nike contractor factory in Indonesia. In 1992, she and several others led almost all of the 6,500 workers to strike over wages and working conditions. The normal work day was ten and a half hours with forced overtime three times a week. Pay was about $2.10 a day in U.S. dollars (Bissel, 1997). These workers were fired and blacklisted so they cannot find further employment (Rhodes, 1997c).

The "neutral" position taken by Nike was to leave such matters to the Indonesian Supreme Court, meaning that Cicih may not live to see her case decided. In 1997, the Court ruled on only 24 cases out of 2,000. Nike claims to pay above the minimum wage. But to attract investment, Indonesia, like many other nations, sets the minimum wage below the poverty line (Rhodes, 1997c). Here, structural violence is appalling but insidious: The global corporations do not inflict the harsh treatment directly. They merely encourage harm by investing capital where such conditions bring the best returns.

DEHUMANIZING WORK IN DEVELOPED AND DEVELOPING COUNTRIES

Free trade agreements affect community well-being on both sides of the U.S.-Mexican border. In 1997, U.S. President Clinton paid a visit to Mexico on Cinco de Mayo to promote the next phase of the North American Free Trade Agreement (NAFTA). He spoke to thousands of Mexican businessmen about the success of free trade. Like the United States, Mexico has a new group of millionaires. Unemployment, however, has reached an all-time high.

The Mexican military needed massive numbers of soldiers to buttress police efforts in clearing out a protest that appeared immense enough to bring Mexico City, the largest city in the world, to a close. Military backup and virtual press blackouts are not surprising when one considers the corporate stakes on both sides of the border. Real wages in Mexico have dropped since the General Agreement on Trade and Tariffs was signed in 1995. The number of workers, called "maquiladoras," working just over the border has increased by 45 percent, while their average earnings have dropped from one dollar an hour to 70 cents. The extent of desperation leads to violence. Within the past decade, the peasants of Northern Tabasco organized a hunger strike until death, while the Zapatistas arose to rebel against harsh military suppression of displaced workers in Chiapas and Guerara (Harvey, 1998).

Meanwhile, the Alfred Angelo Company, founded in 1940 in Philadelphia, demonstrates the ugly brutality of structural violence produced by globalism. For generations, a skilled and dedicated workforce helped the Piccione family become a premiere bridal gown company, supplying the best-known labels and marketing through the J.C. Penney catalog. Annual sales for this company rose from $45 million in 1985, when Piccione acquired the license to produce and market "Christian Dior" bridal gowns, to $59 million in 1996. The company eliminated most of its U.S. jobs, including the 70 workers in the unionized Philadelphia-area cutting and handling center, and over 200 workers in shops in New York City (Rhodes, 1997d). Some of the gowns made with the Alfred Angelo label are being sewn in Guatemala and China. It is difficult to know the conditions under which the clothes were made in China. However, in April 1997, a survey of three factories in Guatemala producing for Alfred Angelo revealed widespread violations of that country's laws, including use of child labor, illegal wage and hour schedules, and life-threatening safety conditions. Fourteen- and 15-year-olds worked ten and eleven hours a day, earning less than minimum wage. Some worked until 2:00 A.M. and had to return at 7:00 A.M. the same day for a full shift. This schedule violated Alfred Angelo's own code of conduct for foreign vendors as well as Guatemalan laws requiring time off for children to go to school. Two years earlier, workers in one factory attempted to organize and there were mass firings (Rhodes, 1997d).

The company claimed "business reasons" to explain its elimination of jobs in the United States. The reason is similar to that offered by Phillips Van Heusen (PVH), a major producer of apparel for export, for choosing to close the only factory in Guatemala that had finally secured a collective bargaining agreement after a six-year struggle. PVH is the leading U.S. marketer of men's shirts, and owns not only the Van Heusen label but also Izod, Gant, Geoffrey Beene, Bass, and others. In neither the PVH nor the Angelo case were the labor cuts needed to stay in business. The cuts were made because the companies could make more profit through contractors and because their competition could be expected to do the same. The PVH situation has resulted in protests across the United States. Some of the Philadelphia community rallied behind the Alfred Angelo workers. Local newspapers have written editorials in support of the workers' fight to save their jobs. In speeches and rallies, Alfred Angelo employees have allied themselves with the exploited workers in Guatemala and China, demanding an end to exploitation of workers in sewing factories in the United States and abroad.

But the people of Philadelphia will not be able to find legal support for economic pressure to keep their jobs when restrictions on trade are eliminated. The rights of municipalities to engage in boycotts, like those which helped to end apartheid in South Africa, or which oppose brutal dictatorial practices in Burma, are currently being viewed as restrictions on trade. The Multilateral Agreement on Investments is soon likely to make nations and local governments liable for any restrictions upon foreign investments that might result from such protective regulations as environmental safety or living wage requirements

(Campaign for Labor Rights, 1998; Rauber, 1998).

GLOBALIZATION'S STRUCTURAL VIOLENCE ON WOMEN'S HEALTH

Wherever the global economy expands into poor areas and replaces the means for local livelihood, HIV spreads among poor women (Daily, Farmer, Rhatigan, Katz, & Furin, 1995). Lacking decent legal employment, the women become involved with drug traffickers and prostitution. Prostitution is an outgrowth of structural violence. The United Nations estimates that in 1997, there were 57 million women and child prostitutes. Thirty thousand "hospitality girls" are registered in the Philippines, but the actual number of prostitutes is about 75,000 (Rosenfeld, 1997). Originally, these prostitutes served two large American military bases, welcomed in the Philippines under the dictatorial regime of Ferdinand Marcos. After Marcos was forced from power, Subic Air Force Base was turned into a free-trade zone, bringing in 150 large corporations (Barry, 1995; Rosenfeld, 1997). The Asia-Pacific Economic Forum considered the Philippines the best place for investment among ten Asian Pacific countries. The benefits, however, have not reached the women, who continue to sell their bodies even with the increased risk of HIV infection.

Meanwhile, the Ukraine has surpassed Thailand as the center of the global business in trafficking women. Young European women are in demand, and the Ukraine, economically devastated by its entrance into the global economy, has provided the supply. Thirty applicants compete for every job in the Ukraine. The average salary today is less than thirty dollars a month, but only half that in the small towns where criminal gangs recruit women with promises of employment in other countries (Specter, 1998).

In Southeast Asia, sub-Saharan Africa, and U.S. cities, the livelihood choices open to poor women are restricted. The HIV epidemic is spreading rapidly among poor women of color. The incidence is high wherever the global economy replaces the means for local livelihood (Daily et al., 1995). The increase is combined with minimal access to treatment, which is also limited by the low tax base needed to lure global capital.

"Since 1987, AIDS has been the leading cause of death among 15–45-year-old Black and Latina women in NYC" (Simmons, Farmer, & Schoepf, 1995, pp. 42–43). Between seven and ten thousand American children are orphaned each year when their mothers die from AIDS (Gardner & Preator, 1996).

GLOBAL FACTORS IN DOMESTIC TERRORISM

When decent working-class jobs move from the United States to countries with cheap labor and less environmental regulation, displaced workers seek scapegoats. This loss has led to acts of terrorism. People like Timothy McVeigh, charged with the 1995 bombing of a U.S. Federal Building in Oklahoma, and bombers of Black churches, are depicted by the media as deranged. This portrayal conceals similarities in their ideologies and in their options. Many of these former workers blame the government's affinity for racial minorities and immigrants, who are getting jobs deserved by "true Americans." One common view is that wealthy Jewish bankers control government policies in a conspiratorial effort to create a world government that would prevent people from defending themselves (Abanes, 1996; Lamy, 1996). But for the fact that some of these extremists have guns and military training, one might dismiss them as sociopaths unable to find a useful purpose. There is, however, no useful purpose open to them.

Half the U.S. working population has suffered falling or stagnant wages for about 20 years. The media tell us that the good life can be purchased on credit. But millions lack the education to participate in a global economy. Former Labor Secretary Robert Reich confronted the inability of government to provide such education. However, his "Putting People First," the populist plan to train people for skilled jobs, has been sacrificed. Balancing the budget, setting interest rates to satisfy Wall Street, and reducing trade barriers are policies that require cutting the safety net (Reich, 1997a; 1997b). In many cases, corporation lobbyists write legislation, manage press releases, and establish as much access as can be bought in Washington (Domhoff, 1971; Seager, 1994; Silverstein, 1998). Hence we can see why the Senate has yet to ratify the International Covenant on Economic, Social, and Cultural Rights, a worldwide treaty that has been ratified by 136 other countries, including the G-7 nations. The treaty outlines a range of civil and human rights principles, including "fair wages," "right to work," and nondiscrimination—all constraints upon economic expansion (Rauber, 1998). Corporation-friendly laws do not reflect an evil scheme. They are consequences of the limited place left for government in a global economy.

A GLOBAL MONOCULTURE OF THE MIND

Perhaps the greatest challenge posed by globalism is how to retain the vital diversity of human voices and communities. Factory piece-workers do the same assembly work the world over. One can buy identical products from similar chain stores around the

globe. Uniform standards for people and products increase profitability. Standardization yields low overhead costs, less customer service, and greater profits. The benefits of this efficiency are not well-distributed. Three-quarters of the money spent locally for a universally marketed fast food hamburger will leave the community, subsidizing global corporations with local resources (Gour & Gunn, 1991; Hanauer, 1998).

Centralized control of the media contributes to skepticism that local voices can be heard (Pilisuk, Parks, & Hawkes, 1987). Similar global economic factors are considered important in explaining the lack of involvement by adolescents in social issues (Damon, 1998). Under globalization, the opportunity for distinctive voices to be heard is reduced, yet the voices of local residents are needed to address issues raised by global expansion.

ANOTHER GLOBAL SOCIETY EMERGING TO PREVENT GLOBAL STRUCTURAL VIOLENCE

Fortunately, an international global network of nongovernmental organizations (NGOs) and local groups has risen dramatically in the nineties. NGOs are creating another global society based upon hearing local community voices (Pilisuk, McAllister, & Rothman, 1996). For example, near San Francisco, California, the voice of Tri-Valley Citizens (TVC) Against a Radioactive Environment exemplifies a spirit of local participation that refuses to give in to forces of the global economy. TVC resides in the community built around the nearby Lawrence Livermore National Laboratories, one of the centers of research on nuclear weapons and nuclear energy. A contract between the Department of Energy and the University of California provides a screen of legitimacy for highly paid scientists to do secret classified work perpetuating the development of nu-clear weapons. Major corporations such as Bechtel, Westinghouse, Raytheon, and General Electric have been beneficiaries of nuclear weapons contracts and secrecy protects their work. TVC was organized in the apartment of one of the local residents to address concerns about risks to health and safety from the work at Livermore. These local citizens were concerned as well with the laboratory's mission of creating nuclear weapons. By leafleting and talking to neighbors, TVC gained support, including some assistance secretly provided by Livermore employees. Through diligent efforts, the group uncovered numerous violations of health and safety standards. They testified at various legally mandated hearings called by the Department of Health, the Department of Energy, and the Environmental Protection Agency.

Demonstrating the increasingly effective networking of NGO groups, TVC joined the Livermore Environment and Peace Association, a coalition consisting of approximately 20 Bay Area peace and environmental groups who help with press releases, demonstrations, and legal actions. TVC is also part of the Military Production Network, a national coalition providing information for each the 18 nuclear weapons facilities in the United States. TVC has also maintained contact with an international network of nuclear weapons survivors, from Kazakhstan to islands in the South Pacific, including veterans groups and down-winders from Utah and Nevada. Several of the laboratory's more dangerous projects have been delayed or canceled, and the dissenting actions have brought an end to the incineration of radioactive wastes. The director of the laboratory was fired. TVC's objective of converting the giant laboratory to a center for environmental and medical research has not yet been achieved, but the group has

reached many people and has demonstrated the possibility of thinking globally and acting locally (Pilisuk, 1996).

The Borneo Project offers another creative response to the global economy. Borneo's indigenous communities have cared for their home in the world's oldest rainforest for thousands of years. In return, the forest has provided the communities with resources needed to survive. These well-established but fragile relationships are now in jeopardy. Ignoring land claims by native peoples, logging companies and oil palm plantations are clear-cutting the forest. It is impossible to guess the costs to future generations from the depletion of the earth's oxygen and extinction of medicinal plant species and other genetic resources. Immediate costs to communities are, however, apparent. Rivers have been contaminated and forests eroded. The abundant resource base upon which a people have depended for the past millennium is diminishing (Pilisuk, 1998).

The village of Uma Bawang, in Malaysian Borneo, has become a center of attempts to bring social and environmental justice to their region. In 1991, Berkeley, California and Uma Bawang became sister communities and launched the nonprofit Borneo Project. The project's volunteers use citizen diplomacy, direct assistance, and cultural exchange. The project enables local villages to secure traditional land claims, network with international NGOs, and monitor violations of human and land rights. The project also educates the public on these issues. Finally, the group raises funds that go directly to support the Uma Bawang Residents Association (Earth Island Institute, 1997). If the project succeeds in saving some of the rainforest, it will become a model for communities everywhere. A tribal leader in Sarawak explained the importance of this approach:

. . . in our race to modernize we must respect the ancient cultures and traditions of our peoples. We must not blindly follow that model of progress invented by European wealth; we must not forget that this wealth was bought at a very high price. The rich world suffers from so much stress, pollution, violence, poverty, and spiritual emptiness. The wealth of the indigenous communities lies not in money or commodities, but in community, tradition, and a sense of belonging to a special place. (Earth Island Institute, 1997, p. 3)

CONCLUSION

The Sarawak example not only demonstrates the increasing effectiveness of global activism to reduce structural violence, but also brings us back to the initial distinction between caring and marketability. Markets are the primary arena for economic entrepreneurship and technical innovation. They do not, however, instruct people with large incomes to consume only their rightful share of natural resources. Markets do not prevent retailers from selling guns to children or require producers to recycle their waste. They give no priority for the allocation of resources to meet basic needs of those in poverty before providing luxuries for those with great wealth. Civil societies create governments to establish and maintain rules that might restrict the forces of the market and permit the expression of caring (Makhijani, 1992).

The Sarawak example has important implications for psychology. Globalization, with its complex demands upon the individual psyche, is upon us. Our Western psychology has long focused on finding logical answers to specific questions, often based upon understanding the rewards to individuals for specific behaviors. But this analysis shows that we will need to reestablish the human community's capacity for caring. This transformation will require the best of our discipline. Vaclav Havel notes that "without a global revolution in consciousness, nothing will change for the better in the sphere of our being as humans, and the catastrophe toward which we are headed . . . will be unavoidable" (as cited in Lasley, 1994, p. 3).

Surely a psychology that is more global in its understanding and better able to appreciate the contributions from non-Western and from indigenous thought is needed (Marsella, 1998). The current condition of globalism presents a challenge. We live with the threat of biological or nuclear terrorism (see Britton, this volume). Much of the world has experienced interminable intrastate or regional wars that stem from unequal access to resources, water scarcity, endless waves of refugees, and overcrowded cities at risk for dangerous epidemics (see Winter, Christie, Wagner, & Boston, this volume).

But the process of globalization has also come with unprecedented opportunities for communication, an increase of contact among different cultures, and a growth of nongovernmental international structures that monitor and regulate the consequences of our changed world. Globalism has also brought to the fore the need for universal protections of basic human rights, and an awareness of the values of cultural and environmental diversity. These potentials for healthy psychological and social development in a global community are illustrated in the Borneo and Livermore Projects and in thousands of others like them. Hopefully, our new global opportunities for contact with people and places can provide openings for informed action in constraining structural violence and redirecting the powerful forces of globalism.

CHAPTER 14

HUMAN RIGHTS VIOLATIONS AS STRUCTURAL VIOLENCE

M. Brinton Lykes

Psychologists have been involved in multiple efforts to end war and other conditions that contribute to human rights violations (Smith, 1999). They have also worked extensively with survivors of human rights abuses (Graça Machel/ *UN Study on the Effects of War on Children,* 1998; Lykes, Brabeck, Ferns, & Radan, 1993; Lykes & Liem, 1990). Much of the work has focused on the effects of direct violence and on the consequences of violating individuals' civil and political rights (called first-generation human rights).

In this chapter, however, I am concerned about later generations of human rights and their impact on the way we think and practice as peace psychologists. Whereas first-generation rights refer to civil and political rights, second-generation rights focus on social, economic, and cultural rights. Third-generation rights refer to "solidarity rights," such as the right to development, self-determination, peace, and a clean environment. Fourth-generation rights refer to the rights of indigenous peoples. After discussing the historical formulations of these rights, I then show how several recent psychological theories, including liberation psychology, cultural psychology, and social constructivism elucidate this extended thinking about human rights. I will argue that examining

these extended human rights helps us illuminate the chronic and hidden structural violence produced by armed conflict. I will then describe how the cases of Argentina and Guatemala demonstrate a "shift toward the social and structural" within selected areas of psychological and human rights discourse. Finally, I will describe community peace-building that focuses on the structural violence produced by violations of these extended human rights.

FOUR GENERATIONS OF HUMAN RIGHTS

Many human rights scholars and social scientists have adopted the language of "generations of rights"[1] to refer to the historical development of formulated rights (*No hiding place: Human rights—A world report,* 1998; Messer, 1995). Within this understanding, first-generation rights (civil-political rights)

[1]Those who critique the language of "generations of rights" argue, in contrast, that it is not a useful distinction because conventions such as the Elimination of Discrimination against Women (approved in 1979) and the Rights of the Child (approved in 1989) cut across these "supposed generations," integrating individual and group rights (see, for example, Oloka-Onyango & Tamale, 1995). Despite this critique, in this chapter I have used the language of generations of rights to develop my argument.

were developed in the seventeenth and eighteenth centuries, and second-generation rights (social, economic, and cultural rights) were developed in the nineteenth century. First- and second-generation rights were embodied by the original Universal Declaration of Human Rights (1948) and made legally binding in the Conventions on Civil and Political Rights and on Economic, Social, and Cultural Rights, both approved by the United Nations in 1966. In contrast, third-generation rights refer to "solidarity rights," such as the right to development, self-determination, peace, and a clean environment; fourth-generation rights refer to the rights of indigenous peoples. These latter rights date from the twentieth century and are embodied in later declarations and conventions.

Differences in prioritizing among these various rights have persisted, as evidenced in the failure of the former Soviet Union and other socialist countries to accept individual political rights, despite their having signed the covenants (Messer, 1997). The United States, in contrast, has neither ratified nor implemented treaties on social or economic rights (Katz, 1998; Messer, 1997; Rosemont, 1998). As significantly, most Unitedstatesians[2] typically think of human rights abuses primarily in civil or political terms, that is, as violations of our rights to free speech, or as arbitrary arrest, or cruel, inhuman, or degrading treatment or punishment. Implicit within this articulation of rights is the assumption that it is the rights of individuals that are being asserted and/or protected. Few countries from Africa,

Latin America, or Asia belonged to the United Nations during the period in which the initial human rights declaration was drafted. Many were still under colonial rule. It is not, therefore, surprising that the views of the "majority world" were not well represented in the initial documents (Messer, 1997).

The end of the Cold War has brought dramatic political changes, creating new alliances and giving voice to formerly marginalized and/or nonexistent states. Some of these countries achieved liberation from European colonial rule while new countries also formed as ethnic/national groups asserted their independence. Leaders within these countries, as well as women and indigenous groups throughout the world, have fought to expand the two original human rights covenants to include demands for the rights of women, children, and indigenous peoples (see *http://www.un.org* for copies of the Convention on the Rights of the Child, 1989; the Convention on the Elimination of Discrimination Against Women, 1979; and the Draft Declaration on the Rights of Indigenous Peoples, 1994). The works of Kam (1998), Menchú Tum (1998), Nagengast (1997), Oloka-Onyango & Tamale (1995), Rao (1995), Wells (1998), and Zechenter (1997) describe important struggles at the grassroots level, and among academics and policy-makers, that concluded in the extension rights. For example, the draft declaration of indigenous rights establishes collective rights, that is, "a right that adheres to certain groups *because* it is not reducible to individuals" (Thompson, 1997, p. 789; italics in original). These collective rights are known as fourth-generation rights. Collective rights raise potential challenges for Westerners, whose assumptions about rights typically are grounded in the belief that the locus of rights is the autonomous individual.

[2]The term is a translation of the Spanish term "estadounidense" (see Gugelberger, 1996, p. 4, also Note 4, p. 119). It is used here rather than the more common "American" since this latter term includes reference to all citizens of the Americas, that is, of Canada, Mexico, Central and South America, and the United States of America.

Thompson (1997), an anthropologist, distinguishes between collective and group rights, recognizing that the latter have a long tradition within the U.S. legal system. He further distinguishes among ethnic minorities, the nation, and the state, hoping thus to clarify the declaration's meaning of collective rights and its implications for international human rights. Thompson's argument parallels similar developments within psychology that have emphasized the social and collective dimensions of individuality while critiquing assumptions of individualism underlying many Euro-American notions (Sampson, 1993). The Draft Declaration on the Rights of Indigenous Peoples also raises critical concerns about the importance of the environment and the multiple ways in which indigenous identity is constructed in relationship with the earth (Menchú Tum, 1998).

In addition, third- and fourth-generation rights challenge the assumed universal character of the initial human rights declarations. They emphasize the importance of social context, that is, of culture, the environment, and of history in the very definition of human rights and to whom they belong. Specifically, third- and fourth-generation rights affirm the collectivity as an important locus of rights. Debates about indigenous peoples' rights challenge the presumed universality of human rights by emphasizing the relative positions of different collectivities in relation to power and resources (see *Universal human rights vs. cultural relativity: Special issue*, 1997). This expanded understanding of human rights thus confirms that denial of civil-political rights as well as economic, cultural, social, and collective rights constitute human rights violations and abuses. It focuses attention on the individual and the collective and the systemic and structural forces in which they are socially embedded.

PSYCHOLOGICAL CONTRIBUTIONS TO AN EXPANDED UNDERSTANDING OF RIGHTS

Although psychologists have not yet explicitly addressed the nature of human rights, several recent theoretical developments contribute to understanding the implications of expanded human rights for peace psychologists and others seeking to work with human rights violations. These developments complement the dominant assumptions in psychology, which are positivist, universalistic, objective, and laboratory-based. I briefly describe some of these ideas to elucidate how they help us understand extended human rights violations as structural violence.

Liberation Psychology in Contexts of War

Ignacio Martín-Baró (1990), a Salvadoran social psychologist and Jesuit priest, argued that the aftereffects of political repression carried out by governments was one of the thorniest problems confronting Latin American states hoping to establish democratic governments. He emphasized that in addition to damage to personal lives, harm had been done to the social structures themselves—to the norms, values, and principles by which people are educated, and to the institutions that govern the lives of citizens. "Social trauma affects individuals precisely in their social character; that is, as a totality, as a system" (Martín-Baró, 1994, p. 124).

Martín-Baró's formulation of liberation psychology draws on Latin American liberation theology and pedagogy (Freire, 1970, 1973; Gutiérrez, 1973/1988) and includes (1) a focus on the liberation of a whole people (i.e., the collectivity), as well as personal liberation; (2) a new epistemology wherein the truth of the popular majority is not to be found, but created, that is, wherein truth is constructed "from below"; and (3) a new praxis, wherein we place ourselves within the research-action process alongside the dominated or oppressed rather than alongside the dominator or oppressor (Martín-Baró, 1994). He argued that taking sides is not bias but rather an ethical choice, grounded in the truths of reason and compassion. As is evident in his description, liberation psychology is clearly political in that it seeks to change power relations.

Martín-Baró's psychology of liberation is not totally new within Western psychology and psychiatry. It echoes earlier work by Franz Fanon (1967; see Dawes, this volume, for a fuller description of Fanon's liberation psychology/psychiatry). African American or Black psychology draws heavily on the works of Black liberation theology and/ or Africanist traditions and is also echoed in Martín-Baró's work. Thomas Gordon (1973) compared "White and Black psychology," raising ethical and political concerns, conceptual limitations, and methodological weaknesses within White, i.e., Euro-American psychology. Gordon challenged Black psychology to give priority consideration to, among other things, developing research that proceeds "from real life needs rather than from theoretical imperatives" (p. 94). He urged the development of collaborative relations with Black communities and suggested that psychologists would need new research competencies and roles, including those of advocates, lobbyists, information resource persons, and watchdogs that "facilitate the advancement of our collective interests" (p. 94). An important point of agreement among the liberation psychologies of Fanon and Martín-Baró and Black psychology is the shift of psychologists' attention to the systemic or structural dimensions of the identified problem or concern,

rather than its more typical focal point, the individual person abstracted from a multi-layered social, historical, and cultural context.

Within this alternative framework, trauma is not primarily or exclusively an intrapsychic phenomenon, but rather is conceived of as a psycho-social event. Psychosocial trauma reflects a dialectic process, that is, it "resides in the social relations of which the individual is only a part" (Martín-Baró, 1994, p. 124). Martín-Baró suggested further that "psychosocial trauma can be a normal consequence of a social system based on social relations of exploitation and dehumanizing oppression" such as those in wartime El Salvador (p. 125). Trauma becomes a usual event, not an aberration. In the context of war, trauma is an everyday part of life. During conditions of peace, the slaughter of individuals, the disappearance of loved ones, the inability to distinguish what is one's experience from what others say it is (and, when one does, the fear to speak one's point of view), the militarization of institutions, and the extreme polarization of social life are seen as abnormal. But in wartime El Salvador, for example, people came to accept these experiences as normal. Martín-Baró offers liberation psychology as one response for psychologists who seek to accompany local populations in responding to and redressing these extreme violations and their effects.

Constructivist and Cultural Interpretations: Symbolic Aspects of Terror

Psychologists who have documented the effects of extreme trauma and torture in war, have typically focused on the events of direct violence and their immediate consequences for the individual. More specifically, those working with survivors of war have termed the constellation of symptoms suffered by many survivors as Post Traumatic Stress Disorder (PTSD) and developed wide-ranging treatment and intervention strategies (Herman, 1992). In contrast, social constructivists argue that the meanings we make of a phenomenon are not adequately represented by this labeling of symptoms (Aron, Corne, Fursland, & Zewler, 1991). Rather, meanings are co-constructed by those who experience them in relationships in a particular socio-historical time, culture, and place (Agger, 1994; Gergen, 1994, 1997). Dialogue and engagement are critical strategies for constructing knowledge and understanding which are inherently value-laden, rather than value-neutral. This point of view is part of a post-modern emphasis on inquiry and action (Reason & Rowan, 1981) and calls our attention to the multiple meanings that are made of war and human rights violations by survivors. This meaning-making process is best understood through the thick descriptions of events constructed by the survivors in dialogue and/or interaction with those who accompany them (Lykes, 1996).

Anthropologists and cultural psychologists who have explored the meanings of human rights violations and their effects have suggested that in addition to the effect of terror on the immediate consequences for individuals, terror has symbolic effects on entire communities and across generations (Danieli, 1998). I have argued previously (Lykes, 1996) that terror not only destroys the present but forces a rethinking of the past and deeply threatens the future through its destructive effects on the next generation's capacity to culturally affirm itself. My field work in Guatemala, as well as the work of others in Argentina, further clarifies the implications of seeing extended human rights violations as structural violence.

ARGENTINA AND GUATEMALA: STRUCTURAL VIOLENCE AS HUMAN RIGHTS VIOLATIONS

Human rights activists and social scientists who have worked with survivors of state-sponsored violence and war in Argentina and Guatemala argue that horrific violations of individual human rights in Argentina (Suárez-Orozco, 1992) and Guatemala (CEH, 1999; ODHAG, 1998; Schirmer, 1998) can be traced, in part, to the world-views of the Latin American elite who controlled these countries. Institutionalization of political and economic structural violence sustained those views. More specifically, the military juntas that perpetrated human rights abuses were supported by wealthy landowners and a Roman Catholic hierarchy in Argentina from 1976 to 1983 and in Guatemala from 1954 to 1986. These military units developed counter-insurgent strategies against civilian populations and justified them in the name of preserving national identity and internal state security (CEH, 1999; *Nunca Más*, 1986; ODHAG, 1998). A brief discussion of life within each of these countries during the most intense periods of political repression suggests that the broader human rights of all citizens were consistently violated and that this structural violence was justified in the name of protecting the civil-political rights of a small elite.

The "Dirty War": 1976 to 1983

In Argentina as many as 30,000 people, over 80 percent of whom were between the ages of 16 and 35, were detained, tortured, and disappeared[3] (*Nunca Más* [*Never Again*],

---

[3]The term disappeared (desaparecido) refers to the process developed within Latin America during twentieth-century dictatorships whereby individuals were kidnapped by security forces or paramilitary organiza-

1986) between 1976 and 1983. The military presented itself as defenders of tradition, family, and property; criticism of them through word or deed was deemed non-patriotic, subversive behavior that should be crushed to protect the nation (Frontalini & Caiati, 1984). Those who challenged dominant definitions of nationhood, often by simply seeking to feed, clothe, or house the poor (that is, the majority of Argentineans), were defined as "subversive" and accused of threatening to destabilize national security; they were tortured, murdered, and/or disappeared. Although several guerrilla groups disrupted social life through kidnappings and bombings during the late 1960s and early 1970s, extensive documentation including the government's own report (*Nunca Más*, 1986) demonstrate definitely that these groups were quashed long before the disappearances began. General Videla, one of the dictators at this time, claimed that the repression was directed against a minority that was not even Argentinean. He thereby justified violations of the human rights of his victims by defining them outside of the realm of citizenry (Frontalini & Caiati, 1984) all the while maintaining the rhetoric of rights when talking to the "good citizenry." Doing so represents a good example of exclusionary justice (see Opotow, this volume).

The military also removed children of those considered subversives, subsequently gifting them to "good" families, that is, those of the military and upper class (Suárez-Orozco, 1987; also see Puenzo, 1985, *The Official Story*, for a film version). General Camps, head of the police of the

province of Buenos Aires when numbers of children were kidnapped, justified this practice: ". . . Personally, I did not eliminate any children. What I did was to give some of them to beneficent organizations so that they would find new parents for them. Subversives educate their children into subversion. That has to be stopped" (cited in Barki, 1988, p. 241; see Arditti & Lykes, 1992; Arditti, 1999, for a fuller discussion of these points).

Such violations of human rights are direct acts of violence in that they are episodic and are perpetrated against individuals (see Wagner, this volume). However, if we situate the individuals affected within the historical, socio-political context described briefly above, the violations are reconfigured. They were not only acts against individuals, but embedded in and sustained by the linguistic and political systems of the state. National leaders used everyday language like rhetoric of rights to subvert their declared objectives and arrest the people they claimed to protect. (Graziano, 1992; Feitlowitz, 1998). As such, they not only deprived many of their civil-political rights but terrorized into silence the vast majority of the Argentinean population for nearly six years (Simpson & Bennett, 1985).

In Argentina, the Grandmothers of the Plaza de Mayo, one of a small number of human rights organizations that did protest the violations described here, sought to recover their kidnapped grandchildren and to tell them the stories of their families of origin. Local psychologists accompanying them supported these efforts. However, François Dalto, a renowned French child psychiatrist, upon learning of the work of the Grandmothers, argued that they were provoking a second trauma in these children by taking them from the families that they had known, into which some had been adopted at infancy. In contrast, psycholo-

---

tions. They were often tortured and then brutally murdered and the bodies tossed into the seas or otherwise disposed of. However, because the bodies did not reappear, family members, friends, and colleagues did not know if they were alive or dead (*Nunca Más*, 1986; ODHAG, 1998).

gists in Argentina working from the liberationist perspective described above, urged authorities to consider the meaning for these children of being raised by the murderers of their biological parents. These psychologists argued for the children's rights to know their identities, that is, the stories of their birth parents and the history of Argentina for which their birth parents fought and/or were murdered (Fariña & Lykes, 1991). Such stories would only be shared if the Grandmothers succeeded. The Grandmothers of the Plaza de Mayo thus asserted a child's right to his or her identity within the Declaration on the Rights of the Child, and hoped to use Argentina's signing of the Declaration to support its work for the recovery of these abducted children (see Arditti & Lykes, 1992; Arditti, 1999).

Although these issues are very complex, the example suggests that a broadened understanding of the structural contexts in which abuses are embedded resituates the description of "the problem" from one focused on the rights of solitary individuals to one which engages consideration of the broader society and cultural context. Ironically, shortly before her death, Dalto, who had accepted an invitation of the Grandmothers to visit them and see their work, changed her position and supported their ongoing efforts to reconnect their grandchildren with their collective identity (Arditti, 1999; Fariña & Lykes, 1991).

Mayan Indigenous Rights in Guatemala

The case of Guatemala further exemplifies the importance of collective rights. Both the Archdiocesan-sponsored report on violations of human rights (ODHAG, 1998) and the official U.N.-sponsored report of the Commission for Historical Clarification (CEH, 1999) have documented thousands of violations of human rights, including the murder of more than 100,000 people, the displacement of more than 1 million people at the peak of this violence, the disappearance of more than 60,000 people, and the destruction of hundreds of rural villages over the 36-year period of the war. In addition, between 100,000 and 250,000 Guatemalan children lost one or both parents between 1981 and 1984, the peak of the government's "scorched earth" policy (see Melville & Lykes, 1992 and Lykes, 1994 for a more extensive discussion of these violations).

Although the violence affected rural and urban populations throughout the country, the weight of its impact was experienced by indigenous groups living within rural communities of the Guatemalan Highlands (Americas Watch Committee, 1984; Amnesty International, 1987). These groups have historically been discriminated against and marginalized from power, resources, and decision-making within Guatemala; the gross violations of this 36-year war are the most recent manifestation of such violence (see, e.g., Amnesty International, 1992; Carmack, 1988).

Michael Richards (1985) interviewed a group of Guatemalan military officers in 1983 and 1984 who were stationed in the Ixil triangle, a remote area within the Guatemalan countryside (Carmack, 1988; Stoll, 1993). Richards quotes officers and soldiers describing the Maya in subhuman categories, such as "lacking reasoning capacity," "lost," "not able to progress," and having "closed thinking" (1985, p. 101). Military personnel that he interviewed concluded that the Maya had been duped by the guerrillas. By labeling these indigenous peasants subhuman, military personnel legitimated their mass murder, extensive enough to become a "partial extermination" of the rural indigenous peoples (Falla, 1984).

After the massive destruction described above, the Guatemalan military's counterinsurgent strategy (ODHAG, 1998; Richards, 1985) shifted to a "guns and beans" program. Survivors of the extermination plan were organized into strategic villages and provided food. The movement of nearly 60,000 people (approximately 12.5 percent of the Highland population, ODHAG, 1998) was controlled in these villages, where they also experienced indoctrination programs that sought to legitimate the army's repressive techniques and convert the civilian population to their side. Analyses of military documents and testimonies gathered by peasants forced into these hamlets confirm the racism implicit in the military's beliefs about the Maya described by Richards (ODHAG, 1998).

To control the rural population through direct and indirect militarization, the army organized men between 18 and 60 years old into the country's civilian defense patrol in the final days of 1981 (America's Watch Committee, 1990; Jay, 1993; ODHAG, 1998). Although alleged to be voluntary, failure to perform weekly duties, which included military and intelligence tasks of the army, had potential deadly consequences for rural boys and men. ODHAG (1998) estimates that by 1982 to 1983 more than 900,000 men were organized in the civilian defense patrols comprising approximately "80 percent of the male populations in rural indigenous zones" at the time. Suárez-Orozco (1990) described the Guatemalan situation as a "culture of terror (Taussig, 1986/1987), with its own vocabulary of sorrow (*desaparecidos* [disappeared]; *torturados* [torture victims]; *huérfanos* [orphans]) and underlying structure [that] managed consensus through violence and intimidation" (p. 361). An America's Watch Report added that Guatemala in the first half of the 1980s was a country where "political terror has

firmly established itself as the principal means of governance" (Brown, 1985, cited in Suárez-Orozco, 1990, p. 361). In the cases of both Argentina and Guatemala the protection of the civil-political rights of an elite citizenry were invoked to legitimate the killing of others, defined as threats to the security of the nation and/or as non-citizens or, in the case of Guatemala, non-humans. Worse, these clearly repressive policies were legitimated and presented as humanitarian using a rhetoric of human rights manipulated by the state.

Amnesty International (1992), among others, has characterized violations of human rights within Guatemala as abuses of Mayan civil and political rights. But I argue here that these direct acts of violence were rooted in ideologies which denied the Maya their humanity. Rhetoric which institutionalized and normalized violence made possible these gross violations of human rights, that as such, illustrate structural violence. The massacres had an impact beyond the sum total of the individuals whose rights were violated. The Maya as a people were violated, in their character as a collectivity. Violence against collective identity also occurs when the environment of traditional peoples is destroyed, because their very identity is rooted in the land, as evidenced in the Maya's self-naming as "people of corn" (Lykes, 1996; see also Winter, 1998).

Messer (1995) has argued that Guatemala "seems to illustrate most vividly the synergisms of political violence, socioeconomic marginalization, and cultural discrimination" (p. 56). The assertion of indigenous rights and the pressure to establish the Draft Declaration as part of the U.N. covenants are important strategies that, if successful, could offer critical protections to the beliefs and social organizations of indigenous people, as well as safeguarding the lands which define who they are.

PEACEBUILDING WITH EXTENDED HUMAN RIGHTS

Peace negotiations culminating in accords signed between the Guatemalan government and Guatemalan National Revolutionary Unity (URNG/guerrilla forces) on December 29, 1996 "ended" more than 36 years of war in Guatemala. The 13 documents that make up the accords confirmed in December, 1996, include agreements on human rights, identity and indigenous rights, procedures for resettling and protecting those uprooted by the armed conflict, socioeconomic and political reforms, and the establishment of a commission to "clarify with objectivity, equity and impartiality, the past human rights violations and acts of violence connected with the armed confrontation that have caused suffering among the Guatemalan people (CEH, 1999). Each accord reflects important negotiations between the former opposition groups, and taken as a whole, they seek to create the conditions necessary for a more democratic political order within Guatemala. The accords have afforded new spaces in which survivors can voice their versions of the horrific violence they experienced, including massacres, military occupation, internal displacement, extreme poverty, and exile to religious and human rights-based commissions established to take these testimonies.

Others, such as women of the Association of Maya Ixil Women—*Ak' saqb' eb'al* [New Dawn] in Chajul, Guatemala, seek more local strategies for telling their stories, hoping to do so within the context of ongoing community programs that will not only heal the psychological wounds from 36 years of war and state-sponsored repression but also establish new social structures to improve their lives and the lives of their children. Within this rural context where I

have worked for eight years, I have been challenged by local women not only to contribute to clarifying contemporary, culturally situated meanings of human rights violations, but to join them in implementing strategies that transform their material and social realities, including extreme poverty and psychosocial trauma. The association's current activities are running a corn mill and community store; conducting an afterschool program in language acquisition and psychosocial assistance for local children ages six to twelve; administering a revolving loan fund in the association; developing a local library; and developing a participatory action research project using photographic and interview techniques. These projects emerged through cross-cultural and transnational interethnic organizing and leadership (see Lykes et al., 1999).

As rural indigenous women, their efforts to redress social injustice and marginalization are embedded in creative workshops that respond directly to their psychosocial trauma, and those of their children (Lykes, 1994). They have also developed a project that combines photography and interview techniques (Wang & Burris, 1994) which actively assists the co-construction of meanings about their experiences of violence and the roots of their oppression. This work includes the development of action plans for change in the local community while facilitating increased control over representations about local community life among the Ixil, thereby enhancing their sense of agency. These women are creating opportunities for sharing among themselves and in ever-widening circles of Maya women, rupturing years of silence, and developing skills and resources to confront some of the individual and collective effects of war, terror, and violence. This work also transforms traditional gender roles within the community. It exemplifies psychological work that creates experiences of material, social, and psychological healing and reparation.

The four generations of human rights described at the outset of this chapter are affirmed by this work of the Association of Maya Ixil Women—*Ak' saqb' eb'al* [New Dawn]. Narrating their stories of the multiple violations of their civil, political, economic, and cultural rights through storytelling, dramatization, and photography, these women heal themselves, their children, and their community. This work constitutes a new praxis, focusing on their actions and their critical reflections upon these actions, which promotes healing, enhances their self-esteem, and rebuilds and transforms Mayan community. These Ixil women are reclaiming the past while creating community-based economic and educational programs in the present. As an "outsider" psychologist, I am privileged to "stand-under" these experiences, accompany these women as they cross cultural, educational, ethnic, linguistic, and geographic borders to envision new understandings of violence and its wake.

There are many other examples of concrete experiences among indigenous peoples that challenge us to explore more carefully the intersection of the four generations of human rights and what it means to harmonize them in theory and through practice. The rights to economic development and a safe environment are clearly evident in the community-based work described which assumes the worldviews of indigenous communities. Future work by psychologists in these contexts could fruitfully explore indigenous and collective rights and how they might inform the reparatory processes that follow peace accords at the end of overt conflict (see Winter, 1998, for a further discussion of the environment and war's effects).

Although the perspectives and experiences presented here offer no easy solutions to violations of human rights described in this chapter, they do sketch promising psychological theories and practices that have contributed alongside an expanded understanding of human rights to clarify how they constitute structural violence. I have argued that a developing liberation psychology, cultural and constructivist perspectives, and praxis with local communities shifts the object of psychological reflection to a social and community level. Recognizing and responding to the abuse of these rights as structural violence is critical if psychologists want to contribute to peacebuilding among the majority of the world's peoples. I am not recommending deserting the important work of defending civil-political rights and protesting their violation. Rather, I have drawn on psychological theory and my own field practice to argue a broader understanding of rights violations as structural violence. My hope is that this analysis will promote work which would improve the social, psychological, and material well-being in communities throughout the world, particularly in zones of ongoing or recent armed conflict.

SECTION III

PEACEMAKING

Introduction by
Richard V. Wagner

In the second half of this volume, we present a series of chapters dealing with ways of responding to violent conflict, real or threatened. We have distinguished between direct and structural violence, the former being episodic and direct from aggressor to target, the latter being indirect and embedded in the social, political, and economic fabric of society. We also distinguish between two major forms of response: *peacemaking* and *peacebuilding*. Peacemaking, the focus of this section, refers to various means of handling direct, episodic violence. Peacebuilding, the focus of the fourth and final section of the book, refers to ways of handling structural violence.

There is a third type of response to violence—*peacekeeping*—which we consider in one chapter in this section. Both peacemaking and peacekeeping refer to procedures that reduce the likelihood that people will engage in violent actions. In peacemaking, however, we try to establish mechanisms that preclude the need for future violence between parties, at least with respect to the particular issues in dispute. Such is the case when a mediator, for example, helps battling parties reach an agreement allowing each to attain an acceptable goal. The next time a dispute arises, they may have learned not to repeat the process of battling to satisfy their respective interests. Of course if they have not, then peacemaking will be necessary again. In peacekeeping, on the other hand, the effort is confined to preventing the parties from engaging in continuing violence, essentially by containing them, keeping them from coming together violently. Peacekeeping can have constructive long-term results: keeping parties apart may give them time to consider the advantages of alternate, nonviolent ways of handling their conflict. But, often the antagonism remains: with the destructive activity suppressed, the pressure to find solutions is removed, leaving the antagonisms in place. Such has been the case in Cyprus: a U.N. peacekeeping force has provided a buffer between Greek and Turk Cypriots since 1964. Neither side has taken the opportunity to find ways of peaceful coexistence, so the peacekeepers must remain to prevent future violence between the adversaries.

POSITIVE AND NEGATIVE APPROACHES

Peacekeeping as a response to episodic violence has sometimes been referred to as a negative approach to peace: only the peacekeeper's presence prevents the violence from recurring. Peacemaking is a more positive approach: building mechanisms that lead people to cooperate in positive, peaceful interaction (Kimmel, 1985). The difference is important because of its implications for peace, be it peace in the family, in the neighborhood, or in the world community (Wagner, 1988). The negative goal, peacekeeping, is essentially reactive and limited by the necessity to operate in a context defined by the adversaries. The ways of keeping peace are few and concrete (Plous, 1988): keeping the parties apart and if possible, disarming them, figuratively or literally. The positive technique of peacemaking, on the other hand, is not so limited and can be innovative. A mediator as peacemaker may help a couple battling over custody of their children to recognize that as permanent co-parents, they share a concern for their children's welfare. The mediator, then, is in a position to work with the couple to create a cooperative agreement that maximizes the children's access to both parents, rather than constantly worrying about how to keep the battlers from sabotaging each other's contact with the children.

CONFLICT RESOLUTION, MANAGEMENT, AND TRANSFORMATION

Conflict resolution, a theme that pervades much of the theory and practice of peacemaking, should be distinguished from conflict management and conflict transformation, terms used in several chapters. Sanson and Bretherton define conflict resolution as a process that "provides techniques to deal with disputes in a manner which is nonviolent, avoids dominance or oppression by one party over the other, and, rather than exploiting one party, aims to meet the human needs of all" (this volume, p. 193). Conflict management may refer to more economic, negotiated procedures for handling disagreement and is sometimes used in the sense of peacekeeping, that is, containing the overt display of conflict without the parties actually ever reaching agreement. Conflict transformation, which appears in several chapters, generally refers to a process of guiding the disputants to a new vision and understanding of the conflict, one in which they not only attain their goals but develop a new, constructive relationship with one another, boding well for the peaceful resolution of future disagreements. Conflict transformation is a basic aspect of the process of peacebuilding. Nevertheless, at times in this section on peacemaking, we will find authors referring to conflict transformation in recognition of the fact that peacemaking often provides only temporary relief from hostilities. Many of them present a vision for the twenty-first century in which conflict is transformed and parties no longer see one another as obstacles to their own goal attainment but rather as partners in the effort to provide a sustainable existence for all.

CULTURE

It is noteworthy that almost every chapter in this section contains an explicit discussion of the cultural relativity of peacemaking techniques. Cultural differences can be seen, for example, on the grand scale comparing Western and non-Western approaches to peacemaking (Pedersen, this volume; Wall & Callister, 1995). They can be seen regionally, for example, within Europe (Shapiro, 1999) or within Latin America (Comas-Díaz, Lykes, & Alarcón,1998; Lykes, this volume). They can be seen within a single society, such as the different ethnic responses to conflict in Bosnia (Agger, this volume) or the differences in the laws governing violence in the ex-slave states and other southern and western states in the United States (Cohen, 1996).

The discussion of culture and peacemaking in this section is rich and varied. Pedersen, for example, presents an extensive discussion of how Western and non-Western peacemaking differs on certain critical dimensions and how these differences can affect the resolution of conflict between people from diverse backgrounds. Sanson and Bretherton agree and note that the conflict resolution processes they describe are predominantly Western. But rather than seeing the cultural difference as *restricting* peacemaking efforts, they argue that the differences should become an integral part of the resolution process, informing the parties about alternate ways of reaching agreement. Coleman and Deutsch, in their proposal for introducing conflict resolution procedures into schools, come to a similar conclusion. They acknowledge that theirs is a Western, male model and recommend that we explore how universal such techniques are and frame our proposals accordingly. Wessells and Monteiro note that Western methods pervade many international efforts to handle conflict, often undermining effective indigenous ways of responding to violent conditions. Similarly, Agger describes the deep ethnic divisions in Bosnia and how inappropriate traditional Western therapeutic procedures have been in the treatment of trauma caused by the war in that nation. All of these authors, then, emphasize that peacemakers should be sensitive to cultural differences in handling conflict. Only in the context of such an understanding can they be truly effective in preventing violence and promoting the peaceful resolution of conflict.

ORGANIZATION OF THE SECTION

The chapters in this section on peacemaking can be divided into three groups: peacekeeping, conflict resolution, and post-war reconstruction. Harvey Langholtz and Peter Leentjes' chapter on U.N. peacekeeping describes the traditional peacekeeping role of the United Nations, i.e., serving as a buffer between warring entities, sometimes between nation states (Egypt and Israel in the Gaza region) and sometimes within states (Greek and Turk Cypriots). However, they continue with a discussion of the additional agendas that have emerged in the past decade, agendas that sound much more like peacemaking: taking an active role in efforts to implement agreements and settlements.

More specific proposals for peacemaking appear in the succeeding four chapters, all of which consider means of resolving conflict constructively. Paul Pedersen's analysis of the cultural context of peacemaking provides a valuable framework for evaluating the generalizability of processes described in succeeding chapters. Pedersen focuses on important differences between Western and non-Western approaches to conflict and its resolution and suggests some non-Western procedures that might be appropriately applied in Western peacemaking. In the next chapter, Ann Sanson and Di Bretherton provide an excellent, detailed overview of principles and processes of conflict resolution as they have evolved in the Western world. The juxtaposition of the Pedersen and Sanson and Bretherton chapters allows for an interesting comparison of procedures used in vastly different cultural settings.

Johan Galtung and Finn Tschudi's chapter on the "transcend" approach to conflict proposes certain strategies for improving quarreling parties' communication, thereby increasing the chances that they will be able to resolve their conflict constructively. While much of their discussion deals with the conscious, cognitive processes involved in dialogue between combatants, they remind us that emotive and subconscious processes can strongly affect the outcome of efforts to reach a satisfactory, nonviolent resolution of conflict.

Recently, Nelson, Van Slyck, and Cardella (1999) concluded from their review of a variety of school programs that "peace education curricula . . . have a potentially significant role to play in the development of peaceful people" (p. 170). In their chapter, Peter Coleman and Morton Deutsch provide a model for introducing such programs into schools. They argue that, for the greatest success, programs must be implemented at five different levels of the educational system: the student disciplinary process, the curriculum, pedagogy, the school culture, and the community. They provide excellent illustrations of how such programs can be realized.

The final three chapters in this section consider how peace psychologists can contribute to reconciliation and reconstruction in the aftermath of violent conflict. Inger Agger describes many of the difficulties confronting the well-meaning psychologist in her captivating chapter on reducing trauma under war conditions in Bosnia. Cheryl de la Rey calls on her experience and understanding of reconciliation, describing the work of the Truth and Reconciliation Commission in South Africa. Both authors highlight the importance of relationships in the process of reconciliation. Agger describes the seemingly irreversible loss of trust among members of different ethnic groups in Bosnia and de la Rey argues that re-establishing relationships must be at the core of any successful attempt to further reconciliation in a society that has endured protracted violent conflict.

Michael Wessells and Carlinda Monteiro echo many of the points made by Agger and de la Rey. They discuss the value of integrating Western and traditional psychosocial interventions to heal the deep wounds caused by over three decades of war in Angola. The task is daunting, given the competing demands of rival militia factions and of citizens traumatized and impoverished by endless bloodshed. Wessells and Monteiro describe a number of reconstruction programs and ultimately focus on the task of reintegrating child soldiers, who have been socialized into a system of violence. Reestablishing relationships is the crux of attempts to reconstruct a society devastated by war.

To summarize, Section III covers a variety of methods for peacemaking and delineates many of the difficulties that the peace psychologist will confront in attempting to help people resolve their conflicts and rebuild relationships. We reiterate our caveat that the principles described should not be applied without giving due consideration to limits in their applicability in different cultures and at different levels of analysis. When successful, peacemaking can set the stage for the more arduous but essential task of building a peaceful society in which the structural institutions are designed to promote human welfare, the theme that will be considered in the fourth and final section of this volume.

CHAPTER 15

U.N. Peacekeeping: Confronting the Psychological Environment of War in the Twenty-first Century

Harvey J. Langholtz and Peter Leentjes

United Nations peacekeeping evolved following the founding of the United Nations in 1945. Throughout the Cold War, U.N. peacekeeping developed as a series of ad hoc responses to individual crises, although the superpowers were always careful to constrain U.N. peacekeeping operations to a limited set of actions to be undertaken only under certain specified conditions. It was not the purview of these peacekeepers to use force themselves or to participate in the conflict. The end of the Cold War brought a period where the superpowers and the world community were willing to see the United Nations attempt more complex and ambitious peacekeeping missions under more difficult conditions and in environments of war and chaos. These more difficult conditions called for a different set of psychological approaches, which included armed peacekeepers using threats, coercion, or force, and sometimes engaging in the fighting.

The attempts by the United Nations to intervene in these demanding environments met with a mixture of success and failure. Soldiers of all nations are trained to

prevail in combat over a clearly defined foe and the traditional soldier's psychology is one of force and intimidation. Soldiers serving on traditional U.N. peacekeeping operations are called upon to use a different set of psychological approaches. Instead of using force to achieve their ends, they use the tools of persuasion and trust to limit fighting between the armies engaged in the conflict. However, recent conflicts have been characterized more often by a complicated mixture of paramilitaries, ethno-political rivalries, humanitarian emergencies, and civilian refugees, than by two clearly defined armies sent to war by sovereign leaders. These complex emergencies present a different psychological environment from earlier conflicts and call for different forms of peacekeeping.

In this chapter, we will trace the development of peacekeeping from the founding of the United Nations to the end of the Cold War, and we will discuss how the close of the Cold War ushered in an era where new approaches to peacekeeping might be undertaken. We will review some of the structural components that contributed to the success or failure of these recent missions, and we will suggest the direction U.N. peacekeeping may take during the early part of the twenty-first century.

THE ORIGINS AND EVOLUTION OF U.N. PEACEKEEPING

The Origins of the United Nations

The United Nations was founded during the closing days of World War II, and it was the goal of the United Nations to prevent a reoccurrence of wars of the scale and scope of the two World Wars. The Charter of the United Nations, which came into force on October 24, 1945, proposed

> To save succeeding generations from the scourge of war which twice in our lifetime has brought untold sorrow to mankind, and to reaffirm faith in fundamental human rights, in the dignity and worth of the human person, in the equal rights of men and women and of nations large and small, and . . . to promote social progress and . . . to ensure that armed force shall not be used, save in the common interest. (United Nations, 1945, pp. 1–2)

However, peacekeeping was never mentioned in the U.N. Charter, but came to be defined through evolution, rather than deliberate planning. United Nations peacekeeping falls somewhere between the pacific settlement of disputes as proposed in Chapter VI of the U.N. Charter, and joint military actions discussed in Chapter VII. The accepted practices of U.N. peacekeeping are known as the unwritten "Chapter six and a half" and are based on the concept of impartial soldiers from neutral nations applying the techniques of conflict resolution to contain and limit violence.

Superpower Limitations and the Evolution of Traditional Peacekeeping

Throughout the Cold War, the two superpowers were reluctant to see the United Nations assume too strong a role in international affairs. If a proposed U.N. peacekeeping mission offered any possible strategic advantage to either the United States or the Soviet Union, the other would veto the resolution in the U.N. Security Council. During these years, therefore, peacekeeping was constrained to a limited range of activities (United Nations, 1990) that would not raise the superpowers' objections. The United Nations would only deploy peacekeepers with the consent of the warring nations, when a cease-fire was in place and the armies disengaged. United Nations peacekeeping was to be a *temporary* measure to maintain a cease-fire while diplomats sought more permanent solutions to fundamentally political problems (Mackinlay & Chopra, 1993). Between 1948 and 1988, the United Nations established only 13 peacekeeping or observer forces (Roberts, 1996), despite more than 80 wars that were fought between nations (and not including the smaller intrastate conflicts) with a toll of 30 million deaths (James, 1990).

The Close of the Cold War and a New Willingness: An Agenda for Peace

With the close of the Cold War and the breakup of the Soviet Union, the political differences that had served to constrain U.N. peacekeeping for over 40 years vanished. In 1992, world leaders gathered at the United Nations for a Security Council Summit and called upon U.N. Secretary General Dr. Boutros Boutros-Ghali, to draft a paper proposing his view of the emerging role the United Nations should play in peacekeeping and international security.

In *An Agenda for Peace,* Boutros-Ghali (1992) proposed that the United Nations and the international community should not simply wait for the outbreak of violence before taking action, but instead should undertake both preventive measures early to avert war, and remedial steps following a cease-fire to hasten a return to a durable peace. He called for a greater willingness to address the basic economic, social, political, and ethnic causes of conflict. *An Agenda for Peace* also called for a greater readiness for the international community to support the United Nations in the use of force when necessary to end violence by imposing peace on behalf of a civilian population in the face of war.

THE 1990s AND A NEW PEACE OPERATIONS ENVIRONMENT

Following *An Agenda for Peace,* a wider scope of U.N. peacekeeping missions were undertaken in the absence of an agreed-upon cease-fire, when the conflicts were intranational, not international, and without the consent of the parties to the conflict. Several general types of operations emerged.

1. *Traditional Peacekeeping Operations,* functioning as they did throughout the Cold War. Unarmed or lightly armed peacekeepers would be deployed with the consent of the parties to the dispute to monitor an agreed-upon cease-fire.
2. *Implementation of Complex Agreements and Settlements,* the U.N. force supervising or monitoring agreements which include not just military, but also extensive civilian components.
3. *Preventive Deployment,* the positioning of armed peacekeepers, without the consent of one or both nations involved, to serve as a preventive military barrier and discourage cross-border aggression.

4. *Observing a Non-U.N. Peacekeeping Force,* a way for the United Nations to assist a regional organization or other local force to maintain peace. This is a way for the United Nations to decentralize the maintenance of peace and security while ensuring the legitimacy and international standards of the peacekeeping force.
5. *Providing Humanitarian Aid,* where soldiers are deployed to provide security and transportation for aid workers, and to escort refugees to safety.
6. *Peace Enforcement,* the use of military force to impose the will of the international community on violators of the peace.

Changing Precepts of Peacekeeping

These newer, more assertive peace interventions require a new set of precepts from those that were operative for traditional peacekeeping.

First, the original requirement that peacekeepers would only be deployed with the consent of the participants to the conflict, is no longer observed. Experience has shown that consent may be a fundamental condition for the eventual success of a peacekeeping mission but it may be possible for the presence of peacekeepers to bring about an *induced consent,* which can lead to peace.

Second, today there is a willingness to abridge the precept of sovereignty, especially when internal conditions have deteriorated catastrophically.

Third, impartiality remains an important precept of modern peacekeeping, especially where an agreement has been signed by the parties in conflict.

Fourth, peacekeeping may now include early measures to avert escalation into a violent conflict, steps to contain a conflict geographically once it begins, and measures to hasten a reconciliation and a return to a stable peace.

Fifth, there may be time constraints and limits on the resources, political effort, and military sacrifice the United Nations and the international community will be willing to expend on a conflict.

Sixth, peacekeeping may now require a willingness to take military action.

Some Successes and Some Failures: Is It Better to Have Tried?

As the United Nations has attempted to intervene in increasingly chaotic and demanding environments there has been a mixture of both success and failure. The U.N. mission in Haiti reintroduced free elections and legitimate self-governance to the nation and helped with the reestablishment of Haiti's own police force and law-enforcement institutions. The U.N. missions in Mozambique succeeded in holding democratic elections and the U.N. interventions in Cambodia helped bring factions together, ending armed conflict. Only time will tell if these successes prove to be the initial steps to durable solutions or if they will subsequently be viewed as well-intended efforts that collapsed shortly after the peacekeepers left.

There have also been some well-publicized failures. The U.N. peace force in Yugoslavia could not prevent atrocities from occurring even in so-called safe havens. The U.N. peacekeeping force in Cyprus, originally intended to be a temporary measure, continues after more than three decades (United Nations, 1996). The U.N. force in Somalia was able to provide humanitarian aid to famine-torn regions but in Mogadishu was capable of doing little more than guarding itself.

These new and messy conflicts brought enormous challenges to the United Nations and the international community, and the struggle to come to grips with these chaotic situations was tentative. Would it have been better to sit by and wait for these conflicts to take a form that would suit traditional peacekeeping, or was it better to attempt constructive interventions? The United Nations, and the nations that contributed troops to these missions, paid a high price, both in terms of casualties to peacekeeping personnel, damage to the reputation of the United Nations, and the amount of support a skeptical public was willing to provide.

This dilemma is likely to be among the most fundamental questions to face the institution of peacekeeping during the first part of the twenty-first century. There may be little point in the United Nations insisting that a conflict conform to a rigid set of prerequisites before a peacekeeping mission is attempted. In the next section, we will discuss lessons the United Nations could learn from the challenges of these recent missions and how it can prepare itself to cope more effectively with such situations in the future.

LESSONS LEARNED

Indispensable Ingredients: Mandate, Outcome, Means, Intelligence, and Media

There has been much interest in identifying the reasons for the success or failure of recent peacekeeping missions (Durch, 1996; Maren, 1997; Roberts, 1996; Schear, 1996; Vaccaro, 1996). It is difficult to draw any conclusive generalizations about what may cause peacekeeping missions to succeed or fail but it is worth exploring five of the key findings generated by the U.N. Lessons Learned Unit.

First, mandates of peacekeeping operations need to be clear and precise, yet flexible and based on the realities that exist in the conflict situation. "Only on the basis of accurate information should a practicable mandate be formulated or a determination made of whether the United Nations should even establish a peacekeeping operation" (Stiftung, 1996, p. 5).

Second, there is a need to determine the political outcome that will stem from the successful pursuit of the mandate. In the Somalian mission, no overall plan of action was ever clearly established. In Eastern Slavonia, on the other hand, the mandate for the operation was relatively clear and precise, and specifically included several nonmilitary interventions, such as monitoring the voluntary return of refugees and establishing and training a transitional police force. This clear and detailed mandate permitted the U.N. Special Representative of the Secretary General to formulate the strategic plan for the mission with confidence.

Third, there must be sufficient resources and mandates must be matched with the means to implement them. The mismatch of the forces vis à vis the mandate in Somalia, where the U.N. mission tried to achieve the impossible, and the failure to provide sufficient resources to the mission in Rwanda, are glaring examples of what happens when the mandate exceeds the means for implementation. United Nations peacekeepers in Somalia could not address the social and political complexities of fighting war lords, and in Rwanda the international community was simply not willing to provide the military force that would have been needed to prevent the slaughter of a half a million Tutsis and moderate Hutus in the genocide of 1994. In contrast, the provision of needed levels of resources in Namibia, Mozambique, Haiti, and Eastern Slavonia represent the alternate approach. More than adequate resources—equipment, money, and personnel—were pro-

vided, allowing the United Nations to undertake its mandate with relative success.

Fourth, intelligence must be included as an essential component of peace operations. Although the concept of "military intelligence" may carry an undeserved sinister association for some, U.N. peacekeeping requires an in-depth understanding of the conflict, based on ample intelligence from member states and solid political analysis. Only on that basis can a clear mandate be formulated and the operational means assembled to achieve it. From the Congo operation, where the intelligence service did not exist, to Eastern Slavonia, where there was a staffed military component within the mission staff, the development of an information/intelligence capacity has assisted commanders in better managing their operations, reacting to possible threats, and better understanding the political, military, and social environment of their area of responsibility.

Fifth, an effective public information strategy should be established by the United Nations to provide a direct channel of communications with the local population as soon as a peacekeeping mission is deployed. Experience has shown correlations between the presence of information strategy and mission success. The U.N. radio station in Cambodia was judged instrumental in the education of the population and in convincing them to vote. The responsible agency, staffed by expatriate Kmer language and culture experts, would go out among the people in the remotest regions of the country and explain to them what the United Nations was doing there, why, and how long it would remain (Ahlquist, 1996). In contrast, the U.N. mission in Somalia, although the best-covered U.N. operation from the media viewpoint, lost the media war. Radio, the key in the Somali oral society, was not set up and proved to be a serious shortfall in getting the U.N. message out (Giuliani et al., 1995).

What If There Is No Political Will?

Political motivation and political persuasion are critical elements in a peace process. When the parties are genuinely interested in a settlement, mountains can be moved in the interests of peace. However in chaotic conditions in which power has devolved to splinter factions which have no real interests in peace, there are palpable limits to what the international community can accomplish. A sense of community—the will to reconcile—cannot be imposed. (United Nations, 1997, p. 2)

Comprehensive peace agreements should be the foundation of any deployment of a peace operation. Consent of the parties is ideal such as occurred with the deployment of the U.N. operations in Mozambique and Angola. Yet in the confused situations found in many war-torn regions, particularly during intra-state conflicts, consent may be fleeting. At this point inducement may be the answer.

Inducement operations are conceived . . . to restore civil society by two methods where it has broken down: (1) the use of positive incentives (rewards) to induce, in the first instance, consent and cooperation with the peace operation and, beyond that, reconciliation; and (2) the threat of coercion to gain the consent and cooperation, however grudging of those who are unresponsive to positive incentives. (Annan, 1996, p. 3)

Civilian, Military, and Diplomatic: Integrative Approaches

To achieve maximum effectiveness, the civilian and military components in a peacekeeping operation must work together and coordinate their joint efforts toward shared goals. Recent complex emergencies have seen a need for the integration and coordination of military resources and humanitarian nongovernmental organizations (NGOs). Twenty-eight different NGOs provided humanitarian aid during the Kurdish crisis of 1991, 78 participated in Somalia, 170 in Rwanda, and over 400 in Haiti (National Defense University, 1996). In cases such as these, a common vision needs to be established within the broad context of the mission to coordinate military and humanitarian efforts. This should be based on a consensus on how to proceed without stripping individual agencies of their independence or autonomy. Military and civilian components need to be cognizant of the operating parameters of the other. Both face serious operating constraints with civilian agencies no longer seen as neutral or facing any less dangers than the military.

Diplomatic activity is central to peace operations. The importance of diplomatic success may be seen in essentially all peacekeeping missions but was most clear in Cambodia and the former Yugoslavia (Perkins, 1998). Perhaps the greatest challenge in the political realm is defining objectives at the strategic level to which all the players can subscribe. There will rarely be complete agreement by all parties on end-states, but for effective interagency coordination, the extent to which there is a commonly pursued goal must be made clear at the highest level (Last & Vought, 1994).

Peacekeeping can no longer be treated as a distinct element that is undertaken in isolation from peacemaking and peacebuilding. Patrick Rechner of the Canadian Pearson Peacekeeping Centre makes an important argument:

. . . the key to linking peace making, peacekeeping and peace building functions is to do so both at the macro and micro levels, working pro-actively at both levels and shifting the focus of efforts between the two as obstacles crop up or local leaders become intransigent. Moreover each of these three functions must be directed at specific aspects of a conflict structure. (Rechner, 1998, p. 5)

From this integration devolve some of the absolutely vital tasks that must begin immediately as a peacekeeping operation is deployed. These include demilitarization, disarmament, demining, law and order training and monitoring of a local police force, human rights monitoring and reintegration of public institutions. They must be considered constituent elements of a secure environment.

Today, security is increasingly understood not just in military terms, and as far more than the absence of conflict. It is in fact a phenomenon that encompasses economic development, social justice, environmental protection, democratization, disarmament and respect for human rights. These goals—these pillars of peace—are interrelated. (Annan, 1997b, p. 4)

THE FACE OF FUTURE PEACEKEEPING: A NEW PARADIGM

Dealing with Complex Humanitarian Emergencies

Although the threat of interstate conflict will not disappear over the foreseeable future, the operating environment for peace operations will clearly focus on intrastate conflict.

These intra-state ethnic conflicts are not going to disappear—they may be the pattern of the future which will be marked on the one hand by the creation of large economic and even political spaces in which internal boundaries will be practically meaningless and, on the other hand by internal conflict and fragmentation of states, usually states in transition, with much bloodshed. (Annan, 1996, p. 3)

These can best be described as complex humanitarian emergencies, and the threats they produce include civil strife; mass dislocations of people both internally and externally; economic collapse; famine; starvation; epidemics; disease; and gross violations of human rights. Within this context, any future paradigm for action must include not only the military capability to impose order in an environment of chaos, but also the humanitarian capability to provide protection, food, water, and shelter to refugees, and the capacity to assist with the full recovery and rebuilding of society in the aftermath of war.

To succeed in bringing relief and order to such chaotic environments, many future U.N. peacekeeping operations will straddle the boundary between peacekeeping and peace enforcement. These types of missions with elements from the enforcement side of the spectrum have presented new problems for the United Nations and the controversial missions in Bosnia, Somalia, and Rwanda have helped to generate conservatism in member states. The United Nations will continue to be asked to conduct multidimensional missions and indications are that the Security Council will continue to ask the Secretary General to perform operations outside the boundaries of traditional peacekeeping. The United Nations must face the problems it is presented and solve them with the appropriate tools, procedures and resources.

In the new paradigm, the scope of peace operations in the twenty-first century will remain broad and incorporate some of the tools previously available: embargoes, blockades, and "all means necessary" for the military enforcement of peace. Forces will be equipped and mandated to accomplish more robust tasks, including preventive deployment, peace enforcement, and other tasks that call on peacekeepers to use the force of arms to impose peace. Enforcement measures may be taken proactively, or may be used under more limited rules of engagement and only to ensure compliance with consent-based agreements. Another progressive step may be the utilization of more technologically advanced equipment to monitor these agreements in order to reduce the need to use force.

Future peacekeeping will almost certainly be a joint venture by a variety of organizations: political, democratic, diplomatic (Perkins, 1998), humanitarian (Wessells, 1998), human rights, media, military, civilian police (Vaccaro, 1998), and electoral (Pagani, 1998). Peacekeeping will also be carried out under conditions of uncertainty and great personal danger to the participants. Political leadership, the military, civilian police, humanitarian agencies, civilian support staff, and developmental staffs must all act in concert during complex multidimensional humanitarian emergencies if success is to be achieved.

The Component Chiefs—both military and civilian—of future missions must recognize there will be no simple military solution to conflict. Military operations can buy time, jump-start an operation, and respond more quickly in a crisis to reduce the levels of violence, disorder, or starvation. But these procedures must be accompanied by long-term political and humanitarian efforts designed to resolve the bases of the conflict.

Another danger for the leaders and planners of future peacekeeping missions is that when the military arrives, other components may be inclined to stand down until it is their turn again. Political efforts must continue while troops are on the ground to ensure their contribution is not wasted. Other components have roles to play in order to reestablish stability and put the peace process back on track. In the former Yugoslavia, the political efforts needed to implement the terms of the 1995 Dayton Peace Accord seemed to slow to a crawl with the arrival of NATO's Implementation Force (IFOR). The presence of a force is a tool in the integrated peace process, not a solution. What happens when the forces are withdrawn? Will this lead to another failed effort? To achieve a coordinated outcome and avoid failure, the mission management structure must integrate efforts of all the mission components simultaneously.

Operations are and will continue to be multidimensional in nature. Future missions will almost always include aspects of many tasks. Tasks performed within the framework of traditional peacekeeping will continue and traditional techniques will continue to be applicable. In the end, the basic principles of peacekeeping doctrine remain as important as they ever were, but perhaps the emphasis and how they are applied has changed as a result of the new paradigm. A brief examination is in order:

Unity of Purpose—Leadership is the key to achieving this goal. Doctrinal conflicts between mission participants, linguistic barriers, different levels of capability, and different levels of training will all impact on the unity of purpose. A principal challenge for leaders in peace operations will be to overcome these internal obstacles in the organization and operation of the mission.

Use of Force—The use of force needs to be considered in the context of the mission area. The use of force may range from the use of coercion, sanctions, or embargoes, to the simple presence of the peacekeeper on the ground, to the application of lethal force by appropriately equipped military units. The decision to use the force needs to balance with the end-state goals of the integrated mission. However, the critical aspect is that peacekeeping must always be backed up with credible force. "You can do a lot with diplomacy, but of course you can do a lot more with diplomacy backed up by fairness and force" (Annan, 1998).[1]

Consensus Planning—In this multidimensional environment, the need to utilize an integrated planning process to ensure that the unity of purpose is woven into all aspects of the plan will be crucial to success. Trying to plan a series of military activities without consideration for the impact on humanitarian or other operations in the mission area may incite disputes ranging from the allocation of resources to a lack of trust and confidence between agencies in the area.

Simplicity—Complex operations need to be broken down into clear achievable tasks, which will make the goals of the mission more apparent to the parties of the conflict and other agencies in the mission area. Additionally, clearly stated goals avoid the "CNN effect" whereby sympathetic viewers worldwide call for the United Nations to undertake more than may be possible in terms of peacekeeping and humanitarian interventions (Jakobsen, 1996).

It is improbable that the Security Council will take a traditional, retrenching approach to peace operations in the future. The overall change in the global context of peacekeeping presents the United Nations with a new ideal that requires a shift from traditional peacekeeping to a refinement in the planning, management, and execution of complex, multi-dimensional operations. There must be a focus on political solutions or achievable end states supplemented by forces mandated and resourced to accomplish them.

How Is the U.N. Community Responding to Changes in the Operational Environment?

It is clear that the Member States of the United Nations have realized that change is occurring rapidly. Although few new missions were authorized by the Security Council during the period 1996 to 1998, troop-contributing nations have been preparing themselves with the expectation that this may change. Training has improved and includes multinational exercises held to teach soldiers methods and techniques for the conduct of peacekeeping operations. Self-paced correspondence courses are offered to instruct peacekeepers world-wide on procedural, conceptual, legal, and administrative aspects of peacekeeping (Langholtz, 1998).

Strengthening of the mechanisms for planning and management, human rights monitoring, humanitarian relief, rapid deployment—all indicate that the community, whether individual member state, agency, or secretariat department are voting through action. Annan (1997a) believes that the U.N. community will be better prepared in the future because they have a clearer understanding of the limits and continuing usefulness of peacekeeping. Past setbacks have demonstrated the risk of dispatching peacekeepers with inadequate resources. Finally, Annan asserts, the U.N. member states recognize that inaction is not an acceptable response to massive violence that threatens international peace and security.

---

[1]Quotes from Annan (1998) can be found in "The Quotable Kofi Annan, Selections from Speeches by the Secretary General," New York: The Department of Public Information, p. 12.

CONCLUSION

The United Nations was built upon the ashes of World War II and was designed to avert a repeat of the scale of wars that had twice plagued the world during the first half of the twentieth century. Peacekeeping was not written into the U.N. Charter but evolved nevertheless throughout the Cold War for use only under certain conditions and only when the nature of the conflict fit with what traditional peacekeeping could offer.

The end of the Cold War brought a willingness for the community of nations to attempt more risky peacekeeping missions, while fighting is still going on, where boundaries and sovereignty are not clearly defined, and where the psychological environment is characterized by polarization, hatred, revenge, and suspicion. "Where in the past (wars) generally arose from aggression across national frontiers, the wars of the 21st century will more likely be between ethnic, religious, ideological, or tribal factions within the same country" (Schlesinger, 1997, p. 12). "The sources of conflict and war are pervasive and deep. To reach them will require our utmost effort to enhance respect for human rights and fundamental freedoms" (Boutros-Ghali, 1992, p. 2).

There is every reason to believe that the first part of the twenty-first century will witness a continuation of these intranational conflicts. It will not be possible to define, control, or understand these conflicts using the political and psychological assumptions that were suitable for peacekeeping operations from the founding of the United Nations to the close of the Cold War. Instead, the twenty-first century is likely to see multidimensional military and civilian peacekeeping missions deployed in settings of war and anarchy, not only to impose peace, but also for the purposes of peacemaking, peacebuilding, demining, humanitarian aid, election monitoring, and assisting with the reinstitution of the fabric of civil life that will nurture an enduring and self-sustaining peace.

CHAPTER 16

THE CULTURAL CONTEXT OF PEACEMAKING

Paul B. Pedersen

Conflict is a natural aspect of any relationship. Conflict may be positive or negative, that is, functional or dysfunctional. Whereas negative conflict threatens to erode the growth and development of a relationship, positive conflict can actually strengthen relationships, especially when the parties in conflict share fundamental values.

One of the major difficulties peacemakers confront in conflicts between groups from different cultures is the uncertainty about cultural values. Peaceful resolution of intercultural conflict often involves the parties acknowledging their shared values and mutually appreciating their cultural differences. However, in intercultural conflict resolution even when different cultural groups share the same values, their behavioral expression of these values may differ. Not only can different behaviors have the same meaning, the same behavior can have different meanings. Therefore, it is important to interpret each behavior in its cultural context. In order to intervene constructively in intercultural conflict, it is essential that a peacemaker understand both the basic values of the cultures and the behavioral expressions of these values. The peacemaker is then in a good position to help the parties empathize with one another and to gauge how best to approach

them in the context of their own conflict resolution processes.

A consistent weakness of many international peacemaking efforts derives from the cultural insularity of the practitioners, especially the insensitivity of Western peacemakers to the cultural context of non-Western groups in conflict. Lund, Morris, and LeBaron-Duryea (1994) suggest that culture-centered models which incorporate a culturally sensitive approach to conflict may be more appropriate than any universal ("one-size-fits-all") model of intervention. It is the purpose of this chapter to explore, clarify, and propose methods of meeting the critical need to incorporate cultural understanding into the peacemaking process. In the first section, I present a culture-centered perspective on conflict. Then, I compare Western and non-Western models of peacemaking, contrasting the collectivist model invoked in the Asia-Pacific region with the individualistic model of the West. In the third section, I describe in detail certain features of the Chinese and Hawaiian conflict resolution systems to exemplify some non-Western peacemaking procedures which could prove useful in the West. In the fourth section, I present the Cultural Grid, a model that helps identify the complexity of culture and guides the training of people to manage conflict in multicultural settings. Finally, I turn to prospects for the future, noting the growing importance of cultural understanding and certain cultural fictions that must be set aside if we are to promote peace effectively in the twenty-first century.

A CULTURE-CENTERED PERSPECTIVE ON CONFLICT

The ways that conflicts between groups are managed reflect each group's culturally acquired patterns of attitudes and beliefs. These patterns may involve punishing wrongdoers, repairing strained or broken relationships, depending on courts or legal systems or relying on informal social pressure through teasing, gossip, exclusion, and supernatural forces. These typical ways of perceiving and responding to conflict are so natural to ingroup members of a culture that they assume their perspectives can be applied in other cultures (Fry & Bjorkqvist, 1997).

The impact of culture on conflict has important implications. First, misunderstandings may occur as groups in conflict interpret the behavior of outsiders according to the cultural rules of insiders. Second, conflict may not be resolved when groups in conflict seek quick and easy answers by forcing their own cultural perspective on one another. Third, a better understanding of the impact of culture on conflict may allow us to adapt others' peacemaking strategies to enlarge our own repertoire.

Peacemaking requires that both parties to a conflict be able to accurately understand the conflict from the other side's point of view. In a failing conflictual process, two groups are frustrated in their efforts to achieve agreement by an inability (or unwillingness) to accurately interpret or understand each other's perspective. In contrast, when conflicting groups adopt a culture-centered perspective, they actively seek meaning in the other's actions and proactively try to make their own actions understandable to the other (Dubinskas, 1992). By jointly constructing cultural meaning, the cultural differences are not erased. Instead, the cultural integrity of all parties is preserved and a new basis for intercultural cooperation and coordination is constructed as a metaphoric bridge to an island of common ground for both sides of the dispute.

WESTERN AND NON-WESTERN MODELS OF PEACEMAKING

Individualistic vs. Collectivistic Cultures

Non-Western cultures have typically been associated with "collectivistic" perspectives, while Western cultures have typically been associated with "individualistic" value systems (Kim, Triandis, Kagitcibasi, Choi, & Yoon, 1994). One difference between the two value systems is that individualism describes societies where the connections between people are loose, and each person is expected to look after him or herself. Collectivism describes cultures where people are part of strong cohesive ingroups which protect them in exchange for unquestioned lifetime loyalty (Hofstede, 1991). Differences on the individualism-collectivism dimension can lead to problems. For instance, the concept of individual freedom is a reflection of an individualistic value and it would be improper to impose such a value on a collectivistic society.

A second difference is that in non-Western collectivistic cultures, one of the ways to manage disagreement between people is through the use of quoted proverbs or stories that give guidance on how to manage power differentials, handle disputes, locate mediators or go-betweens, and how to achieve mutually satisfactory settlements (Augsburger, 1992). For example, Watson-Gegeo and White (1990) describe how Pacific Islanders prefer the term "disentangling" over the more individualistic notions of conflict resolution or dispute management. Disentangling is more a process than an outcome and the image of a tangled net or line blocking purposeful activity has a practical emphasis as well as implying the ideal state where the lines of people's lives are "straight." Katz (1993) likewise talks about "the straight path" as a healing tradition of Fiji with spiritual dimensions of health for the individual and for society.

A third difference is the notion of self. In Western societies, the self is grounded intrapsychically in self-love, self-definition, and self-direction. In the solidarity of a collectivistic setting, the self is not free. It is bound by mutual role obligations and duties, structured and nurtured in an ongoing process of give-and-take in facework negotiations. In the West, there must be high consistency between public face and private self-image. In the East, the self is not an individual but a relational construct" (Augsburger, 1992, p. 86).

High and Low Context Cultures

Another way of distinguishing cultures is the degree to which context matters.

> Low context cultures generally refer to groups characterized by individualism, overt communication and heterogeneity. The United States, Canada and Central and Northern Europe are described as areas where low context cultural practices are most in evidence. High context cultures feature collective identity-focus, covert communication and homogeneity. This approach prevails in Asian countries including Japan,

China and Korea as well as Latin American countries. (Hall, 1976, p. 39)

Gudykunst and Ting-Toomey (1988) have made similar distinctions: Low-context cultures are likely to emphasize the individual rather than the group, be concerned about autonomy rather than inclusion, be direct rather than indirect, take a controlling style of confrontation rather than an obliging style, and be competitive rather than collaborative. To illustrate, Hall (1976) contrasts the American (low-context) with the Japanese (high-context) perspective regarding justice. In a Japanese trial, the accused, the court, the public, and the injured parties come together in a collaborative effort to settle the dispute. In the United States, the function of a trial is to focus on the crime, confront the perpetrator, and affix blame in a way that the criminal and society see the consequences.

Gudykunst and Ting-Toomey associate high- and low-context with collectivism and individualism, respectively. While low-context persons view indirect conflict management as weak, cowardly, or evasive, members of high-context cultures view direct conflict management as impolite and clumsy. While low-context persons separate the conflict issue from the person, high-context cultures see the issue and person as interrelated. While low-context persons seek to manage conflict toward an objective and fair solution, high-context cultures focus on the affective, relational, personal, and subjective aspects which preclude open conflict. While low-context cultures have a linear and logical worldview which is problem-oriented and sensitive to individuals, high-context cultures see the conflict, event, and all actors in a unified, holistic context. While low-context cultures value independence focused on autonomy, freedom, and personal rights, high-context cultures value inclusion, approval, and association.

Table 16.1   Differences between Low- and High-context Cultures

Low Context	High Context
Individual participants must first accept and acknowledge that there is a conflict before resolution/mediation can begin.	Traditional groups must first accept and acknowledge that there is a conflict before resolution/mediation can begin.
Conflict and resolution/mediation process must often be kept private.	Conflict is not private and must be made public before the resolution/mediation process can begin.
Conflict management trains an individual to negotiate/mediate or resolve conflict reactively.	Social conflict management emphasizes monitoring or mediating stress in a proactive manner.
Resolution and mediation are individually defined by the individuals involved in the conflict.	Conflict and its resolution/mediation are defined by the group or culture.
Settlements are usually devoid of ritual and spirituality.	Settlements are most often accompanied by ritual and spirituality.
Negotiations are face-to-face and confidential.	Negotiations are indirect (through intermediaries) and public.
Preference for court settlements.	Relying on courts to resolve/mediate conflict is regarded as a failure.

Using data from a 1994 conference on "Conflict resolution in the Asia Pacific Region," Pedersen and Jandt (1996) developed some hypotheses about how high- and low-context cultures experience conflict differently. These hypotheses are presented in Table 16.1.

Western cultures have typically been associated with more individualistic perspectives with less emphasis on the importance of context. Non-Western cultures have typically been more collectivistic with more emphasis on the importance of context. Of course, neither of these two perspectives is right or wrong or exclusively Western or non-Western. Nevertheless, in any conflict involving parties from different cultures, peacemakers need to be sensitive to the different rules that apply to peacemaking in each culture. An examination of conflict in a high-context culture located in the Asian-Pacific region of the world, can help illustrate many of the principles of peacemaking across cultures.

CONFLICT IN AN ASIAN-PACIFIC CONTEXT: A CASE STUDY

The Asian-Pacific perspective is unique in several ways, as described by a Chinese mediator. "We who engage in mediation work should use our mouths, legs and eyes more often. This means we should constantly explain the importance of living in harmony and dispense legal education. We should also pay frequent visits to people's houses and when we hear or see any symptoms of disputes we should attempt to settle them before they become too serious" (Barnes, 1991, p. 26).

The Concept of "Face"

Conflict management in the Asian context has been described as face maintenance, face saving, face restoration, or face loss (Duryea, 1992). The concept of "face" is Chinese in origin as a literal translation of the Chinese term *lian,* representing the confidence of society in the integrity of moral character. Without moral character, individuals cannot function in their community (Hu, 1945). One loses face when an individual or group or someone representing the group fails to meet the requirements of their socially defined role or position. Face can become more important than life itself as the evaluation of the self by the community is essential to identity. What one thinks of self is less important than what one thinks *others* think. Ting-Toomey (1994) defines the concept of face in conflict management as important in all communications.

The traditional Chinese approach to conflict resolution is based on saving face for *all* parties by the choices each makes regarding personal goals and interpersonal harmony. This approach follows the Confucian tradition in which the choice between personal goals and interpersonal harmony depends on the particular *nature* of the relationship between conflicted parties (Hwang, 1998). When a subordinate is in conflict with a superior he or she must protect the superior's face to maintain interpersonal harmony. Opinions are expressed indirectly, and any personal goal must be achieved privately while pretending to obey the superior.

When the conflict involves horizontal relationships among "ingroup" members, they may communicate directly, and to protect harmony they may give face to each other through compromise. If, however, one insists on his or her personal goal in spite of the feelings of the other, the fight may continue for a long time. If both parties insist on their conflicting personal goals, they may treat the other as an "outgroup" member and confront that person directly, disregarding harmony and protecting their own face. A third party might be required to mediate this conflict and it may result in destroying the relationship.

Hwang (1998) describes the Confucian relationships of father/son, husband/wife, senior/junior brother, and superior/subordinate in a vertical structure emphasizing the value of harmony. "When one is conflicting with someone else within his or her social network, the first thing one has to learn is *forbearance* . . . In its broadest sense, forbearance means to control and to suppress one's emotion, desire and psychological impulse" (p. 28). Therefore a subordinate must obey and endure the superior's demands, relying on indirect communication from some third party in their social network to communicate with the superior. Because Confucian rules of *politeness* require both sides to "care about the other's face" at least superficially, conflict among ingroup members may not be evident to outsiders. In a family, for example, members take care of each other's face in front of outsiders to maintain superficial harmony by obeying publicly and defying privately (Gao & Ting-Toomey, 1998)

Ho'oponopono

One Pacific Islands model for peacemaking and managing conflict is through *ho'oponopono,* which means "setting to right" in the Hawaiian language. The traditional Hawaiian cultural context emphasizes cooperation and harmony. The extended family, or *ohana,* is the foundation of traditional Hawaiian society, . . . [and] successful maturation of a person in the Hawaiian culture thus requires that an individual cultivate an accurate ability to perceive and attend to other people's needs, often without being asked" (Shook, 1985, p. 6). Unregulated conflict disrupts balance and harmony, requires self-scrutiny, admission of wrongdoing, asking forgiveness, and restitution to restore harmony. Illness becomes a punishment that occurs when one ignores the social pressure against taking negative actions or having negative feelings toward others.

The traditional *ho'oponopono* approach to problem solving and conflict management begins with prayer, asking God for assistance and placing the process in a cosmic or spiritual context. This is followed by identification, which means sharing strength to solve the family's problems by reaching out to the persons causing disruption to establish a favorable climate. The problem is then described in a way that ties the person who was wronged and the wrongdoer together in an entanglement. Then the many different dimensions of the entanglement problem are explored and clarified, one by one. As each aspect is identified through discussion, the layers or tangles of the problem are reorganized until family relationships are again in harmony. Individuals who have been wronged are encouraged to share their feelings and perceptions and to engage in honest, open self-scrutiny. If the group discussion is disrupted by emotional outbursts, the leader may declare a period of silence for family members to regain harmony in their discussion. Following this is the sincere confession of wrongdoing, where the wrongdoer seeks forgiveness and agrees to restitution. Untangling the negative then joins both the wronged and the wrongdoer in a mutual release and restores their cosmic and spiritual harmony. A closing spiritual ceremony reaffirms the family's strength and bond.

Attempts to adapt *ho'oponopono* to Westernized contexts have applied those aspects of (1) recognizing the importance of conflict management in a spiritual context, (2) channeling the discussion with sanctions of silence should disruption occur, and (3) bringing the wrongdoer back into the community as a full member with complete restitution and forgiveness. Understanding a radically different dispute resolution system should help peacemakers become more sensitive to whatever cultural differences they encounter in their work.

THE CULTURAL GRID

Hines and Pedersen (1980) introduced and developed The Cultural Grid to help identify and describe the complexity of a cultural context in a way that would suggest research hypotheses and guide the training of people to manage conflict in multicultural settings. Table 16.2 presents the Within-Person Cultural Grid. The grid provides a conceptual framework that demonstrates how cultural and personal variables interact in a combined context, linking each behavior (what you did) to expectations, each expectation to values (why you did it), and each value to the social system (where you learned to do it). Each cultural context is complicated and dynamic so that each value is taught by many teachers, with different values becoming salient in different situations. Multicultural self-awareness means being able to identify what you did (behavior), why you did it (expectation and value), and where you learned to do it (culture-teachers).

The Within-Person Cultural Grid is intended to show the complex network of culturally learned patterns behind each behavior in a chain of logic from teachers to values and expectations to the behavior. The dangers of interpreting behaviors "out of context" are apparent once the contextual linkage of behaviors to expectations, values, and social systems has been demonstrated. Cultural conflict can arise when the context of behavior is not interpreted appropriately. For example, our cultural teachers may have taught us the value of being fair and might have communicated that we should "do unto others as you would have them do unto you." Someone from an-

Table 16.2   Within-Person Cultural Grid

Cultural Teachers	Personal Variables		
	Where you learned to do it (teachers)	Why you did it (values and expect.)	What you did (behavior)

1.Family relationships
   relatives
   fellow countrypersons
   ancestors
   shared beliefs			

2. Power relationships
   social friends
   sponsors and mentors
   subordinates
   supervisors and
      superiors			

3. Memberships
   co-workers
   organizations
   gender and age
      groups
   workplace colleagues			

4. Non-family
      relationships
   friendships
   classmates
   neighbors
   people like me			

other culture might share the same value (i.e., being fair), but there may be differences in which behaviors are viewed as indications of fairness. If you focus only on the behavior out of context, a misunderstanding may occur.

In order to examine interpersonal processes, we now consider another cultural grid. The Between-Persons Cultural Grid is illustrated in Table 16.3. This grid describes the relationship between two people or groups by separating what was done (behaviors) from why it was done (expectations).

The Between-Persons Cultural Grid includes four quadrants. Each quadrant explains parts of a conflict between two individuals or groups, recognizing that the salience of each quadrant may change over time and across situations (Pedersen, 1993). In the first quadrant (same behavior, same expectation), two individuals have similar behaviors and similar positive expectations. The relationship is congruent and harmonious and there are positive shared expectations behind the behavior. Both persons are smiling (behavior) and both persons expect

Table 16.3   Between-Persons Cultural Grid

Why It Was Done (expectation)	What Was Done? (behavior)	
	Same action	Different action
Perceived same and positive reason		
Perceived different and negative reason		

friendship (expectation). There is little conflict in this quadrant.

In the second quadrant, two individuals or groups have different behaviors but share the same positive expectations. There is a high level of agreement in that both persons expect trust and friendliness. However, if behavior is interpreted out of context, it is likely to be incorrectly seen as different and possibly hostile. This quadrant is characteristic of cultural conflict in which each person or group is applying a self-reference criterion to interpret the other person's or group's behavior. Both expect respect but one shows respect by being very formal and the other by being very informal. In another example, two people may both expect harmony but one shows harmony by smiling a lot and the other by being very serious. If the behaviors are not perceived as reflecting shared, positive, common-ground expectations, the conflict may escalate as each party perceives the other as hostile. The conditions described in the second quadrant are very unstable and, unless the shared positive expectations are quickly found and made explicit, the salience is likely to change toward the third quadrant.

In the third quadrant, the two persons have the same behaviors but now they have different or negative expectations. The similarity of behaviors gives the appearance of harmony and agreement, but the hidden expectations are different or negative and are not likely to bode well for the relationship. While you may have cross-cultural conflict when the behaviors are the same and expectations are different, the salient feature here is no longer the shared cultural value, meaning, or expectation, but rather the similar behaviors outside their cultural context. When I interpret your behavior from my own cultural perspective, I impose my culture on you and interpret your behavior out of context. Although both persons are now in disagreement this may not be obvious or apparent to others. One person may continue to expect trust and friendliness while the other person is now distrustful and unfriendly, even though they are both behaving similarly, both smiling and glad-handing. If these two people can be guided to remember an earlier time when they shared positive expectations, they might be able to return to the second quadrant and reverse the escalating conflict between them. If the difference in expectations is ignored or undiscovered, the conflict may move to the fourth quadrant.

In the fourth quadrant, two people have different and/or negative expectations and they stop pretending to be congruent. The two persons are at war with one another and may not want to increase the harmony in their relationship any longer. Their disagreement is now obvious and apparent, and they may just want to hurt one another. This condition would describe intimate violence, hate crimes, ethnopolitical violence, terrorism, and other extreme forms of conflict.

It is very difficult to retrieve conflict from the fourth quadrant because one or both parties have stopped trying to find shared positive expectations. Unfortunately, many conflicts between people and groups remain undiscovered until reaching the fourth quadrant. An appropriate prevention strategy would be to identify the conflict in behaviors early in the process when those differences in behaviors are in a context of shared positive expectations, allowing both parties to build on the common ground they share without forcing either party to lose integrity.

Therefore, two people may both share the positive expectation of *trust* but one may be loud and the other quiet; they may share *respect* but one may be open and the other closed; they may both believe in *fairness* but one may be direct and the other indirect; they may value *efficiency* but one may be formal and the other informal; they may seek *effectiveness* but one may be close and the other distant; or they may want *safety* but one may be task-oriented and the other relationship-oriented. Only when each behavior is assessed and understood in its *own* context does that behavior become meaningful. Only when positive shared expectations can be identified will two individuals or groups be able to find common ground without sacrificing cultural integrity.

CULTURALLY BASED CONFLICT MANAGEMENT IN THE TWENTY-FIRST CENTURY

There are many reasons for conflict across cultures. Different needs and wants, different beliefs, competing goals, different loyalties, values, ideologies, and geopolitical fac-

tors provide opportunities for conflict. Limited resources and wealth, the availability of technological solutions, disparities in power across social groups and classes all provide reasons for disagreement.

The United States offers one example of the increasing importance of a culture-centered perspective on conflict and the need to develop more adequate culture-sensitive tools for managing conflict. Demographic changes in the United States, with some minority groups growing more rapidly than others, will change the nature of community disputes so that issues of race, national origin, and ethnicity are more likely to be important considerations in the twenty-first century. The culture-based approach emphasizes that although cultures may embrace the same core values, the expression of these values in observable behaviors may differ dramatically, thereby increasing the likelihood of misunderstanding. Those seeking to mediate or manage community disputes will need to know more about the cultural background of the people involved. Culturally defined tools and strategies will become necessary not only to understand the disputes, but also to assist and resolve them (Kruger, 1992).

Sunoo (1990) provides seven guidelines for mediators of intercultural disputes.

1. Anticipate different expectations.
2. Do not assume that what you say is being understood.
3. Listen carefully.
4. Seek ways of getting both parties to validate the concerns of the other.
5. Be patient, be humble, and be willing to learn.
6. Apply win-win negotiating principles to the negotiation rather than traditional adversarial bargaining techniques.
7. Dare to do things differently.

These recommendations parallel ten guidelines by Cohen (1991), who suggests that the negotiator study the opponent's culture and history, try to establish a warm personal relationship, refrain from assuming that others understand what you mean, be alert to indirect communication, be sensitive to face/status issues, adapt your strategy to your opponent's cultural needs, be appropriately flexible and patient, and recognize that outward appearances are important.

Lund, Morris, and LeBaron-Duryea (1994) note that culture is complicated and dynamic with considerable diversity within each cultural group. Culture provides a metaphor for respecting the complicated and dynamic diversity within and between cultural groups while also defining the common ground that connects the groups. Finding common ground without giving up integrity and without resorting to simplistic stereotypes or overgeneralizations is the primary challenge.

Dominant-culture methods of conflict resolution are based on culture-bound assumptions and incorporate values and attitudes not shared by members of minority groups. These culture-bound assumptions are implicit or explicit in many of the models of mediation and negotiation originating in the West. It is important to separate fact from fiction in these models and to make peacemakers aware of culturally bound assumptions.

Fictions

One fiction is that conflicts are merely communication problems and if effective communication can be facilitated, then the conflict will be solved. In fact, the cultural context mediates all communications between groups and must be attended to in all conflict management.

A second fiction is that there is a middle ground which both parties must reach through compromise to get some of what they want. In fact, the conflict may not fit a win-lose model and compromising may be less effective than reframing the conflict so that both parties gain without losing integrity.

A third fiction is that the optimal way to address conflict is to get both of the parties in the same room and facilitate an open, forthright discussion of the issues. In fact, direct contact in many cultural contexts may be destructive, especially in contexts where conflicts are managed indirectly.

A fourth fiction is that parties in conflict should emphasize their individual interests over collective values of family, community, or society. In fact, the collective interests may be more important than individual interests in some cultures.

A fifth fiction is that any third-party mediator must be a neutral person with no connections to any of the conflicting parties. In fact, neutrality may be impossible or even undesirable when it requires going outside the group to find a third party.

A sixth fiction is that good procedures for conflict resolution should be standardized according to fair, reasonable, and rational formats and policies. In fact, the expectation of fairness, reasonableness, and rationality may be expressed quite differently by each culture.

Peacemaking between ethnocultural groups has become an urgent need in recent times and promises to be a major priority of the twenty-first century. By better understanding the positive contribution that a culture-centered approach to peacemaking provides, we might be better prepared to promote the sustainable satisfaction of human needs for security and a high quality of life on a global scale for the twenty-first century.

CHAPTER 17

CONFLICT RESOLUTION: THEORETICAL AND PRACTICAL ISSUES

Ann Sanson and Di Bretherton

INTRODUCTION

Conflict resolution is a broad term referring to a range of forms of resolving disagreements which may be manifested at different levels of society. Research into conflict resolution fits into our definition of *peace psychology* in that it seeks to elucidate psychological processes involved in the prevention and mitigation of destructive conflict (see introductory chapter). The practice of conflict resolution aims to utilize knowledge of psychological processes to *maximize the positive potential* inherent in a conflict and to *prevent its destructive consequences.*

Conflict resolution provides techniques to deal with disputes in a manner which is nonviolent, avoids dominance or oppression by one party over the other, and, rather than exploiting one party, aims to meet the human needs of all. In relation to the positive mission of peace psychology (Christie, 1997), conflict resolution can be seen as a set of strategies which can be used to foster the satisfaction of human needs for security, identity, self-determination and quality of life for all people involved in a conflict. An important feature of conflict resolution within the arena of peace psychology is that it bridges theory and practice, moving from a theoretical understanding of psychological processes

into practical strategies for translating ideals into realities in a wide number of arenas. Furthermore it does this in situations which are fraught with difficulty and often seem to tax our commitment to peace values.

There are models of conflict resolution which are descriptive, outlining how negotiators and mediators actually do behave, and models which are prescriptive, recommending the adoption of a set of procedures which negotiators and mediators ought to use to resolve conflicts. We will not attempt to describe the substantial literature that exists on the theory and practice of conflict resolution. Rather, our aims in this chapter are to identify how conflict resolution differs from other approaches to conflict, to discuss the underlying principles, to present one model, and to highlight points of contact and divergence between this and other models. We will go on to discuss the extent to which such a model can be applied, considering whether the Western origins of most conflict resolution models compromise their effectiveness for conflicts in other cultures. We will explore some of the views of knowledge which underlie conflict resolution research and practice. We will end by pointing to some of the areas where further development is necessary if conflict resolution is to contribute to

193

the peaceful resolution of the complex problems of the twenty-first century.

WHAT IS CONFLICT?

There are multiple *definitions of conflict,* including perceived differences in interests, views, or goals (Deutsch, 1973); opposing preferences (Carnevale & Pruitt, 1992); a belief that the parties' current aspirations cannot be achieved simultaneously (Rubin, Pruitt, & Kim, 1994); and the process which begins when one party perceives that another has frustrated, or is about to frustrate, some concern of theirs.

While for many people the idea of conflict has negative connotations, it can be argued that conflict itself is better seen as "value-neutral." Whether *outcomes are positive or negative* will depend on the way in which the conflict is handled (Deutsch, 1973). Conflict *can* have damaging consequences. It can create suspicion and distrust, obstruct cooperative action and damage relationships, escalate differences in positions, and even lead to violent confrontation. But, conflict can sometimes have *positive* effects. It can open up issues for analysis, leading to greater clarity and improving the quality of problem-solving. It can encourage more spontaneous and open communication leading to growth in the parties and in their relationship.

In conflict resolution, the aim is not to avoid conflict but rather to deal with it in a way which minimizes the negative impact and maximizes the positive potential inherent in conflict within the framework of the values of peace. That is, both the solutions which are sought, and the means by which they are sought, are judged against the criteria of being *against* violence, dominance, oppression, and exploitation, and *for* the satisfaction of human needs for security,

identity, self determination and quality of life for all people.

The course of any conflict, be it between individuals, groups, or nations, will be shaped by the *social context* in which it takes place. From an ecological perspective, conflict can be analyzed at a number of different levels, which, though differing in complexity, can have underlying similarities. "Whether we are dealing with interpersonal, community, ethnic [or] international relations, we are dealing with the same ontological needs of people, requiring the same processes of conflict resolution" (Burton, 1991, p. 63). Systematic research on conflict and its resolution has occurred at all levels but most has focused on organizational settings (especially relating to industrial relations), international conflicts, and more recently interpersonal conflicts and disputes (e.g., neighborhood disputes, marital conflict). As research develops in these separate streams, further studies will be needed to check the assumption of the invariance of processes across fields. The variety of terms deriving from different approaches can be confusing.

THE PRINCIPLES
OF CONFLICT RESOLUTION

Four basic principles underlie most approaches to conflict resolution: (1) conflict resolution is a cooperative endeavor, (2) the solutions sought are integrative ones, (3) the foundation is an understanding of all parties' interests, and (4) both the process and its outcome are nonviolent. We will discuss each of these principles, illustrating both the principles and the practice of conflict resolution, using the following scenario:

Mark, Tran, Saida, and Jane are students who share a house. They each have their own room, which includes a desk and study area, but have a communal lounge room, kitchen, and bathroom. One evening Mark asks his new girlfriend, Tracy, whom he wants to impress, home for an evening meal. Unfortunately the kitchen is very untidy. There are unwashed dishes piled high in the sink. A distasteful fishy odor emanates from the trash, which has not been emptied for some time. The refrigerator needs defrosting and is stuffed full of food which is past its recommended "use by" date. Mark is embarrassed, and Tracy suggests they go out to eat.

Cooperation

A key feature of conflict resolution is the focus on *cooperation* rather than competition. The parties see the problem facing them as one on which they can collaborate to find a solution that suits them both. In our scenario, it is apparent that to make their living arrangements work, the students will need to cooperate. If in his anger Mark uses hostile strategies, he may well evoke hostility from the others.

Integrative Solutions

Follett (1940) first referred to the search for *integrative solutions,* that is, solutions which meet the interests and needs of all parties, by offering a personal anecdote. She and another woman disagreed about whether to open or close a window. The compromise solution, that is, having it half open, would satisfy neither of them. Eventually they discovered that one wanted the window open to increase the fresh air, while the other wanted it closed to prevent a draught, which led to the cooperative, integrative or "win-win" solution of opening a window in an adjoining room. This notion was later elaborated as integrative bargaining by Walton and McKersie (1965)—the process by which parties attempt to explore options to increase the size of the joint gain without respect to the division of payoffs.

> When thinking about the solutions to the problem, Mark should not think only of compromises, such as agreeing that the dishes are to be washed every second day. By enlisting the support of the others and approaching the conflict with an open mind, a more creative solution might be found.

Integrative bargaining most commonly occurs either as a direct *negotiation* between the parties in conflict, or through *mediation* where a neutral third party is brought in to facilitate the process. Of course negotiators are often motivated to achieve a solution where they "win" and the other party "loses" (win-lose, zero sum, or distributive negotiations), but the term *conflict resolution* normally covers only negotiations where the goal is an integrative (or win-win) solution. While it is possible to think of other strategies for conflict resolution, mediation and integrative negotiation are the most often used and will be the main foci of discussion here.

> Although an issue such as household chores would as a rule be a matter for negotiation, there might be instances where mediation is called for. If, for example, there is a history of disputes in the group, the students could decide to ask a mutual friend to act as a third party during discussions.

To help clarify what is distinctive about the cooperative, integrative process of problem-solving which characterizes conflict resolution, it may be useful to contrast it with two other approaches: a *rights-based* approach and a *power-based* approach (Ury et al., 1989; Wertheim et al., 1998). In the rights-based approach, decisions are made by reference to legal rules. Such methods include formally taking the conflict to a court of law for judgement, or referring it to an arbitrator who has the power to impose a decision. Informally, a rights-based approach might consist of arguing for a favored position because "it is my right." In each case, the conflict is set up so a party either wins or loses the case, constructing a win-lose situation.

> Mark might assert his right to be able to bring a friend home without feeling embarrassed, or find out whose turn it was to wash the dishes so as to argue that he or she is at fault. Or he might argue that a lack of hygiene is wrong, and so on. We might well sympathize with him and think he has a point but would the other students think so? Would this approach motivate the other students to take responsibility for finding a cooperative solution? Or would it begin an argument about the rights and wrongs of the situation?

An important distinction between a cooperative and a rights-based approach is in terms of the *location of control:* control for defining the problem, for determining the process and for reaching the solution. In a rights-based approach, definition of the issue(s) to be decided, the process of reaching settlement, and the solution are all in the hands of the arbitrator. In contrast, in cooperative negotiation, the control lies entirely with the parties themselves. They decide how to define the conflict, determine how, where, when and how often negotiations should take place, and mutually agree upon the final solution. In mediation, although the neutral third party controls the process, the definition of the conflict and the finding of a solution are still largely in the hands of the parties themselves.

In the power-based approach to conflict, a party attempts to resolve the conflict in its own favor through assertion of power over the other party. The source of power, and how it is used, will vary from one context to another. For example, it may be military or economic power in international contexts, the power to "hire and fire" in organizational settings, or physical strength or emotional coercion in interpersonal conflicts. Violence, domination, oppression, and exploitation, the abuses mentioned in our definition of peace psychology, might be seen as abuses of power over others. Conflict resolution not only argues specifically against these abuses but more fundamentally rejects the use of power as an approach to conflict.

In his initial anger Mark might well use a power-based approach.

> He could yell at Jane, threaten to say insulting things about Tran to Tran's girlfriend, slam doors, tip the rubbish into Saida's bedroom, and the like.

An Interest-based Approach

In both rights-based and power-based methods, each party assumes that they know what is the "best" or "winning" solution for them. The process of resolution revolves around each party trying to impose its solution or position on the other party. However, these positions are only one possible solution. Positional bargaining locks both parties into contemplation of only their opposing positions, discourages any analysis of underlying issues, and discourages the emergence of more creative solutions. The best solution that can be hoped for is a compromise between each party's initial positions.

In contrast, conflict resolution approaches focus on the deeper issues or interests underlying the conflict, pursuing a new and creative solution that is better than either of the parties' initial positions. This is known as an *interest-based* approach. The underlying interests behind a conflict can include needs, wants, fears and concerns, and emerge through a process of "unpacking" the conflict and each party's initial positions.

Ury, Brett and Goldberg (1989) argue persuasively that the costs of using power- and rights-based methods for resolving conflicts are high, and the probability of achieving a lasting settlement is low. Rights-based approaches typically entail high financial and time-related costs, since they tend to involve legal processes, and they impose significant emotional strains on participants. Because the conflict tends to be narrowly defined in legalistic terms, underlying issues are unlikely to be dealt with, and, because the solution is imposed by a third party and is typically distributive (win-lose) in form, at least one of the parties is likely to be unhappy with the solution and eager to reopen the conflict at a later date. The costs of using power-based methods are also typically high in both financial and emotional terms, and the process tends to be protracted in terms of time. In the worst case, of course, they are expensive also in terms of loss of life, property, and environmental damage, as well as injuring innocent third parties.

In contrast, the process of working together on the problem, exploring underlying interests and finding a solution which meets both parties' main interests involves little or no financial cost, less emotional cost, and tends to take less time than the other approaches. Further, it often strengthens rather than damages relationships, and, since it deals with the underlying sources of the conflict, it is likely to result in a long-lasting agreement that is satisfactory to both parties. Ury et al. (1989) conclude that, "in general, it is less costly and more rewarding to focus on interests than to focus on rights, which in turn is less costly and more rewarding than to focus on power" (p.169).

A commitment to interest-based methods does not imply that rights are irrelevant. Rights-based procedures may sometimes be preferable, from an individual and/or societal perspective, on matters of principle. For example, the 1992 "Mabo" Australian High Court decision granting land rights to the traditional owners of Murray Island effectively overturned the doctrine of "terra nullius" ("empty land") which had previously been used to justify denial of land rights to Australian indigenous people (Pearson, 1996). This legal decision had greater weight of authority than a negotiated agreement between the government and the Murray Islanders, as well as going beyond this particular case to have deep significance for all of Australia.

Nonviolence

Implicit in the discussion thus far is another key principle underlying conflict resolution: a commitment to the values of peace and nonviolence. Although one commonly talks about "conflict resolution," what is usually implicit is more fully expressed as "nonviolent conflict resolution." "Resolving" a conflict through the use of arms, for example, is not considered a form of conflict resolution.

Extensive bodies of literature on violence, for example in psychology, criminology, and law, can inform our thinking about the nature and incidence of violence and how it might be prevented or responded to. The peace theorist Johan Galtung (1969; see also Galtung & Tschudi in this volume) suggests that violence is a structural phenomenon, a feature of social arrangements characterized by dominance, oppression, exploitation, and exclusion. Recognizing the structural nature of violence, a major feature of this volume, brings into focus the importance of attending to patterns of inequality such as gender, class, and race. Processes which settle immediate problems but serve, in the longer term, to erode human rights, may appear efficient but would not be considered conflict resolution.

FROM PRINCIPLES TO PRACTICE

As a way of showing how the basic principles articulated above can be put into practice in the resolution of conflicts, we present here one model of *interest-based* conflict resolution. The model depicts certain key stages in the interest-based approach to conflict resolution that merit elaboration.[1] The basic model is represented in Figure 17.1. The feedback loops should be noted.

Building a Cooperative Orientation

Because cooperation is a key feature of conflict resolution, a preliminary task before commencing negotiation (or mediation) is to ensure that parties are in a frame of mind to work together for an integrative solution. According to the *dual-concern model* (Ruble & Thomas, 1976; Lewicki et al., 1992), not all orientations to conflicts lean towards integrative solutions. An individualistic orientation (exclusive concern with one's own outcomes), an altruistic orientation (exclusive concern for the other party's outcomes) or a competitive orientation (characterized by a desire to do better than other party) are mismatched with the search for integrative solutions. A cooperative orientation (concern for both outcomes) is needed.

[1]The model is based on the work of Psychologists for the Promotion of World Peace, an interest group of the Australian Psychological Society and Wertheim and her colleagues (Wertheim et al., 1998) who were in turn inspired by the Harvard Negotiation Project approach (Fisher & Ury, 1996). Our model contains some modifications, extensions, and variations in emphasis based upon our practical experience in conflict resolution in the Asia Pacific region.

Most negotiators enter negotiation believing one party will win, the other lose, and fail to notice integrative possibilities (Thompson, 1990). To build win-win expectancies, negotiators are encouraged to view conflict as normal, inevitable, and solvable, with the viewpoint that it is possible and preferable for all parties to "win." They should note that initial cooperative moves by one party help induce cooperation from the other party, in line with Deutsch's (1973) "crude law of social relations": Competition leads to more competition; cooperation leads to more cooperation.

To build a cooperative orientation Mark could begin by resisting the temptation to yell at his housemates and organize a time for them to talk about the situation. In introducing the issue, he could use language which emphasizes the belief that a mutually satisfactory outcome can be found. For example, rather than talking about "my girlfriend" he could talk about "our visitors."

Active Listening for Interests

An interest-based approach requires that both parties are willing and able to take the perspective of the other party, and this requires careful listening. As noted above, most parties enter a dispute or conflict with a position, their desired outcome for the conflict. In the conflict resolution process, these "positions" in the conflict are first acknowledged, but then the interests underlying those positions are explored (Burton, 1987; Fisher & Ury, 1996). Good active listening skills, involving empathy, reflection, summarizing, and attentive body language (Bolton, 1992), are needed by the "listening" party in order to help the other party articulate the interests involved and to recognize that they have been heard.

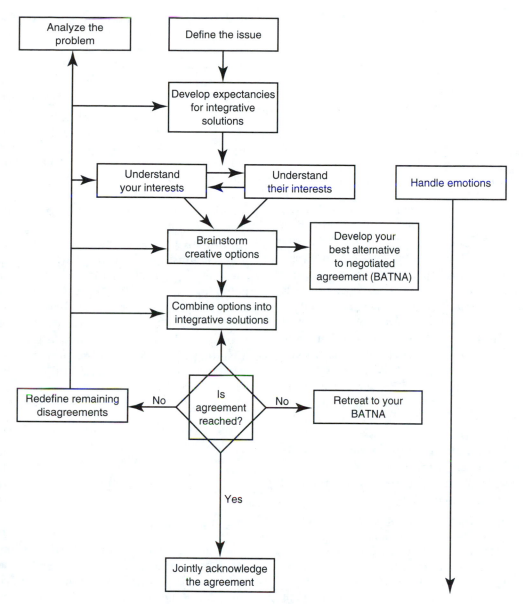

Figure 17.1   Flowchart of the conflict resolution process. Adapted from Littlefield et al. (1993, p. 81).

Before he can find a solution, Mark needs more information. Active listening will help him answer questions such as the following: How do the others feel about the state of the kitchen? What are their needs? Perhaps some members of the group feel that they have in the past done all the work and have given up trying.

Analysis and Communication of One's Own Needs

The initial impetus to use a conflict resolution approach often comes from one party, and there is a good chance the second party may not be a skilled active listener. Thus, the first party will need to articulate its interests without relying on help from the second party. Communicating one's own interests requires some careful thinking and analysis of one's own interests, often better done in advance. To avoid blaming or criticism of the other party, it is often helpful to use "I statements" ("One thing I want/need is . . .", "I am worried about . . ."), which focus attention on the interests involved, rather than "you" statements ("You always/never . . ."), which can produce defensiveness. Because high information exchange promotes the development of integrative solutions (Carnevale & Pruitt, 1992), parties are encouraged to be as open as possible.

> Mark needs to analyze and communicate his own needs. For example he might say, "I was embarrassed when Tracy came into the kitchen. I'm afraid that she won't go out with me again. There were unwashed dishes piled high in the sink, a smell from the trash, and the 'fridge was full of old food. I want to be able to bring people home and have a relaxed time with them in pleasant surroundings."

Brainstorming

A basic assumption of a conflict resolution approach is that the optimal solution is cre-

ated from a consideration of both sets of interests. Further, joint ownership of the solution leads to more satisfaction with it (Wertheim et al., 1998). A joint creative problem-solving process is therefore recommended. After both parties' interests have been identified and listed, they are encouraged to generate as many creative options for resolving the conflict as possible, using brainstorming principles (Burton, 1987). This requires creativity, flexibility, and openness of thinking. D'Zurilla (1988) identified three principles for generating creative options: deferrment of judgment (to prevent premature rejection, to protect the relationship between parties, and because even poor-quality ideas can stimulate better ones); quantity (because later ideas tend to include those of higher quality); and variety. Therefore, parties are instructed to devise as many ideas as possible, including wild and humorous ones, without evaluating or criticizing any. Brainstorming should not stop until each interest has been addressed in at least one brainstormed idea.

> Some of the ideas that the group might brainstorm are: *schedule roster turns at housework, use paper plates, buy better rubbish bins, hire someone to clean up the house, and decide to learn to live with the mess.*

The Role of Emotions

Many authors have noted that *emotions* play a central role in problem-solving and conflict resolution, with the potential to derail the process at any stage (D'Zurilla, 1988). However, as Littlefield et al. (1993) note, little attention has been given to the specific ways in which emotions affect the conflict resolution process. Several authors (e.g., Fisher & Ury, 1996) appear to adopt a "hydraulic theory" of emotions, in which feelings "build up," creating pressure or tension which needs to be released or vented. They therefore advocate giving parties the opportunity to "vent" before proceeding with negotiations. Others (e.g., Wertheim et al., 1998) point out that negative emotions (hurt, anger, depression, fear, anxiety) tend to fix attention on the people involved instead of on the problem and its solution, and therefore they should be controlled and expressed only in a responsible manner.

> Mark might tell himself to stay calm and not get too angry. Sharing his sense of vulnerability and insecurity, and his need to impress his girlfriend, is likely to elicit empathy and cooperation from the others whereas anger and blame might provoke a hostile response.

While strong emotions can disrupt the conflict resolution process, the expression of emotion may provide valuable information about a person's inner state. Recognizing the emotional signals can help parties come to an understanding of the conflict and the interests behind it. Acknowledging feelings is a crucial part of active listening; if only "facts" are heard, the speaker rarely feels fully understood. Feeling may also play a more positive role. Feelings of hope, trust, and goodwill, for example, are assets. Therefore, listening for feelings, acknowledging them, and encouraging their responsible expression is desirable.

Creating Solutions

The final stage involves combining those options which meet the key interests of the parties into integrative or win-win solutions. Forming multiple solutions increase the likelihood that one acceptable to everyone will be found. This stage requires a more disciplined and logical form of problem-solving. Fisher and Ury (1996), Pruitt and Rubin (1986), and Wertheim et al. (1998) have all suggested various strategies for find-

ing integrative solutions, for example: bridging solutions, which go beyond the original positions of the parties to find new solutions; "expanding the pie" where the apparently limited resource "pie" can be "expanded" by including other previously unconsidered resources; cost-cutting to limit the costs of the party who is achieving less; compensation by providing another valued outcome for the "losing" party; and log-rolling, where each party concedes on their lesser-valued issues. If an integrative solution cannot be found, it may be necessary to loop back to previous stages, e.g., to see if some key interests were not identified.

> The group might decide to have a job roster (with the consequences of failure to meet responsibilities clearly understood) as a long-term solution. In the meantime, they may decide to have a meal together once a week during which they can discuss problems before they reach frustrating levels.
> In terms of the positive value of conflict, they might have discovered that one of the students has an under-recognized culinary talent, or knows of cheaper vegetable markets. Through the process of solving their problem together, their relationships might be strengthened.

The Role of Best Alternatives to a Negotiated Agreement (BATNAs)

Despite good intentions, negotiations do not always lead to mutually acceptable solutions. Fisher and Ury (1990) recommend considering in advance what to do if negotiations fail, by developing a "best alternative to a negotiated agreement" or BATNA. A BATNA is the best solution the party can develop which does not rely on any cooperation from the other party, and it is developed using very similar methods to reaching a win-win solution except that it is done alone (or with someone other than the other party). As Wertheim et al. (1998)

note, focusing on your BATNA involves shifting from an integrative, cooperative frame of mind to a distributive, competitive one, and may therefore slow or stop progress on the conflict resolution process. We think a BATNA should not be formulated as a routine precaution, but only when serious difficulties in the negotiations suggest it is needed.

> Mark might decide that if the group cannot arrive at a fair system for doing the chores then he would be better off to move out. Thus his BATNA is to find new accommodations.

Mediation: The Role of Third Parties

The model in Figure 17.1 is designed principally for negotiation between two or more parties. However, many of the processes apply equally to *mediation,* where a neutral third party is involved, controlling the process but not the content or the outcome of the negotiation. Carnevale and Pruitt (1992) note that mediation involves identifying issues; uncovering underlying interests and concerns; setting an agenda; packaging; sequencing; and prioritizing issues; interpreting and shaping proposals; and making suggestions for possible settlement.

The presence of a mediator can serve several useful purposes: The mediator can encourage and model active listening for the identification of interests; reduce the level of tension between parties; keep the negotiation focused without side-tracking caused by parties' inexperience with negotiation, high emotions, or their other agendas coming into play. A mediator can also promote early agreements on simple issues to increase momentum, help parties save face when conceding, and advance a proposal which would be rejected if it came from the other party. In cross-cultural conflicts, the mediator can act as a cultural in-

terpreter, explaining the cultural meanings of behavior to the other party (Cohen, 1996). For example, during the war that we call the Vietnam War (the one that the Vietnamese call the American War), Americans particularly resented the fact that Vietnamese witnesses to physical abuse and torture might respond with laughter. This was seen as proof of their callous attitudes. Someone who has spent time with Vietnamese people could explain that fear, embarrassment, and helplessness might evoke a nervous giggle. A mediator could suggest to a party that he or she should keep an open mind as to the meaning of the other's laughter; that while it may signal amusement, it may also signal fear.

Reviews of research on mediation suggest that when it is effective, participants are usually satisfied, and compliance with the agreed solution is usually high. As would be expected, characteristics of the conflict, the parties, and the mediator all influence effectiveness (Carnevale & Pruitt, 1992). Mediation is more effective when conflict is moderate rather than intense, when the issues don't involve general principles, and where there is not a severe resource shortage. It is more successful when parties are highly motivated to reach a resolution, are committed to mediation, trust the mediator, and are relatively equal in power. It helps if parties have positive working relationships and a sense of mutual dependence. In terms of mediator characteristics, use of a friendly style, perceived neutrality, and perceived power, which sometimes stems from reputation and authority, also influence effectiveness.

Dealing with Difficulties

Using Deutsch's crude law it could be assumed that the other party to a negotiation or mediation would follow the example of the person initiating the conflict resolution process and act cooperatively in the search for an integrative solution. However, in practice the other party may not be committed to integrative negotiation, or may start cooperatively but revert to power-based methods when the going gets tough. For instance, the party may use threats, personal attacks, inaccurate information, and avoidance, or revert to positional bargaining. A variety of approaches have been suggested for dealing with these situations (see Fisher & Ury, 1996; Wertheim et al., 1998). Space precludes a detailed description of these here.

> If the characters in our scenario are going to use attacks, inaccurate information, and other "dirty tricks," it is likely that any problem that comes up will be difficult to deal with and the group will find it difficult to stay together for very long. However, if one of them "names the game" when dirty tricks are used, or notes that the discussion has drifted off course and attempts to get the negotiation back on track, they may have more success.

Other Models and Perspectives

There are multiple models of conflict and conflict resolution. Even within the domain of organizational conflict, Lewicki, Weiss, and Lewin (1992) identified 44 major models of conflict, negotiation, and third-party processes (e.g., mediation and arbitration). They note that the emphasis in the field has been on creating models rather than the equally important task of evaluating them, with the result that no models have received definitive empirical support. Models are either descriptive (how negotiators actually behave) or prescriptive (such as the one outlined above, articulating how to go about the process). Among prescriptive models, some are distributive (how to maxi-

mize your own gains), others integrative. To give a flavor of the alternatives available, we briefly outline five other prescriptive integrative models, each of which has been shown to be useful in at least some contexts. Since they all adhere to the basic principles described earlier, there are many similarities among them, with differences often being more in emphasis than in actual content or practice.

Fisher and Ury's (1996) much-used *principled negotiation* model involves a four-fold approach, the first three of which are common to the model described above: Separate the people from the problem; focus on interests; and invent options for mutual gain. The fourth aspect is the one which gives this model its name: Insist on objective criteria to judge solutions. Objective criteria seem to fall into two groups: rules about how to distribute resources (on the basis of equality, equity, need, etc.) and those about procedures for decision-making (using precedent, flipping a coin, etc.). Littlefield et al. (1993) note that the use of these criteria is more akin to a rights-based approach. Too much emphasis on objective criteria carries the danger of deflecting parties from problem-solving based on interests. It is often possible, however, to incorporate principles or objective criteria into conflict resolution by considering them as legitimate interests which need to be met (e.g., "I am concerned that we use principles of equity in deciding on a solution.")

Pruitt and Rubin's (1986) *creative problem-solving* model is distinguished by setting reasonably high aspirations for one's own gains in the resolution of a conflict, and pursuing these with firmness and commitment. Carnevale and Pruitt (1992) similarly emphasize the need for high aspirations. They argue that effective problem-solving requires negotiators to be both firm and flexible. If both parties are afraid of conflict and therefore not firm, research has shown they achieve lower joint benefit in their solutions. But flexibility is needed about the means to achieve these interests, seeking options which are acceptable to the other party as well as oneself.

Three workers have developed models of conflict resolution which are specifically applicable to large-scale conflicts. Burton's (1987) *problem-solving conflict resolution* model has been applied principally to deeply rooted conflicts such as the intra-state conflicts in South Africa and Fiji. It starts with carefully analyzing parties and issues. Then the parties are brought into a facilitated interactive situation in which relationships are analyzed in depth, without entertaining proposals or engaging in bargaining or negotiation. When there is an agreed definition of the problem, exploration of possible options begins. "Controlled communication," a form of abstract problem-solving in which groups meet in private to discuss conflict analytically, is intended to correct misperceptions and thus improve communication.

Kelman's *problem-solving workshops* (e.g., Kelman, 1997) were developed particularly to address the inter-ethnic conflict in Israel-Palestine. The workshops provide a setting where processes central to conflict resolution such as empathy, insight, creative problem-solving, and learning can take place. The workshops involve politically involved but unofficial representatives of the conflicting parties, take place under academic auspices and are facilitated by social scientists knowledgeable about the conflict, groups/ cultures involved, and group process. Briefly, the process is, first, to understand and acknowledge both sets of concerns, then to engage in joint problem-solving to develop new ideas for resolving the conflict that would satisfy fundamental needs and allay fears of both parties.

Ronald Fisher (1994) has also focused on ethnic conflict, particularly in Cyprus, Canada, and New Zealand. For him, conflict resolution refers to the *transformation* of a mutually destructive situation to one that is "self-supporting, self-correcting and sustainable for the foreseeable future" (p. 59). He focuses on peace building as an important bridge between peacekeeping and peacemaking. His five goals for conflict resolution are based on humanistic and democratic values: Conflict resolution must transform conflicts in an enduring way (not simply settle disputes or suppress differences); it should use a range of complementary methods suitable to the particular issues; it must address basic human needs and build sustainable relationships between groups; it must be infused into decision making and policy making processes to prevent the causes and escalation of destructive conflict; and it must create social structures involving equity among groups.

A variety of other approaches to conflict resolution rely on creativity. Such workers as Boulding (1983) and Macy (1983) stress creative problem-solving and creative thinking, using creative visualization, diagramming, movement and role-playing, to address conflict in environmental, peace and feminist contexts. Fogg (1985) presents a wide array of potentially integrative, effective, and creative nonviolent strategies that can be used in diverse situations.

This brief overview makes apparent the extensive overlap among models. Kelman (1997) summarized the situation by pointing out that, despite the diversity in levels and domains of conflict, and in the intellectual origins of the models, certain common insights and approaches to practice emerge: a non-adversarial, cooperative framework; an analytic approach; a problem-solving orientation directed towards an integrative solution; direct participation of the parties involved in shaping a solution; and (some-times) facilitation by a trained third party.

CULTURE: AN ISSUE IN APPLYING CONFLICT RESOLUTION MODELS

It can be argued that models of conflict res-olution share common assumptions because they share a common cultural deriva-tion. Lewicki et al. (1992) note that com-mon assumptions underlie most descriptive and prescriptive models. For example, re-searchers share the idea that conflict origi-nates from a variety of sources, follows a predictable course, is manifested in many ways and may have positive and negative consequences. Most assume that all types of problems are negotiable and all parties want and are able to negotiate. The litera-ture assumes that there is a definitive way to negotiate well. Responses to conflict are di-chotomized into either distributive (win-lose) or integrative (win-win) types, ignor-ing the possibility of a mix. Models tend to be for two parties, with statements about multilateral negotiations being simplistically extrapolated from bilateral negotiations.

These common assumptions may well reflect a view of knowledge that is Western-ized. Most models of conflict resolution have been developed in North America and might be expected to reflect the values and norms of the culture from which they are derived. The tendency to dichotomize, ob-jectify and deal rationally with problems in-herent in the conflict resolution literature might be seen as reflecting a monocultural view.

The fact that cultural variation has been neglected is reflected in Carnevale and Pruitt's (1992) review which has only one paragraph on cultural differences in negoti-ation behavior and preferences for dispute resolution procedures, plus a discussion concluding that laws governing negotiation

are different under individualistic and co-operative orientations. Kimmel (1994) cri-tiques conflict resolution approaches and notes the lack of awareness of intercultural differences and objectives.

Research on the relationship between culture and conflict tends to be oriented to-ward managing difference. The work of Hofstede (1989, 1994; see also Pedersen, this volume) who categorizes cultures on four dimensions—collectivism-individualism, masculinity-femininity, power distance, and uncertainty avoidance—has been influen-tial. Different cultures can be empirically in-vestigated as to their preference for conflict resolution style (e.g., Fletcher, Olekalns & De Cieri, 1998). A shortcoming of the cul-tural difference approach though, is that it could unwittingly reinforce stereotypes. The Chinese, for example, might be stereotyped as being compliant because they are from a power-distant culture. An Asian researcher would not only be aware of the individual and situational variability in degree of com-pliance in the face of conflict but also view the Chinese response as normal civilized be-havior. The more direct and assertive re-sponse recommended in prescriptive con-flict resolution models may seem downright rude.

It is informative to see culture as a process which guides and shapes our view-points. Encounters with a different culture present an opportunity to examine our own hitherto unchallenged cognitions. Because culture is a framework "for shaping and guiding the thoughts, the actions, the prac-tices as well as the creativity of its members" (Komin, 1991, p. 17), cultural groups tend to share perceptions in a way that does not lead to critical self-reflection.

Hall (1959) describes cultural activities as existing on three levels: formal, informal, and technical. *Formal cultural activities* are based in tradition, are learnt from early childhood and over time come to be seen as natural and admitting no possible alternative: A taboo is either kept or broken. It is very important to be aware of the strength and relevance of cultural differences in this domain. We have been to conflict resolution conferences when these taboos are broken. For example, the serving of roast suckling pig at the opening ceremony of an Asian Conflict Resolution Conference was offensive to many participants whose religions forbade pork. On another occasion, despite careful negotiation with catering staff to avoid serving alcohol when Muslim participants were attending, the after-dinner chocolates contained alcoholic liqueur fillings. There are myriad ways in which a visiting Western mediator might unwittingly be discourteous in South East Asia, such as patting people on the head, sitting barefoot so one's soles are pointed towards the Buddha, touching a Muslim with the left hand, or (if the mediator is female) passing an article to a monk.

Informal cultural learning takes place through imitation. Whole clusters of behavior are learned at one time, often without awareness that learning is taking place or that there are patterns or rules operating. However, if the tacit rules are breached, discomfort and anxiety may result. Much of our conflict resolution behavior can be learnt in this way, through interactions at home, at school, or in the workplace. Conflict resolution courses can capitalize on this type of learning by using stories drawn from people's lives, role plays, and other techniques that draw from the participants themselves how they deal with conflict in real life situations.

Technical learning is transmitted in explicit terms from the teacher to the student and is characterized by the suppression of feeling, since emotion tends to interfere with effective functioning at this level. Technical changes are specific, readily observed, talked about and transmitted to others. It is easy for conflict resolution courses and models of negotiation and mediation to focus at this level and to neglect the importance of the other forms of learning.

Technical skills and knowledge as a negotiator, mediator or conflict resolution trainer are not sufficient preparation for working in other cultures. Each step of the conflict resolution process is shaped by cultural knowledge that is not necessarily conscious. Even to define a situation as a "conflict" represents a cultural framing. For example, there is no Indonesian word that means conflict, whereas the Chinese would use different words to describe family conflict and national conflict. Let us look at several common conflict resolution techniques.

The use of active listening to uncover feelings or concerns presupposes an ability and wish to directly articulate issues which may normally be dealt with in more tacit and indirect ways within that culture. For example, Sri Lankan people we have worked with prefer to show their concern through bringing special teas or foods rather than saying, "I care about you." One woman commented that the banning of English had a strong impact on her bilingual family because her adolescent children always discussed their relationships in English, since Sinhala lacked the vocabulary for such conversations.

Expressing your own interests on your own behalf may seem to violate cultural sanctions against selfishness. For example, Confucian-influenced cultures exhort people to think more of the harmony of the group and less of individualistic concerns. In such cultures, delicate hints may be used to convey one's real wishes, hints which may be lost on a Westerner who is not attuned to picking them up.

Brainstorming creative options or packaging workable solutions will not come easily in cultures that emphasize the need to refer problems to the appropriate authority.

Different cultures may have different understanding of key concepts such as confidentiality and neutrality. An example of such a misunderstanding occurred in Australia when an (Anglo) mediator who had agreed to keep certain issues confidential found himself in a group situation where it became clear that everyone in the (Aboriginal) group knew about these matters. He assumed the need to keep silent no longer held and joined in the conversation. His Aboriginal clients were deeply shocked, felt betrayed and insisted he be taken off the case. For them confidentiality has to do with who is empowered to speak about particular matters. The fact that the matters were known did not give him the right to talk about them.

The notion of neutrality may be also be relatively culturally specific. For example, every Aboriginal person belongs to a web of relationships, and every dispute affects the community. Any Aboriginal mediator can thus be seen as an involved insider, rather than an impartial outsider, though of course greater and lesser degrees of distance can be apportioned.

The point we wish to make here is that experience and familiarity with the culture are important. There is a risk that visiting experts in negotiation or mediation will have insufficient knowledge of the formal and informal cultural domains. They will then interpret the behavior of the parties in terms of their limited experience. We need to be very careful in applying prescriptive models across cultures, to remain open to learning from the other and to be prepared to undertake much more research into how other cultures do actually resolve conflicts. As Tjosvold (1998) points out, "In addition to the present need to manage conflict across cultures, studying conflict in different contexts can challenge and refine present understanding of conflict management. Incorporating ideas and practices of other cultures can develop more robust, elegant theories" (p. 301).

VIEWS OF KNOWLEDGE

Power, rights, and interest-based approaches to conflict draw on different views of knowledge. Most people are used to thinking about conflict in terms of power-based approaches. Some have moved to a predominantly rights-based orientation. To teach and learn conflict resolution may demand a fundamental shift in thinking. In this chapter we have challenged you, the reader, to think differently: for example, suggesting that there are not just two sides to a question, that there may not be a right answer, that a good solution is one which incorporates multiple partial views of reality. In suggesting that conflict resolution approaches depend on a view of knowledge which allows for some degree of subjectivity we are drawing links between peace psychology and some of the traditional areas of psychology, such as "cognition" and "perception."

Power and rights-based approaches are objective. Power-based approaches depend on being able to collect information, analyze the sources of power and estimate the probable consequences of strategies in a particular context. Effective rights-based approaches necessitate the collection and weighing of evidence in relation to a set of rules and making judgements which take precedent and community expectations into account.

Effective interest-based approaches have a subjective element and view knowledge as constructed or created. Melville

(1998) has drawn attention to the importance of critiques of *positivist* views of knowledge for conflict resolution theory and the difficulty of determining the "facts." The idea that knowledge has a subjective element does not mean that reality is denied, but rather that conclusions about the nature of reality are seen as tentative working hypotheses open to revision in the light of new information. Good conflict resolution practitioners recognize that knowledge is partial, so different perceptions may be equally valid.

FUTURE DIRECTIONS

In thinking about the applicability of conflict resolution models to the future, it is first necessary to consider what the future might hold. On this basis of current trends, we might plan for a world in which there is an increasing degree of globalization with interdependent economic arrangements served by electronic communication networks enabling the rapid transfer of information. We might welcome increasing democratization among nations but see the power of democratically-elected national governments limited by the economic sway of multinational businesses and the political clout of international government and non-government organizations. In a postcolonial world we might expect diverse voices to be raised, from people or groups who have experience of more than one culture, from people who come from diverse geographical regions and different social positions. We might also anticipate the formalization of regional structures. For example, processes such as the discussion of common values, which underpinned the formation of the European Union, are now taking place in the Asian region. The "realist" view of international relations which saw nations as unitary actors negotiating bilateral arrangements with a view to maximizing national security and gains becomes increasingly abstracted from the living reality.

The implications of these projections for conflict resolution are even now emerging. Currently most conflicts are intrastate rather than between nation-states. They cut across national lines, and have resonance within Diaspora communities, who can keep in touch through television, fax and Internet and play a significant role. In a talk in Sri Lanka, Galtung (1994) pointed out that thinking about conflict as a two-party dispute over a single issue is a conceptual oversimplification: "I know of no real life conflicts of that type. Real life conflicts have m parties and n issues, and mn can be quite high at times" (p. 3). As the power of nation-states declines, relative to that of intrastate and transnational bodies, the use of power based methods becomes increasingly difficult and less clear-cut. Thus we might predict a move toward the greater use of rights and interest-based methods of conflict resolution at all levels of society, from the personal through the global.

Another way to arrive at a picture of the future is to use visioning exercises to examine alternative possible futures. In asking our students to undertake a meditation exercise and then to draw a picture of the future, we have found that they have a deep concern with environmental degradation and have fears of technology taking over and pushing human beings out. In envisaging an ideal world students have an opportunity to form a positive image of peace and find ways to depict harmony in human relationships and explore their own visions of peace. This exercise of imagination points to disjunction between our model of conflict resolution and the future our students envisage. Conflict resolution models can be very abstract and might be used without locating parties in a physical environment.

For example, the assumption that negotiation occurs indoors is captured by the phrase "putting issues on the table," whereas Aboriginal people often prefer an outdoor setting. Further, conflict resolution approaches can be very task-oriented and "business like." They can view people as possessors of problems to be resolved rather than as entities who feel fear and hope, who have dreams and visions. People from a number of cultures that give a higher priority to spiritual issues, and the role of ceremony in their indigenous conflict resolution systems, make a similar critique.

To meet the challenge posed by the future, peace psychologists need to develop more sophisticated models of analyzing conflict to recognize its multilevel and multiparty nature. We have suggested that there is a need to more clearly articulate the role that conflict resolution has in sustaining interdependent relationships. We have indicated that there is a need for research into multiple perspective taking and the development of multiple, flexible, fluid identities which link us not only with human groups but also with the natural environment. In doing this there are opportunities to learn from other cultures. There is also a need to reconcile ourselves with feelings, and see them not only as possible obstacles to a conflict resolution process, but also as an integral part of humanity and a valuable human resource. Cognitively the demand for flexibility and creativity, for working in teams and learning from others, suggests the need to develop a different view of what intelligence is. Research into the use of communication technology to improve conflict resolution processes should also be a high priority. There is much that already exists within psychology which is not currently seen as connected to conflict resolution, but that can be of value in developing more sophisticated models. Thus a research agenda for the future will involve us not only reaching out to disciplines other than psychology but also in grounding our work in a deeper critical understanding of, and central connection with, our own.

CHAPTER 18

CRAFTING PEACE: ON THE PSYCHOLOGY OF THE TRANSCEND APPROACH

Johan Galtung and Finn Tschudi

INTRODUCTION: SOME BASIC ASSUMPTIONS

Conflict is ubiquitous, violence is not. Hence the Big Question: How can we approach conflict in a nonviolent way? Here is one trend of thought, a trail of ideas, suggesting one answer:

1. The root of a conflict is incompatible goals, within an actor (dilemmas), among actors (disputes), or (usually) both.

2. The conflict appears to the parties as a block: Something stands in the way of attaining goals; their other goals and/or the goals of other parties. Other term: knot.

3. Blocked goal-attainment is also known as frustration, but the range of reactions go beyond aggression,[1] and include: A: attitudes, cognitive and emotive; ranging from glowing hatred of Self or Other to denial, from inner boiling to inner freezing. B: behavior, physical and verbal; ranging from deliberate efforts to hurt and harm Self or Other to withdrawal, ranging from outer boiling to outer freezing.

4. The inner and outer reactions are not necessarily at the same temperature (murder in cold blood, "boiling inside").

5. We then add C: contradiction, the root incompatibility of goals, and get the

Note: Johan Galtung's writing is difficult to understand and challenging for those who are new to his work. His writing often does not fit into the usual academic mainstream and many of his ideas are very original. The rewards are great for those who are patient and grapple with his ideas. More information about the TRANSCEND method can be found at the website: http://www.transcend.org/

conflict triangle, the three corners being A, B, and C, for attitudes, behavior, and contradiction. Causal flows can start anywhere, but generally in C, the contradiction.

6. A contradiction left unresolved leads to accumulation of negative energies in the A and B corners: to violence ("war" for collective actors) sustained by genuine hatred; to mutual isolation sustained by apathy; to the self-hatred of nations that have suffered major trauma, including being defeated, like Jews, Germans, Japanese after World War II (Serbs? Iraqis?).

7. From the root conflict the conflict has now spread, metastasized, to the A and B corners as people react to having their needs insulted by hatred and violence. Parties and media will focus on the meta-conflicts built around being hated and/or hurt and harmed; they are much more dramatic, newsworthy. Thus, in an unpublished study for his master's thesis Dylan Scudder reports that the *International Herald Tribune* for July 1998 had 44 reports on violence in Kosovo and two on possible solutions. This also plays into a tendency to psychologize the conflict, focusing on A, cognitions/emotions of the actors, and not on C.[2]

8. A focus on violence, "troubles," is often accompanied by inability to explore the root problems veiled in taboos. Efforts to break the taboos are strongly resented. The discourse permitted is inadequate to dissolve the problem by dialogue (dia = via, logos = word.) Violence, with its simple winner-looser logic, is promoted by focusing on violence.

9. One basic assumption at this point would be that people are more able to discuss a root problem when they sense a solution somewhere. A glimmer of light at the end of the tunnel makes it considerably more easy to admit that we are in a tunnel. With no light, better not mention the tunnel; truth becomes unbearable. The all-too-human fact that at the end of the tunnel there is another tunnel (all the way, actually) does not make truth easier to bear, except with some light shafts.

10. The second basic assumption is that if we manage to develop a perspective on a transformation of the root conflict, then that opening in the C-corner may drain negative energies in the A and B corners, normalizing inner and outer relations.

Our argument is in favor of recovering the primacy of the root conflict, the contradiction, the incompatibility itself. To soothen hurt egos and teach non-aggressive behavior is good. But hard, root issues have to be approached, coached in deep emotions, the basic one being hatred of the other side for not "seeing the light," i.e. yielding, and for being violent.

Three basic, and frequent, mistakes in conflict practice follow from the failure to take into account the whole triangle:

- The *A-mistake,* the liberal fallacy, focusing on attitudes only, making people more loving (religious), aware of their own mental baggage (psychological). No contradiction is unravelled.

- The *B-mistake,* the conservative fallacy, modifying behavior only by putting a lid on aggressive action. No block disappears.

- The *C-mistake,* the Marxist fallacy, focusing only on the contradiction between labor and capital, regardless of costs to mind and body. We know what happened: The negative energies in A and B caught up with Soviet achievements, and destroyed them.

THE TRANSCEND DIALOGUE METHOD FOR CONFLICT TRANSFORMATION

The method[3] is based on trained conflict workers meeting the parties in a conflict, singly, not combined, one-on-one, typically in a conversation-style setting. One experience[4] is that high-level conflict parties are usually intelligent, articulate, charming people, with high capacity for leadership. There is little doubt that, by and large, they believe what they say, and they are not posturing, at least not after some quiet dialogue disarms their defenses. Nor are they necessarily longing to use violence regardless of the situation; readiness to do so is something else. They are wedded to their positions, but not necessarily inflexible, a characteristic they tend to attribute to the Other. They should not be psychiatrized, nor criminalized; they are not sicker or more criminal than most.

The basic point is that they see no way out, are blocked, tied up in knots partly of their own making. The TRANSCEND method, based on dialogues with all conflict parties one at a time, is an effort to expand their spectrum of acceptable outcomes. The method is not based on arguing positions closer to the other parties, e.g., compromise. That they can do themselves in a process known as negotiation. But the experience is that *direct contact* may exacerbate conflicts for several reasons: because of the verbal violence often used in verbal encounters, because compromise means accepting some of the Other, and because of the absence of creativity when Other is present. In one-on-one conversation-style dialogues, the task is to stimulate creativity, develop new perspectives, and make the conflict parties "ready for the table."

The First Round: Five Processes

Generally, the following five processes are designed to encourage disputing parties to refrain from calcifying their respective positions and moving them each toward new and creative perspectives on the problem.

1. *A first process* will have to probe the negative goals (fears) and positive goals (hopes), exploring beyond public posturing. Thus, Protestant fears in Northern Ireland may be less about religion and more about "being absorbed in tear-dripping Irish sentimentality and emotionalism," mirrored by Catholic fears of "cold English so-called rationality"; not to mention the fears of unemployment (Catholic) and of being killed (both). The positive goal is to be surrounded (and confirmed!) by one's own kind, in a setting of economic and physical security.

2. *A second process* will in no way try to dissuade the party from their goals, but probe more deeply into the nature of the goals. Goals are many-dimensional. Thus, the "Korean conflict" is not only over political-military, but also over cultural-economic issues. The broader the vision of the goal, the more likely that some perspective can be developed, *ceteris paribus*.

3. *A third process,* the kernel, will open cognitive space to new outcomes not envisioned by the parties. These outcomes will relate to the range of goals seen by the parties, allaying the fears, satisfying the hopes, but from another angle. At this stage, much creativity is needed. This is where positive outcomes can be enlarged by creatively arriving at positive goals that overlap for both sides.

For example, in the conflict in and over Korea (including the United States and neighbors), it might be useful to put the complex and incompatible political-military goals on the sideline, and proceed from a cultural-economic angle. There is the rich, shared Korean culture and history. Opening rail and road lines would unleash enormous economic potentials, connecting North Korea–China–Vietnam with South Korea–Japan–Taiwan. Military-political issues can come later, or even better: wither away.

In another example, Northern Ireland, a possible Ulsterite identity could be built on the richness of both cultures, being an enclave of high tech, owned by neither one nor the other, relating positively to both Ireland and England, to Wales and Scotland, in a process of devolution that ultimately may lead to a Confederation of the British Isles. Again, the point is not so much to be for or against any formula as to know that there are formulas further down the road, not uncharted wilderness.

4. *A fourth process* will have each conflict party and conflict worker together construct a new cognitive space, seeing the old goals as suboptimal, simplistic, and formulating broader goals. "Don't be so modest, go in for something better than what you used to demand!"

5. *A fifth process* will explore whether all parties embrace the same points in the new cognitive space. If they do in Korea, there are still conflicts. NAFTA/EU will fear East Asian markets with free flow of goods and services. The Koreas will fear free flow of persons and ideas. There will be quarrels over costs and benefits. But all of this can be handled without violence.

The dialogue between each conflict party and conflict worker ends when they have successfully completed the last two processes: discourse/*Gestalt* enrichment, com-

plexification; and a change in *cathexis* toward new points in the cognitive space.

The conflict worker then goes to the other conflict party, or shares the findings with team members who dialogued with other parties. The latter may be preferable lest conflict party number 2 sees the conflict worker as an envoy for conflict party number 1. In either case, the process with number 2 has to start from the beginning, not using the outcome from number 1 as a starting point for number 2. The process is new for number 2 even if it is not for the conflict worker.

At the end of this first round, the dialogue processes of both parties have to be compared, which is simplest with only one conflict worker. Not only the outcomes, but also the processes leading to those outcomes have to be "processed" for new and shared perspectives.

The Second Round: Sustainability of Outcomes

In the second round, the new cognitive space is handed back to the parties. The space should be complex, having more than one point, but the points should not be spelt out in too much detail. The second round should not be a copy of what conflict parties often do: This is the position, take it or leave it.

If the first round has been done well, mutual acceptability has already been built into the new cognitive space by taking into account all kinds of objections. The task of the second round is to probe for *sustainability*, together with the parties. What could make outcomes of these types stick? What are the vulnerabilities, the weak points? The five processes will be about the same as those employed in the first round.

The Third Round: Coming Together

In the third round, parties meet to negotiate the details of a transcending outcome, not a compromise, now presumably being "ready for the table," equipped with expanded cognitive spaces. Or, even better, one of them makes an opening move and the other follows. For this process they may not even have to meet, the conflict may simply have "evaporated" like what happened to the Cold War with its countless dialogues.

To open the cognitive space, forgotten parties and goals may have to be included so as to have more cognitive complexity to work with. A common goal can then be identified—transcending, going beyond, the original goals—expressed in short, evocative formulations, preferably only one to four words, difficult to reject.[5] Concrete steps will then have to be identified for all parties.

Obviously, this work is difficult, requiring experience, sheer intelligence in the IQ sense, the capacity to internalize vast amounts of emotional/cognitive material and to make that quantum jump to a new image/perspective with sufficient clarity, combined with the wordsmith's ability to find the right words.

PSYCHOLOGICAL PROCESSES IN THE TRANSCEND APPROACH

Two psychological processes seem to be involved: one more cognitive, cognitive expansion and reframing, and one more emotive, a shift in cathexis toward new goal-states.

Cognitive Expansion and Reframing

This happens when a simple two-points discourse, like status quo vs. independence with totally incompatible goals, yields to a more complex discourse with goals at the time held by nobody; like giving the disputed object away (*res nullius*) or sharing it (*res communis*). The original positions are still on the map, but in a context of new po-

sitions that at a first glance may look strange, but worth exploring. As cognitive reframing breaks open a simple Gestalt, providing building blocks for another and more complex Gestalt, emotive suffering and cognitive pain may be high.

A shift in the viewing angle or perspective on the conflict is a part of the process known as reframing in psychotherapy.[6] The terms disembedding/re-embedding are more evocative, however. The conflict, and the accompanying discourse, have come to rest, been "embedded," usually in a dualistic framework. One way of disembedding brings in more goal-dimensions with or without clashes, more actors and more concerns. Sexual infidelity looks different when four other ways of being unfaithful are also considered: of the mind (the secret love), the spirit (no concern for the partner's life project), socially (no social support), economically (having a secret account, "just in case"). Options like separation/divorce look different when children, grandparents, friends, and neighbors enter the cognitive space, not only the couple defining themselves as the center of the universe, wrapped around their fight over sexual monopoly.

Creating Cognitive Dissonances and New Consonances

The point of departure is usually a two-point, dualist discourse reflecting a polarized conflict formation. There is cognitive consonance: Other and his position are both viewed negatively, Self and own position are glorified, the positive identification of each party with their positions is highlighted. To move from this ultra-stable position, dissonances or cognitive inconsistencies have to be introduced.

One approach is to move the dialogue from a concern with the present (diagnosis) to the future (prognosis). Ask what the positions taken will lead to. The answer "only by being firm can we find a solution" can be followed up by the question "what if Other thinks he also has to be firm?" A silence in the dialogue may indicate a recognition of the possibility of endless revenge cycles that may spell disaster to Self. The assumption would be that "peace by peaceful means" has some attraction.[7] And that is where the expanded cognitive space and the new angles may enter: "What would happen if we proceeded along the following lines?" "How would life be for your children, grandchildren?"

This process is not a Socratic "dialogue" where the conflict worker knows in advance what s/he wants as a conclusion. The process is mutual, also taking place inside the conflict worker. For her or him the negative goal, fear, is the violence and the positive goal, hope, some constructive outcome for all parties, that history moves on. If the conflict worker is hardened, refusing to budge, closed to new facts, theories, and values, s/he may have to yield that position to somebody else. The task is to elicit, suggest, propose, not to impose. Sentences end with the question mark typical of a dialogue, not with the exclamation signs typical of a debate.[8]

A dialogue should be between equals. They meet away from the power paraphernalia of the conflict party (seals, titles, flags) or of the conflict worker (books, titles, awards). The conflict worker knows more about general conflict theory, the conflict party more about this specific conflict. The conflict worker ought not to be too well prepared on the specific conflict lest s/he becomes too overwhelming, looming too high, well above the conflict party, both on generalities and specifics. Exchanging general and specific knowledge is not a bad basis for equality.

But there is another inequality lurking. Conflict party and conflict worker are both exploring new outcome spaces for exits. The conflict worker is bound to the principle of hope: Somewhere there is some exit. The conflict party may share that hope but also be convinced, in head-brain or gut-brain, that there is no such point, thereby vindicating the position taken. Violence is legitimated negatively: There is no alternative! Hopes for confirmation makes for blindness to transcendence.

A way out is to use the diagnosis-prognosis-therapy formula creatively. Each of them defines a dialogue mode, a discourse. Diagnosis and prognosis are both descriptive, of past and future, respectively (past because facts that have become data reflect the past). Therapy is prescriptive, of the future. That map reveals an unexplored spot: the therapy of the past.

The question, "what went wrong, when, where, and what could have been done at the time?" is designed to make the party reflect on the past to the point of owning the past, coming on top of history rather than permitting history to come on top of Self; giving in to fate, to destiny. Counterfactual history, in the subjunctive rather than the indicative, has to be elicited.

In our experience, after some reluctance, conflict parties are willing to engage in history "as if." History is distant, or they can make it distant, pointing to events that occurred a long time ago, far beyond their current responsibility horizons. Suggestions usually emerge, creating a discourse that is more creative, less filled with terrible "facts" that lead us nowhere. "Maybe at that point in history we should have. . . ."

The conflict worker would elicit maximum creativity, and then move across both dimensions, from past to future, and from the prescriptive to the descriptive: "What do you think is going to happen now?" Obviously, this would be an effort to provide a positive anchoring in some hope, some perspective emerging from the "therapy of the past" (with the great advantage that it cannot be subjected to the test of reality), and a negative anchoring in the fear, of a dark prognosis come true. But what if they say, "We want only one thing, to win"? Extend the time horizon by asking: "What if they take revenge, in twenty years"?

The conflict worker has two major tasks. The positive task is, through dialogue, to elicit a new conflict perspective and a positive anchor or goal to which both parties are attracted, learning from the parties, contributing own ideas, until something creative and solid emerges. The general method is to expand the cognitive space so that the old conflict positions are still identifiable, yet a new transcending position has emerged. The conflict is disembedded from its old "bed," and re-embedded at a new place.

Second, the negative task is to open for the full spectrum of invisible consequences of violence, the "externalities."[9] Just as in the "science" of economics keeping major effects invisible as "side-effects" or "externalities" makes it easier to engage in exploitative economic practices, the military HQ approach in terms of numbers killed, wounded, and material damage only, nothing about side effects, such as structural and cultural damage, glorification of violence and urge for revenge makes it easier to engage in violent conflict practices.

An important question is where this approach places the conflict worker on the dialogue-debate axis. Conflict workers have a double goal: starting with the therapy of the past, then moving to the prognosis, then risking a joint exploration to arrive at a diagnosis, then making an effort to identify therapies of the future. And then, the same process again. And again, until something fruitful emerges, if necessary by replacing both the conflict parties and the conflict workers.

The process is only meaningful if the dialogue is a genuinely mutual brainstorming process, looking like a cross between a good conversation in a saloon and a lively university seminar. If the conflict worker in fact is pushing a specific position, then she/he is ripe for replacement.

The crisis over UNSCOM inspection in Iraq, February 1998, may serve as an example. That the United States and United Kingdom wanted to bomb Iraq "to the table," or punish Iraq for non-compliance, was clear. But Kofi Annan, the U.N. Secretary General, went to Baghdad and came back with a perspective that looked "reasonable to reasonable men and women." The basic idea was to attach a diplomat to every team so that verbal encounters could be more according to diplomatic protocol. An important point was the difference between plain, colloquial American English and an Arabic richly endowed with honorifics; literal translation would sound even more insulting and "undiplomatic" to Arabs. The perspective became a shared point of reference and built a consensus which in the end was joined also by the United States and United Kingdom.

But why not leave the processes to the parties in a direct encounter? Fine, if they manage. The experience is that in a hard conflict they do not. They are emotionally overwhelmed by their hatred for each other and fear of what may happen if they can be seen as yielding on some point. And they are cognitively blinded by their efforts to defend untenable positions rather than searching for something new. Creativity is at a minimum. Having the "enemy" three feet away does not serve to open up cognitive spaces or to let dissonances in, let alone permit them to start dismantling their entrenched configurations.

Anger may well be a dominant emotion if the conflicting parties are prematurely brought together. No emotion is likely to be more contagious. Trying to create a dialogue when anger prevails is like trying to erect a tent in a tornado.[9] The storm has to settle down before the tent can be made to stay up. That is where the conflict worker, enters: calming the parties down by talking with them one at the time. There may be no time to lose before violence.

With only negative affects towards each other the parties are likely to stick to their positions, and real listening will be minimal. What they hear will sound like well-known tape-recordings and only serve to elicit defenses of their own position. At best it leads to debates that quickly degenerate into quarrels, but not to real dialogue. Real dialogue requires emphatic listening, not so much concern for the other as concern for the total, inclusive "system" (like "Europe" in a broad sense during the Cold War, "the subcontinent" in any Indo-Pak encounter), and willingness to take a fresh look instead of running up and down fixed grooves of thought.

Access to prominent niches in public space is essential. That access will probably be controlled or attempted controlled by State (censorship) or Capital (corporate media), lest a perspective should serve as a war-blocker when that war is wanted for some reason. The more a war seems to be imminent, and the higher the status of the country in the international community, the more closed are major mass media to perspectives on conflict transformation by peaceful means. To break this invariance is no doubt a major task in this field. The Internet does not quite solve the problem: It is publicly accessible, but it is not public knowledge who possess that public knowledge. Big powers prefer perspectives developed behind closed doors, producing a heavy pluralistic ignorance (ignorance about where the plurality stands) and a wait-and-see attitude in the public.

A meta-script seems to be at work here, driving not only the media but also the diplomats. A good story starts up softly, then builds up to a dramatic peak, builds down, and flattens out, to quiet, the End. Let in early violence, let it escalate, let it peak; then time is ripe/mature. People are begging for "peace," handed down to victims and bad (violent) boys, by the intervention of big (powerful) boys, putting an end to conflict.

The idea of an ending already spells disaster. Violence may end, but a conflict always has residues. Violence will be reproduced if the causes are not sufficiently uprooted. Was the agreement really accepted by all parties? Is it really self-sustainable or does it have to be propped up from the outside? In that case, for how long? Has there been any reconciliation? Any professional would know this. Interstate or -nation conflicts are not handled with much professionalism.

DEEPER PSYCHOLOGY OF THE TRANSCEND APPROACH

Of course what has been said above, essentially some Gestalt theory and cognitive dissonance theory, taking note of the emotions accompanying complex cognitive processes, is heavily biased in favor of conscious and cognitive processes. If we try a division of psychology, individual as well as collective, into four fields, then so far we have favored the northwestern corner (see Table 18.1).

Table 18.1   A Division of the Field of Psychology

	Cognitive processes	Emotive processes
Conscious processes	IDEOLOGY True vs. False	LOVE/HATE Good/Right vs. Bad/Wrong
Subconscious processes	COSMOLOGY Deep cognitions	GLORY/TRAUMA Deep emotions

At the conscious level there is awareness or easy retrieval, a test being ability to verbalize. At the subconscious level there is no awareness, retrieval is difficult/painful, and not possible under normal circumstances. Professional help may be needed to construct a map of the subconscious from manifest indicators. Psychoanalysis in the Freudian tradition has had a tendency to focus on the individual, the subconscious, the emotive and the traumatic; a needed, but also narrow approach.

The southeast corner is needed to correct for the northwest corner bias. Dialogues have been explored in order to re-arrange cognitive structures, using emotionally positive and negative anchors. But that is only part of the story. We may enter the deep personality of conflict parties and conflict workers, but it should be noted that in political and particularly geopolitical conflicts, the conflict party is a representative, a diplomat. Consequently, Table 18.1 has to be read as reflecting collective, meaning shared, psychological processes.

The terms in the table are already adjusted to fit also the collective level of analysis.[11] The two subconscious categories add up to the deep culture of that collectivity; which could be a collectivity shared by the representatives/diplomats.

Corresponding to glory/trauma at the collective level would be pride/shame. These deep emotions, especially shame, have been neglected in the literature. An exception is Tomkins:[12]

> While terror and distress hurt, they are wounds inflicted from outside, but shame is felt as an inner torment, a sickness of the soul. The humiliated one who has been shamed feels naked, defeated, lacking in dignity and worth.

No wonder that shame, perhaps more than sexual and aggressive feelings, has been ignored both in everyday life, and in the literature. The more a society is based on exploitation and oppression, the more intolerable shame will be for the oppressor. Shame and fear are instilled in the oppressed, while anger and contempt dominate for the oppressor.

Scheff has drawn attention to how unacknowledged shame may lead to anger, and how spirals of shame-anger figure prominently, not only in quarrels but also in international relations, and how war may be a way to reduce chronic shame. Nathanson has a broader perspective on shame, and one powerful strategy to evade the experience of shame is to "attack others."[13]

Healthy pride, enjoying one's own accomplishments, is a joy to see in children. But the dangers of extracting undue glory from deeds vicariously earned, as in celebrating yesterday's battle victories or "our" team in sports, are ubiquitous. Hubris, false pride, is a well-known human affliction. We hypothesize that the stronger that pride, the more vulnerability to shaming, and shaming will then likely lead to escalating anger. As collectively shared sentiment, this cycle may become dangerous.

Insight in the collective deep culture would seem to be essential for the conflict worker; insight in the deeper layers of the personality of the specific conflict party perhaps less so. Representatives come and go; the deep culture stays about the same, even for *la longue duree* (Braudel), the longer run.

To take an example: Imagine a conflict party (a major country) and a representative (a major person). There is a dialogue with the conflict worker, and a high level of verbal agreement about both the positive and the negative anchors is brought about. Yet there is no acceptability in the sense of acting upon that consensus. There is unarticulated resistance.

Imagine now that in the collective subconscious of that country, in the deeper recesses of that collective mind, two ideas are lurking: [1] no perspective on a conflict is valid unless it can be seen as originating with us (written US?), the center of geopolitics; and [2] no transformation of a conflict is valid unless military power has played a major role.

Whether those beliefs are consciously present and the conflict party prefers not to articulate it, or absent from consciousness and unarticulated, may be less important. The conflict worker has an array of choices: bringing such tacit assumptions out in the open as a dialogue theme; taking the assumptions into account without explicitly saying so.

The first course of action is preferable, but maybe in a roundabout way: "Sometimes there are countries that have a tradition of feeling that _____. What do you think?" To ask that question, however, the conflict worker must have the ability to hear the inaudible, that which has not been said, and to see the invisible, the (too) well-controlled body language. This model becomes more complicated if we think in terms of two persons aiming at conflict transformation. Three cases are:

- two conflict parties, known as negotiation
- one conflict party and one conflict worker, known as dialogue
- two conflict workers, known as a seminar

However, whenever two psyches are meeting, four layers interact:

- the collective conscious, meaning the role behavior
- the personal conscious, meaning the personal outlook
- the personal subconscious, meaning the personal baggage
- the collective subconscious, meaning the deep culture

To start with the conflict worker: no doubt s/he should know more than his role repertory, as spelt out in manuals. Through experience s/he should develop the personal touch, adding and subtracting from prescribed repertory, like any psychotherapist, social worker, mediator, or diplomat would do. S/he should also have some insight in the deeper forces at work at the personal and collective levels, not pretending to be a *tabula rasa*. Any conflict worker, like any other human being, has a biography. Like a psychoanalyst having psychoanalysis as part of her training, the conflict worker may have conflict transformation at the personal level as hers.

This knowledge cannot be demanded of any conflict party. The only thing that should be demanded is conflict worker awareness of such factors, as indicated in the example above.

But the conflict worker might also do well to consider her or his own personality, especially at the subconscious level of deep emotions. Could there be some shame, some false pride? How about compatibility with the conflict party, with regard to the taste for anecdotes, humor, knowledge display, etc.?

How do two conflict parties participate in a negotiation? Their verbal exchange is a debate, not a dialogue; a verbal duel. There is winner and loser, according to whose position best survives the battle. There is mobilization of conscious and subconscious energies to fulfill the collective program, delivering the cultural script intact into the final document.

A critical and very often neglected point is the role of the collective subconscious in this connection. Consider these four possible outcomes:

	Identical collective subconscious	Different collective subconscious
Verbal agreement	A	B
Verbal disagreement	C	D

In Case A, the agreement is unsurprising, assuming that the collective subconscious dictates 90 percent of the positions, making the agreement pre-programmed (e.g., the European Union treaties).

In Case B, the agreement is more interesting, bridging gaps in underlying assumptions. Sustainability of the agreement may be questioned, however (e.g., the U.S.–Japan security treaties).

In Case C, the disagreement is interesting, reflecting genuine ideological disagree-

ment, questioning the sustainability of the disagreement under pressure (e.g., France and NATO in 1965–1966).

In Case D, the disagreement is unsurprising if we assume that the collective subconscious dictates 90 percent of the positions taken, making disagreements pre-programmed (e.g., U.S.–China relations).

An agreement may be little more than a celebration of the collective subconscious, not backed by real dialogue. "Good chemistry" between individuals may bridge gaps. But be skeptical: Such agreements may be based on false assumptions.

CONCLUSION: TOWARD A CONFLICT TRANSFORMATION CULTURE

Conflict releases, and builds, human and social, individual and collective, energy; the problem is how to channel that energy in constructive rather than destructive directions. Look at the faces, at people's eyes when in conflict: Some show dullness and apathy; others have beaming eyes, ready to go. The question is where—to the battlefield or to scale peaks of human creativity?

We have not tapped the psychology of creativity,[14] focusing on the (often lonely) creative individual and how insight comes as a flash, through analogic rather than logic. An exception is provided by Edward deBono[15] and his "lateral thinking" to arrive at fresh perspectives. We are, however, looking more for how people can be creative together, like in the Somalian *shir*:[16]

> . . . a traditional conflict resolution structure that brings together all the mature men in the clans involved in a conflict. Women, children and young hot-blooded warriors are excluded. Men lounge under the thorn trees during the hot, dry day. They chat and drink tea. They also spend long hours chewing qat, the mildly euphoric drug grown in the Horn of Africa, smoking, greeting each

other, delighting in the pleasure of meeting old friends—or old foes. . . . At some point, things will jell. The various pieces that make up the main issue for which the *shir* was called will fall into place because a social climate conducive to a solution will have slowly emerged. The result will be proper peace—a peace felt from the inside—a peace that will have nothing in common with the quick-fix conferences in air-conditioned hotels in Addis Ababa organized by the UN . . .

In short, a conflict market filled to the brim with dialogues! There is no assumption that the model described in this chapter is easy.[17] We would like to emphasize the intellectual effort involved in developing fruitful conflict perspectives. No attention to the emotive and the subconscious, however warranted, should detract from this intellectual aspect, and whether conflicts mobilize sufficient numbers of people with the talents needed. The verdict of this century is a resounding no. We have much to learn, and to do, to handle conflicts better.

NOTES

1. Dollard and Miller, *Frustration and Aggression.* New York: Yale University Press, 1939; Berkowitz, L. "Frustration-aggression hypothesis: Examination and reformulation," *Psychological Bulletin,* 1989, 106, 59–73.

2. It would be unfair to classify the problem-solving workshops of the Yale learning school, the Harvard interactional school and the London communication/human needs school under the A and B corners, failing to take C into account, but not too wrong. But their rebuttal might be that the TRANSCEND transformation approach is singlemindedly focused on C, which is true and is also why TRANSCEND has eleven other programs. For a fine analysis, see Tarja Vaeyrynen, "Problem-Solving as a

Form of Conflict Resolution," Rutherford College, University of Kent, UK, 1992.

3. Johan Galtung, *Conflict Transformation by Peaceful Means,* United Nations, 1998, the "mini-version," in English, French, Spanish, Russian, Arabic and Chinese. A "maxi-version" is coming, available on the TRANSCEND home-page, *www.transcend.org.* For some of the theoretical background, see Johan Galtung, *Peace by Peaceful Means* (London, New Delhi, Thousand Oaks: Sage, 1996), Part II, particularly Chapter 3. For other works, see: John Paul Lederach, *Preparing for Peace: Conflict Transformation Across Cultures,* Syracuse: Syracuse University Press, 1995. "Dialogue" is neither in the table of contents nor in index. There is a fine comparison of the prescriptive and Lederach's own famous elicitive approach (TRANSCEND is in-between); Mari Fitzduff, *Community Conflict Skills,* third ed. Belfast: Community Relations Council Publications, 1998, analyzes "Third Party Roles—Mediation," but "dialogue" is not found in the detailed table of contents (no index); and Friedrich Glasl, Konflikt-Management, *Ein Handbuch fuer Fuehrungskraefte,* Beraterinnen und Berater, Bern: Paul Haupt, 1997. Dialogue is neither in the contents nor in the index.

4. TRANSCEND is today working in and on Chiapas/Guatemala, Colombia, Peru/Ecuador, Northern Ireland, the Basque situation, Gibraltar-Ceuta-Melilla, Yugoslavia, Cyprus, the Middle East, the Kurdish situation, Caucasus, Afghanistan, Kashmir, China-Tibet-Taiwan, Okinawa, Hawaii and the Pacific in general, to mention some conflict arenas. See *www.transcend.org.*

5. Good examples would include "common security" (Palme Commission), "sustainable development" (Brundtland Commission). TRANSCEND has used "Middle East Helsinki Process" for the Israel-Palestine and the Gulf conflicts, "equal right to

self-determination" for Yugoslavia, "condominium," or "joint sovereignty" or "binational zone" for the Ecuador-Peru border issue, "Switzerland of East Asia" for Okinawa, "2+3" for Korea (meaning the two Koreas with Japan, China, and Vietnam, the Mahayana-Buddhist countries), etc.

6. Watzlawick, P., Weakland, J., and Fisch, R., *Change,* New York: W. W. Norton, 1978.

7. This is spelled out in some detail in Johan Galtung, *Peace By Peaceful Means,* London, New Delhi, Thousand Oaks: Sage, 1996. Part II, Ch. 3.

8. For an excellent exploration of the difference, see Deborah Tannen, *The Argument Culture: Moving From Debate to Dialogue,* New York: Random House, 1998.

9. For a presentation of that spectrum, see Johan Galtung, *After Violence: 3R, Reconstruction, Reconciliation, Resolution;* Geneva: TRANSCEND, 1998; also at *www.transcend. org.*

10. We are grateful to Jim Duffy for suggesting this metaphor.

11. For an exploration of the cognitive collective subconscious, see Johan Galtung, *Peace By Peaceful Means,* London, New Delhi, Thousand Oaks: Sage, 1996. Part IV, particularly p. 213, and for an analysis of the emotive collective subconscious see Johan Galtung, *Global Projections of Deep-Rooted U.S. Pathologies,* Fairfax, VA: ICAR, George Mason University, 1996.

12. Silvan S. Tomkins, *Affect, Imagery, Consciousness,* Vol. 2, New York: Springer, 1963, p. 118.

13. Thomas J. Scheff, *Bloody Revenge. Emotions, Nationalism, and War,* San Francisco: Westview, 1994. Scheff discusses the role played by shame-rage in the origin of World War I and II. Donald, L. Nathanson,

Shame and Pride, New York: Norton, 1992. This carries further Tomkins's pathbreaking work on emotions.

14. James L. Adams, *Conceptual Blockbusting,* Toronto: McLeod, 1974, may serve as an introduction to creative problem-solving, and since the root of a conflict is an incompatibility we are certainly in the field of problem-solving. His references are: George F. Kneller, *The Art and Science of Creativity,* New York: Holt, Rinehart and Winston, 1965; S. J. Parnes and H. F. Harding, *A Source Book for Creative Thinking,* New York: Scribner's 1962; Arthur Koestler, *The Act of Creation,* New York: Dell, 1967; H. H. Anderson, ed., *Creativity and its Cultivation,* New York: Harper & Row, 1959; J.S. Bruner, J.J. Goodnow and G.A. Austin, *A Study of Thinking,* (New York: Wiley, 1957); Sigmund Freud, *On Creativity and the Unconscious,* New York: Harper & Row, 1958; Carl Jung, *Man and His Symbols,* New York: Doubleday, 1964; Lawrence S. Kubie, *Neurotic Distortion of the Creative Process,* New York: Farrar, Strauss and Giroux, 1966; F. Perls, R. Hefferline, and P. Goodman, *Gestalt Theory: Excitement and Growth in the Human Personality,* New York: Dell, 1951.

15. See Edward DeBono, *Serious Creativity: Using the power of lateral thinking to create new ideas,* London: HarperCollins Business, 1992.

16. See Gerard Prunier, "Somaliland Goes It Alone," *Current History,* May 1998, pp. 225–228; the quote is from p. 227.

17. Thus, see James Scott, *Seeing Like A State: How Certain Schemes to Improve the Human Condition Have Failed,* New Haven, CT: Yale University Press, 1998 (for a review see C. R. Sunstein, "More is Less," *The New Republic,* May 18 1998, pp. 32–37).

CHAPTER 19

INTRODUCING COOPERATION AND CONFLICT RESOLUTION INTO SCHOOLS: A SYSTEMS APPROACH

Peter Coleman and Morton Deutsch

Families and schools are the two most important institutions influencing the developing child's predispositions to hate and to love. Although the influence of the family comes earlier and is often more profound, there is good reason to believe that the child's subsequent experiences in schools can modify or strengthen the child's earlier acquired dispositions. In this chapter, we shall outline a program of what schools can do to encourage the development of the values, attitudes, knowledge, and skills which foster constructive rather than destructive relations, which prepare our children to live in a peaceful world.

Many schools do not provide much constructive social experience for their students. Too often, schools are structured so that students are pitted against one another.

They compete for the teacher's attention, for grades, for status, and for admission to prestigious schools. In recent years, it has been increasingly recognized that our schools have to change in basic ways if we are to educate children so that they are *for* rather than *against* one another, so that they develop the ability to resolve their conflicts constructively rather than destructively, so that they are prepared to contribute to the development of a peaceful and just world. This recognition has been expressed in a number of interrelated movements in education such as "cooperative learning," "conflict resolution," "violence prevention," and "education for peace." Viewing schools from a systems perspective can allow us to see how these movements may complement each other and work in concert to transform our schools at five levels: the disciplinary, the curricular, the pedagogical, the cultural, and the community.

COOPERATION AND CONFLICT RESOLUTION IN PEACE EDUCATION

In her book, *Comprehensive Peace Education* (1988), Betty Reardon states that the general purpose of peace education is "to promote the development of an authentic planetary consciousness that will enable us to function as global citizens and to transform the present human condition by changing the social structures and the patterns of thought that have created it" (p. x). This statement emphasizes the role of peace education in transforming the thinking and the values of students around social interdependence and social justice, in a manner that moves them to become agents for the constructive transformation of the larger society. In this sense, peace education must be a core concern of peace psychologists as they endeavor to identify and promote conditions that favor the sustainable satisfaction of human needs for security, identity, self determination and quality of life for all people (Christie, 1997).

We see cooperation, conflict, and constructive, nonviolent approaches to the resolution of conflict as processes that are central to the broader mission of peace education. Deutsch (1994) defined peace education as "educating people to learn to live in a cooperative world, to learn to manage the inevitable conflicts that occur in a constructive rather than destructive way" (p. 6). In order to accomplish this most effectively, schools must undergo a basic restructuring of the way in which they function. They must become collaborative institutions which are experienced as such by students and teachers in their day-to-day

functioning. The ways of working together and the ways of dealing with the inevitable conflicts which emerge must incorporate this change. Most schools, in the United States anyway, are not such institutions, and the people within them, teachers and administrators, are not adequately prepared to function that way. This must be a core concern for educators.

The emphasis of this book on the relationship of structural violence (poverty, institutionalized racism, and sexism, etc.) to sustainable peace highlights an important question regarding conflict resolution that has been expressed by some in the peace education movement. Essentially they ask, "Doesn't 'resolving' conflicts in fact put out small fires that perhaps should be fanned into major conflagrations to aid in awakening a sense of injustice and identifying a need for more fundamental social change?" (Lawson, 1994). We believe this depends on how conflict resolution processes are put to use and agree with Stephens's (1994) view of conflict resolution as midway along a continuum extending from social system change to social system maintenance (see Figure 19.1).

Social change is unlikely without conflict. The question is under what circumstances will the conflict take a violent or nonviolent course? Some will argue that violence is necessary to overthrow those in power who don't want to change because they are benefiting from the status quo. Others will argue that there are many nonviolent methods (see Sharp, 1971) for developing both positive and negative incentives to motivate those in power to acquiesce to fundamental social change.

In the abstract, one can never rule out the possibility that, in a specific situation, violence may be necessary to remove a brutal, oppressive despot. However, two important

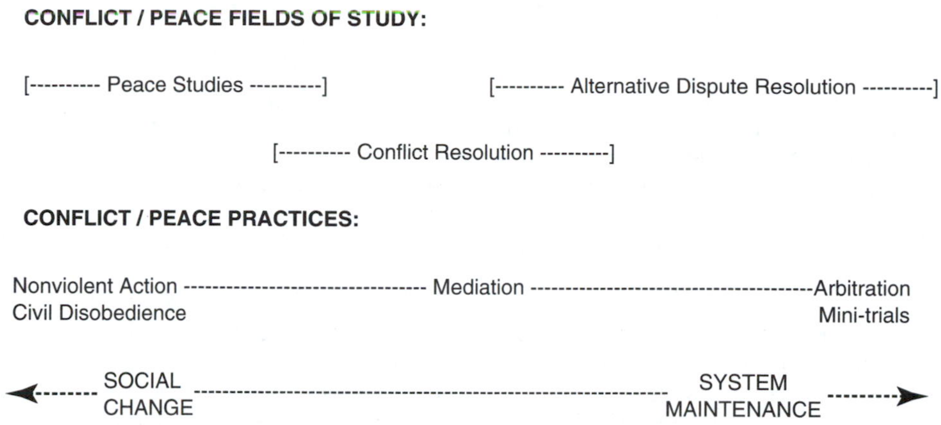

CONFLICT / PEACE FIELDS OF STUDY:

[---------- Peace Studies ----------]   [---------- Alternative Dispute Resolution ----------]

[---------- Conflict Resolution ----------]

CONFLICT / PEACE PRACTICES:

Nonviolent Action --------------------------------- Mediation ---------------------------------------Arbitration
Civil Disobedience   Mini-trials

◄-------- SOCIAL --- SYSTEM --------►
             CHANGE   MAINTENANCE

Figure 19.1   Conflict Resolution: Midway between social change and system maintenance. From J.B. Stephens. (1994). Gender Conflict. In A. Taylor and J.
Berstein Miller (Eds.) *Conflict and Gender*, 217–235. Cresskill, NJ: Hampton Press, Inc.

points must be made. First, violence is too frequently resorted to before other courses of nonviolent social action are adequately considered. Second, even a revolutionary group must have well-developed skills in collaboration and constructive conflict resolution if it is to function well and to manage its internal conflicts effectively.

A SYSTEMIC APPROACH TO COOPERATION, CONFLICT RESOLUTION, AND PEACE EDUCATION IN SCHOOLS

Systemic approaches to conceptualizing conflict processes and intervening in intense conflicts have been gaining increasing attention in the field for conflicts at the individual level (e.g., Pruitt & Olczak, 1995), in schools (e.g., Louis & Miles, 1990; Crawford & Bodine, 1997), in other organizations (e.g., Ury, Brett, & Goldberg, 1988; Costantino & Merchant, 1996), and in or between nations (e.g., Rouhana & Kelman, 1994; Lederach, 1997). This emphasis on

systems reflects the recognition that individuals are members of groups: They affect the groups and are affected by them; groups are components of organizations which affect them and which they affect; a similar two-way causation exists between the organizations and their communities.

Raider (1995) proposed that there are four levels of school systems through which one can introduce cooperation and conflict resolution concepts, skills, and processes: Level 1, the student disciplinary system; Level 2, the curriculum; Level 3, pedagogy; and Level 4, the school culture. We suggest that adding a fifth level—Level 5, the community—will enhance the view of the school system as an "open system" embedded in a larger communal system which can aid in the sustainability of school system change (see Figure 19.2). Interventions at these five levels differ considerably, but all are aimed at change at both the individual and systems level and are centered on the values of empowerment, positive social interdependence, nonviolence, and social justice.

Case Study 1: Conflict and Change

In 1995, our Center (The International Center for Cooperation and Conflict Resolution) was contacted by a newly appointed supervisor of a kindergarden through sixth-grade school district who requested our assistance with managing conflict and change in his new district. The school community was experiencing severe growing pains because of the spread of a more diverse, urban population into what had been a rather small and exclusively white rural community. The district was growing rapidly and was in the process of acquiring a local high school.

These changes had led to an increase in student-student, teacher-parent, and teacher-administration conflicts. Our approach began with a series of group interviews with key stakeholders in the district (teachers, union reps, board members, parents, etc.). These interviews assessed each of the groups' current concerns, their sense of "typical" and "ideal" conflict processes within the district, and their goals for the schools.

These data were then categorized and fed back to all of the interviewees as a group during a day-long feedback and planning session. This group, together, decided on a "whole systems" intervention in the district which included: classroom activity trainings for the teachers (which included training in constructive controversy), peer mediation trainings for the students (third grade and up), adult collaborative negotiation training for *all* staff (including the administration, lunch aides, bus drivers, etc.), and "turn-key" trainings for a select group of staff that, in time, took over the training process. Both anecdotal and empirical evidence have indicated that the intervention has been effective in establishing a safer, more collaborative climate in the district.

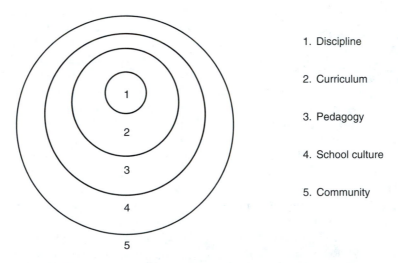

1. Discipline

2. Curriculum

3. Pedagogy

4. School culture

5. Community

Figure 19.2   A systemic approach to transforming schools.

Level 1: The Student Discipline System—Peer Mediation Programs

When there are difficult conflicts which the disputing parties are not able to resolve constructively themselves, it is useful to turn to the help of third parties such as mediators. In schools, such conflicts can occur between students, between students and teachers, between parents and teachers, between teachers and administrators, etc. *Mediation programs* have been established in a number of schools, often in response to an increase in student disciplinary problems, incidents of violence, or to the threat of violence in schools. As a result of their relative low-cost, student-centeredness, and reported effectiveness, peer mediation programs have emerged as one of the most widely used conflict resolution programs in schools (Crawford & Bodine, 1997). However, they are usually brought into a school to enhance the overall disciplinary system of a school, not replace it.

Typically, in these programs students as well as teachers are selected and given between ten and 30 hours of training and follow-up supervision to prepare them to serve as mediators. Oftentimes the student mediators are nominated by their peers. Training focuses on the principles of constructive conflict resolution as well as how to serve as a mediator. They are also given a set of rules to apply during the mediation process. Students as young as ten years as well as high school and college students have been trained. The mediation centers in schools get referrals from deans and teachers as well as students. The services of these centers are usually introduced into the school culture by classroom visits with role plays by mediators, posters and flyers detailing the services, and other ways of persuading the administrators, faculty, and student body of the value of the center's services.

Several evaluation research studies have been conducted over the past ten years which show a consistent pattern of positive effects of peer mediation programs (Craw-

---

Case Study 2: A Fight at P.S. 18

A fight broke out in school today between James, an African-American student, and Luis, a Hispanic student. Luis claims that he was standing around with his friends between periods when he saw James standing against the other wall looking at him with a bad look. One of Luis's friends said in Spanish, "What's his problem?", and then they laughed and joked with each other. Then, for no reason, James got in his face and shoved him. Luis said he knew that James was trying to start something so he took a swing at him. Then the security guard came over. James claims that "these Hispanic kids" are always standing around, talking Spanish and looking at him. Today he heard one of them say "Moreno," which means "Black," and then saw them laughing and joking. James said he knew they were either trashing him or his people. He decided to get out of there, but Luis got in his way so he gave him a shove. Then, for no reason, Luis lunged at him and started a fight.

This case was referred to peer mediation by the dean, and *you* have been asked to mediate it. The word in school is that the fight is going to continue after school between James's and Luis's friends.

ford & Bodine, 1997). At the individual level, a high level of satisfaction is often reported with the mediation process by both the disputants and the mediators. Beyond this, in a recent study (Jones, 1998), the researchers found that " . . . exposure to peer mediation reduces personal conflict and increases prosocial values, decreases aggressiveness, and increases perspective taking and conflict competence" (p. 18). Mediation programs appear to have the most positive effects on the student mediators themselves; positively affecting their self-confidence, self-esteem, assertiveness, and general attitudes towards school (Crawford & Bodine, 1997).

At the school level, mediation programs appear to result in a significant drop in disciplinary referrals, detentions, and suspensions in schools. This, of course, reduces the amount of time that teachers and administrators have to spend dealing with these conflicts. Mediation programs also result in more positive perceptions of school "most notably . . . the development of a productive learning environment, maintenance of high standards, creation of a supportive and friendly environment, and development of positive overall climate" (Jones, 1998, p. 18). Finally, there is some indication from the Jones study that "whole school" mediation programs (schools receiving curriculum training, conflict skills training for staff, and peer mediation training) may better prepare disputants for mediation than cadre programs (peer mediation training only) by creating a "broader knowledge of mediation and constructive conflict behavior" (1998, p. 27). Generally, it is our assessment that mediation programs alone, although useful, are not sufficient to bring about the paradigmatic shift in education that we are proposing is needed to prepare students to live in a peaceful world.

Level 2: Curriculum—Conflict Resolution Training

Conflict is an inevitable feature of all social relations. Conflict can take a constructive or destructive course; it can take the form of enlivening controversy or deadly quarrel.

Case Study 3: The Morning Community Meeting

At a laboratory school outside of Dallas, Texas, Mrs. Jennings's kindergarten class begins each day with a morning meeting. The meeting begins with the teacher asking, "Does anyone have any problems that we should talk about this morning?" Several hands shoot up. Mrs. Jennings tosses a "Koosh ball" to one student, who answers: "We're running down the stairs to lunch too fast!" "Okay," replies Mrs. Jennings, "What could happen if we run down the stairs too fast?" The group then discusses the perils of stairwell accidents. After this, the teacher asks, "How can we help each other to walk more safely to the lunchroom?" The group then brainstorms suggestions. Together they decide that if any student runs down the stairs, he or she will be asked to return to the classroom and will eat lunch apart from the others for one day. This becomes temporary class policy and is written on the board. The next week the policy is reviewed for effectiveness. If it is working, it becomes formal class policy.

Problem identification, an orderly process for discussion, a mutual framing of the problem, an understanding of consequences, brainstorming, agreements, and an implementation check: These are the seeds of community problem-solving and mediation.

There is much to suggest that there is a two-way relation between effective cooperation and constructive conflict resolution. Good cooperative relations facilitate the constructive management of conflict; the ability to handle constructively the inevitable conflicts that occur during cooperation facilitates the survival and deepening of cooperative relations.

Schools and school districts are bringing conflict resolution concepts and skills into the curriculum, either as a course that stands alone or as a unit within existing programs. These curricula provide lessons and activities for preschoolers through university graduates and are focused on such themes as understanding conflict, communication, dealing with anger, cooperation, affirmation, bias awareness, cultural diversity, conflict resolution, and peacemaking. There are many different programs and their contents vary as a function of the age of the students being trained and their background.

Some common elements run through most programs. They derive from the recognition that a constructive process of conflict resolution is similar to an effective, cooperative problem-solving process (where the conflict is perceived as the mutual problem to be solved) while a destructive process is similar to a win-lose, competitive struggle (Deutsch, 1973). In effect, most conflict resolution training programs seek to instill the attitudes, knowledge, and skills that are conducive to effective, cooperative problem-solving and to discourage the attitudes and habitual responses which give rise to win-lose struggles. From a school system perspective, these trainings establish and reinforce a basic frame of reference and language for collaboration, and orient students to a process and skills that are familiar but underutilized. Below, we list the central elements which are included in many training programs, but we do not have the space to describe the ingenious techniques that are employed in teaching them. The sequence in which they are taught varies as a function of the nature of the group being taught.

1. *Know what type of conflict you are involved in.* There are three major types: the zero-sum conflict (a pure win-lose, conflict), the mixed-motive (both can win, both can lose, one can win and the other can lose), and the pure cooperative (both can win or both can lose). It is important to know what kind of conflict you are in because the different types require different types of strategies and tactics (see Lewicki & Litterer, 1985; Walton & McKersie, 1965). The common tendency is for inexperienced parties to define their conflict as "win-lose," even though very few conflicts intrinsically are. But if you misperceive it to be such, you are apt to engage in a competitive, destructive process of conflict resolution.

The strategies and tactics of the different types of conflict differ. In a zero-sum conflict one seeks to amass, mobilize, and utilize the various resources of power to bring to bear more effective, relevant power than one's adversary; or if this is not possible in the initial area of conflict, one seeks to transform the arena of conflict into one in which one's effective power is greater than one's adversary. Thus, if a bully challenges you to a fight because you won't "lend" him money and you cannot amass the power to deter, intimidate, or beat him, you might arrange to change the conflict from a physical confrontation (which you would lose) to a legal confrontation (which you would win) by involving the police or other legal authority. Our emphasis is on the strategy of cooperative problem-solving to find a solution to the conflict which is mutually satisfactory and upon the development and application of mutually agreed-upon fair principles to handle those situations in which the aspirations of both sides cannot be equally realized. The strategy and tactics of the resolution of cooperative conflicts involve primarily cooperative fact-finding and research as well as rational persuasion.

2. *Become aware of the causes and consequences of violence and of the alternatives to violence, even when one is very angry.* Become realistically aware of how much violence there is and how alcohol and drugs contribute to violence. Become aware of what makes you very angry. Learn the healthy and unhealthy ways you have of expressing anger. Learn how to actively channel your anger in ways that are not violent and are not likely to provoke violence from the other. Learn alternatives to violence in dealing with conflict. Prothrow-Stith (1987) and others (see Eron, Gentry, & Schlegal, 1994 for a description of many programs) have developed very helpful curriculum for adolescents on the prevention of violence.

3. *Face conflict rather than avoid it.* Recognize that conflict may make you anxious and that you may try to avoid it. Learn the typical defenses you employ to evade conflict, e.g., denial, becoming overly agreeable, rationalization. Become aware of the negative consequences of evading a conflict—irritability, tension, persistence of the problem, etc. Learn what kinds of conflicts are best avoided rather than confronted—e.g., conflicts that will evaporate shortly, those that are inherently unresolvable, win-lose conflicts that you are unlikely to win.

4. *Respect yourself and your interests, respect the other and his or her interests.* Personal insecurity and a sense of vulnerability often lead people to define conflicts as "life and death," win-lose struggles even when they are relatively minor, mixed-motive conflicts. Helping students develop a respect for

themselves and their interests enables them to see their conflicts in reasonable proportion and facilitates their constructive confrontation.

5. *Avoid ethnocentrism: Understand and accept the reality of cultural difference.* Be aware that we live in a community, a nation, a world in which there are people from many different cultures who differ in myriad ways including ways of thinking about conflict and negotiation. What you take to be self-evident and right may not seem that way to someone from a different cultural background and vice versa. Expect cultural misunderstandings; use them as an opportunity for learning rather than as a basis of estrangement.

6. *Distinguish clearly between "interests" and "positions."* Positions may be opposed but interests may not be (Fisher & Ury, 1981). The classic example from Follett (1940) is that of a brother and sister, each of whom wanted the only orange available. The sister wanted the peel of the orange to make marmalade; the brother wanted to eat the inner part. Their positions ("I want the orange") were opposed; their interests were not. Often when conflicting parties reveal their underlying interests, it is possible to find a solution which suits them both.

7. *Explore your interests and the other's interests to identify the common and compatible interests that you both share.* A full exploration of one another's interests increases empathy and facilitates subsequent problem-solving.

8. *Define the conflicting interests between yourself and the other as a mutual problem to be solved cooperatively.* Define the conflict in terms of specific behavior rather than about who is a better person. Diagnose the problem clearly, and then creatively seek new options for dealing with the conflict that lead to mutual gain. However, not all conflicts can be solved to mutual satisfaction even with the most creative thinking. Here,

agreement upon a fair procedure that determines who gets his or her way, or seeking help from neutral, third parties may be the most constructive resolution possible under the circumstances.

9. *In communicating with the other, listen attentively and speak so as to be understood: This requires the active attempt to take the perspective of the other and to check continually your success in doing so.* The feeling of being understood, as well as effective communication, enormously facilitates constructive resolution.

10. *Be alert to the natural tendencies to bias—misperceptions, misjudgments, and stereotyped thinking—that commonly occur in yourself as well as the other during heated conflict.* These errors in perception and thought interfere with communication, make empathy difficult, and impair problem-solving. These include black-white thinking, narrowing of one's range of perceived options, and the *fundamental attribution error* (the tendency to attribute the aggressive actions of the other to the other's personality while attributing one's own aggressive actions to external circumstances such as the other's hostile actions).

11. *Develop skills for dealing with difficult conflicts so that you are not helpless nor hopeless when confronting those who are more powerful, those who don't want to engage in constructive conflict resolution, or those who use dirty tricks.* Fisher and Ury (1981) have discussed these matters very helpfully in the final three chapters of their well-known book, *Getting to Yes*. We shall not summarize their discussion but rather emphasize several basic principles. First, it is important to recognize that you become less vulnerable to intimidation if you realize that you usually have a choice: You don't have to stay in the relationship with the other.

Second, it is useful to be open and explicit to the other about what he or she is doing that upsets you and to indicate the effects that these actions are having on you. If the other asserts that you have misunderstood or denies doing what you have stated, and if you are not persuaded, be forthright in maintaining that this remains a problem for you: Discuss with the other what could be done to remove the problem (your misunderstanding of the other, your need for reassurance, or the other's noxious behavior).

Third, it is wise to avoid reciprocating the other's noxious behavior and to avoid attacking the other personally for his or her behavior (i.e., criticize the behavior and not the person); such reciprocation often leads to an escalating vicious spiral.

A phrase that we have found useful in characterizing the stance you should take in difficult (as well as easy) conflicts is to be "firm, fair, and friendly." *Firm* in resisting intimidation, exploitation, and dirty tricks; *fair* in holding to your moral principles and not reciprocating the other's immoral behavior despite his or her provocations; and *friendly* in the sense that you are willing to initiate and reciprocate cooperation.

12. *Know yourself and how you typically respond in different sorts of conflict situations.* Different people deal with their anxieties about conflict in different ways. Being aware of your predispositions may allow you to modify them when they are inappropriate in a given conflict. We have found it useful to emphasize six different conflict reaction patterns to characterize a person's predispositions to respond to conflict.

a) *Conflict avoidance vs. excessive involvement in conflict.* Conflict avoidance is expressed in denial, repression, suppression, avoidance, and continuing postponement of facing the conflict, as well as in premature conflict resolution. Excessive involvement in conflict is sometimes expressed in a "macho" attitude, a chip on one's shoulder, a tendency to seek out conflict to demonstrate that one is not afraid of conflict. Presumably, a healthy predisposition involves the readiness to confront conflict when it arises without needing to seek it out or to be preoccupied with it.

b) *Hard vs. soft.* Some people are prone to take a tough, aggressive, dominating, unyielding response to conflict fearing that otherwise they will be taken advantage of and be considered soft. Others are afraid that they will be considered to be mean, hostile, or presumptuous, and as a consequence, they are excessively gentle and unassertive. A more appropriate stance is firm support of your own interests combined with a ready responsiveness to the interests of the other.

c) *Rigid vs. loose.* Some people immediately seek to organize and to control the situation by setting the agenda, defining the rules, etc. At the other extreme, some people are aversive to anything that seems formal, limiting, controlling, or constricting. An approach which allows for both orderliness and flexibility in dealing with the conflict seems more constructive than one that is either compulsive in its organizing or in its rejection of orderliness.

d) *Intellectual vs. emotional.* At one extreme, emotion is repressed, controlled, or isolated so that no relevant emotion is felt or expressed. At the other extreme, there are some people who believe that only feelings are real and that words and ideas are not to be taken seriously unless they are thoroughly soaked in emotion. The ideal mode of communication combines thought and affect: The thought is supported by the affect, and the affect is explained by the thought.

e) *Escalating vs. minimizing.* At one extreme, some people tend to experience any given conflict in the largest possible terms. The issues are cast so that what is at stake involves one's self, one's family, one's ethnic group, precedence for all-time, or the like. At the other extreme are people who tend to minimize the seriousness of their conflicts. The result can produce serious misunderstandings and insufficient effort needed to resolve the conflict constructively.

f) *Compulsively revealing vs. compulsively concealing.* At one extreme are people who feel a compulsion to reveal whatever they think and feel about the other, including their suspicions, hostilities, and fears in the most blunt, unrationalized, and unmodulated manner. Or they may feel they have to communicate every doubt, sense of inadequacy, or weakness they have about themselves. At the other extreme are people who feel that they cannot reveal any of their feelings or thoughts without seriously damaging their relationship to the other. You, in effect, should be open and honest in communication but, appropriately so, taking into account realistically the consequences of what you say or do not say.

13. *Finally, throughout conflict, you should remain a moral person—i.e., a person who is caring and just—and should consider the other as a member of your moral community—i.e., as someone who is entitled to care and justice.* In the heat of conflict, there is often the tendency to shrink your moral community and to exclude the other from it: This permits behavior toward the other which you would otherwise consider morally reprehensible. Such behavior escalates conflict and turns it in the direction of violence and destruction.

There has been increased research on the effects of conflict resolution training in schools, but much of it is confounded by the effects of other interventions such as programs on mediation and cooperative learning. The results generally echo many of the findings of mediation programs in schools. However, two important studies should be mentioned. A two-year longitudinal field study in an alternative high school was conducted by our center, *The International Center for Cooperation and Conflict Resolution,* on the effects of training in conflict resolution and cooperative learning on at-risk students from an alternative urban high school (Deutsch, 1993). This study found that training in these processes had a variety of positive effects. Trained students ". . . exhibited improvement in the management of personal conflicts, experienced increased social support, and felt less victimized by others. Enhanced relationships with others led to increased self-esteem and more frequent positive feelings of well-being among these students, as well as a decrease in feelings of anxiety and depression. Higher self-esteem, in turn, produced a greater sense of personal control and . . . led to higher academic performance (p. 42). Again, this study speaks to the benefits in school systems of combining conflict resolution training with other types of training, such as cooperative learning.

Other interesting findings emerged in a recent evaluation study in elementary schools of the *Resolving Conflict Creatively Program* in New York City (Roderick, 1998). These researchers found that, irrespective of their participation in the RCCP training, all children in the study got *worse* in the course of the school year in terms of how they thought about conflict and the behavioral strategies they exhibited. The children participating in the study showed, on average, "higher mean levels of aggressive fantasies, hostile attributional biases, aggressive strategies, and conduct problems and lower mean levels of competent strategies . . ." (p. 4). What they also found, however, was that in the classrooms where teachers taught the most RCCP lessons, children got worse *at a slower rate.* This study also indicated that there are significant problems in schools with implementing training at the classroom level (in terms of teachers effectively training students and committing to the trainings for the long-term) and with more general organizational readiness (in terms of long-term administration, teacher, and student "buy-in" and commitment).

Level 3: Pedagogy

To further enhance the learning of conflict resolution skills from specific units or courses, students can practice these skills in their regular subject areas with two teaching strategies—cooperative learning and academic controversy.

Cooperative Learning.   Although cooperative learning has many ancestors and can be traced back for at least 2,000 years, it is only in this century that there has been development of a theoretical base, systematic research, and systematic teaching procedures for it. Five key elements are involved in cooperative learning (Johnson, Johnson, & Holubec, 1986). The most important is *positive interdependence.* Students must perceive that it is to their advantage if other students learn well and that it is to their disadvantage if others do poorly. This can be achieved in many different ways—e.g., through mutual goals (goal interdependence); division of labor (task interdependence); dividing resources, materials, or information among group members (resource interdependence); and by giving joint rewards (reward interdependence).

In addition, cooperative learning requires *face-to-face interaction* among students in which their positive interdependence can be expressed in behavior. It also requires *individual accountability* of each member of the cooperative learning group to one another for mastering the material to be learned and for providing appropriate support and assistance to each other. Further, it is neces-

---

Case Study 4: Hate Speech on Campus

In September of 1993, a student committee at Trenton State College in New Jersey invited Khallid Abdul Muhammad to speak at the college during African American History month. This invitation came just after Mr. Muhammad had delivered a "vicious anti-Semitic, anti-White attack" during a speech at Kean College in New Jersey. As a result, the college erupted into turmoil for several months. A schism emerged amongst students, faculty, and the administration. Several public protests were held, both in opposition to and in support of the proposed speaker. The media became a constant presence on campus and served to provoke the divisions. One student leader began to receive death threats. On the one hand, such speakers are the glory of academe: The embodiment of free speech and free inquiry. Yet they also embody a classic tension in a free society between free speech and provocation, exposure of issues needing debate, and collusion in spreading harmful ideas

Ultimately, Mr. Muhammad was allowed to speak, but the event was framed constructively by student leaders and administrators as part of a larger educational experience for the college. The college held several events in the weeks following the speech that gave students the opportunity to air their views and discuss the issues raised by Mr. Muhammad. In the end, the issues were thoroughly articulated and more deeply understood.

---

sary for the students to be trained in the *interpersonal and small group skills* needed for effective cooperative work in groups. Finally, cooperative learning also involves providing students with the time and procedures for *processing* or analyzing how well their learning groups are functioning and what can be done to improve how they work together.

Hundreds of research studies have been done on the relative impact of cooperative, competitive, and individualistic learning experiences (see Johnson & Johnson, 1983, 1989). The results are quite consistent. Students develop considerably greater commitment, helpfulness, and caring for each other regardless of differences in ability level, ethnic background, gender, social class, or physical disability. They develop more skill in taking the perspective of others, emotionally as well as cognitively. They develop greater self-esteem and a greater sense of being valued by their classmates.

They develop more positive attitudes toward learning, toward school, and toward their teachers. They usually learn more in the subjects that they are studying by cooperative learning and they also acquire more of the skills and attitudes that are conducive to effective collaboration with others. Moreover, when used by skillful teachers, cooperative education can help children overcome an alienated or hostile orientation to others which they have developed as a result of their prior experiences.

However, it is important to realize that although the concept of cooperative learning is simple, its practice is not. Changing a classroom and school so that they emphasize cooperative learning requires that teachers learn many new skills, among them: ways of teaching students cooperative skills; how to monitor and intervene in the student work-groups to improve students' collaborative skills; how to develop curriculum materials to promote positive interdependence;

and ways of integrating the cooperative learning with competitive and individualistic learning activities. Commonly, it takes three or four years before teachers feel well-skilled in the use of cooperative learning.

Sometimes parents and teachers have misconceptions about cooperative learning which make them resistant to it initially. There are several myths that it is well to confront (see Johnson, Johnson, & Holubec, 1986, for a more extensive discussion):

1. *Cooperative learning does not prepare students for the adult world, which is highly competitive.* There are two points to be made: (a) the ability of people to work cooperatively is crucial to building and maintaining stable marriages, families, communities, friendships, work careers, and a peaceful world. The reality is that individual as well as corporate success depends on effective cooperation and teamwork (Kohn, 1986); (b) schools, even with extensive cooperative learning, would provide much experience with individual and group competition. The issue is not to eliminate competition and individualism from the schools but to provide a more appropriate balance with cooperation. Furthermore, our impression is that schools rarely teach in a systematic way generalizable skills in how to be an effective competitor.

2. *High-achieving students are penalized by working in heterogeneous cooperative learning groups.* The research evidence (see Johnson & Johnson, 1989) clearly indicates that high-achieving students learn *at least* as much in cooperatively structured classrooms as they do in the more traditional ones. They frequently learn more: especially because teaching less able students often solidifies their own learning. It should also be recognized that cooperative learning does not imply that high-achievers must learn and work at the same pace as low-achievers.

Nor does it imply that high-achievers will lack ample opportunities to work alone or to work cooperatively with other high-achievers.

3. *Grading is unfair in cooperative learning.* Group grading is one way of creating positive interdependence. But, even when group grades are used, individual grades may also be used. Although students sometimes complain about grades, complaints appear to be less frequent in cooperative learning classrooms than in the more traditional ones.

4. *The good students do all the work. The lazy students get a free ride.* A central feature in cooperative learning is individual accountability. If a student is "goofing off," this becomes a problem for the group which, with encouragement and appropriate help from the teacher, the group can usually solve. In solving the problem, the group learns a great deal and the poorly motivated, alienated, withdrawn, or reclusive student often benefits enormously as he or she becomes an active participant in cooperative learning.

Level 4: The School Culture

Most training and intervention concerning cooperation and conflict resolution in schools throughout the country focuses primarily on children. This focus denies the reality that most adults working in the school systems have had little preparation, training, or encouragement to conduct their own work collaboratively or to manage their own conflicts constructively. A culture of competition, authoritarianism, coercion, and contention still appears to reign supreme in schools in this country (Glasser, 1992; Raider, 1995).

In order for school systems to take full advantage of the gains brought by peer mediation programs and cooperation and

Case Study 5: Melting Pot or Salad Bowl?

The J. P. Rockefeller High School is a relatively new school, initially organized as an elite science research school designed to attract science-oriented students. For the first ten years, it achieved this purpose, winning countless scholarships, awards, and commendations for its students. Recently the school experienced a demographic shift from a predominantly White student body to one which is now predominantly composed of students of color. The present student population is approximately 40 percent African-American, 30 percent Latino-American, 25 percent European-American, and 5 percent Asian-American. The faculty is 90 percent European-American and 10 percent African-American. The Parents Association is 100 percent European-American.

Last year the staff decided to become part of the city-wide Site Based Management initiative. The new SBM committee is composed of 18 members consisting of the principal, the union chairperson, a representative from the Parents Association, a student, and elected teachers' representatives from each academic department.

At the last SBM meeting, the teacher from the math department proposed that an official voting seat be designated for an African-American teacher. After much heated discussion, the proposal was voted down. But the problems raised did not go away. Much personal bitterness ensued. Many members of the SBM committee felt that it would be unfair to give a special seat to the Black teachers without opening up other seats for Latino teachers, Jewish teachers, etc. They also deeply resented the implication that they were racist because they voted against the measure. Members of the Black Teachers Caucus (BTC) felt that the school's leadership had been unresponsive to the changes reflected in the student body and that the SBM needed their input to shape the future of the school.

An external conflict resolution consultant was brought into the school to help address the conflict. After a series of initial interviews, the consultant implemented a three-stage approach. First, she addressed the divisive climate of the school by holding several ethnic celebrations in an attempt to broaden cultural awareness within the school. Second, she offered training in collaborative negotiations skills to members of the SBM in preparation for addressing the conflict. Finally, the SBM worked together to design a process for the committee that they were comfortable with. They designated one seat a "multicultural" seat, which would be filled by a Committee on Multiculturalism (which was also established through this conflict) and represent the largest minority group present in the school on any given year.

conflict resolution curricula, the adults in schools also must be trained. Despite significant resistance, adult training can be accomplished through two means: individual-level training in collaborative negotiation skills and work to restructure the school's adult dispute-management system. Collaborative negotiation training for adults often parallels the training offered to students, but focuses on problems that are more germane to the personal and professional life of adults. We stress that all adults in schools should be trained: teachers, administrators, counselors, bus drivers, lunch room aides, para-professionals, librarians, coaches, etc. Such extensive training can be expensive, but the costs can be significantly reduced by the training of in-house staff initially, who then become trainers themselves for other school personnel. Such training engenders commitment from the adults. In so doing, it can help to *institutionalize* the changes through adult modeling of the desired attitudes and behaviors for the students, and by encouraging the development of new norms and expectations around conflict and conflict management throughout the school community.

Level 5: The Broader Community

Collaborative trainings and processes need not and should not stop at the school doors. In fact, many of the student conflicts originate outside of school, at home, on the school bus, or at social events. Parents, caretakers, local clergy, local police officers, members of local community organizations, and others should be trained in conflict resolution and involved in the overall planning process for preventing destructive conflict among children and youths. In Case Study 6, the youth officer's awareness of the school's mediation program allowed for the possibility of the conflict being handled by the school and not by juvenile court. As an example of this type of community involvement, staff from our center have been train-

ing the parents and day care staff at several pre-schools on the East Coast as part of a larger research project. Preliminary findings have been very promising (Horowitz, Boardman, & Cochran, 1998). We encourage school administrators and conflict resolution practitioners to envision the school system as embedded in a larger community system that, ideally, can be brought into this change process in order to better stabilize school change.

CONCLUSION

Efforts to transform schools towards more peaceful and collaborative systems present several challenges for theorists, researchers, and practitioners. First, there is the issue of readiness. Research has shown that unless schools and districts are sufficiently motivated to embrace a change initiative such as this, it is likely to fail (Sarason, 1982; Roderick, 1998). This readiness must exist for a majority of the system, including regents, board members, superintendents, principals, teachers, other professional staff, students, and parents. One method for assessing organizational readiness in schools is being used in the Learning Communities Project, initiated by New York

---

Case Study 6: New York City Youth Officer

Recently, a conflict that began in a high school in New York City spilled out into the street. Earlier in the day, some members of an Asian gang and some members of an Hispanic gang had gotten into a screaming match in the hallway of the school over one youth "sucking his teeth" in the direction of another. Later, on the street, a member of the Hispanic gang flipped a piece of ice onto a member of the other gang. A fight immediately ensued, which was broken up by the local precinct's youth officer. Because the officer was familiar with the mediation program at the school and trusted the competence of the director of the program, he chose to bring the conflict back to the school for mediation instead of to the precinct and the juvenile justice system. This allowed for an agreement between the youths involved that would have been unlikely if the incident had gone to court.

City's Resolving Conflict Creatively Program (Roderick, 1998). For a school to be included in the project, the faculty must vote 70 percent or more in favor of its implementation. This approach could be taken for entire school districts or even for state-wide school initiatives. Administrators and conflict practitioners need to work to develop more innovative methods of fostering readiness throughout school systems (see Coleman, 1997, for a discussion of fostering readiness).

There is also an emerging concern about whether the current models in use in most conflict resolution trainings in schools are implicitly oriented toward Western males and are therefore not sufficiently sensitive and respectful of "difference" (gender, race, culture, class, etc.). For example, Kolb and Coolidge (1991) contend that many of the commonly prescribed conflict resolution processes (such as recommending to "separate the people from the problem," taking a problem-solving orientation to conflict, and the emphasis in integrative negotiation on interests and rights) are gendered and neglect women's preferences for processes such as dialogue (enhanced understanding through interaction) and for an ethic in conflict focused more on relational harmony and care. They recommend an approach to conflict based on: 1) a relational view of others, 2) a view of individual agency which is embedded in relationships, 3) an approach to controlling a situation through the empowerment of others, and 4) problem-solving through dialogue.

Similar concerns have been raised regarding the introduction of Western conflict resolution ideas and methods across cultures. Faure (1995) has argued that the Western psychological paradigm that frames our thinking about conflict resolution is based on certain assumptions about constructs such as *conflict, aggression, time,* and *cause and*

effect that are not universally shared by members of other cultures. He has called for a radical "re-problematization" of our thinking on conflict resolution which would entail: abandoning prior theorizing and research and starting afresh, integrating cross-cultural perspectives at the beginning of the process, emphasizing non-American data, and using non-verbal instruments. Responding to comparable concerns of Western bias in training approaches, Lederach (1995) argues that the traditional "prescriptive" approaches to training, which view the trainer as the expert and participants as passive recipients of predetermined knowledge, models, and skills, are often inappropriate for application in diverse settings. Instead, the context expertise of the participants should be emphasized, where the trainer and the participants together create a new model of conflict resolution specifically suited to the resources and constraints of the context. Our view on this issue is that scholars and practitioners need to begin to better distinguish between those elements of conflict resolution that are universal and therefore applicable across cultures from those that are not. For example, Deutsch (2000) has proposed that certain human values (such as reciprocity and nonviolence) and the relationship between certain theoretical constructs (such as cooperation and constructive conflict resolution) are universal. The cross-cultural value of these more fundamental elements must be seen as separate from the benefits of certain prescribed processes (such as "separating the people from the problem," the open expression of needs, or analyzing issues), which are likely to vary considerably across cultures.

A third area of interest for scholars and practitioners is in better assuring the age-appropriateness of training in conflict resolution. We must devise more developmentally appropriate models for training youth (Crawford & Bodine, 1997). For example, younger students often lack the basic social skills which are necessary to resolve conflicts, and so need training in these skills (communication, cooperation, affirmation, and bias awareness) prior to training in conflict resolution or problem-solving. Repeated experiences with problem-solving are designed as part of the conflict resolution training in order to promote the acquisition and stabilization of skills, language, and emotion relevant to managing conflict.

Finally, there is increasing recognition of the problems of implementing any lasting change in schools of any sort and the need to identify the processes and conditions which give rise to a successful implementation (Roderick, 1998). Introducing cooperation and conflict resolution concepts and practices into schools often involves significant systemic change. It requires, in a sense, a paradigm shift in how people see and approach problems. Fostering this type of fundamental change in the norms and practices of a system requires that people have the necessary skills to motivate and persuade, organize, mobilize, and institutionalize the change. These skills need to be more adequately integrated into the training of school system personnel.

In emphasizing cooperation and conflict resolution processes as the core of any comprehensive program for a peaceful world, we have been guided by the view that it takes more than a single course to bring about fundamental change. Students need to have continuing experiences of constructive conflict resolution as they learn different subject-matters and an immersion in a school environment which provides these experiences. The school should also act for the students as a model of cooperative relations and constructive resolution of conflicts. This pervasive and extended experience, combined with training in the concepts and principles of cooperative work and of conflict resolution, should enable the student to develop generalizable attitudes and skills which would be strong enough to resist the countervailing influences that are so prevalent in their non-school environments. Hopefully, by the time they become adults, they would have developed the attitudes, the knowledge, and the skills which would enable them to cooperate with others in resolving constructively the inevitable conflicts that will occur among and within nations, ethnic groups, communities, and families.

CHAPTER 20

REDUCING TRAUMA DURING ETHNO-POLITICAL CONFLICT: A PERSONAL ACCOUNT OF PSYCHO-SOCIAL WORK UNDER WAR CONDITIONS IN BOSNIA

Inger Agger[1]

INTRODUCTION

When I told a colleague with whom I had worked in Sarajevo that I was going to write a chapter on trauma reduction in Bosnia, he said that if I only had one chapter, I should just cite Bosnian poems. Otherwise, how would I be able to convey the pain and the beauty of people who before the war were living together, one might even say as a married couple, but were now separated and divided by fear and mistrust, while still longing for each other. The bitter betrayals of the war left the marriage scattered; we were many from the outside, from the "international community" who tried to help the partners get back together and rescue the marriage. The question was, however, whether that was also the wish of the partners themselves at that time.

I will follow the advice of my colleague and quote the final lines of the poem, "Burning Skyscraper," written during the war by a Bosnian poet (Alikadic, 1995):

> After the fire, there is no illusion
> scene of fire, ash,
> emptiness is starting.
> If I am a poet after all this evil
> my poetry is a cry.

After the war, there is no illusion, there is an emptiness, as the poet expressed it. During the war, the main task was to help

[1]I wish to convey my gratitude to the Area for Gender and Social Inequality at the Center for Development Research, Copenhagen, for providing me with office facilities and financial support during the writing of this chapter.

the population survive—attempt to reduce trauma—and psycho-social assistance had the form of crisis therapy. After the war, the slow process of healing the trauma following evil perpetrated by neighbor against neighbor, brother against brother, must start from ashes: a painful process of healing the psychological and social trauma caused by ethno-political warfare where the fighting crossed ethnic identity lines.

However, it is necessary to grasp the specific dynamics of ethno-political trauma in order to understand how new cycles of violence can be interrupted. In Bosnia it was evident that trauma from the Second World War played an important role in the psychological reactions seen fifty years later. At that time, not much attention was given to trauma reduction, to transforming the violent narrative constructions from the war into reconciliatory narratives when the post-war socialist society was built. On the contrary, certain narratives were suppressed (those telling about the atrocities committed by Tito's side) while others were turned into heroic stories (those telling about the atrocities committed by the fascist side). Naturally, the suppression of "wrong" narratives did not make them disappear from people's memories, nor did this suppression heal the wounds, which became open and sore again fifty years later.

In the following, I will first try to convey the core of this trauma by relating some case stories illustrating how people in Bosnia felt the impact of ethno-political warfare on their lives. I will end this first part by summarizing the insights I developed into ethno-political trauma during my four years of work in the region. In the last part of the chapter, I will focus on some of the methods that were developed to reduce trauma during the war and in its immediate aftermath.

THE TRAUMA OF ETHNO-POLITICAL CONFLICT

Just after the war ended, I met with a Bosnian woman in one of the major towns of Bosnia. She worked in an international humanitarian aid project helping refugees return to their homes. She was a psychologist, and she was in a so-called "mixed marriage," that is, she and her husband belonged to different ethnic groups. Together with their son they had fled to the town where we met a year after the war started. I asked her if she wanted to return now to their hometown. "No," she said, "I am glad I left that town, I never want to return to that place." "But why," I asked, "what happened to you there?"

> In our hometown both my husband and I belonged to minority groups, but we had never thought about that before the war. We had many friends in the town, good jobs, and a nice apartment. When the war started, our friends suddenly stopped calling us. When we called them, they made excuses for not being able to see us: We are sorry, we are so busy, they said. We had many problems just getting the food most necessary for survival, and none of our former friends helped us. Well, there was actually *one* family that helped us, and I will never forget that, but that was the only example. When my father became ill, they would not send an ambulance from the hospital; it doesn't matter, we were told, he is just a (and then they mentioned the ethnic group to which my father belonged).

> "During a certain period, I had to stand at the market and sell our things to buy food for us. I will never forget the humiliation of that. After a while, the situation became unbearable; we felt that we did not have any future in that town, so we exchanged apartments with a minority family from this city and that has worked OK. Now we are in a place where my husband belongs to the ma-

jority group, we both have jobs, and our son is well. We have not told him that his mother belongs to a minority group.

Now, after the war has ended, our friends from the hometown have begun calling us and sending us letters. How are you, they ask, but I don't trust them anymore. *They have shown me their real faces.* If I ever visit my hometown again, I am going to tell them, but I don't think they will understand; they will have lots of excuses. I will never forget all the pain we went through. I never thought that I would have the strength to live through all that happened to us in this war, but I did have the strength. That was something I discovered from this tragedy.

This woman had not lost any of her close family members during the war, or been in a prison camp; she had not had the type of traumatic experiences associated with the war in Bosnia. But her story is typical of the post-war situation in a traumatized society, so vividly illustrated by her statements about former neighbors and friends: "They have shown me their real faces." This sense of betrayal and mistrust pervades the environment wherever one goes; "betrayal" is at the core of the trauma.

Shortly after I met this woman, I was actually scheduled to visit her hometown and give a lecture on the "testimony method" (Agger, 1994; Agger & Jensen, 1996)[2] to a group of psychologists, psychiatrists, and so-

cial workers who were participating in a training program on post-traumatic therapy. I talked about the importance of not using testimonies to increase tensions among ethnic groups, and I said: "Now at a time when Bosnia has been in a process of peace for more than a year, the main issues are related to confidence-building, dialogue, and reconciliation among the three ethnic groups who fought each other." I could hardly finish the sentence because of the uproar which started among the participants. The trigger words were: "the three ethnic groups who fought each other." They shouted angrily at me, and I felt the impact of their aggression as a wave coming towards me to silence me.

According to their model of the world, there were not three ethnic groups who had fought each other. There was an aggressor and a victim, and the aggressor was evil while the victim was good. How could the international community expect the victim to reconcile with the perpetrator? Such efforts showed a contempt for the victim and the suffering. And so it went for a while. There were 35 people in the room, and maybe ten of them spoke angrily; the others were silent and looked uncomfortable.

After the lecture (which I was finally allowed to continue), I had a long talk with my interpreter. She was a journalist from that town, and she told me that she was a child of a mixed marriage and had herself been in a mixed marriage which was destroyed by the war. She had in her writings tried to change the black-and-white image which was so dominant among the leading class in the town, but now she had stopped trying to change anything. She just wanted to live quietly with her mother. The response I had gotten, she told me, was typical of people with positions in the system. To get such positions it was usually necessary to be on good terms with the ruling ethno-

[2]The Testimony Method was developed by Chilean psychologists during the dictatorship. Originally, the testimony was meant to document human rights violations, but while working with this, psychologists discovered the therapeutic value of giving testimony. Actually, the testimony method is a unique method which combines both private and political realms, documentation and catharsis, legal and psycho-therapeutic objectives. In Denmark, we have further developed the method for psycho-social work with refugees.

nationalistic party whose power was based on the vote of "their own" ethnic group. Those in power needed the enemy images of the other ethnic groups to boost support for their party. Ordinary people, she said, were much more tolerant and wanted to greet their old neighbors again. They actually longed for them, but many were also afraid. Jobs were scarce, and no one wanted to risk their jobs by having views that differed from that of the ruling nationalist party, so they preferred to be silent. At the end of our talk she talked about "forgiveness." That is the key word, she said. "That is something all religions emphasize, the Orthodox, the Catholic, and the Muslim, along with acknowledging one's own evil side, acknowledging that the victim can also become the aggressor."

From the story about the woman who fled the indirect repression she experienced in her town, we know those who perceived themselves as victims in that town were also seen as aggressors by others. In the journalist's model of the world, there was no black-and-white split, no narcissistic regression as a defense against the threat, but she was sad and felt hopeless about the prospects for peaceful reintegration of the divided ethnic groups. She was a child of a mixed marriage and had herself been in a mixed marriage. This is significant and can contribute to the explanation of her more tolerant and mature viewpoint.

To understand the social and psychological factors behind "ethnic cleansing"[3]

and persecution of mixed marriages, one must examine the concept of ethnicity in more detail. Usually, ethnicity denotes a certain cultural, social, and psychological identity, something which is fluid and dynamic. So it was in Bosnia before the war. However, if one wants to find an important cultural indicator of ethnicity in the Balkan context, one must look at religion: Serbs are Orthodox, Croats are Catholic, and Bosnians are Muslim.[4] The confusing factor is that many people were not religious at the start of the war. During the war there was a new religious surge which was associated with post-Communist politics, but probably also with a need for spiritual help and protection in an insecure wartime and post-war situation.

In the new "ethnic nationalism" which tried to equate ethnicity with nationality, we find a very static concept of ethnicity. This type of nationalism claims "that an individual's deepest attachments are inherited, not chosen" (Ignatieff, 1993, p. 4), and it "legitimizes an appeal to blood loyalty and . . . blood sacrifice" (p. 6). In the political and economic crisis which developed with the breakup of Yugoslavia as a nation-state, "people wanted to know who to trust, and who to call their own. Ethnic nationalism

[3]The term "ethnic cleansing" was coined during the recent war in Bosnia and denotes the direct or indirect expulsion by one ethnic group of other ethnic groups from a certain territory. While the term is new, the act of ethnic cleansing is not a novel strategy. It has been applied in many previous conflicts around the world.

[4]In the countries which are now Bosnia (Bosnia-Herzegovina), Croatia, and Yugoslavia (Serbia-Montenegro), and which before the war were part of the Federal Republic of Yugoslavia, the main ethnic groups are the Croats, the Serbs, and the Muslims. Although these three ethnic groups lived among each other and intermarried in all three countries, there were a majority of Croats in Croatia, and of Serbs in Yugoslavia. In Bosnia-Herzegovina, there was a real mixture of all three ethnicities: Bosnian Croats, Bosnian Serbs, and Bosnian Muslims. However, while the Bosnian Croats and Bosnian Serbs had a "motherland" in Croatia and Yugoslavia, the Muslims primarily lived in Bosnia, which thereby became their only motherland. Ethnic cleansing in Bosnia became especially vicious because of its multi-ethnic composition.

provided an answer that was intuitively obvious: only trust your own blood" (p. 6). Nationalism is the most basic form of belonging; "there is no other form of belonging—to your family, work or friends—which is secure" (p. 6) if you do not have the protection of your own ethnic group.

The loss of trust in a safe and predictable world engendered by betrayal by one's previously friendly neighbors is one important traumatic experience. However, the feeling of having been betrayed by one's own family is yet another, and much deeper, trauma experienced by many people in mixed marriages. A number of children from mixed marriages "felt that some of their family members were dangerous and threatening. Unfortunately, they had to take sides. Even when parents stayed together, there were always relatives fighting on different sides" (Ispanovic-Radojkovic et al., 1993, p. 63).

According to a census taken in 1981, 16 percent of all children in Bosnia were from mixed marriages (Oeberg, 1996). Some sources say that 40 percent of marriages in Sarajevo were mixed before the war (Petrovic, 1996). If we take the former Yugoslavia as a whole, 12 percent of all marriages were mixed according to censuses taken from 1962 to 1982 (Botev & Wagner, 1993). Mixed marriages represent the most radical negation of the ideology of ethnic purity and ethnic cleansing. Therefore, such marriages are of course dangerous and in danger in a nationalistic environment. The present statistics of mixed marriages are not known, but probably a large percentage of the 800,000 people who fled to Western Europe, the United States, and other countries during the war were of mixed ethnic origin or living in mixed marriages.

Almost one-third of the population fled from Bosnia during the war, and a similar amount became displaced within Bosnia.

This means that 60 percent of the population had to leave their homes after the war broke out (Media Plan, 1996), and more than half of the population lost their homes. Trauma in Bosnia is about these types of events: the loss of home, the loss of trust, all the injuries which must be healed. Therefore, the return of the refugees and the displaced to their homes, which is a significant part of the Peace Agreement signed in Dayton in November 1995, is of great importance to the peace process and for the society to heal.

However, only a small percentage of the refugees and displaced have actually returned to their homes—far less than expected—and almost all of those who have returned have gone back to an area where their ethnic group is in the majority. Most local authorities simply do not want minority people to return, but many people told me that they were sick and tired of the official separatist propaganda beamed daily by the state-controlled media. They said that they actually missed the times when one's ethnicity did not matter.

In fact, people on all sides in Bosnia despised the entire concept of ethnic purity. But even after the war, powers were trying to prevent the return process—ethnonationalist politicians and their followers profited economically from upholding the ideology of ethnicity, ethnic cleansing, and purity. With a few exceptions, such as mixed communities in Sarajevo and Tuzla, there have been numerous, well-documented instances of overt discrimination or violence; incidents commonly cited include forced evictions from homes, beatings, and arbitrary arrests and detention.

The war meant loss of home to more than half of the population, but it also meant loss of life to many. Although it is very difficult to obtain reliable statistics about the loss of life during a war, according to a research institute in Sarajevo, 6 percent of the population are estimated to have been killed, or to be missing (Media Plan, 1996). This of course affects a large number of family members. The relatives of the almost 20,000 missing (mostly men) are mostly women and children (wives, mothers, sons, and daughters) and are a vast mental health challenge in themselves. In post-war Bosnia we see many experiences among these relatives similar to what we saw in the families of the missing in Latin America. This is a situation of impossible choices. As long as it has not been proven that the missing person is actually dead, the family cannot go through a mourning process, say good-bye to the person and move on in their lives. If, on the other hand, the family members make the decision themselves that the disappeared is dead, this can, psychologically speaking, feel as if they are "killing the person." Latin American therapists have worked extensively with this problem and developed special therapeutic approaches to it (Agger & Jensen, 1996).

In an investigation made at the end of the war (Agger & Mimica, 1996), 2,500 women who were receiving assistance in psycho-social programs funded by the European Union reported the following distribution of traumatic experiences: 80 percent had had life-endangering experiences; 75 percent had lost their home and property; 60 percent had suffered hunger and thirst; 50 percent had felt betrayed by their neighbors; 30 percent had been physically ill; 25 percent had suffered torture or extremely bad treatment; 20 percent had felt betrayed by family and friends; 10 percent had suffered severe physical harm or injury; and 3 percent had been raped. From these answers we concluded that the most frequent traumatic experiences were those related to ethnic cleansing: the life-threatening expulsion from and loss of home; the flight which included periods of hunger and thirst; and the betrayal by neighbors who often actively helped with the expulsion. Of these experiences, the betrayal is often mentioned by the women as the most damaging experience. This "Judas motif" (Schwartz, 1996) is pervasive and fundamental for understanding the hatred and the trauma following ethnic cleansing in this war. However, to these stories of betrayal should be added the traumatic residues of the Second World War in which "the theme of betrayal runs like a bitter stream" (Schwartz, 1996, p. 24).

From the Second World War there was a "powerful reservoir of traumatic memory" (Denich, 1994, p. 367) of the atrocities committed, which also at that time were fueled by ethnic ideology. After the war, when Tito became President it was forbidden to speak publicly about the atrocities—especially those committed by the partisans that had been led by Tito. When the present war started in 1991, it was as if these memories that had been preserved in the icebox of history (Parin, 1994) became defrosted, and began emanating the taste and smell of all the pain, sorrow, guilt, shame, and anger that had been conserved so well by a policy of taboo and repression during the previous fifty years. After war broke out, these feelings could be exploited by nationalist propaganda and become a vehicle for ethnic cleansing.

The women also reported that they felt lonely, frightened, sad, bitter, lost, and restless. Many reported suicidal thoughts. Maybe their state could best be described as one of "demoralization" characterized by helplessness (no one will help me) and hopelessness (no one can help me), accompanied by anxiety, depression, and feelings of isolation. Because an important feature of this emotional state was the belief that "no one can or will help me," it often required a major effort by psycho-social assistance programs to motivate women to even enter the program.

The arrival of many international teams of experts on Post Traumatic Stress Disorder (PTSD),[5] led to posting the symptoms of PTSD on blackboards all over Bosnia. Although many national mental health professionals tired of learning about these symptoms, some national high-ranking doctors were very happy about the PTSD diagnosis: Now there was a medical diagnosis for the misery.

This was not always the feeling of the survivors. Although PTSD is regarded as a normal reaction to an abnormal event, it is a diagnosis, and it may well be felt stigmatizing by the survivors. As I heard some Bosnian refugees express it: "First we lose our home, then we have to live as refugees in a camp, and now they say that we are crazy." Essentially they were saying: "Don't also deprive us of our sanity." As Chilean colleagues have expressed it: Giving medical diagnoses to victims of state terrorism can be viewed as "blaming of the victim" (Agger & Jensen, 1996). The Bosnians were not ill, they were suffering from the war.

There was no doubt about the "traumatizing"[6] effects of the war. It was traumatizing to not only the ordinary people, but also the mental health professionals trying to help them, including the international humanitarian aid workers living in the war zone, often under dangerous and exhausting circumstances (Smith et al., 1996). However, it is my impression that the loss of trust brought about by betrayal was the most serious and most difficult trauma to integrate in a post-war peacebuilding context. The external consequences of the betrayal—the life-threatening ethnic cleansing, loss of family members, loss of home and property, and loss of job—were all serious factors which added bitterness, hate, and hopelessness to the loss of trust in humankind.

METHODS FOR REDUCING THE TRAUMA

Both national and international mental health professionals were feeling overwhelmed and helpless as the war developed and the refugee crisis intensified. How should one approach trauma and healing in this new war context? In what ways were the trauma similar and different from what we already knew, and what were the best ways to help the traumatized people? As a therapist from one Bosnian women's center told me: "We had no knowledge of trauma and how to deal with it. Often, we ourselves did not know how we should cope with our own traumatic experiences, or how we should protect ourselves internally against the terrible stories we heard every day. In retrospect, we often ask ourselves where we got the strength and the courage to do this work, but we were needed, and we could not and would not sit around doing nothing surrounded by this madness. Who was going to help these women, if we did not do it?"

Knowledge about trauma was definitely needed, but the war necessitated other

---

[5]Post Traumatic Stress Disorder (PTSD) was included as a category of the mental disorders in 1980 in the third edition of the *Diagnostic and Statistical Manual of Mental Disorders* (DSM-III) of the American Psychiatric Association. The condition that PTSD defines was previously known as traumatic neurosis, shell shock, combat fatigue, K-Z syndromes, or other names (Wilson & Raphael, 1993).

[6]Trauma means "wound," and the war was certainly wounding the heart and soul of the people who experienced it. I am using "trauma" and "traumatization" in this sense. That does not imply that I regard the whole population as mentally ill. Rather, it would be abnormal *not* to react to the sick context of ethno-political warfare. I do not think that the symptoms of PTSD can adequately describe the wound, although some people, of course, did experience PTSD symptoms.

types of interventions than are usual under peaceful North American or Western European circumstances. The Bosnian mental health professionals had to find their own way, the way most appropriate to the Bosnian culture and to the specific conditions of war and ethnic cleansing. Many psycho-social programs were started to help the traumatized, and various approaches were tried.

There was a constant discussion as to what was the right type of psycho-social assistance for the war-traumatized. Many psychologists and psychiatrists argued that the correct type of assistance was psychotherapy. However, the thousands of traumatized people made this option unrealistic. The multitude of nongovernmental psycho-social programs being developed in the region worked mainly with other types of interventions: self-help groups, occupational activities, counseling, and basic social support such as the establishment of day care and kindergartens to help depressed mothers who were not able to take care of their children.

The discussions about the right type of interventions could be illustrated in the "problem of the wool" which was debated heatedly in the beginning of the war among staff members in the various psycho-social programs. Most of the programs were targeting women (the men were at the frontline), and it was a problem to motivate many of the rural women to participate in the psycho-social programs. There was then, as now, a general attitude of shame connected to consulting psychologists and psychiatrists, which is associated with being crazy. As a result, many programs began contacting women by inviting them to participate in knitting groups where coffee was served—a traditional form of self-healing practiced by Bosnian women.

The coffee ritual is an important feature of Bosnian culture. For centuries, during coffee drinking and knitting traditional Bosnian socks, trauma stories have been told, listened to, and acknowledged by a group of female friends and family. Most psycho-social programs soon learned to copy this procedure. As most of the women were refugees without means, the program had to supply them with wool and knitting needles. Some staff members felt that this was tantamount to buying their clients off. Traditionally, patients pay therapists for help, not the other way around. "The problem of the wool" was gradually solved as staff of psycho-social programs accepted that distribution of wool was not hindering their therapeutic efforts, but was, instead, a practical way of establishing trust and group feeling and of providing useful activities for those women who did not want or need more intensive types of interventions.

Many of the war survivors who sought help in psycho-social assistance programs wanted contact, help, and comfort. Some also came to receive material support, to have something to do, or to avoid thinking of the war. Occupational activities or receiving material aid could provide an acceptable excuse for entering a psycho-social program, and the need and motivation for psychological help would develop gradually as a trusting relationship was built between the survivor and the staff. Trust, which is always an issue in psychotherapy, had a special significance in the Bosnian war context where feelings of betrayal were so pervasive. Providing material aid and occupational activities were important elements in creating a trusting environment. Ultimately, with the exception of only the most hard-line psychoanalytically oriented staff members, it was generally accepted that a psycho-social program also offered material assistance.

PSYCHO-SOCIAL ASSISTANCE UNDER WAR CONDITIONS

So, what was healing under war conditions? Eventually, it was recognized that little healing could happen during the war. The best one could hope for was survival or prevention of a deterioration of the survivors' psychological and social status. We arrived at the following definition of psycho-social emergency assistance: *the aim of psycho-social emergency assistance under war conditions is to promote mental health and human rights by strategies that support the already existing protective social and psychological factors and diminish the stressor factors at different levels of intervention* (Agger, Vuk, & Mimica, 1995).

The concept "levels of intervention" proved to be useful in the debate about "right" or "wrong" types of practice. It was not a question of right or wrong but rather an acknowledgment of the level at which one should or could intervene. The best psychotherapeutic intervention would be to stop the war, but that was not in our power. We could only try to intervene on various levels of psycho-social interventions. The different levels of interventions were defined as follows: (1) *political, economic, and physical survival* interventions, which were at the baseline; (2) *community development* interventions, such as the establishment of an orphanage for homeless or unaccompanied children; (3) *task-oriented* interventions, such as organizing knitting groups, language courses, or other types of occupational or educational activities; (4) *psychologically oriented* group interventions, such as organizing women's self-help groups; (5) *counseling* interventions, such as providing individual or group consultation with a social worker around present problems and dilemmas; (6) *intensive psychotherapy* interventions, such as providing individual or group therapy by psychologists and psychia-

trists in which deeper emotional problems were addressed.

The use of this model facilitated the understanding of what was actually being done in a certain program, as well as the choice of new methods. With this model it was possible to conceptualize interventions, to evaluate the target group and the resources, and to implement the methods most appropriate in the given context.

It was an important aspect of this model that no type of intervention *per se* was better than any other. Many therapists, of course, tended to think that intensive psychotherapy interventions were "better" than psychologically oriented group interventions. But in psycho-social projects under war conditions, whether it was counseling, group therapy, provision of social services, or community work, we were entering new territory. Mostly, mental health staff had to rely on themselves as the best tool available with whatever amount of maturity or strength they possessed. The only other guidelines they had for choosing which actions to take derived from their theory about the world, which enabled them to understand the daily problems they were facing.

PSYCHO-SOCIAL ASSISTANCE UNDER POST-WAR CONDITIONS

When the peace agreement was signed in Dayton, the conditions for psycho-social work changed radically. While the focus during the war was on survival by supporting the already existing protective factors and diminishing the stressor factors as much as possible, the focus in the post-war period had to shift toward peacebuilding and healing. A definition of the aim of psycho-social assistance under post-war conditions could be formulated in the following way: *The aim of psycho-social assistance under post-war conditions is to promote mental health and human rights by therapeutic strategies that promote dialogue, confidence-building, and reconciliation, and diminish ethnic tensions at different levels of intervention.*

Under post-war conditions, mental health and human rights can be promoted by these new therapeutic strategies at a number of levels: 1) *community-oriented interventions,* such as organizing meetings for ethnically mixed groups discussing neutral topics of mutual interest; 2) *task-oriented interventions,* such as organizing education in human rights; 3) *psychologically-oriented group interventions,* such as creating self-help groups for family members of the missing; 4) *counseling interventions,* such as providing individual or group consultation around present dilemmas concerning the return process; 5) *intensive psychotherapy interventions,* such as providing individual or group therapy in which deeper emotional problems are addressed such as the mourning of loss, and the process of forgiveness.

The war survivors were suffering from war-related human rights violations. In this perspective, I built on my experiences from field work in Chile. Although the Chilean context is quite different from the Balkans— in Chile during the dictatorship they were fighting a mostly socio-political struggle, while in the Balkans they were mainly fighting an ethno-political war—there were also a number of similarities: to *divide,* to *victimize,* to *destroy,* and to *silence* the voices of opposition were fundamental strategies of state terrorism in Latin America as well as of ethnic cleansing in the Balkans.

Ethnic cleansing brought about identity conflicts in individuals of mixed-ethnic origin and division in mixed families, communities, and the whole country. It victimized individuals, families, and communities of the "wrong" ethnicity. It destroyed individuals, families, and communities by killing them or expelling them to a life as refugees. And it persecuted voices of opposition.

Within this overall perspective I also saw the development of healing and peacebuilding strategies. On the psycho-social levels of intervention, the main focus of strategies should relate to counteracting the destructive processes of war and ethnic cleansing. Healing processes should, therefore, aim at *unifying* the divided, *empowering* the victimized, *rebuilding* social networks, and *denouncing* human rights violations. The political point of departure would be a critical stance towards the ideology of ethnic cleansing, regardless of who practices it.

In the immediate post-war period, this was not an easy task. Even after one year of peace, people were not ready to enter into any positive dialogue with their former foes. They needed more time. They needed to mourn their losses. During the second year, one could liken the situation to a divorce: It seemed as if the separated marital partners were beginning to be ready to start a dialogue, but they were still cautious and defensive. They could talk about neutral subjects, but it was still too dangerous to get close to the traumatic areas, such as the feelings of betrayal.

A Bosnian therapist told me about a group therapy she had led with refugee women. One woman began an angry monologue about how bad the other ethnic group was, how bad she and her family had been treated, and how much she hated this ethnic group. During several sessions the woman had the need to express these aggressive feelings and receive sympathy from the group. Gradually, the therapist was able to direct the woman in another direction. Maybe the neighbor who had advised her to leave her home had actually tried to protect her and her family against a worse fate. At last the woman was able to see that some people from the other ethnic group had actually tried to help her. The black-and-white split was overcome, the ethnic stereotypes were left, and the woman was in the more mature position of sadness over the losses everyone had suffered—on all sides of the conflict.

It is important in the post-war healing process also to find examples of good and positive deeds. There is a tendency to focus on war crimes, on all the injustices. Naturally, these acts should not be forgotten, but an effort should also be made to remember the positive events that happened during the war. In the first case story about the woman in a mixed marriage who had to flee her hometown, there was actually one family from the majority group who had helped her. To follow the divorce metaphor, the good parts about the "spouse" must also be integrated before the marital partners can be reconciled.

But we cannot demand "forgiveness" of separated partners who are not yet ready for it. Before that stage, the partners probably need to recover their feelings of security in the community at large, to recover their life-project, and to recover their trust in a safe world. This will be of tremendous importance for peace in the twenty-first century, which could otherwise be threatened by new violent cycles of conflict instigated by those who seek revenge. Thus, building peace includes a psychological and social process of reconciliation within individuals and families, as well as between individuals, families, and groups. However, social and economic development is also needed in order to reduce exploitation and repression—the basis on which ethno-nationalist leaders can recruit the discontented for their dubious cause.

CHAPTER 21

RECONCILIATION IN DIVIDED SOCIETIES

Cheryl de la Rey

Reconciliation is a complex concept. As is the case with many concepts that describe human interaction, it cannot be easily defined. Reconciliation has been interpreted in many different ways, and it has been given form through a range of structures and processes that vary across contexts and boundaries. This chapter provides a mapping of the complexities of its meaning, identifying points of clarity and consensus while also pointing to areas that require further explication. Exploration of the meanings of a concept such as reconciliation is not a mere semantic exercise, for as Kriesberg (1998) has suggested, understanding these variations is critical to developing theories, policies, and practices that promote peaceful societies. Moreover, mapping the meaning of reconciliation is central to the mission of peace psychology as envisioned in this volume, namely, that peace psychology seeks to develop theories and practices that elucidate psychological processes involved in the prevention and mitigation of violence.

CHARACTERISTICS OF DIVIDED SOCIETIES

One of the reasons that it is so difficult to arrive at a single definition of reconciliation is that its interpretation seems to vary depending upon the specific dynamics within a social context. For example, Hamber and van der Merwe (1998) have distinguished five ways in which people in South Africa have interpreted reconciliation. Chief among these five is what they term the *non-racial ideology of reconciliation*. This interpretation sees the reconciliation as decreasing the salience of racial identities that formed the basis of the old apartheid system. This may be appropriate in a context like South Africa where race discrimination between black and white people has been the primary source of conflict, but it may not be applicable in a context such as Northern Ireland, where the divisions are political and religious. Therefore, a good starting point for an analysis of the multiplicity of meanings of reconciliation with a view to identifying commonalities is to identify the characteristics that create the *need* for reconciliation. At a meta-level, or across the variations of context, what are the defining features of contemporary conflicts across the globe? Using the analysis carried out by Lederach (1995), the following key characteristics may be listed:

- structural injustice such as poverty and oppression
- the lines of conflict typically coincide with group identities where one group has been oppressed by the other

- the conflicts have long histories across generations
- conflicting parties are in close geographical proximity
- there has been direct, physical violence

As is evident from this list, the concept of *relationship,* albeit conflictual, is often central to the divisions in contemporary societies. It makes sense then, that any policies established to promote reconciliation must focus on *changing the relationship* between the parties in conflict. On this aspect, there is consensus.

While the notion of relationship is central, there are several other aspects of reconciliation that are considered below in the section on mapping meaning. Then I discuss the preconditions for reconciliation, continuing with a brief overview of some of the methods for reconciliation, followed by the conclusion of the chapter. To illustrate many of the issues, the case of South Africa, my native country, is frequently cited. A short overview of the South African Truth and Reconciliation Commission (TRC) follows to provide a context for the examples used throughout the chapter.

SOUTH AFRICA'S TRUTH AND RECONCILIATION COMMISSION

A central question faced by societies whenever an era of oppression has ended is how does one achieve closure of the past and set the scene for a peaceful future? The first-ever democratic elections in South Africa in April 1994 marked the end of legislated racism, known as *apartheid,* which had begun in 1948. Under the apartheid system of government, all South Africans were classified in terms of one of four main racial categories: Black, White, Asian (mostly people of Indian descent), and colored (mixed race). These racial classifications determined where the individual lived, worked, what kind of job s/he could do, and whom s/he could marry. Apartheid was a complete system of racial segregation which determined life circumstances and access to opportunity. Only people classified as White had the vote and thus controlled the government, the economy, and the entire society. This system of minority rule (Whites comprise only 13 percent of the population) was enforced by a web of state security which included the army and the police. All peaceful resistance was brutally crushed through detentions, torture, and murder. Consequently, political organizations opposing apartheid, such as the African National Congress, were forced into exile. A protracted struggle for liberation ensued both inside and outside the country. By the early 1990s, the extent of the political resistance and international pressure exerted through measures such as economic sanctions had increased such that the demise of apartheid seemed imminent.

The elections in 1994 were a culmination of a four-year process of negotiations in which the key players were the African National Congress in alliance with other liberation parties on the one side, and the Nationalist Party/South African government on the other side. The South African Government of National Unity (GNU) elected into office in April 1994 ended White minority rule and faced the tricky question of how to confront the wrongs of the past while simultaneously pursuing national reconciliation, unity, and peace. In answer to this question, South Africa turned to the concept of a truth commission. The Promotion of National Unity and Reconciliation Bill establishing the Truth and Reconciliation Commission (TRC) was signed by President Mandela in May 1995, and it became an Act of Parliament in July of the same year.

Four key words encapsulate the objectives of the TRC: truth, forgiveness, healing, and reconciliation. In broader terms, the tasks of the TRC were to:

- establish as complete a picture as possible of the causes, nature, and extent of the gross violations of human rights committed during the years of apartheid.

- facilitate the granting of amnesty to persons who make full disclosure of all relevant facts relating to acts with a political objective.

- establish and make known the fate of victims, restore their human and civil dignity by granting them an opportunity to relate their own accounts of the violations, and make recommendations on reparation measures in respect of the violations.

- compile a comprehensive report of the activities and findings of the TRC together with recommendations of measures to prevent future violations of human rights.

It was believed that through the process of meeting these objectives, the commission would restore the moral order of South African society, create a culture of human rights and respect for the rule of law, and prevent the past abuses happening again.

After a process of consultation, the President appointed 17 TRC commissioners, with Archbishop Desmond Tutu as the chairperson. The criteria for the appointment of the commissioners were that they had to be fit and proper persons who were seen as impartial and who did not have a high political profile. The composition of the commissioners as a group showed sensitivity to both race and gender. Seven women were appointed, and all race groups were represented.

The commissioners presided over three committees: the Committee on Human Rights Violations, the Committee on Amnesty, and the Committee on Reparation and Rehabilitation of Victims. Each of these three committees had different tasks which were executed with the assistance of specific support structures such as an investigations arm, a research unit, and a media department. The Committee on Human Rights Violations was responsible for conducting public hearings throughout the country. The purpose of these public hearings was to provide survivors of human rights abuses the opportunity to tell their stories and thereby come to terms with the pain and trauma of the past. The task of the Committee on Amnesty was to consider applications for amnesty from those who had committed political crimes. A condition for granting amnesty was that the perpetrator had to first disclose the full details of the abuse, and the act of abuse had to be within the definition of a political crime. The Committee on Reparation and Rehabilitation was to make recommendations to the government on how to implement a reparations policy.

The TRC was not wholly a judicial process. It was not fully constituted as an institution of law, but it did follow some procedures of law, for example, the use of legal representatives and cross-examination procedures. It could name perpetrators and grant amnesty without a trial and conviction in a court of law. However, the TRC could not carry out prosecutions nor could it sentence. Wilson (1995) noted that the legal system and the TRC had to be seen as "complementary and working in tandem, with the latter compensation for the limitations and deficiencies of the former" (p. 42).

In South Africa, the formation of the Truth and Reconciliation Commission created a great deal of public debate on the meaning of reconciliation. Many of these debates were facilitated by the TRC itself in a concerted effort to achieve its task. References to these debates and the TRC processes appear throughout this chapter with an eye to illuminating the complexities involved in reconciliation.

MAPPING THE MEANING OF RECONCILIATION

Reconciliation as Process and Outcome

Overall, reconciliation is widely seen as a process undertaken to restore relationships, rather than as an event (e.g., Kriesberg, 1998; TRC Report, 1996). Based on an analysis of the use of the term in everyday language, Cohen (1997) concludes that reconciliation is used to refer both to a process *and* a state that is the outcome of the process. To illustrate, she offered the example of the release of political prisoners which, she suggests, may be understood as a step in a process designed to achieve a state of reconciliation between conflicting parties.

Kraybill (1992) offers another version of reconciliation. He very specifically defines reconciliation as a process that unfolds in stages over time. According to his model, each stage poses new challenges and dilemmas to be addressed. Therefore, the process is complex. Kraybill's model differs from many others in that he views reconciliation as a cyclic process; namely, a process that will be repeated many times to transform the differences in relationships.

Reconciliation as Relationship Building

There is widespread agreement that reconciliation necessarily involves the *restoration* of relationships that have been fractured. Moving from strife or antagonism to a more positive relationship is a defining feature of

reconciliation. But there are variations in the type of relationship necessary for reconciliation to occur. Kriesberg (1998) explains that one meaning is to bring people who have had some history of conflict into a harmonious relationship. Another meaning may be to bring people *into agreement* on a set of historical events or circumstances. Or reconciliation may just involve developing the capacity to live with one another, according to TRC Commissioner, Wynand Malan (TRC, 1998a).

Whatever the nuances in meaning, reconciliation is undoubtedly a relational concept. This statement then begs the question: relationship between whom? One way of answering this question is to import the categorization scheme used by Tavuchis (1991) in his work on apology and reconciliation. Applied to reconciliation, it would read as follows:

- interpersonal reconciliation between one individual and another (one to one)
- reconciliation between an individual and a collectivity (one to many)
- reconciliation between a collectivity and an individual (many to one)
- reconciliation between one collectivity to another (many to many)

This means that reconciliation may vary in terms of units of analysis. As Kriesberg (1998) observes, it may be achieved between individuals, families, officials, groups, or any combination thereof. However, in the context of a deeply divided society these units of interaction, be they individuals or collectivities, would more than likely have had a long history of experience where some people would have been in a position of power or privilege over others. Given Lederach's characteristics of divided societies, they are also likely to have had experience of direct physical violence. Thus individuals or collectivities would enter into reconciliation not simply as individuals or collectivities but with a history of relationships, as perpetrators or victims and/or as beneficiaries or victims. This brings into play the role of the past in reconciliation.

RECONCILIATION: PAST, PRESENT, AND FUTURE

In South Africa throughout the TRC process, the need to address the past was emphasized. On signing the legislation that created the TRC, President Nelson Mandela proclaimed "We can now deal with our past." du Toit (1996) has explained that dealing with the past is an historical act of interpretation through which we try to understand and explain ourselves personally and nationally.

This explanation hinges on the understanding that in divided societies the past would have had a negative impact on the identity of people as humans. In whatever ways the lines of power differentials were drawn, be it race or ethnicity or religion, there would have been consequences for all, be they beneficiaries or victims. Frye (1992) has used the image of a bird in a cage to illustrate the impact of a system of oppression. She makes the point that barriers, such as the wires of a birdcage, are restrictive to those within the cage and those outside of it. Of course, the meaning is different if one is inside. For the bird in the cage, it is immobilization; those outside control the lock and keys. This metaphor highlights the significance of power inequalities; the wires of the cage cut people off from one another as humans in relationship with other humans.

The *dehumanizing* impact of a system of oppression on those who seemingly benefit from the system is illustrated in the final TRC report (1998b). In one of the testimonies, a victim of torture asked the perpetrator: "When you do those things, what happens to you as a human being?" He responded: " . . . as long as I was one of the Whites, the privileged Whites who had an education, who had a house, I couldn't see it being taken away. If you ask me what type of person is it that can do that, I ask myself the same question" (p. 15).

Cohen (1997) uses the concept *alienation* to describe the estrangement from other human beings experienced during prolonged periods of conflict and structural violence. In her terms, we become estranged or disaffected from another person when we see them as outside of our moral community. She says that this is the type of dehumanization that makes it possible for enemies to inflict torture and to kill. Another feature of this type of alienation, explains Cohen, is that it is accompanied by a corresponding splitting within oneself. This is perhaps seen in the following testimony given during the TRC public hearings: A man describes how after the death of his brother at the hands of the White army, " . . . anti-White obsession grew, and I would dream about burning down White businesses and farms. . . . I then began to fantasize and, while this may seem laughable, I sincerely prayed to God to make me invisible for just one day so that I could do the things I dreamed of, and when God did not comply, I reduced the time to one hour, and in that hour I was determined to go to Parliament and shoot every cabinet minister" (TRC, 1998b, p. 19).

We see in these accounts that there are sound psychological reasons for dealing with the past to attain reconciliation in divided societies. Through a reinterpretation of the past, people may work toward changing themselves and in this way build a future of community. Reconciliation is, therefore, poised in relation to three time frames: a very specific form of relationship building that necessitates a linking of *past* with *future* through the *present.*

Reconciliation and Truth

An additional reason for dealing with the past is that in many situations of prolonged oppression and resistance, numerous individuals seemingly disappear or die under mysterious circumstances. As a result, many people are left simply not knowing what happened to relatives and loved ones. In such situations, an undertaking to deal with the past is likely to become a search for the truth. Such was the case in South Africa. Throughout the TRC process, establishing the truth has been one of "the principal paths South Africans have taken to deal with their dark past" (Hamber, 1997, p. 1). But the TRC experience has shown that this is a complex task subject to political contestation.

A central point of contention concerns the question "What is truth?" At one level there is factual truth: Did something happen or not? But there is also truth as interpretation. In psychology, we have seen the emergence of post-structuralism, a theoretical framework which rejects the idea of an absolute truth in favor of a multiplicity of truths. At a very simple level, this is a view that incorporates the significance of perspective in definitions of what is true. Rothman (1998) spells it out as follows: "When conflicting parties in identity conflict do describe its significance in historical terms, observers may believe different histories are being told. In many ways this is so. . . . One side's freedom fighter is very often another side's terrorist" (p. 231)

Truth may be *factual* evidence, but it may also be *subjective* account. The complex-ity of the question of what is truth is powerfully illustrated in the following statement made to the TRC (1998b):

> Coming from the apartheid era at my age, 43, I was never a supporter, an active supporter of apartheid. But it's something that you grew up with, and things changed quite fast in the last couple of years. All of a sudden you start hearing from the blacks how they've been ill-treated, exploited, all kinds of words and all of a sudden you start seeing the bad side of it. . . . coming from a background where everything was fine for all these years, now all of a sudden . . . the police were the baddies. (p. 8)

In this statement, we see that what someone understands as truth may be shaped by his or her position within a social system; we also see how versions of truth may change as social and historical circumstances shift over time.

Is truth necessary for reconciliation? A nuanced answer is provided in Hamber's (1997) observation that "Some victims may be satisfied by knowing the facts. . . . but for others, truth may heighten anger and calls for justice rather than lead to feelings of reconciliation" (p. 2). He further points out that there is a possibility that truth may produce revenge rather than reconciliation. The tensions around the meaning of truth emerged during the TRC process even though the Commission tried to be accommodating. On the one hand, people were allowed to tell their version of events without being subjected to cross-examination, but on the other hand there was an investigative unit which worked at establishing the facts. Answers to the question of how this tension is to be bridged in the reconciliation process may perhaps best be derived through careful consideration of why the truth is important. The accuracy of the historical record may be one reason, but another is the importance of merely *acknowl-*

edging and validating the hurtful experiences of the past.

Reconciliation as Acknowledging the Other

Acknowledgment of the other is widely viewed as critical to reconciliation. Lederach (1995), in fact, argues that it is decisive in the reconciliation dynamic. The exclusion of the other, someone who does not belong to one's own group, from the scope of a moral framework is a key factor in violence between groups. Earlier in this chapter, Cohen's (1997) concept of alienation was outlined to explain the psychology of dehumanization. Toscano (1998), on the other hand, refers to a particular form of identity known as narcissistic identity, to explain the psychological processes involved in denying of the humanity of the other. He has aptly named it "erasing the face of the other" (p. 67). *Narcissistic group identity* occurs when one's own group is perceived as so superior to any other group that the others are seen as outside the moral code of one's community.

A widely supported idea is that if reconciliation is to be attained, the different sides of the conflict must relate to one another as *humans in relationship.* The traditional African concept of *ubuntu* describes the philosophy that a person is a person through other persons or "I am human because you are human. If I undermine your humanity, I dehumanize myself" (Gevisser, 1996, p. 103).

Acknowledging the existence of the humanity of the other after a protracted period of conflict is necessarily emotional. Toscano (1998) distinguishes three components that are involved in the process he calls "the reconstruction of the face of the other." The first component is cognitive—knowing the other; the second component is emotive—valuing the other; and the third

component is behavioral—getting closer to the other. In distinguishing cognition from the other two components, Toscano draws attention to reconciliation as an *emotional activity.* We acknowledge the other through understanding the harm that has occurred through our actions, either directly or indirectly. This is cogently illustrated in the TRC testimony of a man who said that he felt the peace of reconciliation when he placed himself "in the other person's shoes" and considered ". . . how would I have felt about it. How would I have liked not to be able to vote, not to have any rights, and that kind of thing. So I realized that I would not have liked it, so I realized how it must have felt for them."

Throughout the TRC hearings there was much talk of the pain and suffering that people had experienced. Many psychologists have emphasized that reconciliation necessarily involves the expression of pain, guilt, anger, and sorrow (e.g., Edelstein & Gibson, 1993; Statman, 1995). Mechanisms that provide the space and opportunity for people on both sides to express their experiences of pain and loss can be a significant means towards a mutual acknowledgment of the moral reality of the other. But whether this should lead to apology and forgiveness is a question over which there is little consensus.

Reconciliation, Apology, and Forgiveness

In considering the role of apology and forgiveness in reconciliation, Cohen (1997) notes that several scholars, such as Brummer (1992) and Tavuchis (1991), virtually make reconciliation equivalent with apology and forgiveness. In South Africa many researchers would seem to agree. Villa-Vicencio (1995), the head of research in the TRC, has stated that "Forgiveness, contrition, penance, repentance, restitution and reconciliation are an integrated whole" (p. 121). However, there is no agreement on this issue. Cohen also considers the work of other scholars, such as the anthropologist Gulliver (1979), who do not believe that apology and forgiveness is a central issue in reconciliation.

The meanings, nature, and functions of apology are explored in great detail in Tavuchis's work, which draws attention to the very specific requirements of an apology. At a minimal level, it incorporates an *admission* that there has been a violation and an expression of *regret*. Forgiveness would mean that the offended party accepts the offender's acknowledgment of the wrong together with the expression of sorrow. In this way both parties, the offender and the offended, are brought into a common moral community. A woman whose son had been killed by the police during the apartheid era, when asked how she saw the concept of reconciliation, responded:

> What we are hoping for when we embrace the notion of reconciliation is that we restore the humanity to those who were perpetrators. We do not want to return evil by another evil. . . . I think that all South Africans should be committed to the idea of re-accepting these people back into the community. . . . We want to demonstrate humaneness towards them, so that they in turn may restore their own humanity. (TRC, 1998b, p. 13)

Thus we see a view of reconciliation that relies on the mutual recognition of humans as moral agents.

Hamber and van der Merwe (1998) note a second approach—the human rights approach—that seeks to establish a new order but typically through the establishment of democracy and legal and civil rights. Even though the moral and the human rights approaches are competing models, they can co-exist. Indeed, the final report of the TRC suggests that a weak or limited form of reconciliation that emphasizes peaceful co-existence may often be the most realistic goal for societies trying to overcome decades of conflict, especially at the beginning of the peacemaking process.

Reconciliation, Reparation, and Justice

Apology and forgiveness clearly try to deal with the wrong that has been done; another form of acknowledging that wrong has been committed may be achieved through *reparation* or making amends in some way. Tangible forms of reparation may include financial compensation, memorials, policies and procedures offering protection against future violations, or even some type of punishment for the perpetrators. It raises images of making things right or rectifying wrong.

Justice is about fairness and equality. Boesak (1996) makes a distinction between two forms of justice that may enter into reconciliation. The first form is punitive or *retributive justice*. The second is *compensatory justice*. Reparations are a form of the latter and can be distinguished from restitution. Whereas reparations refer to compensatory measures, restitution refers to measures aimed at restoring the dignity and humanity of victims (and sometimes their families).

Reparations may be both the responsibility of the state and of the perpetrators. In South Africa, the TRC recommended that the state pay reparations as a way for the nation to show sorrow for the victims. In some cases, the perpetrators themselves undertook some form of reparation. Examples included setting up a trust fund for victims, participation in community work, and cooperation with the authorities to expose further abuses. Whether it is from the state or the perpetrators themselves, reparations may take many different forms, from symbolic to legal and administrative measures. Tavuchis (1991) raises the possibility that apology itself, if offered and accepted, may constitute sufficient restitution.

The TRC hearings showed that the needs of people are likely to be varied. First, as Tavuchis suggests, acknowledgment and apology is sufficient for some. Others want financial assistance, and yet other people simply want symbolic measures. Then, there are those who, as Kriesberg (1998) points out, want punishment for the perpetrators. In sum, there are no reconciliation procedures that are guaranteed to be successful in every instance. People's needs differ, as do the circumstances underlying the conflict they have been engaged in.

PRECONDITIONS FOR RECONCILIATION

What circumstances are most conducive to the initiation of the reconciliation process? Very little is known definitively in answer to this question, for we are still developing our knowledge about the process of reconciliation in practical terms. In the absence of such a body of knowledge, we may turn to related fields, such as conflict transformation and peacebuilding, to explore lessons to be learned.

Reconciliation generally begins when a relationship of conflict between groups shifts to a new phase of lessened conflict, typically through an agreement of some type. Zartman (1985) used the concept of the "ripe moment" to talk about opportunities that offer hope for the resolution of conflict. But as de Silva and Samarasinghe's (1993) review demonstrates, peace accords and agreements that result from mediation often fail to bring about reconciliation. Lederach (1995) identifies the critical element as the *role of relationship:* In the negotiations

and peace talks which often occur between conflicting groups, *do the parties take serious account of the need for developing relationship, not only at the top level of leadership but also at the middle-range and grassroots levels?* He argues that without incorporating the dynamics of and space for relationship building, peace accords and agreements will not translate into reconciliation.

Lederach's propositions are still to be subjected to systematic study. Richardson Jr. and Wang (1993) point out that amongst authors who have done case studies there is no consensus on the essential preconditions for peace; there is no list that guarantees successful relationship building.

METHODS AND MECHANISMS FOR RECONCILIATION

The chapter now turns to the praxis of reconciliation. In this section, I present a short overview of some mechanisms used in the reconciliation process, to overcome the conflict of the past and to restore social harmony.

Storytelling and Testimony

Psychologists such as Gergen (1989) and Bruner (1990) have promulgated the idea that people use narrative to make sense of themselves and their experiences within a socio-historical context. In their view, narrative or storytelling is central to the construction of the individual's self-perception and worldview. This proposition is evident in Botman's (1996) statement that people "communicate, confess, forgive and reconcile in the form of stories" (p. 37).

Public storytelling in the form of giving testimony was the primary mechanism used in the South African TRC process. As explained in an article by de la Rey and Owens (1998), the South Africans were strongly influenced by the Chilean experience in turning to testimony as a mechanism for reconciliation. Public hearings were held in venues across the country where people told their stories of pain, suffering, and loss. The public nature of the event—having an audience, having the story reported in the media and recorded as written text—permitted the reconstruction of private, individual trauma as part of a larger social-political process. Botman (1996) described it as follows:

> Victims and perpetrators and those who thought that they were just innocent bystanders, now realize their complicity, and have an opportunity to participate in each other's humanity in story form. (p. 37)

The value of storytelling has also been endorsed by Rothman (1998), who has argued that storytelling is particularly significant in identity-based conflict. This makes sense, given the idea that self-perceptions are constructed through stories. In evaluating the TRC process of public testimony, Hamber (1997) concluded that providing space for the telling of stories was clearly useful.

Dialogue

A common assumption about deeply divided societies is that an absence of dialogue is at the source of the conflict. Communication is then presented as the antidote. But as Rothman (1998) points out, in many divided societies there is dialogue even when there is intense conflict. Thus not all types of dialogue may be useful in attaining reconciliation. Rothman has identified several distinct dialogue approaches. If dialogue is used as a method for reconciliation, which approach should be used?

Reflexive dialogue, which allows disputing parties to articulate to each other and discover the meeting points in their narratives, best fits the requirements of reconciliation as outlined in this chapter. It is an approach in which participants "reframe their perceptions and analyses of each other and their own identities; . . . they learn to articulate their own voice and recognize each other's as valid" (Rothman, 1998, p. 234). During the course of the dialogue, questions are posed for the purposes of clarification and mutual understanding until it is possible to see one another as humans. It therefore resonates with the core components of reconciliation as outlined in this chapter.

Traditional Institutions

Honwana (1997), in discussing reconstruction in Mozambique, argues that the process of community rebuilding needs to take into account the worldview of the local population. For the reconciliation process, this may mean making a space for the role of traditional institutions and practices. Honwana describes a number of rituals that are aimed at self-renewal, healing, and restoration. Among the mostly rural population of Mozambique, chiefs, healers, spiritualists, and diviners are significant role-players in the lives of the people. In South Africa, the TRC tried to incorporate rituals to signify loss, death, and closure. Ritual activities may include washing of clothes, slaughtering of animals, and communal feasts. Symbolically they refer to concepts such as confession, forgiveness, and apology.

The role of religion as a traditional institution is another important mechanism for reconciliation. Prayers and religious services are used for forgiveness, guidance, and, generally, to restore relationships. These activities may be meaningfully used in the reconciliation process *if* they are consistent with the worldviews of the particular communities.

Legislation and Policies

There is the view that change of relationships, although vital to reconciliation, by itself is not enough. It needs to be accompanied by changes in social structure (Statman, 1997). The *creation of a human rights culture* is widely viewed as pivotal to reconciliation in modern societies. This usually involves introducing new legislation and policies, as well as measures to safeguard these initiatives. Many of these *structural* methods are described in Section IV of this volume.

Although the TRC is probably South Africa's most well-known mechanism for reconciliation, a number of structural methods have been implemented since the advent of democracy in the society. A constitution with a bill of rights is one; others have included a human rights commission, a gender equality commission, and a youth commission. Together these structures are aimed at creating a society in which there is a culture of human rights. Through monitoring and acting on complaints from citizens, these structures enhance the possibility of sustainable peaceful co-existence, noted in a previous section as a form of reconciliation.

An important component of reconciliation is the reduction of inequalities between groups. Policies such as affirmative action and specific equal opportunity programs may be used to reduce inequalities (Kriesberg, 1998). Another method listed by Kriesberg is the use of superordinate goals and the fostering of common identities. The creation of a new sense of nationhood through a new national anthem and other national symbols, such as a flag, is often a way to foster a common identity among formerly divided societies. In many instances the country may also be renamed. In South Africa a new flag was chosen through a public participation process in which individuals could submit designs. These were then published in the mass media for comment before the flag was finally chosen.

CONCLUSION

As we move into the twenty-first century, we are confronted with a number of ethnic-based conflicts in different parts of the world; some, such as in Northern Ireland, Israel, and Palestine, show signs of abating, but others, such as in Sri Lanka, do not. A pivotal challenge for peace psychologists as we enter the twenty-first century is the further development of our knowledge base on reconciliation in both theory and practice. There is a dire need for systematic empirical research on issues such as the identification of the minimum conditions for reconciliation practices that work. We need answers to questions such as what are the basic requirements for relationship building, what strategies are most likely to be effective, and how can positive beginnings such as the TRC be translated into sustainable social harmony in contexts of diversity. Furthermore, given the variation across contexts, there is a particular need for research across boundaries of ethnicity, nationhood, and culture. Finally, although developing our knowledge base is critical, we also need to take steps to ensure that the accumulated knowledge is widely disseminated and put into practice where required.

CHAPTER 22

PSYCHOSOCIAL INTERVENTION AND POST-WAR RECONSTRUCTION IN ANGOLA: INTERWEAVING WESTERN AND TRADITIONAL APPROACHES

Michael Wessells and Carlinda Monteiro

The intra-state wars that now comprise the dominant form of armed conflict in the world (Wallensteen & Sollenberg, 1998) cause immense physical, psychological, and social damage, and create profound obstacles to peace. Since the fighting occurs in and around communities, civilians constitute nearly 90 percent of the casualties, in contrast with the situation at the beginning of this century when combatants comprised the majority of war casualties (Garfield & Neugut, 1997; Sivard, 1991). Many of the intra-state conflicts of the 1990s are protracted: nearly 40 percent are ten or more years old, and 25 percent are over 20 years old (Smith, 1997). These conflicts have devastated local infrastructure and amplified already severe problems of poverty and displacement. Lacking well-defined end-points and defying tidy distinctions between relief and development (*World Disasters Report*, 1996), they have created complex humanitarian emergencies that entail mass needs for food, clean water, and basic health services. Typically, they place societies at risk of continuing cycles of political and criminal violence. In protracted conflicts, poverty and violence exist in a mutually supportive spiral, violence becomes normalized, and violence in communities and families continues long after the signing of a ceasefire.

These situations, exemplified in countries such as Angola, Guatemala, Rwanda, Somalia, and Uganda, require *post-war reconstruction* (also called *post-conflict reconstruction*), defined as efforts to assist the transition from widespread violence to peace.

Comprehensive post-war reconstruction is not simply social rehabilitation but a *proactive* step toward conflict prevention and interruption of ongoing cycles of violence. Following decades of economic, political, and ecological distress, effective assistance in rebuilding often comes from nongovernmental organizations (NGOs), U.N. agencies, and intergovernmental institutions such as the World Bank (Minear & Weiss, 1993; Weiss & Collins, 1996).

Peace psychology has much to contribute to efforts toward post-war reconstruction. Psychologists' role in post-conflict reconstruction, however, has seldom been articulated and is not widely appreciated, particularly among policy-makers who make decisions about handling complex emergencies. The purpose of this chapter is twofold. First, it aims to show that psychosocial reconstruction is an integral part of wider, multidisciplinary processes of post-war reconstruction. Second, it examines a national program for psychosocial reconstruction in Angola conducted by Christian Children's Fund (CCF), an international NGO. The program addresses two main elements of psychosocial reconstruction: healing the wounds of war and demobilizing and socially reintegrating former child soldiers. The focus on Angola is timely because the scale of human needs there is immense and because Angola remains trapped in recurrent cycles of violence. To make its maximum contribution, psychological methods must be shown to apply under the most dire conditions. The program discussed here fits within the definition of peace psychology since it aims to help prevent violence. Further, Angolan cosmology and traditional practices challenge the assumptions of Western peace psychology, offer an opportunity for intercultural learning and integration, and work in a partnership mode.

TASKS AND CHALLENGES OF POST-WAR RECONSTRUCTION

Post-war reconstruction entails interrelated tasks of economic, political, and social reconstruction (Ball, 1997; Kumar, 1997). Economic reconstruction tasks include rebuilding damaged infrastructure, including homes, roads and bridges, health centers, and schools; currency stabilization and monetary reform; demining; agricultural reestablishment; job creation; and means of addressing poverty, which war amplifies. Political reconstruction tasks include creating a legitimate (typically integrated) government; regularly conducting elections; demilitarizing and demobilizing soldiers; constructing law and order through civilian police and a functioning justice system; political discourse; building norms of political participation; and settling political disputes. Social reconstruction tasks include rebuilding civil society; resettling displaced peoples; revitalizing the community; establishing awareness of and support for basic human rights; and creating social trust across the lines of conflict. In all of these tasks, a high priority is the establishment of *social justice*, transforming patterns of exclusion, inequity, and oppression that fuel tensions and fighting.

Psychosocial intervention is a small but essential part of post-conflict reconstruction (Wessells, 1998a; 1998b). Although the signing of a peace accord may be an important step, it does not constitute peace because a system of violence is what often remains on the ground. The "wronged victims" identity thwarts peace, invites revenge, and provides convenient rationalization for acts of violence and oppression that might typically be regarded as immoral. War also creates powerful fears and exaggerated enemy images of the diabolical Other (White, 1984), all of which heighten the risk of ongoing cycles of violence and present powerful obstacles to national reconciliation and the construction of civil society. Protracted conflicts often normalize violence and draw large numbers of youth into soldiering (Brett & McCallin, 1996; Cairns, 1996; Wessells, 1997). In the aftermath of armed conflict, violence often saturates families and communities, and a shift may occur from political to criminal violence. Exposure to violence at various social levels impedes development, as violence-affected children may experience difficulties in school and violence-affected adults may not be in a good position to make decisions about health, governance, and the future.

In these situations, psychosocial intervention is needed to interrupt cycles of violence and to provide a psychological climate in which peacebuilding, reconciliation, and sustainable development processes can take root. More than a means of reducing suffering, psychosocial intervention is a key component of conflict prevention. Important tasks of psychosocial reconstruction include healing wounds of war; the social reintegration of former soldiers; community mobilization; social integration of displaced people; assistance to mine victims and mine-awareness training; cross-conflict dialogue and cooperation; fear-reduction; tolerance building; truth-telling; forgiveness and reconciliation; and the reestablishment of normal patterns and routines, among others.

Significant challenges, however, confront efforts at psychosocial reconstruction. First, few roadmaps exist for rebuilding psychologically on a national scale following long-term war in an environment where money and psychological expertise are in short supply. Second, cultural differences thwart efforts to apply Western models "off the shelf," and attempts to use Western methods exclusively can silence local knowledge, block the recovery of traditional methods, and promote psychological imperialism (Dawes, 1997). Third, the very definition of "reconstruction" is problematic. To define it as the rebuilding of what had been present before the fighting had erupted is to risk supporting a status quo that may violate human rights, privilege particular groups, and in the long run, encourage conflict. If external actors define reconstruction, problems of dependency and external domination arise. If internal elites define reconstruction, they may construct programs to advance their own political purposes, making reconstructive efforts a political tool. Fourth, psychologists are trained as specialists, but effective psychosocial reconstruction must be holistic and integrated with wider efforts toward political, economic, and social reconstruction (Wessells, 1998a; Wessells & Kostelny, 1996).

These challenges admit no simple answers and demand that psychosocial reconstruction work be initiated in a manner that encourages dialogue, mutual learning, and power-sharing; puts culture at the center; integrates psychosocial work into wider programs of reconstruction; and stimulates critical reflection about the goals, methods, and processes used. The program described in this chapter attempts to meet these challenges through the use of a community-based approach that blends Western and traditional methods and works collaboratively with a large number of local communities and agencies. To see the context for the program, it is necessary to sketch briefly the Angolan context.

WAR, STRESSES, AND HEALING IN ANGOLA

War raged in Angola for nearly 35 years, from 1961 to 1994, and new fighting on a wide scale erupted at the end of 1998. The first stage of war, a liberation struggle against the Portuguese colonial regime, began in 1961. Although independence came in 1975, internal groups struggled for power. The Angolan civil war soon joined the ranks of the proxy wars in the global struggle between the United States and the Soviet Union (Minter, 1994). The Angolan socialist government, which received extensive aid from the Soviet Union and troops and military support from Cuba, fought against the opposition forces of UNITA (the National Union for the Total Independence of Angola), headed by Jonas Savimbi and backed by the United States and apartheid South Africa. The end of the Cold War, coupled with the defeat of South African forces in the 1988 battle of Cuito Cuanavale, undermined outside support for the warring parties. A stalemate in fighting and rising international pressures for peace led in May, 1991, to the Bicesse Peace Accords, establishing a ceasefire and enabling national elections.

The ceasefire, however, was short-lived. In national elections held in November, 1992, the current president, Eduardo dos Santos narrowly failed to achieve the required 50 percent of the vote over Jonas Savimbi. UNITA denounced the elections, and fighting re-erupted October 31, 1992. This time—late 1992 through May, 1994—the fighting was particularly intense and claimed heavy civilian casualties. A U.N. Consolidated Appeal estimated that 3.3 million people were in need of emergency assistance. The number of internally displaced people rose from 344,000 in May, 1993 to 1.2 million people by September, 1994. Both sides used landmines extensively, leaving Angola with approximately 6 million landmines and ranking her with Cambodia and Afghanistan as one of the world's most heavily mined countries.

A stalemate in the fighting, coupled with international pressures, led to the sign-ing in November, 1994, of the Lusaka Protocol, which established a ceasefire, enabled disarmament and demobilization, an integrated army, and the formation in April, 1997 of a new Government of National Unity and Reconciliation. However, tensions remained high. Weak governmental and civil institutions and grinding poverty and desperation spurred rising crime and pervasive hopelessness. These factors may also have set the stage for the renewed fighting that began in late 1998.

IMPACT ON CHILDREN

Programs of post-war reconstruction in Angola must attend to the needs of children, who comprise nearly half the population and are key future resources yet who have grown up in a situation in which war is a daily reality. The war killed nearly 500,000 children, and it created nearly 15,000 "unaccompanied" children (separated from their families). Hunger, disease, and the destruction of health facilities boosted morbidity rates. By 1993, UNICEF estimated that 320 out of 1,000 children died before they had reached the age of five years.

In numerous provinces, children experienced singly or in combination chronic poverty, attack, loss of loved ones, uprooting, and community destruction. To assess children's war experiences and their psychosocial impact in provinces where extensive fighting had occurred, the Christian Children's Fund team used Exposure and Impact Scales, respectively, developed initially by Nancy Dubrow and Magne Raundalen and modified to fit the Angolan context. Figure 22.1 shows the Exposure Scale data for a sample of 100 randomly selected children (59 male and 41 female) between seven and 18 years of age. Large percentages of children had experienced attack and starvation, seen dead and wounded

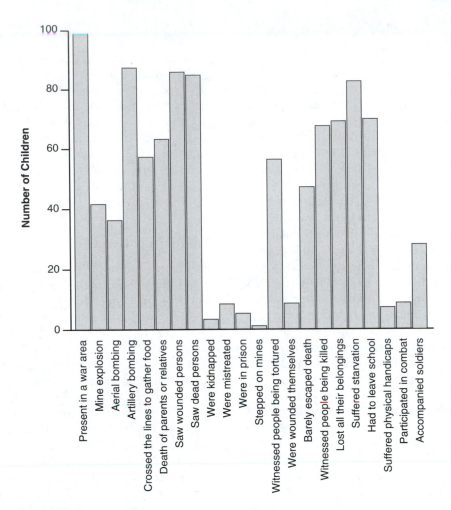

Figure 22.1   War experiences of children.

people, or suffered loss of relatives and belongings. The strong psychological impact is evident in Figure 22.2, which shows data from the Impact Scale for the same sample of children. Many children experienced fears, disturbed dreams, concentration difficulties, and exhibited heightened aggression and chronic isolation. In viewing these data, two caveats are noteworthy. First, there are no pre-war baseline data regarding

these behaviors. Second, the effects may owe not only to children's war experiences but also to the related experience of post-war violence in the family or community.

Psychosocial impacts are evident also in mine victims, mostly children, who suffered loss, disfigurement, disability, and stigmatization (Dastoor & Mocellin, 1997). Because of the extreme poverty, the anarchic environment in many rural areas, and the in-

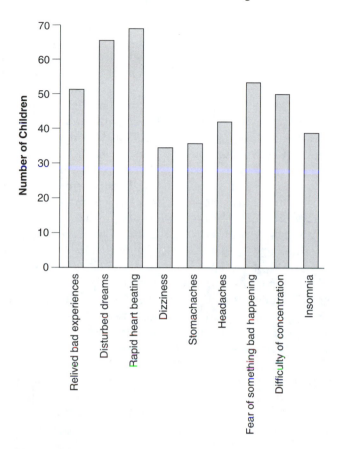

Figure 22.2   Psychological and physiological impact
of exposure to violence.

volvement of many education-deprived youths in the military, many youths have turned to banditry, which remains one of the biggest security problems in Angola today. Socialization for fighting is both a psychosocial impact of war and a source of continued violence.

TRAUMA, CULTURE, AND HEALING

Western-trained psychologists tend to enter war zones focusing on clinical problems such as trauma. Although many Angolan children present symptoms characteristic of Post-Traumatic Stress Disorder (PTSD; for

useful reviews, see Friedman & Marsella, 1996; van der Kolk, McFarlane, & Weisaeth, 1996), Western-defined diagnostic categories should be used judiciously. For many children, the biggest problem is poverty, and impoverished children who do not meet the formal criteria for PTSD may nonetheless be war-affected and in need of assistance (Dawes & Donald, 1994). In addition, war is profoundly political and social, yet terms such as "trauma" tend to medicalize and individualize the problem (Martín-Baró, 1994; Punamäki, 1989) and to focus intervention work excessively on individuals rather than on communities. Further, concentrating on trauma can pathologize entire populations, portraying people as victims, overlooking the significant resilience that often exists, and downplaying the importance of individual differences (see Agger, this volume).

The wider problem, however, is cultural. As constructed in Western psychology, terms such as "trauma" usually have few spiritual connotations. But in Angola, as in many Bantu areas of Africa, spirituality is at the center of life, and spiritual attributions regarding life events have profound psychological implications (Wessells & Monteiro, 2000). In Angolan cosmology, the visible world is fused with the world of the ancestors, who protect and participate in the life of the community. Significant events such as loss of loved ones are typically attributed to spiritual discord or failure to honor the ancestors through practice of appropriate rituals and traditions.

In this belief system, the spiritual dimensions of terrible life events have great salience and may be the primary source of stress. If, for example, a soldier had killed innocent people, he might experience strong guilt, but the greater stress might be his perception that he is haunted by the unavenged spirits of those he had killed. Stress may also stem from community rejection, as local people may believe that he is spiritually contaminated and that his return home would visit spiritual pollution on the community. Similarly, a child whose village had been destroyed and whose parents had been killed might experience great stress as a result of having fled without having conducted the culturally appropriate burial rite for the parents. The local belief is that without these rites, the parents' spirits cannot make transition to the realm of the ancestors, staying in a restless state and causing problems among the living. In both cases, the spiritual discord, which is communal rather than individual, threatens the vital linkage between the living and the ancestral community. Western-trained psychologists might overlook these spiritual, communal dimensions and might not learn about them from local people, who may withhold their traditional beliefs to avoid appearing backward. To be effective, work on healing must fit local beliefs about life and death, illness and health.

In this context, healing entails the conduct of culturally appropriate rituals to restore spiritual harmony. Nearly every community has a traditional healer who is trained in the performance of these rituals and who takes a holistic approach that interconnects physical, spiritual, and social elements of healing. Traditional healing in Angola remains poorly documented and must be approached cautiously and without romanticizing or essentializing it (Dawes, 1997; Wessells & Monteiro, 2000). Having a strong cultural foundation and extensive roots in local communities, it constitutes a valuable, sustainable resource for programs of healing and reconstruction.

A MULTI-PROVINCE PROGRAM FOR ADDRESSING WAR STRESSES

Coming to terms with the pain of the past is an essential first step toward a positive future. In Angola, the wounds of war are communal, so approaches to healing should also be communal. Much distress stems not only from spiritual discord but also from uprooting, community destruction, and the disruption of traditions and patterns of daily living. In addition, problems of hopelessness and futurelessness are communally constructed and shared phenomena. After so many years of war, many communities have lapsed into a state of diminished planfulness and activity. Many people find it difficult to imagine conditions other than war, heightening their vulnerability to political manipulation. To promote healing and hope, it is essential to revitalize communities, to strengthen traditions that provide a sense of continuity and support, and to build processes of dialogue and participation that strengthen civil society.

Community-based approaches to healing are indicated also by considerations concerning culture, local capacity, and sustainability. Individual approaches do not fit well the collectivist, group orientation of Angolan culture and are unaffordable in dire economic circumstances. Further, local communities embody local cultural practice and can assist in the construction of culturally grounded approaches to healing. Communities have a broad understanding of their needs, mitigating against programs that are not holistic and well integrated with community life. Since there are few trained psychologists in Angola, the emphasis should be on building local capacity and on scaling up to assist large numbers of war-affected people. By weaving this capacity into the fabric of communities, one increases sustainability, an immense concern in a country having very long-term needs that may outlast donors' interest.

The hallmarks of *community-based approaches* are that they honor local people and culture, using elicitive methods (Lederach, 1995) that stimulate mutual learning and working in a spirit of participation, dialogue, and partnership. It was in this vein that CCF/Angola initiated in September, 1995, a three-year training of trainers program that mobilizes communities around providing psychosocial assistance to war-affected children. The program worked in eight provinces most severely affected by war and it aimed to train 4,000 adults to assist 320,000 war-affected children.

To build local capacity, the program was led not by expatriates but by Angolans who knew the local situation, culture, and languages and who were selected for their leadership, commitment to children's well-being, strong relationship with local communities and organizations, background in social service, and flexibility in solving difficult problems. A five-person national team oversaw the program and selected and trained a team of three people in each province. Guidance for the trainings came from a situation analysis, the conduct of which enabled community entry and began a process of relationship building and partnership to assist children.

SITUATION ANALYSIS AND RELATIONSHIP BUILDING

In tandem with a pilot project conducted in Luanda from 1994 to 1995 (Wessells, 1996), the national team collected data from UNICEF, government ministries, and various NGOs to identify the provinces that had been most severely affected by war and that had the fewest services for providing psychosocial assistance to children. Within these provinces, work began with a *situation analysis* to identify children's needs, map the available local resources for assisting children, and pinpoint the communities in greatest need of assistance.

Sensitization (consciousness-raising) and relationship building were important elements of the local situation analyses. Since war had been a constant reality and the press of daily circumstances had made it difficult for local people to step back and reflect on their war experiences, there was little awareness of how children had been affected by the war. Most adults viewed problems such as children's aggression as signs of disobedience and did not connect them with children's experiences of war and violence. To build awareness, the provincial team typically met first, following

Angolan custom, with the local *soba* or tribal chief and male elders, including traditional healers. The team asked about the community's war experiences and whether youth experienced problems such as sleep disturbances, chronic isolation, and heightened aggression. Having noted possible association with children's war experiences, they talked about ways other communities had addressed children's needs through various methods, including traditional healing methods. Deeply concerned about their children and feeling valorized by the interest in local healing methods, most communities rapidly expanded the dialogue to include women and community members who worked extensively with children. Dialogue often led to joint agreement that the CCF teams and the local community should collaborate on work to assist children.

COMMUNAL SELECTION AND TRAINING

Adults were selected for training by their communities on the basis of their commitment to children's well-being and their ability to assist significant numbers of children. To integrate the intervention fully into community life, an attempt was made also to include people from different sectors such as health, education, and church and also to achieve gender balance.

Working in pairs, members of the provincial teams conducted week-long training seminars for 20 to 25 adults. The curriculum included basic concepts in five areas: children's psychosocial development, the impact of war on children, rites of death and mourning, methods of healing, and nonviolent conflict resolution. Emphasizing dialogue, the trainers built sessions around questions such as "What do children need to develop in a healthy manner?" Discussion revealed that war stresses were increasing

the levels of family violence, and it made little sense to address impacts of violence without also working to prevent additional violence. For this reason, the expanded curriculum included material on conflict resolution in families.

Conducted in a participatory style, the seminars enabled adults to talk about their own war experiences, and many reported that this was the first time they had engaged in such dialogue. The seminars also evoked much dialogue about traditional beliefs and local methods of healing. To teach specific activities that could be used to advance healing in children, the trainers emphasized Western methods of emotional expression in a secure, supportive environment. The seminars emphasized expressive arts such as drawing, drama, storytelling, and dance. In addition, organized sports were presented as a means of building cooperation and teamwork and of learning to handle conflict and frustration nonviolently. The seminars encouraged discussion about how to mix Western and traditional methods and about the strengths and weaknesses of various approaches.

ACTIVITIES AND PRELIMINARY RESULTS

Following the training seminars, trainees arranged in their communities a variety of expressive arts activities, sporting events, and educational dialogues. They also networked with traditional healers and, when appropriate, they encouraged the use of traditional healing methods for children.

To foster emotional expression in children, trainees used free-drawing methodology, giving children blank sheets of paper and crayons and asking them to draw whatever came to mind. Many children drew pictures related to their war experiences, enabling discussion with the trainer. Trainees also conducted structured group activities such as singing, dancing, sports, and informal educational dialogues. Within the community, trainees served as children's advocates who mobilized healers, teachers, elders, and others in assisting children. They arranged community discussions on children's needs, on ways in which the community could best meet these needs, and on policy changes that would assist children. Trainees received periodic follow-up visits and support from the trainers, who in turn received periodic follow-up visits and support from members of the national team.

Recognizing the close interconnection in a situation of poverty between psychosocial well-being and economic development, the province-based teams and trainees assisted communities in planning and implementing projects to assist children. For example, communities that planned to build a school could apply for a grant of approximately 10,000 U.S. dollars. The communities selected for funding, provided by the Dutch government, the World Bank, and other sources, used the money to purchase building materials and donated the labor themselves. In this manner, communities became agents of their own reconstruction.

By the end of the project, 172 training seminars had been conducted for a total of 4,894 adults, well in excess of the goal of training 4,000 adults. Although systematic data from pre- and post-tests are not yet available, focus group discussions indicated that the training seminars have increased awareness of children's psychosocial needs, of connections between children's war experiences and their current behavior, and of how the war affected adults and communities. In some communities, demand for additional seminars was high since participation had become a symbol of one's commitment to children (Green & Wessells,

1997). Adults reported that the training seminars had boosted their self-esteem by validating the traditional aspects of culture that had been suppressed during the colonial regime.

Focus group discussions with community leaders, parents, and trainees revealed that the intervention (training plus activities) had numerous positive impacts on children: improved child-child and adult-child relationships; improved behavior and cooperation in the classroom; diminished isolation behavior; less evidence of war-related games or toys; reduced violence and aggressive behavior between children; fewer concentration problems; decreased hypervigilence; and increased school attendance (Green & Wessells, 1997).

In communities, the intervention stimulated both awareness and mobilization around children's needs. Focus group discussions indicate that community influentials were more likely to understand the impacts of war on children and to interpret children's negative behavior not as unruly or disobedient but as related to their war experiences. In addition, communities provided for children more structured activities through soccer teams, dance groups, community kindergartens, theater groups, and handiwork groups. The most striking results occurred in communities that had initiated construction projects such as building a school or a community center. Community leaders, trainees, and trainers agreed that these projects had helped to build effective planning and reestablished a sense of control and hope, all of which are vital elements of resilience. As the structures were built, they became visible monuments of the community's empowerment, movement beyond its past, and efficacy in shaping its own future. These results suggest the importance of integrating psychosocial and economic reconstruction, thereby opening a pathway for wider processes of community development.

THE REINTEGRATION OF UNDERAGE SOLDIERS PROJECT

Worldwide, approximately a quarter of a million children participate in military activity, often as the result of victimization, coercion, or economic desperation (Brett & McCallin, 1996). Many have killed or witnessed tortures, executions, and deaths. In Angola in 1994, there were over 9,000 child soldiers, most of whom had been forcibly recruited at age 13 to 14 years.

Child soldiers pose one of the greatest obstacles to post-war reconstruction since they have been socialized into a system of violence and deprived of education, job training, and normal family life (Wessells, 1997). Communities may not welcome them home out of fear, remembrance of the bad things they had done, or concern that they will be trouble-makers. While youth between the ages of twelve and 18 years have the combination of physical stature and intellectual ability to cause much social turmoil, they are also in a position to make key choices about how to live their lives. In this post-war environment, work on demobilization and reintegration of former child soldiers is a high priority.

To complement the project on healing, CCF/Angola, with funding from USAID, conducted concurrent work with UNICEF on the demobilization and reintegration of underage soldiers in seven provinces. Of the 5,171 children who were demobilized, 4,104 children were demobilized into the areas where CCF and UNICEF were working.

Using a community-based approach, the provincial teams worked through a network of over 200 *activistas,* local influentials, many of whom were connected with the local church and were recognized by their communities as having been in a good position to assist returning youth. The provincial teams trained the *activistas* on the psychosocial impacts of child soldiering and on methods of enabling the reintegration of former soldiers. The training seminars, however, were oriented toward partnership and mutual learning. The *activistas* provided valuable information about views of their local communities toward returning soldiers, the problems they would likely encounter, and means of preparing for successful integration.

Preparation

The *activistas'* work in regard to a particular underage soldier occurred in three phases: preparation, re-entry, and social integration. While the recently demobilized youth were retained in quartering areas, *activistas* helped identify the youths accurately and to trace and notify their families, immediate or extended. To set the stage for re-entry, the *activistas* listened to family members' concerns, educated them about the situation of child soldiers, and advised them on how to aid the family and community reintegration of the youth. *Activistas* also worked to increase understanding that possible behavioral problems such as disobedience may relate to the youth's war experiences. For example, youth who had exercised command responsibilities or made life and death decisions might have difficulty submitting to parental authority subsequently.

Re-Entry

The *activistas* also provided assistance in re-uniting children with their families and in mobilizing communities to receive the former child soldiers. This work was dangerous and fraught with problems, as tensions remained high in the rural areas. There were reports that groups of demobilized youths had been re-recruited, and some youth had disappeared en route to meeting their families. Frequent logistic failures occurred because of last-minute changes in the transportation dates and destination points, route changes necessitated by damage to roads and bridges, and problems of families knowing when and how to reach the designated meeting points.

Under these conditions, logistics support constitutes a form of psychosocial assistance, one of the most basic elements of which is family reunification. Helping with logistics, the *activistas* succeeded in reuniting 2,153 former child soldiers with their families. They also arranged community receptions for the former child soldiers. This was an important first step in reconciling former child soldiers with their communities, as no one had known how communities would react. Fortunately, families and communities greeted the returning youth with great joy and relief. Reunion occasioned much singing, dancing, and traditional re-entry rituals in which adults sprinkled the youths' faces and heads with flour or water.

Social Reintegration

For particular children, spiritual cleansing is a necessary first step toward reintegration back into the community. In rural areas, people believe that soldiers who have engaged in unjustified acts of killing are spiritually contaminated by the unavenged spirits of those killed. Local communities fear that the former soldiers will pollute spiritually the entire community, rupturing the bond with the ancestors that constitutes the foundation of the living community. Western-based interventions such as counseling are ill-suited for addressing this situation. When leaders or healers see the need for spiritual cleansing, *traditional purification rit-*

uals conducted by traditional healers are needed to restore spiritual harmony.

In one village, while the purification rituals are taking place, the women dance around the child, gesturing with hands and arms to ward away undesirable spirits or influences, sending them behind and away from him. Afterwards, they each touch him with both hands from head to foot to cleanse him of impurities.

When the ritual is complete, the child is taken to his village, where the villagers celebrate his return. A party is held in his home where only traditional beverages are served, principally to the village chiefs. The child must be formally presented to the chiefs by his parents. During the party, the child sits beside the chiefs, drinking and talking to them, thereby marking his changed status in the village.

Later, the village elders make plans with the young man about his future. They discuss whether he wants to stay in that village, what kind of work he would like to do, whether he prefers to live with his parents or to build his own home, and whether the elders should allocate some land for him to cultivate.

In a spiritually centered culture, this purification ritual is of considerable importance. The process, however, also has key social elements, as it communalizes recognition and acceptance that the young person is no longer a soldier but a citizen of the village. Individual approaches would not address these communal elements effectively.

To date, 158 traditional ceremonies have been conducted for returning young soldiers, and over 20 have been documented by CCF teams, working with Dr. Alcinda Honwana, a social anthropologist at the University of Cape Town. Much work remains to be done in the documentation of the rituals and their psychological effects on individuals and communities. Through documentation, one may identify potentially valuable local resources for healing and reintegration that complement the tools provided by Western psychology. The documentation process itself is an essential part of psychosocial reconstruction since it helps to reclaim traditions that had been damaged by colonialism but that provide a sense of support, identity, and self-esteem.

In communities, *activistas* have assisted social reintegration by helping to identify school, job, and vocational training placements. These are vital for building hope for the future and giving young people skills that will enable them to support themselves. From a psychosocial perspective, these placements are useful since participation in culturally appropriate patterns of activity provides a sense of normalcy, continuity, and social meaning (Gibbs, 1997). Unfortunately, although most of the youth have only three or four years of education, many have chosen not to return to school because of problems such as shortages of teachers and schools and embarrassment over having to take classes with young children in primary school. Many of the demobilized youths have returned to mostly agricultural communities, and approximately one-third of the youths listed their occupation in early 1998 as "helping the family in farming." Because family lands are often limited, it is significant that some youths have purchased their own farm land through funding provided by the World Bank. In addition, the national team has administered a program that provides small grants for quick-impact projects, such as small business start-up. Much additional work, however, is needed to create viable paths through which youths make a living.

In many areas, both elders and parents report that overall, returning underage soldiers were reintegrating into their families and communities. Integration, however, is a long-term process, and many difficulties have been encountered. Family members reported that returning minors often did not want to work, had problems communicating, or displayed anger frequently. The youth themselves reported that they got sick frequently, thought often about their experiences, angered easily, and had difficulty sleeping. It is too early to gauge the success of youths' reintegration.

In addition, powerful macrosocial barriers to integration exist, not least of which is the re-eruption of fighting. Reports of re-recruitment are not uncommon, and *activistas* have lost contact with some minors. Even in the absence of fighting, obstacles exist in the form of extreme poverty and lack of educational access. Extreme inflation and shortages of food and basic materials tempt youth to use violence to obtain what they want. Collectively, these barriers provide a reminder that although peace must be built at the grassroots level, the achievement of peace requires structural changes and the transformation of larger social systems.

TOWARD THE FUTURE

Looking foward in this new millennium, war prevention remains a very high priority. To prevent war, it is essential to have viable models of post-war reconstruction that break ongoing cycles of violence. This chapter describes a model that builds local capacity through training local trainers and integrates psychosocial work into the larger project of post-conflict reconstruction. Although the particulars of the model would need to be tailored to the realities of specific cultures and situations, it has several generalizable features. First, it is holistic and avoids the individualism and fragmentation that has attended many humanitarian projects. Second, it is community-based and emphasizes participation and leadership by local people.

Third, it is culturally grounded and supports and utilizes community psychosocial resources that fit with local beliefs and practices. It avoids the application of Western methods in a colonial mode, and it invites intercultural dialogue and joint learning that can significantly enrich peace psychology. Fourth, it entails systematic documentation and evaluation processes. These are important not only for donor accountability but also for enabling communities to take stock of how they are doing, to improve program effectiveness, to plan effectively, and to present data that may influence policy decisions. We believe the model, applied with cultural sensitivity and critical awareness, could be used to assist war-affected children and communities worldwide.

In the future, psychosocial assistance will need to be applied on a wide scale to respond effectively to societal crises such as those in Bosnia, Rwanda, and other intrastate conflicts. Failure to include psychosocial assistance in programs of post-war reconstruction is likely to leave wounds and social cleavages that invite additional conflict. This said, one must humbly appreciate the limits on what psychosocial assistance and peace psychology can accomplish. As indicated by the case of Angola, which is moving once again toward internal war, psychosocial assistance alone cannot build peace. There must also be political will for peace, and this has been sorely lacking on UNITA's side. If psychosocial assistance is to be more than patching up people so they can fight more, it must be integrated thoroughly with wider programs of political and economic reconstruction. In this respect, the future challenge is to develop multidisciplinary, highly integrated aproaches to the reconstruction of war-torn societies.

SECTION IV

PEACEBUILDING: APPROACHES TO SOCIAL JUSTICE

Introduction by
Daniel J. Christie

Peace psychologists are not only developing theories and practices aimed at the prevention of *direct violence,* but are also working to mitigate *structural violence,* which means the reduction of hierarchical relations within and between societies. Hierarchical relations privilege those on the top while oppressing, exploiting, and dominating those on the bottom. Framed positively, we can conceptualize peacebuilding as movement toward social justice which occurs when *political structures* become more inclusive by giving voice to those who have been marginalized in decisions that affect their well-being, and *economic structures* become transformed so that those who have been exploited gain greater access to material resources that satisfy their basic needs.

Although the chapters in this section focus mainly on structural transformation, peacebuilding has both structural and cultural dimensions (Galtung, 1976; 1996). While structure refers to external, objective conditions of a social system, culture refers to internal, subjective conditions of collectivities within a social system. When people share subjectivities that justify and legitimize inequitable power relations in political and economic structures, *cultural violence* is taking place (Galtung, 1996). For example, *Just World Thinking* is a belief shared by some people that rationalizes disparities in power and wealth by assuming the world is fair; therefore, people get what they deserve (Lerner, 1980). Cultural violence and hierarchical societal structures are mutually reinforcing and highly resistant to change.

In contrast to cultural violence, the subjectivities associated with peacebuilding are characterized by an awakening of critical consciousness (Freire, 1970) in which the powerless begin to critically analyze and break through dominant cultural discourses that support oppression. It is the awakening and enacting of a critical consciousness that is central to this section on peacebuilding.

WHY PEACEBUILDING MATTERS

Peacebuilding matters because those with few resources have severe restrictions in everyday choices about health, education, child care, and other matters that affect their well-being. Peacebuilding redresses these inequalities and promotes the realization of human potentials for all members of a society.

In addition, other peaceful approaches, such as peacekeeping and peacemaking, tend to be reactive and may fail to deal with power differentials. Emphasis on *peacekeeping* by threatening to remove or actually eliminate violent people from society, without attending to the structural roots of violence, can lead to acceptance of "law and order" societies (Galtung, 1969) where individuals who commit criminal offenses are incarcerated and macro-level structural changes are ignored. *Peacemaking* is also limited in part because those who have power can insist on peaceful means of resolving disputes, while ignoring socially unjust ends.

PEACEBUILDING THEMES IN SECTION IV

Peacebuilding Challenges Dominant Cultural Discourses

Several chapters offer thought-provoking critiques of discourses that support structural violence. Webster and Perkins critically analyze the field of psychology when they argue that structural violence is inherent in any discipline that locates the source of a problem in the individual without due consideration of structural factors in a society. They point out that poverty is related to child maltreatment; however, by ignoring the relationship, it is possible to locate the source of the problem inside the abuser instead of dealing with both the abuser and the structures of a society that generate enormous differences in material well-being. Similarly, Dawes is critical of the ideology that underlies psychology, an ideology that is greatly influenced by the tenets of capitalism, emphasizing individual freedom and psychological constructs of self (e.g., self-actualization) over equality and collective well-being.

McKay and Mazurana's critique of dominant discourses extends to peace psychology, arguing that the field is patriarchal or male dominated, as exemplified by the largely invisible contributions of women to peacebuilding, which they explore in their research. Steger discusses how Gandhi's successful experiments in nonviolent structural change challenges the dominant assumption in the field of international relations that "power" can only be derived from the capacity to do violence on others. For Gandhi, major social change was accomplished by nonviolent means.

Peacebuilding Honors Multiple Voices and the Co-construction of Social Change

Nearly all of the authors are sensitive to the possibility of peace psychologists unwittingly committing *ideological violence*, which can occur when mainstream Western psychological approaches are exported to cultures that operate with different cosmologies of peace and social justice. These indigenous understandings may be regarded as inferior to the scientific approach used in the West (see especially the chapters by Dawes and by Wessells, Schwebel, and Anderson).

Webster and Perkins cite the problem that arises when policymakers fail to honor local voices and co-opt the language of empowerment while having little or no impact on those who are unempowered. Dawes is emphatic about the value of a *relativistic perspective* which recognizes that the meaning of social justice can only be understood when situated in a particular cultural context. Not surprisingly, nearly all of the chapters emphasize the importance of peace practitioners listening to local people, becoming contextually sensitive, honoring different perspectives, and forming partnerships so that social change is co-constructed.

An Activist Agenda Is Essential to Knowledge Generation

All of the authors in the peacebuilding section endorse an activist agenda, which nonviolently changes structures of violence to structures of peace. Moreover, the knowledge and skills used by practitioners for peacebuilding purposes are often learned through activism, what Gandhi referred to as "experiments in truth," rather than through traditional academic training. As Mayton and Steger note in their chapters, Gandhi's political theory of peacebuilding was developed inductively, through the accumulation of concrete encounters with oppression.

Montiel's chapter on peacebuilding is also problem-driven and informed by her experiences as an activist psychologist during the "people power movement" in the Philippines, a large-scale peacebuilding movement in which the Filipino people transformed political structures and gained greater representation and voice. Wessells, Schwebel, and Anderson also address activism as one of several specific avenues through which psychologists can contribute to public policy. They note that peace psychologists have training in mobilizing people and changing attitudes. Dawes also favors an activist agenda, but his approach more directly addresses social transformation. Steeped in the struggle against apartheid, Dawes offers insight on psychological processes involved in moving people toward democratization.

Empowerment Is Central to the Peacebuilding Process

Webster and Perkins define *empowerment* as individual and group efforts to gain control over their destiny. They shed light on the dynamics of empowerment at various levels, beginning with the individual and moving to the level of a whole society. Similarly, McKay and Mazurana assert that women's peacebuilding efforts at the grassroots level are empowering as women seek solutions to local problems. Dawes addresses empowerment from the framework of a *liberation psychology* that is unabashedly political and aspires to work in partnership with those who are oppressed and exploited. The goal is empowerment and emancipation of the powerless.

Peacebuilding as the Sustainable Satisfaction of Basic Human Needs

The satisfaction of basic human needs for all people is central to many analyses of peacebuilding. Montiel views structural peacebuilding as the transformation of societal structures toward a configuration in which "all groups have more equitable control over politico-economic resources needed to satisfy basic needs." Webster and Perkins view empowerment as a process through which people gain control over the environment and their ability to satisfy basic material needs through adequate housing, health care, education, and employment. McKay and Mazurana note that many grassroots women's groups emphasize psychosocial and basic human needs, such as safety, food, and shelter. According to Steger, Gandhi's perspective on peacebuilding was tantamount to the nonviolent pursuit of socially just ends where the ends referred to the sustainable satisfaction of human needs for all people.

Wessells, Schwebel, and Anderson note that sustainable societies meet "the needs of the current generation without compromising the ability to meet the needs of future generations"; in other words, intergenerational justice. At the same time, Wessells and colleagues caution that warfare also satisfies human needs. Reiterating William James's treatise on war, they note that war meets a variety of needs, such as the need for heroism and excitement. It follows that one task for peace psychologists is to find ways to present constructive alternatives for satisfying war-related needs. Dawes is critical of any human needs approach that aspires to a hierarchical construction. He points out that Western liberal values put a premium on political rights, but in some societies there are greater needs for good nutrition and other material need satisfiers.

Taken together, although the precise number, kind, and order of human needs vary across cultures, many of the authors view the sustainable satisfaction of human needs for all people as coterminous with social justice.

ORGANIZATION OF THE CHAPTERS

The lead chapter by Cristina Montiel, "Toward a Psychology of Structural Peacebuilding," frames the concept of peacebuilding. Drawing on two historical cases from the Filipino context, Montiel illustrates the political and economic dimensions of peacebuilding. The chapter makes the powerful point that unlike the harmony that is sought in peacemaking processes, peacebuilding engenders enormous levels of tension and discomfort, often resulting in psychological distress, pain, and sometimes even death.

The second chapter by Andy Dawes takes us to South Africa where psychologists participated in dismantling apartheid, a system of legal racial discrimination that lasted until 1994 when democracy was achieved. Dawes offers a provocative and critical analysis of the hidden values built into mainstream Western scientific psychology with its focus on the autonomous individual. The chapter offers an alternative, liberation psychology, a form of peace psychology that seeks to use psychological knowledge to socially transform societies. Dawes discusses the emancipatory agenda of liberation psychology in the South African context as he recounts some of the struggles that psychologists faced during the apartheid era.

After examining peacebuilding in the Filipino and South African contexts, we turn to Gandhi's pursuit of social justice in India under colonial rule in the middle of the twentieth century. Dan Mayton offers an introduction to the key concepts in Gandhi's political philosophy from a social psychological perspective. He notes that principles of truth, nonviolence, and personal suffering are central to Gandhi's goal of political self-determination for the Indian people. Mayton's introduction to Gandhian principles lays the groundwork for Manfred Steger's chapter, which pits Gandhi's political theory of nonviolence against a *realist philosophical framework* that equates power with the capacity to do violence. For anyone who clings to the view that nonviolence cannot be a powerful force for social change, the case studies that Steger presents should leave naysayers with greater humility. One case even takes on what some might regard as the ultimate test of nonviolent power, the successful application of nonviolent social change procedures in the context of Nazi Germany.

Ilse Hakvoort and Solveig Hägglund give voice to arguably the most marginalized group in the world, children. In their cross-cultural study, Dutch and Swedish children express their views on the nature of peace and strategies to attain peace. Hakvoort and Hägglund demonstrate the diversity of children's concepts of peace and relate them to the varying contexts within which children are socialized.

Linda Webster and Doug Perkins turn our attention to social injustices in the United States, emphasizing the effects of structural violence on children and families. These authors give a great deal of clarity to what can be a murky construct, "empowerment," and delineate how it operates at various levels of aggregation, from individual empowerment to the empowerment of whole societies.

Susan McKay and Diane Mazurana pick up on the theme of peacebuilding and argue for "gender-aware and women-empowering political, social, economic, and human rights." Feminist ideology is asserted and the centrality of gender equity in the peacebuilding process is emphasized. Global in scope, the McKay and Mazurana chapter surveys the many and varied ways in which women contribute to the reduction of direct and structural violence. Consistent with feminist views, they offer a critical analysis of the narrow conception of peace, as the absence of war, and note that women's peacebuilding efforts extend to the social justice arena. The authors define women's peacebuilding broadly, as activities that contribute to a "culture of peace."

The concept *cultures of peace* is central to the last chapter in the peacebuilding section by Mike Wessells, Milt Schwebel, and Anne Anderson. The chapter is highly integrative and proactive, setting out a long-term agenda and delineating elements of cultures of peace that psychologists can actively pursue in the interest of preventing direct violence and diminishing structural violence. They discuss multiple venues for psychologists who want to make a difference in the public arena. Readers should come away from this chapter with an appreciation for the depth and breadth of peace psychology as well as a greater awareness of meaningful ways of contributing to cultures of peace.

CHAPTER 23

TOWARD A PSYCHOLOGY OF STRUCTURAL PEACEBUILDING

Cristina Jayme Montiel

This chapter describes concepts related to the process of changing structures of violence to structures of peace, a *transformative* process called structural peacebuilding. I will begin with two stories depicting structural peacebuilding in the Philippines.

A STRUCTURAL VIEW OF VIOLENCE AND PEACE

Two Social Narratives

The first account illustrates a group's efforts to transform structures of economic injustice. Seventeen farmers engaged in a hunger strike, struggling against the economically exploitative conditions of landlessness (Lasay & Macasaet, 1998a, 1998b). The second narrative talks about political oppression. After 14 years under dictatorial rule, millions of Filipinos banded together in a mass-based movement called People's Power to dismantle structures of political authoritarianism (Licuanan, 1987; Magno, 1986; Mercado, 1986).

Against Economic Exploitation: Farmers Hunger Strike for Land. The hunger strike story started when the Philippine government awarded 144 hectares to the landless farmers, in an effort to distribute agricultural land more equitably. The

landowner was a multimillionaire who owned other vast lands outside this contested estate. He refused to give up the 144 hectares and hired paramilitary forces to guard the farm peripheries (Lasay & Macasaet, 1998a). At this point, the farmers considered three options. First, they could give up the land and go landless. Going underground with the New People's Army and facing the landowner's military strength with their own armed force constituted a second option. The final choice was to embark on a hunger strike until either the land was given to them or they died of hunger. In late 1997, they decided to go on a hunger strike.

To generate support from sympathetic groups the farmers began networking with nongovernment organizations (NGOs) in MetroManila.[1] I first met them at this juncture when they consulted with me about the psychopolitical strategies of a hunger strike. We planned some media coverage to mobilize public pressure, and talked about what happened to one's mind and body when one stopped eating. We also discussed the psy-

---

[1]MetroManila refers to the primary metropolitan area of the Philippines where national government offices, media stations, financial centers, and leading universities are located.

chological and political implications of an irreversible-till-death commitment. Then their hunger strike began. They set up camp in front of the Department of Agrarian Reform, and called daily press conferences. After a few days, the weaker ones collapsed and were hospitalized. As more farmers collapsed from hunger, Philippine President Fidel Ramos intervened in the conflict, granting one-third of the land to the single landowner, and the remaining two-thirds of the estate to the 17 farmers. The farmers saw this allocation as a victory, so they called off their strike, celebrated, thanked their NGO allies, and returned home to their land (Lasay & Macasaet, 1998a). I will stop my story here, but add that the farmers' "victory" was only short-lived, and their peaceful saga for land ownership continues (Lasay & Macasaet, 1998b).

Against Political Oppression: People's Power for Democratic Structures.

The second narrative details the People's Power movement to dismantle authoritarian political structures (Mercado, 1986). In September 1972, after Philippine President Ferdinand Marcos declared martial law, thousands of prodemocracy Filipinos were arrested, tortured, and killed. In 1983, Marcos's political archrival Senator Benigno Aquino returned from his U.S. exile to persuade Marcos to grant more freedoms to the nation. After Senator Aquino's plane landed, military men pulled him out of the plane, shut the door behind them, and in a few seconds Aquino's dead body lay on the tarmac. The Marcos administration blamed the local communists for the brutal slaying, but almost every Filipino knew otherwise (Mercado, 1986).

The burial march of Senator Aquino, attended by millions, marked the first massive but peaceful show of collective anger against Marcos's rule. This nonviolent display of force by MetroManilans set the political tone for the next three years in which citizens were no longer paralyzed by fear. Under the leadership of Senator Aquino's widow Corazon Aquino, Filipinos poured out of their homes to join the escalating protest rallies, braving the hazards of arrests, police beatings, snipers, tear gas attacks, and water cannons (Mercado, 1986).

As soon as Marcos announced his presidential bid in the snap national elections in early 1986, oppositionists from various ideological positions united behind the dictator's electoral rival, Senator Benigno Aquino's widow, Corazon. Marcos then declared himself the victor in an election widely perceived as rigged. The public anger against rampant electoral cheating ripened the atmosphere for sociopolitical change.

In February 1986, Marcos's longtime allies Defense Minister Juan Ponce Enrile and Armed Forces Vice Chief of Staff Fidel Ramos announced over the radio that they no longer supported the Marcos government. In a few hours, hundreds of thousands of pro-Aquino civilians surrounded the military camps where the breakaway military faction of Enrile and Ramos fortified their armed defense. The unarmed swarm of Filipinos functioned as human shields between the Marcos tanks and the Enrile-Ramos military wing. The throng of nonviolent protesters sat, ate, sang, prayed, and slept on the main highway in front of the military camps. On the fourth day of what became popularly known as "People's Power," Marcos escaped to Hawaii by helicopter. He was toppled without much bloodshed. In a few days, Corazon Aquino set up office as the new President of the Republic of the Philippines (Mercado, 1986). In the next twelve months, the new democratic government appointed local government heads to replace the Marcosian minions throughout the country. A year after the peaceful upheaval, Filipinos went to the polls to elect their local leaders, causing the Philippine authoritarian political structure to become more egalitarian.

The stories of the farmers' hunger strike and the Philippine People's Power movement can be used to elucidate concepts about social structure. The discussion below refers to the two social narratives to concretize some structural ideas.

Social Structure

Social structure pertains to patterns of relatively permanent hierarchical relations among groups or collectivities in a social system (Parsons, 1961). This definition highlights three properties of social structure. First, social systems are the primary *unit of analysis,* not interpersonal relations (Blau, 1969). For example, in the hunger strike, the structural basis of the incident was the configuration of relations between the landless and the landed in the Philippines, not the interpersonal relations between the landowner and the 17 farmers. A second property of social structure is that it is marked by *social differentiation* that is not only heterogeneous but also unequal (Blau, 1977). This means that differences among collectivities in a structure are not horizontal but vertical in nature (Galtung, 1978) with those on the top having the most wealth and power. A structural perspective is sensitized to *social power differentials* between groups. A third characteristic of social structure is its invariance or tendency to resist change, even though there may be lower-amplitude shorter-time-duration alterations in a social system (Parsons, 1961). For example, in the Philippines, the unequal intergroup relations based on land ownership have been embedded in the social system for about four centuries.

Structural Violence

A social structure is violent when its vertical arrangement of inequality prevents huge numbers of collectivities from satisfying basic human needs (Christie, 1997; Galtung, 1975, 1978, 1980a, 1980b, 1996). Resources are controlled by a privileged few. Massive deprivations underneath a layer of elite overindulgence characterize structurally *violent social configurations.*

Galtung (1980a) separates the sources of violence into two types: actors and structures. For example, if students who lead a prodemocracy march are beaten up and then detained by government forces, the youths' needs for security and freedom are blocked by specific armed individuals. The violence on the protesters is interpersonal and is traced to the people in the military who behaved aggressively. Peace workers who focus on the individual actor tend to employ strategies aimed to change the mental processes and/or behaviors of aggressive persons, and may remain oblivious to the goal of restructuring vertical intergroup relations embedded in the social system.

The primary aim of peace workers with a structural perspective is to restructure *vertical systems* toward more equal systemic configurations. For instance, an unequal distribution of agricultural land ownership in a country gives rise to economic misery. Likewise, a system of political authoritarianism squashes self-determination needs and alienates the citizenry from their own government. The challenge of structural peace work remains as long as social inequalities persist in the social system, even when direct violence and other human rights violations are no longer manifest.

Variables related to structure-dependent deprivations are unlike the variables of violence that psychologists traditionally examine within an intrapersonal or interpersonal framework (Berkowitz, 1993). Structural violence lacks intent, subject, object, and inter-personal action (Galtung, 1975). For example, collective identity deprivations caused by an authoritarian system arise from the hierarchical intergroup relations between the military forces and ordinary citizens. This pervading *vertical configuration of political powers* cannot be described as possessing aggressive intent because the problem is embedded in a system and is not due to the motivation of an individual or collectivity.

Violent conditions that are actor-dependent and structure-dependent can be separated from each other only on an abstract analytical plane. In real life, structure-related violence and individual actions support each other. An episode of interpersonal violence may occur in which a military officer hits a student. On one level, the violence is between two actors. On another level, the violence is supported by the vertical arrangement of power.

Structural Peace

The absence of structural violence is structural peace (Galtung, 1975). *Structural peace* is a *utopic system* (i.e., it does not exist in its pure form in the real world) marked by egalitarian configurations, wherein decision-making powers over resource allocation are distributed equally in a society. Structurally peaceful social systems are marked by equitably-distributed decision-powers in the production, allocation, and utilization of economic, political, and cultural resources. Structural peace conditions contain social differentiation, but the intergroup variations are horizontal rather than vertical.

Mallman (1980) clarifies the relationship between resource control, structural peace, and access to need satisfiers. He explains that when the distribution of available need-satisfiers are controlled by the elite, an inequitable sharing of satisfiers tends to arise and produce massive deprivations among those at the bottom of the system. By definition, when decision-making over vital resources is distributed *horizontally*, each group will protect its interests but at the same time will have to make its interests compatible with other groups' interests. The process of equally-shared decision-making brings about a more equitable distribution of basic needs satisfiers and lessens conditions of massive need deprivations that mark structural violence.

Let us use the farmers' narrative to illustrate structural peace. In the Philippines, land is inequitably distributed and the landowning elite decide how to utilize their land resources. Predictably, unilateral decisions of the landowner in the hunger strike case favored self-interest and resulted in chronic poverty among the landless tillers (Lasay & Macasaet, 1998a, 1998b). In a utopic condition of structural peace, landowners would possess less land and farmers would acquire a greater portion of the land through cooperatives owned collectively and managed by themselves. Tillers of the soil would then have more decision-making powers over the land harvests. In the hunger strike story, the farmers were already organized into a cooperative called *Mapalad* (Blessed), as they prepared alternative peaceful structures and struggled to transform the inequitable system (Lasay & Macasaet, 1998a, 1998b).

STRUCTURAL PEACEBUILDING

Building peace entails changing structures of violence to structures of peace. More specifically, *structural peacebuilding* is (a) a social psychological process of transforming (b) relatively permanent unequal relationships among collectivities in a social structure (c) to new sets of intergroup relations where all groups have more *equitable control over politico-economic resources* needed to satisfy basic needs.

Structural Peace Is Not Structural Peacebuilding

Structural peace is very different from structural peacebuilding. First, peacebuilding is a means while structural peace is an end. Second, peacebuilding is characterized by disequilibrium and strain, as collectivities disengage from a structurally violent system. On the other hand, structural peace is an attribute of a utopic social structure, marked by equilibrium and harmony. Finally, peacebuilding is dynamic while structural peace is relatively invariant. I will now expound on the nature of structural peacebuilding.

Building Social Strain

Since structural peacebuilding necessitates systemic transformation, one needs to take a closer look at sources of structural change. From where does change originate? Structural shifts usually arise from strains internal to the system (Godelier, 1978; Merton, 1968; Parsons, 1961). *Structural strain* exists in relationships between groups in a system when there is pressure to change the relationships to new ones incompatible with the *dominant structure* (Parsons, 1961).

Paradoxically, the route to creating *horizontal structures* includes the production of strain within vertical systems. Structural change arises as the social system seeks ways to reduce the pervasive strain. There are other ways to lessen strain, such as bringing back full conformity with the dominant structure, or some accommodation, but these efforts do not result in *structural transformation* (Parsons, 1961). Since vertical structures are deeply embedded in social systems, structural peacebuilding involves the creation (not the cessation) of social strain, conflict, and disequilibrium between two or more structural collectivities, producing movement toward more horizontal rela-

tions. The idea of increasing conflict to produce transformative strain in structural peacebuilding disagrees with current conflict resolution and peacemaking strategies that seek to reduce strain (Rubin et al., 1994).

Structural change transforms inequitable relationship patterns in the social configuration. When structural strain is resolved too early and equilibrium is restored prematurely, the "peaceful" process rebuilds full or partial conformity with inequitable structures. Structural peacebuilding is hindered by such circumstances. For example, at one point in the hunger strike, the Philippine government's Office of the Presidential Adviser for the Peace Process (OPAPP) met with the protesting farmers. One official from OPAPP pleaded with the strikers to stop their hunger strike for the sake of peace but the farmers refused. If farmers had agreed, the landowner would have retained all 144 hectares of the agricultural plot.

As psychologists and peace activists carry out peace work in the midst of social conflict, they confront the invisible danger of prematurely restoring structural equilibrium, even when peacebuilding requires precisely the opposite, *systemic disequilibrium.* Strain resolution, or what psychologists may refer to as conflict resolution (Rubin et al., 1994), may interrupt the ripening structural change process with untimely calls for intrapersonal forgiveness and interpersonal reconciliation.

Discussion of the effectiveness of strain resolution begs the question: when the structural status quo is restored in the name of forgiveness and reconciliation, which structural groups stand to gain? I am not purporting that there is no room for forgiveness and reconciliation in the broader scenario of structural peace and peacebuilding. Only that untimely forgiveness and reconciliation may be the new "opium of the people" (Marx, 1844/1975, p. 175), and cause people to disengage from the strain and disequilibrium involved in structural peacebuilding.[2]

Groups in the dominant structure tend to control local arsenals and use these to resist attempts to change systemic configurations. For example, the landowner in the farmers' situation hired local paramilitary troops to barricade the peripheries of the controversial land. Likewise, during the rise of nonviolent demonstrations in the Philippines, military forces fought the rallyists with tear gas and bullets. Margarita Cojuangco (1986), a Filipina prodemocracy activist, recorded her experience during an armed military street offensive with these words:

> I'm writing you while events are still vivid in my mind . . . I am writing about the Quezon Boulevard rally . . . I had a borrowed gas mask. The others brought theirs too, along with lemon juice and water to protect their faces from tear gas . . . We locked our arms tightly to keep from breaking ranks . . . Suddenly, the water hoses were turned on us . . . A few minutes later, I heard (tear gas) cans fall on the pavement . . . Suddenly, a composite[3] shouted: "Armalites!" . . . I saw a long gun behind a military man's shield . . . I took a deep breath and remained unafraid. I cannot explain how I mustered all that courage. Then, fire trucks and truncheon-and-shield-bearing soldiers came at us . . . Gunshots were fired. The order came:

"Run!" My partner[4] Guila Maramba and I ran, arm in arm. (pp. 35–36)

Persistent systemic resistance and the relatively invariant nature of social structures make structural peacebuilding a formidable challenge to human societies. As a protective counterforce to structural invariance, the production and management of strain necessitates some kind of social power. The following section explains some social psychological ideas related to social power and structural peacebuilding.

Structural Transformation Is Possible

Social structures are implemented through *embedded power systems*. Blalock (1989) defines *power* in terms of *dependency*. Party X is dependent on Y to the degree that Y controls X's access to X's valued goals. The power of Y over X is the degree to which X's dependence on Y exceeds Y's dependence on X. Structural verticality means the elite at the top hold power over the production, allocation, and utilization of resources needed to satisfy basic needs (Galtung, 1975; Mallman, 1980; Parsons, 1961). For example, in the farmers' story, the landowner claimed economic monopoly over the land resources needed to alleviate the farmers' misery. Similarly, under martial law's authoritarian structure, Philippine military forces controlled the political resources needed by the citizenry for *self-determination*, which means political representation and voice in matters that affect their well being. But social power is implemented through human action. The nature of human action carries the key to the possibility of structural change despite structural rigidity and resistance.

---

[2]Karl Marx (1844/1975) claimed that religion was the opium of the people because beliefs in the supernatural and the afterlife artificially satisfied poor people and pushed them to accept their earthly destitutions without much discontent. Similarly, premature calls for forgiveness and reconciliation may result in artificial social harmony, enticing structural victims to accept the predominant vertical structures instead of changing the systemic violence.

[3]Seasoned street protesters, usually from the ranks of the students or urban poor.

[4]For safety, street marchers were required to arm-lock with a buddy or partner at all times, even when running away from military firing.

Action is a behavior that is purposive and cognitively informed (Porpora, 1987). The mental facilities of purpose and cognition make it possible to disconnect human action from the deterministic hold of oppressive and exploitative social structures. These mental abilities place importance on one's subjective facilities as distinct from the objective structural conditions surrounding the action. When the farmers chose to go on a hunger strike to obtain agricultural land, they made a subjective choice outside the boundaries of a structural reaction that would have kept them subservient and locked in the position of landless structural victims. Accompanied by subjective purpose and cognition, the farmers' action became structurally transformative and disconnected from an automatic (human) response to (structural) stimuli.

Producing Force: Networking, Mobilizing, Conscientizing.

What is the basis of the force of hunger strikes, People's Power, and other structural peacebuilding methods? Certainly the force is not attributed to the traditional power-bases of a violent social structure, which concentrates capital, land, and military arsenals. The social power of peaceful structural transformation emanates from collective human actions, mobilized into a synchronized social force, purposefully directed toward disequilibrating vertical structures and building new egalitarian systems. To produce systemically transformative power, structural peacebuilders face three concrete tasks: networking, mobilizing, and political education.

Networking involves creating an alternative collectivity outside the oppressive structure, by building organizational links with sympathetic individuals and groups. For example, when the farmers decided to go on a hunger strike, they networked with nongovernment groups in MetroManila. The prodemocracy movement during the Marcos dictatorship established an extensive web of sympathizers among church workers, students, laborers, business leaders, and—more discretely—even within the ranks of military institutions.

The human potentials available in the counterstructure networks do not generate social power until the groups are mobilized into a single coordinated social force. *Mobilization* aims to produce collective action where the networked individuals operate in unison to oppose the actions emanating from the vertical structure. Among the farmers, the mobilized action was their hunger strike, while prodemocracy activists consolidated their networks during mass protest actions.

Political education pertains to the discussion of underlying structural issues related to the mobilized action. Networking and mobilization aim to change verticality in the objective structure, while education transforms the corresponding subjective verticality within one's consciousness. Political education functions to create a collective cognition and purpose directed toward disequilibrating exploitative systems and creating alternative peaceful structures. The pedagogical style of political education should promote nonverticality, or else a new *hierarchical culture of intellectual domination* may rise out of the peacebuilding movement. Filipinos working for structural transformation often used Paolo Freire's (1970) process of nonvertical education called *conscientization*, where the emphasis is on relationships that are horizontal instead of authoritarian and hierarchical.

My own peacebuilding experiences during the Marcos dictatorship included networking and mobilizing tasks, though most of my energies went to running political education workshops around the Philippines. We facilitated conscientization sessions covering topics such as structural analysis, vision of person and society, Philippine political spectrum, active nonviolence, and strategies for change. Understandably, the military forces grew suspicious of our seminars. At one workshop in a rural town in the Ilocos Region, as we held our discussions under a huge mango tree, two military tanks came down the road and parked a few meters away in an attempt to harass us. We felt afraid, but continued our political discussions, and were much relieved when the tanks rolled away without harming anyone in the workshop.

Creative Social Power and Structural Roles. The production and management of a peacebuilding force demands three social psychological processes related to roles. First, a conscientization process is experienced as people grow *aware* of their respective structural roles. Second, individuals *disentangle* from the behaviors and cognitions prescribed by their positions in the embedded inequitable system. Third, individuals *acquire* new roles needed to create and utilize social disequilibrium. These three requirements apply across-status, regardless of one's structural position in the *exploiter-victim relationship.*

For example, when landlords and landless farmers interact, they may either play out their structurally determined roles or choose to step out of these roles. Those who opt to remain in their structural roles do not produce any social strain and may even obtain rewards for such behaviors. For instance, it was widely rumored that farmers who remained subservient and did not join the hunger strike received cash incentives from the landowner. On the other hand, the 17 hunger-striking farmers demonstrated the possibility of stepping out of their subservience roles in the structure, as

they took more strain-producing counter-structure roles vis-à-vis the landowner.

In another example of structure-free creative actions, civilians who joined protest actions showed that it was possible to step out of structural roles at the juncture where citizens interacted with their military role partners. Creative action is not limited to victims; the top dog can do likewise. For example, during street rallies where police beat up protesters, a police officer would occasionally intervene and ask for mercy in the name of the victim. And even at the height of martial law, I had the personal experience of having a prison guard smuggle out a letter to me from a political prisoner who was being held incommunicado inside a military camp.

In summary, the *forcefulness of structural peacebuilding* comes from: (a) creative—i.e., not structure-determined—action (b) skilled in the production and management of *nonviolent social strain* (c) collected or mobilized into *conscientized social power* (d) purposefully directed by the dual goals of removing structural inequities and crafting more equitable structural configurations. These procedural requirements open up systemic transformation to the positive contributions of structure-sensitive psychologists. The following section explores some psychological aspects of structural peacebuilding.

APPLYING PSYCHOLOGY TO STRUCTURAL PEACEBUILDING

Producing Nonviolent Social Strain

The production of nonviolent strain includes at least three psychological ingredients: a sense of sacrifice and shared spirituality among participants, practical politico-organizational tactics while facing a militarized enemy, and leadership which is ascetic, pragmatic, and decentralized.

Sense of Sacrifice and Shared Spirituality. Stepping out of one's structural role expectations usually produces negative consequences for those who do so. At the very least, the vertical system fails to reward role-deviant behaviors materially, psychologically, and/or professionally; at worst, the deviance is punished. In our example of the land distribution controversy, the 17 hunger-striking farmers were ostracized by other community members who followed the wishes of the landowner. Furthermore, the act of disequilibrating embedded structures, while simultaneously refraining from countermilitary offensives, demands much personal sacrifice from the peacebuilders. The siren call of counterviolence is constantly present. For example, the protesting farmers could have joined the New People's Army to fight the landowner. Instead, they chose to embark on a hunger strike—a collective act that destabilizes a system through *group self-sacrifice.* Likewise, during the People's Power Revolution in the Philippines, large numbers of unarmed civilians placed their bodies in front of military tanks. Engaging in structural peacebuilding often calls for a readiness to lay down one's life if things do not go well. In a sense, it is this openness to pain and/or death that helps bring forth the human force to dismantle a structure without creating additional violence.

In structural peacebuilding, sacrifice is not an individual behavior, but rather a collective act by a group determined to produce its own purposive social force. Usually, the collective activity is accompanied by a sense of *shared spirituality* among the participating members. For example, the hunger-striking farmers requested spiritual reflection sessions at the height of their struggle.

One biblical phrase that caught their attention was that a person does not live "on bread alone" (Matthew 4:4, The New American Bible). To this, one of the farmers responded, "We can continue going hungry until we get justice." At the People's Power rallies, street protesters celebrated masses and prayed the rosary through their political vigils. In prayer sessions during critical political times, Filipinos petitioned the resurrected Christ to be beside them in case they got killed. Belief in the Resurrection helped the protesters become more courageous as they faced the military tanks and the possibility of death. In other new democracies, there are many examples of the blending of spirituality with structural peacebuilding efforts: Cambodia's Walk-for-Peace led by Buddhist monk Venerable Maha Ghosananda (Mahoney, 1998; Moser-Puangsuwan, & Maure, n.d.; Mydans, 1998 September); and Eastern Europe's Lutheran church-based candle-lit protests that sparked the implosion of the Soviet Empire (Schoensee & Lederer, 1991). A spiritual orientation provides the psychological strength needed to engage in nonviolent structural transformation. Furthermore, when a group triumphs in their structural peacebuilding efforts and obtains transformative power, a spiritual disposition may likewise help members remain detached from the seductive attractions of personal ambition, material extravagance, and post-conflict revenge.

Psychological Dimensions of Facing the Militarized Enemy. Creating a social force for restructuring requires that individuals act collectively and purposefully. When a group produces social strain, individuals in the system may react with direct violence. It becomes a challenge to continue managing social strain in an active nonviolent way, without either backing out or engaging in direct counterviolence. Some social psychological features of *collective active nonviolence* are a high level of psychological tolerance for the enemy, knowledge of and insistence on one's human rights, the *buddy or partner system* (i.e., always being with one other person to deter abduction by military agents), unquestioned obedience to the group's security marshals, and protective, not offensive collective behaviors in case of physical violence (e.g., lying down and taking cover instead of standing up or going against water cannons, explosives, and tear gas; see box on p. 292).

Collective nonviolence likewise requires an attempt to win over the goodwill of the militarized enemy. Examples of such behaviors are offering symbols of peace like flowers, candies, and cigarettes, to the front-line police forces or tank personnel; or speaking gently to the military to persuade them to join the street protesters. The Philippine experience has shown that military forces are less angry and fearful toward women and religious leaders. Therefore, individuals from these subgroups were the most effective rally frontliners in persuading the military to receive flowers and other gifts of peace.

One reason why structural peacebuilding is a collective rather than an individualistic process is that different individuals are needed at different points of the structural peacebuilding process. Many protesters involved in structural disequilibration (e.g., during the bleak days of authoritarianism) are too psychologically scarred with *traumatic memories*. When it is time to build *alternative peaceful structures,* they are unable to shed their fears and anger which makes it difficult for them to undertake structural change in a forceful but nonviolent manner.

A personal incident showed me how past fears may interfere with collective nonviolence. At a People's Power rally, I was a security marshal. I had previously instructed the marchers under my care that in case of violent dispersal, they were to sit down rather than run. During the rally, I saw my friend, who was around 15 meters away from me, being snatched by a plainclothes intelligence agent. I screamed out my friend's name to catch the attention of our fellow rallyists. Seeing the military snatch my friend triggered fears associated with my past military-caused traumas, so I automatically began to run away from the intelligence agents. I failed to follow my own instructions not to run away in case of violence. Luckily, when I began to run, I was arm-locked with my rally buddy, and he shouted at me "Don't run. Sit!" After he said this, I realized that everyone else was sitting on the pavement and I sat down, too. Because we were seated, the agents did not chase us (with their truncheons!), but instead engaged in peaceful negotiations with our rally leaders. At this juncture both victims and oppressors had stepped out of their structural role scripts and began to relate with each other in new ways.

Leadership. Often, *structural peacebuilding leaders* fuse contemporary *asceticism* with practical political power. Their social influence emanates not from their ability to wield brute force, but from a capacity for self-sacrifice and kind acts effectively coupled with pragmatic political tactics. As we begin the twenty-first century, examples of world-recognized peacebuilders are Cambodia's Venerable Maha Gosanda, Burma's Aung San Suu Kyi, South Africa's Nelson Mandela, and the Philippines' Corazon Aquino.

If one were to look more closely at the structural peacebuilding process, however, one would realize that there is not a single leader but many leaders who take on various responsibilities in the struggle for structural change. Leadership roles are not centralized for pragmatic reasons. The collective spirit of a huge protest movement is

Reminders for Rally Participants *

What to do when:

1. There are provocateurs:
   a) There may be attempts to taunt rally participants so that there will be trouble. Provocateurs may infiltrate the ranks or may pose as bystanders who may taunt participants by shouting invectives, throwing stones, and using other physical methods to instigate trouble.
   b) Do not retaliate or do anything that may cause trouble. Maximum tolerance is the rule. Notify marshals or line leaders if you see agitators or if anybody in the ranks has reached the point of blowing up.

2. There is dispersal:
   a) Wait for instructions from the marshals.
   b) Do not break the ranks or leave your line or buddy. "Kapitbisig" (arm-locking) can be done to prevent the ranks from splitting up.
   c) If there is need to withdraw, be sure you know where the rendezvous point is. Do not move alone.

3. You are detained/picked up:
   a) Make sure you are not alone. It is important that the buddy system is maintained.
   b) Shout if you have to call the attention of others in the group.
   c) Ask for the identification of the person detaining you.
   d) Insist on your rights. You cannot be detained without charges.
   e) Report cases of physical abuse by the police/government forces (secure a certification from a doctor regarding the extent of physical damage as soon as possible).

4. There is tear gas:
   a) Cover mouth and nose with a wet handkerchief.
   b) Crouch low to avoid inhaling the fumes.
   c) Do not break the ranks, this will only create confusion and may open the ranks to infiltration or illegal detention. Follow instructions of the marshals.

5. Facing water cannons:
   a) Follow instructions of the marshals and do not run away from the ranks.
   b) Keep down. Do not stand up against the force of the water cannons.

6. An explosion takes place:
   a) Lie down and take cover when an explosion takes place.
   b) Do not run without your group. Await instructions from the marshals where to regroup.
   c) Notify the medical team in case you see casualties.

*An Example of Practical Instructions for Collective and Peaceful Force—Excerpt from a Leaflet Handed out during a People's Power Rally more resilient when leadership is diffused rather than resting on a single person. Hence, even if some influential personalities are detained or killed, the process of peacebuilding tends to move onward. Furthermore, the psychological requirements of self-sacrificial readiness constitute a choice that cannot be imposed by centralized leadership. Self-sacrifice is a daily personal decision that is carried out in the context of a small group.

SUMMARY

This chapter used two social narratives to illustrate the concept of structural peacebuilding as a process of transforming unjust social systems into more peaceful structures. Structures work through social power which, in turn, is implemented through human action. Structural peacebuilding involves stepping out of structural roles, building social strain, and creating forceful collective actions by mobilizing and conscientizing large networks of people. Networking and mobilization transform external vertical structures while conscientization (Freire, 1970) changes the corresponding subjective verticality in an individual's consciousness. The transformation of objective and subjective verticalities affect each other reciprocally and are equally important in structural change. A sense of spirituality, skillful confrontation of the militarized enemy, and appropriate leadership styles help produce effective but nonviolent structural change. I will end this chapter with a look at what psychologists can contribute to structural peacebuilding in the twenty-first century.

TOWARD THE FUTURE

As humankind welcomes the twenty-first century, populations are wracked with social antagonisms related to inequalities between conflicting groups. Amidst these conditions of inequality, effective ways of structural peacebuilding will continue to evolve. In the new century, psychology can make significant contributions through applied and theoretical work related to the nature of structural violence and the process of structural peacebuilding. Psychological advances related to systemic violence in a variety of countries include work on *structural victimization* (Lavik et al., 1994; Pilisuk, 1997; Schwebel, 1997) and *cultural inequalities* such as prejudice (Brown, 1995; Dovidio & Gaertner, 1986; Ehrlich, 1973; Stephan et al., 1994; Swim & Stangor, 1998), ethnocentrism (Brewer, 1986; Grant, 1992; Grant & Brown, 1995; Greeson, 1991; Smith, 1992; Triandis, 1990), stereotypes (Karim, 1997; Stephan et al., 1994) and group bias (Bar-Tal, 1990; Karim, 1997; Mullen et al., 1992).

The conceptual difficulty of psychology vis-à-vis peacebuilding is in the understanding that the social system's configuration is not only a cause of human behaviors and mental processes but also an effect. Psychologists tend to focus on individuals' structural victimization, but not on the discovery of social psychological processes involved in changing social configurations. A paradigm expansion is needed.

Beyond observing the psychological ramifications of injustice and asking how humans are victimized by inequalities, a new question in the twenty-first century can be this: What psychological factors are involved in equalizing power relationships in a social structure? There are examples of structural peacebuilding in different parts of the world, especially among the disadvantaged groups in violent structures. Peacebuilding narratives are evolving out of the experiences of the oppressed groups in the First World, in Third World societies, and in new democracies. For example, the phenomenon of *People's Power* demonstrates how large groups can use peaceful but forceful means to disequilibrate well-oiled authoritarian political structures. Recent People's Power experiences in Indonesia (Kristof, 1998; Landler, 1998; Mydans, 1998 May, 1998 November), Philippines (Licuanan, 1987; Magno, 1986; Mercado, 1986), and Eastern Europe (Schoensee & Lederer, 1991) show that it is possible to restructure authoritarian rule in a forceful but bloodless manner.

Psychologists may also want to begin looking at restructuring global inequities. In the global context, structural peace is an international configuration of political and economic equitability (Galtung, 1980b). *Global structural peacebuilding* refers to human-based processes that distribute power and wealth more equitably among the different nations and regions of the world.

Psychologists need not shy away from the theoretical and practical challenges of structural change. There are numerous psychology-related issues that can be explored. To cite a few examples, there is little known about the mental processes activated during and after structural destabilization, psychological resources of peacebuilders while undergoing external and internal strain, cognitions and affects of participants engaged in the production of nonviolent social force, and building a collective culture of forceful nonviolence.

Indeed, psychology holds a vital key to structural peacebuilding, to the crafting of a more *forceful peace*. But perhaps psychologists are looking in a different direction. We search for peace through interpersonal harmony. We avoid social strain and remain insensitive to power inequities. And as long as we pursue harmony and avoid strain, we may remain disconnected from a majority of the world populations that bear the yoke of structural inequities.

CHAPTER 24

PSYCHOLOGIES FOR LIBERATION: VIEWS FROM ELSEWHERE

Andy Dawes

In this chapter, I will introduce some ideas that may not be familiar to those who have learned about psychology in modern Western societies. I will begin with an examination of the *ideology* that underpins both peace psychology and what I call *"mainstream" psychology.* Mainstream psychology is a body of knowledge that claims its truth value largely on the basis of its adherence to the research tradition of modern *empiricism,* the belief that sensory experience is the only valid source of knowledge. In addition to embracing empiricism, peace psychology has *liberal humanist* values, which emphasize democratic structures and individual freedom. At the core of both the philosophy of empiricism and the value of liberal humanism is the concept of the *autonomous individual.* I will demonstrate how coupling these two systems of ideas, emphasizing individualism and freedom, can lead to a form of *ideological violence* when peace psychologists seek to address direct and structural violence in parts of the world. Ideological violence occurs when the ideas and practices of a particular group are negated, and unfamiliar ideas and practices that are held to be superior are introduced.

The second half of this chapter will focus on liberation psychologies. Liberation psychologies (there are several approaches) developed independently of the peace psychology movement. They had their roots in the responses of mental health workers to freedom struggles in the politically repressive societies of Latin America, Africa, and the Pacific region. Working at both the individual and the larger group level, liberation psychologists have sought to assist survivors of structural and direct political violence. More radically, their psychological work has been linked to political activism that has social transformation as its goal. I will use the South African case as an example of one approach to liberation psychology that evolved in response to the structural violence of apartheid prior to the attainment of democracy in 1994.

PEACE PSYCHOLOGY, PEACEBUILDING, AND IDEOLOGY

Peace psychologists in the post–Cold-War period have begun to engage with a new agenda of peacebuilding. Their work potentially entails a more radical orientation, because it addresses the structural roots of episodic violence, and promotes social and institutional change as the route to lasting peace and social justice (Galtung, 1990;

Comas-Díaz, Lykes, & Alarcón, 1998; Mays, Bullock, Rosenzweig, & Wessells, 1998). Peacebuilding seeks to create a platform for the establishment of social justice by moving beyond interventions at the individual level to structural interventions that improve life conditions for all.

Some of the inspiration for peacebuilding initiatives is drawn from various declarations of rights by the United Nations (U.N.). The argument is that the advancement of respect for basic rights can redress many of the conditions that promote direct and structural violence. These principles reflect core values of liberal humanism that emerged in Europe in the period following Rousseau's treatise on individual human rights. These values include the promotion of social justice founded on the principle of equality for all, a respect for individual self-determination (freedom of choice) and the protection of individual rights (Collins, 1992; Hayek, 1975). A central focus is on the *individual*.

In contrast, as Lykes points out in Chapter 14, many societies see the rights of the individual as subordinate to those of the community. For example, strict Hindu societies do not have the same views as North Americans on the natural rights of individual liberty and choice (Shweder, Mahapatra, & Miller, 1990). The life choices of the individual are circumscribed according to their gender and caste position. For example, a lower-caste person may not choose to marry a high-caste person. In such a case, the matter of individual freedoms does not even arise as a consideration. The choices of those involved are ignored in the interest of adhering to the natural law that informs caste practices. The Hindu system is seen as just because it is thought to be determined by natural law, driven as it were by an innate morality rather than civil law.

Another ideological element of peace psychology is the emphasis placed on *political rights*. In some communities that lack many basic resources such as adequate nutrition, one may argue that the satisfaction of these basic needs is a greater priority than civil liberties, which are political rights espoused in the West. These differences raise many challenges for peace psychologists informed and influenced by the political rights consciousness of the West.

A third ideological element intrinsic to peace psychology is the acceptance of the modern Western image of individuality, which underpins mainstream psychology, itself a product of the Enlightenment (Ingleby, 1995). The central point is that this individual is presented by psychology as *natural* and *universal*, and as *revealed* by a particular way of conducting scientific inquiry. In contrast, critics such as Ingleby maintain that this person (and her supposed psychological mechanisms) is not universally representative. Rather, the psychology we have produced is mainly a description of the individual in a particular historical context, which is greatly influenced by the tenets of capitalism with its emphasis on individual freedom. This person has been *created* rather than revealed, and has been *misrepresented* as universal. The argument is that as psychologists, we are embedded in, rather than have, an existence independent of this ideological universe, so our subject matter and practice will reflect our ideology.

One version of psychology's image of the individual is evident in the work of theorists such as Carl Rogers (1973) and Abraham Maslow (1968). They present their personality theories as universally applicable. However an analysis of their constructs reveals that they have developed theories of the personality that are quite culture-bound. For example, they both stress the importance of the autonomy of the self for psychological health, and Maslow in particular sees self-actualization as an important drive and goal. The idea of the actualizing self embraces many of the values of modern Western societies including the idea of the psychologically autonomous individual, who can make her own informed decisions in life relatively unfettered by the demands of family and community (Jacoby, 1975).

Many communities do not share this view (Dawes & Cairns, 1998; Lykes, 1994). Some do not have a concept of the "the self" at least in the sense that Rogers uses the term. Instead, individual identity is seen as co-extensive with the natural environment, kin, and deceased ancestors (Honwana, 1997). Because of their more sociocentric, rather than individually-centered, orientation, they also have a different view of individual rights. Rights are seen as properties of social positions associated with ancestry, gender, and age. These structural arrangements are supported by cultural narratives that express shared beliefs that are very different from the Western narratives where individual freedoms and rights are regarded as natural, no matter what social position the individual occupies. Conditions that peace psychologists would see as structurally violent are regarded in these communities as "normal" social arrangements.

For example, in many African communities, male elders have traditionally held considerable power over their communities. The chief allocates land to the people, the senior men adjudicate in disputes between individuals, and the rights of women are curtailed under patriarchal control. In South Africa, until 1998, women in African customary marriages (those which took place according to African custom and not through the civil courts) were regarded as the property of the husband and his family.

In essence an adult woman had the status of a minor child (Bennett, 1991). If she did not live up to the expectations of her husband and his parents, she could be sent home to her family with no compensation or rights. Here the rights of the individual woman are clearly compromised by rules that confer fundamentally unequal power to men and women. While these patterns are changing with the globalization of rights conventions, at the community level they are often still regarded as normal and proper—particularly by the men whose interests they serve. A serious problem that arises under such conditions, is that when women are regarded as subordinate chattels, they frequently become victims of abuse, particularly under conditions of severe poverty and political oppression (Campbell, 1995).

Constructs of selfhood, values, and justice therefore vary across the world, and they do not always match those that underpin the activities of Western peace psychologists. If we impose Western approaches of psychological functioning and treatment on communities that have different ideologies of selfhood and rights, we commit *ideological violence*. There are many ways in which this can occur. For example, in African war zones it has been common for Western psychologists to train local health workers in trauma work. There is sometimes little reflection by Western psychologists on the cultural relevance of the methods and concepts they are exporting. The very fact that the trainers are deployed to give skills to local workers rests on the assumption that the latter need to be skilled because their indigenous knowledge of trauma work is inadequate. Also, trainers have considerable power in providing jobs for local health workers in areas where the aftermath of war ensures that little work exists. If they are sensible, the trainees will be inclined to suppress their indigenous knowledge in favor of demonstrating their newly acquired skills (Dawes & Honwana, 1998). From this example, it is evident that nothing is directly forced upon the community. Rather a new set of ideas, which may or may not fit well with existing cosmologies, is introduced through the greater power of the psychologist to shape the discourse of distress and healing. Where the fit is not good, there is the risk that health workers' responses to trauma will not meet local needs (Dawes & Cairns, 1998).

Another example drawn from the work of Reynolds (1997) in Zimbabwe, touches more on issues of rights. Reynolds tells the story of the Zimbabwian *inyanga* (healer) who decided that an adolescent girl should be given in marriage to a father in compensation for the loss of his son during the liberation war. A member of the girl's family had been broken under torture, revealing the whereabouts of freedom fighters to the army. This led to the son's death and caused great tension in the village. The *inyanga* decided that harmony would be restored by the marriage, as the girl would bear sons to continue the line. Clearly from a Western perspective, the girl's *individual* rights were violated.

These examples raise complex issues, and easy answers are not readily available. While embracing the values of peace psychology, I have to be aware that my commitment to these values is a function of my position as someone socialized in the ideological climate of the modern Western world. There are other possible social systems in which the individual has a different place for reasons that are understandable. It is therefore necessary to negotiate with the groups with whom we work, and this may mean suspending, or even altering, some of the constructs which normally inform our activities. This is why many in this field rec-

ognize the importance of *co-constructing change* with, rather than for, communities (Martín-Baró, 1989; Comas-Díaz, et al., 1998; Gilbert, 1997). Such a position does not imply capitulation to conditions of structural violence out of respect for local ways. Indeed direct confrontation may be appropriate as the examples of South Africa and Latin America illustrate. However, the co-construction of change does recognize the importance and role of different ideologies and psychologies as they influence social arrangements and individual functioning. Apart from being disrespectful, to ignore these differences is to reduce the possible success of one's intervention.

PEACEBUILDING AS LIBERATION PSYCHOLOGY: THE SOUTH AFRICAN CASE

As has been stressed throughout this volume, peace psychology seeks to develop theories and practices that elucidate the processes involved in the prevention and mitigation of direct and structural violence. Liberation psychology, as a form of peace psychology, may be construed as an approach that seeks to use psychological knowledge and practice to bring about change in structurally violent societies, and to address the psychological needs of oppressed individuals. Liberation psychology is overtly political, has a clear social emancipation agenda, and works in the interests of the politically and economically oppressed. The interests of the oppressed may vary but would commonly include a desire for political freedom, democracy and economic justice. Liberation is also used to refer to the psychological freeing of individuals from the negative conceptions of self and community that are common psychological correlates of oppression. An example is the negative own-group identification experienced by blacks in racist societies (Foster, 1994). Psychological liberation also involves freeing the oppressor from the psychological orientations toward those who he or she oppresses, or preventing the development of such orientations. Prejudice reduction and anti-racist education initiatives would be examples (Eyber, Dyer, Versfeld, Dawes, Finchilescu, & Soudien, 1997).

My particular consideration of liberation psychology will draw on the South African situation. I will begin with a brief consideration of structural violence on the African continent. Some of these conditions gave rise to the first anti-colonial liberation psychology developed by Frantz Fanon (1967a, 1967b). His work influenced Latin American liberation psychologists (see Lykes in this volume), as well as those in apartheid South Africa.

Some History

According to leading Africanists such as Davidson (1992) and Mamdani (1996), the political, ideological, and local cultural forces operating before and during the colonial period have played a major role in the production of structural and direct violence in modern Africa. Space restricts me to a few points, and I will draw principally on the work of these authors.

To untangle one of the roots of ethnic and political conflict, we need to go back to the slave trade. The practice not only caused immeasurable suffering, but played a role in shaping ethnic relations that remain apparent today. Davidson (1992) observes that responses by Africans to slavery included the development of kin-based participation in the trade as a form of resistance to capture. Communities linked by language, clan, and kin connections would group together to form units that would participate in the subjugation of less powerful groups, who would

then be captured and sold into slavery. In this way, some could resist being captured. With the advent of colonization, existing territorial boundaries of indigenous groups were ignored as states were created and new boundaries cut across ethno-linguistic communities. On many occasions, groups with a history of hostility were thrust together, or political arrangements during colonialism caused intergroup friction.

It was common for local cultural structures to be used by the colonial administrations to extend their control over the native people. Subnational ethnic identities and boundaries were further strengthened as a result. For example, the authorities would appoint chiefs to administer the local populace on their behalf. This was often to the advantage of these men (it was always men), who could entrench their power. Indigenous groups were therefore not entirely passive in these processes, with more powerful members benefiting as far as possible from their position as puppets of the colonial state, or in the case of South Africa, the white government.

After independence, arrangements such as these sometimes led to border disputes, as in the case of Eritrea and Ethiopia, or attempts at secession in the cases of Eritrea and Biafra (in southern Nigeria). In part, these conflicts were attempts to establish political autonomy based on ethno-linguistic commonality.

Additional threats to stability in African states include underdevelopment, desperate poverty, huge disparities in wealth, corruption, and foreign debt. In recent years, structural adjustment policies of the World Bank and the International Monetary Fund aimed at cutting government spending in return for trade and aid, have been associated with reductions in social services, a decline in health and literacy levels, and renewed political tensions (George, 1992).

Some Psychological Considerations

Intergroup Relations and Ethnicity.

A common way for ordinary people involved in intergroup conflict to explain their situation is to construct the narrative in terms of ethnic identities. For them, ethnic division is experienced as real. Psychological aspects of ethnic identity construction are therefore important factors to consider when explaining the generation of conflict. Ethnic identity is a form of social identity. Once groups are formed, comparisons between people who are assigned to them become possible (Hogg & Abrams, 1988). Social identities clarify group boundaries, and normally involve groups being accorded differential status, which in turn makes it easier for the persecution of lower status ethnic groups to be justified. Ethnic groups typically share a sense of common cultural identity, symbols, language, and a narrative of origins (Thornton, 1988). Their collective ethnic memories usually contain images of heroism and violence, as well as the historic relations between one's own and other groups (Cairns & Darby, 1998; Mare, 1992). Ethnic identities also can be used as a basis for both structural and direct violence.

South Africa's apartheid system is an exemplary case of structural violence. The architects of the system both constructed and drew on existing ethnicities and used them for purposes of White political and economic domination. Race classification underpinned all practices. For example, impoverishment of those not classified as Whites was achieved by reserving 86 percent of the land for Whites and limiting educational and job opportunities for Blacks. Systematic efforts were made to construct and entrench ethnic histories and practices, so as to justify racial separation. These were sometimes taken up and used for personal power and ethnic mobilization by ethnic chiefs appointed to oversee the Black population. The legacy of this project is evident in the Kwazulu-Natal region of South Africa, where Zulu traditionalist sentiment continues to be used to support violent acts against those who reject tribal authority (Mare, 1992).

Individual Subjectivity and Its Liberation.

Frantz Fanon, a black psychiatrist who worked in Algeria, was the first African mental health worker to articulate a psychology of liberation which could inform revolutionary action against the structural violence of the French colonists (Fanon, 1967a; 1967b; 1968). Fanon's work is extensive and space precludes elaboration beyond a few central points.

He argued that individual psychological health was inseparable from political liberty, and that under conditions of structural violence, a situation of national psychological distress was present. For Fanon, the structural violence of colonization (and one could add apartheid), produces a *Manichean* psychological state, which is characterized by the defense mechanism of splitting. Internal psychological constructions of people and social groups are separated into distinct categories of good and bad. One of the key violences of colonization was the colonization of subjectivity, whereby the native takes on the subjectivity and values of the colonizer, and rejects his or her own heritage (and color). Splitting ensures that the worldview and cultural goods of the colonizer are viewed as positive, while those of the native are considered to be negative and to be denied.

To achieve both individual and national liberation, Fanon held that the colonized person had to challenge the colonizer both internally and externally. First the native had to purge her or his psychology of the destructive elements of mental colonization, and regain self-respect through the reversal of the internalized negative view of self and culture (see also Comas-Díaz et al., 1998). This theme was also taken up within the liberation strategy of the *Black Consciousness Movement* (BCM) among African Americans (Burlew, et al., 1992), South African Blacks (Biko, 1978), and in Latin America. Fanon (and the other liberation psychologies to which I have referred), rejected psychotherapy as the route to restoring positive Black identity. There were several reasons, not the least of which was its elite connections, its unavailability to the masses, and its unlikely role in promoting revolution.

The second leg of Fanon's argument was his belief that the oppressed would be psychologically freed by confronting the colonizer with violence. This was because he argued that the latter relied on violence to rule, and did not understand reasoned arguments for liberation. In this regard, Bulhan remarks that:

"Experience (as a liberation fighter) led him to reformulate the problem and the solution . . . The oppressed who were dehumanized by the violence of the oppresor. [They could] regain their identity, reclaim their history, reconstitute their bonding, and forge their future through violence. Through violence they remove the primary barrier to their humanity and they rehabilitate themselves." (Bulhan, 1985, p. 144).

This argument has been highly controversial. For example, Couve (1986), agrees with much of Fanon's position, but faults him on theoretical (psychoanalytic) grounds for his conclusion that a violent catharsis on the part of the colonized against the oppressor will be psychologically healing. Freud rejected the role of emotional catharsis as a key source of psychological recovery, which Fanon did not seem to recognize. Couve also mounts a materialist (Marxist) critique of Fanon for his overemphasis on a White

master–Black subject dialectic as explaining oppressed subjectivity, and his neglect of the role of class forces in the production of the social arrangements that underpin the shape of racial ideologies and individual psychology. Oppression is therefore not as color-coded as Fanon's psychological and classless analysis would have it. Nor is violent conduct therapeutic. Indeed, the recent continuing political repression and violence in Algeria (where Fanon worked) would suggest that the violent catharsis of the revolution did not lay to rest the hatred that had been bred under colonialism. Fanon's most lasting and useful contribution, which has made its mark in Latin America, South Africa, and the United States, is probably his writing on Black or indigenous identity, and the role of political resistance in its reclamation.

LIBERATION PSYCHOLOGY AND THE DISMANTLING OF APARTHEID

South Africa emerged from colonialism at the beginning of the twentieth century but it was not until 1994 that the country threw off the shackles of four centuries of White minority rule. This section of the chapter will outline the response of liberation psychologists in South Africa to the structural violence of their society. Sporadic and individual attempts to address the psychological impact of apartheid have taken place since the late 1940s. The work of MacCrone (1947) on attitudes, Manganyi (1973) on Black subjectivity, and Lambley (1980) on links between authoritarian personality structure and support for apartheid policy, are some examples. More collective and sustained efforts commenced in the early 1980s, and continued until the demise of apartheid in 1994. My commentary will reflect struggles with the issue of ethnicity, and ethical neutrality during what amounted to a low-level civil war. The full history of this time has not been told, but several commentaries exist (Flisher et al., 1993; Louw & van Hoorn, 1997; Louw, 1987; Cooper, Nicholas, Seedat, & Statman, 1990; Nicholas 1990; Seedat, 1997; Swartz, Gibson, & Swartz, 1990).

South African psychologists who identified with the need to liberate their country from racial oppression, drew on a variety of strategies common to peace psychology (see Wessells, Schwebel, and Anderson, in this volume). Theory and research were used to both understand and address conflict, as well as to attend to the needs of those who had suffered the consequences of oppression. In addition, a cornerstone of the work that often is not associated with peace psychology was the attempt to use psychological knowledge to inform political action (see Montiel's chapter in this volume). In the following sections, I outline how professional organizations, research programs, and direct interventions contributed to the reduction of structural violence during the apartheid era.

Prior to 1994, organized South African psychology was itself affected by the divisiveness of the political life of the country. Psychology was split into a majority conservative and a small progressive sector that was actively opposed to the apartheid regime. The conservative Psychological Association of South Africa never took a position on social transformation (Cooper, Nicholas, Seedat, & Statman, 1990). Rather, as Cooper and his colleagues note, organized psychology and its members were active in both the design of the apartheid system and in its later maintenance. Because the Association declared itself politically neutral, military officers and members of a police force were members.

In contrast, the small progressive sector (perhaps 15 percent of professional psycho-logists) was split along political/ideological lines; some psychologists aligned with the South African Black Consciousness Movement (BCM) and responded to apartheid as a Black group reclaiming its identity. A key feature of their position was the recognition that Black psychologists needed to develop solidarity and a positive identity free from the limiting gaze of Whites who dominated the profession (Seedat, 1997). The link to the ideas of Fanon and South African Black Consciousness leader Steve Biko was evident here. A second faction of the progressive movement was known as the *Organization for Appropriate Social Services in South Africa* (*OASSSA*), which served to unite anti-apartheid mental health workers across professions and the color line. These mental health workers used their professional skills to challenge the regime. Both these factions can be termed liberation psychologies. Like Martín-Baró in Latin America, both factions argued that the apartheid structure and the direct violence that kept it in place were damaging to the well-being of South Africans. It was therefore necessary to engage the mental health disciplines to fight for change and publicly take a political stand against the State.

Sections from the OASSSA Statement of Principles, formulated in 1983, are worth quoting (see italics below) as they illustrate several central features of a liberation psychology, similar to those developed in Latin America by Comas-Díaz et al. (1998):

> We are aware that in South Africa there are specific *economic and political structures which contribute to most social and personal problems.* Apartheid and economic exploitation provide the base for poor living conditions, work alienation, and race and sex discrimination which are antithetical to mental health. *Our commitment as social service workers demands that we continually expose the effects of these conditions and participate in efforts to*

change the structures that underlie them. In order to properly serve our community, *we must work for the sharing of knowledge and skills with the community at large and, ultimately, for an economically just and democratic society.*

Unlike the Latin American progressive psychologists described by Comas-Díaz et al. (1998), the South Africans did not emphasize the role of cultural factors in responses to stress and healing under political repression. Instead, the policy of liberation movements in South Africa emphasized national unity so as to bind all South Africans to the struggle for a non-racial state, regardless of their ethnic identity. Progressive psychologists supported this position and used social identity theory (SIT) to inform their views of the situation (Hogg & Abrams, 1988). SIT and related research shows that if ethnic group identities are made highly salient and if groups are compared unfavorably with one another, the likelihood of intergroup conflict increases. Also, the simple practice of focusing on national sub-group identities, makes it more difficult for people to imagine themselves as part of one nation; hence, the emphasis on national identity.

Progressive psychologists were also influenced by prevailing socialist discourse which stressed the superiority of materialist (class) analyses over race relations theories in explaining the South African situation (Wolpe, 1988). The *materialist argument* was that apartheid policy had little to do with race relations but was based on a white capitalist strategy to control economic power. To achieve this aim, whites had to control the land, the natural resources, and the economy, which they succeeded in doing. Progressives therefore downplayed the role of culture because they had problems with its adequacy as an explanation of apartheid policy, and because they did not wish to reinforce the divisions and cultural racism of apartheid. The class argument was the subject of extensive debate in progressive mental health circles (Swartz & Foster, 1984).

Research

While not conducted under the auspices of a progressive movement, the work of Foster, Davis, and Sandler (1987) on political imprisonment and torture, stands as exemplary research in the interests of justice. The work was conducted at a time when psychologists were being asked to give expert testimony in the courts on the admissibility of confessions made by captured members of anti-apartheid movements. Commonly these people were tortured and held in solitary confinement for long periods with no access to anyone other than their captors. The defendants claimed that their confessions were made under duress and were false. This defense was repeatedly rebutted by the State, on the grounds that there was no independent evidence of the allegations against the state (Foster et al., 1987).

Foster and his colleagues interviewed several hundred ex-detainees and obtained self-reports about their treatment in prison. If common findings of maltreatment and negative psychological sequellae were found, this evidence could be used to challenge the admissibility of confessions made under such conditions. In addition, the authors wished to draw public attention to the psychological harm caused by torture and solitary confinement, if the results supported such a conclusion. The study found overwhelming evidence of systematic and brutal maltreatment. When the study was released to the public, Foster was attacked by the government and right-wing social scientists. He also suffered attacks on his home by persons unknown—probably state hit squads.

The so-called "torture report" led to an increase in awareness among those members of the White public who were prepared to listen. The report also raised international pressure against South Africa. However, it had no significant impact on the legal process, because no court accepted the psychological claim that the South African version of solitary confinement was harmful. Also, the law continued to require the defendant to demonstrate ill-treatment, an impossible task when there were no witnesses to the events other than the security police. Nonetheless, Foster's work constitutes an example of thorough psychological research being put to work in an attempt to improve the delivery of justice, and also to challenge politically repressive practice.

Other projects, research findings, and clinical knowledge about the effects of police harassment, torture and imprisonment were published in popular form as pamphlets and handbooks written in local languages. The literature was disseminated free among communities affected by repression. One example was a self-help booklet on symptoms of stress and how to cope with them. Readers were informed in simple language about what symptoms to expect following torture and imprisonment so as to render their reactions less disturbing. They and their families were also given suggestions on techniques that could be employed to relieve distress, and who to contact for more assistance.

Direct Intervention. Direct intervention took the form of clinical consultations with individuals, families, and groups (Dawes & de Villiers, 1989; Dawes, 1992). Lay community members were also trained to offer basic supportive services under supervision (Swartz, Dowdall & Swartz, 1986). In the last case, interventions were similar to those described by Metreaux (1992) and Langer (1989) in Nicaragua, where professionals "multiplied" the effects of psychological in-

terventions by training local lay therapists appointed by the community. Although the South Africans knew nothing of the Central American work until later, the two initiatives were driven by a wish to develop "appropriate" services for the politically oppressed and the poor (Flisher, Skinner, Lazarus, & Louw, 1993).

As in the work of the Latin Americans, progressive and "appropriate" services in South Africa often challenged many accepted clinical practices, such as ethical neutrality. For example, members of the South African security forces were deliberately excluded from services. As I have discussed elsewhere (Dawes, 1992), there were two main reasons for this decision. The political reason was that we decided that offering services to the security forces would be tantamount to assisting "the enemy," thereby compromising the campaign to end the structural violence of apartheid. The practical reason was that in order to win the trust of people who had suffered at the hands of the security forces, and lived in fear of informers, clinicians had to make their opposition to the government clear. Therapists were sometimes asked to disclose their own political ideology, and if this served to facilitate the process of therapeutic engagement, then some therapists did so. But even disclosure was often not enough. Also necessary was being known in resistance circles as a member of a progressive organization and an activist against repression. The political and the psychological were thus quite closely interwoven, with members of progressive mental health groups defying bans on public gatherings, and speaking at rallies about the psychological effects of apartheid and repression.

While many interventions took place in clinics, others took place outside in informal settings. Dawes and de Villiers (1989), for example, report how they met to work with families and their teenage children (who had been sentenced to prison for public violence) in their homes, or in a supposedly safe room at the back of a cinema. Eventually, when the children went into prison, their therapists accompanied them and community members to the prison gates before all were chased away by the riot police.

CONCLUSIONS

The practices that developed during the South African liberation struggle raise many questions, not least, the ethical decision to work only for those involved in the liberation struggle. In our view at the time, the fundamental feature of the structural violence of South Africa was the absence of democracy for the majority of the people. The system within which they had to live was unjust and compromised their mental health. For these reasons, OASSSA mental health workers and those within the grouping of Black psychologists, aligned themselves with efforts to remove apartheid. As far as I can determine, no organized group of progressive psychologists ever took a public stance on the issue of violence against oppressors. That matter was left to individual conscience. However, as has been the case in other repressive contexts, such as the Philippines (Montiel, 1995), it was common to offer psychological assistance to people who had committed violence as part of the political struggle. In the case of South Africa, socialist language as well as materialist analysis was present in the rhetoric of the time (e.g. Couve, 1986; Dawes, 1986). Therefore, South African liberation psychology is probably best described as a broad anti-apartheid initiative with socialist leanings. An examination of documents such as the OASSSA Statement of Principles, indicates that there was a strong con-

viction that future economic policy should spread the wealth of the nation more evenly to reduce poverty, support public health, enhance welfare services, and increase the life chances of all.

While democracy has been achieved in South Africa, the goals of a redistribution of wealth and socialized public services have not. At the end of the 1990s, as is the case in the rest of Africa, the vast majority of South Africans remain impoverished. Tight macroeconomic policies, which have led to limits on social spending, and South Africa's vulnerable economic position relative to the major industrial powers and currencies, are likely to ensure that poverty will remain a significant force for instability and episodic violence in the twenty-first century.

Political conflict between ethnic groups is not as marked in South Africa as elsewhere on the continent, where political parties and contesting groups have commonly had an ethnic base (e.g. Nigeria, Zimbabwe, and Angola). A major reason for the lack of such conflict is probably the unifying approach of the largest and currently ruling party, the African National Congress (ANC). The ANC has never had a local ethnic base, and has a long established policy of stressing national unity in a context of cultural diversity. The party always mobilized around the common experience of Black political and economic oppression. Also, as du Preez (1997) argues, under apartheid it was not the practice to play one African ethnic group off against the other as was the case in Rwanda and elsewhere. However, people of mixed racial descent and Asians did hold more political and economic rights than members of African ethnic groups. In the post-apartheid situation, tensions between these groups and other Black South Africans are becoming evident (Finchilescu & Dawes, 1998). Racism is commonly accelerated under conditions of structural inequality, and because these conditions continue to prevail, racism will remain a major threat to peace.

Direct violence is perhaps the most prominent feature of the psychological legacy of apartheid, one of the most oppressive political designs of modern times. As I have noted, Fanon spoke of the *Manichean* psychologies of the colonies (and apartheid), that emphasized differences between rulers and indigenous groups. A further central component of apartheid ideology was the dehumanization of those deemed to be inferior. Apartheid made a banal art of the construction of differences between groups. Initially supposed racial characteristics and later cultural markers, were used to emphasize inferiority and difference (Nicholas, 1993). The dehumanization that formed part of this process legitimized the use of structural and direct violence in the pursuit of power, and "peace" (i.e. racial harmony through separation) [Foster, 1998; Truth and Reconciliation Commission (TRC), 1998].

South Africa is awash with weapons, another legacy of the liberation struggle and regional wars that were sponsored by the apartheid regime (South African Institute of Race Relations, 1997). There is much talk of South Africa enduring a "culture of violence" in which violent responses to conflict have become normalized (Dawes, 1994). As much as it is present in the streets, gender oppression rooted in cultural practices of male hegemony in both Black and White communities ensures that violence is also present in the home. Poverty conditions and alcohol abuse contribute further to domestic violence, as unemployed men strike out against women in reaction to the loss of their status as patriarchs (Campbell, 1995).

It is now necessary to shape a post-apartheid psychology designed to liberate South Africans and meet these difficult challenges. That work has begun, and embraces elements of the progressive program of the 1980s. Among other projects, research is being conducted to address the impact of poverty and violence (Barbarin, Richter, de Wet, & Wachtel, 1998); the position of women (de la Rey & Owens, 1998; Finchilescu, 1995); mental health service transformation (Foster et al., 1997); culturally appropriate forms of intervention (Dawes & Cairns, 1998); and the promotion of intergroup tolerance (Eyber et al., 1997). Psychologists have also been active in the processes of the Truth and Reconciliation Commission, which was designed to uncover past abuses of human rights, and consider reparations for victims (de la Rey & Owens, 1998; also see de la Rey in this volume).

For an effective and committed liberation psychology to emerge in democratic South Africa, psychologists will have to highlight the impact of economic structural adjustment on individual lives. Psychological research on the impact of poverty will need to continue to be brought to the attention of policy makers, in support of the concerns of those who have few opportunities to give voice to their difficulties. They will also have to confront the powerful with the risks their economic policies pose to the consolidation of a hard won democracy. As one individual commented recently at a forum on poverty: "We now have a Rainbow Nation (Nelson Mandela's term for multi-cultural South Africa), but you can't eat Rainbows!" In order for the people of Africa to be able to enjoy all that their rainbow nations have to offer, peace psychologists will need to become involved in promoting a social justice morality at local *and* international levels. For the peace of the poor nations of the world is intricately and structurally bound to the wealth of the rich.

CHAPTER 25

GANDHI AS PEACEBUILDER: THE SOCIAL PSYCHOLOGY OF *SATYAGRAHA*

Daniel M. Mayton II

On a cold night over a hundred years ago in Maritzburg, South Africa, Mohandas K. Gandhi was thrown off a train when he refused to move from his first-class seat. Gandhi's presence in that seat offended a white passenger because it was not appropriate for a "coloured person" to travel first class. This discrimination was a defining moment in Gandhi's life as it led him to develop the resolve needed to remove the injustice of color prejudice that was pervasive in South Africa at that time (Gandhi, 1957/1927).

Over the next five decades Gandhi became a peacebuilder. He developed and tested methods that produced political change and reduced social injustices. Gandhi's teachings and actions had a profound effect on those around him, his coun-

try, and, in many respects, the world. In this chapter, I will outline the philosophy of Gandhi and the actions he used and advocated to establish social justice. Following this, I will outline the psychological dynamics that contributed to making his peacebuilding efforts effective.

THE GOAL AND PRINCIPLES GUIDING GANDHI'S ACTIONS

Gandhi's overarching goal throughout his life was *sarvodaya* which translates to "the welfare of all" (Bose, 1987, p. 23) or "uplift of all" (Bondurant, 1965, p. 6). To achieve this goal, three main principles guided his writings and actions. The Indian terms describing these principles are *satya* (truth), *ahimsa* (nonviolence), and *tapasya* (self-suffering) (Bondurant, 1965; Gandhi, 1951; Pelton, 1974).

Satya or Truth

Satyagraha, as discussed and used by Gandhi, can be understood on at least two levels. First, it refers to the process of developing an understanding of any situation and the points of view of all individuals who are involved with it. *Satyagraha,* which can be translated to mean "Soul Force," serves in this regard as a process to vindicate the truth. In trying to understand the validity of each viewpoint, Gandhi was well aware of his limitations and those of any human being trying to establish absolute truth. Given these limitations, he believed we can never be sure if we, as one side of a conflict, are correct in our position or if our adversaries, on the other side of a conflict, have truth on their side. Therefore, while Gandhi viewed the pursuit of truth as an ongoing aspect of life which was never fully achievable in a complete sense, *satyagraha* was an important orientation to maintain on an individual level.

The second interpretation for the term *satyagraha* is as a positive peacebuilding strategy on a larger societal level; here, *satyagraha* is a process of civil disobedience or nonviolent resistance. It is *satyagraha* in this second sense which helped India attain independence from Great Britain and which had a profound impact on other peacebuilders such as Martin Luther King, Jr. Later in this chapter, I will describe the characteristics of a *satyagraha* movement from this perspective, and then I will provide a concrete example, the Salt *Satyagraha* campaign of 1930 to 1931. However, to fully understand the *satyagraha* method, a close look at two other principles in Gandhi's philosophy is essential.

Ahimsa or Nonviolence

An integral part of Gandhi's philosophy and life's work is the notion of *ahimsa,* which literally means "non-injury" or "nonviolence." For Gandhi, *ahimsa* was the belief in the sacredness of life and the refusal to do harm to living things (Bose, 1987; Nakhre, 1982), an interpretation that was based on the deep-rooted Hindu tradition of not doing harm.

Ahimsa was vital to Gandhi's peacebuilding efforts for several reasons. First, *ahimsa* means not harming others either in thought or deed. Second, Gandhi viewed *ahimsa* as also having a more dynamic and positive state which is love (Gandhi, 1951). Pelton (1974) describes this love as active goodwill and it also bears similarity to the Rogerian concept of unconditional positive regard. This love serves as the means to get to the ends of truth. Third, a means which uses nonviolence to reveal truth has advantages to Gandhi because only relative truth can be attained for certain. Given this human limitation, the nonviolent means to realize one's goal guarantees that individuals will not hurt any adversary in a conflict who might be closer to the absolute truth than they themselves are. Excluding the use of violence is best, because humans are not capable of knowing the absolute truth and therefore are not competent to punish (Nakhre, 1982).

Throughout his life, Gandhi insisted that the means to get to any goal must be carefully selected or the attainment of the goal might be short-lived or ultimately subverted. For instance, he wanted to obtain India's independence using nonviolent means while others advocated violent rebellion. Gandhi believed the leaders who would emerge if India followed the violent path to independence would be just as tyrannical as the British leadership which they would replace. Therefore, the end result of independence would have very little impact on the common citizen of India and would not be as desirable as the leadership which would emerge if the principle of *ahimsa* was followed in the struggle for independence.

Tapasya or Self-Suffering

Tapasya translates to "self-suffering" and is the third major principle in Gandhi's belief system. Gandhi viewed self-suffering as a viable maneuver to confront the violence that is often leveled at those who work to remove social injustices. The willingness to endure suffering instead of retaliating for a violent act with a violent act breaks the cycle of violence. While those fighting social injustices might suffer more than those who work to maintain the status quo, Gandhi believed that in the long run the world as a whole will witness less total violence.

The ability to engage in self-suffering requires considerable courage and self-control. In fact, Gandhi describes the self-discipline required of someone who follows his principles as being akin to those of a military soldier. Like soldiers, individuals who practice *tapasya* require extensive training to establish the needed discipline when violence is leveled at them.

Gandhi's Value System

Human values are transsituational goals which vary in importance and serve as guiding principles in people's lives (Schwartz, 1992, 1994). An analysis of the value system of an individual can help explain the actions of an individual in a range of social and political situations (Rokeach, 1973, 1979). Schwartz (1994) has identified ten value types which have implications for understanding political orientation and politi-

cal action. Closely examining the goals and principles which Gandhi considered important can shed some light on his actions.

Based on the goals and principles of Gandhi, outlined above, his values seem to fall into three of the value types identified by Schwartz (1994). The notion of the welfare of all (*sarvodaya*) and the concern about truth and wisdom (*satya*) directly corresponds to the two self-transcendent value types of universalism and benevolence. The emphasis placed on self-discipline corresponds to the value type of conformity as defined by Schwartz. This is consistent with the research of Mayton, Diessner, and Granby (1996), who found that individuals with predispositions to nonviolent behavior placed more emphasis on universalism, benevolence, and conformity values than individuals more predisposed to violence.

GANDHI'S USE OF *SATYAGRAHA* TO OBTAIN POLITICAL GOALS

Satyagraha as a Peacebuilding Strategy

Satyagraha is a method whereby grievances could successfully challenge an established political order. Bondurant (1965) has outlined the steps of a typical *satyagraha* movement, which is an activity of civil disobedience designed to confront unjust laws and policies. It would start with an effort to resolve the conflict through established channels and accepted protocol. Should these methods prove ineffective, systematic planning for the group to take direct action would begin. Following an active propaganda campaign involving demonstrations, parades, etc., a final strong appeal or ultimatum to one's opponent would be made which would explain the steps that will be undertaken if no agreement can be reached. Depending on the nature of the grievances and the specific situation, the subsequent actions taken may involve boycotts, strikes, and other forms of noncooperation such as nonpayment of taxes. Those who take part in the movement are called *satyagrahi*.

The Salt *Satyagraha*

The Salt *Satyagraha* was a national movement throughout India that began early in 1930 and lasted for over a year (Bondurant, 1965). Its immediate goal was the removal of the salt tax which exploited the peasants and symbolized the unjust nature of British rule. The Salt Act made it a crime to possess salt not purchased by the British salt monopoly (Fischer, 1954).

Following the initial planning of the specific actions, Gandhi sent a letter to the Viceroy describing the grievances regarding the Salt Act and indicating the specific nature of the plan for civil disobedience. When this ultimatum was ignored, Gandhi and other *satyagrahis* began their historic march to the sea. Careful planning and the training of the *satyagrahis* in self-restraint and crowd control made this a peaceful event. The march took over three weeks and was widely covered in the press, making the injustice of British rule known throughout the world. Shortly after arriving at the beach, Gandhi purposely broke the law outlined in the Salt Act by making salt. With his act he opened the door for others to engage in the same type of civil disobedience. Estimates of the number of Indians jailed for breaking the Salt Act exceed sixty thousand (Fischer, 1954). As the salt tax was still in place, additional levels of civil disobedience were planned and executed.

In a second letter to the Viceroy, Gandhi explained how the *satyagrahis* would demand possession of the Dharsana salt works. While this letter led to Gandhi's arrest, the march on the salt works still took place. Over two thousand *satyagrahis* took part in the nonviolent raid on the salt works. The leaders of the Salt *Satyagraha* admonished the *satyagrahis* to not resist nor raise a hand even to ward off the inevitable blows from the police. Webb Miller, a journalist for United Press, witnessed the raid and reported

> In complete silence the Gandhi men drew up and halted a hundred yards from the stockade. A picked column advanced from the crowd, waded the ditches, and approached the barbed-wire stockade. Suddenly, at a word of command, scores of native policemen rushed upon the advancing marchers and rained blows upon their heads with their steel-shod lathis. Not one of the marchers even raised an arm to fend off the blows. They went down like ten-pins. From where I stood I heard the sickening whack of the clubs on unprotected skulls. The waiting crowd of marchers groaned and sucked in their breath in sympathetic pain at every blow. Those struck down fell sprawling, unconscious or writhing with fractured pain or broken shoulders . . . Although everyone knew that within a few minutes he would be beaten down, perhaps killed, I could detect no sign of wavering or fear. They marched steadily, with heads up, without the encouragement of music or cheering or any possibility that they might escape injury or death. . . . There was no fight, no struggle, the marchers simply walked forward until struck down (as quoted by Fischer, 1954, p. 101).

The raids and the carnage continued for days with stretcher bearers carrying bleeding men to the first aid station.

While the raids on the salt works ended with the approaching monsoons, civil disobedience continued in the form of boycotts and intentional acts that broke unjust laws and ordinances (Bondurant, 1965). Eventually, the salt regulations were modified in ways which removed much of the injustice forced on the poor. The impact of the thousands of localized campaigns which were part of the Salt *Satyagraha* had been successful in following the guidelines for a *satyagraha* and were effective in reaching the immediate goal.

PSYCHOLOGICAL EXPLANATIONS FOR THE SUCCESS OF *SATYAGRAHA*

Gandhi implemented *satyagraha* successfully in many contexts (Gandhi, 1951, 1957/1927). In his "experiments with truth" Gandhi field-tested and applied numerous psychological constructs in very effective ways. How can we explain the success of this method Gandhi called a *satyagraha*? The next sections of this chapter will draw on research and theory in social psychology in an attempt to explain the positive outcomes of *satyagraha*.

Attribution Theory

From Gandhi's point of view the goal of *satyagraha* was to awaken the conscience of the opponent (Nakhre, 1982). Social psychologists have observed that people make attributions or try to determine the causes of their own and other people's behavior all the time (e.g. Brehm, Kassin, & Fein, 1999). According to attribution theory, when we try to understand why others are behaving the way they are, we often focus on the situation. However, when their behavior is vastly different from what we would expect of people in their situation, then our tendency is to attribute their behavior to their disposition. We learn a lot about people's disposition when their behavior deviates markedly from our expectation (Jones & Davis, 1965). Ordinarily, we would expect the *satyagrahis* to respond violently to the violence of the British. Because the *satya-*

grahis' nonviolent behavior deviates from the norm or what we would expect of people in their situation, we are likely to attribute their nonviolence to the disposition of Gandhi and his fellow Indians.

Not only were the peaceful *satyagrahis* viewed favorably according to world opinion, but there were additional psychological dynamics that could have influenced the British to focus on the unjust nature of the Salt Acts. Social psychologists have identified a set of biases and errors that people make in looking for causes of behavior. The *self-serving bias* involves the tendency of people to take less credit for failures than they do for their successes. When the *satyagrahis* provoked the British to enforce the unjust law and to engage in violent action, self-serving attributional biases would predict the British would continue to view themselves favorably by attributing their violent actions to external situational factors. Therefore, instead of denigrating themselves for inflicting pain on the Indians who had positive dispositional characteristics, they would attribute their violent behavior to the external situation and focus on the law that required them to commit acts which were unjust. With each additional aspect of the Salt *Satyagraha* as well as subsequent acts of civil disobedience, which were nonviolent, the self-attributions of being on the moral high ground gave way to the focus on the socially unjustice policies created by the British. Fischer (1954) characterized the effects of the Salt *Satyagraha* in a manner consistent with this attributional interpretation when he said "it made the British aware that they were subjugating India" (p. 102).

Attitude Change Variables

Gandhi succeeded in getting support for his efforts from the Indian people as well as the world community. Gandhi capitalized on many of the factors identified as efficacious by researchers of persuasive communication. In particular, three factors that are found in models of persuasive communication are noteworthy.

First, Gandhi's *charismatic leadership* clearly worked in his favor. Gandhi spent considerable time traveling around India observing and listening to the concerns of the common citizen. Subsequently, he was able to address issues of significance in succinct ways that could be easily understood. Gandhi had a message of independence for India and the removal of social injustices, which were inspirational to nearly all Indians.

A second source characteristic of the communication model of persuasion which helped Gandhi was his *similarity* with the common people of India. He dressed and lived in the manner of an Indian peasant which made him a positive role model. He was very knowledgeable about diverse religious beliefs present in India and abroad and used this knowledge to express his nonviolence in terms of Hindu, Moslem, and Christian doctrine. From the Bhagavad-Gita, to the Koran, to the "Sermon on the Mount" in the Bible, Gandhi was comfortable with many different audiences. His use of traditional terms to explain his procedures and concerns increased the support he received.

Third, Gandhi engaged people in his thoughtful analysis of social injustice. Petty & Cacioppo (1986) have developed the elaboration likelihood model. This model proposes that the central route to persuasion, which engages the person being persuaded in serious thought to the relevant points, results in more long term attitude change than the peripheral route, which appeals to emotion and results in lower cognitive engagement. Gandhi's efforts utilized the central route to persuasion in several ways. Because *satyagraha* was so different from what people expected, the focus on the content of the message was enhanced and thus more serious thought was given to the message and a more enduring change was a result.

Negotiation Methods

Gandhi's way of dealing with the British utilized behaviors which foreshadowed the method of principled negotiation discussed by Fisher, Ury, and Patton (1991). The notions of separating the people from the problem and focusing on interests and not positions, are mainstays of principled negotiation (Fisher, Ury, & Patton, 1991). In separating the people from the problem, Gandhi was quick to remind his *satyagrahis* to distinguish the unjust laws from those who enforced them, and when harm did befall any of the British he was deeply troubled by it. Gandhi harbored no animosity toward any British individual and, on the contrary, his compassion for the hardship his actions had on the British were very genuine (Fischer, 1954). The outcome of the Salt *Satyagraha* serves as a good example of how Gandhi focused on interests of all parties instead of digging in and holding onto a position. While the initially stated objective was the repeal of the Salt Act, when the British agreed to modify the salt regulations so that much of the injustice forced on the poor ended, he modified his position and accepted their proposal as it satisfied the interests of this *satyagraha* (Bondurant, 1965).

Psychological Lessons from Gandhi

From the time he was thrown off the train in South Africa until he fell from an assassin's bullet in India, Gandhi acted to rid his country of social injustice. His peacebuilding efforts were strongly based on self-transcendent values combined with a commitment to principle which reflected a conservative value emphasis. The search for truth combined with tolerance and self discipline made him an ethical model who many wanted to emulate. He utilized good communication with his allies and his opponents at the interpersonal level as well as via the written word. Gandhi never lost sight of the fact that all were humans cut from the same cloth by God, and gave unconditional positive regard to all. He was an applied social scientist who used some very effective psychological principles to reach his goals.

CHAPTER 26

PEACEBUILDING AND NONVIOLENCE: GANDHI'S PERSPECTIVE ON POWER

Manfred B. Steger

Mahatma Gandhi's theory of nonviolent power represents a much-needed perspective from which to criticize contemporary dominant modes of representing power primarily in terms of violence. His understanding of power offers both a theoretical and a practical approach to the problem of peacebuilding in today's global society. This chapter makes its arguments in three parts. First, I point to some shortcomings of the dominant discourse of power rooted in Thomas Hobbes' early modern view of human nature. Second, I introduce Gandhi's contrasting perspective on power and nonviolence based on his idea of "searching for *satya*" (truth, being) through the practice of *ahimsa* (nonviolence). Third, I examine particularly difficult historical cases in which the employment of nonviolent means actually produced socially transformative ends.

I am sensitive to critical voices who have rightly urged theorists of nonviolence to provide more precise definitions of their key terms. I must admit that I use the term "nonviolence" only reluctantly because it signifies for many people the *total* absence of both "direct" (physical) and "indirect" (structural) forms of violence. Yet, even for Gandhi, absolute nonviolence remained a moral ideal which might only be approximated in the world of politics. Indeed,

Gandhi himself sometimes engaged in such extreme actions as fasting-unto-death and harsh physical discipline, which could be interpreted as weapons of psychological coercion (Borman, 1986). Moreover, in *Hind Swaraj,* his sole sustained treatise on political theory, published in 1909, Gandhi relied on the conceptual violence of constructing a "pure" Indian identity defined against a tainted British "Other." Thus, throughout the essay, I will therefore limit the use of the term "nonviolence" to mean the opposite of open, physical forms of violence. After all, the earliest English usages of violence (from the Latin *violentia*) describe it as "the exercise of physical force" against someone who is thereby "interrupted or interfered with rudely or roughly" (Keane, 1996).

THOMAS HOBBES AND THE DOMINANT DISCOURSE OF POWER

Our ideas about social phenomena are closely connected to the way we construct and use language. We make sense of social reality through *discourses* and *narratives* that reflect shared images, ideas, values, beliefs, and ideals. Discourses provide individuals and social groups with a coherent orientation in time and space.

Political discourses tend to focus on the meaning and legitimate exercise of power (Ricoeur, 1986). With the seventeenth-century rise of *liberalism* as a political doctrine challenging *feudalism* and the king's *divine right* to rule in an autocratic fashion, Western political discourses acquired new meanings, most importantly the idea that power rested in individuals and their ability to apply violence and coercion. To this day, this central assumption is reflected in the standard definition of the *liberal agency model of power:* "A has power over B to the extent that he can get B to do something that B would not otherwise do" (Dahl, 1957, pp. 203–204). This understanding of power derives from philosophical and psychological assumptions made by early modern thinkers, most notably by the English political theorist Thomas Hobbes (1588–1679). His ideas about human nature and political institutions gave rise to an understanding of power which emphasized "natural" aggression, looming violent disruptions, and other "imaginings and threats of force, disorder, and pain" (Sarat & Kearns, 1995, pp. 1–2). Indeed, Hobbes's influential writings greatly contributed to the invention of the modern "realist" political discourse which was later termed *Realpolitik.* This German term refers to the idea that the essence of politics consists of a ceaseless struggle for power, material goods, and the control of the means of violence.

In order to better understand the fundamental psychological and political assumptions inherent in Realpolitik's equation of power and violence, it is useful to examine in some detail Thomas Hobbes's view of human nature. In *Leviathan,* his major treatise on political theory published in 1651, Hobbes puts at the center of his analysis a particular understanding of the individual as an isolated, self-contained being who interacts with other individuals in mechanical fashion. As Donald Tannenbaum and David Schultz (1998) point out, Hobbes' atomistic conception of the individual has a clear psychological basis, rooted in three motives. First, all individuals are amorally selfish and controlled by their hedonistic desires and physical appetites. They are absorbed in their personal interests as they compete for scarce or limited goods such as wealth. Second, they are impelled by the desire to seek power and domination of others to protect themselves and their goods. As Hobbes notes, "I put as a general inclination of all mankind a perpetual and restless desire of power after power that ceases only in death" (1985, p. 161). This is due to what Hobbes calls "diffidence," or mistrust of others. Finally, individuals desire glory, the good opinion of others which makes them seem superior and more praiseworthy (Tannebaum & Schultz, 1998).

For Hobbes, "reason" merely functions as a calculating device in the service of passion which leads the individual toward pleasure and the avoidance of pain. However, the raging competition among appetitive individuals for the same goals results in a state of violent anarchy—a "natural state of war" bereft of civility, friendship, and compassion. In Hobbes' state of nature, "the life of man is solitary, poor, nasty, brutish, and short" (Hobbes, 1985, p. 186). On one hand, their irrational desires prompt individuals to behave like solitary beasts who feel no natural obligation to others and are guided solely by the urge for power and self-satisfaction. On the other, however, they seek to use reason to escape the "continual fear and danger of violent death" lurking in the chaotic state of nature. It is this fear of death, born of their own primordial violent tendencies that ultimately serves as the incentive for calculating individuals to create an artificial "civil society" which ends the state of nature and allows for the maximizing of pleasures while minimizing the possibility of violent death. Through a *social contract*, individuals transfer their "natural right" to exercise power through violence to a common sovereign authority (the state) which claims a monopoly on the use of violence.

Relying on a model of human nature based on an individualized psychology of primordial violence and fear, Hobbes was the first modern thinker to argue for the creation of a more "rational" and therefore more "economical" order of violence backed by popular consent rather than divine right. While Hobbes' contract theory opened the door for the later development of more democratic models of self-government based on popular sovereignty, it also provided the rationale for modern *Realpolitik* and its claim that the exercise of political power inevitably involved the capacity to unleash violence. The creation of a civil society through the social contract merely centralized violence in the hands of a powerful state: "Covenants without the sword are but words, and of no strength to secure a man at all" (Hobbes, 1985, p. 223). Evident in Hobbes' connection between "strength" and the "sword," the sovereign's power was ultimately grounded in force and violence, not persuasion and communication.

As I will show below, Gandhi's model of power fundamentally challenged such dominant "realist" discourses of power. Unfortunately, modern thinkers in the West have failed to respond to Gandhi's challenge of Hobbes' one-dimensional conception of power as bringing violence to bear on someone else's person or possessions. Seen as hopelessly utopian and politically impotent, alternative models of power such as Gandhi's hardly ever impact the contemporary debates on democracy and social justice. As a result, liberal democratic discourses of power perpetuate the belief in the naturalness of violence, and a new generation of citizens resigns itself to the "fact" that the maintenance of our individual liberties as well as our political institutions of representative democracy inevitably involve some forms of violence. In the end, political thinkers in the Hobbesian tradition remain suspended in discursive and cultural practices that simultaneously encourage, limit, and redistribute the violence of its origins. Thus, it is not hard to concur with John Keane's (1996) observation that the reasons for political theory's frozen political imagination about violence and power and its consequent glum silence about nonviolence derive from the "confused and confusing mélange of unspoken prejudices and significant assumptions" of the Hobbesian paradigm.

MAHATMA GANDHI'S NONVIOLENT SEARCH FOR TRUTH

The most valuable contribution of Gandhi's theory of nonviolent power lies in its critique of dominant discourses of power based on a psychology of fear which equates power with violence. Gandhi emphasized the crucial role of moral reason in a politically anchored, nonviolent search for truth. Gandhi's defense of radical political action directed against oppression corresponded to his preference for a conception of theory as a "critical program" designed to charge political systems and their institutions with violating universal human rights. From a Gandhian perspective, *nonviolent direct action*—the withdrawal of popular obedience—is the most effective way of frustrating unaccountable power networks. Gandhi and his followers thus considered both a philosophical and a pragmatic "search for truth" as an indispensable means for challenging the violence of colonialism and other forms of oppression.

Before discussing the basic elements of Gandhi's political thought—*satya* (truth, being), *agraha* (firmness, force, power), and *ahimsa* (nonviolence)—we must remember that he considered himself primarily a spokesman for the marginalized and downtrodden, such as the Indian caste of *dalits* ("Untouchables"). Gandhi's writings and speeches can hardly be detached from their cultural context, reflecting the concreteness of his political location within an intricate web of existing power relations which routinely undermined a sense of human dignity and cultural self-expression. Thus, it was only through concrete political struggles that he developed his new model of political power as the nonviolent search for truth (*satyagraha*). Yet, nonviolent resisters (*satyagrahis*) could not unilaterally impart privileged philosophical knowledge to the masses; rather, they developed their own theoretical understanding of nonviolent political power out of their daily interactions with those social groups most exposed to the effects of colonial power. Indeed, Gandhi's political theory represents less a cognitive affair than a problem-driven, theoretical extension of concrete experiences of domination and resistance at the level of everyday existence. The violence of racism, for example, was embodied by the colonial policeman who threw the young Indian barrister out of the first-class cabin of a train bound for Maritzburg or the English barber in Pretoria who refused to cut the hair of a "bloody coolie" (Gandhi, 1948).[1] Such moments of intense suffering served as the crucial catalysts for Gandhi's formidable challenge to the dominant Hobbesian discourse of power.

Deeply influenced by the Jain philosophy of *anekantavada*—the *many-sidedness of all phenomena*—Gandhi defended throughout

his life the importance of an ethical and spiritual pluralism rooted in the fragmentariness of our understanding of *satya* (Chatterjee, 1983). Noting the derivation of the term from the Sanskrit verb *sat* ("to be" or "to exist"), Gandhi opted for an "experimental" basis of truth which differed sharply from Cartesian rationalism and its various philosophical offshoots. In other words, while explaining truth as epistemological (truth as "factual correctness"), pragmatic (truth as "selfless political action"), psychological (truth as "honesty"), and religious (truth as "God"), Gandhi remained nonetheless firmly wedded to the skeptic's position regarding the difficulty of ever grasping *satya* in its fullness (Iyer, 1973).

In spite of the complexity of moral choices, the political activist was called upon to continue the struggle for a political realization of *satya* through the employment of *nonviolent* means: *negotiations, demonstrations, strikes, civil disobedience,* and *other nonviolent forms of non-cooperation.* Deeply concerned with the practical applicability of truth, Gandhi insisted on a tight connection between theory and practice; this allowed him to address head-on the practical difficulties associated with the notorious political ineffectiveness of rational discussion and the ensuing moral problem of the proper relationship between means and ends in instances where reason had fallen silent. "I have found that mere appeal to reason does not answer where prejudices are age-long and based on supposed religious authority. Reason has to be strengthened by suffering and suffering opens the eyes of understanding" (Gandhi in Bose, 1948, p. 222).

But what exactly did Gandhi mean by "strengthening reason through suffering"? Wasn't it much more "reasonable" to avoid suffering and pain at all cost, especially in times of crisis when the thin garments of civility were stripped away and naked impera-

---

[1]For an interpretation of Gandhi's spirituality as attention to the details of social and political life, see Brown (1989); Chatterjee (1983); and Green (1993).

tives for self-preservation prevailed? It was precisely in such situations that the Hobbesian model of violent retaliation seemed to offer commonsensical, practical guidance for eliminating human suffering caused by arbitrary acts of violence.

For Gandhi, a genuine process of peacebuilding had to involve the use of nonviolent *means* to secure a sustainable satisfaction of human needs of security, identity, self-determination, and quality of life. His most serious challenge to the dominant Hobbesian discourse of power becomes apparent in his conscious break with the assumption that the nature of political power was to be found in the capacity to unleash violence, and thus, that the exercise of political power inevitably involved employing violent means of physical coercion. Instead, he offered a compelling rationale for why the principle of *ahimsa* might constitute the core of an alternative model of power:

> [It] is a method of securing rights by personal suffering; it is the reverse of resistance by arms. When I refuse to do a thing that is repugnant to my conscience, I use soul-force. For instance, the Government of the day has passed a law which is applicable to me. I do not like it. If by using violence I force the Government to repeal the law, I am employing what may be termed body-force. If I do not obey the law and accept the penalty for its breach, I use soul-force. It involves sacrifice of the self. (Gandhi, 1938, p. 71)

As Dennis Dalton (1993) noted, the term "power" appears to be a much better translation for *satyagraha* than "soul-force," because "force" is usually associated with "violence." After all, it was precisely this supposedly natural connection between power and violence that Gandhi wished to challenge in his assertion that *satyagraha* represented power "born of Truth and Love or nonviolence" (Gandhi, 1958, Vol. 29, p. 92). For

Gandhi, the infliction of violence on another person presumed society's ability to pass ultimate judgment in terms of right and wrong; but since there was never absolute certainty as to the truth of one's own position, there could be no "natural right" or competence to punish: "In the application of *satyagraha,* I discovered in the earliest stages that pursuit of Truth did not admit of violence being inflicted on one's opponent, but that he must be weaned from error by patience and sympathy. For what appears to be Truth to one may appear false to the other" (Gandhi, 1958, Vol. 19, p. 46). Even forms of corrective violence undertaken by agents of the state or other "legitimate" claimants of authority amounted to the dogmatic posture of violently enforcing one's partial understanding of truth. Thus, Gandhi insisted that the practice of arriving at uncoerced, consensual truth through the practice of *ahimsa* represented the only rationally defensible course of action. Employed as nonviolent direct action, such as in Gandhi's famous 1930 Salt March when he and his followers defied the British monopoly on salt-making, *satyagraha* overcame the dilemma of political impotence without violating its theoretical emphasis on nonviolence. It allowed for a settling of conflicts which did not involve the elimination of enemies or the application of physical force. As Joan Bondurant (1988, p. 195) has put it, "The claim for *satyagraha* is that through the operation of nonviolent action the truth as judged by the fulfillment of human needs will emerge in the form of a mutually satisfactory and agreed-upon solution." This practical reconciliation of self-interest and other-interest could only be consistently applied through the practice of *satyagraha:* "Means and ends are convertible terms in my political philosophy" (Gandhi, 1958, Vol. 25, p. 480).

But the firm adherence to such an ethic was not an easy option for the fainthearted.

To put up a determined resistance to British troops and their deadly firepower without resorting to violence required tremendous courage of the sort that seemed to ignore the biological imperatives of self-preservation. Once again, Hobbes' psychologically effective story of the omnipresent danger of society's descent into war seems to make the more convincing argument for basing political order on the ineradicable persistence of fear and violence. For Hobbes, to be alive meant to experience the fear of violent death. Early modern political thinkers skillfully interwove their influential postulations of natural imperatives for self-preservation with the development of a psychology of fear in which the horrors of physical pain and violent death were the essential components constituting human identity. Political leaders who disregarded fear in favor of love were seen by realists as fools blind to the "commonsensical" claim that without violence, politics had to come to a halt, for politics was essentially a commerce with violence.

Gandhi never denied the existence of fear in the face of the unsettling possibility of having to endure physical pain, torture, and violent death in the course of nonviolent direct actions. But it was precisely *because of* his clear recognition of the pivotal role of fear that he refused to go along with Hobbes' conclusion. For Gandhi, any attempt to exclusively link fear to a discourse of power as violence merely served as a means to disrupt dialogue.

Gandhi insisted on the possibility of overcoming fear with the result of realizing self-rule in both a political and psychological sense. The traditional Hindu virtue of *abhaya* (fearlessness) in the face of violence, repression, and even impending death was a quality which the *satyagrahi* could gradually develop through rigorous spiritual, political, and social training in *ahimsa*: "Just as

one must learn the art of killing in the training for violence, so one must learn the art of dying in the training of nonviolence. . . . The votary of nonviolence has to cultivate the capacity for sacrifice of the highest type in order to be free from fear. . . . He who has not overcome all fear cannot practice *ahimsa* to perfection" (Gandhi, 1958, Vol. 72, p. 416).[2] Undoubtedly, Gandhi's familiarity with Indian philosophies and religions facilitated his adroit utilization of self-suffering as a method for simultaneously transforming one's own fear and morally persuading one's oppressor.

THE PSYCHOLOGY OF FEAR[3]

In the previous chapter on Gandhi by Dan Mayton, some social psychological explanations for the effectiveness of nonviolent action were hypothesized. In this section, the control of fear through cognitive mediation and learning is discussed.

Gandhi argued that fear need not be linked to violent behavior. This insight is supported by psychological work on the emotion of fear. Stressful environmental stimuli trigger the *fight or flight mechanism,* whereby physiological responses in the nervous system arouse the body and prepare it for action. Any situation that is interpreted as dangerous can activate a range of chemical and hormonal changes throughout the brain and muscular system, changes which stimulate the muscles for action. Specifically, the hypothalamus controls the sympathetic system, releasing neurotransmitters to activate various organs and smooth muscles, such as heart rate and pupil dilation. Simultaneously, chemical transmitters are released into the

---

[2]For a discussion of the traditional Indian cardinal moral virtues, see Datta, 1953, pp. 86–104.

[3]This section was contributed by Deborah Du Nann Winter, Laura Boston, Sara Houck, and Matthew Lee.

bloodstream to elevate blood sugar levels that prepare muscles for quick action. The combined effect of these chemical and muscular changes is a heightened probability of fight or flight, and the accompanying emotional experience of anger and/or fear.

Therapists have developed a range of techniques to lower the stress response in their patients and reduce the likelihood of fight or flight, thereby supporting Gandhi's claim that fear need not lead to violence. For example, patients suffering from a *phobia,* or excessive fear, can be classically conditioned to emit alternative responses to anxiety-provoking stimuli. Just as a patient who is deathly afraid of snakes can be taught to breathe deeply and gradually learn to enjoy playing with one, so training for nonviolence teaches political activists to stay calm, resist the temptation to run or fight, and stay near a buddy who can monitor one's actions (see Montiel's chapter, also in this section). Rehearsals and drills for nonviolent actions are important features of the method's success, demonstrating the behavioral approach to changing stress responses.

Cognitive therapy also offers insights. Fight or flight behavior is most likely when thoughts about danger are unexamined, leading to self-protective strategies. However, Gandhi teaches that suffering is a crucial feature of truth, and that self-protection is less important than ultimate truth, which addresses the human needs of more people than the self. Thus attributing one's personal suffering to a necessary struggle against unjust social conditions helps activists endure discomfort and personal pain. Clear recognition of the justness of one's cause fortifies nonviolent activists to remain steadfast, rather than cave in to fight or flight. Again, training in nonviolence is necessary because thoughts and cognitions about risks and physical pain are important in mediating fight or flight.

The psychology of fear might be seen as indirect evidence for Hobbes. After all, we are physiologically wired for fight or flight, and must be taught to resist these actions when chemically aroused. Without the cortical areas of the brain, Hobbes' view might prevail. However, the fact that we can be taught to resist violence, as well as the fact that we have to be taught to emit it (as in the strenuous training procedures of boot camp for military institutions), demonstrates that the human propensity for violence greatly depends on learning, thinking, and even spiritual dimensions. The ability to endure personal suffering for the greater good is a spiritual capacity which Gandhi and other great religious leaders, including Christ, have demonstrated.

In summary, then, Gandhi's conceptualization of power as seeking truth through the practice of *ahimsa* challenges the dominant discourse of power as the ability to inflict violence. He opted for a model favoring the idea of common people exercising power nonviolently through voluntary self-suffering and sacrifice for a cause they consider to be just and true according the standard of fulfillment of human needs. As such, Gandhi's ideas are clearly reflective of a position espoused by the authors in this volume—a peace psychology that seeks to elucidate psychological processes involved in the prevention and mitigation of destructive conflict, violence, dominance, oppression, and exploitation.

DOES NONVIOLENCE "WORK"? TWO CASE STUDIES

Gandhi's perspective has served as an inspiration to other twentieth-century proponents of nonviolence, such as Martin Luther King, Jr., Nelson Mandela, Vaclav Havel, and Aung San Suu Kyi. Still, many critics have questioned the practicality of nonviolent power to redress social injustices, arguing that Gandhi's nonviolent campaigns or the Civil Rights Movement under Martin Luther King, Jr. merely represent exceptional cases which show that nonviolence will only "work" with principled oppressors such as Great Britain or the United States. Inevitably, such skeptics point to more difficult cases of oppressive authoritarian governments that are not bound by a democratic logic. George Orwell (1950) most clearly captures this common objection: "It is difficult to see how Gandhi's methods could be applied in a country where opponents of the regime disappear in the middle of the night and are never heard of again" (p. 101).

Drawing on two extreme cases, I will argue that Orwell's assertion is open to serious challenges. The nonviolent resistance of the Mothers of the Plaza de Mayo against the murderous Argentine military dictatorship of the 1970s, and the little-known 1943 Berlin Rosenstrasse Protest of ordinary Germans against the genocidal policies of the Nazi state show that the power of *satyagraha* can be successfully employed even against the most repressive political regimes in modern history.

Mothers of the Plaza de Mayo

During the Argentine junta's 1976 to 1983 "Dirty War" against political "subversives," whose crimes consisted of demanding Argentina's return to democracy and the government's adherence to human rights, tens of thousands of ordinary citizens were abducted and tortured, often disappearing forever in the secret prisons of the military dictatorship (Guzman Bouvard, 1994). The power of the junta rested on its total control of the coercive state apparatus and the mass media. Moreover, its virulent anti-Communist rhetoric secured the tacit support of the

United States and heightened a sense of general helplessness and all-pervading fear on the part of the population.

Beginning in 1977, a small group of middle-aged women—most of whom were homemakers who had never before actively participated in politics—formed the core of a growing dissident movement in Argentina which resolved to "speak truth" to the military government. Known as the Mothers of the Plaza de Mayo, these women gathered regularly at the central square of Buenos Aires and publicly demanded from the regime that it disclose the whereabouts of their abducted sons and husbands. Circling the Plaza de Mayo arm-in-arm and wearing white shawls which symbolized the innocence of their children, the Mothers broke through the wall of fear and passivity in spite of mounting repressive measures employed by the police. Employing Gandhian methods of nonviolent struggle—demonstrations, strikes, and noncooperation—the Mothers defied police barricades, tear gas, attack dogs, arrests, and even assassinations. Undeterred, they continued their weekly display of solidarity, motherly care, and nonviolent power. By the late 1970s, the Mothers had built an impressive network of support that included church leaders, human rights activists, labor unionists, and other ordinary citizens who felt inspired by the women's ongoing political dialogue on truth. Having acquired an international reputation and a distinct identity as nonviolent protectors of human life against brute force, the Mothers' activities ultimately proved to be instrumental in bringing down the military dictatorship in the wake of Argentina's 1982 war with England over the Falkland Islands.

The impressive example of the Mothers of the Plaza de Mayo shows the efficacy of nonviolent power even in struggles against brutal oppressors who refuse to identify with the logic of liberal democracy. In particular, three important lessons can be drawn from this Argentine case. First, the Mothers proved that the values and language of militarism can be successfully challenged by a nonviolent, maternal discourse of life, family, love, and trust. Emphasizing the continuity between the private sphere and public responsibility, the Mothers ingeniously employed traditional concepts of maternity for their own revolutionary purpose without resorting to violent or immoral tactics. Second, like Charter 77—Vaclav Havel's dissident organization in communist Czechoslovakia—the Mothers represented the ever-present possibility of a moral regeneration of society through the nonviolent creation of a resistance movement within an oppressive society. Founded on principles of self-management, shared responsibility, and direct democracy, the Argentine dissident organization demonstrated the awesome power of solidaristic, nonviolent action. Third, the Mothers provided another impressive example of a new political consciousness of women challenging male conceptions of power and strength. Seemingly one of the most powerless groups in society, these middle-aged women took control of their lives and moved beyond their culture's restraints and expectations, in the process enlarging the political sphere of all Argentine women. Organized around the Gandhian principle of *ahimsa,* the Mothers of the Plaza the Mayo united feeling, thinking, and acting in their powerful display of maternal love and individual responsibility.

Rosenstrasse Protest

Let us now turn to the most difficult case: Nazi Germany at the height of its power. Nathan Stoltzfus' study, *Resistance of the Heart* (1996) charts the lives of ordinary Germans who married Jews in the context of Nazi persecution and social harassment. Using interviews with surviving resisters and thousands of Nazi records never before examined in detail, Stoltzfus brings into sharp focus the frequently neglected issue of German-Jewish intermarriages in Nazi Germany. In December 1942, with the "Final Solution" at its height, there were still close to 30,000 intermarried couples in the German Reich and its Czech protectorate area. Given that the large majority of intermarried Germans were women, the story of opposition by intermarried Germans is largely (but not only) the story of German women married to Jewish men (Stoltzfus, 1996, p. xxvii).

The existence of these intermarried couples was disturbing to Nazi ideology for a variety of reasons. First, under the Nazi logic of "racial purification," intermarried Jews should have been the first Jews to be isolated and deported. Yet, it proved to be impossible for the regime to forcibly break up these marriages without undermining social traditions such as the "sanctity of marriage," fervently supported by Nazi ideology. Second, intermarried couples gave birth to a "polluted mixture of Master Race and Jew" called *Mischlinge.* Third, their noncompliance with racial laws and their unwillingness to divorce their spouses directly challenged Nazi power and its propaganda of flawless German unity and the people's unquestioned loyalty to concepts of racial purity and superiority.

The sole known mass demonstration against Nazi racial policies, the 1943 Berlin "Rosenstrasse Protest," involved hundreds to thousands of Germans protesting the mass arrest of intermarried Jews. Stoltzfus explains not only why the demonstrations ended successfully in the release of the detained Jews, but he also offers a compelling narrative framework that shows the power of nonviolent resistance. For six days, hundreds of German women engaged in public demonstrations. Demanding their husbands, sons, and brothers back, they defied menacing guards and refused to comply with Hitler's Total War decree ordering them to register for work. Joseph Goebbels was ultimately forced to order the release of the Jewish prisoners, because he realized that Nazi power rested, first and foremost, on popular accommodation ranging from enthusiastic support to passive acceptance. A withdrawal of accommodation touched off by the Rosenstrasse Protest could cause serious problems for the regime. The Nazi dictatorship feared social unrest more than it feared compromising its racial ideology or even rescinding its racist initiatives. The successful Rosenstrasse protest is extremely significant, for it proves that nonviolent opposition to the Nazi state was possible and that limits could have been placed even on the most notorious aspect of the regime—genocide. On Rosenstrasse, the protesters expressed the nonviolent power of "living in truth"—the willingness to live according to one's own conscience and reason, in the process defying the most murderous regime in the twentieth century (Stoltzfus, 1996).

CONCLUSION

Rejecting the dominant discourse of power based on Hobbes' psychology of fear which equates power and violence, Gandhi instead provided a model of political power based on fearlessness and *ahimsa*. Emphasizing the crucial connection between political theory and social practice, Gandhi's perspective on nonviolent power appeals to the kind of "practical wisdom" that can actually be used and applied by peace activists. The reassertion of such a problem-driven approach reinvigorates the critical impulse to understand and address concrete political problems in the world. By raising the crucial question of how political power can be conceptualized *and* practiced in *nonviolent* ways, Gandhi focused on the importance of linking social theory to the concrete task of diffusing violence in society. Thus, his perspective on power and nonviolence contains a strong injunction to link morality and politics without abandoning the great Enlightenment ideal of individual self-realization. At the end of a long century of violence, Gandhi's perspective on power and nonviolence indeed offers an appealing vista for the twenty-first century.

CHAPTER 27

GIVING VOICE TO CHILDREN'S PERSPECTIVES ON PEACE

Ilse Hakvoort and Solveig Hägglund

You are really interested in what I have to say about peace! I enjoy talking to you. I do have a lot of thoughts about peace, war, and solving conflicts but nobody ever asked me about it.

This comment was made by a 13-year-old Dutch girl who participated in an interview study. In this chapter, the concept of peace and strategies to attain peace will be addressed from the perspective of children and adolescents. By listening to what children have to say about these issues, we have access to what they internalize through various kinds of interactions with their environment (Bronfenbrenner, 1979).

In order to give voice to children's ideas about peace, we will present some results from a cross-cultural research project initiated in the middle 1990s (cf. Hägglund, Hakvoort, & Oppenheimer, 1996). An international group of researchers (i.e., from Australia, Croatia, India, Israel, Latvia, Lithuania, Malaysia, the Netherlands, Northern Ireland, Philippines, South Africa, and Sweden) collaborated in this ongoing endeavour. In this chapter, voice is given to children from two relatively peaceful European countries with a long tradition of democratic political systems: the Netherlands and Sweden.

We begin by presenting children's reflections on the concept of peace and their ideas about strategies they think will promote peace. Four themes will emerge: communication, interpersonal relationships, human values, and nature. In the following sections, we elaborate on these four themes and then we present developmental considerations, focusing on the increasing compexity of children's conceptions of peace. Throughout, we emphasize the diversity of children's conceptualizations which is caused by the varying contexts in which children are socialized. We conclude with some thoughts about children's conceptions of peace and implications for training children in conflict management in the twenty-first century.

From our perspective, children's conceptions of peace and strategies to attain peace are products of their interactions with the social, cultural, political, and physical environment (cf. Durkin, 1995; Winegar &

Valsiner, 1992a, 1992b; Woodhead, Light, & Carr, 1991). Accordingly, we begin by highlighting some features of the contexts in which Dutch and Swedish children live and grow.

CHILDREN'S CONCEPTIONS OF PEACE IN TWO SOCIETIES

The Netherlands and Sweden

The Netherlands and Sweden represent two different but overlapping contexts for socialization and development (Hakvoort, Hägglund, & Oppenheimer, 1998). Both countries are positioned in northwestern Europe and are members of the European Union. While the total Swedish territory covers 449,964 square kilometers (173,732 square miles), the Dutch territory is much smaller, covering 41,526 square kilometers (16,033 square miles). The populations show a reverse order: The Netherlands has a population of 15,499,000 people, while Sweden has a population of 8,564,000 people. The Netherlands and Sweden both have democratic political systems and both are monarchies (i.e., the monarch is the formal head of the state—a hereditary title—and a prime minister is the head of the government). The voting age in both countries is 18 years of age. The Netherlands represents a mixed Catholic and Protestant tradition (i.e., 39 percent no religion; 33 percent Roman Catholic; 23 percent Protestant; 3 percent Muslim; 2 percent other). Until recently Sweden had a State church in the Protestant tradition to which the majority of the population (88 percent) belonged.

Children in both countries face comparable standards of social and economic development in education, health care, child care, and social welfare. Moreover, Dutch and Swedish children can expect similar prospects for future education and employment. Basically, both have identical experiences with regard to information in the mass media (i.e., news about world events, fashion, and music). Generally, peace and democracy tend to be regarded as stable and unthreatened in these countries though there are some tensions between immigrants and national groups.

The most obvious difference between the two countries is the historical fact that the Netherlands was directly involved in the Second World War in defending its borders and finally repelling the invading Germans, while Sweden was only indirectly involved by supplying arms and information to both sides of the conflict. Hence, Dutch children are raised in a context of collective memories and symbols related to the war (e.g., war cemeteries, parents and grandparents telling about the war, annual memorial services for the fallen, and liberty and peace celebrations). Swedish children rarely, if ever, have experienced these kinds of cultural manifestations and memories of peace and war.

Assessing Children's Conceptions of Peace

Individual, semi-structured interviews were conducted with a total of 207 Dutch and 209 Swedish children, aged seven to 17. These children presented their ideas about peace and war, and strategies to attain peace (cf. Hakvoort et al., 1998). We wanted them to think about peace from various perspectives, including their own personal role in peace processes, and what they would do to take care of peace if they were the boss of their country and the boss of the world. During the interviews we experienced how the children were constructing their thoughts while talking to us.

THEMES

Communication

At all ages, Dutch and Swedish children referred to the absence of war and the absence of war activities (e.g., the absence of fighting) when asked about peace. Stopping and preventing wars were mentioned as ways of making peace. This tendency for children to equate absence of war (i.e., negative peace) to the concept of peace has been shown consistently in many different studies (for a review, see Hakvoort & Oppenheimer, 1998).

Dutch and Swedish children also discussed *how* negative peace could be attained. Typically the children first mentioned who they thought should be involved in stopping or preventing wars and secondly what actions should be undertaken. Most children did not think that they themselves were able to take the responsibility for actions to stop wars. They repeatedly suggested that someone in a power position (e.g., country leaders, kings, or the United Nations) should do so by using talking strategies, including negotiations with enemies, discussions with other leaders, and talks with their own soldiers. Previous research has shown that such a "personalization" of political responsibility is common among children (Torney & Hess, 1971). For example, Torney and Hess reported that young children "view political systems as if they consisted of one or two persons to whom personal relationships can be formed" (p. 472). As children get older, they learn to understand that political structures and political institutions exist without a particular person.

It seemed as if the Dutch and Swedish children were confident in having trustworthy and competent leaders around. By suggesting various kinds of "talking strategies" the children expressed an implicit knowledge about the importance of communication and dialogue. We would argue that this knowledge is a momentous prerequisite to attain and maintain peace.

Interpersonal Relationships: Having Friends

When peers were included in their thoughts about making or maintaining peace, the seven- to 13-year-old Dutch and Swedish children regarded themselves as active participants in making or maintaining peace. They frequently referred to interpersonal relationships in their ideas about strategies to make peace and they seemed to have developed knowledge and skills to build and maintain positive relationships with their friends and age-mates (Hägglund, 1999). Even though the Dutch and Swedish children literally referred to situations that would be defined as negative peace (i.e., avoiding or stopping interpersonal conflicts), they, at the same time, described activities and strategies aimed at maintaining and developing positive relationships with friends: "When I have a quarrel with my friend, I would go to him to shake hands and tell him that he can come to my place and borrow my bike this afternoon." They also mentioned helping their mother, playing with friends, and being nice and kind to classmates.

Clearly, in their concepts of peace and in their ideas about how to attain peace, friendship seemed to play a significant role. We regard this as an illustration of the fact that peer groups constitute important social settings for the development of social knowledge. This is in line with research showing that peer groups offer natural social settings in which norms, values, and attitudes are elaborated and practiced (Corsaro, 1990; Frønes, 1995; Piaget, 1932). In short, children's conceptions of peace are not merely the absence of something negative but also include actions that contribute to interpersonal cooperation and harmony.

Human Values: Equality and Social Justice

In contrast to younger children, adolescents (13 to 17 years) did not refer to individually oriented activities when describing ways of making peace. Instead, they spoke about values such as equality and solidarity between human beings. When proposing strategies to establish equality, Dutch adolescents expressed views different from the Swedish adolescents. The Dutch 13 to 17 year olds talked about reducing discrimination, increasing tolerance, and, to a lesser extent, strengthening democratic processes. They thought this could be done by informing and educating people via, for example, media and pamphlets. In contrast, the Swedish adolescents more frequently emphasized the importance of international collaboration and sharing their own welfare with poor people in other countries. For example, they suggested sending clothes, money, and medicine to Third World countries. They also referred to the membership of the European Union as a way to attain peace. Clearly, the Dutch adolescents were more attuned to addressing peace in their own society, while the Swedish adolescents expressed a more global orientation in which peace in other societies was the focus (Hakvoort et al., 1998).

When compared to children, adolescents demonstrate an enlarged repertoire of ideas about peace which include not only peacekeeping and peacemaking but also social justice. In view of the monuments and other remembrances of World War II, it is not surprising that Dutch children mention actions that diminsh the likelihood of war when they discuss the meaning of peace. In addition, a social justice orientation is apparent in their conceptions of peace, especially when they describe activities that would strengthen non-oppressive societal structures.

Similarly, Swedish adolescents include social justice in their repertoire. However, Swedish adolescents have an international orientation, referring to the promotion of non-oppressive structures globally. Clearly, both Dutch and Swedish adolescents are keenly aware of the importance of social justice; they differ in their unit of analysis: intranational for Dutch adolescents and international for Swedish adolescents.

Nature and Sustainability

Some children in our study, in particular, Dutch boys, referred to nature and ecological issues when asked about peace and strategies to attain peace (Hakvoort, 1996). These ideas were emphasized even more when they discussed strategies to attain or maintain peace. They mentioned, for example, preserving rainforests, closing polluting industries, and stopping the usage of cars or airplanes. In recent decades, an increase in attention to the natural environment in which humans live has been noted in the Netherlands. The media, interest groups and associations, and political organizations show an increase in their concern for these issues. In a country like the Netherlands, with so many people and so little space, information about sustainability is of widespread interest.

DEVELOPMENTAL CONSIDERATIONS: COMPLEXITY AND DIVERSITY IN CHILDREN'S RESPONSES

Evidence is accumulating which suggests that some features of children's thinking can be generalized quite widely. As children develop, their conceptions of peace become increasingly multidimensional, complex, and dynamic, not unlike the complex and divergent ways in which peace researchers operationalize the construct of peace (cf. Brock-Utne, 1989; Galtung, 1996; Rinehart, 1995).

Indeed, previous studies (for review see Hakvoort & Oppenheimer, 1998) have demonstrated that older children and adolescents continue to include references to the absence of direct violence (i.e., negative peace) when they conceptualize peace, just as younger children do. In addition, adolescents enlarge their "cognitive repertoire" by including ideas about positive peace (e.g., respect, tolerance, democracies, and univeral rights).

In short, our work suggests that children's growing ability to understand the complexity of peace issues is likely to be a universal phenomenon due to the child's increasingly sophisticated means of processing information. On the other hand, the content of their ideas about peace varies considerably, reflecting diversity, because children do not learn about peace and strategies to attain peace in a vacuum. Instead, they learn in particular cultural and historical contexts. Hence, when we look at children's conceptualizations across time and place, divergent meanings emerge and contextual diversity becomes our main interest (cf. Aspeslagh & Burns, 1996). By contextual diversity we mean that children's ideas and beliefs about peace and strategies to attain peace are developed in varying contexts. For example, children in the Netherlands grow up in a context where memories of the Second World War and the celebration of peace are salient, while in Sweden, discourses about peace and war are relatively rare.

TOWARDS THE FUTURE

From our perspective, children and adolescents are actively and continuously involved in the process of conceptualizing peace. Moreover, their conceptions of peace, while following a developmental course toward increasing complexity, are nuanced by the contexts within which children grow and develop. In some countries, for example, peace education and conflict resolution programmes are part of the school curriculum, while in countries like Liberia, Uganda, and El Salvador, children must face their "responsibility" as child soldiers. In some places, children are prepared to become citizens by learning about democratic elections and their responsibility to influence political decisions; in other countries children are taught to kill their neighbors. Finally, in some countries children may percieve that they participate in peace processes by writing letters to heads of state, while their agemates in other countries participate in peace by demonstrating in the streets.

Because children's conceptions of peace depend on context, their notions do not neatly conform to Western models of peace and the means to attain peace. For instance, while there has been a proliferation of programs to teach children conflict resolution skills in the West, the inductive approach we are employing would suggest a "one size fits all" approach might not easily be exported to children who are growing up in vastly different contexts (see also Pedersen in this volume). Moreover, in view of the increasing interdependency of the world, considerations of the context-sensitive nature of peace are likely to become more important in the future.

Because children's understanding of peace and strategies to attain peace are contextually informed, their views are good indices of the prevailing norms, values, and attitudes towards peace in their society (cf. Hakvoort, 1996). By listening to children, we can gain insights into the norms, values, and attitudes a particular society holds. Insights into the developmental substrates of children's ideas, combined with an understanding of how their conceptions vary across contexts, should help us assess the state of peace in the world and should give us some indication of its changing nature as we move through the twenty-first century.

CHAPTER 28

REDRESSING STRUCTURAL VIOLENCE AGAINST CHILDREN: EMPOWERMENT-BASED INTERVENTIONS AND RESEARCH

Linda Webster and Douglas D. Perkins

Structural violence occurs when political and economic systems are organized in ways that oppress, exploit, and dominate certain segments of a population while privileging others who hold power and wealth. When violence is built into the structures of a society, some people are deprived of food, shelter, health care, and other resources that are necessary for normal human growth and development (Christie, 1997). In this chapter, we look at structural violence in the United States and give special attention to the problems faced by women, children, and minorities. We focus on policies that support structural violence and then review empowerment-based approaches designed to mitigate structural violence.

In the United States, the problem of structural violence is reflected in the gap be-

tween the rich and poor, a gap that is greater in the United States than in most other industrialized nations (Gottschalk & Smeeding, in press). The discrepancy between the haves and have-nots is justified by the myth of the "American Dream" which implies that there *is* equal opportunity for every individual to pursue wealth and happiness. It is implicit in the myth that those individuals who do not achieve this dream fail to do so out of choice; they are lazy and morally bankrupt, and therefore deserve their fate.

Children in all societies have the least voice, power, and control over their own lives, and as such, are extremely vulnerable to abuses in power relationships. When poverty is introduced into the equation, the results are often disastrous, and can take the form of being forced to work in sweatshops, or sold as sex slaves in some countries (Pilisuk, 1998). The United Nations Universal Declaration of Human Rights proclaims that "childhood is entitled to special care and assistance" (United Nations General Assembly, 1989). Unfortunately, many poor children are viewed as the troublesome by-products of undeserving people, and not as the result of the politics and economics of structure-based inequalities in the way resources are distributed (Polakow, 1993).

Moreover, many so-called "interventions" to help those with few resources are actually misuses of power, designed to elicit desired outcomes from recipients which are in accordance with the organization's interests and serve to substantiate the moral ideologies and mythologies of those in power (Hasenfeld, 1992). For example, in the United States, the "Welfare Reform" movement of the 1990s had the implicit assumption that a lack of personal responsibility was the principal cause of poverty and unemployment. Accordingly, interventions were geared towards punishing or fixing those individuals. This position, codified in the Personal Responsibility and Work Opportunity Reconciliation Act of 1996, ignored the underlying issues that perpetuate the problem such as economic shifts away from medium- and high-wage blue-collar jobs, poor education, the lack of affordable child care for the working-class and single-parent families, mental health problems, and so on. Instead, the movement supported the government's agenda to cut aid to the "undeserving" (American Psychological Association, 1998).

Even among those who receive human services, there are social class differences. Poorer clients tend to receive poorer services, whether the services are housing, health care, education, or social services (Hasenfeld, 1992), and they have little or no real choice in the matter. In the following section, we examine injustices in the human services sector.

STRUCTURAL VIOLENCE IN HUMAN SERVICE SECTORS

Housing and Homelessness

For many Americans, the word "homeless" evokes a picture of a derelict and transient male individual. In fact, children and families make up the fastest growing segment of the homeless population. The typical homeless family of today consists of an unmarried, 20-year-old mother with one or two children under the age of six. It is most probable that she never completed high school and never worked to support her children. There is a one in five chance that she was in foster care as a child. If that was the case, she is more than twice as likely as other homeless mothers to have an open case of child abuse or neglect with a child welfare agency. Her children are three times more likely to be placed in remedial education programs, and four times more likely to drop out of school. Over one-third of homeless families have an open case for child abuse or neglect, and one in five have lost at least one child to foster care. Nearly half of homeless children have witnessed or been subjected to violence (Homes for the Homeless, 1998).

The homeless are merely the "tip of the iceberg" when it comes to the affordable housing crisis. Housing conditions of low-income families and children have worsened over the past 25 years (Children's Defense Fund, 1998). The cost of rents has increased while income has declined. The ratio of rent to income for low-income families has increased in recent years. Although the U.S. Department of Housing and Urban Development assumes that families should pay no more than 30 percent of their income on housing, many now spend well over 40 percent. Poor families also spend a substantial proportion of their meager incomes to pay for child care, averaging between 17 and 32 percent of their total income (Bassuk, Brown, & Buckner, 1996; Brooks & Buckner, 1996; Cherlin, 1995). When these two proportions are taken together, it is readily apparent that the money spent on housing and childcare significantly reduces the amount of money left for meeting other pressing basic needs such as food and clothing, and children pay the price. The lack of adequate, affordable housing has serious ramifications for children, and results in homelessness, or the need to constantly move from one dilapidated place to another. This, in turn, is related to poor health, missed school and academic failure, emotional damage, and the potential for lead poisoning in older housing.

Despite this dire and worsening situation, low-income housing appropriations have declined precipitously over the past 20 years. Seventy percent of the total federal housing subsidy now goes, not to low-income renters, but to middle- and upper-income homeowners mostly in mortgage interest tax deductions. Some families may qualify for federally-funded housing which pays a portion of rent for families, but as rents increase, so does the family's share of cost. Also, some landlords will not accept federally-funded renters, and the demand for such housing always exceeds supply, which results in waiting lists of two to three years in some areas. This places landlords in the position of being able to pick and choose to whom they will rent. Although anti-discrimination laws exist, they are difficult to enforce and few poor families have the time, energy, finances, or education necessary to pursue a complaint. The situation has become a power-dependence rela-

tionship whereby families are forced to conform to the organization's expectations (such as family size and exclusion of extended family) and interests in order to obtain necessary services, in this case housing. Housing agencies may employ strategies designed to discourage use, including waiting lists and intrusive intake procedures or rigid eligibility requirements (Lorenzo & Adler, 1984; Parker & McDavis, 1989; Takeuchi, Leaf, & Hsu-Sung, 1988). This may result in engaging only the most motivated and resourceful clients, or alternately the most devious.

Health Care

Health care for the nation's five million children and infants living in poverty has been inadequate in the United States for decades. According to a report released by the National Center for Children in Poverty (1991), poor children are more likely than nonpoor children to be born too soon or too small; to die in the first year of life; to experience acute illness, injuries, lead poisoning, or child abuse or neglect; and to suffer from nutrition-related problems and chronic illnesses—many of which are preventable. The United States is the only major Western country without national health insurance or a system of family allowances. In infant mortality, the United States ranks seventeenth among Western nations. The rate for African Americans, which is 17.6 per 100,000, is more similar to the rate for individuals living in a Third World country (O'Hare, Pollard, & Mann, 1991).

Education

Education has consistently has been the preferred strategy to eradicate poverty (Katz, 1994; also see Schwebel & Christie in this volume). Unfortunately, the plight of poor children, many of whom are ethnic and language minorities, is grim. A critical factor in success for these children is the willingness of various funding sources to invest in education. The Department of Education (1997) found that schools with the highest proportion of poor children have markedly fewer resources than schools that enroll more affluent children. Schools serving large numbers of poor children have fewer books and supplies, and have teachers with less training and lower average salaries.

In addition, schools in the poorest communities are also in the highest state of disrepair. Schools in central cities and those with over 50 percent minority enrollment are more likely than others to have insufficient technology and unsatisfactory environmental conditions. Poor environmental conditions are associated with poorer academic outcomes (Children's Defense Fund, 1998), thus perpetuating the cycle of poverty.

Although the U.S. government has stressed the importance of education for the nation's workforce and for national well-being ("Clinton reaffirms," 1997), the new welfare law of the 1990s drastically limited the number of adult recipients who could participate in education because the law mandated a "work first" policy (American Psychological Association, 1998). Although education has been and continues to be one of the most secure routes out of poverty, many of those in poverty will be required to take any available job, and therefore will have little likelihood of earning an income sufficient to raise them out of poverty. This position is in direct contrast to studies which have demonstrated that empowering the poor through higher education improves not only their incomes and job prospects, but also has a profound effect on their children's overall development and performance in school (American Psychological Association, 1998).

Child and Family Services

A large number of individuals and families in the United States rely on the resources and services of county departments of social services to meet their daily basic needs for shelter, food, clothing, and security. In accordance with the myth that the individual alone is responsible for being in poverty, public policy has tried to reduce poverty by changing the behavior of poor people, and has done little to address the reasons why so many young healthy people (especially women with children) are in poverty (Axinn & Stern, 1988; Duncan, 1984).

A second myth is the pervasive belief about the role and responsibility of elites for supervising the behavior of the poor. The assumption is that these helpless and passive dependent people need the assistance of outsiders (in power) to lift them out of poverty, and further, that they should be grateful for this help.

These myths are compounded by a long-standing distinction between the "deserving" and "undeserving" poor. Historically, the deserving poor fell into two classes: clearly helpless and dependent people (e.g., the aged or infirm), and those who were rendered dependent through no fault of their own, *and* were willing to work for the amount of public support they might receive. The most deserving were widows who kept their children clean, taught them manners, sent them to school, and were willing to spend hours per day sewing or scrubbing for tiny wages. The undeserving poor were dependent because of their own lazy, irresponsible, and immoral behavior. Not only did they burden the taxpayer but they threatened the safety of others. Katz (1994) argues that these themes resemble contemporary views of the underclass.

Agencies thus use their power to maintain and strengthen these historical interests in several ways, preferring clients who represent the "deserving" poor and who reflect positively on evaluation criteria used by key external legitimizing, political, and funding bodies. Program success is frequently measured by the large number of clients served (and graduated from the agency) with the least amount of cost. In this way, a homeless program may prefer those individuals or families that are most likely to quickly attain and maintain independence from the program. Hence, preference would be given to individuals without a psychiatric illness, drug and alcohol condition, or physical handicap conditions which might prolong their need and use of the agency's resources. Unfortunately, in this way the very conditions that increase the most vulnerable population's need for services are often used as a means to deny or limit access to services. Clients with their own power resources, particularly education and income, are better able to obtain the services they want and are more likely to influence the process to suit their needs and interests (Hasenfeld, 1992). The agency naturally wants its clients to make successful use of its resources; however, the result is a system that favors those with more income and education, while the most needy clients are paradoxically bypassed.

The ability to choose, and the range of available choices are the core of power. The constriction of choices is at the core of poverty. Persons with financial resources and education are in a much better position to obtain the services they want compared to persons in poverty. Take, for example, the case of a family whose child is removed from the home and placed in foster care because of the parents' drug abuse. It would not be unusual in this situation for the Department of Social Services to require the parents to undergo drug testing, drug counseling, parenting classes, individual and couples' therapy, and a series of supervised visits in order to reunify the parents with their child. Parents with money and education are in a much better position to access and pay for the services needed to fulfill the reunification plan. They may choose and pay for (or their employer may pay for) their counselors and drug rehabilitation programs, while their poverty-stricken counterparts must rely on services provided at a low fee or at no cost. Low-cost services are frequently underbudgeted and understaffed which often results in a waiting list and/or restriction of services provided. It may take the parents three or more months to obtain services, which may result in their loss of their opportunity to regain custody of their child. The child may then become a veteran of the system and be at significantly higher risk for poverty him or herself.

Agencies are also structured to prefer clients who conform to its historical moral assumptions about human behavior. For example, clients who are physically and emotionally capable of gainful employment, and who are not encumbered by the need for child care will likely experience greater success under the new welfare reform law. When agency goals are not met, welfare recipients may be unfairly labeled as "lazy" (i.e., undeserving poor) when in actuality the ongoing stress and chaos of poverty combined with a lack of resources may effectively prevent participation in a welfare-to-work program (American Psychological Association, 1998).

Pelton (1978) has asserted that child maltreatment is related to class, and that attempts to portray it as classless are motivated largely by two factors. A classless perspective supports psychodynamic medical models which dissociate personal problems from poverty, thereby locating the problem intrapsychically. Second, an association of child maltreatment with poverty makes it appear to be a problem of the underclass, and thus of less pressing concern to politicians and the middle class.

Denying association between poverty and child maltreatment "undermines the development of effective approaches to deal with the real and difficult problems [of the poor], and directs us towards remedies more oriented to the middle class" (Pelton, 1978, p. 614). This is a subtle but important point. If researchers, teachers, theorists, and students are convinced that child maltreatment is economically democratic in its distribution, then new practice interventions are unlikely to be centered around problems associated with poverty.

The close association between poverty and child maltreatment suggests that the most effective way to prevent child abuse would be to reduce the numbers of families in poverty. Thus, primary prevention efforts might best target the underlying political, social, and economic structures which perpetuate poverty (American Psychological Association, 1998). This philosophy is in keeping with a peace psychology approach to counter structural violence (Christie, 1997; Pilisuk, 1998).

EMPOWERMENT: A PSYCHOLOGICAL APPROACH TO STRUCTURAL CHANGE

The powerlessness that those in poverty experience is manifest in the lack of access to resources that guarantee survival, reduce suffering, and enable one to control one's environment. Similar to the notion of learned helplessness (Seligman, 1975), powerlessness is a process of alienation which frequently becomes self-perpetuating, as the poverty-stricken members of society come to accept the power structure, externalize their locus of control, and reduce their expectations of their quality of life accordingly (Kroeker, 1995).

The concept of empowerment is based on the assumption that the capacity of people to improve their lives is determined by their ability to control their environment. Zimmerman (1995) argues that empowerment involves individual and group efforts to gain control over their own destinies, access to resources, and an understanding of the sociopolitical context. This is a process through which even poor families and children may obtain resources that would enable them to gain greater control over their environment (Hasenfeld, 1992), and ensure the satisfaction of basic needs. Implicit is a responsibility to shift from a victim-blaming person-centered focus of service delivery to one that takes as its core activity and philosophy the formulation of policy and strategies to empower the impoverished segments of society (Ryan, 1976). Interventions which are empowerment-oriented focus on health and wellness while at the same time focusing on remediating problems, and engaging professionals as collaborators as opposed to authoritative experts (Perkins & Zimmerman, 1995). For professionals, this entails involving community members in the development, implementation, and evaluation of interventions, as well as creating opportunities for community members to develop skills which foster independence as opposed to dependence upon the professional (Zimmerman, 1995). A thorough discussion of the vast and growing empowerment literature is beyond the scope of this chapter. Some critical issues and case studies which demonstrate ideas and possibilities are worth exploring, however.

Empowerment as a Multilevel Construct

In the literature on empowerment, there is an increasing understanding that empowerment is multilevel: affecting the individual, the organization, the community, and possibly even the society at large. Moreover, the four levels are interrelated in that psychological empowerment (including a sense of personal responsibility and collective effi-cacy) may be a necessary condition for com-munity and organizational empowerment (Perkins, Brown, & Taylor, 1996), which are the basis for societal empowerment, which entails broad-based social and political movements. At the same time, true grass-roots movements (as opposed to "astroturf," or artificial, grassroots organizations) can result in community, organizational, and in-dividual empowerment (Kroeker, 1995; see Wessells, Schwebel, & Anderson on psychol-ogy and public policy in this volume; also see Dawes on liberation psychology in this volume).

Individual and Family-level Empower-ment.   At the personal level, empower-ment is focused on acquiring access to re-sources and increasing control. A goal for the poverty-stricken segments of the popula-tion is to begin to meet their material needs by obtaining housing, health care, edu-cation, and employment (Albee, Joffe, & Dusenbury, 1988; Alinsky, 1946; Friere, 1970). However, while meeting material goals is necessary, it is not sufficient for em-powerment as it does not necessarily lead to an increase in feelings of value, self-efficacy, and control (Kroeker, 1995).

Unfortunately, it is in this psychological arena that many child and family services organizations fall short of empowerment. Liddie (1991) describes a program for low-income mothers of children in an urban day-care center which illustrates how a group of mothers can increase their power, control, and respect. In this program, moth-ers began to increase their sense of material empowerment by establishing a food co-op, and they later participated in a march to protest day-care cuts. However, the mothers felt oppressed by the staff at the day care, and frequently complained about feeling harassed by the staff's criticism of how their children were dressed or their "unruly" be-havior, and of their parenting skills in gen-eral. The mothers decided to request a meeting with the staff in order to become part of the decision-making process regard-ing their children's care at the center. The results were remarkable in that not only were the women able to induce changes in staff attitudes, cooperation, and respect, but their process served as a model for staff to empower themselves and confront mem-bers of the administration regarding issues related to service delivery. This is an excel-lent example of how *individuals* were able to attain a sense of psychological empower-ment that was not dependent upon the beneficence of the organization, and they were also able to alter the structure of the agency so that it was more empowering to its participants.

At the family level, one model of em-powerment is *family-centered service delivery* which includes family involvement and col-laboration, a focus on family strengths, and informed family choice including flexibility and accessibility (Allen & Petr, 1998). In fact, the movement came more from dissat-isfied parents than from professionals. At the organizational level, agencies adopting a family-centered approach to service deliv-ery must undertake thorough reviews of their policies, procedures, and practices, and modify them as necessary to comply with the principles inherent in the model (Friesen & Koroloff, 1990). Involvement of consumers at all levels of decision-making is essential to ensuring that program develop-ment and evaluation truly reflect the prefer-ences of families, while also providing a means of strengthening their sense of con-trol and self-efficacy.

Organizational-level Empowerment. At the organizational level, empowerment focuses on changing belief systems, roles and power relationships, support systems, and leadership styles (Maton & Salem, 1995) of a group in order to increase its efficacy, self-sufficiency, and the legitimacy of its members in the organization and/or society. A popular example of organizational empowerment in education is Project Head Start, which had from its inception a major goal of directly empowering poor communities, parents, and children through its philosophy on parent participation (Zigler & Muenchow, 1992). Local centers were given control over planning and operation, as well as major hiring and firing decisions of key personnel. In this way, the process of organizing themselves and sharing responsibilities, enhances psychological empowerment and facilitates societal empowerment (Kroeker, 1995). But their variation and autonomy also mean that Head Start represents organizational rather than societal-level empowerment.

Empowerment is also a focus of many school-based parent involvement programs. But to be successful, it is critical for such programs to look beyond individual or family-level empowerment and work toward empowering organizational (school) or even institutional-level (e.g., school board) changes (Gruber & Trickett, 1987).

Community-level Empowerment.

Tremendous variation exists among communities in their levels of structural violence, coping resources, and resilience (Wandersman & Nation, 1998). Thus, it makes sense that there are a wide variety of community-level empowerment strategies to address local housing, health care, urban and rural development, crime, environmental hazards, and other problems (Perkins, 1995; Perkins, Brown, & Taylor, 1996; Rich, Edelstein, Hallman, & Wandersman, 1995). For example, the Pacific Institute for Community Organizations (PICO) is a commu-

nity organizing network with organizations in 25 cities across the United States. Speer and Hughey (1995) argue that "PICO organizations strive to become capable of competing adeptly in their community on issues within their organizational self-interest" (p. 732). This is accomplished by forming coalitions in communities and gathering large numbers of individuals to work together on a common purpose. Speer and Hughey (1995) describe an example in which a community organization discovered a financial link between dilapidated housing structures owned by absentee landlords and the local department of social services. By researching funding sources, making public this discovery, and strategically applying public pressure, the organization was able to demand that the housing be improved to comply with city building, fire, and health codes.

The community is an especially appropriate level at which to organize housing programs geared toward empowering low-income residents. A good example of this is the "community household model" of limited equity co-op apartments that have turned squalid, abandoned buildings in some of the poorest and most distressed neighborhoods in New York City into opportunities for home ownership and inspirational stories of individual, family, and community empowerment (Saegert, 1989; Saegert & Winkel, 1996). An even more surprising example is the organization of unions of homeless people in cities all over the United States (Yeich, 1996). These demonstrate that even the most destitute and disenfranchised among the poor can be empowered to organize, educate, demonstrate, and advocate on their own behalf.

In recent years, empowerment-oriented coalitions and partnerships for health promotion and substance-abuse prevention have been organized across multiple communities in many cities and states. Fawcett et al. (1995) identified at least 33 different enabling activities conducted by such coalitions in support of community empowerment. However, it is especially important at the community and coalition levels to make sure that at the individual and organizational levels, empowerment is also occurring (McMillan, Florin, Stevenson, Kerman, & Mitchell, 1995) and actual conditions are improving. These coalitions operate at a level between individual communities and the whole society. This may well be the widest practical level of empowerment intervention in the United States at present.

Societal-level Empowerment. Societal empowerment targets the larger social structures and institutions that keep people in positions of powerlessness and poverty, and may be targeted in an effort to sustain the other levels of empowerment and resolve problems associated with poverty (Kroeker, 1995). Perkins (1995), however, finds a clear pattern of co-optation of empowerment ideology, or at least language, at the societal level of national and international policy-making, with little-to-no specificity regarding the meaning of empowerment and little-to-no impact on empowerment at other levels. But outside the United States, more successful empowerment-based political and economic development programs which do manage to connect individuals, families, communities, and local organizations with larger governmental and nongovernmental structures (Friedmann, 1992) may provide more promising models for addressing structural violence in any society.

Kroeker (1995) describes the Nicaraguan cooperative movement as a model organization that grew out of principles of empowerment. In the 1980s, severely disadvantaged peasants organized themselves into more than 3,000 voluntary agricultural cooperatives, which were later nationally encouraged by the government. The members typically share a land deed, its work, responsibilities, and rewards. In turn, the cooperative provides various benefits including education, housing, and land for personal farming in addition to occasional supplies such as wood, fruit, milk, or meat. The Contra war weakened many cooperatives, but they remained an integral and necessary component of the national economy. Kroeker argues that the cooperatives fostered empowerment on the personal, organizational, and societal levels. They also addressed material needs such as jobs, food, and housing, and facilitated autonomy through collective land ownership. The members chose and elected their own leadership, which allowed for direct participation in decision-making and increased the sense of organizational empowerment. Many cooperatives also participated in working with and challenging national institutions and policies, which afforded some a sense of societal empowerment. Kroeker's work also demonstrated, however, that local and national relations, policies, and events had a powerful influence, at times both enhancing and deterring the development of empowerment. Implementation of any empowerment program must then, take these elements into consideration when planning, modifying, and evaluating the program.

RECOMMENDATIONS AND CONCLUSIONS

Housing and Homelessness

Psychologists and policy-makers must recognize that the primary causes of homelessness are not personal vulnerabilities, such as mental illness or substance abuse. As important as those problems are to address, they are merely selection factors determining who will be homeless. The primary causes are poverty and the scarcity of affordable housing (Shinn, 1992). Ideally, housing services would go beyond the provision of shelter and include the education and training that families need to build independent lives, and to develop jobs which address the serious lack of jobs for the unemployed, possibly by increasing public services. "Sweat equity," low-income limited equity housing co-ops (Saegert & Winkel, 1996), and other mechanisms for tenant control, management, and ownership which have proven to be a successful empowerment strategy should be expanded. Families should be encouraged to organize and define the boundaries of the family such that if a family is caring for elderly parents, or cousin, brother, or aunt they will not be denied housing nor benefits on those grounds, but on the contrary be rewarded for their efforts, which ultimately reduce the need for governmental services. Although low-income tenants and the homeless may be difficult to organize politically, it is possible to do so (Yeich, 1996) and important to try so that they may develop a greater sense of self worth and self-efficacy.

Health Care

Poverty remains the leading health risk for children. Children in poverty are less likely to receive annual check-ups, less likely to be current on their immunizations, and less likely to receive health care when they are sick (National Center for Children in Poverty, 1991). Clearly, all children should be ensured a regular source of ongoing health, mental health, and social care. To that end, health care and promotion programs should be decentralized, and efforts made to organize and support local collaborative partnerships of patients/citizens, community leaders, health care professionals, and researchers (Fawcett et. al., 1995; McMillan et al., 1995). The formation and expansion of local support and information groups for specific health problems and self-help/mutual assistance referral centers should be supported at the local, state, and national levels.

Education

Empowerment strategies in the area of education should aim to improve student success, de-emphasize bureaucracies, and emphasize the collaboration amongst professionals, parents, and the community towards the common goal of academic achievement for all children (Schorr, 1997). In this spirit, schools should expand parental involvement programs and broad-based local control of schools and school governance in the manner of Head Start (Zigler & Muenchow, 1992) and the Comer project (Comer, 1993; Ramirez-Smith, 1995).

Funding should be increased so that the mission of the educational setting can be expanded to include after-school programs designed to help older children "catch-up" to their appropriate grade-level, help parents complete their GED (graduation equivalency), and provide poor families with on-site job training for job readiness and workplace skills. Schools are also natural environments to house family literacy programs designed to foster literacy development for the entire family and stimulate family involvement in their children's learning. Schorr (1997) argues that schools have a prominent place in encouraging school, family, and community collaboration to promote the success of all children, but that the burden cannot rest solely on schools for initiation and success, and thus neighborhood and family involvement and responsibility are essential.

Finally, time limits on welfare for adults should be flexible to accommodate those adults who are actively enrolled in job training and educational services which will provide them with long-term self-sufficiency. Caseworkers should be allowed flexibility in making decisions about eligibility in this regard (American Psychological Association, 1998).

Child and Family Services

The National Commission on Children (1991) concluded that the current child and family welfare system was essentially a frustrating and ineffective system for children and families. Child and family welfare services clearly need to be developed in ways that support the self-determination of the individual, family, and community by including educational opportunities for both children and families, as well as the provision of culturally relevant and proven psychological interventions to prevent spousal and child abuse, and substance abuse. To promote this ideal, linkages should be established between various agencies which promote the integration of services and which serve to decrease the disempowering bureaucratic maze which functions as an obstacle for access to services for families with multiple needs (American Psycololgical Association, 1998). A focus on a community orientation which promotes comprehensive neighborhood-based partnerships between child protective agencies, community agencies, and local foster parent associations to support troubled families and protect children may be particularly empowering, cost-effective, and may also minimize trauma for children (Schorr, 1997).

Standards for the training of social workers and caseworkers should be expanded beyond the "traditional" model of social work towards a model which focuses on integrating cultural diversity, family strengths and empowerment in the best interests of the child and preservation of the family.

Finally, families need more control under welfare reform and should have access to grievance and appeals processes which are timely and responsive, and which provide due process guarantees.

Lawmakers and officials who write rules and regulations need to work to ensure that family-centered principles based upon empowerment are integrated into new laws and programs. The degree of family choice and of focus on family strengths operative in a policy, service, or program should be key components in the evaluation of the success of family-centered practice. Communities must also be taken into consideration, as they have profound influence on families and children, and, if organized, developed, and empowered, can be valuable resources to lead efforts to fulfill a broad vision of health, education, and equity for disadvantaged young children and families.

Structural violence operates at every level of society and so demands a multi-level solution. Truly empowering strategies are not easy to implement well. And everyone involved in empowerment programs—participants, staff, administrators, and evaluators—must be careful not to substitute perceived gains in empowerment for real material gains in people's lives (Saegert & Winkel, 1996). But empowerment strategies represent perhaps the only solution that explicitly addresses the structural aspects of violence at every level in which it occurs.

CHAPTER 29

GENDERING PEACEBUILDING

Susan McKay and Dyan Mazurana

This chapter introduces the reader to characteristics of *gendered thinking*, its neglect within psychology and peace psychology, and discusses how peacebuilding as commonly defined lacks a gender perspective. We argue that feminist analysis contributes to a more comprehensive meaning of peacebuilding than a non-gendered analysis. We describe results of our research on women's international peacebuilding initiatives, underscoring the emphases women give to psychosocial processes such as healing, reconciliation, and cooperation. We characterize distinct ways women build peace at grassroots (local) levels and within nongovernmental organizations (NGOs). Finally, we discuss the United Nations (U.N.) Platform for Action which is an important global feminist document that provides important directions for women's peacebuilding.

FEMINIST PERSPECTIVES IN PEACE PSYCHOLOGY

Gendered thinking, which considers the perspectives and behaviors of both men and women, has not characterized psychology in general or peace psychology in particular. *Gendering peace psychology* means that peace psychology has not, in the past, been sufficiently conscious of gender biases, biases derived from the predominance of men's thinking and perspectives. Therefore the discipline has *patriarchal,* or male-biased, assumptions and perspectives that need to be challenged through incorporation of feminist perspectives and thinking (McKay, 1996).

Gendered thinking illuminates similarities and also substantial differences between male and female perspectives. An example of how thinking about war and peace is not sufficiently gendered is the following: Think about who is injured and who dies during wars—who comes to mind? Most people, both men and women, follow patriarchal thought by identifying combat soldiers who are mostly men. In fact, the predominant casualties of today's wars, estimated to be as high as 95 percent, are civilians—the majority of whom are women and children (Levy & Sidel, 1997; U.N., 1996a). Another example occurs when thinking about who are peacemakers and peacebuilders during and after conflicts. Many people have images from popular media of high-profile political male figures such as George Mitchell forging the May 1998 peace accords in Northern Ireland, or of U.N. Secretary-General Kofi Annan, who has been instrumental in peace negotiations in 1998 in Eritrea, Ethiopia, and Iraq. Far fewer know of instrumental women peacemakers and peace-builders such as Hanan Ashwari (1995) of Palestine who has been a leading spokeswoman for brokering peace in the Middle East, or Monica McWilliams of Northern Ireland who founded the Northern Ireland Women's Coalition (NIWC). Nor do people often imagine the multiple venues in communities and nations in which women act to build sustainable peace. Women have long been integrally involved in peacemaking and peacebuilding processes (see Bennett, Bexley, & Warnock, 1995; Cock, 1993; El-Bushra & Mukarubuga, 1995; Enloe, 1993; Sharoni, 1994; U.N., 1996a; Utting, 1994). Their activities at community and regional levels are extensive and often within the aegis of NGOs and grassroots (local) women's organizations.

Feminism is an ideology that purports men and women are of equal value and their equality should be recognized by all societies (Reardon, 1990). This point of view recognizes that women throughout the world suffer from sex-based discrimination or *sexism*. Feminism seeks to challenge the dynamic of domination at all levels, from the home to the military, and to demand a world based more on cooperation than on conquest (Bunch, 1987). For example, feminist peace theorist Birgit Brock-Utne (1989) incorporates gender perspectives in her definitions of positive and negative peace. Thus authentic peace and security require *positive peace,* a society in which there is no indirect or structural violence such as gender inequality. *Negative peace* occurs when personal, physical, and direct violence such as armed conflict, rape, and spousal battering are absent. Peace psychologists share with feminists their concern for authentic peace and security for all humans, a focus infrequently found in governmental and intergovernmental definitions of security, which typically are framed within the

limits of states' boundaries and interests (McKay, 1996).

A Critical Analysis of Peacebuilding

Feminist analysis looks at the world by gathering and interpreting information through the eyes and experiences of women as subjects. It separates itself from a patriarchal world view and the constraints of male-dominated theoretical analyses (Young, 1992), seeking to explain the importance of women's oppression in terms of their unequal status in society at large. In terms of *women's peacebuilding,* feminist analysis identifies women's specific concerns about peacebuilding, approaches peacebuilding from women's perspectives, welcomes pluralistic voices and diverse methods. Using feminist analysis, critical questions are asked about peacebuilding such as: what does building peace mean to women across cultures? Who are the women talking about peacebuilding? Do their perspectives and practices about peacebuilding coincide with definitions of the United Nations, states, or NGOs? A question of particular interest to feminist peace psychologists is to what extent do the United Nations, various States, NGOs, and grassroots organizations emphasize in their peacebuilding human processes such as reconciliation and restoration of relationships, as compared with institutional and structural rebuilding? (Mazurana & McKay, 1999).

To build peace requires visioning the components of peace and security across cultures, nationalities, ethnicities, and between men and women. There is no unitary construct called "peacebuilding" to which everyone subscribes. Governmental, U.N., NGO, and grassroots organizations often have widely differing notions of peacebuilding. One of the most commonly-referenced definitions of peacebuilding is that of former U.N. Secretary-General Boutros-Ghali whose *An Agenda for Peace* (U.N., 1992) has become a pivotal document to describe U.N. meanings of peacekeeping, peacemaking, and peacebuilding. In it, peacebuilding is defined as occurring in post-conflict societies: "rebuilding the institutions and infrastructures of nations torn by civil war and strife and building bonds of peaceful mutual benefit among nations formerly at war" (U.N., 1992, p. 8). Most peace operations of U.N. states and NGOs focus upon peacekeeping, peacebuilding, and providing humanitarian aid. Peacebuilding within women's grassroots groups emphasizes relational behaviors, reconciliation and healing of psychological wounds (Mazurana & McKay, 1999).

The remainder of this chapter describes women's peacebuilding approaches within international grassroots groups and NGOs and uses data we have gathered and analyzed (Mazurana & McKay, 1999). We stress women's meanings of peacebuilding and peacebuilding work they do. We emphasize some distinct approaches of women, especially at grassroots levels. Importantly, to avoid imposing Western thinking about what constitutes peacebuilding, we stress recognizing culturally-specific views and methods of peacebuilding within and between various women's groups.

WOMEN'S GRASSROOTS PEACEBUILDING

The real work of peacebuilding requires that local people seek solutions in their communities, regions, and nations rather than outsiders imposing their approaches. Grassroots women's peace groups tend to center peacebuilding actions upon nonviolence; recognition of, and respect for, human rights; promotion of intercultural tolerance and understanding; and women's empowerment in economic, social, cultural and political spheres. Women's full participation is stressed in all these processes.

Grassroots women's groups may involve themselves in peacemaking and peacebuilding because of concerns for their families' survival and knowledge that women and children are the primary casualties of indirect and direct violence during armed conflict. They emphasize the centrality of psychosocial (psychological responses situated within the context of community) and basic human needs, such as food, shelter and safety, far more than governmental organizations, NGOs, and the United Nations usually do (Mazurana & McKay, 1999). For many grassroots women's groups, peacebuilding means securing food for the family and a future for children (Susanne Thurfjell, personal communication, November 4, 1997). Issues of structural violence such as the economics of poverty and the degradation of the environment are of primary concern for many grassroots women.

Women's grassroots peacebuilding is frequently personal, interpersonal, creative and political. It may use imaginative activities to protest violence and advocate peace such as the wearing of black to protest violence, employing street theater, holding demonstrations, vigils, peace camps, and peace walks. In some instances where the most creative approaches are employed, conditions are very dangerous. For example, the Women in Black in Belgrade (former Yugoslavia) demanded accountability and an end to violence, protesting when no other groups dared (Cynthia Enloe, personal communication, January 24, 1998).

Grassroots women's group often work through networks and coalitions whereby women meet to strategize, gain energy, and push for peace at regional and global levels. Above all, grassroots peacebuilding is practical. It may mean stopping the fighting, and women's groups may organize towards this aim. The Sudanese Women's Voice for Peace, for example, is made up of women from the warring factions in the North and South, seeking solutions to women's and men's violence (United Nations Development Fund for Women/African Women in Crisis [UNIFEM/AFWIC], 1995).

The rationale for grassroot women's organizing is often based on beliefs that women are by nature—often because they are mothers—more caring, peaceful, and nonviolent (i.e., Agosin, 1993; Ruddick, 1982, 1990; Women for Life Without Wars and Violence!, 1996). We contend that there is nothing inherently (biologically) more peaceful about women than men although women may be socially conditioned to exhibit more peaceful qualities. Patriarchy works through various race, ethnic, and class lines, religions, and nationalism to encourage and involve women in violence. History has shown women are often essential to the perpetration of violence, and they have acted to support and encourage it (i.e. Afkhami, 1995; African Rights, 1995; Basu, 1993; Cock, 1992; Enloe, 1988, 1993; Human Rights Watch/Asia Watch, 1993).

Women's Spiritual Beliefs and Grassroots Peacebuilding

Both secular and religious women's groups work for peace at the grassroots level. The role of churches in preventing and ameliorating the effects of destructive conflict is significant because churches are frequently well placed to mediate conflict and advocate for peace. Churches are close to local communities and understand the human costs of conflicts. They may have more resources than NGOs. Also, their personal contacts are important—for example, newsletters, pastoral sermons and visits, and often they are a public site of gathering and strength for women. Because spiritual beliefs of women's religious

peacebuilding groups are a foundation for their actions, activities to promote forgiveness and reconciliation are often emphasized. Despite this, in their peacebuilding work, women's religious groups frequently critique patriarchal behaviors fostered by religion, such as the domination of women by men within the church hierarchy. Similarly, secular women's peacebuilding groups may critique patriarchal practices perpetuating the war system.

Reconciliation

Grassroots women's organizations, whether religious or secular, often emphasize reconciliation although their foci may differ. *Spiritual reconciliation,* a "change of heart," emphasizes atonement and forgiveness. In contrast, *secular reconciliation* more often emphasizes justice, a key issue for women who seek gender justice through the prosecution of perpetrators and the acknowledgment of governments' wrongdoing because of rapes, sexual slavery, and other forms of violence against women. For instance, grassroots groups have worked for gender justice in the aftermath of massive rapes that occurred in the 1990s during the war in the former Yugoslavia and, for several decades, have sought redress and apology from the Japanese government for the sexual slavery of Korean women during World War II (McKay, 1999).

Reconciliation includes bringing together former enemies to make peace, learning to coexist in peace, and defusing enemy imaging. Women's grassroot groups often play instrumental roles. In Mali, East Africa, for example, the national Women's Movement for Securing Peace and National Unity (MNFPUN) organized meetings of military officers, high-level politicians, and diplomats. The eventual result was the 1991 National Pact to stop the war. Women worked to humanize the face of the conflict by emphasizing the situation of victims. They also served as mediators. More recently, women have sought to diffuse tensions between various ethnic groups, in particular, encouraging local women to take pro-active roles in conflict prevention. A major objective has been making women's concerns a priority at the national level and increasing women's numbers within the National Assembly as well as strengthening their effective participation (International Fellowship of Reconciliation, 1998).

In Burundi, Africa, with the sponsorship of a United States-based peace group, Search for Common Ground, a women's peace center was established in January 1995. The goal of the center, where typically 200 Hutu and Tutsi women visit weekly, was to reduce ethnic conflict, encourage reconciliation, and establish a cadre of women trainers in conflict resolution methods. Hutu and Tutsi women have met there to work on common goals, and the Center has served as a resource on gender issues. It has organized round tables to promote coordination and collaboration among various women's groups. Additionally, support has been provided for local women's groups and women in displaced camps (International Fellowship of Reconciliation and International Peace Bureau, 1997).

Militarism

Within grassroots women's peace organizations, a persistent theme is the issue of *militarism* and its effects. Militarism refers to processes through which individuals, groups, and social, economic, and political systems increasingly become reliant upon, or dominated by the military (Enloe, 1993). Grassroots women have organized to ameliorate the effects of militarism such as domestic violence, violence against women, sex trafficking, and degradation of the environment. Further they act to bring attention to concerns such as the global proliferation of

light arms, militarization of children's toys and games, difficulties in reintegrating ex-combatants into their societies—particularly child-soldiers—and land demining (IFOR, 1998; Rebera, 1992).

An effort to combat militarism and promote peace occurred with the gathering of a Christian Conference of Asian Women's Concerns when women from many countries in the region gathered to document and analyze violence in their societies, particularly in the form of militarism. Together they discussed methods based on past and future work about how to best move towards cultures of peace (Rebera, 1992). Other examples are women's peace groups in Algeria, Chile, and the Philippines, which have asked for the voluntary dumping of war toys. The groups have held ceremonial burnings, have buried these destructive toys, and have worked to help children reject games of torture and violence (Agosin, 1993; Rebera, 1992). Women in the Russian Federation and their counterparts in Chechenya have challenged militaries' practice of forced conscription. Organized as a Committee of Soldiers' Mothers, they have hidden, lied about, and physically resisted the forced conscription of their sons in Chechenya. They also have pressured the Russian government for a nonviolent solution to the conflict, challenged the military authority of the State, and demanded radical reform of the Russian Army (Women for Life Without Wars and Violence!, 1996).

Women's Participation in Decision-making

Another focus of some grassroot women's peace groups has been to increase women's numbers and strengthen their effective participation in decision-making bodies. These efforts are deemed critical to enhancing women's peacebuilding initiatives and capacities for achieving a just peace. The simple presence of women in international, regional, or national decision-making bodies is not, however, likely to have an impact without recognition of causes and processes of women's disempowerment and ways in which diverse women are oppressed. This knowledge must be followed by actions that facilitate women's empowerment. For example, the Burmese Women's Union was formed in 1995 by female students in Burma (now called Myanmar) to promote women's voices in politics, increase the recognition and practice of women's human rights, and prompt women's voices in building peace and democracy (IFOR & IPB, 1997).

Stopping Violence in the Home

A U.S.-based grassroots woman-led organization, Peace Links, works to empower local people toward achieving and sustaining peace through nonviolent forms of conflict resolution and violence prevention in their families, communities, nations and world. Although the United States is not characterized by open warfare, structural and direct violence—especially violence against women—is widespread (Schuler, 1992). Western countries, too, must analyze ways in which violence occurs in their own homes and societies, and their countries' perpetuation of violence on others and also actively engage in peacebuilding. Thus initiatives by organizations such as Peace Links to address violence in the United States are also essential to peacebuilding.

NONGOVERNMENTAL ORGANIZATIONS AND PEACEBUILDING

Nongovernmental groups often work in conjunction with local grassroots movements or they may involve themselves at multiple levels from international to local. NGOs, because of their linkages to both grassroots groups, governmental, and U.N. bodies have important potential for influencing peacebuilding, particularly through the formation of coalitions. NGOs at local levels (as compared with international NGOs) have grassroots knowledge of the psychological dimensions of conflicts, and they possess know-how for local conflict resolution. NGOs thus can be pivotal agents facilitating the capacities of locals to build peace, and these are often women.

Coaltition Building

One of the ways NGOs are most effective is through building coalitions, thus linking resources of States, the United Nations, and civil society (Kunugi, Boulding, & Oberg, 1996). Peace researcher Elise Boulding (1993) observed that in order for peacebuilding to be viable it must have roots in local peace concerns and the often-invisible peace culture of family, neighborhood, and community. Thus, peacebuilding should not be a process only supporting those in power but must empower ordinary people. Further, although governments can speed up peace processes, they do not invent them; local people do (Boulding, 1993).

In coalition building, the *process* of building peace is emphasized more than are specific outcomes. Peacebuilding is thus approached as a dynamic and complex process made up of roles, function, and activities and involving interactions of many actors with varying skills (Lederach, 1995a; Lederach, 1995b). Unfortunately, what may happen is outside donor organizations (for example, international NGOs and humanitarian aid programs) establish product-oriented agendas that tend to control peacebuilding agendas. These organizations initiate little consultation with local goverments and people; that is, they eschew networking and coalition building (UNRISD, 1994). Since women so often work through networks and coalitions, their initiatives can consequently be marginalized when NGOs' "outcome agendas" overshadow emphasis on peacebuilding *processes*.

An example of coalition building occurred when NGOs came together with governmental and intergovernmental organizations and the United Nations during a 1997 networking meeting sponsored by the Peace Team Forum of the Swedish Peace Council and the Swedish Ministry for Foreign Affairs. Invited representatives of nearly 40 international and national NGOs and government officials from ten countries, the European Union, and the United Nations, convened at a conference on "Government-NGO Relations in Preventing Violence: Transforming Conflict and Building Peace" (Consortium on Peace Research, Education and Development [COPRED], 1997).

Women's NGO Peacebuilding

A limited number of NGOs are starting to develop programmatic focus on how they can facilitate women's peacebuilding. An important challenge to NGOs engaged in peacebuilding is to more thoroughly integrate gendered thinking into their work and recognize the critical importance of psychosocial processes, such as healing from trauma and relationship building, as integral to effective peacebuilding initiatives. Other NGOs have always focused upon women and peace. For example, the Women's International League for Peace and Freedom (WILPF) links issues of peace with women's oppression, inequality, and empowerment. Founded in 1915, its activities are global in scope. WILPF has long advocated for women's fuller participation in all stages of peace processes and negotia-

tions. Another woman-focused NGO is the Centre for Strategic Initiative for Women (CSIW) which, in addition to its original human rights emphasis, has extended its mission to include women's leadership roles in peacebuilding.

Other NGO Contributions to Peacebuilding

In addition to fostering activism and coalition building, NGOs can be influential in supporting research, policy development and capacity building. In Canada, the International Development Research Centre (IDRC) is an autonomous (NGO) Canadian organization created by the Parliament of Canada. IDRC's perspective is that research on and for peacebuilding can play a catalytic role in facilitating processes of dialogue, consensus and coalition building, and policy development; it supports country-specific, regional and global projects. In 1996 IDRC established its Peacebuilding and Reconstruction Program Initiative (PBR PI). The PBR PI focuses on developmental challenges of post-conflict societies. Emphasizing that gender is integral, all IDRC-funded research must consider the differential impact change will have on the lives of both men and women. Also, gender mainstreaming, that is "thinking gender" about every program and project, is supported in all of the programs of the Centre.

An NGO that fosters action research in peacebuilding is Life and Peace Institute (LPI), based in Uppsala, Sweden. Founded by the Swedish Ecumenical Council, its principal aim is to support the work of churches in the fields of peace, justice and reconciliation. LPI views the central process of both conflict transformation and peacebuilding as empowering people within societies affected by conflict so they become owners of the peace process. LPI asserts that peace must be grown from inside if it is to be sustainable. Its extensive peacebuilding work in Somalia had as one emphasis the empowerment of women, within a broader aim of enabling women and men to work together for a new and peaceful Somali society (Heinrich, 1997). Although women in Somalia do not have prominent decision-making and public affairs roles or equal access to education, health services, and economic resources, they do play crucial roles in managing conflict and building peace. An aim of LPI was to support women in these new and often difficult roles—for example as mediators between clans and in reestablishing communication between hostile groups. Thus LPI stressed capacity building for women, such as giving support to women members of local administrative councils and sponsoring workshops that focused upon topics such as conflict transformation, peace and justice, human rights issues, leadership roles, and democracy.

Jerusalem Link is an NGO consisting of Israeli and Palestinian women who work for peace at the grassroots level. Activities are organized around several major areas: human rights education and advocacy, peace education, dialogue groups of Israeli and Palestinian women, youth and young women making peace, and the engagement of women political leaders on both sides. Most activities are joint efforts, but sometimes they are conducted for either Palestinian or Israeli women. One project of Jerusalem Link is a media campaign. Jerusalem Link has recognized the critical role domestic and international media play in shifting public opinion and has published petitions and joint letters, focusing upon both print and electronic media. Significantly, ability to access and use electronic media is critical for women's effectiveness in peacebuilding

and is increasingly a focus of international attention.

THE U.N. PLATFORM FOR ACTION'S (PFA) IMPACT UPON WOMEN'S PEACEBUILDING

The PFA, adopted in Beijing, China by the Fourth World Conference on Women on September 15, 1995 with the consensus of 181 nations, provides a blueprint of peacebuilding actions for many global women's coalitions and networks (McKay & Winter, 1998; United Nations, 1996b). Many sections of the PFA address issues of central importance to peace psychologists—violence against women, women and the environment, women and the media, and human rights of women, to name a few. The PFA is of substantial interest to feminist peace psychologists because of its identified strategies that can be used by men and women throughout the world to improve the status of the world's women. The PFA places emphasis on ending direct violence and also on seeking to ameliorate structural (indirect) violence so that societies are transformed to more equitable and peaceful ones. A section on women and armed conflict and women's initiatives to build more peaceful societies emphasizes nonviolence, equality between women and men, gender justice, recognition and honoring of women's human rights, reduction in military expenditures and international trade, trafficking in and proliferation of weapons, women's contributions as peace educators and in fostering a culture of peace, cooperative approaches to peace and security with women's participation in power structures, and women's involvement in all efforts to prevent and resolve conflicts (United Nations, 1996b). The PFA is a guiding document for many grassroots and NGO women's organizations that do peacebuilding.

CONCLUSION

In this chapter we have presented examples of ways women build peace and some distinct approaches they may use. Women's peacebuilding may be informed by views of "natural peacefulness," religious beliefs, a mother's sense of responsibility to protect her family, or analyses which connect militarism with violence.

Information about women's best practices of peacebuilding is not yet well known. This is because learning about women's peacebuilding has not been viewed with much interest by governmental and nongovernmental organizations or researchers. Also, because local women often work without recognition and use indigenous methods, they have been marginalized. Their actions converge on some issues, such as increasing women's presence in decision-making bodies. Women's initiatives are also divergent, reflecting particular cultural, historical and material contexts. Importantly, through their peacebuilding practices, women are pushing "acceptable" gendered practices and spaces, and often they bring women together from diverse backgrounds and classes to work to end violence and build peace.

We believe that women's peacebuilding practices can be of particular interest to peace psychologists because women emphasize processes such as relationship building, reconciliation, cooperation, and networking and other intrapersonal and interpersonal processes. A challenge for peace psychologists for the twenty-first century is to incorporate gendered thinking into scholarship and practice. This will require evaluating patriarchal biases with respect to the acquisition and use of psychological knowledge but will substantially enrich peace psychology's knowledge base and practice.

CHAPTER 30

Psychologists Making a Difference in the Public Arena: Building Cultures of Peace

Michael Wessells, Milton Schwebel, and Anne Anderson

Inevitably, analyses of peace and social justice raise practical questions about what can be done. Left unanswered, these questions invite hopelessness and feelings of futility about changing a world grown accustomed to a culture of war. In this chapter, we offer a framework for action and identify four specific venues for action on a wide basis: sensitization, consultation, activism, and policy work. We also attempt to situate our ideas in historic context and to raise critical consciousness about work in the public arena. Through ongoing critical review of their work, peace psychologists help to ensure that their actions in the public arena embody the values they seek to nourish in the world.

Throughout the twentieth century, psychologists of many different orientations have worked in the public arena for peace.

Early on, William James (1910/1995), the philosopher-psychologist, advocated that since war meets human needs for heroism, sacrifice, and excitement, those who seek peace must construct nonviolent, morally acceptable outlets for those needs. In 1945, near the end of World War II, psychologists such as Gordon Allport and E. C. Tolman distributed publicly a statement on human nature that underscored the preventability of war (Jacobs, 1989). During the Cold War, psychologists such as Ralph White, Herbert Kelman, Morton Deutsch, and Brewster Smith suggested psychologically informed policies for reducing superpower tensions and the threat of nuclear war. Charles Osgood's (1962) suggestion of GRIT (Graduated Reciprocal Initiatives in Tension Reduction) may even have encouraged President Kennedy to unilaterally propose a ban on atmospheric nuclear testing in 1963 (Jacobs, 1989).

Although some have viewed work for peace as something to be done "after hours" and as citizens, others have made cogent arguments that work to advance human well-being in the public arena is a matter of *professional responsibility*. Alfred Adler, for example, saw social responsibility as "fundamental to the practice of psychology" (Rudmin & Ansbacher, 1989, p. 8), saying, in 1935 that

> The honest psychologist cannot shut his [sic] eyes to social conditions which prevent the child from becoming part of the community and from feeling at home in the world, and which allow him to grow up as though he lived in enemy country. Thus psychologists must work against nationalism when it is so poorly understood that it harms mankind as a whole; against wars of conquest, revenge, and prestige, against unemployment which plunges people into hopelessness; and against all other obstacles which interfere with the spreading of social interest in the family, the school, and society at large. (Adler, 1935/1956, p. 454)

These brief examples provide an historical context for considering the evolving challenges and opportunities that peace psychologists encounter in their work in the public arena. In the past, particularly during the Cold War, peace researchers and practitioners have frequently reacted to problems such as the nuclear threat, environmental destruction, or whichever current war happened to be most devastating. Reactive approaches, although often necessary, can neither address effectively the root causes of war nor transform the war system into a peace system. Building peace requires prevention and long-term, proactive work (Christie, 1997; Wagner, de Rivera, & Watkins, 1988) for changing cultures of violence into cultures of peace (Adams, 1995; Galtung, 1996). Even short-term reactive responses to particular crisis situations can prove to be more effective if they have been chosen within the framework of building positive peace.

THE CULTURES OF PEACE FRAMEWORK

A useful description for positive peace has been adopted by the U.N. General Assembly. Recognizing the long term nature of the work, the U.N. General Assembly (Resolution 52/15) declared the year 2000 as the International Year for the Culture of Peace. Broadly, *cultures of peace* include seven core elements that vary in form across cultures, yet are universals of positive peace. These elements may be envisioned as spokes of a wheel, a weakness in any one of which may produce systemic weakness or collapse. The elements are:

- *Social justice:* institutionalized equity in distribution and access to material, social, and political resources; truth-telling, reparations, and penalties for infractions; full participation and power-sharing by different groups; gender justice and full participation by women;
- *Human rights:* rule of law and adherence to human rights standards;
- *Nonviolence:* institutionalized arrangements for nonviolent conflict resolution and reconciliation; values and attitudes of civility; norms and processes that promote human security, cooperation, interdependence, and harmonious relationships at all levels;
- *Inclusiveness:* respect for difference; participation by different groups; meeting identity needs; cultural sensitivity;
- *Civil society:* strength and diversity of civic groups in sectors such as health, business, religion, and education; commu-

nity action, support, and hope through these venues, full citizen participation in government;

- *Peace education:* formal and informal, experiential education for peace at all levels; socialization of values, attitudes, and behaviors conducive to peace and social justice.
- *Sustainability:* preservation of global resources; meeting the needs of the current generation without compromising the ability to meet the needs of future generations.

Psychologists may contribute to the construction of cultures of peace through work at many levels. Therapists who help to reduce family violence and to build equitable, nonviolent relationships in families contribute to cultures of peace. Educators who teach skills of nonviolent conflict resolution or work for social justice at the community level also contribute to the construction of cultures of peace. Ultimately, however, large-scale, systemic social change is needed to build cultures of peace. To be maximally effective, psychologists may take their work into the public arena, reaching larger numbers of people, constructing social policies that help institutionalize social justice and end oppression, and enlarging the potential scale on which they can make a difference in effecting peace and social justice.

Although many peace psychologists recognize the potential benefits and importance of work in the public arena, numerous concerns limit their involvement. Many feel overwhelmed by the vast number of issues and the complexity involved in producing large-scale change. Many feel helpless and uncertain about how one can make a difference. In addition, multifaceted issues of peace and social justice require multidisciplinary work, which exceeds the specialized training of many psychologists. Fur-

ther, psychologists may worry that by working in the public arena on political issues, they may politicize the discipline and damage its credibility, fall prey to role confusion, or go beyond what is known or what can legitimately be said on scientific grounds (Suedfeld & Tetlock, 1992).

Although complex, these questions should neither block action nor lead one to forget that inaction itself is a choice that has profound implications. Nowhere is this more apparent than in regard to issues of science and the practice of psychology.

SCIENCE, VALUES, AND ACTION

Science and Values

Although science has often been portrayed as an objective, value-neutral enterprise, it is suffused with the values of a dominant order that has institutionalized war and injustice. For researchers to raise questions about the adverse effects of the nuclear arms race during the height of the Cold War was to risk being labeled "unpatriotic." The neutrality myth fails to consider that it is people and social agencies who set the research agendas, which are socially constructed and inherently value-laden. Which questions seem most important to ask and which problems one chooses to address reflect societal values. Further, science often tracks funding, and in the United States following World War II, over half the funding for scientific research came from defense-related sources (Melman, 1985). Resource allocation for scientific research is guided by societal values, in this case a dominant social order that institutionalized war, drained resources away from peaceful activities designed to meet basic human needs, and caused much pollution and environmental damage (McKenzie-Mohr & Winter, 1992). It is not a question, then, whether values will influence psychological research but rather which values and whose values.

Consistent with the cultures of peace framework outlined above, peace psychology embraces values associated with nonviolence, human rights, and social justice. However, peace psychology is not inherently more value-laden than other areas of psychology, though it may appear to be so by virtue of its explicit emphasis on peace and its opposition to the values of the dominant war system. Nor is peace psychology inherently pacifist. Some peace psychologists believe that a commitment to building a nonviolent world does not preclude the use of force when circumstances afford no other realistic options. Indeed, many prominent peace psychologists have records of distinguished military service. In addition, peace psychology is not monolithic and includes people who hold disparate assumptions and views about how to cope with tyrants like Saddam Hussein as well as the misguided leaders in their own respective countries. Both the values of peace psychology and their relationship to science and action are topics of ongoing dialogue and reflection, as is appropriate to any field, especially a nascent one.

From the standpoint of peace psychology, the values of inclusiveness, diversity, and equity are important in regard to research and practice (Kimmel, 1995; Wessells, 1992). If research in peace psychology were dominated by Western approaches, the result would be not only culturally biased concepts and tools but also social injustice within the field of peace psychology that would likely be reflected in the marginalization of local voices, the privileging of Western approaches as more "scientific" or prestigious, and in inequitable distribution of resources such as publication space and funding. This power asymmetry represents a form of neo-colonialism (Wessells, 1992)

or cultural imperialism (Dawes, 1997). Although the asymmetry exists de facto by virtue of the wider economic and political privileging of Western countries, psychologists in the Western world can take systematic steps to include the voices and perspectives of psychologists from different countries, thereby enriching the field, enhancing cultural relevance of psychological theory and method, and building equity within the house of psychological science.

Science and Action

Traditionalists, who view science as truth-seeking and as independent of the arena of political discourse and action, have eschewed speaking out in the public arena or taking positions on controversial issues (Suedfeld & Tetlock, 1992). In this view, scientists should stick strictly to science. The problem, however, is that although one can conduct relatively "pure" research without any interest in application or action, knowledge is a social commodity, and others may use the knowledge in objectionable ways. The inadequacy of the view that scientists have no responsibility for what they develop through research is apparent to anyone who has studied Nazi science, which was thoroughly state-controlled and the results of which were used for purposes of genocide. Further, inaction on the part of scientists serves as a warrant for the perpetuation of the status quo, an objectionable situation in a socially unjust system. To have conducted pure research on psychophysics during the Nazi regime, for example, would have been tantamount to complicity in genocide through one's silence.

A more appropriate view for peace psychology is that science is inevitably an extension of socially constructed political agendas, often left unstated. In addition, scientists bear responsibility for their discoveries and tools and how they are used. In this sense, peace research is intimately connected with action for social justice. The questions asked should address issues of peace and social justice, and what is learned from the research should inform actions in the public arena. Of course, difficult questions remain about when it is appropriate to speak out, what can legitimately be said, and how scientific results will be used. These issues are examined further in the sections below.

VENUES FOR ACTION

Sensitization

In work on *sensitization* or consciousness-raising, psychologists may contribute to public dialogue through agenda-setting. Not infrequently, the public agenda is set by people trained in disciplines such as law and political science who may not recognize or have the expertise to handle psychological dimensions of social justice issues. For example, an essential part of peacebuilding in the former Yugoslavia is the conduct of war crimes tribunals, including those for perpetrators of gender-specific war crimes such as rape. Initial plans of procedures for women to give testimony, however, did not adequately consider the profound psychological implications of the very act of giving testimony about one's experience of being raped nor provide appropriate witness support and protection. Through the efforts of an international group of mental health professionals, including Anne Anderson of Psychologists for Social Responsibility, working through the Coordination of Women's Advocacy, procedures were changed and psychological supports were improved (Anderson & Richter-Lyonette, 1997). Similarly, in work on issues such as discrimination, psychologists have been instrumental in

calling attention to the psychological damage resulting from discrimination even as long ago as the 1940's, when Kenneth and Mimi Clarke's (1947) study demonstrated the effects of racism on the self-concept of young black children.

A key part of work on sensitization is the dissemination of psychological knowledge and tools. This can be particularly important in addressing issues of human nature or in correcting misuse of psychological knowledge. As Doris Miller (1972) has noted, the public discourse contains many presumed psychological "truths" that psychologists ought to examine critically:

> Economists, politicians, physicists, editorialists, munitions manufacturers and "philosophers" have not hesitated to advise society on problems of social motivation, the inevitability of war as "inherent in human nature" and the like. What psychologists have come forth to substantiate or refute these "psychological" laws? These are important psychological questions per se; that their answers may have important implications does not make them less so and should not frighten us away from them. (p. 221)

In this spirit, psychologists and scholars from other disciplines wrote the widely disseminated Seville Statement on Violence (1987), which challenged the view of war as genetically determined. The publication of the statement elicited a new round of research and discussion on the causes of war which continues today.

A particularly useful sensitization strategy is to target policy leaders, enabling psychological information to enter policy dialogue. A salient example is the work of Ralph K. White in regard to the Middle East peace process. Following the wars of 1967 and 1973 and the entrenchment of U.S. policy to oppose the spread of communism in the Middle East, Arab-Israeli relations had become saturated with misperceptions, black and white thinking, and mutual lack of empathy. In 1977, White published a paper that pointed out the divergent historical realities of Israelis and Arabs, identified damaging, self-sustaining misperceptions, and emphasized the need to address these misperceptions (White, 1977). This paper, circulated to approximately 100 U.S. embassies around the world, likely helped to establish a psychological climate favorable to peacemaking activities such as the 1978 Camp David process which built peace between Egypt and Israel. It is significant that White's paper did not call for particular policies. By raising awareness of the psychological dimensions, White helped to reframe problems that had been thought of mostly in historical, political, and economic terms. He also helped to redefine the peace agenda.

Reframing issues in light of psychological knowledge and situating issues in psychological perspective often helps to break out of conventional modes of thought, to challenge underlying assumptions, and to bring previously neglected dimensions into sharp relief. Even in the absence of hard data on particular policies, the reframing of issues constitutes one of the most valuable contributions peace psychologists make in the public arena (Smith, 1986). It was in this spirit that Herbert Kelman (1977) helped to mobilize in 1952 a small group of social scientists who established the Research Exchange on the Prevention of War. In turn, the Exchange led to the formation of the *Journal of Conflict Resolution,* which has included psychological and multidisciplinary issues related to conflict.

Since building cultures of peace is a global process and issues such as gender equity are global in scope, sensitization efforts often rely on tools such as networks and mass media. Through networking, one potentially creates multiple venues for carry-ing messages to a wide audience. The Internet and other tools make it possible to deliver messages more widely and immediately than ever before. Accordingly, the UNESCO Culture of Peace Programme has focused its work for the Year 2000 on the establishment of an Internet worldwide peace news network that helps to redefine what counts as "newsworthy" (Adams, 1998).

Mass media such as radio and television provide excellent venues for taking messages to a wide public audience. To establish social justice in countries in Africa, Search for Common Ground, a non-governmental organization (NGO) based in the United States, has developed a series of radio programs that feature drama and psychologically informed discussions to encourage tolerance and understanding across lines of conflict. Radio is still the most accessible medium in many areas of Africa. In developed nations such as the United States, television plays a central role in defining social reality, and television images are widely believed to have helped mobilize public support for particular policies.

Peace psychologists have only begun to use television for purposes of sensitization, in part because war is more sensational and the communications industry has reflected the priorities and values of the war system. Many psychologists are wary because they have had their material misused or have been uncomfortable reducing complex issues into "sound bites." Some harbor negative stereotypes of media they see as having helped to normalize violence and social inequities. Others struggle with ethical issues, fearing, for example, that interviews conducted on camera with victims in war zones may violate confidentiality or jeopardize the security or the community acceptance of interviewees.

Although these complexities warrant careful attention, they should not be allowed to exercise a chilling effect. Many of the problems can be addressed through careful preparation and by working with psychological organizations, subjecting ideas to be presented on camera to peer review. The transformation of public media is an essential part of building cultures of peace, and peace psychologists should do their part to criticize inappropriate media imagery and the misuse of psychological material, to get peace and social justice issues on the media agenda, and to encourage programming that encourages values, attitudes, and behaviors conducive to cultures of peace.

Consultation

Psychologists are often asked to provide expert advice at different social levels in addressing issues of social justice and peace. To improve race relations, communities may look to psychologists for help in analyzing problems, moderating dialogues, designing and conducting research, or developing and implementing strategies of intervention and prevention. Similarly, schools that want to improve gender equity or to address problems of violence may look to peace psychologists for advice. Not infrequently, psychologists are called upon to give expert legal testimony on issues such as the psychological damage inflicted by family and community violence, the community impacts of nuclear weapons development and testing, or the effects of gender discrimination in the workplace. Systematic work at different social levels, even if conducted with little public attention, is needed to build cultures of peace.

Since building peace is a global project and injustices within one country are frequently interconnected with injustices in other countries and regions, it is vital for peace psychologists to work internationally. In addition, many countries, ravaged by long histories of colonialism, poverty, and war, require external assistance. Global work on humanitarian assistance, peace, and sustainable development is often conducted by governmental organizations, NGOs, and United Nations (U.N.) agencies, which frequently receive financial support from donor governments and agencies such as the U.S. Agency for International Development.

Consultation within the U.N./NGO system constitutes an increasingly important venue for peace psychologists working to make a difference in the public arena. Indeed, significant numbers of psychologists serve as consultants to international and local NGOs on projects such as addressing war trauma, making women more central in development projects, providing psychosocial support and care for refugee and internally displaced peoples, and reconstructing communities for peace, to name only a few. On the ground, psychologists often provide consultation and services via training, education, program design, evaluation, and human rights monitoring. Psychologists also advise via NGO committees to the United Nations and by working directly with particular U.N. agencies. Here psychologists may help to develop appropriate standards, integrate psychosocial perspectives and establish comprehensive programs of development, and offer psychologically informed criticism of U.N. activities.

Significant risks centered around power and culture attend consultation efforts. Because of the dominance of Euro-American psychology, most consultants have Western training and have Ph.D. degrees, which carry significant prestige in the developing world. Typically, they enter difficult situations as consultants for international NGOs or U.N. agencies that provide money, food, health care, housing, and other resources. Because of extreme poverty and enormous human needs locally, a significant power asymmetry exists between local communities and the psychologists and the agencies for which they work (Wessells & Kostelny, 1996). In this context, local people may be excessively deferential to the external "experts" and may either embrace or give the appearance of embracing the methods and projects they suggest. Eager to avoid appearing backward, local people may not mention or may keep on the margins centuries-old practices that could contribute to psychosocial well-being in the community. This situation marginalizes local voices and continues the injustices of class, wealth, power, and ethnicity that are deeply embedded in global North-South relations.

Thus, psychology can become a tool of cultural imperialism (Dawes, 1997; Wessells, 1998) that derogates local culture and undermines traditions that might provide a sense of continuity and support under difficult circumstances. The sad irony, of course, is that Western-derived concepts and tools, although useful in many settings, may not apply "off the shelf." Embodiments of Western cultural assumptions and values, these concepts and tools may not fit local beliefs, values, and practices, severely limiting both their efficacy and their sustainability. As one example, Giller (1998) tells of having been invited to Uganda in the late 1980s to set up a center for victims of torture. Although her Western background led to a focus on trauma, she soon realized that poverty was the larger problem, that "trauma" in that context correlated poorly with social function, and that individualized counseling approaches were culturally inappropriate. Wisely, she decided to learn from local people and to develop culturally grounded approaches.

Giller's example points out the importance of working self-critically in a collabo-rative spirit of dialogue and power sharing. Aware of the potential problems, Western consultants may temper the hierarchical role of "experts" who presumably hold solutions to difficult problems, opting instead for a role of partnership in addressing difficult issues. This role entails careful listening to local people, learning about local customs, regarding local people and traditions as resources, and encouragement of local leadership and ownership of programs. The emphasis is on building local capacity and culturally relevant interventions rather than on seeking external solutions to problems. Working in this partnership mode, consultation is a process of mutual dialogue and problem-solving. This approach is at the heart of community-based programs (see Wessells & Monteiro, this volume). It is also at the center of the Culture of Peace Programme (cf. Adams, 1995) of UNESCO (the U.N. Educational, Scientific, and Cultural Organization), which laid the foundation for the International Year of the Culture of Peace in 2000.

Activism

Activism is a process of mobilizing people for action, where the action may support a particular position (e.g., writing Congress-people in support of a Comprehensive Test Ban) or may be nonpositionally oriented (e.g., urging people to vote in the next U.S. presidential election). Activism is central to the project of social change since public mobilization is often needed to move leaders towards actions that help to build peace and social justice. Without public support, leaders may feel constrained politically from peace-promoting steps toward which they may be inclined personally.

Peace psychology stands to contribute much to projects of activism to build cultures of peace. Psychologists have a wealth of relevant tools and concepts pertaining to attitude change, motivation, nonviolent options, and organization, among many others, that can be used to assist the work of peace organizations (Wollman, 1985). Psychologists are in a position to build understanding of activism, of how to empower people and keep them involved in the face of adversity, and of what leads to activism within the system or outside of it (Schwebel, 1993). In addition, peace psychologists may offer key insights that help to mobilize people on particular issues. For example, the work of White (1984), Deutsch (1983), Bronfenbrenner (1961), Keen (1986), Silverstein (1989) and others suggested that processes of excessive fear, enemy imaging, and related problems of misperception and judgmental biases made the policy of nuclear deterrence imperfect and dangerous. Via networks with peace organizations and the Enemy Images Project of Psychologists for Social Responsibility (PsySR), which produced the manual *Dismantling the Mask of Enmity,* these insights entered public dialogue. The psychological critique of nuclear deterrence was not universally accepted, but it did contribute to public discourse, an important form of action without which leaders are potentially at liberty to engage in folly (Tuchman, 1984). Similarly, during the Cold War, psychologists worked to mobilize people in discussing the nuclear threat and its implications for families (e.g., Greenwald & Zeitlin, 1987), communities (Albee, 1992; Pilisuk & Parks, 1986), and for nations and civilizations (Jacobs, 1989; Mack, 1982; White, 1984). This strategy of stimulating critical discourse at multiple levels is essential for enabling large-scale social change.

An important form of activism by peace psychologists is the construction of effective psychological organizations. These organizations mobilize their own discipline for peace with regard to structure and activities such as research, training, education, and practice. Historically, activist psychology organizations in the United States included the Committee on Psychology in National and International Affairs, the SPSSI Committee on Arms Control and Disarmament, and American Psychologists for Social Action (Jacobs, 1989). The work of the Society for the Study of Peace, Conflict, and Violence: Peace Psychology Division of the American Psychological Association (Division 48) helps to build social justice within the world's largest psychological association and also encourages psychologists to do their share in building peace both locally and globally. Related peace psychology organizations exist in many different countries, and one of the key tasks of activating psychology for peace is to build effective networks among these organizations (Harari, 1992; Wessells, 1992). To assist in building these networks, the Committee for the Psychological Study of Peace, which works under the auspices of the International Union of Psychological Science, convenes biennially an International Symposium on the Contributions of Psychology to Peace.

In guiding action in the wider public arena, activist organizations are significant in defining the issues, deciding what to say, whom to target, etc. For the past 15 years, PsySR, facilitated by its national coordinator, Anne Anderson, has been the activist arm of psychology in the United States. Although PsySR works extensively on peacebuilding and prevention (e.g., its current main project is Building Cultures of Peace), it has also served as a rapid-response network that attempts to bring forward the best psychological knowledge in times of crisis. When a hot issue such as the Gulf Crisis of 1991 arises, PsySR begins an inclusive dialogue within its national Steering Committee and Advisory Board, which includes distinguished psychologists possessing diverse orientations. It also launches an intensive search through its international networks for issue-relevant expertise. This process targets key issues, identifies what is known and what is not, and often leads to a position that takes into account diverse viewpoints and the collective wisdom of many professionals. In this manner, PsySR speaks for many psychologists and potentially has an impact beyond that achievable by individuals acting alone.

Education for peace, which is not an armchair endeavor but a process of education and mobilizing people for peace (Brocke-Utne, 1989), is of central importance in activism. Peace education in schools is valuable and draws significantly on psychological concepts and tools (Coleman & Deutsch, this volume). But education for peace also includes informal education, including learning by doing and social action. Psychologists stand to contribute significantly to this multi-level work through activities such as conducting community-based training to oppose racism (as in the PsySR "US & THEM: The Challenge of Diversity" project), developing effective facilitated processes that improve communication about controversial subjects, encouraging parents' groups to speak out on the quantity and graphic nature of violence on television (Hesse, 1989; Carlsson-Paige & Levin, 1990), and mobilizing to improve the status of women, such as participating in the follow-up to the fourth U.N. Conference on Women to implement the National Action Agenda (Stanley Foundation, 1997).

Influencing Policy

Peace psychologists have a number of important roles to play in regard to public policy. As researchers, they may conduct policy-relevant research that helps to inform policy decisions (Suedfeld & Tetlock, 1992; Tet-

lock, 1986). In the role of the local opposition and using the cultures of peace elements outlined above as a compass, they may offer psychologically informed critiques of existing policies, discuss problems of current policies with policy leaders, or help to *mobilize public opposition* to psychologically damaging policies (DeLeon, O'Keefe, VandenBos, & Kraut, 1996).

Psychologists may also serve as monitors, reporting on social injustice and human rights abuses that they see in their field work and that stem from particular policies. This monitoring role is particularly important in regard to the *abuse of psychological knowledge and tools.* For example, repeated field reports and recently declassified documents suggest that Latin American military personnel, trained in the United States at the School of the Americas in Fort Benning, Georgia, had committed numerous atrocities and had also used psychological methods for purposes of interrogation and torture. Although peace psychologists diverge in their views on the necessity for and utility of covert operations, wide agreement exists that it is unethical to use psychological tools for purposes of torture. Ethical issues of this nature outstrip the guild codes of ethics of most professional associations such as the American Psychological Association. In this context, it is vital for peace psychologists to monitor and report publicly on abuses observed, to educate policy makers about the damage inflicted by psychological torture, and to work within the discipline to oppose the development of psychological instruments of torture and to encourage psychologists to be vigilant in regard to how their methods are actually used (Psychologists for Social Responsibility, 1997). Psychologists' responsibilities do not end with the development of psychological tools.

Policy advocacy is an essential element of work toward cultures of peace. In some cases, peace psychologists can advocate policies that are based upon established psychological knowledge. For example, to assist Angolan children who had been separated from parents or who were "orphans," the Angolan government had developed by 1994, a practice of placing unaccompanied children in institutions or orphanages, which operated under extreme conditions of poverty, overcrowding, and understaffing. An extensive psychological literature attests to the ill effects of rearing children in such institutions, where inattention and lack of stimulation are prevalent (Bowlby, 1979). Accordingly, the Angolan psychological staff of Christian Children's Fund advocated publicly in meetings with Angolan government officials on behalf of scaling back on institutionalizing children while using precious funds for purposes of documentation, tracing, and family reunification. In Angola, extended family is nearly always available for assisting children, and families are in the best position to provide an environment conducive to children's healthy psychosocial development. Fortunately, the Angolan government had a genuine interest in children's well-being, and this advocacy contributed to a national deemphasis on institutionalization of children.

Policy advocacy within the United States is of special importance since the U.S. government has powerful influence worldwide and has resources that can make a difference in many regions. Arguably, U.S. government policies have contributed strongly to war and injustice in many parts of the world as well as to social injustice within U.S. borders. During the Cold War, for example, the U.S. military expenditures were approximately $300 billion annually, and such vast defense spending drained scarce resources away from meeting widespread needs for health care, housing, and employment (Sivard, 1986). In fact, the United States has spent more on nuclear weapons since 1940 than on all other budget cate-

gories besides Social Security and nonnuclear defense, according to a Brookings Institution report. Total cost since 1940 in nuclear weapons and infrastructure is $5.5 trillion (as of 1996, adjusted for inflation; see Schwartz, 1998).

To strengthen emphasis on peace, psychologists such as Paul Kimmel, the first APA Public Policy Fellow, advocated on behalf of the establishment of a U.S. Institute of Peace (USIP), which could enhance national security through the development and application of concepts and tools of nonviolent conflict resolution. Kimmel "has attributed the concepts formulated by Jerome Frank, Charles Osgood, Morton Deutsch, and Ralph K. White in the sixties as those which laid the foundation of the Peace Academy Campaign" (Jacobs, 1989, p. 80) that culminated in the establishment of the USIP. The expertise of distinguished psychologists such as Herbert Kelman (1996) is now prominent in USIP-sponsored books, conferences, and policy dialogues.

Work on public policy faces difficult issues of how to make a difference, what can be said, which issues to focus on, etc. As discussed above in connection with activism, one may address these issues by working through socially responsible organizations that have credibility and provide peer review and inclusive dialogue. A persistent problem in this work is the focus on crises, which are omnipresent. Although perhaps too much has been made of the "CNN effect," it is true that public attention and the work of peace psychology organizations has tended to track the hottest crises. As one example, work on nuclear weapons policies within peace psychology and the wider peace community diminished following the end of the Cold War. But the 1998 nuclear testing and tensions between India and Pakistan put these policies back in the spotlight. The problem, one that peace psychologists ought to attend to, is that nuclear policies and threats are long-term and are associated with related issues of weapons development, cultural, political, and economic militarization, and problems of conversion and unemployment, to name only a few. If policy work is to be an effective means of prevention, this work itself must have a long-term, systems orientation toward analysis and change.

Issues of culture and power also pose significant challenges. For example, who determines what constitutes human rights? As recognized in the Universal Declaration on Human Rights, it is vital to have global standards for protection. In practice, however, Western nations have led the dialogue on "human rights," leading to collisions between Western values and those of local people in non-Western cultures. The world's most widely endorsed human rights instrument—the *UN Convention on the Rights of the Child (CRC)*—prohibits the military recruitment of youth under 15 years of age, and most signatories of the CRC support an Optional Protocol to boost the minimum age to 18 years. Intended to prohibit the exploitation of children through soldiering, this limit embodies Western definitions of childhood. In many Bantu cultures in Africa, a young male of twelve or 13 years is regarded as an adult following passage through the culturally scripted rites of manhood (Wessells, 1998). This case and many others raise issues about who defines childhood and whether it is appropriate to impose universal standards on local peoples.

Although these issues admit no easy answers, two points are particularly noteworthy. First, against concerns about cultural imperialism, one must weigh the need for moral accountability and the importance of avoiding extreme *cultural relativism,* which can create an "anything goes" mentality. For example, some local practices such as female infanticide are unacceptable to the vast majority of peoples and need to change. Second, full participation and ongoing dialogue are essential in the construction of policy standards. Social injustice arises when any small group of nations sets the human rights agenda or limits participation in the construction of policies. Standards and policies are dynamic, and full participation helps to ensure that they will evolve in ways that advance social justice and peace. Thus psychologists have a responsibility to advance this inclusive, participatory dialogue in their own work in the policy arena.

TOWARD THE FUTURE

A glimpse at the past shows great promise for peace in the future and considerable need for the services of psychologists in nurturing cultures of peace. The twentieth century has no equal in the blood that has been spilt and in a record of being the most inhumane in history, with a trail of warfare directed at civilian targets, atrocities against women and children, extreme racism, and ethnic slaughter and genocide.

Alongside that lurid history is another, its diametric opposite, a record that reveals a steadily rising trajectory toward the peaceful resolution of conflict, culminating in its last decade in the drive to transform a culture of war to a culture of peace. The century has witnessed the establishment of the first international organizations aimed at the maintenance of world peace, the League of Nations and the United Nations. The latter has endured many trials, outlasted predictions of its early demise, and appears, now at the dawn of the twenty-first century, to be a permanent feature of global life.

Most strikingly has been the change in the consciousness of people and in their collective actions. The helplessness of adults has been displaced by the power of people all over the world who insisted on their independence, as in India and former colonies throughout Africa. In much of the world, as in the United States, oppressed people, including women, have demanded equality, and many have won a share of it. And worldwide, most people have rejected, and demonstrated and voted against, the nuclear arms race. That is why the concept of "cultures of peace" has such wide appeal.

Not surprisingly, during the half century that has seen the rapid rise of the peace trajectory, psychologists have increasingly participated in efforts to introduce peaceful means of conflict resolution in family and community life, in organizations and institutions, and in national and international af-

fairs. There is increasing appreciation that peace is systemic and that the construction of peace requires efforts at various levels such as marital counseling, community dispute resolution, interethnic mediation, and international diplomacy.

What is called for now, all the more, is the creative genius of psychology to generate new approaches to propel the transformation to cultures of peace. There is, at the same time, the need for psychologists in virtually all of its many fields—e.g., developmental, cognitive, clinical, counseling, educational, organizational—to situate their theory, research and practice in such a culture.

Conclusion: Peace Psychology for the Twenty-First Century

Deborah Du Nann Winter, Daniel J. Christie,
Richard V. Wagner, and Laura B. Boston

Peace psychology at the turn of the millennium has greatly expanded since its inception during the Cold War. With the collapse of the Soviet Union in the early 1990s, the planet's bipolar international organization changed dramatically, as did the nature of war. The dyadic relationship between two superpowers no longer captures the psychological complexity of armed conflict in its many forms. At the beginning of the new millennium, war is no longer a matter of ideological struggle between two rival economic systems, and the global system of nation/states is no longer viewed as a set of dominoes falling to one side or another. War is not even primarily a matter of interstate conflict, since the vast majority of wars are fought within states. Instead of traditional military theaters with emphasis on extended deterrence and defense of borders (see Introduction), armed violence is now ubiquitous, occurring not only in jungles and villages, but in urban streets (see Kostelney & Garbarino, this volume), and households of all economic classes (see Abrahams, this volume).

As the settings for armed conflict have expanded, so has the number of victims increased. War-related deaths, especially to civilians, have steadily grown throughout the twentieth century. An average of twelve wars per year were conducted in 1950s; by the 1980s that figure had risen to 40 (Renner, 1999). Concomitantly, civilians have borne an increasing proportion of deaths from war (see Table 1). As Wessells, Schwebel, and Anderson (this volume) have noted, the twentieth century is clearly the bloodiest on record.

The twentieth century also ushered in new levels of affluence and an enlargement of choices for some people, and new levels of deprivation with a narrowing of choices for many

Table 1   Largest Armed Conflicts since 1945 (from Renner, 1999, p. 17)

Conflict	Time Period	Number Killed (thousand)	Civilian Victims (percent)
China (civil war)	1946–1950	1,000	50
N. vs. S. Korea (international intervention)	1950–1953	3,000	50
N. vs. S. Vietnam (United States intervention)	1960–1975	2,358	58
Nigeria (Biafra civil war)	1967–1970	2,000	50
Cambodia (civil war; foreign intervention)	1970–1989	1,221	69
Bangladesh (secession from Pakistan)	1971	1,000	50
Afghanistan (Soviet intervention)	1978–1992	1,500	67
Mozambican (civil war)	1981–1994	1,050	95
Sudan (civil war)	1984–present	1,500	97

others. As we begin the twenty-first century, peace psychology is confronting the structural roots of direct violence. Many forms of direct violence can be traced to structure-based inequalities, exacerbated by ethnic tensions, environmental degradation, and economic desperation, which powerful leaders exploit (Hauchler & Kennedy, 1994; Homer-Dixon, 1993; Renner, 1996).

But the twentieth century in general, and the last few decades in particular, presented unprecedented opportunities for peace, and demonstrated some impressive accomplishments in peacemaking, peacekeeping, and peacebuilding. For example, the world has been astonished by the *peacemaking* achieved by South Africa in its relatively nonviolent end to apartheid; by the "velvet revolution" of the Czech Republic; and in the relatively bloodless process in which the Soviet Union dissolved into independent nations. In international *peacekeeping*, the United Nations was established in 1945 and has taken an increasingly important role in protecting peace agreements in the last decade (see Langholtz & Leentjes, this volume). The United Nations's *peacebuilding* efforts are even more extensive, including human rights conventions, and agencies which promote education, health, and sustainable development (see below). Meanwhile, the world witnessed the proliferation of non-governmental organizations (NGOs) which give representation and voice to a wider spectrum of citizen needs; the establishment of women's suffrage and civil rights; the growth of democracy; the promotion of compulsory education; and a general improvement in the quality of life for the average world citizen. Paradoxically, *both* the omnipresence of armed violence, and the prospects for peace, have never been greater than at the turn of the millenium.

FOUR-WAY MODEL

In this book, we have attempted to map the vast expansion of topics in peace psychology with a four-way model. Our model distinguishes direct from indirect violence, and direct from indirect peace. For example, forms of direct violence such as genocide (see Staub, this volume), domestic violence (see Abrahams, this volume), hate crimes (see Murphy, this volume), and ethnic violence (Niens & Cairns, this volume) are salient and episodic. But indirect structural violence, such as global economic oppression of third world citizens (see Pilisuk, this volume), violations of indigenous rights (see Lykes, this volume), and excessive militarization (see Britton, this volume; Winter, Pilisuk, Houck, & Lee, this volume) is chronic and insidious.

On the peace side, we have differentiated direct peacemaking from indirect peacebuilding. Conflict resolution and mediation techniques (see Sanson & Bretherton, this volume; Coleman & Deutsch, this volume), and peacekeeping (see Langholtz & Leentjes, this volume) create peace directly, whereas peacebuilding is a long term process of restructuring society's institutions to reduce oppression and create equality. Peacebuilding will require increasing rather than decreasing tension (see Montiel, this volume), redressing poverty (see Dawes, this volume), and the large scale project of building cultures of peace (see Wessells, Schwebel, & Anderson, this volume).

While our model allows us to map a vast terrain of topics under these four categories, there are, of course, many topics which we have failed to include, simply because no one single volume can include everything. Notably missing are the issue of terrorism and how it impacts national security (White, 1998), the problem of media violence and how it feeds a culture of violence (Bok, 1998), reemerging fascism and militia movements (Lee, 1997), warlords (Reno, 1999), the psycholinguistics of language which lead to conflict and violence (Tannen, 1998), the problematic marketing of light weapons (Renner, 1998), and arms control (Renner, 1994).

Furthermore, by assigning our chapters to these four sections, we have stressed the distinctions rather than the connections between categories. But we also realize that our distinctions are often more conceptual than concrete. Direct and structural violence are reciprocal processes, in that they exacerbate each other. Peacemaking will not last long if peacebuilding isn't also addressed, and most forms of violence have both direct and structural features. Direct violence usually stems from structural violence because structured inequalities are predisposing conditions for outbreaks of violent episodes.

For example, we can understand incidences of neighborhood violence as an integrated system of direct and structural violence. In April of 1999, two boys from Columbine High School in Colorado, United States, killed twelve students and one teacher. These boys were widely known among their classmates as social outcasts. The brutality and scope of this massacre led many to focus on the psychopathology of the two perpetrators, and we certainly do not deny their emotional distress. But noting the systemic ways in which structural violence and direct violence interact leads us also to examine the adolescent subculture of high schools in the United States, where athletes rank much higher than non-athletes in status, respect, and popularity. Taunting and social isolation are forms of structural violence and often lead to anger, resentment, and direct violence. The U.S. economy, which makes guns easily available to children, enabled these boys to translate their fantasies of revenge and their frustration with the school's differential power structure into direct violence with dire consequences.

As this example clearly demonstrates, indirect structural violence and direct violence are highly interdependent. Social injustices fuel social unrest, often leading to a "malignant spiral of hostile interaction," to borrow an image from Deutsch's (1983) analysis of the nuclear arms race. Attempts to halt violent conflict require recognition that opponents' needs must be met if long-term solutions are to be successful.

PEACE PSYCHOLOGY: TENSIONS IN THE TWENTY-FIRST CENTURY

Our model implies several tensions that will shape peace psychology in the coming years. These tensions include activism vs. analysis, univeralism vs. relativism, proaction vs. reaction, and peaceful means vs. peaceful ends. We phrase these issues as tensions because they operate as dilemmas, where it is difficult to maximize both ends at the same time. Let us elaborate what we mean in each case.

Activism vs. Analysis

We believe that lasting peace requires active political confrontation against socially unjust institutions and traditions. Until human needs are met on a fairly equitable basis, prospects for peace will be slim. Our call to confront social injustice is a controversial (though not original) plea to psychologists. The bylaws of the American Psychological Association state that the APA exists to promote human welfare (APA Bylaws I.1, *http://www.apa.org/about/mission.html*). Throughout psychology's history, great thinkers have urged us to find ways to alleviate human suffering. George Miller admonished us to "give psychology away" (1969). B. F. Skinner (1971) believed that psychology should be applied to solve humankind's pressing problems. More recently, George Albee (1996, 1998) argued that prevention of mental illness and distress requires psychologists to address the economic and political structures that create suffering, especially poverty. And most recently, Martin Seligman's APA Presidential Initiative on ethno-political conflict focused psychologists' attention on what we can do to "understand, predict, and even prevent such warfare" (1998, p. 2).

Just as practice and science constitute the larger discipline of psychology, we assert that peace psychology should be based on both activism and analysis. While the idea of political activism is not new, psychology students are not currently trained to practice and pursue it. Political participation is left to individual choice, rather than programmatic design, as if the political actions of psychologists are irrelevant to their work. Little wonder, then, that the voice of psychology is seldom heard by political leaders (Blight, 1987).

Will psychologists apply our knowledge to confront and change unjust social institutions? Because public policy is a psychological issue, we believe that students should be trained how to think about, research, lobby, and affect peace. We agree with Dawes (this volume) that peace is a political process and psychologists cannot abdicate the political dimension of our work. Our roles as scientists do not require us to remain politically neutral. Science itself is value laden; feigning neutrality is intellectually dishonest and socially irresponsible.

Thus, for several reasons, we believe that peace psychologists should be activists. First, because peace cannot wait until all the data are in; second, because we learn from our ideas as we apply them; third, because we are likely to be better practitioners if we simultaneously test our ideas. Just as the Boulder Model (Raimy, 1950) urges that clinicians base their practices on the process of science, so do we as peace psychologists see the importance of empirical research in providing foundations for our work as practitioners.

Universalism vs. Relativism

Political activism brings with it the complicated question of universal values. To what extent can we assume that our claims about human rights and our conception of the elements of "cultures of peace" (see Wessells, Schwebel, & Anderson, this volume) are universal? We recognize that a great risk in doing peace psychology is that most psychologists are trained in a particular culture and Zeitgeist that supports capitalism and Western-style democracies (see Dawes, this volume). If we naively ignore our own situated, arbitrary, and limited worldview, we undermine our own effectiveness, as well as those we attempt to help (see Agger, and Pederson, this volume). The planet has watched the rapid spread of Western traditions and values during the last few centuries (see Pilisuk, this volume). Peace psychologists must be careful to avoid the colonial process of replacing traditional cultures with Western assumptions that promulgate capitalism and democracy as the only legitimate economic and political models of social organization.

Our discussion of structural violence assumes that equality and human rights are both universal values. But many values are not universally shared and we risk being ethnocentric as we articulate our values. For example, people in patriarchal societies assume that men deserve more resources than women (see Mazurana & McKay, this volume) and feminists who promote equality between the sexes are frequently seen as ethnocentrically operating through a narrowly Western set of lenses. In countries like China, where governments cope with huge numbers of people, human rights are not embraced, and those Westerners who raise questions about human rights are called ethnocentric. Some African cultures endorse involuntary clitorectomy, the surgical removal of young women's sexual organ. Although we risk being called ethnocentric, we believe that enforced annihilation of female sexuality is wrong. Similarly, we believe that equitable distribution of human resources is a necessary step for creating peace, even though we recognize that many, both inside and outside our culture, would disagree with us.

To what extent is the promotion of equality and human needs in our definition a product of our naïve ethnocentrism? This difficult question defies easy answers. We cannot blithely assume that our definition is universal, but we cannot abandon the project of defining values simply because they are difficult to generalize and we are afraid of overstating our terms. All we can do is promote one definition as the best we have right now, staying aware of the risks involved in putting it forward, and assuming that we will learn more about how to improve it. Building peace requires us to take some uncomfortable stands: to practice activism alongside analysis, and to sincerely embrace and promote certain values, while continuously investigating the appropriateness of their universal application.

Pro-action vs. Reaction

Closely related to the activism issue is the question of pro-action vs. reaction. From the outset, peace psychology was reactive, originating in the 1980s as a reaction to the Cold War and the threat of nuclear annihilation. Reactive approaches to peace focus on violence which either breaks out, or seems imminent. In contrast, proactive approaches aim at the pursuit of social justice, the mitigation of oppressive and exploitative structures that can be predisposing conditions for episodes of direct violence. Proactive approaches treat peace and social justice as indivisible, and take a long view of peace, committing resources to social changes that embrace the principles of equity and inclusion (Wagner, 1988). Given the reactive origins of peace psychology, will we be distracted in the future whenever major violent episodes occur? Or will peace psychologists also fix their attention on the structural roots of violent episodes, and take a long range view to the project of building peace?

Peaceful Means vs. Peaceful Ends

Although every author who addressed the issue of social justice endorsed the value of pursuing socially just ends, there is less consensus in peace psychology on whether the means toward peaceful ends should always be nonviolent. In the present volume, Wessells, Schwebel and Anderson point out that while nonviolence is a value in peace psychology, some peace psychologists (for example, White, 1998) find force necessary under certain conditions. In contrast, the Gandhian perspective, as articulated in the chapters by Steger and Mayton, endorses not only socially just ends, but peaceful means. Gandhi's view explicitly rejected violence of any kind. From his perspective, means and ends could be distinguished conceptually and temporally, but not morally (Ostergaard, 1990).

In the current volume, Montiel also endorses using only nonviolent means and notes that when violence is used, the actors merely switch roles in the dominant-subservient relationship. Both Steger and Montiel point out that nonviolence requires courage, and when used with commitment, is a powerful technique which produces change. Although peace psychologists do not endorse violence, they differ in the degree to which they see nonviolence crucial for effecting peace.

CHALLENGES FOR THE TWENTY-FIRST CENTURY

Our treatment of peace psychology via this four-way model means that peace psychologists will be challenged in important ways. Because peace is not a simple, unidimensional process, peace psychologists in the twenty-first century need to analyze conflict systemically, examine multiple levels of analysis, transform peace education, and work on building sustainable communities. We discuss these challenges one by one.

Peace Psychologists as Systems Analysts and Practitioners

One implication of our model is that the interface between direct and indirect peace and violence prompts peace psychologists to inquire about both aspects in any conflict situation. Individuals will likely have preferences and training that lead them to give priority to one dimension over the other. Indeed, as a field, psychology trains its students to disregard the structural features of societies, in favor of focusing on individual responses to them (Sampson, 1983, 1993). For example, because most high school students are not outcasts and do not go on killing rampages, both the media and psychologists can easily focus on the individual psychopathology of those who do. Psychologists can no longer afford to work *simply* on the individual level, though of course, they are particularly well-trained to address individual responses. Long-term solutions require that we illuminate the systemic connections between direct and indirect levels of violence as well as between individuals and their communities. Treating only the individual's reactions to social injustice is analogous to fixing a flood by removing a teaspoon of water at a time, instead of shunting the water off at its source.

Building peace and ending conflict in the twenty-first century require that we begin to notice the ethnocentric bias of traditional Western psychology. In most developing countries, where collectivist thinking is more common than individualist thinking, Western psychology's excessive individualism makes it unsuitable for application (Moghaddam, 1987; Sloan, 1990). For example, reconstruction after war in African societies (see Wessells & Monteiro, this volume), as well as in Latin America (Lykes, this volume; also, Lykes, 1999) requires that psychology address community structures which give meaning to individual identity. Thus, the individual cannot be separated from the collective.

Pushing the Limits of our Knowledge: The Levels of Analysis Problem

Addressing both direct and structural features returns us to the question of how well we can generalize from individuals to families, communities, nations, and societies. As we noted in the Introduction, peace psychology during the Cold War tended to ignore levels of analysis, and presumed that processes that apply to individuals generalize easily to larger units, such as social groups and nations. The bipolar world of two superpowers vying for prestige and security invited psychologists to think about the Cold War as a bad dyadic relationship: ineffective communication resulted from distorted perceptions, giving rise to mirrored enemy images (White, 1984). These phenomena were observed between the Soviet Union and the United States, just as they were between distressed couples.

In the post–Cold War world, however, we are invited to question whether principles of dyadic relationships can be generalized to other levels of analysis. Rubin and Levinger (1995) listed some important differences between couples and nations. First, international conflict tends to involve more than two parties and more than one issue, clearly challenging the dichotomized Cold War view. Second, unlike conflict in marriages and friendships, international conflict offers no opportunity for exit—countries can't divorce each other the way spouses can. Third, chronic power asymmetries tend to endure in international systems; a small, newly independent nation can't ask for the equivalent of "spousal support" because its economy suffers the disadvantages of a century or more of colonial exploitation. Because of these dissimilarities, international relations tend to be less fluid than interpersonal relationships. Communication difficulties are compounded by cultural differences, bureaucratic inertia, and lessened opportunity for trust.

Clearly, families, neighborhoods, high schools and embassies have different levels of complexity, different sets of competing values, different degrees of flexibility, and different opportunities for face-to-face contact. Yet, the premise of our book suggests that examining peace and conflict across these domains yields important insights. In particular, we posit that the chapters here demonstrate the importance of considering human needs across levels of analysis. Although countries are different from families, human needs operate in both units. If India and Pakistan are locked in an arms race, their needs for national security in the face of their neighbor's threat, and their needs for prestige in the world community, are comparable to a street gang's need to defend its territory and reputation. Both sets of players portray the human need for security and respect, and violence can be expected until those needs are satisfied.

On the other hand, it is also true that some phenomena cannot be generalized, and we must not ignore crucial differences that have an impact on our ability to facilitate peace in larger units of analysis. The bigger the unit of analysis, the more complicated and difficult is the resolution of conflict because of the heterogeneous constituencies whose interests are at stake in any decision (Kelman, 1999). Nevertheless, we claim that conflict and war are human behaviors that have human needs at their root. Our ability to track differences between levels is aided by attention to the psychological needs that various groups carry. We will say more about the importance of considering human needs in the final section of this chapter.

Transforming Peace Education: From Conflict Resolution to Societal Transformation

Traditional approaches in peace psychology have focused on conflict resolution and nonviolence. But to the extent that conflict resolution eclipses power differences, peace psychology will unwittingly contribute to the status quo, colluding with social injustice. In contrast, if peace psychology develops emancipatory aspirations, we join other pedagogies that address the empowerment of the oppressed. Peace psychology has much to learn from liberatory pedagogies, the central purpose of which is the empowerment of individuals and communities to challenge and change the world rather than adapt to unjust situations (Freire, 1993; Martín-Baró, 1994).

Transforming peace education to address social justice presents challenges. First, there may be little consensus about what constitutes social justice, in which case, the most productive education might result from simply raising issues, pointing to social injustice in settings where the topic has never been raised before(see Opotow, this volume). Second, the education process is a multilevel enterprise, in which student culture, pedagogy, administrative decisions, and community values are relevant (see Coleman & Deutsch, this volume). Changes at one level, if they are at all substantive, will likely affect other levels and constituents. For example, if a public school teacher unilaterally introduces a peace education segment in a social studies course, especially a segment that focuses on social injustice, questions about values and politics are likely to come from parents, administrators, and community members. The problem is that a curriculum that attempts to transform peace education to address issues of social justice is itself embedded in socially unjust structures of society.

Promoting Sustainable Communities and the Satisfaction of Human Needs

Because we see the equitable satisfaction of human needs as a crucial element of effective peacebuilding, we close our discussion by examining the long-term prognosis for peace as a function of building sustainable cultures. Instead of assuming that military muscle will deliver peace, we find that it often leads to violence and war. Rather than focusing simply on national security, peacebuilding in the twenty-first century will require that we pay careful attention to human security, and to our sustainable potential to satisfy human needs.

As the planet industrializes, hope for a better life becomes available for billions of people. At the same time however, we are quickly approaching the earth's carrying capacity. Key limits in the twenty-first century will be fresh water, range-lands, forests, oceanic fisheries, biological diversity, and the global atmosphere (Brown & Flavin, 1999). As Homer-Dixon (1993) and Renner (1996) have both shown, ecological stresses are common causes of armed conflict around the world, and we can expect wars to increase as environments continue to deteriorate. Indeed, some have made a persuasive case for the proposition that in the twenty-first century, environmental security will replace national security as a primary strategy for preventing war (Myers, 1993). Environmental security requires international cooperation because ecological damage does not respect national borders. Global treaties to protect environmental indicators will become as important as military alliances are now.

Education is crucial for building environmental security. Limiting population growth depends on education, since research has shown that minimal schooling for girls (fourth grade or above) is the best predictor of lowered fertility rates (Jacobson, 1992). Education for more extensive "ecological literacy" (Orr, 1992) is making progress in developing as well as industrialized nations. Ecological literacy requires that we educate in order to connect and integrate knowledge about the physical world with the decisions we make in our social institutions and personal lives. Ecological education means helping people assume responsibility and consciousness about the environmental impacts of their own households, organizations, governments, and militaries. A peaceful world will require a populace educated for civic life, committed to environmental responsibility, and determined to build a peaceful world.

Crucial in this regard is the growing importance of grassroots peacebuilding (see Pilisuk, this volume). Education does not necessarily have to move from the top down. "Bottom-up" information sharing, through non-governmental organizations (NGOs) and grassroots groups, can be just as effective, if not more, than government-approved educational programs. In many nations, NGOs and local groups are working together to effect change and create both sustainable societies and peace.

There are many paths to peace: arms reduction and gun control, guaranteed livable wage, a stronger United Nations willing and able to intervene in early signal situations, a World Court to try war criminals, a powerful international agency for dispute mediation, effective and sophisticated peacekeeping forces. But we highlight the dimension of sustainable development here, for unless we learn to build sustainable cultures, the world cannot expect to see lasting peace. Natural resource scarcity will lead to war in the twenty-first century even more often than it has led to war in previous centuries; as population continues to increase and resources become increasingly rare and unevenly distributed, conflict over them will become more frequent and intense. Human security is, in the long run, environmental security. We will never build lasting peace until we design cultures that sustain themselves without oppressing either their neighbors or their progeny.

CONCLUSION

In conclusion, peace psychologists, as well as citizens around the world, are recognizing that peace depends on ending poverty and making a commitment to justice and insuring environmental security. Meeting human needs in the twenty-first century means that we begin building sustainable cultures immediately. Human security will require our best creativity, commitment, compassion, and idealism. It will also require that we continually ask difficult questions about activism vs. analysis, universalism vs. relativism, pro-action vs. reaction, levels of analysis, nonviolent means and ends, and sustainable use and distribution of resources.

Peace psychologists can provide important leadership, analysis, activism, and support for the crucial task of building sustainable peace. Analyzing the causes of violence, rebuilding war-torn communities, lobbying for social justice and arms control, teaching and practicing nonviolent conflict resolution, sensitizing ourselves to our own ethnocentrism, consulting with peacekeeping operations, ensuring gender parity, addressing ethnic identities and hostilities, empowering alternative voices, and building environmental security are just a few of the myriad ways peace psychologists can contribute to building a peaceful world. Our work building peace will in turn build peace psychology. Hopefully, the twenty-first century will bring vigorous development of both. Peacebuilding is no small task—but, we ask, what else is more important?

REFERENCES

Abanes, R. (1996). *American militias: Rebellion, racism and religion.* Downers Grove, IL: Intervarsity Press.

Aber, L., Brown, J., & Henrich, C. (1999). *Teaching conflict resolution: An effective school-based approach to violence prevention.* New York: National Center for Children in Poverty.

About Project Ploughshares. (1997). [WWW document]. Available: *http://watserv1.uwaterloo.ca/~plough/ppabout.html.* [1999, June 18].

Abrahams, N. (1998). *Abused by the law: Discursive frames for domestic violence in the courts.* Presented at the Annual Meeting of the American Sociological Association, San Francisco, August 21–25.

Adams, D. (1995). *UNESCO and a Culture of Peace: Promoting a global movement.* Paris: UNESCO Culture of Peace Programme.

Adams, D. (1998). Personal communication, June 7.

Adas, M., Schwartz, S.B., & Stearns, P.N. (1996). *World civilizations: The global experience, Volume 2, 1450 to the present.* New York: HarperCollins.

Adler, A. (1956). *The individual psychology of Alfred Adler* (H.L. & R.R. Ansbacher, Eds.). New York: Basic Books.

Adomeit, H. (1981). Consensus vs. conflict: The dimension of foreign policy. In S. Bialer (Ed.), *The domestic context of Soviet foreign policy* (pp. 271–334). Boulder, CO: Westview Press.

Adorno, T.W., Frenkel-Brunswik, E., Levinson, D., & Sanford, R.N. (1950). *The authoritarian personality.* New York: Harper & Row.

Afkhami, M. (Ed.). (1995). *Faith and freedom: Women's human rights in the Muslim world.* Syracuse, NY: Syracuse University Press.

African Rights. (1995). *Rwanda: Not so innocent, when women become killers.* London: African Rights.

Agger, I. (1994). *The blue room: Trauma and testimony among refugee women—a psycho-social exploration.* London: Zed Books.

Agger, I., & Jensen, S.B. (1996). *Trauma and healing under state terrorism.* London: Zed Books.

Agger, I., & Mimica, J. (1996). *Psycho-social assistance to victims of war in Bosnia-Herzegovina and Croatia: An evaluation.* Brussels: ECHO.

Agger, I., Vuk, S., & Mimica, J. (1995). *Theory and practice of psycho-social projects under war conditions in Bosnia-Herzegovina and Croatia.* Brussels: ECHO.

Agosin, M. (Ed.). (1993). *Surviving beyond fear: Women, children and human rights in Latin America.* New York: White Pine Press.

Ahlquist, L. (1996). *Co-operation, command and control in U.N. peacekeeping operations: A pilot study from the Swedish War College.* Stockholm: Swedish War College.

Ainsworth, M. (1982). Attachment: Retrospect and prospect. In C. Parkes & J. Stevens-Hinde (Eds.), *The place of attachment in human behavior* (pp. 330–334). New York: Basic Books.

Ainsworth, M.D.S., Blehar, M.C., Waters, E., & Wall, S. (1978). *Patterns of attachment: A psychological study of the strange situation.* Hillsdale, NJ: Erlbaum.

Alaimo, K., Briefel, R.R., Frongillo, E.A., & Olson, C.M. (1988). Food insufficiency exists in the United States: Results from the third national health and nutrition examination survey (NHANES III). *American Journal of Public Health, 88,* 419–425.

Albee, G.W. (1992a). Powerlessness, politics, and prevention: The community mental health approach. In S. Staub & P. Green (Eds.), *Psychology and social responsibility: Facing global challenges* (pp. 201–220). New York: New York University Press.

Albee, G.W. (1992b). Saving children means social revolution. In G.W. Albee, L.A. Bond, & T.V. Cook Monsey (Eds.), *Improving children's lives: Global perspectives on prevention* (pp. 311–329). Newbury Park, CA: Sage.

Albee, G.W. (1996). Revolutions and counterrevolutions in prevention. *American Psychologist, 51*, 1130–1133.

Albee, G.W. (1998). The politics of primary prevention. *Journal of Primary Prevention, 19*, 117–127.

Albee, G.W., Joffe, J.M., & Dusenbury, L.A. (Eds.). (1988). *Prevention, powerlessness and politics: Readings on social change.* Newbury Park, CA: Sage.

Alexander, C. (1979). *The timeless way of building.* New York: Oxford University Press.

Alexander, C., Ishikawa, S., Silverstein, M., Jacobson, M., Fiksdahl-King, I., & Angel, S. (1977). *A pattern language.* New York: Oxford University Press.

Alikadic, B. (1995). City of courage. *Why—Publication for Human Rights and Peace, Sarajevo: War Issue.*

Alinsky, S.D. (1946). *Reveille for radicals.* Chicago: University of Chicago Press.

Allen, R.I., & Petr, C.G. (1998). Rethinking family-centered practice. *American Journal of Orthopsychiatry, 68*, 4–15.

Allport, G. (1979). *The nature of prejudice.* (25th Anniversary Edition). Reading, MA: Addison-Wesley.

Allport, G.W. (1954). *The nature of prejudice.* Cambridge, MA: Addison-Wesley.

Altemeyer, B. (1981). *Right-wing authoritarianism.* Winnipeg: University of Manitoba Press.

American Psychological Association. (1998, October 23). *Making 'Welfare to Work' Really Work* [Report of the Task Force on Women, Poverty, and Public Assistance posted on the World Wide Web]. Washington, DC: Author. Retrieved October 23, 1998 from the World Wide Web: http://www.apa.org/pi/wpo.html

America's Watch Committee. (1984). *Guatemala: A nation of prisoners.* New York: Author.

America's Watch Committee. (1990). *Messengers of death: Human rights in Guatemala, November 1988–February 1990.* New York: Author.

Amir, Y. (1969). Contact hypothesis in ethnic relations. *Psychological Bulletin, 71*, 319–342.

Amnesty International. (1987). *Guatemala: The human rights record.* London and New York: Amnesty International Publishers.

Amnesty International. (1992). *Human rights violations against indigenous peoples of the Americas.* London and New York: Amnesty International Publishers.

Anderson, A., & Richter-Lyonette, E. (1997). The war crime of rape. *Reconciliation International 12 (3)*, 20–21. Alkmaar, The Netherlands: International Fellowship of Reconciliation.

Anderson, B. (1991) *Imagined communities: Reflections on the origin and spread of nationalism.* New York: Verso.

Annan, K. (1996). *Peace operations and the United Nations: Preparing for the next century.* Unpublished manuscript.

Annan, K. (1997a). Address at Cedar Crest College, Allentown, Pennsylvania, 13 September 1997 (SG/SM/6325). New York: United Nations.

Annan, K. (1997b). *Renewal amid transition: Annual report on the work of the organization,* 3 September 1997 (A/52/1). New York: United Nations.

Annan, K. (1998). Joint Press Conference with Deputy Prime Minister of Iraq Tariq Aziz, Baghdad, 23 February 1998.

Anthony, E., & Cohler, B. (1987). *The invulnerable child.* New York: Guilford Press.

Arblaster, A. (1987). *Democracy.* Milton Keynes, UK: Open University Press.

Archer, D. (1985). Social deviance. In G. Lindzey & E. Aronson (Eds.), *The handbook of social psychology* (3rd ed., Vol. 2, pp. 743–804). New York: Random House.

Arditti, R. (1999). *Searching for life: The Grandmothers of the Plaza de Mayo and the disappeared children of Argentina.* Berkeley, CA: University of California Press.

Arditti, R., & Lykes, M.B. (1992). "Recovering identity": The work of the Grandmothers of the Plaza de Mayo. *Women's Studies International Forum, 15*, 461–471.

Arkin, W.M., & Fieldhouse, R.W. (1985). *Nuclear battlefields: Global links in the arms race.* Cambridge, MA: Ballinger.

Aron, A., Corne, S., Fursland, A., & Zewler, B. (1991). The gender-specific terror of El Salvador and Guatemala: Post-traumatic stress disorder in Central American refugee women. *Women's Studies International Forum, 14*, 37–47

Ashbury, J. (1993). *Violence in families of color in the United States.* In R.C. Hampton, T.P. Gullotta, G.R. Adams, E.H. Potter, & R.P. Weissberg (Eds.)., *Family violence: Prevention and treatment* (pp. 159–178). Newbury Park, CA: Sage.

Ashwari, H. (1995). *This side of peace.* New York: Simon & Schuster.

Aspeslagh, R., & Burns, R.J. (1996). Peace education and the comparative study of education. In R.J. Burns & R. Aspeslagh, (Eds.), *Three decades of peace education around the world: An anthology* (pp. 3–23). New York: Garland.

Augsburger, D.W. (1992). *Conflict mediation across cultures.* Louisville, KY: Westminister/John Knox Press.

Austin, W., & Hatfield, E. (1980). Equity theory, power, and social justice. In G. Mikula (Ed.), *Justice and social interaction* (pp. 25–61). New York: Springer Verlag.

Axinn, J., & Stern, M.J. (1988). *Dependency and poverty: Old problems in a new world.* Lexington, MA: Lexington Books.

Baker-Brown, G., Ballard, E.J., Bluck, S., de Vries, B., Suedfeld, P., & Tetlock, P.E. (1992). The conceptual/integrative complexity scoring manual. In C.P. Smith (Ed.), *Motivation and personality: Handbook of thematic content analysis* (pp. 400–418). Cambridge: Cambridge University Press.

Balakian, P. (1997). *The black dog of fate: A memoir.* New York: Basic Books.

Ball, N. (1997). Demobilizing and reintegrating soldiers: Lessons from Africa. In K. Kumar (Ed.), *Rebuilding war-torn societies: Critical areas for international assistance* (pp. 85–105). Boulder, CO: Lynne Rienner.

Bandura, A. (1991). Social cognitive theory of moral thought and action. In W.M. Kurtines & J.L. Gewirtz (Eds.), *Handbook of moral behavior and development. Vol. 1: Theory* (pp. 45–103). Hillsdale, NJ: Erlbaum.

Bandura, A. (1997). *Self efficacy: The exercise of control.* New York: Freeman.

Barbarin, O., Richter, L., de Wet, T., & Wachtel, A. (1998). Ironic trends in the transition to peace: Criminal violence supplants political violence in terrorizing South African Blacks. *Peace and Conflict: Journal of Peace Psychology, 4,* 283–305.

Barki, I. (1988). *Pour ces yeux-la* [For those eyes]. Paris: Editions La Decouverte.

Barnes, B. (1991). *Mediation in the Pacific Pentan-gle (PCR).* Working Paper. Honolulu: University of Hawaii Press.

Barnett, O.W., & LaViolette, A.D. (1993). *It could happen to anyone: Why battered women stay.* Newbury Park, CA: Sage.

Barry, K. (1995). *Prostitution of sexuality.* New York: New York University Press.

Bar-Tal, D. (1990). Causes and consequences of delegitimization: Models of conflict and ethnocentrism. *Journal of Social Issues, 46*(1), 65–81.

Bassuk, E.L., Browne, A., & Buckner, J.C. (1996, October). Single mothers and welfare. *Scientific American, 275*(4), 60–67.

Basu, A. (Ed.). (1993). Women and religious nationalism in India. *Bulletin of Concerned Asian Scholars, 25*(4).

Basu, A. (1997). *The challenge of local feminisms: Women's movements in global perspective.* Boulder, CO: Westview Press.

Baumrind, D. (1972). Socialization and instrumental competence in young children. In W.W. Hartup (Ed.), *The young child: Reviews of research* (pp. 202–224). Washington, DC: National Association for the Education of Young Children.

Bazilli, S. (Ed.). (1991). *Putting women on the agenda.* Johannesburg: Ravan Press.

Beck, A.T. (1976). *Cognitive therapy and the emotional disorders.* New York: International Universities Press.

Beck, A.T., Rush, A.J., Shaw, B.F., & Emery, G. (1979). *Cognitive therapy of depression.* New York: Guilford Press.

Bedrossyn, M.D. (1983). *The first genocide of the twentieth century: The perpetrators and the victims.* Boyajian, Armenia: Voskedar Publishing Co.

Bee, H. (1997). *The developing child.* New York: Addison-Wesley Longman.

Belenky, M.F., Clinchy, B.M., Goldberger, N.R., & Tarule, J.M. (1986). *Women's ways of knowing: The development of self, voice and mind.* New York: Basic Books.

Bell, C. (1991). Traumatic stress and children in danger. *Journal of Health Care for the Poor and Underserved, 2,* 175–188.

Bellah, R.N., Madsen, R., Sullivan, W.M., Swidler, A., & Tipton, S.M. (1986). *Habits of the heart.* Berkeley, CA: University of California Press.

Belsey, M., & Royston, E. (1987). *Overview of the health of women and children.* Paper presented at the International Conference on Better Health for Women and Children Through Family Planning, Nairobi, Kenya.

Bem, D. (1981). Gender schema theory: A cognitive account of sex typing. *Psychological Review, 88,* 354–364.

Bennett, O., Bexley, J., & Warnock, K. (1995). *Arms to fight—arms to protect.* London: Panos.

Bennett, T. (1991). *A sourcebook of customary law for Southern Africa.* Cape Town: Juta.

Benson, D.E., & Trew, K.K. (1995). Facets of self in Northern Ireland: Explorations and further questions. In A. Ooterwegel & R.A. Wicklund (Eds.), *The self in European and North American culture: Development and processes* (pp. 291–307). Dordrecht, the Netherlands: Kluwer Academic Publishers.

Berghahn, V.R. (1984). *Militarism: The history of an international debate, 1861–1979.* Cambridge: Cambridge University Press.

Berk, R.A., Berk, S.F., Loseke, D.R., & Rauma, D. (1983). Mutual combat and other family violence myths. In D. Finkelhor, R.J. Gelles, G.T. Hotaling, & M.A. Straus (Eds.), *The dark side of families: Current family violence research* (pp. 197–212). Beverly Hills, CA: Sage.

Berk, R.A., Boyd, E.A., & Hamner, K.M. (1992). Thinking more clearly about hate-motivated crimes. In G.M. Herer & K.T. Berrill (Eds.), *Hate crimes: Confronting violence against lesbians and gay men* (pp. 123–349). Newbury Park, CA: Sage.

Berk, S.F. (1985). *The gender factory: The apportionment of work in American households.* New York: Plenum.

Berke, R.L. (1998, August 2). Chasing the polls on gay rights. *New York Times,* p. 3

Berkowitz, L. (1993). *Aggression: Its causes, consequences and control.* San Francisco: McGraw-Hill.

Berkowitz, M.W., Guerra, N.G., & Nucci, L. (1991). Sociomoral development and drug and alcohol abuse. In W.M. Kurtines & J.L. Gerwirtz (Eds.), *Handbook of moral behavior and development, Vol. 3* (pp. 35–54). Hillsdale, NJ: Erlbaum.

Berrill, K.T. (1992). Anti-gay violence and victimization in the United States: An overview. In G.M. Herer & K.T. Berrill (Eds.), *Hate crimes: Confronting violence against lesbians and gay men* (pp. 19–45). Newbury Park, CA: Sage.

Berrill, K.T., & Herek, G.M. (1992). Primary and secondary victimization in anti-gay hate crimes: Official response and public policy. In G.M. Herek & K.T. Berrill (Eds.), *Hate crimes: Confronting violence against lesbians and gay men* (pp. 289–305). Newbury Park, CA: Sage.

Berry, J.W. (1984) Multicultural policy in Canada: A social-psychological analysis. *Canadian Journal of Behavioral Science, 16,* 353–370.

Bienen, H. (1995). Ethnic nationalisms and implications for U.S. foreign policy. In C.A. Kupchan (Ed.), *Nationalism and nationalities in the New Europe* (pp. 158–179). Ithaca, NY: Cornell University Press.

Biko, S.B. (1978). *I write what I like.* London: Bowerdean Press.

Billig, M., & Tajfel, H. (1973). Social categorization and similarity in intergroup behavior. *European Journal of Social Psychology, 3,* 27–52.

Birrell, D. (1972). Relative deprivation as a factor in conflict in Northern Ireland. *Sociological Review, 20,* 317–343.

Bissel, T. (1997, April 24). *Nike Packet, parts 1–7. Campaign for Labor Rights.*

Blake, R.R., & Mouton, J.S. (1979). Intergroup problem solving in organizations: From theory to practice. In W.G. Austin & S. Worchel (Eds.), *The social psychology of intergroup relations* (pp. 19–23). Monterey, CA: Brooks/Cole.

Blalock, H.M. (1989). *Power and conflict: Toward a general theory.* Newbury Park, CA: Sage.

Blau, P. (1969). Objectives of sociology. In R. Bierstedt (Ed.), *A design for sociology: Scope, objectives and method* (pp. 43–71). Philadelphia: American Academy of Political and Social Science.

Blau, P. (1977). *Inequality and heterogeneity.* New York: Free Press.

Blight, J.G. (1987). Toward a policy-relevant psychology of avoiding nuclear war: Lessons for psychology from the Cuban missile crisis. *American Psychologist, 42,* 1–18.

Blight, J.G., & Lany, J.M. (1995). Burden of nuclear responsibility: Reflections on the critical oral history of the Cuban missile crisis. *Peace and Conflict: Journal of Peace Psychology, 1,* 225–264.

Block, R., & Block, C. (1993). *Street gang crime in Chicago.* Research in Brief. Washington, DC: U.S. Department of Justice.

Boesak, W. (1996). Truth, justice and reconciliation. In H.R. Botman & R.M. Petersen (Eds.), *To remember and to heal: Theological and psychological reflections on truth and reconciliation* (pp. 65–69). Cape Town: Human & Rosseau.

Bok, S. (1998). *Mayhem: Violence as public entertainment.* Reading, MA: Perseus.

Bolton, R. (1992). *People skills.* New York: Prentice Hall.

Bond, D., & Vogele, W. (1995). Profiles of international "hotspots." Unpublished Manuscript. Program on Nonviolent Sanctions and Cultural Survival, Center for International Affairs, Harvard University.

Bondurant, J.V. (1965). *Conquest of violence: The Gandhian philosophy of conflict.* Berkeley, CA: University of California Press.

Bondurant, J.V. (1988). *Conquest of violence: The Gandhian philosophy of conflict,* (Rev. ed.). Berkeley, CA: University of California Press.

Bonham, G.M., & Shapiro, M.J. (1986) Mapping structures of thought. In I.N. Gallhofer, W.E. Saris, & M. Melman (Eds.), *Different test analysis procedures for the study of decision making* (pp. 125–139). Amsterdam: Sociometric Research Foundation.

Bordin, J. (1998, August). Psycho-social pathologies in political and military decision-making: An analysis of U.S. military officers' intelligence assessments of a terrorist attack on a U.S. embassy. Paper presented at the 24th International Congress of Applied Psychology, San Francisco, CA.

Borman, W. (1986). *Gandhi and non-violence.* Albany, NY: SUNY Press.

Bose, A. (1987). *Dimensions of peace and nonviolence: The Gandhian perspective.* Delhi: Gian Publishing House.

Bose, N.K. (Ed.). (1948). *Selections from Gandhi.* Ahmedabad: Navajivan Publishing House.

Botev, N., & Wagner, R.A. (1993). Seeing past the barricades: Ethnic intermarriage in Yugoslavia during the last three decades. *Anthropology of East Europe Review [Special Issue], 11,* 27–35.

Botman, R.H. (1996) Narrative challenges in a situation of transition. In H.R. Botman & R.M. Petersen (Eds.), T*o remember and to heal: Theological and psychological reflections on truth and reconciliation* (pp. 37–44). Cape Town: Human & Rosseau.

Boulding, E. (1983). Teaching in the nuclear age. (Series of workshops co-sponsored by Teaching in a Nuclear Age Advisory Committee and Educators for Social Responsibility, held at Friends House in Philadelphia.) Cambridge, MA: Educators for Social Responsibility.

Boulding, E. (1993, December). *Notes on the strengthening of peacebuilding resources for Palestinians and Israeli.* Paper presented for UNESCO Roundtable on Peace in the Middle East, Granada, Spain.

Boutros-Ghali, B. (1992). *An agenda for peace.* New York: United Nations.

Bowers v. Hardwick, 478 U.S. 186 (1986).

Bowlby, J. (1973). *Separation.* New York: Basic Books.

Bowlby, J. (1979). *The making and breaking of affectional bonds.* London: Tavistock.

Bradley, R., Whiteside, L., Mundfrom, D., Casey, P., Kelleher, K., & Pope, S. (1994). Early indications of resilience and their relation to experiences in the home environments of low birthweight, premature children living in poverty. *Child Development, 65,* 346–360.

Brehm, S.S., Kassin, S.M., & Fein, S. (1999). *Social psychology* (4th ed.). Boston: Houghton Mifflin.

Brenner, M.H. (1976). *Estimating the social costs of national economic policies: Implications for mental and physical health and criminal violence* (Report for the Joint Economic Committee of Congress). Washington, DC: U.S. Government Printing Office.

Brett, R. & McCallin, M. (1996). *Children: The invisible soldiers.* Vaxjo, Sweden: Rädda Barnen.

Brewer, M.B. (1968). Determinants of social distance among East African tribal groups. *Journal of Personality and Social Psychology, 10,* 279–289.

Brewer, M.B. (1979a). Ingroup bias in the minimal intergroup situation: A cognitive-motivational analysis. *Psychological Bulletin, 86,* 307–324.

Brewer, M.B. (1979b). The role of ethnocentrism in intergroup conflict. In W.G. Austin & S. Worchel (Eds.), *The social psychology of intergroup relations* (pp. 71–84). Monterey, CA: Brooks-Cole.

Brewer, M.B. (1986). The role of ethnocentrism in intergroup conflict. In S. Worchel & W.G. Austin (Eds.), *Psychology of intergroup relations* (2nd ed.) (pp. 88–102). Chicago: Nelson-Hall.

Brewer, M.B., & Kramer, R.M. (1985). The psychology of intergroup attitudes and behavior. *Annual Review of Psychology, 36,* 219–243.

Brewer, M.B., & Silver, M. (1978). Ingroup bias as a function of task characteristics. *European Journal of Social Psychology 8,* 393–400.

Brock-Utne, B. (1989). Feminist perspectives on peace and peace education. New York: Pergamon Press.

Brody, N. (1997). Intelligence, schooling and society. *American Psychologist, 52,* 1046–1050.

Bronfenbrenner, U. (1961). The mirror image in Soviet-American relations: A social psychologist's report. *Journal of Social Issues, 17*(3), 45–56.

Bronfenbrenner, U. (1979). *The ecology of human development. Experiments by nature and design.* Cambridge, MA: Harvard University Press.

Brooks, M.G., & Buckner, J.C. (1996). Work and welfare: Job histories, barriers to employment, and predictors of work among low-income single mothers. *American Journal of Orthopsychiatry, 66,* 526–537.

Brown, B. (1983). Impact of political and economic changes upon mental health. *American Journal of Orthopsychiatry, 53,* 583–592.

Brown, J. (1989). *Gandhi: Prisoner of hope.* New Haven, CT: Yale University Press.

Brown, L., & Flavin, C. (1999). A new economy for a new century. In L. Starke (Ed.), *State of the world 1999* (pp. 3–21). New York: Norton.

Brown, R. (1988). *Group processes: Dynamics within and between groups.* Oxford: Blackwell.

Brown, R. (1995). *Prejudice.* Oxford: Blackwell.

Browne, A., & Bassuk, S.S. (1997). Intimate violence in the lives of homeless and poor housed women. *American Journal of Orthopsychiatry, 67,* 261–275.

Browning, C.R. (1992). *Ordinary men: Reserve Batallion 101 and the final solution in Poland.* New York: HarperCollins.

Brummer, V. (1992). Speaking of a personal God: An essay in philosophical theology. New York: Cambridge University Press.

Bruner, J. (1990). *Acts of meaning.* Cambridge, MA: Harvard University Press.

Brydon-Miller, M. (1997). Participatory action research: Psychology and social change. *Journal of Social Issues, 53*(4), 657–666.

Bulhan, H. (1985). *Frantz Fanon and the psychology of oppression.* New York: Plenum Press.

Bulloch, J., & Morris, H. (1991). *Saddam's war: The origins of the Kuwait conflict and the international response.* Boston: Faber & Faber.

Bunch, C. (1987). *Passionate politics: Feminist theory in action.* New York: St. Martin's Press.

Bunch, C. (1995). Transforming human rights from a feminist perspective. In J. Peters & A. Wolper (Eds.), *Women's rights human rights: International feminist perspectives* (pp. 11–17). New York: Routledge.

Bunch, C., & Carillo, R. (1998). Global violence against women: The challenge to human rights and development. In M. Klare & Y. Chandrani (Eds.), *World security: Challenges for a new century* (pp. 229–248). New York: St. Martin's Press.

Burlew, A.K.H., Banks, W.C., McAdoo, H.P., & Ajamiya Azibo, D. (Eds.). (1992). *African American psychology.* New York: Sage.

Burn, S.M., & Oskamp, S. (1989). Ingroup biases and the U.S.-Soviet conflict. *Journal of Social Issues, 45*(2), 73–89.

Burns, J.F. (1992, May 3). New, virulent strains of hatred in the Balkans and beyond. The *New York Times,* Sect. 4, p. 3.

Burns, J.F. (1998, May 29). Pakistan, answering India, carries out nuclear test; Clinton's appeal rejected. The *New York Times,* p. 1A, col. 6.

Burris, B.H. (1983). *No room at the top: Unemployment and alienation in the corporation.* New York: Praeger.

Burton, F. (1979). *The politics of legitimacy.* London: Routledge & Kegan Paul.

Burton, J. (1991). Conflict resolution as a political philosophy. *Interdisciplinary Peace Research, 3,* 62–72.

Burton, J.W. (1987). *Resolving deep-rooted conflict: A handbook.* Lanham, MD: University Press of America.

Buss, A.H. (1966). The effect of harm on subsequent aggression. *Journal of Experimental Research in Personality, 1,* 249–255.

Butler, K. (1997, March/April). The anatomy of resilience. *The Family Therapy Networker,* 22–31. Carnegie Commission on the Prevention of Deadly Conflict. (1997). *Preventing deadly conflict: Final report.* New York: Carnegie Corporation.

Butterfield, F. (1998, December 10). Guns blamed for rise in homicides by youths in 80's. The *New York Times,* p. A25.

Buvinic, M., & Yodelman, S.W. (1989). *Women, poverty, and progress in the Third World.* New York: Foreign Policy Association.

Buzuev, A. (1985). *Transnational corporations and militarism.* Moscow: Progress Publishers.

Cairns, E. (1980). The development of ethnic discrimination in young children in Northern Ireland. In J. Harbison & J. Harbison (Eds.), *A society under stress: Children and young people in Northern Ireland* (pp. 115–127). Somerset, UK: Open Books.

Cairns, E. (1982). Intergroup conflict in Northern Ireland. In H. Tajfel (Ed.), *Group identity and intergroup relations* (pp. 277–297). London: Cambridge University Press.

Cairns, E. (1987). *Caught in crossfire: Children and the Northern Ireland conflict.* Syracuse, NY: Syracuse University Press.

Cairns, E. (1996). *Children and political violence.* Oxford: Basil Blackwell.

Cairns, E. & Darby, J. (1998). The conflict in Northern Ireland: Causes, consequences and controls. *American Psychologist, 53*, 754–760.

Cairns, R.B., & Cairns, B.D. (1994). *Lifelines and risks: Pathways of youth in our time.* Cambridge: Cambridge University Press.

Campaign for Labor Rights. (1998). *Sweatshops and debt cancellation,* [on-line]. Available: <clr@igc.apc.org> CLR@igc.org Web site: *www.summersault.com/~agj/clr* [7 Dec. 1998].

Campbell, C. (1995). The social identity of township youth: Social Identity Theory and gender(Part 2). *South African Journal of Psychology, 25*, 160–167.

Campbell, D.T. (1965). Ethnocentral and other altruistic motives. In D. Levine (Ed.), *Nebraska Symposium on Motivation* (pp. 283–311). Lincoln, NE: University of Nebraska Press.

Caporael, L.R., Dawes, R.M., Orbell, J.M., & van der Kagt, A.J.C. (1989). Selfishness examined: Cooperation in the absence of egoistic incentives. *Behavior and Brain Sciences, 12*, 683–739.

Carlsson-Paige, N., & Levin, D.E. (1990). *Who's calling the shots? How to respond effectively to children's fascination with war play and war toys.* Philadelphia: New Society Publishers.

Carmack, R.M. (Ed.). (1988). *Harvest of violence: The Maya Indians and the Guatemalan crisis.* Oklahoma City, OK: University of Oklahoma Press.

Carnevale, P.J., & Pruitt, D.G. (1992). Negotiation and mediation. *Annual Review of Psychology, 43*, 531–582.

Carter Center (1996). The Carter Center: Frequently asked questions (on-line). Available: *http://www.emory.edu/CARTER_CENTER/faq.html.* [June 17, 1999].

Cathcart, K. (1998). Letter to contributors. Available from Lambda Legal Defense and Educational Fund, Inc., 120 Wall Street, Suite 1500. New York, NY.

CEH/Commission for Historical Clarification [Comisión para el Esclarecimiento Histórico]. (February, 1999). Report of the CEH [On-line]. Available: *http://hrdata.aaas.org/ceh.* Guatemala: Author.

Chang, I. (1997). *The rape of Nanking: The forgotten holocaust of World War II.* New York: Basic Books.

Charny, I. (1991). Genocide: Intervention and prevention. *Social Education, 55*, 124–127.

Chatterjee, M. (1983). *Gandhi's religious thought.* Notre Dame, IN: University of Notre Dame Press.

Cherlin, A. (1979). Work life and marital satisfaction. In G. Levinger & O.C. Moles (Eds.), *Divorce and separation* (pp. 151–166). New York: Basic Books.

Cherlin, A.J. (1995). Policy issues of child care. In P.L. Chase-Lansdale & J. Brooks-Gunn (Eds.), *Escape from poverty: What makes a difference for children?* (pp. 121–137). Cambridge: Cambridge University Press.

Children's Defense Fund. (1998). *The state of America's children.* Washington, DC: Author.

Chivian, E., Mack, J.E., Waletsky, J.P., Lazaroff, C., Doctor, R., & Goldenring, J.M. (1985). Soviet children and the threat of nuclear war: A preliminary study. *American Journal of Orthopsychiatry, 55*, 484–502.

Christie, D. (1997). Reducing direct and structural violence: The human needs theory. *Peace and Conflict: Journal of Peace Psychology, 3*, 315–332.

Christie, D.J., & Hanley, C.P. (1994). Some psychological effects of nuclear war education on adolescents during Cold War II. *Political Psychology, 15*, 177–199.

Cialdini, R.B., & Richardson K.D. (1980) Two indirect tactics of image management: Basking and blasting. *Journal of Personality and Social Psychology, 39*, 406–415.

Clark, K.W., & Clark, M. (1947). Racial identification and preferences in Negro children. In T.M. Newcomb & E.L. Hartley (Eds.), *Readings in social psychology* (pp. 169–178). New York: Holt.

Clarke-Stewart, K.A., Gruber, C.P., & Fitzgerald, L.M. (1994). *Children at home and in day care.* Hillsdale, NJ: Erlbaum.

Clinton reaffirms commitment to education as a top priority. (1997, February 25). *USA Today,* p. 30.

Cock, J. (1993). *Women and war in South Africa.* Cleveland, OH: Pilgrim Press.

Cogan, J.C. (1996). The prevention of anti-lesbian/gay hate crimes through social change and empowerment. In E.D. Rothblum & L.A. Bond (Eds.), *Preventing heterosexism and homophobia* (pp. 219–238). Newbury Park, CA: Sage.

Cohen, C.E. (1997). A poetics of reconciliation: The aesthetic mediation of conflict. Unpublished doctoral dissertation, University of New Hampshire.

Cohen, D. (1996). Law, social policy, and violence: The impact of regional cultures. *Journal of Personality and Social Psychology, 70,* 961–978.

Cohen, R. (1991). *Negotiating across cultures.* Washington, DC: U.S. Institute of Peace.

Cohen, R. (1996). Cultural aspects of international mediation. In J. Bercovitch (Ed.), *Resolving international conflicts* (pp. 107–128). Boulder, CO: Lynne Rienner.

Cohn, C. (1987). Sex and death in the rational world of defense intellectuals. *Signs: Journal of Women in Culture and Society, 12,* 687–717.

Cojuangco, M. (1986). Margarita Cojuangco, opposition leader. In M. Mercado (Ed.), *People's power* (pp. 35–36). Manila, Philippines: The James B. Reuter, S.J. Foundation.

Coleman, D.H, & Straus, M.A. (1983). Alcohol abuse and family violence. In E. Gottheil, K. Druly, T. Skoloda, & H. Waxman (Eds.), *Alcohol, drug abuse and aggression* (pp. 104–124). Springfield, IL: Charles C. Thomas.

Coleman, P.T. (1997). Redefining ripeness: A social-psychological perspective. *Peace and Conflict: Journal of Peace Psychology, 3,* 81–103.

Coles, G. (1998). *Reading lessons: The debate over literacy.* New York: Farrar, Straus & Giroux.

Collins, P. (1992): *Ideology after the fall of Communism.* London: Boyers/Bowerdean.

Comaroff, J.L., & Stern, P.C. (Eds.). (1995). *Perspectives on nationalism and war.* International Studies in Global Change, vol. 7. Amsterdam: Gordon & Breach Publishers.

Comas-Díaz, L., Lykes, M.B., & Alarcón, R.D. (1998). Ethnic conflict and the psychology of liberation in Guatemala, Peru, and Puerto Rico. *American Psychologist, 53,* 778–792.

Comer, J. (1993). *Creating learning communities: The Comer process. Experimental session.* Annual Conference of the Association for Supervision and Curriculum Development.

Comstock, G.D. (1991). *Violence against lesbians and gay men.* New York: Columbia University Press.

Connor, W. (1994). *Ethnonationalism: The quest for understanding.* Princeton, NJ: Princeton University Press.

Consortium on Peace, Research, Education, and Development (COPRED). (1997, November). Conference reports. *COPRED Peace Chronicle, 22*(4), 10.

Convention on the Elimination of Discrimination Against Women. (1979). New York: United Nations. (For copies see *http://www.un .org*)

Convention on the Rights of the Child. (1989).

New York: United Nations. (For copies see *http://www.un.org*)

Cooper, S., Nicholas, L., Seedat, M., & Statman, J. (Eds.). (1990). Psychology and apartheid: The struggle for psychology in South Africa. In S. Cooper & L. Nicholas (Eds.), *The psychology of apartheid: Essays on the struggle for psychology and the mind in South Africa* (pp. 1–21). Johannesburg: Vision/Madiba.

Copelon, R. (1994). Intimate terror: Understanding domestic violence as torture. In R. Cook (Ed.), *Human rights of women: International perspectives* (pp. 116–152). Philadelphia: University of Pennsylvania Press.

Corsaro, W.A. (1990). The underlife of the nursery school: Young children's social representations of adult roles. In G. Duveen & B. Lloyd (Eds.), *Social representations and the development of knowledge.* Cambridge: Cambridge University Press.

Coser, L. (1956). *The functions of social conflict.* New York: Free Press.

Costantino, C.A., & Sickles Merchant, C. (1996). *Designing conflict management systems: A guide to creating productive and healthy organizations.* San Francisco: Jossey-Bass.

Cottam, R.W. (1987) State motivation and political realism. Paper presented at the Mershon Center, Ohio State University, October 8, 1987.

Cottrell, L.S., & Eberhart, S. (1948). *American opinion on world affairs in the atomic age.* Princeton, NJ: Princeton University Press.

Couve, C. (1986). Psychology and politics in Manganyi's work: A materialist critique. *Psychology in Society, 5,* 90–130.

Crawford, D., & Bodine, R. (1997). *Conflict resolution in schools.* Washington, DC: National Institute for Dispute Resolution.

Crooks, D. (1995). American children at risk: Poverty and its consequences for children's health, growth, and school achievement. *Yearbook of Physical Anthropology, 38,* 57–86.

Crosby, F.J., & Lubin, E.P. (1990). Extending the moral community: Logical and psychological dilemmas. *Journal of Social Issues, 46*(1), 163–172.

Crosby, J., & Van Soest, D. (1997). *Challenges of violence worldwide.* Washington, DC: NASW Press.

Dadrian, V. (1996). *German responsibility in the Armenian genocide: A review of the historical evidence of German complicity.* Cambridge, MA: Blue Crane Books.

Dahl, R.A. (1957). The concept of power. *Behavioral Science 2*, 201–205.

Daily, J., Farmer, P., Rhatigan, J., Katz, J., & Furin, J. (1995). Women and HIV infection—a different disease? In P. Farmer, M. Connors, & J. Simmons (Eds.), *Women, poverty and AIDS* (pp. 125–124). Monroe, ME: Common Courage Press.

Dalton, D. (1993). *Mahatma Gandhi: Nonviolent power in action*. New York: Columbia University Press.

Damon, W. (1998). Political development for a democratic future: A commentary. *Journal of Social Issues, 54*(3), 621–627.

Danieli, Y. (1985). The treatment and prevention of long-term effects and intergenerational transmission of victimization: A lesson from holocaust survivors and their children. In C.R. Figley (Ed.), *Trauma and its wake* (pp. 295–313). New York: Brunner/Mazel.

Danieli, Y. (Ed.). (1998). *International handbook of multigenerational legacies of trauma*. New York: Plenum.

Darmstadter, J. (Ed.). (1992). *Global development and the environment: Perspectives on sustainability*. Washington, DC: Resources for the Future.

Darwish, A., & Alexander, G. (1991). *Unholy Babylon: The secret history of Saddam's war*. London: Victor Gollancz.

Dastoor, T.J., & Mocellin, J.S.P. (1997). *Mine-related problems in Angola*. New York: UNICEF.

Datta, D.M. (1953). *The philosophy of Mahatma Gandhi*. Madison, WI: University of Wisconsin Press.

Davidson, B. (1992). *The Black man's burden: Africa and the curse of the nation state*. London: James Currey.

Davis, J.A., & Smith, T. (1984). *General social surveys 1972–1983: Cummulative data*. New Haven, CT: Yale University, Roper Center for Public Opinion Research.

Dawes, A. (1986). The notion of relevant psychology with particular reference to Africanist pragmatic initiatives. *Psychology in Society, 5*, 28–48.

Dawes, A. (1992). Psychotherapeutic issues in the context of political repression. *Changes, An International Journal of Psychology and Psychotherapy, 10*(2), 82–89.

Dawes, A. (1994). Political violence and moral conduct. In A. Dawes & D. Donald (Eds.), *Childhood and adversity: Psychological perspectives from South African research* (pp. 200–219). Cape Town: David Philip.

Dawes, A. (1997, July). Cultural imperialism in the treatment of children following political violence and war: A Southern African perspective. Paper presented at the Fifth International Symposium on the Contributions of Psychology to Peace, Melbourne, Australia.

Dawes, A., & Cairns, E. (1998). The Machel study: Dilemmas of cultural sensitivity and universal rights of children. *Peace and Conflict: Journal of Peace Psychology, 4*, 335–348.

Dawes, A., & de Villiers, C. (1989). Preparing children and their parents for prison: The Wynberg Seven. In J. Mason & J. Rubenstein (Eds.), *Family therapy in South Africa today* (pp. 15–23). Congella Durban: South African Institute for Marital & Family Therapy.

Dawes, A., & Donald, D. (1994). *Childhood and adversity: Psychological perspectives from South African research*. Cape Town: David Philip.

Dawes, A., & Honwana, A. (1998). Children, culture and mental health: Interventions in conditions of war. In B. Efraime, P. Riedesser, J. Walter, H. Adam, & P. Steudtner (Eds.), *Children, war and persecution: Rebuilding hope* (pp. 74–81). Maputo, Mozambique: AMOZAPO.

Dawes, R.M. (1991). Social dilemmas, economic self-interest, and evolutionary theory. In D.R. Brown & J.E. Keith Smith (Eds.), *Frontiers of mathematical psychology: Essays in honor of Clyde Coombs*. New York: Springer-Verlag.

de la Rey, C., & Owens, I. (1998). Perceptions of psychosocial healing and the Truth and Reconciliation Commission in South Africa. *Peace and Conflict: Journal of Peace Psychology, 4*, 257–270.

de Silva, K.M., & Samarasinghe, S.W.R. de A., (Eds.). (1993). *Peace accords and ethnic conflicts*. London: Pinter Publishers.

Defiant Hussein threatens UN/ links cooperation to end of sanctions. (1998, January 18). *Newsday*, p. A19.

DeLamater, J., Katz, D., & Kelman, H.C. (1969). On the nature of national involvement: A preliminary study. *Journal of Conflict Resolution, 13*, 320–357.

DeLeon, P.H., O'Keefe, A.M., VandenBos, G.R., & Kraut, A.G. (1996). How to influence public policy: A blueprint for activism. In R.P. Lorion, I. Iscoe, P.H. DeLeon, & G.R. VandenBos (Eds.), *Psychology and public policy* (pp. 263–280). Washington, DC: American Psychological Association.

Demos, J. (1970). *A little commonwealth*. New York: Oxford University Press.

Denich, B. (1994). Dismembering Yugoslavia: Nationalist ideologies and the symbolic revival of genocide. *American Ethnologist, 21*, 367–390.

DeRidder, R., Schruijer, S.G.K., & Tripathi, R.C. (1992). Norm violation as a precipitating factor of negative intergroup relations. In R. DeRidder & R.C. Tripathi (Eds.), *Norm violations and intergroup relations* (pp. 3–37). Oxford: Oxford University Press.

Desforges D.M., Lord, C.G., Ramsey, S.L., Mason, J.A., Van Leeuwen, M.D., & West, S.C. (1991). Effects of structured cooperative contact on changing negative attitudes toward stigmatized social groups. *Journal of Personality and Social Psychology, 60*, 531–544.

Deutsch, M. (1973). *The resolution of conflict: Constructive and destructive processes*. New Haven, CT: Yale University Press.

Deutsch, M. (1974). Awakening the sense of injustice. In M. Lerner & M. Ross (Eds.), *The quest for justice: Myth, reality, ideal* (pp. 19–42). New York: Holt, Rinehart & Winston.

Deutsch, M. (1983). The prevention of World War III: A psychological perspective. *Political Psychology, 4*, 3–31.

Deutsch, M. (1985). *Distributive justice: A social-psychological perspective*. New Haven, CT: Yale University Press.

Deutsch, M. (1993). Conflict resolution and cooperative learning in an alternative high school. *Cooperative Learning, 13*(4).

Deutsch, M. (1994). Education beyond hate. In A. Bjerstedt (Ed.), *Education beyond fatalism and hate* (pp. 7–23). Malmo, Sweden: School of Education.

Deutsch, M. (1995). William James: The first peace psychologist. *Peace and Conflict: Journal of Peace Psychology, 1*, 27–36.

Deutsch, M. (2000). Justice and conflict. In M. Deutsch & P.T. Coleman (Eds.), *The handbook of constructive conflict resolution: Theory and practice* (pp. 41–65). San Francisco: Jossey-Bass.

Dobash, R.E., & Dobash, R.P. (1979). *Violence against wives: A case against patriarchy*. New York: Free Press.

Dobash, R.E., & Dobash, R.P. (1992). *Women, violence, and social change*. New York: Routledge.

Dollard, J., Doob, L.W., Miller, N.E., Mowrer, O.H., & Sears, R.R. (1939). *Frustration and aggression*. New Haven, CT: Yale University Press.

Domhoff, G.W. (1971). How the power elite set national goals. In R. Perrucci & M. Pilisuk (Eds.), *The triple revolution emerging: Social problems in depth* (pp. 210–219). Boston: Little Brown.

Dovidio, J. F., & Gaertner, S.L. (Eds.). (1986). *Prejudice, discrimination, and racism*. Orlando, FL: Academic Press.

Draft Declaration on the Rights of Indigenous Peoples (1994). (For copies see *http://www.un.org*)

Driver, M.J. (1965). A structural analysis of aggression, stress, and personality in an Inter-Nation simulation (Institute Paper No. 97). Lafayette, IN: Purdue University, Institute for Research in the Behavioral, Economic, and Management Sciences.

Druckman, D. (1968a). Ethnocentrism in the Inter-Nation simulation. *Journal of Conflict Resolution, 12*, 45–68.

Druckman, D. (1968b). Prenegotiation experience and dyadic conflict resolution in a bargaining situation. *Journal of Experimental Social Psychology, 4*, 367–383.

Druckman, D. (1986). Stages, turning points, and crises: Negotiating military base rights, Spain and the United States. *Journal of Conflict Resolution, 30*, 327–360.

Druckman, D. (1994). Nationalism, patriotism, and group loyalty: A social psychological perspective. *Mershon International Studies Review, 38*, 43–68.

Druckman, D. (1995). Social-psychological aspects of nationalism. In J.L. Comaroff & P.C. Stern (Eds.), *Perspectives on nationalism and war* (pp. 47–98). International Studies in Global Change, vol. 7. Amsterdam: Gordon & Breach Publishers.

Druckman, D., Ali, F., & Bagur, J.S. (1974). Determinants of stereotypy in three cultures. *International Journal of Psychology, 9*, 293–302.

Druckman, D., & Green, J. (1986). *Political stability in the Philippines: Framework and analysis*. Monograph Series in World Affairs, Volume 22, Book 3, Graduate School of International Studies. Denver: University of Denver.

Dryfoos, J.G. (1997). The prevalence of problem behaviors: Implications for programs. In R.P. Weissberg, T.P. Gullotta, R.L. Hampton, B.A. Ryan, & G.R. Adams (Eds.), *Enhancing children's wellness* (pp. 17–46). Thousand Oaks, CA: Sage.

du Preez, P. (1997). In search of genocide: A comparison of Rwanda and South Africa. *Peace and Conflict: Journal of Peace Psychology, 3*, 245–260.

du Toit, C. (1996). Dealing with the past. In H.R. Botman & R.M. Petersen (Eds.), *To remember and to heal: Theological and psychological reflections on truth and reconciliation* (pp. 118–128). Cape Town: Human & Rosseau.

Dubinskas, F.A. (1992). Culture and conflict: The cultural roots of discord. In D.M. Kolb & J.M. Bartunek (Eds.), *Hidden conflict in organizations* (pp. 187–207). Newbury Park, CA: Sage.

Duckitt, J. (1989). Authoritarianism and group identification: A new view of an old construct. *Political Psychology, 10,* 63–84.

Duckitt, J. (1992). *The social psychology of prejudice.* Westport, CT: Prager.

Dunbar, E.W. (1998, August). Hate crime reporting: Comparison on behavioral and demographic characteristics. Paper presented at the 106th Annual Convention of the American Psychological Association, San Francisco.

Duncan, G.J. (1984). *Years of poverty, years of plenty: The changing fortunes of American workers and families.* Ann Arbor, MI: Institute for Social Research, University of Michigan.

Dunn, S. (1989). Integrated schools in Northern Ireland. *Oxford Review of Education, 15*(2), 121–128.

Durch, W. (1996). Keeping the peace: Politics and lessons of the 1990s. In W. Durch (Ed.), *UN peacekeeping, American policy, and the uncivil wars of the 1990s* (pp. 1–34). New York: St. Martin's Press.

Durkin, K. (1995). *Developmental social psychology: From infancy to old age.* Oxford: Basil Blackwell.

Duryea, M.L.B. (1992). *Conflict and culture: A literature review and bibliography.* Victoria, BC: University of Victoria Institute for Dispute Resolution.

Dutton, D.G. (1995). *The domestic assault of women: Psychological and criminal justice perspectives.* Vancouver: University of British Columbia Press.

Dutton, D.G., & Golant S.K. (1995). *The batterer: A psychological profile.* New York: Basic Books.

D'Zurilla, T.J. (1988). Problem-solving therapies. In K.S. Dobson (Ed.), *Handbook of cognitive behavioral therapies* (pp. 85–135). New York: Guilford Press.

Earth Island Institute. (1997). Why Borneo? The Borneo project (on-line). Available: *http://www.earthisland.org/berkborn/berkborn.html.*

Ebert, T. (1996). *Ludic feminism and after: Postmodernism, desire and labor in late capitalism.* Ann Arbor, MI: University of Michigan Press.

Edelman, M.W. (1983). Death by poverty, arms, or moral numbness. *American Journal of Orthopsychiatry, 53,* 593–601.

Edelstein, I., & Gibson, K. (1993). A psycho-analytic contribution to the concept of reconciliation. *Psycho-analytic Psychotherapy in South Africa, 2,* 12–17.

Edmonds, P., & Castaneda, C.J. (1992, January 16). After the storm, rebuilding at home. *USA Today,* p. 1A.

Edwards, K., & von Hippel, W. (1995). Hearts and minds: The priority of affective vs. cognitive factors in person perception. *Personality and Social Psychology Bulletin, 21,* 996–1011.

Ehrenreich, B. (1997). *Blood rites: Origins and history of the passions of war.* New York: Metropolitan Books.

Ehrlich, H.J. (1973). *The social psychology of prejudice: A systematic theoretical review and propositional inventory of the American social psychological study of prejudice.* New York: Wiley.

Einhorn, B. (1993). *Cinderella goes to market: Citizenship, gender and women's movements in east central Europe.* London: Verso.

Eisenberg, N. (1992). *The caring child.* Cambridge, MA: Harvard University Press.

El-Bushra, J., & Mukarubuga, C. (1995). Women, war and transition. *Gender and Development, 3*(3), 16–22.

Elliot, F. (1977). The neurology of explosive rage: The episodic dyscontrol syndrome. In M. Roy (Ed.), *Battered women: A psychosociological study of domestic violence* (pp. 98–109). New York: Van Nostrand.

Elliott, L. (1996). Women, gender, feminism, and the environment. In J. Turpin & L.A. Lorentzen (Eds.), *The gendered new world order: Militarism, development, and the environment* (pp. 13–34). New York: Routledge.

El-Mouelhy, M. (1992). The impact of women's health and status on children's health and lives in the developing world. In G.W. Albee, L.A. Bond, & T.V. Cook Monsey (Eds.), *Improving children's lives: Global perspectives on prevention* (pp. 83–96). Newbury Park, CA: Sage.

Elshtain, J.B. (1987). *Women and war.* New York: Basic Books.

Enloe, C. (1989). *Does khaki become you? The militarization of women's lives.* Boston: Pandora.

Enloe, C. (1993). *The morning after: Sexual politics at the end of the cold war.* Berkeley, CA: University of California Press.

Entwistle, D., Alexander, K., & Olson, L. (1997).

Children, schools, and inequality. Boulder, CO: Westview Press

Erdley, C.A., & Asher, S.R. (1998). Linkages between children's beliefs about the legitimacy of aggression and their behavior. *Social development, 7,* 321–339.

Eron, L.D., Gentry, J.H., & Schlegal, P. (1994). *Reason to hope: A psychological perspective on violence and youth.* Washington, DC: American Psychological Association.

Eth, S., & Pynoos, R. (Eds.). (1985). *Post-traumatic stress disorder in children.* Washington, DC: American Psychiatric Press.

Etzioni, A. (1967). The Kennedy experiment. *Western Political Quarterly, 20,* 361–380.

Eyber, C., Dyer, D., Versfeld, R., Dawes, A., Finchilescu, G., & Soudien, C. (1997). *Resisting racism: A teacher's guide to equality in education.* Cape Town: Institute for Democracy in South Africa.

Ezrahi, Y. (1997). *Rubber bullets: Power and conscience in modern Israel.* Berkeley, CA: University of California Press.

Fagan, K. (1998, May 1). Hearing explores big gap between wealthy and poor. *San Francisco Chronicle,* A23, A27.

Falla, R. (1984). We charge genocide. In S. Jonas, E. McCaughan, & F.S. Martinez (Eds. and trans.), *Guatemala: Tyranny on trial – testimony of the permanent people's tribunal* (pp. 112–119). San Francisco: Publicaciones Sinthesis.

Fanon, F. (1967a). *Black skin, white masks.* New York: Grove Press.

Fanon, F. (1967b). *Toward the African revolution.* New York: Grove Press.

Fanon, F. (1968). *The wretched of the earth.* New York: Grove Press.

Farer, J. (1996). Intervention in unnatural humanitarian emergencies: Lessons of the first phase. *Human Rights Quarterly, 18,* 1–22.

Fariña, J.J., & Lykes, M.B. (1991). Cuestiones éticas y epistemológicas ante la experimentación psicológica con niños [Ethical and epistemological questions in psychological experiments with children]. *Actas del Congreso Nacional de Itica.* Asociación Argentina de Investigaciones Éticas. Buenos Aires: Universidad de Argentina.

Faure, G.O. (1995). Conflict formulation: Going beyond culture bound views of conflict. In B.B. Bunker & J.Z. Rubin (Eds.), *Conflict, cooperation and justice* (pp. 39–58). San Francisco: Jossey-Bass.

Fawcett, G.M., Heise, L., Isita Espejel, L., & Pick, S. (1999). Changing community responses to wife abuse: A research and deomonstration project in Iztacalco, Mexico. *American Psychologist, 54,* 41–49.

Fawcett, S.B., Paine-Andrews, A.L., Francisco, V.T., Schulz, J.A., Richter, K.P., Lewis, R.K., Williams, E.L., Harris, K.J., Berkley, J.Y., Fisher, J.L., & Lopez, C.M. (1995). Using empowerment theory in collaborative partnerships for community health and development. *American Journal of Community Psychology, 23,* 677–697.

Fein, H. (1993). Accounting for genocide after 1945: Theories and some findings. *International Journal of Group Rights, 1,* 79–106.

Feitlowitz, M. (1998). A lexicon of terror: Argentina and the legacies of torture. New York: Oxford University Press.

Ferraro, K.J., & Pope, L. (1993). Irreconcilable differences: Battered women, police, and the law. In N.Z. Hilton (Ed.), *Legal responses to wife assault* (pp. 96–126). Newbury Park, CA: Sage.

Feshbach, S. (1990). Psychology, human violence and the search for peace: Issues in science and human values. *Journal of Social Issues, 46*(1), 183–198.

Festinger, L., Pepitone, A., & Newcomb, T. (1952). Some consequences of deindividuation in a group. *Journal of Abnormal and Social Psychology, 47,* 383–389.

Feuerstein, R. (1980). *Instrumental enrichment.* Baltimore: University Park Press.

Finchilescu, G. (1995). Setting the frame: Gender and psychology. *South African Journal of Psychology, 25*(3), 133–139.

Finchilescu, G., & Dawes, A. (1998). Catapulted into democracy: South African adolescents' socio-political orientations following rapid social change. *Journal of Social Issues, 54*(3), 563–584.

Fineman, M.A., & Mykitiuk, R. (Eds.). (1994). *The public nature of private violence: The discovery of domestic abuse.* New York: Routledge.

Fingarette, H. (1969). *Self-deception.* New York: Humanities Press.

Finn, P., & McNeil, T. (1987). *The response of the criminal justice system to bias crime: An explanatory review.* (Available from Abt Associates, 55 Wheeler Street, Cambridge, MA 02138)

Fischer, L. (1954). *Gandhi: His life and message for the world.* New York: Mentor Books.

Fisher, R., (1994). *The social psychology of intergroup and international conflict resolution.* New York: Springer-Verlag.

Fisher, R., & Ury, W. (1981). *Getting to yes: Negotiating agreements without giving in.* Boston: Houghton Mifflin.

Fisher, R. & Ury, W. (1996). *Getting to yes.* London: Business Books.

Fisher, R., Ury, W., & Patton, B. (1991). *Getting to yes: Negotiating agreement without giving in* (2nd ed.). New York: Penguin Books.

Fisher, R.J. (1997). *Interactive conflict resolution.* Syracuse, NY: Syracuse University Press.

Fletcher, L., Olekalns, M., & De Cieri, H. (1998). *Cultural differences in conflict resolution: Individualism and collectivism in the Asia Pacific Region.* Department of Management Working Paper in Organisation Studies, No. 2. University of Melbourne, Australia.

Flisher, A., Skinner, D., Lazarus, S., & Louw, L. (1993). Organizing mental health workers on the basis of politics and service: The case of the Organization for Appropriate Social Services in South Africa (OASSSA). In L.J. Nicholas (Ed.), *Psychology of oppression: Critiques and proposals* (pp. 236–245). Johannesburg: Skotaville.

Fogg, R.W. (1985). Dealing with conflict: A repertoire of creative, peaceful approaches. *Journal of Conflict Resolution, 29,* 330–358.

Folger, R. (1987). Reformulating the preconditions of resentment: A referent cognitions model. In J.C. Master & W.P. Smith (Eds.), *Social comparison, social justice, and relative deprivation* (pp. 183–215). Mahwah, NJ: Erlbaum.

Follett, M.P. (1940). Constructive conflict. In H.C. Metcalf & I.L. Urwick (Eds.), *Dynamic administration: The collected papers of Mary Parker Follett* (pp. 1–20). New York: Harper.

Foster, D. (1994). Racism and minority group children. In A. Dawes & D. Donald (Eds.), *Childhood and adversity: Psychological perspectives from South African research* (pp. 220–239). Cape Town: David Philip.

Foster, D. (1998). Perpetrators of gross human rights violations. *Journal of Community and Health Sciences, 4*(2), 1–34.

Foster, D., Davis, D., & Sandler, D. (1987). *Detention and torture in South Africa.* Cape Town: David Philip.

Frank, J. (1986). The role of pride. In R.K. White (Ed.), *Psychology and the prevention of nuclear war* (pp. 220–226). New York: New York University Press.

Frank, J.D. (1967). *Sanity and survival in the nuclear age.* New York: Random House.

Franklin, K. (1998, August). Psychosocial motivations of hate crime perpetrators: Implications for educational intervention. Paper presented at the 106th Annual Convention of the American Psychological Association, San Francisco.

Freire, P. (1970). *Pedagogy of the oppressed.* New York: Seabury Press.

Freire, P. (1973). *Education for critical consciousness.* New York: Seabury Press.

Freire, P. (1993) *Pedagogy of the oppressed* (Rev. ed). New York: Continuum.

Friedman, M.J., & Marsella, A.J. (1996). Posttraumatic stress disorder: An overview of the concept. In A.J. Marsella, M.J. Friedman, E.T. Gerrity, & R.M. Scurfield (Eds.), *Ethnocultural aspects of posttraumatic stress disorder: Issues, research, and clinical applications* (pp. 11–32). Washington, DC: American Psychological Association.

Friedmann, J. (1992). *Empowerment: The politics of alternative development.* Cambridge, MA: Blackwell.

Friesen, B.J., & Koroloff, N.M. (1990). Family-centered services: Implications for mental health administration and research. *Journal of Mental Health Administration, 17,* 13–25.

Frisby, C.L. (1998). Contextual factors of learner-centered principles. In N.M. Lambert & B.L. McCombs (Eds.), *How students learn: Reforming schools through learner-centered education* (pp. 61–79). Washington, DC: American Psychological Association.

Frønes, I. (1995). *Among peers: On the meaning of peers in the process of socialisation.* Oslo: Scandinavian University Press.

Frontalini, D., & Caiati, M.C. (1984). *El mito de la guerra sucia [The myth of the dirty war].* Buenos Aires: CELS.

Fry, D., & Bjorkqvist, K. (1997). Culture and conflict-resolution models: Exploring alternatives to violence. In D.P. Fry & K. Bjorkqvist (Eds.), *Cultural variation in conflict resolution* (pp. 9–23). Mahwah, NJ: Erlbaum.

Frye, M. (1992). Oppression. In M.L. Andersen & P. Hill Collins (Eds.), *Race, class and gender* (pp. 37–41). Belmont, CA: Wadsworth.

Gallagher, A.M. (1989). Social identity and the Northern Ireland conflict. *Human Relations, 42,* 917–935.

Galtung, J. (1969). Violence, peace and peace research. *Journal of Peace Research, 3,* 176–191.

Galtung, J. (1975). Violence, peace, and peace research. In J. Galtung (Ed.), *Essays in peace re-*

search, vol. I. Peace: Research, education, action (pp. 109–134). Copenhagen: Christian Ejlers.

Galtung, J. (1976). Three approaches to peace: Peacekeeping, peacemaking, and peacebuilding. In J. Galtung (Ed.), *Essays in peace research, vol. II, Peace, war and defense:* (pp. 282–304). Copenhagen: Christian Ejlers.

Galtung, J. (1978). Introduction. In J. Galtung (Ed.), *Essays in peace research, vol. III. Peace and social structure* (pp. 21–27). Copenhagen: Christian Ejlers.

Galtung, J. (1980a). The basic needs approach. In K. Lederer (Ed.), *Human needs* (pp. 55–125). Cambridge, MA: Oelgeschlager, Gunn & Hain.

Galtung, J. (1980b). A structural theory of imperialism. In J. Galtung (Ed.), *Essays in peace research, vol. IV. Peace and world structure* (pp. 437–481). Copenhagen: Christian Ejlers.

Galtung, J. (1990). Violence and peace. In P. Smoker, R. Davies, & B. Munske (Eds.), *A reader in peace studies* (pp. 9–14). New York: Pergamon.

Galtung, J. (1994, July). *Third parties in conflict transformation: Conflict facilitators, conflict thieves, both or neither.* Unpublished keynote address to the Social Workers World Conference in Colombo.

Galtung, J. (1996). *Peace by peaceful means: Peace and conflict, development and civilization.* London: Sage.

Galtung, J. (1998). On the genesis of peaceless worlds: Insane nations and insane states. *Peace and Conflict: Journal of Peace Psychology, 4,* 1–12.

Gandhi, M.K. (1938). *Hind Swaraj.* Ahmedabad: Navajivan Publishing House.

Gandhi, M.K. (1948). *Autobiography: The story of my experiments with truth.* Washington, DC: Public Affairs Press.

Gandhi, M.K. (1951). *Non-violent resistance.* New York: Schocken Books.

Gandhi, M.K. (1957/1927). *An autobiography: The story of my experiments with truth.* Boston: Beacon Press.

Gandhi, M.K. (1958–1984). *The collected works of Mahatma Gandhi,* 90+ vols. Publications Division: Ministry of Information and Broadcasting, Government of India.

Gao, G., & Ting-Toomey, S. (1998). *Communicating effectively with the Chinese.* Thousand Oaks, CA: Sage.

Garbarino, J. (1993). *Let's talk about living in a world with violence.* Chicago: Erikson Institute.

Garbarino, J. (1995). *Raising children in a socially toxic environment.* San Francisco: Jossey-Bass.

Garbarino, J. (1999). *Lost boys: Why our sons turn violent and how we can save them.* New York: Free Press.

Garbarino, J., & Associates. (1992). *Children and families in the social environment* (2nd ed.). Hawthorne, NY: Aldine de Gruyter.

Garbarino, J., Dubrow, N., Kostelny, K., & Pardo, C. (1992). *Children in danger: Coping with the consequences of community violence.* San Francisco: Jossey-Bass.

Garbarino, J., & Kostelny, K. (1992). Child maltreatment as a community problem. *Child Abuse and Neglect, 16,* 455–464.

Garbarino, J., & Kostelny, K. (1993). Children's response to war: What do we know? In L. Leavitt & N. Fox (Eds.), *The psychological effects of war and violence on children* (pp. 23–39). Hillsdale, NJ: Erlbaum.

Garbarino, J., & Kostelny, K. (1994). Family support and community development. In S. Kagan & B. Weissbourd (Eds.), *Putting family first: America's family support movement and the challenge of change* (pp. 297–320). San Francisco: Jossey-Bass.

Garbarino, J., & Kostelny, K. (1996a). Child development: What do we need to know to understand children in war? In R. Apfel & B. Simon (Eds.), *Minefields in their hearts: The mental health of children in war and communal violence.* New Haven, CT: Yale University Press.

Garbarino, J., & Kostelny, K. (1996b). The effects of political violence on Palestinian children's behavior problems: A risk accumulation model. *Child Development, 66,* 33–45.

Garbarino. J., & Kostelny, K. (1997a). Coping with the consequences of community violence. In A. Goldstein & J. Conoley (Eds.), *School violence intervention: A practical handbook* (pp. 366–387). New York: Guilford Press.

Garbarino, J., & Kostelny, K. (1997b). What children can tell us about living in a war zone. In J. Osofsky (Ed.), *Children in a violent society* (pp. 32–41). New York: Guilford Press.

Garbarino, J., Kostelny, K., & Barry, F. (1998). Neighborhood-based programs. In P. Trickett & C. Shellenbach (Eds.), *Violence against children in the family and the community* (pp. 287–314). Washington, DC: American Psychological Association.

Garbarino, J., Kostelny, K., & Dubrow, N. (1991a). *No place to be a child: Growing up in a war zone.* San Francisco: Jossey-Bass.

Garbarino, J., Kostelny, K., & Dubrow, N. (1991b). What children can tell us about living in danger. *American Psychologist, 46,* 376–383.

Gardner, W., & Preator, K. (1996). Children of seropositive mothers in the U.S. AIDS epidemic. *Journal of Social Issues, 52*(3), 177–195.

Garfield, R.M., & Neugut, A.I. (1997). The human consequences of war. In B.S. Levy & V.W. Sidel (Eds.), *War and public health* (pp. 27–38). New York: Oxford University Press.

Garmezy, N., & Rutter, M. (Eds.). (1983). *Stress, coping, and development in children.* New York: McGraw-Hill.

Garnets, L., Herek, G. M., & Levy, B. (1990). Violence and victimization of lesbians and gay men. *Journal of Interpersonal Violence, 5,* 366–383.

Garofalo, J. (1997). Hate crime victimization in the United States. In R.C. Davis, A.J. Lurigio, & W.G. Skogan (Eds.), *Victims of crime* (pp. 134–145). Newbury Park, CA: Sage.

Garofalo, J., & Martin, S.E. (1993). *Bias motivated crimes: Their characteristics and the law enforcement response.* (Final report to the National Institute of Justice.) Carbondale: Southern Illinois University, Center for the Study of Crime, Delinquency, and Corrections.

Gelles, R.J. (1974). *The violent home: A study of physical aggression between husbands and wives.* Beverly Hills, CA: Sage.

Gelles, R.J. (1983). An exchange/social control theory. In D. Finkelhor, R.J. Gelles, & G.T. Hotaling (Eds.), *The dark side of families: Current family violence research* (pp. 151–165). Beverly Hills, CA: Sage.

Gelles, R.J. (1993a). Alcohol and other drugs are not the cause of violence. In R. Gelles & M. Straus (Eds.), *Current controversies on family violence* (pp. 182–196). Newbury Park, CA: Sage.

Gelles, R.J. (1993b). Through a sociological lens: Social structure and family violence. In R.J. Gelles & D.R. Loseke (Eds.), *Current controversies on family violence* (pp. 31–46). Newbury Park, CA: Sage.

Gelles, R.J. (1997). *Intimate violence in families* (3rd edition). Thousand Oaks, CA: Sage.

Gelles, R. J., & Straus, M.A. (1979). Determinants of violence in the family: Toward a theoretical integration. In W.R. Burr, R. Hill, F.I. Nye, & I.L. Reiss (Eds.), *Contemporary theories about the family* (Vol. 1, pp. 549–581). New York: Free Press.

Gelles, R. J., & Straus, M.A. (1988). *Intimate violence.* New York: Simon & Schuster.

Gellner, E. (1995) Introduction. In S. Periwal (Ed.), *Notions of nationalism* (pp. 1–7). Budapest: Central European University Press.

George, A.L. (1969). The operational code: A neglected approach to the study of political leaders and decision-making. *International Studies Quarterly, 13,* 251–280.

George, A.L. (1983). *Managing U.S.-Soviet rivalry: Problems in crisis prevention.* Boulder, CO: Westview Press.

George, S. (1992). *The debt boomerang: How Third World debt harms us all.* London: Pluto Press.

Gerbner, G., Morgan, M., & Signorielli, N. (1994). Television violence profile no. 16: The turning point—from research to action. Unpublished manuscript, Annenberg School of Communication, University of Pennsylvania.

Gergen, K. (1989). Warranting voice and elaboration. In J. Shotter & K.J. Gergen (Eds.), *Texts of identity* (pp. 70–81). London: Sage.

Gergen, K. (1994). *Toward transformation in social knowledge* (2nd ed.). Thousand Oaks, CA: Sage.

Gergen, K. (1997). *Realities and relationships: Soundings in social construction.* Cambridge, MA: Harvard University Press.

Gerstenfeld, P.B. (1992). Smile when you call me that!: The problems with punishing hate motivated behavior. *Behavioral Sciences and the Law, 10,* 259–283.

Gevisser, M. (1996). *Portraits of power: Profiles in a changing South Africa.* Johannesburg: David Phillip.

Ghosh, A. (1998, October 26/November 2). In South Asia, nuclear catastrophe in the making. *The New Yorker,* 186–197.

Gibbs, S. (1997). Postwar social reconstruction in Mozambique: Reframing children's experiences of trauma and healing. In K. Kumar (Ed.), *Rebuilding war-torn societies: Critical areas for international assistance* (pp. 227–238). Boulder, CO: Lynne Rienner.

Gilbert, A. (1997). Small voices in the wind: Local knowledge and social transformation. *Peace and Conflict: Journal of Peace Psychology, 3,* 275–292.

Giller, J. (1998). Caring for victims of torture in Uganda: Some personal reflections. In P. Bracken & C. Petty (Eds.), *Rethinking the trauma of war* (pp. 128–145). London: Free Association Books.

Gilligan, C. (1982). *In a different voice: Psychological theory and women's development.* Cambridge, MA: Harvard University Press.

Girard, P. (1980). Historical foundations of anti-semitism. In J.E. Dimsdale (Ed.), *Survivors, victims and perpetrators: Essays on the Nazi Holocaust* (pp. 55–77). New York: Hemisphere Publishing.

Giuliani, F., Eckhart, F., Mawlawi, F., & Bennett, G. (1995). Seminar on Lessons Learned, United Nations Operation in Somalia, New York, 19–20 June 1995.

Gladstone, A.I. (1962). Relationship orientation and processes leading toward war. *Background, 6,* 13–25.

Glasser, W. (1992). *The quality school.* New York: HarperCollins.

Godelier, M. (1978). System, structure and contradiction in "Capital." In D. McQuarie (Ed.), *Marx: Sociology/social change/capitalism* (pp. 77–102). London: Quarter Books.

Goldstein, J.H., Davis, R.W., & Herman, D. (1975). Escalation of aggression: Experimental studies. *Journal of Personality and Social Psychology, 31,* 162–170.

Gondolf, E.W., Fisher, E., & McFerron, J.R. (1988). Racial differences among shelter residents: A comparison of Anglo, Black, and Hispanic battered women. *Journal of Family Violence, 3,* 39–51.

Gordon, T. (1973). Notes on White and Black psychology. *Journal of Social Issues, 29*(1), 87–95.

Gottschalk, P., & Smeeding, T.M. (2000). Empirical evidence on income inequality in industrialized countries. In A.B. Atkinson & F. Bourgignon (Eds.), *Handbook of income distribution.* Amsterdam: Elsevier-North Holland Publishers.

Gour, C., & Gunn, H.D. (1991). *Returning capital: Democratic initiatives and community development.* Ithaca, NY: Cornell University Press.

Gourevich, P. (1998). *We wish to inform you that tomorrow we will be killed with our families.* New York: Farrar Straus & Giroux.

Graça Machel/UN Study on the Effects of War on Children (1998). *Peace and Conflict: Journal of Peace Psychology, 4*(4). Entire issue.

Grant, P.R. (1992). Ethnocentrism between groups of unequal power in response to perceived threat to social identity and valued resources. *Canadian Journal of Behavioural Science, 24,* 348–370.

Grant, P.R., & Brown, R. (1995). From ethnocentrism to collective protest: Responses to relative deprivation and threats to social identity. *Social Psychology Quarterly, 58,* 195–212.

Graziano, F. (1992). *Divine violence: Spectacle, psychosexuality, and radical Christianity in the Argentine "Dirty War."* Boulder, CO: Westview Press.

Green, E.G., & Wessells, M.G. (1997). *Mid-term evaluation of the province-based war trauma team project: Meeting the psychosocial needs of children in Angola.* Arlington, VA: USAID Displaced Children and Orphans Fund and War Victims Fund.

Green, M. (1993). *Gandhi: Voice of a new age revolution.* New York: Continuum.

Greenwald, D.S., & Zeitlin, S.J. (1987). *No reason to talk about it: Families confront the nuclear taboo.* New York: Norton.

Greeson, L.E. (1991). Cultural ethnocentrism and imperialism in citations of American and Scandinavian psychological research. *International Journal of Psychology, 26,* 262–268.

Greider, W. (1998). *Fortress America: The American military and the consequences of peace.* New York: Public Affairs.

Griffith, P. (1989). *Battle tactics of the Civil War.* New Haven, CT: Yale University Press.

Grossman, D. (1996). *On killing: The psychological cost of learning to kill in war and society.* New York: Little, Brown.

Grossman, D. (1998, August). Trained to kill. *Christianity Today,* 31–39.

Gruber, J., & Trickett, E.J. (1987). Can we empower others? The paradox of empowerment in an alternative public high school. *American Journal of Community Psychology, 15,* 353–372.

Gubb, M., Koch, M., Munson, A., Sullivan, F., & Thomson, I. (1993). *The earth summit agreements: A guide and assessment.* London: Earthscan Publications.

Gudykunst, W., & Ting-Toomey, S. (1988). *Culture and interpersonal communication.* Newbury Park, CA: Sage.

Guetzkow, H. (1957). Isolation and collaboration: A partial theory of international relations. *Journal of Conflict Resolution, 1,* 46–68.

Gugelberger, G.M. (Ed.). (1996). *The real thing: Testimonial discourse and Latin America.* Durham, NC: Duke University Press.

Gulliver, P.H. (1979). *Disputes and negotiations: A cross-cultural perspective.* New York: Academic Press.

Gurr, T.R. (1970). *Why men rebel.* Princeton, NJ: Princeton University Press.

Gusterson, H. (1991). *Rituals of renewal among nuclear weapons scientists.* Washington, DC: American Association for the Advancement of Science.

Gutiérrez, G. (1973/1988). *A theology of liberation: History, politics and salvation* (Trans. and ed. by Sister C. Inda & J. Eagleson). Maryknoll, NY: Orbis Books.

Guzman Bouvard, M. (1994). *Revolutionizing motherhood: The mothers of the Plaza de Mayo.* Wilmington, DE: Scholarly Resources.

Hacker, A. (1997). *Money: Who has how much and why?* New York: Scribner.

Hägglund, S. (1999). Peer relationships and children's understanding of peace and war: A socio-cultural perspective. In A. Raviv, L. Oppenheimer, & D. Bar-Tal (Eds.), *How children understand war and peace: A call for international peace education* (pp. 190–207). San Francisco: Jossey-Bass.

Hägglund, S., Hakvoort, I., & Oppenheimer, L. (Eds.). (1996). *Research on children and peace: International perspectives.* Sweden: Göteborg University. Report No. 1996:04.

Haight, M.R. (1980). *The study of self deception.* Atlantic Highlands, NJ: Humanities Press.

Hakvoort, I. (1996). Conceptualizations of peace and war from childhood through adolescence. Unpublished doctoral dissertation. University of Amsterdam, The Netherlands.

Hakvoort, I., Hägglund, S., & Oppenheimer, L. (1998). Dutch and Swedish adolescents' understanding of peace and war. In J.-E. Nurmi (Ed.), *Adolescents, cultures and conflicts: Growing up in contemporary Europe* (pp. 75–105). MSU Series on Children, Youth and Family. New York: Garland Publishing.

Hakvoort, I., & Oppenheimer, L. (1998). Conceptualization of peace and war: A review of developmental psychological research. *Developmental Review. Perspectives in Behavior and Cognition, 18,* 353–389.

Hall, E. (1959). *The silent language.* New York: Anchor Books, Doubleday.

Hall, E.T. (1976). *Beyond culture.* Garden City, NY: Anchor.

Hallie, P .P. (1979). *Lest innocent blood be shed: The story of the village of Le Chambon, and how goodness happened there.* New York: Harper & Row.

Halpern, R. (1990). Poverty and early childhood parenting: Toward a framework for intervention. *American Journal of Orthopsychiatry, 60,* 6–18.

Hamber, B. (1997). Truth: The road to reconciliation? Retrieved August 28, 1998 from the World Wide Web: *http://www.wits.ac.za/wits/csvr/artrcant.htm*

Hamber, B. (1998). The burdens of truth. *American Imago, 55,* 9–28.

Hamber, B., & van der Merwe, H. (1998, March 28). What is this thing called reconciliation? Paper presented at the Goedgedacht Forum "After the Truth and Reconciliation Commission." Retrieved August 28, 1998 from the World Wide Web: *http://www.wits.ac.za/wits/csvr/artrcb&h.htm*

Hamberger, L.K., & Hastings, J.E. (1986). Characteristics of spouse abusers. *Journal of Interpersonal Violence, 1,* 363–373.

Hamberger, L.K., & Hastings, J.E. (1991). Personality correlates of men who batter and non-violent men: Some continuities and discontinuities. *Journal of Family Violence, 6,* 131–147.

Hamner, K.M. (1992). Gay-bashing: A social identity analysis of violence against lesbians and gay men. In G.M. Herek & K.T. Berrill (Eds.), *Hate crimes: Confronting violence against lesbians and gay men* (pp. 179–190). Newbury Park, CA: Sage.

Hanauer, R.L. (1998, March/April). Economic alternatives: An integral part of the agenda for peace and justice. *Fellowship, 64*(3/4), 10–11

Harari, C. (1992). Psychology and international peacemaking in the changing world scene. In U.P. Gielen, L.L. Adler, & N.A. Milgram (Eds.), *Psychology in international perspective* (pp. 30–41). Amsterdam: Swets & Zeitlinger.

Harff, B., & Gurr, T.R. (1990). Victims of the state: Genocides, politicides and group repression since 1945. *International Review of Victimology, 1,* 1–19.

Harris & Associates (1994). Metropolitan Life survey of the American teacher: Violence in America's public schools, Part II. New York: Metropolitan Life Insurance.

Harris, R.A., Proshansky, H.M., & Raskin, E. (1956). Some attitudes of college students concerning the hydrogen bomb. *Journal of Psychology, 42,* 29–33.

Harry, J. (1992). Conceptualizing anti-gay violence. In G.M. Herek & K.T. Berrill (Eds.), *Hate crimes: Confronting violence against lesbians and gay men* (pp. 113–158). Newbury Park, CA: Sage.

Hartigan, P. (1995). California university provides lesson in military conversion. *Boston Globe,* Sept. 1. Retrieved January 23, 1999 from LEXIS-NEXIS on the World Wide Web: *http://web.lexis-nexis.com/universe.*

Hartunian, A. (1968). *Neither to laugh nor to weep.* Boston: Beacon Press.

Harvey, N. (1998). *The Chiapas rebellion: The strug-*

gle for land and democracy. Durham, NC: Duke University Press.

Hasenfeld, Y. (1992). Power in social work practice. In Y. Hasenfeld (Ed.), *Human services as complex organizations.* Newbury Park, CA: Sage.

Hauchler, I., & Kennedy, P.M. (1994). *Global trends: The world almanac of development and peace.* New York: Continuum Publishing.

Hawkins, J.D. (1997). Academic performance and school success: Sources and consequences. In R.P. Weissberg, T.P. Gullotta, R.L. Hampton, B.A. Ryan, & G.R. Adams (Eds.), *Enhancing children's wellness* (pp. 278–305). Thousand Oaks, CA: Sage.

Hayek, F.A. (1975). The principles of a liberal social order. In A. De Crespigny & J. Cronin (Eds.), *Ideologies of politics* (pp. 55–75). Cape Town: Oxford University Press.

Heinrich, W. (1997). *Building the peace: Experiences of collaborative peacebuilding in Somalia, 1993–1996.* Uppsala, Sweden: Life and Peace Institute.

Henton, J., Cate, R., Koval, J., Lloyd, S., & Christopher, S. (1983). Romance and violence in dating relationships. *Journal of Family Issues, 4,* 467–482.

Herek, G.M. (1984). Beyond "homophobia": A social psychological perspective on attitudes toward lesbians and gay men. *Journal of Homosexuality, 19* (1/2), 1–21.

Herek, G.M. (1988). Heterosexuals' attitudes toward lesbians and gay men: Correlates and gender differences. *Journal of Sex Research, 25,* 451–477.

Herek, G.M. (1989). Hate crimes against lesbians and gay men. *American Psychologist, 44,* 948–955.

Herek, G.M. (1992). The social context of hate crimes: Notes on cultural heterosexism. In G.M. Herek & K.T. Berrill (Eds.), *Hate crimes: Confronting violence against lesbians and gay men* (pp. 89–104). Newbury Park, CA: Sage.

Herek, G.M., & Berrill, K.T. (1992). Documenting the victimization of lesbians and gay men: Methodological issues. In G.M. Herek & K.T. Berrill (Eds.), *Hate crimes: Confronting violence against lesbians and gay men* (pp. 270–315). Newbury Park, CA: Sage.

Herek, G M., & Capitanio, J.P. (1996). "Some of my best friends": Intergroup contact, concealable stigma, and heterosexuals' attitudes toward gay men and lesbians. *Personality and Social Psychology Bulletin, 22,* 412–424.

Herek, G.M., Gillis, J.R., Cogan, J.C., & Glunt

F. K. (1997). Hate crime victimization among lesbian, gay, and bisexual adults. *Journal of Interpersonal Violence 12,* 195–215.

Herken, G. (1985). *Counsels of war.* New York: Knopf.

Herken, G. (1992). *Cardinal choices: Presidential science advising from the atomic bomb to SDI.* New York: Oxford University Press.

Herman, E. (1995). *The romance of American psychology.* Berkeley, CA: University of California Press.

Herman, J.L. (1992). *Trauma and recovery.* New York: Basic Books.

Herrenkohl, E.C., Herrenkohl, R.C., & Toedter, L.J. (1983). Perspectives on the intergenerational transmission of abuse. In D. Finkelhor, R.J. Gelles, G.T. Hotaling, & M.A. Straus (Eds.), *The dark side of families: Current family violence research* (pp 305–316). Beverly Hills, CA: Sage.

Hershberger, S.L., & D'Augelli, A.R. (1995). The impact of victimization on the mental health and suicidality of lesbian, gay, and bisexual youth. *Developmental Psychology, 31,* 65–74.

Heskin, K. (1980). *Northern Ireland: A psychological analysis.* Dublin: Gill & Macmillan.

Hesse, P. (1989). *The World is a Dangerous Place: Images of the Enemy on Children's Television.* [Film]. Cambridge, MA: Center for Psychology and Social Change.

Hesse, P., & Mack, J. (1991). The world is a dangerous place: Images of the enemy on children's television. In R. Reiber (Ed.), *The psychology of war and peace: The image of the enemy* (pp. 131–154). New York: Plenum.

Hicks, D., & Walch, K. (1990, April) An analysis of the transition to global security from the perspective of cognitive development. Paper presented at the annual meeting of the International Studies Association, Washington, DC.

Higgins, E.T. (1981). Role-taking and social judgment: Alternative developmental perspectives and processes. In V.H. Flavell & L. Ross (Eds.), *New directions in the study of social-cognitive development.* Cambridge: Cambridge University Press.

Hines, A.B., & Pedersen, P. (1980). The cultural grid: Matching social system variables and cultural perspectives. *Asian Pacific Training and Development Journal, 1,* 5–11.

Hobbes, T. (1985). *Leviathan.* (Ed. C.B. Macpherson) London: Penguin.

Hochschild, A. (1989). *The second shift.* New York: Viking.

Hoff, L.A. (1990). *Battered women as survivors.* New York: Routledge.

Hofstede, G. (1989). Cultural differences in teaching and learning. *International Journal of Intercultural Relations, 10,* 301–302.

Hofstede, G. (1991). *Cultures and organizations: Software of the mind.* London: McGraw-Hill.

Hogg, M., & Abrams, D. (1988). *Social identifications: A social psychology of intergroup relations and group processes.* London: Routledge.

Holloran, R., Gelb, H., & Raines, H. (1981, August 14). Weinberger said to offer Reagan plan to regain atomic superiority. *New York Times,* A1 and A11.

Holmes, D.S. (1968). Dimensions of projection. *Psychological Bulletin, 69,* 248–268.

Holt, R.R., & Silverstein, B. (1989). The image of the enemy: U.S. views of the Soviet Union. *Journal of Social Issues, 45*(2).

Homer-Dixon, T.F. (1993). *Environmental scarcity and global security.* New York: Foreign Policy Association.

Homes for the Homeless. (1998). *Facts on homeless children and their families.* New York: Author.

Honwana, A.M. (1997). Healing for peace: Traditional healers and post-war reconstruction in southern Mozambique. *Peace and Conflict: Journal of Peace Psychology, 3,* 293–305.

Horne, S. (1999). Domestic violence in Russia. *American Psychologist, 54,* 55–61.

Hornung, C., McCullough, B., & Sugimoto, T. (1981). Status relationships in marriage: Risk factors in spouse abuse. *Journal of Marriage and the Family, 43,* 679–692.

Horowitz, S., Boardman, S., & Cochran, K. (1998). *Parent-child conflict resolution: The Peaceful Kids, Safe Kids Program. Report on pilot study: Year 1,* p. 544 (Unpublished report).

Houston, J.E., Crozier, W.R., & Walker, P. (1990). The assessment of ethnic sensitivity among Northern Ireland schoolchildren. *British Journal of Developmental Psychology, 8,* 419–422.

Hovland, C.L., & Sears, R.R. (1940). Minor studies of aggression: Correlations of lynchings with economic indices. *Journal of Psychology, 9,* 301–310.

Hu, H.C. (1945). The Chinese concepts of face. *American Anthropologist, 46,* 45–64.

Huber, J., & Spitze, G. (1983). *Sex stratification, children, housework and jobs.* New York: Academic Press.

Huberman, E., & Huberman, E. (1964). *50 great essays.* New York: Bantam.

Human Rights Watch/Americas. (1996). *Colombia's killer networks: The military-paramilitary partnership and the United States.* New York: Human Rights Watch.

Human Rights Watch/Asia Watch. (1993). *A modern form of slavery: Trafficking of Burmese women and girls into brothels in Thailand.* New York: Human Rights Watch.

Hwang, K.K. (1998). Guanxi and Mientze: Conflict resolution in Chinese society. *Intercultural Communication Studies, 7,* 17–42.

Ignatieff, M. (1993). *Blood and belonging: Journeys into the new nationalism.* London: BBC Books.

In Common. (1999, June 18). Building Peace. [on-line]. Available: *http://incommon.web.net/tenpoint/peace.html.*

Ingleby, D. (1995). Problems in the study of the interplay between science and culture. In N.R. Goldberger and J. Verhoff (Eds.), *The culture and psychology reader* (pp. 108–123). New York: New York University Press.

Insko, C.A., Hoyle, R.H., Pinkley, R.L., Hong, G., & Slim, R.M. (1988). Individual-group discontinuity: The role of a consensus rule. *Journal of Experimental Social Psychology, 24,* 505–519.

International Fellowship of Reconciliation (IFOR) and International Peace Bureau (IPB). (1997). *International Women's Day for Peace and Disarmament: 24 May 1996.* Geneva, Switzerland: IPB.

International Fellowship of Reconciliation (IFOR). (1998, February). *Women's Peacemakers Program.* Alkmaar, The Netherlands: Author.

Isabella, R.A. (1993). Origins of attachment: Maternal interactive behavior across the first year. *Child Development, 64,* 605–621.

Ispanovic-Radojkovic, V., Bojanin, S., Tadic, N., & Rudic, N. (1993). Mental health care of children and adolescents—the victims of war in former Yugoslavia (1991–1993). In P. Kalicinin, J. Bukelic, V. Ispanovic-Radojkovic, & D. Lecic-Tosevski (Eds.), *The stresses of war.* Belgrade: Institute for Mental Health.

Iyer, R. (1973). *The moral and political thought of Mahatma Gandhi.* New York: Oxford University Press.

Jacobs, M.S. (1989). *American psychology in the quest for nuclear peace.* New York: Praeger.

Jacobson, J.L. (1992). *Gender bias: Roadblock to sustainable development* (Worldwatch paper no. 110). Washington, DC: Worldwatch Institute.

Jacoby, R. (1975). *Social amnesia. A critique of con-*

formist psychology from Adler to Laing. Hassocks, UK: Harvester Press.

Jaising, I. (1995). Violence against women: The Indian perspective. In J. Peters & A. Wolper (Eds.), *Women's rights human rights: International feminist perspectives* (pp. 51–56). New York: Routledge.

Jakobsen, P. (1996). National interest, humanitarianism, or CNN: What triggers UN peace enforcement after the Cold War? *Journal of Peace Research, 33,* 205–215.

James, A. (1990). *Peacekeeping in international politics.* London: Macmillan and the International Institute for Strategic Studies.

James, W. (1995/1910). The moral equivalent of war. *Peace and Conflict: Journal of Peace Psychology, 1,* 17–26.

Janis, I.L. (1982). *Victims of groupthink* (2nd ed.). Boston: Houghton Mifflin.

Janis, I.L. (1989). *Crucial decisions: Leadership in policy-making and management.* New York: Free Press.

Janoff-Bulman, R. (1992). *Shattered assumptions.* New York: Free Press.

Jay, A. (1993). *Persecution by proxy: The civil patrols in Guatemala.* New York: Robert F. Kennedy Memorial Center for Human Rights.

Jenness, V., & Broad, K. (1994). Antiviolence activism and the (in)visibility of gender in the gay/lesbian and women's movements. *Gender and Society, 8,* 402–423.

Jenness, V., & Grattet, R. (1996). The criminalization of hate: A comparison of structural and polity influences on the passage of "bias-crime" legislation in the United States. *Sociological Perspectives, 39,* 129–154.

Jervis, R. (1976). *Perception and misperception in international politics.* Princeton, NJ: Princeton University Press.

Johnson, D.W., & Johnson, R.T. (1983). The socialization and achievement crisis: Are cooperative learning experiences the solution? In L. Beckman (Ed.), *Applied Social Psychology Annual 4.* Beverly Hills, CA: Sage.

Johnson, D.W., & Johnson, R.T. (1987). *Creative conflict.* Edina, MN: Interaction Book Company.

Johnson, D.W., & Johnson, R.T. (1989). *Cooperation and competition: Theory and research.* Edina, MN: Interaction Book Company.

Johnson, D.W., Johnson, R.T., & Holubec, E.J. (1986). *Circles of learning: Cooperation in the classroom.* Edina, MN: Interaction Book Company.

Jones, E.E., & Davis, K.E. (1965). From acts to dispositions: The attributional process in person perception. In L. Berkowitz (Ed.), *Advances in Experimental Social Psychology* (Vol. 2, pp. 220–266). New York: Academic Press.

Jones, E.E., & Nisbett, R.E. (1971). *The actor and the observer: Divergent perceptions of the causes of behavior.* Morristown, NJ: General Learning Press.

Jones, T.S. (1998). Research supports effectiveness of peer mediation. *The Fourth R,* Volume 82, March, April. National Institute for Dispute Resolution.

Kagitcibasi, C. (1998, August). Psychology and human potential development. Paper presented at the 26th International Congress of Applied Psychology, San Francisco.

Kam, A.L.N. (1998). Sticks, stones and smoke-screens. *New Internationalist, 298,* 34–35.

Kanner, A., & Gomes, M. (1995). The all consuming self. In T. Roszac, A. Kanner, & M. Gomes (Eds.), *Restoring the earth: Healing the mind* (pp. 77–91). San Francisco: Sierra Club Books.

Karim, K.H. (1997). The historical resilience of primary stereotypes: Core images of the Muslim Other. In S.H. Riggins (Ed.), *Communication and human values: Vol. 24. The language and politics of exclusion: Others in discourse* (pp. 153–182). Thousand Oaks, CA: Sage.

Katz, A. (1998, December 29). Human rights on wheels. *The Nation,* 19–22.

Katz, J.H. (1993). *The straight path: A story of healing and transformation in Fiji.* Reading, MA: Addison-Wesley.

Katz, M.B. (1994). *Improving poor people.* Princeton, NJ: Princeton University Press.

Kaufman, J., & Ziegler, E. (1993). The intergenerational transmission of abuse is overstated. In J.R. Gelles & D.R. Loseke (Eds.), *Current controversies on family violence* (pp. 209–221). Newbury Park, CA: Sage.

Kaufman, P., Chandler, K., & Rand, M. (1998). Indicators of school crime and safety. Washington, DC: U.S. Department of Justice.

Kawakami, K., & Dion, K.L. (1995). Social identity and affect as determinants of collective action. *Theory and Psychology, 5,* 551–577.

Keane, J. (1996). *Reflections on violence.* London: Verso.

Keating, M. (1993). *The Earth Summit's agenda for change: A plain language version of Agenda 21 and the other Rio Agreements.* Geneva, Switzerland: Centre for Our Common Future.

Keefer, R., Goldstein, J., & Kasiarz, D. (1983). Olympic games participation and warfare. In J.H. Goldstein (Ed.), *Sport violence* (pp. 183–193). New York: Springer-Verlag.

Keen, S. (1986). *Faces of the enemy.* New York: Harper & Row.

Kellaghan, T. (1994). Family and schooling. In T. Husen & T.N. Postlewaite (Eds.), *The international encyclopedia of education* (2nd ed., pp. 2250–2258). Tarrytown, NY: Elsevier Science.

Kelley, H.H. (1952). Two functions of reference groups. In G.E. Swanson, T.M. Newcomb, & E.C. Hartley (Eds.), *Readings in social psychology* (pp. 410–414). New York: Henry Holt.

Kelly, L. (1993). *Surviving sexual violence.* Minneapolis, MN: University of Minnesota Press.

Kelman, H.C. (1977). The conditions, criteria, and dialectics of human dignity: A transnational perspective. *International Studies Quarterly, 21,* 529–552.

Kelman, H.C. (1988). Nationalism, national sentiments, and international conflict. Paper prepared for the Workshop on Nationalism and International Conflict, National Academy of Sciences, Washington, DC.

Kelman, H.C. (1990). Applying a human needs perspective to the practice of conflict resolution: The Israeli-Palestinian case. In J. Burton (Ed.), *Conflict: Human needs theory* (pp. 283–297). New York: St. Martin's Press.

Kelman, H.C. (1996). The interactive problem-solving approach. In C.A. Crocker, F.O. Hampson, & P. Aall (Eds.), *Managing global chaos* (pp. 501–520). Washington, DC: United States Institute of Peace Press.

Kelman, H.C. (1997). Group processes in the resolution of international conflicts: Experiences from the Israeli-Palestinian case. *American Psychologist, 52,* 212–220.

Kelman, H.C. (1999). Building a sustainable peace: The limits of pragmatism in the Israeli-Palestinian negotiations. *Peace and Conflict: Journal of Peace Psychology, 5,* 101–116.

Kelman, H.C., & Hamilton, V.C. (1989). *Crimes of obedience.* New Haven, CT: Yale University Press.

Kennedy, P. (1986). *The rise and fall of great powers.* New York: Vintage Books.

Kim, U., Triandis, H.C., Kagitcibasi, C., Choi, S. C., & Yoon, G. (1994). *Individualism and collectivism.* Thousand Oaks, CA: Sage.

Kimmel, P.R. (1985). Learning about peace: Choices and the U.S. Academy of Peace as seen from two different perspectives. *American Psychologist, 40,* 536–541.

Kimmel, P.R. (1994). Cultural perspectives on international negotiations. *Journal of Social Issues, 50*(1), 179–196.

Kimmel, P.R. (1995). Sustainability and cultural understanding: Peace psychology as public interest science. *Peace and Conflict: Journal of Peace Psychology, 1,* 101–116.

Kinzie, J., Sack, W., Angell, R., Manson, S., & Rath, B. (1986). The psychiatric effects of massive trauma on Cambodian children. *Journal of the American Academy of Child Psychiatry, 25,* 370–376.

Kite, M.E. (1984). Sex differences in attitudes toward homosexuals: A meta-analytic review. *Journal of Homosexuality, 19*(1/2), 69–81.

Kite, M.E., & Whitley, B.E. (1998). Do women and men differ in their attitudes toward homosexuality? A conceptual and methodological analysis. In G.M. Herek (Ed.), *Stigma and sexual orientation* (pp. 39–61). Thousand Oaks, CA: Sage.

Klare, M., (1998). The era of multiplying schisms: World security in the twenty-first century. In M. Klare & Y. Chandrani (Eds.), *World security: Challenges for a new century* (pp. 59–77). New York: St. Martin's Press.

Klare, M., & Chandrani, Y. (Eds.). (1998). *World security: Challenges for a new century.* New York: St. Martin's Press.

Kohn, A. (1986). *No contest: The case against competition.* Boston: Houghton Mifflin.

Kolb, D., & Coolidge, G.G. (1991). Her place at the table: A consideration of gender issues in negotiation. In J.Z. Rubin & J.W. Breslin (Eds.), *Negotiation theory and practice* (pp. 261–277). Cambridge, MA: Harvard Program on Negotiation.

Komin, S. (1991). *The psychology of Thai people.* Bangkok: Research Centre of the National Institute of Development Administration.

Koop, C., & Lundberg, G. (1992). Violence in America: A public health emergency. *Journal of the American Medical Association, 267,* 3075–3076.

Korten, D.C. (1995). *When corporations rule the world.* West Hartford, CT: Kumerian.

Korten, D.C. (1999). *Globalizing civil society: Reclaiming our right to power.* New York: Seven Stories Press.

Kostelny, K., & Garbarino, J. (1998). *Evaluation of a violence prevention program for school age children.* Chicago: Erikson Institute.

Kraybill, R. (1992). The cycle of reconciliation. *Track Two, November* issue.

Kreisher, O. (1998, March 2). Military, Congress clash over base closings; Clinton set off sparks on politically sensitive issue. *San Diego Union-Tribune*, p. A1.

Kressel, K., & Pruitt, D. (1989). *Mediation research: The process and effectiveness of third-party intervention*. San Francisco: Jossey-Bass.

Kressel, N.J. (1996). *Mass hate: The global rise of genocide and terror*. New York: Plenum.

Kriesberg, L. (1998). Coexistence and the reconciliation of communal conflicts. In E. Wiener (Ed.), *The handbook of interethnic coexistence* (pp. 182–198). New York: Continuum.

Kristof, N. (1998, April 29). "People Power" unrest on Indonesian campuses. *New York Times*, pp. A1, A6.

Kroeker, C.J. (1995). Individual, organizational, and societal empowerment: A study of the processes in a Nicaraguan agricultural cooperative. *American Journal of Community Psychology, 23*, 749–764.

Kruger, J.A. (1992). *Racial/ethnic intergroup disputing and dispute resolution in the United States: A bibliography and resource guide*. (Available from Judith A. Kruger, P.O. Box #3, Collingswood, NJ 08108.)

Krystal, H. (1988). *Integration and self-healing: Affect, trauma, alexithymia*. Hillsdale, NJ: Analytic Press.

Kumar, K. (Ed.). (1997). *Rebuilding war-torn societies: Critical areas for international assistance*. Boulder, CO: Lynne Rienner.

Kunugi, T., Boulding, E., & Oberg, J. (1996). *United Nations peacekeeping and peoples' peacebuilding: Patterns of partnerships*. Lund, Sweden: The Transnational Foundation for Peace and Future Research.

Kupchan, C.A. (Ed.). (1995). *Nationalism and nationalities in the new Europe*. Ithaca, NY: Cornell University Press.

Kuper, L. (1981). *Genocide: Its political use in the twentieth century*. New Haven, CT: Yale University Press.

Lambert, W.E., & Klineberg, O. (1967). *Children's views of foreign peoples: A cross-national study*. New York: Appleton-Century-Crofts.

Lambley, P. (1980). *The psychology of apartheid*. London: Seeker & Warburg.

Lamison-White, T. (1997). *Poverty in the United States: 1996* (Current Population Report, Series P60–198). Washington, DC: U.S. Government Printing Office.

Lamy, P. (1996). *Millennium rage: Survivalists, white supremacists and the doomsday prophecy*. New York: Plenum.

Landler, M. (1998, May 20). Joyfully, Indonesian students thumb noses at authority. *New York Times*, p. A10.

Lane, V. (1990). *Bias motivated crimes*. St. Paul, MN: Minnesota Board of Peace Officer Standards and Training.

Langer, M. (1989). *From Vienna to Managua: Journey of a psychoanalyst*. London: Free Association Books.

Langholtz, H. (1998). The psychology of peacekeeping: Genesis, ethos, and application. *Peace and Conflict: Journal of Peace Psychology, 4*, 217–236.

Largoza-Maza, L. (1995). The medium term Philippine development plan toward the year 2000: Filipino women's issues and perspectives. In J. Peters & A. Wolper (Eds.), *Women's rights human rights: International feminist perspectives* (pp. 62–66). New York: Routledge.

Larrain, S. (1993). *Estudio de frecuencia de la violencia intrafamiliar y la condición de la mujer en Chile [Study of the frequency of intrafamily violence and the condition of women in Chile]*. Santiago, Chile: Pan-American Health Organization.

Lasay, N., & Macasaet, S. (1998a, January). Chronology of events. *Mapalad (Blessed) Agrarian Reform Monitor*, pp. 1–7.

Lasay, N., & Macasaet, S. (1998b, January). The Mapalad hunger strike and agrarian reform. *Mapalad (Blessed) Agrarian Reform Monitor*, pp. 1–7.

Lasley, T. (1994). *Teaching peace: Toward cultural selflessness*. Westport, CT: Bergin & Gravey.

Last, D., & Vought, D. (1994). Interagency cooperation in peace operations—A conference report, United States Army Command and General Staff College Fort Leavenworth, Kansas, 18–20 October 1994.

Latane, B., & Darley, J. (1970). *The unresponsive bystander: Why doesn't he help?* New York: Appleton-Century-Crofts.

Lavik, N.J., Nygard, M., Sveaass, N., & Fannemel, E. (Eds.). (1994). *Pain and survival*. Oslo: Scandinavian University Press.

Lawson, M. (1994). The teaching of conflict resolution and non-violence in Australian schools: A context for peace education. In A. Bjerstedt (Ed.), *Education beyond fatalism and hate* (pp. 62–73). Malmo, Sweden: School of Education.

Lazarus, R.S., & Folkman, S. (1984). *Stress, appraisal, and coping*. New York: Springer.

Leana, C.R., & Ivancevich, J.M. (1987). Involuntary job loss: Institutional interventions and a research agenda. *Academy of Management Review, 12,* 301–312.

LeBlanc, S. (1991). 8 in 10: A special report of the Victim Recovery Program of the Fenway Community Health Center. Boston: Author. (Available from Fenway Community Health Center, 7 Haviland Street, Boston, MA 02115)

LeBon, G. (1896). *The crowd: A study of the popular mind.* London: Ernest Benn.

Lebow, R.N. (1981) *Between peace and war: The nature of international crisis.* Baltimore: Johns Hopkins University Press.

Lederach, J. (1995a). *Building peace: Sustainable reconciliation.* Tokyo: United Nations University.

Lederach, J. (1995b). *Preparing for peace.* Syracuse, NY: Syracuse University Press.

Lederach, J.P. (1997). *Building peace: Sustainable reconciliation in divided societies.* Washington, DC: United States Institute of Peace Press.

Lee, M. (1998). *The beast reawakens.* Boston: Little, Brown.

Leites, N. (1953). *A study of Bolshevism.* New York: Free Press.

Lemyre, L., & Smith, P.M. (1985). Intergroup discrimination and self-esteem in the minimal group paradigm. *Journal of Personality and Social Psychology, 49,* 660–670.

Leonard, K.E., & Jacob, T. (1988). Alcohol, alcoholism, and family violence. In V.B. Van Hasselt, R.L. Morrison, A.S. Bellack, & M. Hersen (Eds.), *Handbook of family violence* (pp. 383–406). New York: Plenum.

Lerner, M.J. (1970). The desire for justice and reactions to victims. In J. Macauley & L. Berkowitz (Eds.), *Altruism and helping behavior: Social psychological studies of some antecedents and consequences* (pp. 205–229). New York: Academic Press.

Lerner, M.J. (1980). *The belief in a just world: A fundamental delusion.* New York: Plenum.

Lerner, M.J., & Simmons, C.H. (1966). Observers' reaction to the "innocent victim": Compassion or rejection? *Journal of Personality and Social Psychology, 2,* 203–210.

Lerner, S.C. (1981). Adapting to scarcity and change (I): Stating the problem. In M.J. Lerner & S.C. Lerner (Eds.), *The justice motive in social behavior: Adapting to times of scarcity and change* (pp. 3–10). New York: Plenum.

Letellier, P. (1994). Gay and lesbian male domestic violence victimization: Challenges to feminist theory and responses to violence. *Violence and Victims, 9,* 95–106.

Leventhal, G.S. (1979). Effects of external conflict on resource allocation and fairness within groups and organizations. In W.G. Austin & S. Worchel (Eds.), *The social psychology of intergroup relations* (pp. 237–251). Monterey, CA: Brooks/Cole.

Levi, A., & Tetlock, P.E. (1980). A cognitive analysis of Japan's 1941 decision for war. *Journal of Conflict Resolution, 24,* 195–211.

Levin, J., & McDevitt, J. (1993). *Hate crimes: The rising tide of bigotry and bloodshed.* New York: Plenum.

LeVine, R.A., & Campbell, D.T. (1972). *Ethnocentrism: Theories of conflict, ethnic attitude, and group behavior.* New York: Wiley.

Levinger, G., & Rubin, J.Z. (1994). Bridges and barriers to a more general theory of conflict. *Negotiation Journal, 10,* 201–215.

Levy, B., & Sidel, V. (Eds.). (1997). *War and public health.* New York: Oxford University Press.

Lewicki, R.J., & Litterer, J.A. (1985). *Negotiation.* Homewood, IL: Richard D. Irwin.

Lewicki, R.J., Weiss, S.E., & Lewin, D. (1992). Models of conflict, negotiation and third party intervention: A review and synthesis. *Journal of Organizational Behavior, 13,* 209–252.

Lewis, C.S. (1949). *The weight of glory and other essays.* New York: Macmillan.

Licuanan, P. (1987). *People power: A social psychological analysis.* Manila: Development Academy of the Philippines.

Liddie, B. (1991). Relearning feminism on the job. In M. Bricker-Jenkins, N. Hooyman, & N. Gottlieb (Eds.), *Feminist social work practice in clinical settings* (pp. 131–146). Newbury Park, CA: Sage.

Lifton, R.J. (1986). *The Nazi doctors: Medical killing and the psychology of genocide.* New York: Basic Books.

Lifton, R.J. (1997). Reflections on Aum Shin Rikyo. In M. Flynn & C. Strozier (Eds.), *The year 2000: Essays on the end.* New York: New York University Press.

Linton, R. (1936). *The study of man.* New York: Prentice Hall.

Lippmann, W. (1947). *The Cold War: A study of U.S. foreign policy.* New York: Harper and Brothers.

Littlefield, L., Love, A., Peck, C., & Wertheim, E. (1993). A model for resolving conflict: Some theoretical, empirical and practical implications. *Australian Psychologist, 28,* 80–85.

Lorenzo, M., & Adler, D. (1984). Mental health services for Chinese in a community health center. *Social Casework, 65,* 600–609.

Louis, K.S., & Miles, M.B. (1990). *Improving the urban high school: What works and why.* New York: Teachers College Press.

Louw, J. (1987). From separation to division: The origins of two psychological associations in South Africa. *Journal of the History of the Behavioral Sciences, 23,* 341–352.

Louw, J., & van Hoorn, W. (1997). Psychology, conflict and peace in South Africa: Historical notes. *Peace and Conflict: Journal of Peace Psychology, 3,* 233–244.

Lund, B., Moris, C., & LeBaron-Duryea, M. (1994). *Conflict and culture.* Vancouver, BC: University of Victoria Institute for Dispute Resolution.

Lykes, M.B. (1994). Terror, silencing and children: International multidisciplinary collaboration with Guatemalan Maya communities. *Social Science and Medicine, 38,* 453–552.

Lykes, M.B. (1996). Meaning making in a context of genocide and silencing. In M.B. Lykes, A. Banuazizi, R. Liem, & M. Morris (Eds.), *Myths about the powerless: Contesting social inequalities* (pp. 159–178). Philadelphia: - Temple University Press.

Lykes, M.B. (1997). Activist participatory research among the Maya of Guatemala: Constructing meanings from situated know ledge. *Journal of Social Issues, 53*(4), 725–746.

Lykes, M.B. (1999). Doing psychology at the periphery: Constructing just alternatives to war and peace. *Peace and Conflict: Journal of Peace Psychology, 5,* 27–36.

Lykes, M.B., Brabeck, M.M., Ferns, T., & Radan, A. (1993). Human rights and mental health among Latin American women in situations of state-sponsored violence: Bibliographic resources. *Psychology of Women Quarterly, 17,* 525–544.

Lykes, M.B., in collaboration with Caba Mateo, A., Chavez Anay, J., Laynez Caba, A., Ruiz, U., & Williams, J.W. (1999). Telling stories—Rethreading lives: Community education, women's development and social change among the Maya Ixil. *International Journal of Leadership in Education, 2,* 207–227.

Lykes, M.B., & Liem, R. (1990). Human rights and mental health work in the United States: Lessons from Latin America. *Journal of Social Issues, 46*(3), 151–165.

Lynn, J.A. (1984). *The bayonets of the republic.* Urbana, IL: University of Illinois Press.

Maccoby, E.E., & Martin, J.A. (1983). Socialization in the context of the family: Parent-child interaction. In E.M. Hetherington (Ed.), *Handbook of child psychology: Socialization, personality, and social development,* (Vol. 4, pp. 1–102). New York: Wiley.

MacCrone, I.D. (1947). Reaction to domination in a color-caste society. *Journal of Social Psychology, 26,* 69–98.

Mack, J.E. (1982). The perception of U.S.-Soviet intentions and other psychological dimensions of the nuclear arms race. *American Journal of Orthopsychiatry, 52,* 590–599.

Mackinlay, J., & Chopra, J. (1993). *A draft concept of second generation multinational operations.* Providence, RI: Thomas J. Watson Jr. Institute for International Studies.

Macksoud, M., & Aber, L. (1996). The war experiences and psychosocial development of children in Lebanon. *Child Development 67,* 70–88.

Macy, J. (1983). *Despair and personal power in the nuclear age.* Philadelphia: New Society Publishers.

Magno, F. (1986). The political dynamics of People Power. *Kasarinlan (Sovereignty): Philippine Quarterly of Third World Studies, 3,* 13–18.

Mahoney, J. (1998, July 12). *Cambodia patriarch urges peaceful elections* [On-line]. Available at: *http://www.cambodian.com/peace.html*

Makhijani, A. (1992). *From global capitalism to economic justice: An inquiry into the elimination of systematic poverty, violence and environmental destruction in the world economy.* The Council of International and Public Affairs. New York: Apex Press.

Mallman, C. (1980). Society, needs, and rights: A systemic approach. In K. Lederer (Ed.), *Human needs* (pp. 37–54). Cambridge, MA: Oelgeschlager, Gunn & Hain.

Mamdani, M. (1996). *Citizen and subject: Contemporary Africa and the legacy of late colonialism.* London: James Currey.

Mangan, J.A. (1981). *Athleticism in the Victorian and Edwardian public school.* London: Cambridge University Press.

Manganyi, N.C. (1973). *Being black in the world.* Johannesburg: Ravan Press.

Marans, S., & Adelman, A. (1997). Experiencing violence in a developmental context. In J. Osofsky (Ed.), *Children in a violent society* (pp. 202–222). New York: Guilford Press.

Mare, G. (1992). *Brothers born of warrior blood: Pol-*

itics and ethnicity in South Africa. Johannesburg: Ravan Press.

Maren, M. (1997). *The road to hell: The ravaging effects of foreign aid and international charity.* London: Free Press.

Markus, H., & Zajonc, R.B. (1985). The cognitive perspective in social psychology. *Handbook of Social Psychology, Vol. I* (3rd ed., pp. 137–230). New York: Random House.

Markusen, A., & Yudken, J. (1992) *Dismantling the Cold War economy.* New York: Basic Books.

Martin, K. (Producer), & Nash, T. (Director). (1995). *Who's counting? Marilyn Waring on sex, lies, and global economics* [Film]. (Available from Bullfrog Films, P.O. Box 149, Oley, PA 19547).

Martín-Baró, I. (1989). Political violence and war as causes of psychosocial trauma in El Salvador. *International Journal of Mental Health, 18,* 3–20.

Martín-Baró, I. (1990). Reparations: Attention must be paid: Healing the body politic in Latin America. *Commonweal, 117*(6), 184, 186.

Martín-Baró, I. (1994a). War and mental health. In A. Aron & S. Corne (Eds.), *Writings for a liberation psychology: Ignacio Martín-Baró* (pp. 108–121). Cambridge, MA: Harvard University Press.

Martín-Baró, I. (1994b). *Writings for a liberation psychology.* Cambridge: Harvard University Press.

Marx, K. (1975). Contribution to the critique of Hegel's philosophy of law, introduction (J. Cohen, C. Dutt, M. Milligan, B. Ruhemann, D.J. Struik, & C. Upward, Trans.). In M. Shcheglova, T. Grishina, & L. Zubrilova (Eds.), *Karl Marx & Frederick Engels collected works* (Vol. 3, pp. 175–187). Moscow: Progress Publishers. (Original work published in 1844.)

Maslow, A.H. (1968). *Toward a psychology of being.* Princeton, NJ: Van Nostrand.

Maton, K.I., & Salem, D.A. (1995). Organizational characteristics of empowering community settings: A multiple case study approach. *American Journal of Community Psychology, 23,* 631–656.

May, M.A. (1943). *A social psychology of war and peace.* New Haven, CT: Yale University Press.

Mays, V.M., Bullock, M., Rosenzweig, M.R., & Wessells, M. (1998). Ethnic conflict: Global challenges and psychological perspectives. *American Psychologist, 53,* 737–742.

Mayton, D.M., Diessner, R., & Granby, C. (1996). Nonviolence and human values: Empirical support for theoretical relationships. *Peace and Conflict: Journal of Peace Psychology, 2,* 245–253.

Mazurana, D., & McKay, S. (1999). *Women and peacebuilding.* Montreal: International Centre for Human Rights and Democratic Development.

McGranahan, D. (1995). Measurement of development: Research at the United Nations Research Institute for Social Development. *International Social Science Journal, 143,* 39–56.

McKay, S. (1996). Gendering peace psychology. *Peace and Conflict: Journal of Peace Psychology, 2,* 93–107.

McKay, S. (1998). The effects of armed conflict on girls and women. *Peace and Conflict: Journal of Peace Psychology, 4,* 381–392.

McKay, S. (1999). Gender justice and reconciliation. Manuscript submitted for publication.

McKay, S., & Winter, D. (1998). The United Nations Platform for Action: Critique and implications. *Peace and Conflict: Journal of Peace Psychology, 4,* 167–178.

McKenzie-Mohr, D., & Winter, D. (1992). The case for approaching global issues systematically: Militarization and development. *The Peace Psychology Bulletin, 1,* 8–11.

McKibben, B. (1995). *Hope, human and wild.* St. Paul, MN: Hungry Mind Press.

McLoyd, V.C. (1998). Socioeconomic disadvantage and child development. *American Psychologist, 55,* 185–204.

McLoyd, V.C., & Wilson, L. (1991). The strain of living poor: Parenting, social support, and child mental health. In A.C. Huston (Ed.), *Children in poverty: Child development and public policy* (pp. 105–135). Cambridge: Cambridge University Press.

McMillan, B., Florin, P., Stevenson, J., Kerman, B., & Mitchell, R.E. (1995). Empowerment praxis in community coalitions. *American Journal of Community Psychology, 23,* 699–727.

Media Plan. (1996). *Elections B&H '96: Guide for journalists in Bosnia and Herzegovina.* Sarajevo: Media Plan—Development, Research, Training.

Melman, S. (1985). *The permanent war economy.* New York: Simon & Schuster.

Melville, A. (1998). *The role of identity in conflict appraisal.* Unpublished doctoral dissertation, University of Melbourne, Australia.

Melville, M., & Lykes, M.B. (1992). Guatemalan Indian children and the sociocultural effects of government-sponsored terrorism. *Social Science and Medicine, 34,* 533–548.

Menchú Tum, R. (1998). *Crossing borders* (Trans. & ed. by A. Wright). New York: Verso.

Mercado, M. (Ed.). (1986). *People power.* Manila, Philippines: James B. Reuter, S.J. Foundation.

Mercer, G.W., & Cairns, E. (1982). Conservatism and its relationship to general and specific ethnocentrism in Northern Ireland. *British Journal of Social and Clinical Psychology, 20,* 13–17.

Merton, R. (1968). *Social theory and social structure.* Toronto: Collier-Macmillan Canada.

Merton, R.K. (1957) *Social theory and social structure.* New York: Free Press.

Mertus, J. (1995). State discriminatory family law and customary abuses. In J. Peters & A. Wolper (Eds.), *Women's rights human rights: International feminist perspectives* (pp. 135–148). New York: Routledge.

Messer, E. (1995). Anthropology and human rights in Latin America. *Journal of Latin American Anthropology, 1,* 48–97.

Messer, E. (1997). Pluralist approaches to human rights. *Journal of Anthropological Research, 53,* 293–317.

Messick, D.M., & Mackie, D.M. (1989). Intergroup relations. *Annual Review of Psychology, 40,* 45–81.

Messick, D.M., & Sentis, K.P. (1979). Fairness and preference. *Journal of Experimental Social Psychology, 15,* 418–434.

Metreaux, J-C. (1992, January). Training techniques of non-professionals in the framework of a preventive and primary health care programme in mental health (Nicaragua). Paper presented to the Seminar on the Mental Health of Refugee Children Exposed to Violent Environments. Refugee Studies Program, University of Oxford.

Milburn, T.W. (1961). The concept of deterrence: Some logical and psychological considerations. *Journal of Social Issues, 17*(3), 3–11.

Milburn, T.W. (1972) The management of crisis. In C.F. Hermann (Ed.), *International crisis: Insights from behavioral research* (pp. 259–277). New York: Free Press.

Milgram, S. (1974). *Obedience to authority.* New York: Harper & Row.

Miller, D.K. (1972). The activists' corner: Social reform and organized psychology. *Journal of Social Issues, 28*(1), 217–231.

Miller, D.T., & Ross, M. (1975). Self-serving biases in the attribution of causality: Fact or fiction? *Psychological Bulletin, 82,* 213–225.

Miller, W. (1992). Crime by youth gangs and groups in the United States. Washington, DC: U.S. Department of Justice, Office of Juvenile Justice and Delinquency Prevention.

Minear, L., & Weiss, T.G. (1993). *Humanitarian action in times of war.* Boulder, CO: Lynne Rienner.

Minter, W. (1994). *Apartheid's contras: An inquiry into the roots of war in Angola and Mozambique.* London: Zed Books.

Moghaddam, F.M. (1987). Psychology in the third world: As reflected by the crisis in social psychology and the move toward indigenous third world psychology. *American Psychologist, 42,* 912–920.

Moghaddam, F.M. (1998). *Social psychology: Exploring universals across cultures.* New York: W.H. Freeman.

Molotsky, R. (1995, November 18). Admiral has to quit over his comments on Okinawa rape. *New York Times,* p. 1.

Mongella, G. (1994). Change for the last and the least. In P. Adamson (Ed.), *The progress of nations: The nations of the world ranked according to their achievements in child health, nutrition, education, family planning, and progress for women* (p. 31). New York: UNICEF.

Montiel, C. (1995, June). Journey to wholeness. Therapy for underground trauma. Paper presented at the 4th International Symposium on the Contributions of Psychology to Peace, Cape Town, South Africa.

Moore, R.I. (1987). *The formation of a persecuting society.* Oxford: Blackwell.

Morawski, J.G., & Goldstein, S.E. (1985). Psychology and nuclear war: A chapter in our legacy of social responsibility. *American Psychologist, 40,* 276–284.

Morganthau, H. (1972). *Politics among nations.* New York: Random House.

Morgenthau, H.J. (1948) *Politics among nations: The struggle for power and peace.* New York: Alfred A. Knopf.

Morgenthau, H.J., & Thompson, K.W. (1985). *Politics among nations: The struggle for power and peace.* New York: Alfred A. Knopf.

Mortimore, P. (1995). The positive effects of schooling. In M. Rutter (Ed.), *Psychosocial disturbances in young people: Challenges for prevention* (pp. 333–363). Cambridge: Cambridge University Press.

Moscovici, S., Mucchi-Faina, A., & Maas, A. (Eds.). (1994). *Minority influence*. Chicago: Nelson-Hall.

Moser-Puangsuwan, Y., & Maure, M. (n.d.). *Summary of the focus, political highlights, and important results of the Dhammayietras (DY)* [On-line]. Available at: *http://www.igc.apc.org/nonviolence/niseasia/dymwalk/dy3.htm*

Moskos, C.C. (1970). *The American enlisted man*. New York: Russell Sage.

Mueller, J. (1973). *War, presidents, and public opinion*. New York: Wiley.

Mueller, J. (1998). The rise, decline, and shallowness of militant nationalism in Europe. Paper presented at the annual meetings of the International Studies Association, Minneapolis.

Mullen, B., Brown, R., & Smith, C. (1992). Ingroup bias as a function of salience, relevance, and status: An integration. *European Journal of Social Psychology, 22,* 103–122.

Murray, C., & O'Regan, C. (1991). Putting women into the constitution. In S. Bazilli (Ed.), *Putting women on the agenda* (pp. 33–56). Johannesburg: Ravan Press.

Murray, J. (1997). Media violence and youth. In J. Osofsky (Ed.), *Children in a violent society* (pp. 72–96). New York: Guilford Press.

Mydans, S. (1998, May 20). Army out in force to halt protests aimed at Suharto. *New York Times*, pp. A1, A10.

Mydans, S. (1998, June 10). In Jakarta, reports of numerous rapes of Chinese in riots. *New York Times*, pp. A1, A6.

Mydans, S. (1998, September 11). Thousands in streets of Phnom Penh cheer for peace. *New York Times*, p. A10.

Mydans, S. (1998, November 13). Indonesia's students: An unrelenting force for change. *New York Times*, p. A3.

Myers, D.G., & Deiner, E. (1995). Who is happy? *Psychological Science, 6,* 10–19.

Myers, N. (1993). *Ultimate security: The environmental basis of political stability*. New York: Norton.

Nagengast, C. (1997). Women, minorities, and indigenous peoples: Universalism and cultural relativity. *Journal of Anthropological Research, 53,* 349–370.

Nakhre, A.W. (1982). *Social psychology of nonviolent action: A study of three satyagrahas*. Delhi, India: Chanakya Publications.

Narasimhan, S. (1993, February 9–10). The unwanted sex. *New Internationalist*.

Narasimhan, S. (1994). India: From sati to sex-determination tests. In M. Davies (Ed.), *Women and violence: Realities and responses worldwide* (pp. 43–52). London: Zed Books.

National Center for Children in Poverty. (1991). Poverty takes toll on child health. *Child Poverty News and Issues, 1*(1).

National Coalition of Anti-Violence Programs. (1997). *Anti-lesbian, gay, bisexual and transgendered violence in 1996*. New York: Author. (Available from The New York City Gay & Lesbian Anti-Violence Report, 647 Hudson Street, New York, NY 10014–1650).

National Commission on Children. (1991). *Beyond rhetoric: A new American agenda for children and families*. Washington, DC: National Commission on Children.

National Defense University Institute for National Strategic Studies (INSS) Directorate for Advanced Concepts, Technologies, and Information Strategies (ACTIS). (1996, April). Findings of the ACTIS workshop, Humanitarian and Peace Operations: The NGO/Interagency Interface.

National Gay & Lesbian Task Force. (1986). *Antigay violence, victimization, and defamation in 1985*. Washington, DC: Author. (Available from NGLTF, 1517 U Street, NW, Washington, DC 20009).

National Gay & Lesbian Task Force. (1989). *Antigay violence, victimization and defamation in 1988*. Washington, DC: Author (Available from NGLTF, 1517 U Street, NW, Washington, DC 20009).

Neidig, P., Friedman, D., & Collins, B. (1986). Attitudinal characteristics of males who have engaged in spouse abuse. *Journal of Family Violence, 1,* 223–233.

Nelessen, A.C. (1993) *Visions for a new American dream: Process, principles, and an ordinance to plan and design small communities*. Ann Arbor, MI: Edwards Brothers.

Nelson, L.L., Van Slyck, M.R., & Cardella, L.A. (1999). Curricula for teaching adolescents about peace and conflict. *Peace and Conflict: Journal of Peace Psychology, 5,* 169–174.

Nevin, J.A. (1985). Behavior analysis, the nuclear arms race, and the peace movement. In S. Oskamp (Ed.), *International conflict and national public issues: Applied social psychology annual*, (Vol. 6, pp. 27–44). Beverly Hills, CA: Sage.

Newland, K. (1979). *The sisterhood of man*. New York: Worldwatch Institute.

Nicholas, L.J. (1990). The response of South African professional psychology associations to apartheid. *Journal of the History of the Behavioral Sciences, 26,* 59–63.

Nicholas, L.J. (Ed.). (1993). *Psychology of oppression: Critiques and proposals.* Johannesburg: Skotaville.

Nikolic-Ristanovic, V. (1996). War and violence against women. In J. Turpin & L.A. Lorentzen (Eds.), *The gendered New World Order* (pp. 195–210). New York: Routledge.

No hiding place: Human rights—A world report, 1998. (1998, January–February). *The New Internationalist* (298). Entire issue.

Nunca Más [Never Again]—The Report of the Argentine National Commission on the Disappeared. (1986). New York: Farrar Straus & Giroux.

Nyberg, K.L., & Alston, J.P. (1976–77). Analysis of public attitudes toward homosexual behavior. *Journal of Homosexuality, 2*(2), 99–107

O'Hare, W.P., Pollard, K.M., & Mann, T.L. (1991, July). African Americans in the 1990s. *Population bulletin 46* (pp. 13–14). Washington, DC: Population Reference Bureau.

O'Leary, K.D. (1988). Physical aggression between spouses: A social learning theory perspective. In V.B. Van Hasselt, R.L. Morrison, A.S. Bellack, & M. Hersen (Eds.), *Handbook of family violence* (pp. 31–55). New York: Plenum.

O'Leary, K.D. (1993). Through a psychological lens: Personality traits, personality disorders, and levels of violence. In J.R. Gelles & D.R. Loseke (Eds.), *Current controversies on family violence* (pp. 7–30). Newbury Park, CA: Sage.

O'Neil, B. (1989). Game theory and the study of the deterrence of war. In P.C. Stern, R. Axelrod, R. Jervis, & R. Radner (Eds.), *Perspectives on deterrence* (pp. 134–156). Oxford: Oxford University Press.

Oakes, P.J., & Turner, J.C. (1980). Social categorization and intergroup behavior: Does minimal intergroup discrimination make social identity more positive? *European Journal of Social Psychology, 10,* 295–301.

ODHAG/Oficina de Derechos Humanos del Arzobispado de Guatemala [Office of Human Rights of the Archdiocese of Guatemala]. (1998). *Nunca más: Informe proyecto interdiocesano de recuperación de la memoria histórica* [*Never again: Report of the inter-diocescan project on the recovery of historic memory*] (Vols. 1–5). Guatemala: Author.

Oeberg, J. (1996, 23 July). Demokratisk etnisk udrensning (Democratic ethnic cleansing). *Information,* p. 6.

Office of Juvenile Justice and Delinquency Prevention. (1997). 1997 National Youth Gang Survey. Washington, DC: U.S. Department of Justice.

Office of Juvenile Justice and Delinquency Prevention. (1998). Youth gangs: An overview. Washington, DC: U.S. Department of Justice.

Office of Juvenile Justice and Delinquency Prevention. (1998, May). OJJDP Fact Sheet, #79. Washington, DC: U.S. Department of Justice.

Ogden, T.H. (1989). *The primitive edge of experience.* Northvale, NJ: Jason Aronson.

Olds, D., Eckenrode, J., Henderson, C., Kitzman, H., Powers, J., Cole, R., Sidora, K., Morris, P., Pettitt, L., & Luckey, D. (1997). Long-term effects of home visitation on maternal life course and child abuse and neglect: 15 year follow-up of a randomized trial. *Journal of the American Medical Association, 278,* 637–643.

Olds, D., Henderson, C., Tatelbaum, R., & Chamberlin, R. (1986). Improving the delivery of prenatal care and outcomes of pregnancy: A randomized trial of nurse-home visitation. *Pediatrics, 77,* 16–28.

Oloka-Onyango, J., & Tamale, S. (1995). "The personal is political," or why women's rights are indeed human rights: An African perspective on international feminism. *Human Rights Quarterly, 17,* 691–731.

Opotow, S. (Ed.). (1990a). Moral exclusion and injustice. *Journal of Social Issues, 46*(1).

Opotow, S. (1990b). Moral exclusion and injustice: An introduction. *Journal of Social Issues, 46*(1), 1–20.

Opotow, S. (1992, August). *Pluralism and nonviolence.* Paper presented at the annual meeting of the American Psychological Association, Washington, DC.

Opotow, S. (1993). Animals and the scope of justice. *Journal of Social Issues, 49*(1), 71–85.

Opotow, S., & Clayton, S. (1994). Green justice: Conceptions of fairness and the natural world. *Journal of Social Issues, 50*(2), 1–11.

Opotow, S., & Deutsch, M. (1999). Learning to cope with conflict and violence: How schools can help youth. In E. Frydenberg (Ed.), *Learning to cope: Developing as a person in complex societies* (pp. 198–224). Oxford: Oxford University Press.

Opotow, S.V. (1987). Limits of fairness: An experimental examination of antecedents of the scope of justice. *Dissertation Abstracts Interna-*

tional, 48 (08B), 2500. (University Microfilms No. 87–24072.)

Organski, A.F.K., & Kugler, J. (1980). *The war ledger*. Chicago: University of Chicago Press.

Orr, D. (1992). *Ecological literacy: Education and the transition to a postmodern world*. Albany, NY: State University of New York Press.

Orwell, G. (1950). *Shooting an elephant and other essays*. New York: Harcourt, Brace & World.

Osgood, C.E. (1962). *An alternative to war or surrender*. Urbana, IL: University of Illinois Press.

Osgood, C.E., Suci, G.J., & Tannenbaum, P.H. (1957). *The measurement of meaning*. Urbana, IL: University of Illinois Press.

Osofsky, J., Wewers, S., Hann, D., & Fick, A. (1993). Chronic community violence: What is happening to our children? In D. Reiss, J. Richters, M. Radke-Yarrow, & D. Scharff (Eds.), *Children and violence* (pp. 36–45). New York: Guilford Press.

Ostergaard, G. (1990). A Gandhian perspective on development. In P. Smoker, R. Davies, & B. Munske (Eds.), *A reader in peace studies* (pp. 206–209). New York: Pergamon Press.

Pagani, F. (1998).The peace process at its culmination: The reconciliation elections. In H. Langholtz (Ed.), *The psychology of peacekeeping* (pp. 223–238). Westport, CT: Praeger.

Pagelow, M.D. (1981). *Woman-battering: Victims and their experiences*. Beverly Hills, CA: Sage.

Parin, P. (1994). Open wounds: Ethno psychoanalytical reflections on the wars in the former Yugoslavia. In A. Stiglmayer (Ed.), *Mass rape: The war against women in Bosnia-Herzegovina* (pp. 35–53). Lincoln, NE: University of Nebraska Press.

Parker, W., & McDavis, R. (1989). Attitudes of Blacks towards mental health agencies and counselors. In D. Burgest (Ed.), *Social work practice with minorities* (pp. 14–25). Metuchen, NJ: Scarecrow Press.

Parsons, T. (1961). An outline of the social system. In T. Parsons, E. Shils, K. Naegele & J. Pitts (Eds.), *Theories of society: Foundations of modern sociological theory* (pp. 30–79). New York: Free Press.

Partridge, G.E. (1919). *The psychology of nations: A contribution to the philosophy of history*. New York: Macmillan.

Pearson, F. (1994). *The global spread of arms*. Boulder, CO: Westview Press.

Pearson, N. (1996). Eddie Mabo Human Rights Lecture. In J. Wilson, J. Thomson, & A. McMahon (Eds.), *The Australian welfare state:*

Key documents and themes (pp. 140–148). South Melbourne: Macmillan Education Australia.

Pedersen, P. (1993). Mediating multicultural conflict by separating behaviors from expectations in a cultural grid. *International Journal of Intercultural Relations, 17,* 343–353.

Pedersen, P., & Jandt, F.E. (1996). Cultural contextual models for creative conflict management. In F.E. Jandt & P.B. Pedersen (Eds.), *Constructive conflict management: Asia-Pacific Cases* (pp. 3–28). Thousand Oaks, CA: Sage.

Pelton, L. (1978). Child abuse and neglect: The myth of classlessness. *American Journal of Orthopsychiatry, 48,* 608–617.

Pelton, L.H. (1974). *The psychology of nonviolence*. New York: Pergamon Press.

Pennebaker, J.W., & Beall, S.K. (1986). Confronting a traumatic event: Toward an understanding of inhibition and disease. *Journal of Abnormal Psychology, 95,* 274–281.

Pennebaker, J.W., Hughes, C.F., & O'Heeron, R.C. (1987). The psychophysiology of confession: Linking inhibitory and psychosomatic processes. *Journal of Personality and Social Psychology, 52,* 781–793.

Periwal, S. (Ed.). (1995). *Notions of nationalism*. Budapest: Central European University Press.

Perkins, D.D. (1995). Speaking truth to power: Empowerment ideology as social intervention and policy. *American Journal of Community Psychology, 23,* 765–794.

Perkins, D.D., Brown, B.B., & Taylor, R.B. (1996). The ecology of empowerment: Predicting participation in community organizations. *Journal of Social Issues, 52*(1), 85–110.

Perkins, D.D., & Zimmerman, M.A. (1995). Empowerment theory, research, and application. *American Journal of Community Psychology, 23,* 569–580.

Perkins, E. (1998). The psychology of diplomacy: Conflict resolution in a time of minimal or unusual small-scale conflicts. In H. Langholtz (Ed.), *The psychology of peacekeeping* (pp. 41–56). Westport, CT: Praeger.

Perry, B.J. (1998). Defenders of the faith: Hate groups and ideologies of power in the United States. *Patterns of Prejudice, 32*(3), 32–54.

Perry, S.E. (1957). Notes on the role of national: A social-psychological concept for the study of international relations. *Journal of Conflict Resolution, 1,* 346–363.

Petrovic, S. (1996). *Study in reproductive health:*

Self-reported symptoms of gynaecological morbidity in refugee and displaced population of Croatia and Bosnia and Herzegovina. Split: Marie Stopes International, Report.

Pettigrew, T.F. (1997). Generalized intergroup contact effects on prejudice. *Personality and Social Psychology Bulletin, 23*, 173–185.

Pettigrew, T.F. (1998). Intergroup contact theory. *Annual Review of Psychology, 49*, 65–85.

Petty, R.E., & Cacioppo, J.T. (1986). The elaboration likelihood model of persuasion. In L. Berkowitz (Ed.), *Advances in Experimetal Social Psychology*, (Vol. 19, pp. 123–205). New York: Academic Press.

Pharr, S. (1988). *Homophobia: A weapon of sexism.* (Available from The Women's Project, 2224 Main Street, Little Rock, AR 72206.)

Phillips, A. (1991). *Engendering democracy.* University Park, PA: Pennsylvania State University Press.

Phillips, A. (1992). Universal pretensions in political thought. In M. Barrett & A. Phillips (Eds.), *Destabilizing theory: Contemporary feminist debates* (pp. 10–30). Palo Alto, CA: Stanford University Press.

Piaget, J. (1932). *The moral judgment of the child.* New York: Harcourt Brace and Co.

Piaget, J. (1965) *The moral judgment of the child.* Harmondsworth, UK: Penguin.

Pilisuk, M. (1972). *International conflict and social policy.* Englewood Cliffs, NJ: Prentice Hall.

Pilisuk, M. (1996, November/December). Taking on Goliath: The Lawrence Livermore Lab. *Peace Magazine: Science for Peace*, 27–28.

Pilisuk, M. (1997, August). *The hidden structure of violence.* Presidential address for Division 48 presented at the 105th Annual Convention of the American Psychological Association, Chicago.

Pilisuk, M. (1998). The hidden structure of contemporary violence. *Peace and Conflict: Journal of Peace Psychology, 4*, 197–216.

Pilisuk, M. (1999). Addictive rewards and acceptable risks in nuclear weapons develoment. *Peace Review, 11*, 597–602.

Pilisuk, M., McAllister, J., & Rothman, J. (1996). Coming together for action: The challenge of contemporary grassroots community organizing. *Journal of Social Issues, 52*(1), 15–37.

Pilisuk, M., & Parks, S.H. (1986). *The healing web: Social networks and human survival.* Hanover, NH: University Press of New England.

Pilisuk, M., Parks, S.H., & Hawkes, G.R. (1987).

Public perception of technological risk. *Social Science Journal, 24*, 403–413.

Pilisuk, M., & Sklonick, P. (1968). Inducing trust: A test of the Osgood proposal. *Journal of Personality and Social Psychology, 8*, 121–133.

Pizzey, E. (1974). *Scream quietly or the neighbours will hear.* London: Penguin.

Plous, S. (1988). Disarmament, arms control, and peace in the nuclear age: Political objectives and relevant research. *Journal of Social Issues, 44*(2), 133–154.

Polakow, V. (1993). The other childhood: The classroom worlds of poor children. In M.A. Jensen & S.G. Goffin (Eds.), V*isions of entitlement: The care and education of America's children* (pp. 157–174). Albany, NY: State University of New York Press.

Political Ecology Group. (1994). *Toxic empire: The WMX corporation, hazardous waste and global strategies for environmental justice.* San Francisco: PEG/Tides Foundation.

Porpora, D. (1987). *The concept of social structure.* Westport, CT: Greenwood Press.

Posen, B.R. (1993). Nationalism, the mass army, and military power. *International Security, 18*, 80–124.

Prescott, S., & Letko, C. (1977). Battered women: A social psychological perspective. In M. Roy (Ed.), *Battered women* (pp. 72–96). New York: Van Nostrand Reinhold.

Proshansky, H.M., Fabian, A.K., & Kaminoff, R. (1995). Place identity: Physical world socialization of the self. In L. Groat (Ed.), *Readings in environment psychology: Giving places meaning* (pp. 87–114). London: Academic Press.

Prothrow-Stith, D. (1987). *Violence prevention: Curriculum for adolescents.* Newton, MA: Education Development Center.

Pruitt, D.G. (1981). *Negotiation behavior.* New York: Academic Press.

Pruitt, D.G., & Lewis, S.A. (1975). Development of integrative solutions in bilateral negotiation. *Journal of Personality and Social Psychology, 31*, 621–633.

Pruitt, D.G., & Olczak, P. (1995). Beyond hope: Approaches to resolving seemingly intractable conflict. In B.B. Bunker & J.Z. Rubin (Eds.), *Cooperation, conflict, and justice: Essays inspired by the work of Morton Deutsch* (pp. 59–92). New York: Sage.

Pruitt, D.G, & Rubin, J.Z. (1986). *Social conflict: Escalation, stalemate and settlement.* New York: McGraw-Hill.

Prunier, G. (1995). *Rwanda*. New York: Columbia University Press.

Psychologists for Social Responsibility. (1997). *School of the Americas: A human rights problem for psychologists*. Washington, DC: Psychologists for Social Responsibility.

Puenzo, L. (Director). (1985). *La historia oficial* [The official story]. [Film]. Almi Pictures Inc. (Available on video, with English subtitles or dubbed in English.)

Punamäki, R. (1989). Political violence and mental health. *International Journal of Mental Health, 17,* 3–15.

Pynoos, R., & Nader, K. (1998). Psychological first aid and treatment approach to children exposed to community violence: Research implications. *Journal of Traumatic Stress Studies, 1,* 445–473.

Raider, E. (1995). Conflict resolution training in schools: Translating theory into applied skills. In B.B. Bunker & J.Z. Rubin (Eds.), *Cooperation, conflict, and justice: Essays inspired by the work of Morton Deutsch* (pp. 93–122). New York: Sage.

Raimy, V. (1950). *Training in clinical psychology.* Englewood Cliffs, NJ: Prentice Hall.

Ramirez-Smith, C. (1995). Stopping the cycle of failure: The Comer model. *Educational Leadership, 52,* 14–19.

Rand, H.P. (1960). Mental conditioning of the soldier for nuclear war. *Military Medicine, 307,* 744–745.

Rao, A. (1995). The politics of gender and culture in international human rights discourse. In J. Peters & A. Wolper (Eds.), *Women's rights human rights: International feminist perspectives* (pp. 167–175). New York: Routledge.

Raphael, T.D. (1982). Integrative complexity theory and forecasting international crises: Berlin, 1946–1962. *Journal of Conflict Resolution, 26,* 423–450.

Rapoport, A. (1962). The uses and abuses of game theory. *Scientific American, 207,* 108–118.

Rapoport, A., & Chammah, A. (1965). *Prisoner's dilemma.* Ann Arbor, MI: University of Michigan Press.

Rauber, P. (1998, July/August). All hail the multinationals! *Sierra, 83*(3),16–17.

Reardon, B. (1985). *Sexism and the war system.* New York: Teachers College Press.

Reardon, B. (1988). *Comprehensive peace education.* New York: Teachers College Press.

Reardon, B. (1990). Feminist concepts of peace and security. In P. Smoker, R. Davies, & B. Munske (Eds.), *A reader in peace studies* (pp. 136–150). Oxford: Pergamon.

Reason, P., & Rowan, J. (Eds.). (1981). *Human inquiry: A sourcebook of new paradigm research.* Chichester, UK: Wiley.

Rebera, R. (Ed.). (1992). *Sowing the grains of peace, a resource handbook for building peace: Consultation on militarism, Christian conference of Asian women's concerns, 19–25 June 1992.* Okinawa, Japan: Northeast Asia Subregional Women's Consultation.

Rechner, P. (1998, March/April). U.N. peacekeeping and the Yugoslav conflict. *Analysis of Current Events, 10,* Nos. 3–4.

Reiber, R.W., & Kelly, R.J. (1991). Substance and shadow: Images of the enemy. In R. Reiber (Ed.), *The psychology of war and peace: The image of the enemy* (pp. 3–39). New York: Plenum.

Reich, R. (1997a). *Locked in the cabinet.* New York: Knopf.

Reich, R. (1997b, May 6). *Interview on Pacifica Radio,* KPFA Berkeley, CA.

Renne, T. (Ed.). (1997). *Ana's land: Sisterhood in Eastern Europe.* Boulder, CO: Westview Press.

Renner, M. (1990). Converting to a peaceful economy. In L. Brown (Ed.), *State of the world, 1990* (pp. 154–172). New York: Norton.

Renner, M. (1994). *Budgeting for disarmament: The costs of war and peace.* Worldwatch paper #122. Washington, DC: Worldwatch Institute.

Renner, M. (1996). *Fighting for survival: Environmental decline, social conflict, and the new age of insecurity.* Worldwatch Environmental Alert Series. New York: Norton.

Renner, M. (1998a). Curbing the proliferation of small arms. In L. Brown, C. Flavin, & H. French (Eds.), *The state of the world, 1998* (pp. 131–148). New York: Norton.

Renner, M. (1998b). The global divide: Socioeconomic disparities and international security. In M. Klare & Y. Chandrani (Eds.), *World security: Challenges for a new century* (pp. 273–293). New York: St. Martin's Press.

Renner, M. (1999). *Ending violent conflict.* Worldwatch paper #146. Washington, DC: Worldwatch Institute.

Reno, W. (1999). *Warlord politics and African states.* Boulder, CO: Lynne Rienner.

Renzetti, C. (1997). Violence in lesbian and gay relationships. In L.L. O'Toole & J.R. Schiffman (Eds.), *Gender violence: Interdisciplinary perspectives* (pp. 285–293). New York: New York University Press.

Renzetti, C.M., & Miley, C.H. (1996). *Violence in*

gay and lesbian domestic partnerships. New York: Harrington Park,

Reynolds, P. (1997). *Children and traditional healing in Zimbabwe.* Athens, OH: Ohio University Press.

Rhodes, M. (1997a, May 1). *Nike workers strike! Analysis, resources.* [Web document] Campaign for Labor Rights: Washington, D.C. (Available: clr@igc.apc.org, *http://www.compugraph. com/clr.*)

Rhodes, M. (1997b, May 1). *Disney and McDonald's linked to $.06/hour sweatshop in Vietnam.* [Web document] Campaign for Labor Rights: Washington, DC. (Available: clr@igc.apc.org, *http://www.compugraph.com/clr.*)

Rhodes, M. (1997c, May 6). *Day 1 Nike worker tour.* [Web document] Campaign for Labor Rights: Washington, DC. (Available: clr@igc.apc.org, *http://www.compugraph.com/clr.*)

Rhodes, M. (1997d, May 17). *Alfred Angelo threatens to close U.S. bridal gown factories; violates code of conduct in Guatemala* [Web document] Campaign for Labor Rights: Washington, DC. (Available: clr2@igc.apc.org.)

Rhodes, R. (1995). *Dark sun: The making of the hydrogen bomb.* New York: Simon & Schuster.

Rich, R.C., Edelstein, M., Hallman, W.K., & Wandersman, A.H. (1995). Citizen participation and empowerment: The case of local environmental hazards. *American Journal of Community Psychology, 23,* 657–676.

Richards, M. (1985). Cosmopolitan world view and counterinsurgency in Guatemala. *Anthropological Quarterly, 58,* 90–107.

Richardson, J.M., Jr., & Wang, J. (1993). Peace accords: Seeking conflict resolution in deeply divided societies. In K.M. de Silva & de A. Samarasinghe (Eds.), *Peace accords and ethnic conflicts* (pp. 173–198). London: Pinter Publishers

Richters, J., & Martinez, P. (1993). The NIMH community violence project: Children as victims of and witnesses to violence. *Psychiatry, 56,* 7–21.

Ricoeur, P. (1986). *Lectures on ideology and utopia.* New York: Columbia University Press.

Riggs, D.S., & O'Leary, K.D. (1989). Violence between dating partners: Background and situational correlates of courtship aggression. In M. Pirog-Good & J.E. Sets (Eds.), *Violence in dating relationships: Emerging social issues* (pp. 53–71). New York: Praeger.

Rinehart, M. (1995). Understanding the concept "peace": A search for common ground. *Peace*

and Change: Journal of Peace Research, 20, 379–396.

Roberts, A. (1996). The crisis in UN peacekeeping. In C. Crocker & F. Hampson (Eds.), *Managing global chaos, sources and responses to international conflict* (pp. 297–320). Washington, DC: United States Institute of Peace Press.

Roderick, T. (1998). Evaluating the resolving conflict creatively program. *The Fourth R,* Volume 82, March, April. National Institute for Dispute Resolution.

Rogers, C.R. (1973). *Client-centered therapy.* London: Constable.

Rogers, J.D., Spencer, J., & Uyangoda, J. (1998). Sri Lanka: Political violence and ethnic conflict. *American Psychologist, 53,* 771–777.

Rokeach, M. (1973). *The nature of human values.* New York: Free Press.

Rokeach, M. (1979). *Understanding human values.* New York: Free Press.

Roodman, D.M. (1999). Building a sustainable society. In L. Starke (Ed.), *State of the world 1999* (pp. 167–188). New York: Norton.

Rosemont, H., Jr. (1998). Reflections on human rights conflicts: When individual and social rights clash. *RESIST Newsletter, 7*(9), 1–3.

Rosenberg, B.H. (1998, November 15). Chairman of the Working Group on Biological Weapons Verification with the Federation of American Scientists. Personal communication.

Rosenfeld, S. (1997, April 6). Women suffer brutal captivity. *San Francisco Examiner,* pp. A1 and A16.

Ross, L. (1977). The intuitive psychologist and his shortcomings: Distortions in the attribution process. In L. Berkowitz (Ed.), *Advances in experimental social psychology* (Vol. 10, pp. 173–220). New York: Academic Press.

Ross, M., & Fletcher, G.J.O. (1985). Attribution and social perception. In G. Lindzey & E. Aronson (Eds.), *The handbook of social psychology, Vol. 2* (3rd ed.; pp. 73–122). New York: Random House.

Ross, M., Greene, D., & House, P. (1977). The "false consensus effect": An egocentric bias in social perception and attribution processes. *Journal of Experimental Social Psychology, 13,* 279–301.

Ross, M.H. (1991). The role of evolution in ethnocentric conflict and its management. *Journal of Social Issues, 47*(3), 167–185.

Rothman, J. (1992). *From confrontation to coopera-*

tion: *Resolving ethnic and regional conflict.* Newbury Park, CA: Sage.

Rothman, J. (1997). *Resolving identity-based conflict in nations, organizations, and communities.* San Francisco: Jossey-Bass.

Rothman, J. (1998). Dialogue in conflict: Past and future. In E. Wiener (Ed.), *The handbook of interethnic coexistence* (pp. 217–235). New York: Continuum Publishing Co.

Rouhana, N., & Kelman, H. (1994). Promoting joint thinking in international conflict. *Journal of Social Issues, 50*(1), 157–178.

Rounsaville, B.J. (1978). Theories of marital violence: Evidence from a study of battered women. *Victimology, 3,* 11–31.

Roy, A. (1998, September 28) The end of imagination. *The Nation,* pp. 11–19.

Rubenson, D. (1996). Break out of the base closure doldrums. *Los Angeles Times,* March 7. Retrieved on January 23, 1999 from LEXIS-NEXIS, *http://web.lexis-nexis.com/universe.*

Rubin, J.Z., & Levinger, G.L. (1995). Levels of analysis: In search of generalizable knowledge. In B.B. Bunker & J.Z. Rubin (Eds.), *Conflict, cooperation and justice: Essays inspired by the work of Morton Deutsch* (pp. 13–38). San Francisco: Jossey-Bass.

Rubin, J.Z., Pruitt, D.G., & Kim, S.H. (1994). *Social conflict: Escalation, stalemate and settlement* (2nd ed.). New York: McGraw-Hill.

Rubin, Z., & Peplau, L.A. (1975). Who believes in a just world? *Journal of Social Issues, 31*(3), 65–89.

Ruble, T.L., & Thomas, K.W. (1976). Support for a two-dimensional model of conflict behaviour. *Organisational Behaviour and Human Performance, 16,* 143–155

Ruddick, S. (1982). Maternal thinking. In B. Thorne & M. Yalom (Eds.), *Rethinking the family: Some feminist questions* (pp. 76–94). London and New York: Longman Press.

Ruddick, S. (1995). *Maternal thinking: Toward a politics of peace.* Boston: Beacon Press.

Rudmin, F. W., & Ansbacher, H.L. (1989, Fall). Anti-war psychologists: Alfred Adler. *Psychologists for Social Responsibility Newsletter, 8(4).* Washington, DC: Psychologists for Social Responsibility.

Rummel, R.J. (1994). Democide in totalitarian states: Mortacracies and megamurderers. In I.W. Charny (Ed.), *Widening circle of genocide* (pp. 7–9). New Brunswick, NJ: Transaction.

Runciman, W.G. (1966). *Relative deprivation and social justice.* Berkeley, CA: University of California Press.

Rupesinghe, K. (1996). From Civil War to Civil Peace: Multi-Track Solutions to Armed Conflict. Unpublished manuscript. London's International Alert.

Russell, R.W. (Ed.). (1961). Psychology and policy in a nuclear age [Special Issue]. *Journal of Social Issues, 17*(3).

Rutter, M. (1987). Continuities and discontinuities from infancy. In J. Osofsky (Ed.), *Handbook of infant development* (pp. 1256–1296). New York: Wiley.

Ryan, W. (1976). *Blaming the victim.* New York: Random House.

Saegert, S. (1989). Unlikely leaders, extreme circumstances: Older Black women building community households. *American Journal of Community Psychology, 17,* 295–316.

Saegert, S., & Winkel, G. (1996). Paths to community empowerment: Organizing at home. *American Journal of Community Psychology, 24,* 517–550.

Saltzman, L.E., Mercy, J.A., Rosenberg, M.L., Elsea, W.R., Naper G., Sikes, R.K., & Waxweiler, J.J. (1990). Magnitudes and patterns of family and intimate assault in Atlanta, Georgia, 1984. *Violence and Victims, 5,* 3–17.

Sampson, E.E. (1983). *Justice and the critique of pure psychology.* New York: Plenum.

Sampson, E.E. (1993a). *Celebrating the other. A dialogic account of human nature.* Boulder, CO: Westview Press.

Sampson, E.E. (1993b). Identity politics: Challenges to psychology's understanding. *American Psychologist 48,* 1219–1230.

Sampson, S. (1996). The social life of projects: Importing civil society to Albania. In C. Hann & E. Dunn (Eds.), *Civil society: Challenging Western models* (pp. 121–142). New York: Routledge.

Santmire, Tara E., Wilkenfeld, J., Kraus, S., Holley, K.M., Santmire, Toni E., & Gleditsch, K.S. (1998). The impact of cognitive diversity on crisis negotiations. *Political Psychology, 19,* 721–748.

Sarason, S.B. (1982). *The culture of school and the problem of change.* Needham Heights, MA: Allyn & Bacon.

Sarat, A., & Kearns, T.R. (Eds.). (1995). *Law's violence.* Ann Arbor, MI: University of Michigan Press.

Scarr, S., & Eisenberg, M. (1993). Child care research: Issues, perspectives, and results. *Annual Review of Psychology, 44,* 613–644.

Schatz, R. T., & Fiske, S.T. (1992). International reactions to the threat of nuclear war: The rise and fall of concern in the eighties. *Political Psychology, 13,* 1–30.

Schear, J.(1996). Riding the tiger: The United Nations and Cambodia's struggle for peace. In W. Durch (Ed.), *UN peacekeeping, American policy, and the uncivil wars of the 1990s* (pp. 135–192). New York: St. Martin's Press.

Scheer, R. (1992). *With enough shovels: Reagan, Bush and nuclear war.* New York: Random House.

Schell, J. (1998). *The gift of time: The case for abolishing nuclear weapons now.* New York: Metropolitan Books.

Schirmer, J. (1993). The seeking of truth and the gendering of consciousness: The comadres of El Salvador and the Conavigua widows of Guatemala. In S. Radcliffe & S. Westwood (Eds.), *Viva: Women and popular protest in Latin America* (pp.30–64). New York: Routledge.

Schirmer, J. (1998). *The Guatemala military project: A violence called democracy.* Philadelphia: University of Pennsylvania Press.

Schlesinger, A., Jr. (1997). Has democracy a future? *Foreign Affairs, 76*(5), 2–12.

Schmittroth, L. (Ed.). (1991). *Statistical record of women worldwide.* Detroit: Gale Research Inc.

Schoensee, R., & Lederer, G. (1991). The gentle revolution. *Political Psychology, 12,* 309–330.

Schorr, L.B. (1997). *Common purpose: Strengthening families and neighborhoods to rebuild America.* New York: Anchor Books.

Schroder, H.M., Driver, M.J., & Streufert, S. (1967). *Human information processing.* New York: Holt, Rinehart, & Winston.

Schuler, M. (Ed.). (1992). *Freedom from violence against women: Women's strategies from around the world.* New York: UNIFEM.

Schwartz, J.M. (1996). *Pieces of mosaic: An essay on the making of Macedonia.* Hoejbjerg, Denmark: Intervention Press.

Schwartz, S., & Winograd, B. (1954). Preparation of soldiers for atomic maneuvers. *Journal of Social Issues, 10*(3), 42–52.

Schwartz, S.H. (1992). Universals in the content and structure of values: Theoretical advances and empirical tests in 20 countries. *Advances in Experimental Social Psychology, 20,* 1–65.

Schwartz, S.H. (1994). Are there universal aspects in the structure and contents of human values? *Journal of Social Issues, 50*(4), 19–45.

Schwartz, S.I. (Ed.). (1998). *Atomic audit: The costs and consequences of U.S. nuclear weapons since 1940.* Washington, DC: Brookings Institution Press.

Schwebel, M. (1965). *Behavioral science and human survival.* Palo Alto, CA: Science and Behavior Books, Inc.

Schwebel, M. (1982). Effects of nuclear threat on children and teenagers: Implications for professionals. *American Journal of Orthopsychiatry, 52,* 608–618.

Schwebel, M. (1993). What moves the peace movement: Psychosocial factors in historical perspective. In V.K. Kool (Ed.), *Nonviolence: Social and psychological issues* (pp. 59–78). Lanham, MD: University Press of America.

Schwebel, M. (1997). Job insecurity as structural violence: Implication for destructive intergroup conflict. *Peace and Conflict: Journal of Peace Psychology, 3,* 333–352.

Seager, J. (1993). *Earth follies: Coming to feminist terms with the global environmental crisis.* New York: Routledge.

Sears, D.O. (1969). Political behavior. In G. Lindzey & E. Aronson (Eds.), *The handbook of social psychology* (2nd ed.) (pp. 315–458). Reading, MA: Addison-Wesley.

Seedat, M. (1997). The quest for liberatory psychology. *South African Journal of Psychology, 27,* 261–270.

Seligman, M. (1998). Ethnopolitical warfare (President's Column). *APA Monitor, 29*(3), 2.

Seligman, M.E.P. (1975). *Helplessness: On depression, development, and death.* San Francisco, CA: Freeman.

Selznick, G.J., & Steinberg, S. (1969). *The tenacity of prejudice: Anti-Semitism in contemporary America.* New York: Harper & Row.

Sen, A. (1990, December). More than 100 million women are missing. *New York Review,* p. 20.

Senge, P.M. (1990). *The fifth discipline: The art and practice of the learning organization.* New York: Doubleday.

Seville Statement on Violence. (1987). In J.M. Ramirez, R.A. Hinde, & J. Groebel (Eds.), *Essays on violence* (pp. 159–163). Seville: University of Seville.

Shapiro, I. (1999). New approaches to old problems: Lessons from an ethnic conciliation project in four Central and Eastern European countries. *Negotiation Journal, 15,* 149–167.

Sharoni, S. (1994). Gender issues in democracy: Rethinking Middle East peace and security from a feminist perspective. In E. Boulding (Ed.), *Building peace in the Middle East: Challenges for states and civil society* (pp. 99–110). Boulder, CO: Lynne Rienner.

Sharp, G. (1973). *The politics of non-violent action, part one.* Boston: Porter-Sargent.

Sheffield, C.J. (1987). Sexual terrorism: The social control of women. In B.B. Hess & M.M. Ferree (Eds.), *Analyzing gender: A handbook of social science research* (pp. 171– 189). Newbury Park, CA: Sage.

Sherif, M., & Sherif, C.W. (1953). *Groups in harmony and tension.* New York: Harper.

Sherif, M., & Sherif, C.W. (1965). Research on intergroup relations. In O. Klineberg & R. Christie (Eds.), *Perspectives in social psychology* (pp. 153–177). New York: Holt, Rinehart & Winston.

Sherman, L. (1992). *Policing domestic violence: Experiments and dilemmas.* New York: Free Press.

Shields, D.L.L., & Bredemeier, B.J.L. (1996). Sport, militarism, and peace. *Peace and Conflict: Journal of Peace Psychology, 2,* 369–384.

Shinn, M. (1992). Homelessness: What is a psychologist to do? *American Journal of Community Psychology, 20,* 1–24.

Shook, E.V. (1985). *Ho'oponopono.* Honolulu: University of Hawaii Press.

Shweder, R.A., Mahapatra, M., & Miller, J.G. (1990). Culture and moral development. In J.W. Stigler, R.A. Shweder, & G. Herdt (Eds.), *Cultural psychology: Essays on comparative human development* (pp. 130–204). Cambridge: Cambridge University Press.

Sidanius, J. (in press). Ethnic identity, legitimizing ideologies and social status: A matter of ideological asymmetry. *Political Psychology.*

Silverstein, B. (1989). Enemy images: The psychology of U.S. attitudes and cognitions regarding the Soviet Union. *American Psychologist, 44,* 903–913.

Silverstein, B., & Holt, R.R. (1989). Research on enemy images: Present status and future prospects. *Journal of Social Issues, 45*(2), 159–175.

Silverstein, K. (1998). *Washington on $10 million a day.* Monroe, ME: Common Courage Press.

Simmons, J., Farmer, P., & Schoepf, B. (1995). A global perspective. In P. Farmer, M. Connors, & J. Simmons (Eds.), *Women, poverty and AIDS* (pp. 39–90). Monroe, ME: Common Courage Press.

Simpson, C. (1993). *The splendid blond beast.* New York: Grove Press.

Simpson, J., & Bennett, J. (1985). *The disappeared and the mothers of the Plaza: The story of the 11,000 Argentineans who vanished.* New York: St. Martin's Press.

Singer, J.E., Radloff, L.S., & Wark, D.M. (1963). Renegades, heretics, and changes in sentiment. *Sociometry, 26,* 178–189.

Sipes, R.G. (1973). War, sports, and aggression: An empirical test of two rival theories. *American Anthropologist, 75,* 64–86.

Sipes, R.G. (1975). War, combative sports, and aggression: A preliminary causal model of cultural patterning. In M.A. Nettleship, R. Dalegivens, & A. Nettleship (Eds.), *War: Its causes and correlates* (pp. 749–762). The Hague, The Netherlands: Mouton.

Sipes, R.G. (1976). Sports as a control for aggression. In T.T. Craig (Ed.), *Humanistic and mental health aspects of sports, exercise, and recreation* (pp. 46–49). Chicago: American Medical Association.

Sivard, R.L. (1986). *World military and social expenditures* (16th ed.). Washington, DC: World Priorities.

Sivard, R.L. (1988). *World military and social expenditures.* Washington, DC: World Priorities.

Sivard, R.L. (1991). *World military and social expenditures 1991.* Washington, DC: World Priorities.

Sivard, R.L. (1993). *World military and social expenditures 1993.* Washington, DC: World Priorities.

Sivard, R.L. (1996). *World military and social expenditures 1996.* Washington, DC: World Priorities.

Skinner, B.F. (1971). *Beyond freedom and dignity.* New York: Knopf.

Sloan, T.S. (1990). Psychology for the third world? *Journal of Social Issues: 46*(3), 1–20.

Smith, B. (1992). Nationalism, ethnocentrism, and the new world order. *Journal of Humanistic Psychology, 32,* 76–91.

Smith, B., Agger, I., Danieli, Y., & Weisaeth, L. (1996). Emotional responses of international humanitarian aid workers. In Y. Danieli, N.S. Rodley, & L. Weisaeth (Eds.), *International responses to traumatic stress* (pp. 397–424). New York: Baywood Publishing Company.

Smith, D. (1997). *The state of war and peace atlas.* London: Penguin.

Smith, D.N. (1998). The psychocultural roots of genocide: Legitimacy and crisis in Rwanda. *American Psychologist, 53,* 743–753.

Smith, M.B. (1986). War, peace, and psychology. *Journal of Social Issues, 42*(4), 23–38.

Smith, M.B. (1999). Political psychology and peace: A half-century perspective. *Peace and Conflict: Journal of Peace Psychology, 5*, 1–16.

Smith, N.S. (1998). The psychocultural roots of genocide. *American Psychologist, 53*, 743–753.

Smithson, A. (1998, November 15). Senior Associate and Director of the Chemical and Biological Weapons Nonproliferation Project at the Henry L. Stimson Center. Personal communication.

Smoker, P., Davies, R., & Munske, B. (1990). *A reader in peace studies*. New York: Pergamon Press.

Snell, J.E., Rosenwald, R.J., & Robey, A. (1964). The wife beater's wife: A study of family interaction. *Archives of General Psychiatry 11*, 107–113.

Song, Y.I. (1996). *Battered women in Korean immigrant families: The silent scream*. New York: Garland.

South African Institute of Race Relations. (1997). *Race relations survey 1996–1997*. Braamfontein, South Africa: S.A.I.R.R.

Specter, M. (1998, January 11). Traffickers' new cargo: Naive Slavic women. *New York Times*, pp. A1& A17.

Speer, P.W., & Hughey, J. (1995). Community organizing: An ecological route to empowerment and power. *American Journal of Community Psychology, 23*, 729–748.

Spergel, I. (1995). *The youth gang problem: A community approach*. New York: Oxford University Press.

Spillane, L.A. (1994). Hate crimes: A legal perspective. In J.E. Hendricks & B. Byers (Eds.), *Multicultural perspectives in criminal justice and criminology* (pp. 223–257). Springfield, IL: Charles C. Thomas.

Stagner, M., & Richman, H. (1985). *General assistance profiles: Findings from a longitudinal study of newly appointed recipients*. Springfield, IL: Illinois Department of Public Aid.

Stagner, R. (1967). *Psychological aspects of international conflict*. Belmont, CA: Brooks/Cole.

Stanley Foundation. (1997). *Building on Beijing: United States NGOs shape a women's national action agenda*. In cooperation with American Association of University Women, Church Women United, National Association of Commissions for Women, Women's Environment and Development Association. Muscatine, IA: Author.

Statman, J.M. (1995, July). Exorcising the ghosts of apartheid: Memory, identity and trauma in the "New" South Africa. Paper presented at the Eighteenth Annual Meeting of the International Society of Political Psychology, Washington, DC.

Statman, J.M. (1997). No more the miracle? Violence, vengeance, and reconciliation in the New South Africa. *ReVision, 20*(2), 32–37.

Staub, E. (1989). *The roots of evil: The origins of genocide and other group violence*. New York: Cambridge University Press.

Staub, E. (1990). The psychology and culture of torture and torturers. In P. Suedfeld (Ed.), *Psychology and torture* (pp. 49–77). Washington, DC: Hemisphere.

Staub, E. (1996a). Altruism and aggression in children and youth: Origins and cures. In R. Feldman (Ed.), *The psychology of adversity* (pp. 115–146). Amherst, MA: University of Massachusetts Press.

Staub, E. (1996b). The cultural-societal roots of violence: The examples of genocidal violence and of contemporary youth violence in the United States. *American Psychologist, 51*, 117–132.

Staub, E. (1996c). Preventing genocide: Activating bystanders, helping victims and the creation of caring. *Peace and Conflict: Journal of Peace Psychology, 2*, 189–201.

Staub, E., & Pearlman, L. (1996, November). Trauma and the fulfillment of the human potential. Workshop presented at the meeting of the International Society for Traumatic Stress Studies, San Francisco.

Steil, J.M. (1995). Supermoms and second shifts: Marital inequality in the 1990s. In J. Freeman (Ed.), *Women: A feminist perspective* (pp. 149–161). Mountain View, CA: Mayfield.

Steinmetz, S.K. (1977). *Cycle of violence*. New York: Praeger.

Stephan, W.G., Ageyev, V., Coates-Shrider, L., Stephan, C.W., & Abalakina, M. (1994). On the relationship between stereotypes and prejudice: An international study. *Personality and Social Psychology Bulletin, 20*, 277–284.

Stephens, J.B. (1994). Gender conflict. In A. Taylor & J. Bernstein Miller (Eds.), *Conflict and gender* (pp. 217–235). Cresskill, NJ: Hampton Press.

Stiftung, F. (1996). *Comprehensive review on lessons learned from United Nations operation in Somalia, April 1992–March 1995*. Lessons Learned Unit of the U.N. Department of Peacekeeping Operations in cooperation with the Life and Peace Institute, Sweden, and the Norwegian

Institute of International Affairs. New York: United Nations.

Stoessinger, J.G. (1998). *Why nations go to war* (7th ed.). New York: St. Martin's Press.

Stoll, D. (1993). *Between two armies in the Ixil towns of Guatemala.* New York: Columbia University Press.

Stoltzfus, N. (1996). *Resistance of the heart: Intermarriage and the Rosenstrasse protest in Nazi Germany.* New York: Norton.

Straus, M. (1973). A general systems theory approach to a theory of violence between family members. *Social Science Information, 12,* 105–125.

Straus, M.A. (1980). A sociological perspective on the causes of family violence. In M.R. Greed (Ed.), *Violence and the family* (pp. 7–31). Boulder, CO: Westview Press.

Straus, M. A., & Gelles, R.J. (1990). *Physical violence in American families.* New Brunswick, NJ: Transaction.

Streufert, S., & Streufert, S. (1978). *Behavior in the complex environment.* Washington, DC: Winston.

Stringer, M., & Cairns, E. (1983). Catholic and Protestant young people's ratings of stereotyped Protestant and Catholic faces. *British Journal of Social Psychology, 23,* 241–246.

Suárez-Orozco, M. (1987). The treatment of children in the "Dirty War": Ideology, state terrorism and the abuse of children in Argentina. In N. Scheper-Hughes (Ed.), *Child survival: Anthropological perspectives on the treatment and maltreatment of children* (pp. 227–246). Boston: D. Reidel.

Suárez-Orozco, M. (1990). Speaking of the unspeakable: Toward a psychosocial understanding of responses to terror. *Ethos, 18,* 353–383.

Suárez-Orozco, M. (1992). A grammar of terror: Psychocultural responses to state terrorism in Dirty War and post-Dirty War Argentina. In C. Nordstrom & J. Martin (Eds.), *The paths to domination, resistance and terror* (pp. 219–259). Berkeley, CA: University of California Press.

Suedfeld, P. (1992). Cognitive managers and their critics. *Political Psychology, 13,* 435–453.

Suedfeld, P., & Bluck, S. (1988). Changes in integrative complexity prior to surprise attacks. *Journal of Conflict Resolution, 32,* 626–635.

Suedfeld, P., Corteen, R.S., & McCormick, C. (1986). The role of integrative complexity in military leadership: Robert E. Lee and his opponents [Special Issue on Military Psychol-

ogy]. *Journal of Applied Social Psychology, 16,* 498–507.

Suedfeld, P., & Rank, A.D. (1976). Revolutionary leaders: Long-term success as a function of changes in conceptual complexity. *Journal of Personality and Social Psychology, 34,* 169–178.

Suedfeld, P., & Tetlock, P.E. (1992). Psychologists as policy advocates: The roots of controversy. In P. Suedfeld & P.E. Tetlock (Eds.), *Psychology and social policy* (pp. 1–30). New York: Hemisphere Publishing.

Suedfeld, P., Tetlock, P.E., & Ramirez, C. (1977). War, peace, and integrative complexity: UN speeches on the Middle East problem, 1947–1976. *Journal of Conflict Resolution, 21,* 427–442.

Suedfeld, P., Wallace, M.D., & Thachuk, K.L. (1993). Changes in integrative complexity among Middle East leaders during the Persian Gulf crisis. *Journal of Social Issues, 49*(4), 183–199.

Sullivan, D. (1995). The public/private distinction in international human rights law. In J. Peters & A. Wolper (Eds.), *Women's rights human rights: International feminist perspectives* (pp. 126–134). New York: Routledge.

Sullivan, M. (Speaker). (1998, September 12). *Morning edition: Women's bill in India.* Washington, DC: National Public Radio.

Sunoo, J.J.M. (1990). Some guidelines for mediators of intercultural disputes. *Negotiation Journal, 6,* 383–389.

Swartz, L., Dowdall, T., & Swartz, S. (1986). Clinical psychology and the 1985 crisis in Cape Town. *Psychology in Society, 5,* 131–138.

Swartz, L., & Foster, D. (1984). Images of culture and mental illness. South African psychiatric approaches. *Social Dynamics, 10,* 17–25.

Swartz, L., Gibson, K., & Swartz, S. (1990). State violence in South Africa and the development of a progressive psychology. In N.C. Manganyi & A. du Toit (Eds.), *Political violence and the struggle in South Africa* (pp. 234–264). London: Macmillan.

Swartz, M.J. (1961). Negative ethnocentrism. *Journal of Conflict Resolution, 5,* 75–81.

Swim, J.K., & Stangor, C. (Eds.). (1998). *Prejudice: The target's perspective.* San Diego: Academic Press.

Syme, S.L., & Berkman, L. (1976). Social class, susceptibility and illness. *American Journal of Epidemiology, 104,* 1–8.

Tajfel, H. (1969). Cognitive aspects of prejudice. *Journal of Social Issues, 25*(4), 79–97.

Tajfel, H. (1978). *Differentiation between social groups: Studies in the social psychology of intergroup relations* (European Monograph in Social Psychology, No. 14). London: Academic Press.

Tajfel, H. (1981). *Human groups and social categories: Studies in social psychology.* Cambridge: Cambridge University Press.

Tajfel, H. (1982a). Introduction. In H. Tajfel (Ed.), *Social identity and intergroup relations* (pp. 1–11). Cambridge: Cambridge University Press.

Tajfel, H. (1982b). Social psychology of intergroup relations. *Annual Review of Psychology, 33,* 1–39.

Tajfel, H., & Turner, J.C. (1979). An integrative theory of intergroup conflict. In W.G. Austin & S. Worchel (Eds.), *The social psychology of intergroup relations* (pp. 33–47). Monterey, CA: Brooks/Cole.

Tajfel, H., & Turner, J.C. (1986). The social identity theory of intergroup behaviour. In S. Worchel & W.G. Austin (Eds.) *Psychology of intergroup relations* (pp. 7–25). Chicago: Nelson-Hall.

Tajfel, H., & Wilkes, A.C. (1963). Classification and qualitative judgment. *British Journal of Psychology, 54,* 101–114.

Takeuchi, D., Leaf, P., & Hsu-Sung, K. (1988). Ethnic differences in the perception of barriers to help seeking. *Social Psychiatry and Psychiatric Epidemiology, 23,* 273–280.

Tannen, D. (1994). *Gender and discourse.* New York: Oxford University Press.

Tannen, D. (1998). *The argument culture: Moving from debate to dialogue.* New York: Random House.

Tannenbaum, D. & Schultz, D. (1998). *Inventors of ideas: An introduction to Western political philosophy.* New York: St. Martin's Press.

Taussig, M. (1986/1987). *Shamanism, colonialism, and the wild man: A study in terror and healing.* Chicago: University of Chicago Press.

Tavuchis, N. (1991). *Mea culpa: A sociology of apology and reconciliation.* Stanford, CA: Stanford University Press.

Taylor, F. (Ed.). (1983). *The Goebbels diaries: 1939–1941.* New York: G.P. Putnam.

Terhune, K.W. (1964). Nationalism among foreign and American students: An exploratory study. *Journal of Conflict Resolution 8,* 256–270.

Terr, L. (1990). *Too scared to cry.* New York: HarperCollins.

Tetlock, P.E. (1979). Identifying victims of group-think from public statements of decision makers. *Journal of Personality and Social Psychology, 37,* 1314–1324.

Tetlock, P.E. (1981). Pre- to post-election shifts in presidential rhetoric: Impression management or cognitive adjustment? *Journal of Personality and Social Psychology, 41,* 207–212.

Tetlock, P.E. (1983). Cognitive style and political ideology. *Journal of Personality and Social Psychology, 45,* 118–126.

Tetlock, P.E. (1984). Cognitive style and political belief systems in the British House of Commons. *Journal of Personality and Social Psychology, 46,* 365–375.

Tetlock, P.E. (1985). Integrative complexity of American and Soviet foreign policy rhetoric: A time-series analysis. *Journal of Personality and Social Psychology, 49,* 1565–1585.

Tetlock, P.E. (1986). Psychological advice on foreign policy: What do we have to contribute? *American Psychologist, 41,* 557–567.

Tetlock, P.E. (1988). Monitoring the integrative complexity of American and Soviet policy rhetoric: What can be learned? *Journal of Social Issues, 44*(2), 101–131.

Tetlock, P.E., Armor, D., & Peterson, R.S. (1994). The slavery debate in ante-bellum America: Cognitive style, value conflict, and the limits of compromise. *Journal of Personality and Social Psychology, 66,* 115–126.

Tetlock, P.E., & Boettger, R. (1989). Cognitive and rhetorical styles of traditionalist and reformist Soviet politicians: A content analysis study. *Political Psychology, 10,* 209–232.

Tetlock, P.E., & Manstead, A.S.R. (1985). Impression management vs. intrapsychic explanations in social psychology: A useful dichotomy? *Psychological Review, 92,* 59–79.

Tetlock, P.E., & Tyler, A. (1996). Churchill's cognitive and rhetorical style: The debates over Nazi intentions and self-government for India. *Political Psychology, 17,* 149–170.

Thompson, L. (1990). Negotiation behavior and outcomes: Empirical evidence and theoretical issues. *Psychological Bulletin, 108,* 515–532.

Thompson, M. (1994, May 23). The living room war: Rising domestic violence on U.S. military bases. *Time,* p. 48.

Thompson, R.H. (1997). Ethnic minorities and the case for collective rights. *American Anthropologist, 99,* 786–798.

Thornborrow, N.M., & Sheldon, M.B. (1995). Women in the labor force. In J. Freeman

(Ed.), *Women: A feminist perspective* (pp. 197–219). Mountain View, CA: Mayfield.

Thornton, R. (1988). Culture: A contemporary definition. In E. Boonzaier & J. Sharp (Eds.), *South African keywords: Uses and abuses of political concepts* (pp. 17–28). Cape Town: David Philip

Ting-Toomey, S. (Ed). (1994). *The challenge of facework: Cross-cultural and interpersonal issues.* Albany, NY: State University of New York Press.

Tjosvold, D. (1998). Cooperative and competitive goal approach to conflict: Accomplishments and challenges. *Applied Psychology: An International Review, 47,* 285–342.

Tolan, P., & Guerra, N. (1994). *What works in reducing adolescent violence: An empirical review of the field.* Monograph prepared for the Center for the Study and Prevention of Youth Violence. Boulder, CO: University of Colorado.

Tolman, D.L., & Brydon-Miller, M. (1997). Transforming psychology: Interpretive and participatory research methods. *Journal of Social Issues, 53*(4), 597–604.

Toomey, B.G., & Christie, D.J. (1990). Social stressors in childhood: Poverty, discrimination, and catastrophic events. In L.E. Arnold (Ed.), *Childhood stress* (pp. 423–456). New York: Wiley.

Torney, J.V., & Hess, R.D. (1971). The development of political attitudes in children. In G.S. Lesser (Ed.), *Psychology and educational practice* (pp. 466–501). Glenview, IL: Scott, Foresman.

Toscano, R. (1998). The face of the other: Ethics and intergroup conflict. In E. Wiener (Ed.), *The handbook of interethnic coexistence* (pp. 63–81). New York: Continuum Publishing Co.

Toynbee, A.J. (1957). *A study of history.* Abridged and edited by D.C. Somerville. London: Oxford University Press.

TRC. (1996). Human rights violations report. Cape Town: Truth and Reconciliation Commission.

TRC. (1998a). *The Final Report.* Cape Town. Retrieved, November 30, 1998 from the World Wide Web: *http://www.truth.org.za/final/5chap9 .htm*

TRC. (1998b). *A summary of reparation and rehabilitation policy, including proposals to be considered by the President.* Cape Town: Truth and Reconciliation Commission.

Triandis, H.C. (1990). Theoretical concepts that are applicable to the analysis of ethnocentrism. In R.W. Brislin (Ed.), *Cross-cultural research and methodology series: Vol. 14. Applied cross-cultural psychology* (pp. 34–55). Newbury Park, CA: Sage.

Triandis, H.C. (1995). The self and social behavior in differing cultural contexts. In N.R. Goldberger & J.B. Veroff (Eds.), *The culture and psychology reader* (pp. 326–365). New York: New York University Press.

Trost, M.R., Cialdini, R.B., & Maass, A. (1989). Effects of an international conflict simulation on perceptions of the Soviet Union: A FIREBREAKS backfire. *Journal of Social Issues, 45*(2), 139–158.

Truth and Reconciliation Commission of South Africa (TRC). (1998). *Truth and Reconciliation of South Africa Report, 5 Volumes.* Cape Town: CTP Printers.

Tuchman, B. (1984). *The march of folly: From Troy to Vietnam.* New York: Ballantine.

Turner, J.C. (1987). *Rediscovering the social group: A self-categorization theory.* New York: Basil Blackwell.

Turpin, J. (1998). Many faces: Women confronting war. In L.A. Lorentzen & J. Turpin (Eds.), *The women and war reader* (pp. 3–18). New York: New York University Press.

Ulbrich, P., & Huber, J. (1981). Observing parental violence: Distribution and effects. *Journal of Marriage and the Family, 43,* 623–631.

UNDP. (1992). *Human Development Report 1992.* New York: Oxford University Press.

UNDP. (1995). *Human Development Report 1995.* New York: Oxford University Press.

UNDP. (1996). *Human Development Report 1996.* New York: Oxford University Press.

UNDP. (1997). *Human Development Report 1997.* New York: Oxford University Press.

UNICEF. (1998). *State of the World's Children 1998.* New York: UNICEF.

United Nations Children's Fund [UNICEF]. (1994). *The progress of nations: The nations of the world ranked according to their achievements in child health, nutrition, education, family planning, and progress for women.* New York: UNICEF.

United Nations Department of Economic Affairs, Statistical Office. (1953). *A system of national accounts and supporting tables. Studies in methods 2.* New York: United Nations Statistical Office.

United Nations Development Fund for Women (UNIFEM) and African Women in Crisis (AFWIC). (1995). *African women in crisis: Activities of the African women for conflict resolution and peace project of UNIFEM/AFWIC.* New York: UNIFEM.

United Nations Development Fund for Women. (1995, September). *A commitment to the world's women*. United Nations Website [On-line]. Available: United Nations Website.

United Nations Development Program. (1994). *Human Development Report 1994*. New York: Oxford University Press.

United Nations Development Programme. (1997). *Human Development Report 1997*. New York: Oxford University Press.

United Nations General Assembly. (1989, November 17). *Adoption of a convention on the rights of the child*. New York: United Nations.

United Nations Research Institute for Social Development (UNRISD). (1994). *The challenge of rebuilding wartorn societies: Report on the working seminar at Cartigny, Geneva, 29 November–1 December 1994*. Geneva: Author.

United Nations. (1945 and later editions). *Charter of the United Nations and statute of the International Court of Justice*. New York: UN Department of Public Information.

United Nations. (1990). *The blue helmets: A review of United Nations peacekeeping (2nd ed.)*. New York: UN Department of Public Information.

United Nations. (1992). *An agenda for peace*. New York: Author.

United Nations. (1996a). *The blue helmets: A review of United Nations peacekeeping (3rd edition)*. New York: UN Department of Public Information.

United Nations. (1996b). *Impact of armed conflict on children: Report of the expert of the Secretary General of the United Nations Ms. Graca Machel*. (Document A/51/306 & Add. 1). New York: Author. May be ordered from the Public Inquiries Unit, Department of Information, United Nations, New York, NY 10017. Orders may be sent via fax to (212) 963–0071.

United Nations. (1996c). *Platform for action and the Beijing declaration*. New York: United Nations Publications.

United Nations. (1997). Secretary General Annan's address "Adapting to a Changing World: Recent Lessons from U.N. Peacekeeping Operations," 17 November 1997, (SG/SM/6398). New York: United Nations.

Universal human rights vs. cultural relativity: Special issue. (1997). *Journal of Anthropological Research, 53*, 269–381.

Ury, W.L., Brett, J.M., & Goldberg, S.B. (1989). *Getting disputes resolved: Designing systems to cut the costs of conflict*. San Francisco: Jossey-Bass.

U.S. Census Report. (1997a). Money income in the United States: 1996 [Web document] Available: http://*WWW.CENSUS.GOV/PROD/WWW/TITLES.HTML* [Sept. 29, 1997].

U.S. Census Report. (1997b). Poverty in the United States: 1996 [Web document]. Available: *WWW.CENSUS.GOV/PROD/WWW/TITLES.HTML* [Sept. 29, 1997].

U.S. Department of Education. (1997). *Report on the condition of education*. Washington, DC: Author.

U.S. Department of Justice. (1995). *Uniform crime reports for the United States, 1994*. Department of Justice, Federal Bureau of Investigation.

U.S. Department of State. (1971). Nuclear Non-Proliferation Treaty, Article VI, in *United States Treaties and Other International Agreements* (vol. 21, part 1). Washington, DC: U.S. Government Printing Office.

U.S. Department of State. (1996). *Colombia Country Report on Human Rights Practices for 1996*. Washington, DC: U.S. Government Printing Office.

Utne, M.K., & Kidd, R. (1980). Equity and attribution. In G. Mikula (Ed.), *Justice and social interaction* (pp. 63–93). New York: Springer-Verlag.

Utting, P. (1994). *Between hope and insecurity: The social consequences of the Cambodian peace process*. Geneva: UNRISD.

Vaccaro, J.M. (1996). The politics of genocide: Peacekeeping and disaster relief in Rwanda. In W. Durch (Ed.), *UN peacekeeping, American policy, and the uncivil wars of the 1990s* (pp. 367–408). New York: St. Martin's Press.

Vaccaro, J.M. (1998). Creating a durable peace: Psychological aspects of rebuilding and reforming the indigenous criminal justice system. In H. Langholtz (Ed.), *The psychology of peacekeeping* (pp. 167–178). Westport, CT: Praeger.

Valent, P. (1997). Child survivors: A review. In J.S. Kostenberg & C. Kahn (Eds.), *Children surviving persecution: An international study of trauma and healing* (pp. 109–123). New York: Praeger.

van der Kolk, V.A., McFarlane, A.C., & Weisaeth, L. (Eds.). (1996). *Traumatic stress: The effects of overwhelming experience on mind, body, and society*. New York: Guilford Press.

Van Evera, S. (1995). Hypotheses on nationalism and the causes of war. In C.A. Kupchan (Ed.), *Nationalism and nationalities in the New Europe* (pp. 136–157). Ithaca, NY: Cornell University Press.

Villa-Vicencio, C. (1995). Telling one another stories: Towards a theology of reconciliation. In C. Villa-Vicencio & C. Niehaus (Eds.), *Many cultures, one nation* (pp. 105–121). Cape Town: Human & Rosseau.

Volkan, V.D. (1988). *The need to have enemies and allies: From clinical practice to international relationships.* New York: Jason Aronson.

Vygotsky, L.S. (1978). *Mind in society.* Cambridge, MA: Harvard University Press.

Wade, S. (1994, July 21). Ammo plant's boss says nature, industry can co-exist at base. *The Courier Journal,* p. 1A.

Wagner, R.V. (1985). Psychology and the threat of nuclear war. *American Psychologist, 40,* 531–535.

Wagner, R.V. (1988). Distinguishing between positive and negative approaches to peace. *Journal of Social Issues, 44*(2), 1–15.

Wagner, R.V., de Rivera, J., & Watkins, M. (1988). Psychology and the promotion of peace. *Journal of Social Issues, 44*(2).

Walker, I., & Pettigrew, T.F. (1984). Relative deprivation theory: An overview and conceptual critique. *British Journal of Social Psychology, 23,* 301–310.

Walker, L. (1979). *The battered woman.* New York: Harper and Row.

Walker, L. (1989). *Terrifying love: Why battered women kill and how society responds.* New York: HarperPerennial.

Walker, L. (1999). Psychology and domestic violence around the world. *American Psychologist, 54,* 21–29.

Wall, J.A., Jr., & Callister, R.R. (1995). *Ho'oponopono:* Some lessons from Hawaiian mediation. *Negotiation Journal, 11,* 45–53.

Wallace, M.D., & Suedfeld, P. (1998). Leadership performance in crisis: The longevity-complexity link. *International Studies Quarterly, 32,* 439–451.

Wallace, M.D., Suedfeld, P., & Thachuk, K.L. (1993). Political rhetoric of leaders under stress in the Gulf crisis. *Journal of Conflict Resolution, 37,* 94–107.

Wallbaum, A.B.C. (1993). Integrative complexity, international crises, and cognitive management. In K.S. Larsen (Ed.), *Conflict and social psychology* (pp. 34–44). London: Sage.

Wallensteen, P., & Sollenberg, M. (1998). Armed conflicts and regional conflict complexes, 1989–97. *Journal of Peace Research, 35,* 621–634.

Walster, E., & Walster, G.W. (1975). Equity and social justice. *Journal of Social Issues, 31*(3), 21–43.

Walton, R.E., & McKersie, R.B. (1965). *A behavioral theory of labor negotiations: An analysis of a social interaction system.* New York: McGraw-Hill.

Wandersman, A., & Nation, M. (1998). Urban neighborhoods and mental health: Psychological contributions to understanding toxicity, resilience, and interventions. *American Psychologist, 53,* 647–656.

Wang, C., & Burris, M. (1994). Empowerment through photo novella: Portraits of participation. *Health Education Quarterly, 21,* 171–186.

Waring, M. (1988). *If women counted: A new feminist economics.* San Francisco: Harper & Row.

Watson, S. (Ed.). (1990). *Playing the state: Australian feminist interventions.* London: Verso.

Watson-Gegeo, K., & White, G. (Eds.). (1990). *The discourse of disentangling: Conflict discourse in Pacific societies.* Palo Alto, CA: Stanford University Press.

Weiss, T.G., & Collins, C. (1996). *Humanitarian challenges and intervention.* Boulder, CO: Westview Press.

Weitzman, J., & Dreen, K. (1982). Wife-beating: A view of the marital dyad. *Social Casework, 63,* 259–265.

Wells, A. (1998). Human rights in the Asian Pacific: Regional crisis, global threats and struggle for human rights. *RESIST Newsletter, 7*(9), 4–5.

Werner, E. (1990). Protective factors and individual resilience. In S.J. Meisels & J.P. Shonkoff (Eds.), *Handbook of early childhood intervention.* Cambridge: Cambridge University Press.

Werth, J.L., & Lord, C.G. (1992). Previous conceptions of the typical group member and the contact hypothesis. *Basic and Applied Social Psychology, 13,* 351–369.

Wertheim, E., Love, A., Peck, C., & Littlefield, L. (1998). *Skills for resolving conflict.* Emerald, Australia: Eruditions Publishers.

Wertsch, J.V. (1998). *Mind as action.* New York: Oxford University Press.

Wessells, M. (1996). Assisting Angolan children impacted by war: Blending Western and traditional approaches to healing. *Coordinators' Notebook: An International Resource for Early Childhood Development, 19,* 33–37.

Wessells, M. (1997). Child soldiers. *Bulletin of the Atomic Scientists, 53*(6), 32–39.

Wessells, M., & Kostelny, K.K. (1996). *The Graça Machel/UN study on the impact of armed conflict on children: Implications for early child development.* New York: UNICEF Working Paper.

Wessells, M., & Monteiro, C. (2000). Healing wounds of war in Angola: A community-based approach. In D. Donald, A. Dawes, & J. Louw (Eds.), *Addressing childhood adversity* (pp. 176–201). Cape Town: David Philip.

Wessells, M.G. (1992). Building peace psychology on a global scale: Challenges and opportunities. *The Peace Psychology Bulletin, 1*(3), 32–44.

Wessells, M.G. (1995). Social-psychological determinants of nuclear proliferation: A dual-process analysis. *Peace and Conflict: Journal of Peace Psychology, 1*, 49–66.

Wessells, M.G. (1996). A history of Division 48 (Peace Psychology). In D.A. Dewsbury, (Ed.), *Unification through division: Histories of the Divisions of the American Psychological Association, 1* (pp. 265–298). Washington, DC: American Psychological Association.

Wessells, M.G. (1998a). The changing nature of armed conflict and its implications for children: The Graca Machel/UN study. *Peace and Conflict: Journal of Peace Psychology, 4*, 321–334.

Wessells, M.G. (1998b). Children, armed conflict, and peace. *Journal of Peace Research, 35*, 635–646.

Wessells, M.G. (1998c). Humanitarian intervention, psychosocial assistance, and peacekeeping. In H. Langholtz (Ed.), *The psychology of peacekeeping* (pp. 131–152). Westport, CT: Praeger.

White, J.R. (1998). *Terrorism: An introduction.* Belmont, CA: Wadsworth.

White, R.K. (1966). Misperception and the Vietnam War. *Journal of Social Issues, 22*(3).

White, R.K. (1977). Misperception in the Arab-Israeli conflict. *Journal of Social Issues, 33*(1), 190–221.

White, R.K. (1984). *Fearful warriors: A psychological profile of U.S.-Soviet relations.* New York: Free Press.

White, R.K. (1986). *Psychology and the prevention of nuclear war.* New York: New York University Press.

White, R.K. (1998). American acts of force: Results and misperceptions. *Peace and Conflict: Journal of Peace Psychology 4*, 93–128.

Whyte, J. (1990). *Interpreting Northern Ireland.* Oxford: Clarendon Press.

Willis, M., & Cairns, E. (1993). Catholic accounts of rioting in Derry. *Irish Journal of Psychology, 14*, 535–545.

Willis, M.A. (1991). Relative deprivation and political conflict: A Northern Irish case. Unpublished doctoral dissertation, University of Ulster, Coleraine.

Wilson, J.P., & Raphael, B. (1993). *International handbook of traumatic stress syndromes* New York: Plenum.

Wilson, J.W. (1996, August 18). Work. *New York Times Magazine*, pp. 145, 26–52.

Wilson, R. (1995). Manufacturing legitimacy: The Truth and Reconciliation Commission and the rule of law. *Indicator SA, 13*(1), 41–46.

Winegar, L.T., & Valsiner, J.T. (1992a). *Children's development within social context. Volume 1: Metatheory and theory.* Hillsdale, NJ: Erlbaum.

Winegar, L.T., & Valsiner, J.T. (1992b). *Children's development within social context. Volume 2: Research and methodology.* Hillsdale, NJ: Erlbaum.

Winter, D.D. (1996). *Ecological psychology: Healing the split between planet and self.* New York: HarperCollins.

Winter, D.D. (1998). War is not healthy for children and other living things. *Peace and Conflict: Journal of Peace Psychology, 4*, 415–428.

Winter, D.G. (1997, July). Comparing "war" and "peace" crises: The role of motivation, responsibility, and integrative complexity. Paper presented at the meeting of the International Society of Political Psychology, Krakow, Poland.

Winter, D.G., & Molano, J.R.V. (1998, August). Toward a psychological theory of ethno-political war. Paper presented at the 24th International Congress of Applied Psychology, San Francisco.

Wispe, L.G. (1972). Positive forms of social behavior: An overview. *Journal of Social Issues, 28*(3), 1–19.

Wollman, N. (Ed.). (1985). *Working for peace: A handbook of practical psychology and other tools.* San Luis Obispo, CA: Impact.

Wolpe, H. (1988). *Race, class and the apartheid state.* London: James Currey.

Women for Life Without Wars and Violence! (1996, November). *International Conference Women for Life Without Wars and Violence! Rostovon-Don.* Translated by Elena Schetinina.

Woodhead, M., Light, P., & Carr, R. (1991). *Growing up in a changing society.* Child Development in Social Context 3. London: Routledge.

World Commission on Economic Development. (1987). *Our common future.* New York: Oxford University Press.

World Disasters Report 1996. Oxford: Oxford University Press.

World Game Institute. (1997). *What the world wants.* Philadelphia: World Game Institute.

Wright, Q., Evan, W.M., & Deutsch, M. (1962).

Preventing World War III: Some proposals. New York: Simon & Schuster.

Yatani, C., & Bramel, D. (1989). Trends and patterns in Americans' attitudes toward the Soviet Union. *Journal of Social Issues, 45*(2), 13–32.

Yeich, S. (1996). Grassroots organizing with homeless people: A participatory research approach. *Journal of Social Issues, 52*(1), 111–121.

Yllo, K.A. (1993). Through a feminist lens: Gender, power and violence. In R.J. Gelles & D.R. Loseke (Eds.), *Current controversies on family violence* (pp. 47–62). Newbury Park, CA: Sage.

Yllo, K.A., & Bogard, M. (Eds). (1988). *Feminist perspectives on wife abuse.* Newbury Park, CA: Sage.

Young, E. (1992). *Keepers of the history: Women and the Israeli-Palestinian conflict.* New York: Teachers College Press.

Zama, L. (1991). Theories of equality: Some thoughts for South Africa. In S. Bazilli (Ed.), *Putting women on the agenda* (pp. 57–61). Johannesburg: Ravan Press.

Zander, A. (1979). The psychology of group processes. *Annual Review of Psychology, 30,* 417–451.

Zartman, I.W. (1985). *Ripe for resolution: Conflict and intervention in Africa.* New York: Oxford University Press.

Zechenter, E.M. (1997). In the name of culture: Cultural relativism and the abuse of the individual. *Journal of Anthropological Research, 53,* 319–347.

Zechmeister, K., & Druckman, D. (1973). Determinants of resolving a conflict of interest: A simulation of political decision-making. *Journal of Conflict Resolution, 27,* 63–88.

Zigler, E., & Muenchow, S. (1992). *Head Start: The inside story of America's most successful educational experiment.* New York: Basic Books.

Zimbardo, P.G. (1970). The human choice: Individuation, reason and order vs. deindividuation, impulse and chaos. In N.J. Arnold & D. Levine (Eds.), *Nebraska symposium on motivation, 1969* (pp. 237–307). Lincoln, NE: University of Nebraska Press.

Zimmerman, J. (1995). *Tailspin: Women at war in the wake of Tailhook.* New York: Doubleday.

Zimmerman, M. (1995). Psychological empowerment: Issues and illustrations. *American Journal of Community Psychology, 23,* 581–599.

INDEX

TEXT CREDITS

(p. 19) "Intimate Violence," by Naomi Abrahams. Used with permission.

(p. 28) "Anti-Gay/Lesbian Violence in the United States," by Bianca Cody Murphy. Used with permission.

(p. 39) "Intrastate Violence," by Ulrike Niens and Ed Cairns. Used with permission.

(p. 49) "Nationalism and War: A Social-Psychological Perspective," by Daniel Druckman. Used with permission.

(p. 66) "Integrative Complexity and Political Decisions that Lead to War or Peace," by Lucian Gideon Conway III, Peter Suedfeld, and Philip E. Tetlock. Used with permission.

(p. 76) "Genocide and Mass Killing: Their Roots and Prevention," by Ervin Staub. Used with permission.

(p. 87) "Weapons of Mass Destruction," by Michael Britton. Used with permission.

(p. 102) "Social Injustice," by Susan Opotow. Used with permission.

(p. 110) "The War Close to Home: Children and Violence in the United States," by Kathleen Kostelny and James Garbarino. Used with permission.

(p. 120) "Children and Structural Violence," by Milton Schwebel and Daniel J. Christie. Used with permission.

(p. 130) "Women, Girls, and Structural Violence: A Global Analysis," by Dyan Mazurana and Susan McKay. Used with permission.

(p. 139) "Understanding Militarism: Money, Masculinity, and the Search for the Mystical," by Deborah Du Nann Winter, Marc Pilisuk, Sara Houck, and Matthew Lee. Used with permission.

(p. 149) "Globalism and Structural Violence," by Marc Pilisuk. Used with permission.

(p. 158) "Human Rights Violations as Structural Violence," by M. Brinton Lykes. Used with permission.

(p. 173) "U.N. Peacekeeping: Confronting the Psychological Environment of War in the Twenty-first Century," by Harvey J. Langholtz and Peter Leentjes. Used with permission.

(p. 183) "The Cultural Context of Peacemaking," by Paul B. Pedersen. Used with permission.

(p. 193) "Conflict Resolution: Theoretical and Practical Issues," by Ann Sanson and Di Bretherton. Used with permission.

(p. 210) "Crafting Peace: On the Psychology of the TRANSCEND Approach," by Johan Galtung and Finn Tschudi. Used with permission.

(p. 223) "Introducing Cooperation and Conflict Resolution into Schools: A Systems Approach," by Peter Coleman and Morton Deutsch. Used with permission.

(p. 240) "Reducing Trauma during Ethno-Political Conflict: A Personal Account of Psycho-social Work under War Conditions in Bosnia," by Inger Agger. Used with permission.

(p. 251) "Reconciliation in Divided Societies," by Cheryl de la Rey. Used with permission.

(p. 262) "Psychosocial Interventions and Post-war Reconstruction in Angola: Interweaving Western and Traditional Approaches," by Michael Wessells and Carlinda Monteiro. Used with permission.

(p. 282) "Toward a Psychology of Structural Peacebuilding," by Cristina Jayme Montiel. Used with permission.

(p. 295) "Psychologies for Liberation: Views from Elsewhere," by Andy Dawes. Used with permission.

(p. 307) "Gandhi as Peacebuilder: The Social Psychology of *Satyagraha*," by Daniel M. Mayton II. Used with permission.

(p. 314) "Peacebuilding and Nonviolence: Gandhi's Perspective on Power," by Manfred B. Steger. Used with permission.

(p. 324) "Giving Voice to Children's Perspectives on Peace," by Ilsa Hakvoort and Solveig Hägglund. Used with permission.

(p. 330) "Redressing Structural Violence against Children: Empowerment-based Interventions and Research," by Linda Webster and Douglas B. Perkins. Used with permission.

(p. 341) "Gendering Peacebuilding," by Susan McKay and Dyan Mazurana. Used with permission.

(p. 350) "Psychologists Making a Difference in the Public Arena: Building Cultures of Peace," by Michael Wessells, Milton Schwebel, and Anne Anderson. Used with permission.